PAGE FROM AN ILLUMINATED MANUSCRIPT

AN INTRODUCTION TO THE

HISTORY OF WESTERN EUROPE

BY

JAMES HARVEY ROBINSON

PROFESSOR OF HISTORY IN COLUMBIA UNIVERSITY

History is no easy science;
its subject, human society,
is infinitely complex.

FUSTEL DE COULANGES

GINN & COMPANY

BOSTON · NEW YORK · CHICAGO · LONDON

The Athenæum Press
GINN & COMPANY · PRO-
PRIETORS · BOSTON · U.S.A.

PREFACE

In introducing the student to the history of the development of European culture, the problem of proportion has seemed to me, throughout, the fundamental one. Consequently I have endeavored not only to state matters truly and clearly but also to bring the narrative into harmony with the most recent conceptions of the relative importance of past events and institutions. It has seemed best, in an elementary treatise upon so vast a theme, to omit the names of many personages and conflicts of secondary importance which have ordinarily found their way into our historical text-books. I have ventured also to neglect a considerable number of episodes and anecdotes which, while hallowed by assiduous repetition, appear to owe their place in our manuals rather to accident or mere tradition than to any profound meaning for the student of the subject.

The space saved by these omissions has been used for three main purposes. Institutions under which Europe has lived for centuries, above all the Church, have been discussed with a good deal more fullness than is usual in similar manuals. The life and work of a few men of indubitably first-rate importance in the various fields of human endeavor — Gregory the Great, Charlemagne, Abelard, St. Francis, Petrarch, Luther, Erasmus, Voltaire, Napoleon, Bismarck — have been treated with care proportionate to their significance for the world. Lastly, the scope of the work has been broadened so that not only the political but also the economic, intellectual, and artistic achievements of the past form an integral part of the narrative.

I have relied upon a great variety of sources belonging to the various orders in the hierarchy of historical literature ; it is happily unnecessary to catalogue these. In some instances I have found other manuals, dealing with portions of my field, of value. In the earlier chapters, Emerton's admirable *Introduction to the Middle Ages* furnished many suggestions. For later periods, the same may be said of Henderson's careful *Germany in the Middle Ages* and Schwill's clear and well-proportioned *History of Modern Europe*. For the most recent period, I have made constant use of Andrews' scholarly *Development of Modern Europe*. For England, the manuals of Green and Gardiner have been used. The greater part of the work is, however, the outcome of study of a wide range of standard special treatises dealing with some short period or with a particular phase of European progress. As examples of these, I will mention only Lea's monumental contributions to our knowledge of the jurisprudence of the Church, Rashdall's *History of the Universities in the Middle Ages*, Richter's incomparable *Annalen der Deutschen Geschichte im Mittelalter*, the *Histoire Générale*, and the well-known works of Luchaire, Voigt, Hefele, Bezold, Janssen, Levasseur, Creighton, Pastor. In some cases, as in the opening of the Renaissance, the Lutheran Revolt, and the French Revolution, I have been able to form my opinions to some extent from first-hand material.

My friends and colleagues have exhibited a generous interest in my enterprise, of which I have taken constant advantage. Professor E. H. Castle of Teachers College, Miss Ellen S. Davison, Dr. William R. Shepherd, and Dr. James T. Shotwell of the historical department of Columbia University, have very kindly read part of my manuscript. The proof has been revised by my colleague, Professor William A. Dunning, Professor Edward P. Cheyney of the University of Pennsylvania, Dr. Ernest F. Henderson, and by Professor Dana C. Munro of the University of Wisconsin. To all of these I am much indebted. Both in the arduous preparation of the manuscript and in the reading of the proof my wife has been my constant companion, and to her the volume owes innumerable rectifications in arrangement and diction. I would also add a word of gratitude to my publishers for their hearty coöperation in their important part of the undertaking.

The *Readings in European History*, a manual now in preparation, and designed to accompany this volume, will contain comprehensive bibliographies for each chapter and a selection of illustrative material, which it is hoped will enable the teacher and pupil to broaden and vivify their knowledge. In the present volume I have given only a few titles at the end of some of the chapters, and in the footnotes I mention, for collateral reading, under the heading "Reference," chapters in the best available books, to which the student may be sent for additional detail. Almost all the books referred to might properly find a place in every high-school library.   J. H. R.

COLUMBIA UNIVERSITY,
January 12, 1903.

CONTENTS

LIST OF MAPS

x   *List of Maps*

FULL-PAGE ILLUSTRATIONS

INTRODUCTION TO THE HISTORY

OF

WESTERN EUROPE

CHAPTER I

THE HISTORICAL POINT OF VIEW

1. History, in the broadest sense of the word, is all that we know about everything that man has ever done, or thought, or hoped, or felt. It is the limitless science of past human affairs, a subject immeasurably vast and important but exceedingly vague. The historian may busy himself deciphering hieroglyphics on an Egyptian obelisk, describing a mediæval monastery, enumerating the Mongol emperors of Hindustan or the battles of Napoleon. He may explain how the Roman Empire was conquered by the German barbarians, or why the United States and Spain came to blows in 1898, or what Calvin thought of Luther, or what a French peasant had to eat in the eighteenth century. We can know something of each of these matters if we choose to examine the evidence which still exists; they all help to make up history.

The present volume deals with a small but very important portion of the history of the world. Its object is to give as adequate an account as is possible in one volume of the chief changes in western Europe since the German barbarians overcame the armies of the Roman Empire and set up states of their own, out of which the present countries of France, Germany, Italy, Austria, Spain, the Netherlands, and England

have slowly grown.   There are, however, whole libraries upon
the history of each of these countries during the last fifteen
hundred years, and it requires a volume or two to give a
tolerably complete account of any single important person,
like St. Francis, Cromwell, Frederick the Great, or Napoleon.
Besides biographies and general histories, there are many special
treatises upon the Church and other great institutions; upon
the literature, art, philosophy, and law of the various countries.
It is obvious, therefore, that only a very few of the historical
facts known to scholars can possibly find a place in a single
volume such as this.   One who undertakes to condense what
we know of Europe's past, since the times of Theodosius and
Alaric, into the space of six hundred pages assumes a very
grave responsibility.   The reader has a right to ask not only
that what he finds in the book shall be at once true and
clearly stated, but that it shall consist, on the whole, of the
most important and useful of all the things which might have
been selected from the well-nigh infinite mass of true things
that are known.

We gain practically nothing from the mere enumeration of
events and dates.   The student of history wishes to know how
people lived; what were their institutions (which are really
only the habits of nations), their occupations, interests, and
achievements; how business was transacted in the Middle
Ages almost without the aid of money; how, later, commerce
increased and industry grew up; what a great part the Christian church played in society; how the monks lived and what
they did for mankind.   In short, the object of an introduction to mediæval and modern European history is the description of the most significant achievements of western civilization
during the past fifteen hundred years, — the explanation of how
the Roman Empire of the West and the wild and unknown districts inhabited by the German races have become the Europe
of Gladstone and Bismarck, of Darwin and Pasteur.

In order to present even an outline of the great changes during this long period, all that was exceptional and abnormal must be left out. We must fix our attention upon man's habitual conduct, upon those things that he kept on doing in essentially the same way for a century or so. Particular events are important in so far as they illustrate these permanent conditions and explain how the western world passed from one state to another.

We must learn, above all, to study sympathetically institutions and beliefs that we are tempted at first to declare absurd and unreasonable. The aim of the historian is not to prove that a particular way of doing a thing is right or wrong, as, for instance, intrusting the whole government to a king or forbidding clergymen to marry. His object is to show as well as he can how a certain system came to be introduced, what was thought of it, how it worked, and how another plan gradually supplanted it. It seems to us horrible that a man should be burned alive because he holds views of Christianity different from those of his neighbors. Instead, however, of merely condemning the practice, we must, as historical students, endeavor to see why practically every one in the thirteenth century, even the wisest and most tender-hearted, agreed that such a fearful punishment was the appropriate one for a heretic. An effort has, therefore, been made throughout this volume to treat the convictions and habits of men and nations in the past with consideration ; that is, to make them seem natural and to show their beneficent rather than their evil aspects. It is not the weakness of an institution, but the good that is in it, that leads men to adopt and retain it.

We should study the past sympathetically.

2. It is impossible to divide the past into distinct, clearly defined periods and prove that one age ended and another began in a particular year, such as 476, or 1453, or 1789. Men do not and cannot change their habits and ways of doing things all at once, no matter what happens. It is true

Impossibility of dividing the past into clearly defined periods.

that a single event, such as an important battle which results in the loss of a nation's independence, may produce an abrupt change in the government. This in turn may encourage or discourage commerce and industry and modify the language and the spirit of a people. Yet these deeper changes take place only very gradually. After a battle or a revolution the farmer will sow and reap in his old way, the artisan will take up his familiar tasks, and the merchant his buying and selling. The scholar will study and write and the household go on under the new government just as they did under the old. So a change in government affects the habits of a people but slowly in any case, and it may leave them quite unaltered.

All general changes take place gradually.

The French Revolution, at the end of the eighteenth century, was probably the most abrupt and thoroughgoing change in the habits of a nation of which we have any record. But we shall find, when we come to study it, that it was by no means so sudden in reality as is ordinarily supposed. Moreover, the innovators did not even succeed in permanently altering the form of government; for when the French, after living under a monarchy for many centuries, set up a republic in 1792, the new government lasted only a few years. The nation was monarchical by habit and soon gladly accepted the rule of Napoleon, which was more despotic than that of any of its former kings. In reorganizing the state he borrowed much from the discarded monarchy, and the present French republic still retains many of these arrangements.

The unity or continuity of history.

This tendency of mankind to do, in general, this year what it did last, in spite of changes in some one department of life,— such as substituting a president for a king, traveling by rail instead of on horseback, or getting the news from a newspaper instead of from a neighbor, — results in what is called the *unity* or *continuity of history*. The truth that no abrupt change has ever taken place in all the customs of a people, and that it cannot, in the nature of things, take place, is perhaps the most fundamental lesson that history teaches.

Historians sometimes seem to forget this principle, when they claim to begin and end their books at precise dates. We find histories of Europe from 476 to 918, from 1270 to 1492, as if the accession of a capable German king in 918, or the death of a famous French king in 1270, or the discovery of America, marked a general change in European affairs. In reality, however, no general change took place at these dates or in any other single year. It would doubtless have proved a great convenience to the readers and writers of history if the world had agreed to carry out a definite programme and alter its habits at precise dates, preferably at the opening of each century. But no such agreement has ever been adopted, and the historical student must take things as he finds them. He must recognize that nations retain their old customs while they adopt new ones, and that a portion of a nation may advance while a great part of it stays behind.

3. We cannot, therefore, hope to fix any year or event which may properly be taken as the beginning of that long period which followed the downfall of the Roman state in western Europe and which is commonly called the Middle Ages. Beyond the northern and western boundaries of the Roman Empire, which embraced the whole civilized world from the Euphrates to Britain, mysterious peoples moved about whose history before they came into occasional contact with the Romans is practically unknown. These Germans, or barbarians, as the Romans called them, were destined to put an end to the Roman Empire in the West. They had first begun to make trouble about a hundred years before Christ, when a great army of them was defeated by the Roman general, Marius. Julius Cæsar narrates in polished Latin, familiar to all who have begun the study of that language, how fifty years later he drove back other bands. Five hundred years elapsed,

Meaning of the term 'Middle Ages.'

however, between these first encounters and the founding
of German kingdoms within the boundaries of the Empire.
With their establishment the Roman government in western
Europe may be said to have come to an end and the Middle
Ages to have begun.

Yet it would be a great mistake to suppose that this means
that the Roman civilization suddenly disappeared at this time.
As we shall see, it had gradually changed during the centuries
following the golden age of Augustus, who died A.D. 14. Long
before the German conquest, art and literature had begun to
decline toward the level that they reached in the Middle Ages.
Many of the ideas and conditions which prevailed after the
coming of the barbarians were common enough before, —
even the ignorance and want of taste which we associate
particularly with the Middle Ages.

The term *Middle Ages* is, then, a vague one. It will be used
in this volume to mean, roughly speaking, the period of nearly
a thousand years that elapsed between the opening of the
fifth century, when the disorder of the barbarian invasions
was becoming general, and the fourteenth century, when
Europe was well on its way to retrieve all that had been lost
since the break-up of the Roman Empire.

The 'dark
ages.'

It used to be assumed, when there was much less interest
in the period than there now is, that with the disruption of the
Empire and the disorder that followed, practically all culture
perished for centuries, that Europe entered upon the "dark
ages." These were represented as dreary centuries of ignorance and violence in marked contrast to the civilization of
the Greeks and Romans on the one hand, and to the enlightenment of modern times on the other. The more careful
studies of the last half century have made it clear that the
Middle Ages were not "dark" in the sense of being stagnant
and unproductive. On the contrary, they were full of movement and growth, and we owe to them a great many things

in our civilization which we should never have derived from Greece and Rome. It is the purpose of the first nineteen chapters of this manual to describe the effects of the barbarian conquests, the gradual recovery of Europe from the disorder of the successive invasions, and the peculiar institutions which grew up to meet the needs of the times. The remaining chapters will attempt to show how mediæval institutions, habits, and ideas were supplanted, step by step, by those which exist in Europe to-day.

CHAPTER II

WESTERN EUROPE BEFORE THE BARBARIAN INVASIONS

4. No one can hope to understand the Middle Ages who does not first learn something of the Roman Empire, within whose bounds the Germans set up their kingdoms and began the long task of creating modern Europe.

At the opening of the fifth century there were no separate, independent states in western Europe such as we find on the map to-day. The whole territory now occupied by England, France, Spain, and Italy formed at that time only a part of the vast realms ruled over by the Roman emperor and his host of officials. As for Germany, it was still a region of forests, familiar only to the barbarous and half-savage tribes who inhabited them. The Romans tried in vain to conquer this part of Europe, and finally had to content themselves with keeping the German hordes out of the Empire by means of fortifications and guards along the Rhine and Danube rivers.

The Roman Empire, which embraced southern and western Europe, western Asia, and even the northern portion of Africa, included the most diverse peoples and races. Egyptians, Arabs, Jews, Greeks, Germans, Gauls, Britons, Iberians, — all alike were under the sovereign rule of Rome. One great state embraced the nomad shepherds who spread their tents on the borders of Sahara, the mountaineers in the fastnesses of Wales, and the citizens of Athens, Alexandria, and Rome, heirs to all the luxury and learning of the ages. Whether one lived in York

government, for through them the same ideas and culture were carried to even the most distant parts of the Empire.

The Roman government attempted to regulate everything. Let us first glance at the government and the emperor. His decrees were dispatched throughout the length and breadth of the Roman dominions; whatsoever pleased him became law, according to the well-known principle of the Roman constitution. While the cities were permitted some freedom in the regulation of their purely local affairs, the emperor and his innumerable and marvelously organized officials kept an eye upon even the humblest citizen. The Roman government, besides maintaining order, administering justice, and defending the boundaries, assumed many other responsibilities. It watched the grain dealers, butchers, and bakers; saw that they properly supplied the public and never deserted their occupation. In some cases it forced the son to follow the profession of his father. If it could have had its way, it would have had every one belong to a definite class of society, and his children after him. It kept the unruly poorer classes quiet in the towns by furnishing them with bread, and sometimes with wine, meat, and clothes. It provided amusement for them by expensive entertainments, such as races and gladiatorial combats. In a word, the Roman government was not only wonderfully organized, so that it penetrated to the utmost confines of its territory, but it attempted to guard and regulate almost every interest in life.

The worship of the emperor. Every one was required to join in the worship of the emperor because he stood for the majesty of the Roman dominion. The inhabitants of each province might revere their particular gods, undisturbed by the government, but all were obliged as good citizens to join in the official sacrifices to the deified head of the state. The early Christians were persecuted, not only because their religion was different from that of their fellows, but because they refused to offer homage to the image of the emperor and openly prophesied the downfall of the Roman state. Their religion was incompatible with what was then deemed good citizenship, inasmuch as it forbade them to express the required veneration for the government.

As there was one government, so there was one law for all the civilized world. Local differences were not considered; the same principles of reason, justice, and humanity were believed to hold whether the Roman citizen lived upon the Euphrates or the Thames. The law of the Roman Empire is its chief legacy to posterity. Its provisions are still in force in many of the states of Europe to-day, and it is one of the subjects of study in our American universities. It exhibited a humanity unknown to the earlier legal codes. The wife, mother, and infant were protected from the arbitrary power of the head of the house, who, in earlier centuries, had been privileged to treat the members of his family as slaves. It held that it was better that a guilty person should escape than that an innocent person should be condemned. It conceived humanity, not as a group of nations and tribes, each with its peculiar institutions and legal customs, but as one people included in one great empire and subject to a single system of law based upon reason and equity.

The Roman law.

A Fortified Roman Gateway at Treves

Roads and
public works.

Magnificent roads were constructed, which enabled the messengers of the government and its armies to reach every part of the Empire with incredible speed. These highways made commerce easy and encouraged merchants and travelers to visit the most distant portions of the realm. Everywhere they found the same coins and the same system of weights and measures. Colonies were sent out to the confines of the Empire, and the remains of great public buildings, of theaters and bridges, of sumptuous villas and baths at places like Treves, Cologne, Bath, and Salzburg indicate how thoroughly the influence and civilization of Rome penetrated to the utmost parts of the territory subject to her rule.

The same
culture
throughout
the Roman
Empire.

The government encouraged education by supporting at least three teachers in every town of any considerable importance. They taught rhetoric and oratory and explained the works of the great writers. The Romans, who had no marked literary or artistic ability, had adopted the culture of the Greeks. This was spread abroad by the government teachers so that an educated man was pretty sure to find, even in the outlying parts of the great Empire, other educated men with much the same interests and ideas as his own. Everywhere men felt themselves to be not mere natives of this or that land but citizens of the world.

Loyalty to
the Empire
and convic-
tion that it
was eternal.

During the four centuries from the first emperor, Augustus, to the barbarian invasions we hear of no attempt on the part of its subjects to overthrow the Empire or to secede from it. The Roman state, it was universally believed, was to endure forever. Had a rebellious nation succeeded in throwing off the rule of the emperor and establishing its independence, it would only have found itself outside the civilized world.

Reasons why
the Empire
lost its power
to defend
itself against
the Germans.

5. Just why the Roman government, once so powerful and so universally respected, finally became unable longer to defend its borders and gave way before the scattered attacks of the German peoples, who never combined in any general alliance against it, is a very difficult question to answer satisfactorily. The inhabitants of the Empire appear gradually to have lost their energy and self-reliance and to have become less and less prosperous. This may be explained partially at least by the following considerations : (1) the terrible system of taxation, which discouraged and not infrequently ruined the members of the wealthier classes; (2) the existence of slavery, which served to discredit honest labor and demoralized the free workingmen ; (3) the steady decrease of population ; (4) the infiltration of barbarians, who prepared the way for the conquest of the western portion of the Empire by their fellow-barbarians.

It required a great deal of money to support the luxurious **Oppressive taxation.** court of the emperors and their innumerable officials and servants, and to supply " bread and circuses " for the populace of the towns. All sorts of taxes and exactions were consequently devised by ingenious officials to make up the necessary revenue. The crushing burden of the great land tax, the emperor's chief source of income, was greatly increased by the pernicious way in which it was collected. The government made a group of the richer citizens in each of the towns permanently responsible for the whole amount due from all the landowners within their district. It was their business to collect the taxes and make up any deficiency, it mattered not from what cause. This responsibility and the weight of the taxes themselves ruined so many landowners that the government was forced to decree that no one should desert his estates in order to escape the exactions. Only the very rich could stand the drain on their resources. The middle class sank into poverty and despair, and in this way the Empire lost just that prosperous class of citizens who should have been the leaders in business enterprises.

The sad plight of the poorer laboring classes was largely **Slavery.** due to the terrible institution of slavery which prevailed everywhere in ancient times. So soon as the Romans had begun to conquer distant provinces the number of slaves greatly increased. For six or seven centuries before the barbarian invasions every kind of labor fell largely into their hands in both country and town. There were millions of them. A single rich landholder might own hundreds and even thousands, and it was a poor man that did not have several at least.

The villa. Land was the only highly esteemed form of wealth in the Roman Empire, in spite of the heavy taxes imposed upon it. Without large holdings of land no one could hope to enjoy a high social position or an honorable office under the government. Consequently the land came gradually into the hands of the rich and ambitious, and the small landed proprietor disappeared. Great estates called *villas* covered Italy, Gaul, and Britain. These were cultivated and managed by armies of slaves, who not only tilled the land, but supplied their master, his household, and themselves with all that was needed on the plantation. The artisans among them made the tools, garments, and other manufactured articles necessary for the whole community, or "family," as it was called. Slaves cooked the food, waited on the proprietor, wrote his letters, and read to him. To a head slave the whole management of the villa was intrusted. A villa might be as extensive as a large village, but all its members were under the absolute control of the proprietor of the estate. A well-organized villa could supply itself with everything that it needed, and found little or no reason for buying from any outsider.

Slavery brings labor into disrepute. Quite naturally, freemen came to scorn all manual labor and even trade, for these occupations were associated in their minds with the despised slave. Seneca, the philosopher, angrily rejects the suggestion that the practical arts were invented by a philosopher; they were, he declares, "thought out by the meanest bondman."

Slavery did more than bring manual labor into disrepute ; it largely monopolized the market. Each great household where articles of luxury were in demand relied upon its own host of dexterous and efficient slaves to produce them. Moreover, the owners of slaves frequently hired them out to those who needed workmen, or permitted them to work for wages, and in this way brought them into a competition with the free workman which was fatal to him. *Competition of slaves fatal to the freeman.*

It cannot be denied that a notable improvement in the condition of the slaves took place during the centuries immediately preceding the barbarian invasions. Their owners abandoned the horrible subterranean prisons in which the farm hands were once miserably huddled at night. The law, moreover, protected the slave from some of the worst forms of abuse ; first and foremost, it deprived his master of the right to kill him. Slaves began to decrease in numbers before the German invasions. In the first place, the supply had been cut off after the Roman armies ceased to conquer new territory. In the second place, masters had for various reasons begun to emancipate their slaves on a large scale. *Improved condition of the slaves and their emancipation.*

The freed slave was called a *freedman*, and was by no means in the position of one who was born free. It is true that he was no longer a chattel, a mere thing, but he had still to serve his former master,—who had now become his patron,—for a certain number of days in the year. He was obliged to pay him a part of his earnings and could not marry without his patron's consent. *The freedman.*

Yet, as the condition of the slaves improved, and many of them became freedmen, the state of the poor freeman only became worse. In the towns, if he tried to earn his living, he was forced to mingle with those slaves who were permitted to work for wages and with the freedmen, and he naturally tended to sink to their level. In the country the free agricultural laborers became *coloni*, a curious intermediate class, neither slave nor really free. They were bound to the particular bit *The coloni.*

of land which some great proprietor permitted them to cultivate and were sold with it if it changed hands. Like the

mediæval *serf*, they could not be deprived of their fields so long as they paid the owner a certain part of their crop and worked for him during a period fixed by the customs of the domain upon which they lived. This system made it impossible for the farmer to become independent, or for his son to be better off than he. The coloni and the more fortunate slaves tended to fuse into a single class; for the law provided that, like the coloni, certain classes of country slaves were not to be taken from the field which they had been accustomed to cultivate but were to go with it if it was sold.[1]

Moreover, it often happened that the Roman proprietor had a number of dependents among the less fortunate landowners in his neighborhood. These, in order to escape the taxes and gain his protection as the times became more disorderly, surrendered their land to their powerful neighbor with the understanding that he should defend them and permit them to continue during their lifetime to cultivate the fields, the title to which had passed to him. On their death their children became coloni. This arrangement, as we shall find, serves in a measure to explain the feudalism of later times.

When a country is prosperous the population tends to increase. In the Roman Empire, even as early as Augustus, a falling off in numbers was apparent, which was bound to sap the vitality of the state. War, plague, the evil results of slavery, and the outrageous taxation all combined to hasten the depopulation; for when it is hard to make a living, men are deterred from marrying and find it difficult to bring up large families.

In order to replenish the population great numbers of the Germans were encouraged to settle within the Empire, where they became coloni. Constantine is said to have called in

1 There is a short description of Roman society in Hodgkin, *Dynasty of Theodosius*, Chapter II.

three hundred thousand of a single people. Barbarians were enlisted in the Roman legions to keep out their fellow-Germans. Julius Cæsar was the first to give them a place among his soldiers. The expedient became more and more common, until, finally, whole armies were German, entire tribes being enlisted under their own chiefs. Some of the Germans rose to be distinguished generals; others attained important positions among the officials of the government. In this way it came about that a great many of the inhabitants of the Roman Empire were Germans before the great invasions. The line dividing the Roman and the barbarian was growing indistinct. It is not unreasonable to suppose that the influx of barbarians smoothed the way for the break-up of the western part of the Empire. Although they had a great respect for the Roman state, they must have kept some of their German love of individual liberty and could have had little sympathy for the despotism under which they lived.

6. As the Empire declined in strength and prosperity and was gradually permeated by the barbarians, its art and literature fell far below the standard of the great writers and artists of the golden age of Augustus. The sculpture of Constantine's time was far inferior to that of Trajan's. Cicero's exquisitely finished style lost its charm for the readers of the fourth and fifth centuries, and a florid, inferior species of oratory took its place. Tacitus, who died about A.D. 120, is perhaps the latest of the Latin authors whose works may be ranked among the classics. No more great men of letters arose. Few of those who understand and enjoy Latin literature to-day would think of reading any of the poetry or prose written after the beginning of the second century. *Decline of literature and art.*

During the three hundred years before the invasions those who read at all did not ordinarily take the trouble to study the classics, but relied upon mere collections of quotations; and for what they called science, upon compendiums and manuals. *Reliance upon mere compendiums.*

These the Middle Ages inherited, and it was not until the time of Petrarch, in the fourteenth century, that Europe once more reached a degree of cultivation which enabled the more discriminating scholars to appreciate the best productions of the great authors of antiquity, both Greek and Latin.[1]

Preparation for Christianity. In spite of the general decline of which we have been speaking, the Roman world appeared to be making progress in one important respect. During the first and second centuries a sort of moral revival took place and a growing religious enthusiasm showed itself, which prepared the way for the astonishingly rapid introduction of the new Christian religion. Some of the pagan philosophers had quite given up the old idea which we find in Homer and Virgil, that there were many gods, and had reached an elevated conception of the one God and of our duty toward Him. "Our duty," writes the philosopher Epictetus at the end of the first century, "is to follow God, . . . to be of one mind with Him, to devote ourselves to the performance of His commands." The emperor Marcus Aurelius (d. 180) expresses similar sentiments in his *Meditations*,[2] the notes which he wrote for his own guidance. There was a growing abhorrence for the notorious vices of the great cities, and an ever-increasing demand for pure and upright conduct. The pagan religions taught that the souls of the dead continued to exist in Hades ; but the life to come was believed to be a dreary existence at best.

Promises of Christianity. Christianity brought with it a new hope for all those who would escape from the bondage of sin, of which the serious-minded were becoming more and more conscious. It promised, moreover, eternal happiness after death to all who would consistently strive to do right. It appealed to the desires and needs of all kinds of men and women. For every one who

[1] Reference, Adams, *Civilization during the Middle Ages*, Chapter II, "What the Middle Ages started with."

[2] There are a number of editions of this work in English, and selections from Epictetus are issued by several publishers. See *Readings*, Chapter II.

accepted the Gospel might look forward in the next world to such joy as he could never hope to experience in this.

The new religion, as it spread from Palestine among the Gentiles, was much modified by the religious ideas of those who accepted it. A group of Christian philosophers, who are known as the early fathers, strove to show that the Gospel was in accord with the aspirations of the best of the pagans. In certain ceremonies the former modes of worship were accepted by the new religion. From simple beginnings the church developed a distinct priesthood and an elaborate service. In this way Christianity and the higher forms of paganism tended to come nearer and nearer to each other as time went on. In one sense, it is true, they met like two armies in mortal conflict; but at the same time they tended to merge into one another like two streams which had been following converging courses. At the confluence of the streams stands Boethius (d. about 524), the most gifted of the later Roman writers. His beautiful book, *The Consolation of Philosophy*, was one of the most popular works during the Middle Ages, when every one believed that its author was a Christian.[1] Yet there is nothing in the book to indicate that he was more than a religious pagan, and some scholars doubt if he ever fully accepted the new religion.

Christianity and paganism tend to merge into one another.

Boethius

7. We learn from the letters of St. Paul that the earliest Christian communities found it necessary to have some organization. They chose certain officers, the bishops — that is to say, overseers — and the presbyters or elders, but St. Paul does not tell us exactly what were the duties of these officers. There were also the deacons, who appear to have had the care of the poor of the community. The first Christians looked for the speedy coming of Christ before their own generation should pass away. Since all were filled with enthusiasm for the Gospel and eagerly awaited the last day, they did not feel the need of an elaborate constitution. But as time went on

The primitive, or apostolic, church.

[1] There is an English translation of this published by Stock ($1.20).

the Christian communities greatly increased in size, and many joined them who had little or none of the original fervor and spirituality. It became necessary to develop a regular system of church government in order to control the erring and expel those who brought disgrace upon their religion by notoriously bad conduct.

The 'Catholic,' or universal, Church.

A famous little book, *The Unity of the Church*, by Bishop Cyprian (d. 258) gives us a pretty good idea of the Church a few decades before the Christian religion was legalized by Constantine. This and other sources indicate that the followers of Christ had already come to believe in a " Catholic " — i.e., a universal — Church which embraced all the communities of true believers wherever they might be. To this one universal Church all must belong who hoped to be saved.[1]

Organization of the Church before Constantine.

A sharp distinction was already made between the officers of the Church, who were called the *clergy*, and the people; or *laity*. To the clergy was committed the government of the Church as well as the instruction of its members. In each of the Roman cities was a bishop, and at the head of the country communities, a priest (Latin, *presbyter*), who had succeeded to the original elders (presbyters) mentioned in the New Testament. Below the bishop and the priest were the lower orders of the clergy, — the deacon and subdeacon, — and below these the so-called minor orders — the acolyte, exorcist, reader, and doorkeeper. The bishop exercised a certain control over the priests within his territory. It was not unnatural that the bishops in the chief towns of the Roman provinces should be especially influential in church affairs. They came to be

---

[1] Whoever separates himself from the Church, writes Cyprian, is separated from the promises of the Church. " He is an alien, he is profane, he is an enemy, he can no longer have God for his father who has not the Church for his mother. If anyone could escape who was outside the Ark of Noah, so also may he escape who shall be outside the bounds of the Church." See *Readings in European History*, Chapter II.

called *archbishops*, and might summon the bishops of the province to a council to decide important matters.

In 311 the emperor Galerius issued a decree placing the Christian religion upon the same legal footing as paganism. Constantine, the first Christian emperor, carefully enforced this edict. In 325 the first general council of Christendom was called together under his auspices at Nicæa. It is clear from the decrees of this famous assembly that the Catholic Church had already assumed the form that it was to retain down to the present moment, except that there is no explicit recognition of the Bishop of Rome as the head of the whole church. Nevertheless, there were a number of reasons — to be discussed later — why the Bishop of Rome should sometime become the acknowledged ruler of western Christendom. The first of the Roman bishops to play a really important part in authentic history was Leo the Great, who did not take office until 440.[1]

The first general council, 325. Position of the Bishop of Rome during this period.

Constantine's successors soon forbade pagan practices and began to issue laws which gave the Christian clergy important privileges. In the last book of the Theodosian Code, a great collection of the laws of the Empire, which was completed in 438, all the imperial decrees are to be found which relate to the Christian Church and the clergy. We find that the clergy, in view of their holy duties, were exempted from certain onerous offices and from some of the taxes which the laity had to pay. They were also permitted to receive bequests. The emperors themselves richly endowed the Church. Their example was followed by rulers and private individuals all through the Middle Ages, so that the Church became incredibly wealthy and enjoyed a far greater income than any state of Europe. The clergy were permitted to try certain cases at law, and they themselves had the privilege of being tried in their own church courts for minor criminal offenses. This

The Church in the Theodosian Code.

[1] Reference, Adams, *Civilization*, Chapter III, "The Addition of Christianity."

last book of the Code begins with a definition of the Trinity; and much space is given to a description of the different kinds of unbelievers and the penalties attached to a refusal to accept the religion of the government.[1]

The Church survives the Empire.

In these provisions of the Theodosian Code the later mediæval Church is clearly foreshadowed. The imperial government in the West was soon overthrown by the barbarian conquerors, but the Catholic Church conquered and absorbed the conquerors. When the officers of the Empire deserted their posts the bishops stayed to meet the oncoming invader. They continued to represent the old civilization and ideas of order. It was the Church that kept the Latin language alive among those who knew only a rude German dialect. It was the Church that maintained some little education in even the darkest period of confusion, for without the ability to read Latin its services could not have been performed and its officers could not have carried on their correspondence with one another.

The Eastern Empire.

8. Although the Roman Empire remained one in law, government, and culture until the Germans came in sufficient force to conquer the western portions of it, a tendency may nevertheless be noticed some time before the conquest for the eastern and western portions to drift apart. Constantine, who established his supremacy only after a long struggle with his rivals, hoped to strengthen the vast state by establishing a second capital, which should lie far to the east and dominate a region very remote from Rome. Constantinople was accordingly founded in 330 on the confines of Europe and Asia.[2] This was by no means supposed to destroy the unity of the Empire. Even when Theodosius the Great arranged (395) that both his sons should succeed him, and that one should

[1] See *Readings in European History*, Chapter II, for extracts from the Theodosian Code.

[2] An older town called Byzantium was utilized by Constantine as the basis of his new imperial city.

rule in the West and one in the East, he did not intend to divide the Empire. It is true that there continued to be thereafter two emperors, each in his own capital, but they were supposed to govern one empire conjointly and in "unanimity." New laws were to be accepted by both. The writers of the time do not speak of two states but continue to refer to "the Empire," as if the administration were still in the hands of one ruler. Indeed the idea of one government for all civilized mankind did not pass away but continued to influence men during the whole of the Middle Ages.

Although it was in the eastern part of the Empire that the barbarians first got a permanent foothold, the emperors at Constantinople were able to keep a portion of the old possessions of the Empire under their rule for centuries after the Germans had completely conquered the West. When at last the eastern capital of the Empire fell, it was not into the hands of the Germans, but into those of the Turks, who have held it since 1453.

There will be no room in this volume to follow the history of the Eastern Empire, although it cannot be entirely ignored in studying western Europe. Its language and civilization had always been Greek, and owing to this and the influence of the Orient, its culture offers a marked contrast to that of the Latin West, which was adopted by the Germans. Learning never died out in the East as it did in the West, nor did art reach so low an ebb.

For some centuries after the disruption of the Roman Empire in the West, the capital of the Eastern Empire enjoyed the distinction of being the largest and most wealthy city of Europe. Within its walls could be found the indications of a refinement and civilization which had almost disappeared in the Occident. Its beautiful buildings, its parks and paved streets, filled the traveler from the West with astonishment. When, during the Crusades, the western

Constantinople the most wealthy and populous city of Europe during the early Middle Ages.

peoples were brought into contact with the learning and culture of Constantinople they were greatly and permanently impressed by them.

General Reading. — For an outline of the history of the Roman Empire during the centuries immediately preceding the barbarian invasions, see BOTSFORD, *History of Rome*, WEST, *Ancient History to the Death of Charlemagne*, MYERS, *Rome: Its Rise and Fall*, or MOREY, *Outlines of Roman History*, — all with plenty of references to larger works on the subject. The best work in English on the conditions in the Empire upon the eve of the invasions is DILL, *Roman Society in the Last Century of the Western Empire* (Macmillan, $2.00). HATCH, *The Influence of Greek Thought upon the Christian Church* (Williams & Norgate, $1.00), and RENAN, *The Influence of Rome on the Development of the Catholic Church* (Williams & Norgate, $1.00), are very important for the advanced student. The best of the numerous editions of Gibbon's great work, *The Decline and Fall of the Roman Empire*, which covers the whole history of the Middle Ages, is that edited by Bury (The Macmillan Company, 7 vols., $14.00).

CHAPTER III

THE GERMAN INVASIONS AND THE BREAK-UP OF THE ROMAN EMPIRE

9. Previous to the year 375 the attempts of the Germans to penetrate into the Empire appear to have been due to their love of adventure, their hope of enjoying some of the advantages of their civilized neighbors, or the need of new lands for their increasing numbers. And the Romans, by means of their armies, their walls, and their guards, had up to this time succeeded in preventing the barbarians from violently occupying their territory. But suddenly a new force appeared which thrust the Germans out upon the weakened Empire. The Huns, a Mongolian folk from central Asia, swept down upon the Goths, who were a German tribe settled upon the Danube, and forced a part of them to seek shelter across the river, within the boundaries of the Empire. Here they soon fell out with the imperial officials, and a great battle was fought at Adrianople in 378 in which the Goths defeated and slew the emperor, Valens. The Germans had now not only broken through the boundaries of the Empire, but they had also learned that they could defeat the Roman legions. The battle of Adrianople may, therefore, be said to mark the beginning of the conquest of the western part of the Empire by the Germans. For some years, however, after the battle of Adrianople the various bands of West Goths — or Visigoths, as they are often called — were induced to accept the terms offered by the emperor's officials and some of the Goths agreed to serve as soldiers in the Roman armies.

25

Alaric takes
Rome, 410.

Before long one of the German chieftains, Alaric, became dissatisfied with the treatment that he received. He collected an army, of which the nucleus consisted of West Goths, and set out for Italy. Rome fell into his hands in 410 and was plundered by his followers. Alaric appears to have been deeply impressed by the sight of the civilization about him. He did not destroy the city, hardly even did serious damage to it, and he gave especial orders to his soldiers not to injure the churches or take their property.[1]

West Goths
settle in
southern
Gaul and
Spain.

Alaric died before he could find a satisfactory spot for his people to settle upon permanently. After his death the West Goths wandered into Gaul, and then into Spain, which had already been occupied by other barbarian tribes, — the Vandals and Suevi. These had crossed the Rhine into Gaul four years before Alaric took Rome ; for three years they devastated the country and then proceeded across the Pyrenees. When the West Goths reached Spain they quickly concluded peace with the Roman government. They then set to work to fight the Vandals, with such success that the emperor granted them a considerable district (419) in southern Gaul, where they established a West Gothic kingdom. Ten years after, the Vandals moved on into Africa, where they founded a kingdom and extended their control over the western Mediterranean. Their place in Spain was taken by the West Goths who, under their king, Euric (466–484), conquered a great part of the peninsula,

---

[1] St. Augustine, who was then living, gives us an idea of the impression that the capture of Rome made upon the minds of contemporaries, in an extraordinary work of his called *The City of God*. He undertakes to refute the argument of the pagans that the fall of the city was due to the anger of their old gods, who were believed to have withdrawn their protection on account of the insults heaped upon them by the Christians, who regarded them as demons. He points out that the gods whom Æneas had brought, according to tradition, from Troy had been unable to protect the city from its enemies and asks why any reliance should be placed upon them when transferred to Italian soil. His elaborate refutation of pagan objections shows us that heathen beliefs still had a strong hold upon an important part of the population and that the question of the truth or falsity of the pagan religion was still a living one in Italy.

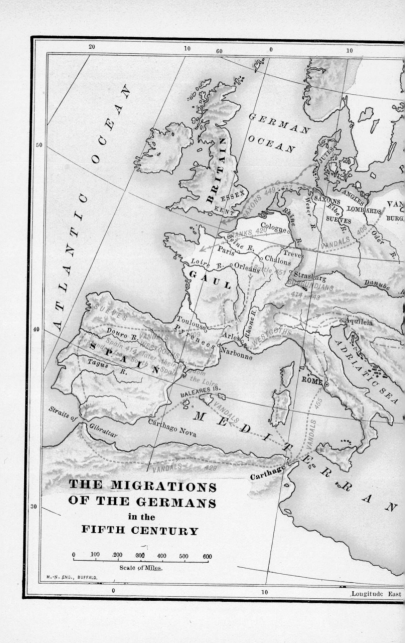

THE MIGRATIONS
OF THE GERMANS
in the
FIFTH CENTURY

Scale of Miles.

0   100   200   300   400   500   600

M.·N. ENG., BUFFALO.

Longitude East

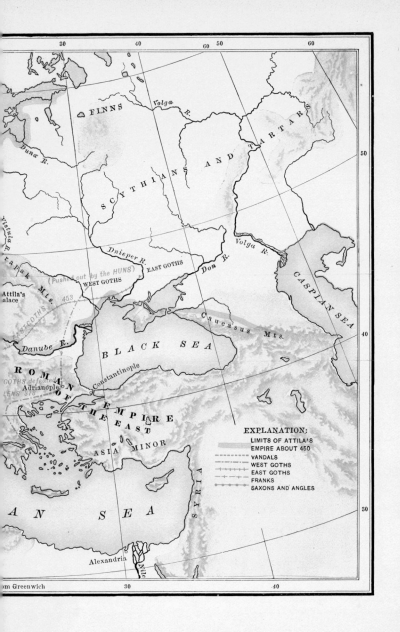

FINNS

Volga R.

SCYTHIANS AND TARTARS

Dunæ R.

50

Vistula R.

Dnieper R.

Rapak Mts.

(Pushed out by the HUNS)

WEST GOTHS   EAST GOTHS

Don R.

Volga R.

CASPIAN SEA

Attila's
Palace

453

EASTGOTHS

40

Danube R.

Caucasus Mts.

BLACK SEA

ROMAN

GOTHS defeated

Constantinople

LENS 378

Adrianople

OF

THE

EMPIRE

THE EAST

ASIA MINOR

EXPLANATION:

LIMITS OF ATTILA'S
EMPIRE ABOUT 450
VANDALS
WEST GOTHS
EAST GOTHS
FRANKS
SAXONS AND ANGLES

AN   SEA

S Y R I A

30

Alexandria

Nile

pretty much at their pleasure, and the German troops in the service of the Empire amused themselves setting up and throwing down puppet emperors.   In 476 the German mercenaries in the Roman army demanded that a third part of Italy be

Odoacer.   given to them.   On the refusal of this demand, Odoacer, their leader, banished the last of the western emperors (whose name was, by the irony of fate, Romulus Augustus the Little) to a villa near Naples.   Then Odoacer sent the insignia of empire to the eastern emperor with the request that he be permitted to rule Italy as the emperor's delegate, thus putting an end to the line of the western emperors.[1]

Theodoric conquers Odoacer and establishes the kingdom of the East Goths in Italy.   It was not, however, given to Odoacer to establish an enduring German kingdom on Italian soil, for he was conquered by the great Theodoric, the king of the East Goths (or Ostrogoths).   Theodoric had spent ten years of his early youth in Constantinople and had thus become familiar with Roman life.   Since his return to his people he had been alternately a dangerous enemy and an embarrassing friend to the eastern emperor.   The East Goths, under his leadership, had harassed and devastated various parts of the Eastern Empire, and had once threatened the capital itself.   The emperor had repeatedly conciliated him by conferring upon him various honors and titles and by making large grants of money and land to his people.   It must have been a great relief to the government when Theodoric determined to lead his people to Italy against Odoacer.   "If I fail," Theodoric said to the emperor, " you will be relieved of an expensive and troublesome friend ; if, with the divine permission, I succeed, I shall govern in your name and to your glory, the Roman Senate and that part of the Empire delivered from slavery by my victorious arms."

The struggle between Theodoric and Odoacer lasted for several years, but Odoacer was finally shut up in Ravenna and

[1] Reference, Oman, *Dark Ages*, Chapter I.

surrendered, only to be treacherously slain a few days later by Theodoric's own hand (493).[1]

The attitude of the East Goths toward the people already in possession of the land and toward the Roman culture is significant. Theodoric put the name of the eastern emperor on the coins that he issued and did everything in his power to insure the emperor's approval of the new German kingdom. ^{The East Goths in Italy.}

Interior of a Church at Ravenna, built in Theodoric's Time

Nevertheless, although he desired that the emperor should sanction his usurpation, Theodoric had no idea of being really subordinate to Constantinople.

The invaders appropriated one third of the land for themselves, but this was done with discretion and no disorder appears to have resulted. Theodoric maintained the Roman laws and institutions, which he greatly admired. The old offices and titles were retained, and Goth and Roman lived

[1] Reference, Oman, *Dark Ages*, Chapter II.

under the same Roman law. Order was restored and learning encouraged. In Ravenna, which Theodoric chose for his capital, beautiful buildings that date from his reign still exist.

The East Goths were Arian heretics.

On his death in 526, Theodoric left behind him an admirably organized state, but it had one conspicuous weakness. The Goths, although Christians, were unorthodox according to the standard of the Italian Christians. They had been converted by eastern missionaries, who taught them the Arian heresy earlier prevalent at Constantinople. This doctrine, which derived its name from Arius, a presbyter of Alexandria (d. 336), had been condemned by the Council of Nicæa. The followers of Arius did not have the same conception of Christ's nature and of the relations of the three members of the Trinity as that sanctioned at Rome. The East Goths were, therefore, not only barbarians,—which might have been forgiven them,—but were guilty, in the eyes of the orthodox Italians, of the unpardonable offense of heresy. Theodoric himself was exceptionally tolerant for his times. His conviction that "we cannot command in matters of religion because no one can be compelled to believe against his will," showed a spirit alien to the traditions of the Roman Empire and the Roman Church, which represented the orthodox belief.

The German kingdoms of Theodoric's time.

11. While Theodoric had been establishing his kingdom in Italy with such enlightenment and moderation, what is now France was coming under the control of the most powerful of the barbarian peoples, the Franks, who were to play a more important rôle in the formation of modern Europe than any of the other German races. Besides the kingdoms of the East Goths and the Franks, the West Goths had their kingdom in Spain, the Burgundians had established themselves on the Rhone, and the Vandals in Africa. Royal alliances were concluded between the reigning houses of these nations, and for the first time in the history of Europe we see something like a family of nations, living each within its own boundaries and

dealing with one another as independent powers.   It seemed for
a few years as if the process of assimilation between Germans
and Romans was going to make rapid progress without
involving any considerable period of disorder and retrogression.

Map of Europe in the Time of Theodoric

But no such good fortune was in store for Europe, which   Extinction
was now only at the beginning of the turmoil from which it   of Latin
                                                             literature.
was to emerge almost completely barbarized.   Science, art, and
literature could find no foothold in the shifting political sands
of the following centuries.   Boethius,[1] whom Theodoric put   Boethius.
to death (in 524 or 525) for alleged treasonable correspondence

1 See above, p. 19.

with the emperor, was the last Latin writer who can be compared in any way with the classical authors in his style and mastery of the language. He was a scholar as well as a poet, and his treatises on logic, music, etc., were highly esteemed by following generations.

Cassiodorus and his manuals. Theodoric's distinguished Roman counselor, Cassiodorus (d. 575), to whose letters we owe a great part of our knowledge of the period, busied himself in his old age in preparing textbooks of the liberal arts and sciences, — grammar, arithmetic, logic, geometry, rhetoric, music, and astronomy. His manuals were intended to give the uninstructed priests a sufficient preparation for the study of the Bible and of the doctrines of the Church. His absurdly inadequate and, to us, silly treatment of these seven important subjects, to which he devotes a few pages each, enables us to estimate the low plane to which learning had fallen in Italy in the sixth century. Yet his books were regarded as standard treatises in these great fields of knowledge all through the Middle Ages. So mediæval Europe owed these, and other text-books upon which she was dependent for her knowledge, to the period when Latin culture was coming to an end.

Scarcely any writers in western Europe during the sixth, seventh, and eighth centuries. A long period of gloom now begins. Between the time of Theodoric and that of Charlemagne three hundred years elapsed, during which scarcely a writer was to be found who could compose, even in the worst of Latin, a chronicle of the events of his day.[1] Everything conspired to discourage education. The great centers of learning — Carthage, Rome, Alexandria, Milan — were partially destroyed by the barbarians or the Arabs. The libraries which had been kept in the temples of the gods were often annihilated, along with the pagan shrines, by Christian enthusiasts, who were not sorry to see the heathen literature disappear with the heathen religion. Shortly after Theodoric's death the eastern emperor withdrew the support

[1] See *Readings*, Chapter III (end), for historical writings of this period.

which the government had hitherto granted to public teachers and closed the great school at Athens. The only important historian of the sixth century was the half-illiterate Gregory, Bishop of Tours (d. 594), whose whole work is unimpeachable evidence of the sad state of intellectual affairs. He at least heartily appreciated his own ignorance and exclaims, in incorrect Latin, "Woe to our time, for the study of letters has perished from among us."

12. The year after Theodoric's death one of the greatest of the emperors of the East, Justinian (527–565), came to the throne at Constantinople.[1] He undertook to regain for the Empire the provinces in Africa and Italy that had been occupied by the Vandals and East Goths. His general, Belisarius, overthrew the Vandal kingdom in northern Africa in 534, but it was a more difficult task to destroy the Gothic rule in Italy. However, in spite of a brave defense, the Goths were so completely defeated in 553 that they agreed to leave Italy with all their movable possessions. What became of the remnants of the race we do not know. They had been too few to maintain their control over the mass of the Italians, who were ready, with a religious zeal which cost them dear, to open their gates to the hostile armies of Justinian. *Justinian destroys the kingdoms of the Vandals and the East Goths.*

The destruction of the Gothic kingdom was a disaster for Italy. Immediately after the death of Justinian the country was overrun anew, by the Lombards, the last of the great German peoples to establish themselves within the bounds of the former Empire. They were a savage race, a considerable part of which was still pagan, and the Arian Christians among them appear to have been as hostile to the Roman Church as their unconverted fellows. The newcomers first occupied the region north of the Po, which has ever since been called Lombardy after them, and then extended their conquests southward. *The Lombards occupy Italy.*

[1] For Justinian, who scarcely comes into our story, see Oman, *Dark Ages*, Chapters V–VI.

Instead of settling themselves with the moderation and wise statesmanship of the East Goths, the Lombards chose to move about the peninsula pillaging and massacring. Such of the inhabitants as could, fled to the islands off the coast. The Lombards were unable, however, to conquer all of Italy. Rome, Ravenna, and southern Italy continued to be held by the Greek empire. As time went on, the Lombards lost their wildness, accepted the orthodox form of Christianity, and gradually assimilated the civilization of the people among whom they lived. Their kingdom lasted over two hundred years, until it was overthrown by Charlemagne.

The Franks; their importance and their method of conquest.

13. None of the German peoples of whom we have so far spoken, except the Franks, ever succeeded in establishing a permanent kingdom. Their states were overthrown in turn by some other German nation, by the Eastern Empire, or, in the case of the West-Gothic kingdom in Spain, by the Mohammedans. The Franks, to whom we must now turn, were destined not only to conquer most of the other German tribes but even to extend their boundaries into districts inhabited by the Slavs.

When the Franks are first heard of in history they were settled along the lower Rhine, from Cologne to the North Sea. Their method of getting a foothold in the Empire was essentially different from that which the Goths, Lombards, and Vandals had adopted. Instead of severing their connection with Germany and becoming an island in the sea of the Empire, they conquered by degrees the territory about them. However far they might extend their control, they remained in constant touch with the barbarian reserves behind them. In this way they retained the warlike vigor that was lost by the races who were completely surrounded by the enervating influences of Roman civilization.

In the early part of the fifth century they had occupied the district which constitutes to-day the kingdom of Belgium, as well as the regions east of it. In 486, seven years before

Theodoric founded his Italian kingdom, they went forth under
their great king, Clovis (a name that later grew into Louis),
and defeated the Roman general who opposed them. They
extended their control over Gaul as far south as the Loire,
which at that time formed the northern boundary of the kingdom of the West Goths. Clovis then
enlarged his empire on the east by
the conquest of the Alemanni, a
German people living in the region
of the Black Forest.[1]

A Frankish Warrior

The battle in which the Alemanni
were defeated (496) is in one respect
important above all the other battles
of Clovis. Although still a pagan
himself, his wife was an orthodox
Christian convert. In the midst of
the conflict, as he saw his line giving
way, he called upon Jesus Christ and
pledged himself to be baptized in
His name if He would help the
Franks to victory over their enemies.
He kept his word and was baptized
together with three thousand of his
warriors. His conversion had the
most momentous consequences for
Europe. All the other German
peoples within the Empire were Christians, but they were
all Arian heretics; and to the orthodox Christians about
them they seemed worse than heathen. This religious difference had prevented the Germans and Romans from inter-
marrying and had retarded their fusion in other ways. But
with the conversion of Clovis, there was at least one barbarian
leader with whom the Bishop of Rome could negotiate as with

Conversion of Clovis, 496, and its consequences.

1 Reference, Oman, *Dark Ages*, Chapter IV.

a faithful son of the Church. It is from the orthodox Gregory of Tours that most of our knowledge of Clovis and his successors is derived. In Gregory's famous *History of the Franks,* the cruel and unscrupulous king appears as God's chosen instrument for the extension of the Catholic faith.[1] Certainly Clovis quickly learned to combine his own interests with those of the Church, and the alliance between the pope and the Frankish kings was destined to have a great influence upon the history of western Europe.

Conquests of Clovis. To the south of Clovis' new acquisitions in Gaul lay the kingdom of the Arian West Goths, to the southeast that of another heretical German people, the Burgundians. Gregory of Tours reports him as saying: "I cannot bear that these Arians should be in possession of a part of Gaul. Let us advance upon them with the aid of God ; after we have conquered them let us bring their realms into our power." So zealous was the newly converted king that he speedily extended his power to the Pyrenees, and forced the West Goths to confine themselves to the Spanish portion of their realm. The Burgundians became a tributary nation and soon fell completely under the rule of the Franks. Then Clovis, by a series of murders, brought portions of the Frankish nation itself, which had previously been independent of him, under his scepter.

Character of Frankish history. 14. When Clovis died in 511 at Paris, which he had made his residence, his four sons divided his possessions among them. Wars between rival brothers, interspersed with the most horrible murders, fill the annals of the Frankish kingdom for over a hundred years after the death of Clovis. Yet the nation continued to develop in spite of the unscrupulous deeds of its rulers. It had no enemies strong enough to assail it, and a certain unity was preserved in spite of the ever-shifting distribution of territory among the members of the royal house.[2]

[1] See *Readings,* Chapter III, for passages from Gregory of Tours.
[2] Reference, Emerton, *Introduction,* 68–72.

The Frankish kings succeeded in extending their power over pretty nearly all the territory that is included to-day in France, Belgium, and the Netherlands, as well as over a goodly portion of western Germany. By 555, when Bavaria had become tributary to the Frankish rulers, their dominions extended from the Bay of Biscay to a point east of Salzburg.

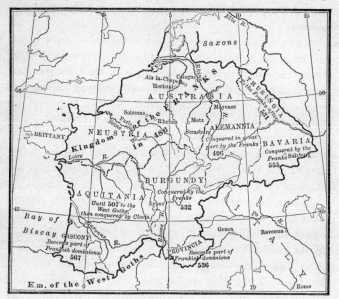

The Dominions of the Franks under the Merovingians

Considerable districts that the Romans had never succeeded in conquering had been brought into the developing civilization of western Europe.

As a result of the divisions of the Frankish lands, fifty years after the death of Clovis three Frankish kingdoms appear on the map. Neustria, the western kingdom, with its center at Paris or Soissons, was inhabited mainly by the older Romanized people among whom the Franks had settled. To the east was

Austrasia, with Metz and Aix-la-Chapelle as its chief cities. This region was completely German in its population. In these two there was the prophecy of the future France and Germany. Lastly, there was the old Burgundian realm. Of the Merovingian kings, as the line descended from Clovis was called, the last to rule as well as reign was Dagobert (d. 638), who united the whole Frankish territory once more under his scepter.

The Frankish nobility. A new danger, however, threatened the unity of the Frankish kingdom, namely, the aspirations of the powerful nobles. In the earliest accounts which we have of the Germans there appear to have been certain families who enjoyed a recognized preëminence over their companions. In the course of the various conquests there was a chance for the skillful leader to raise himself in the favor of the king. It was only natural that those upon whom the king relied to control distant parts of the realm should become dangerously ambitious and independent.

The Mayors of the Palace. Among the positions held by the nobility none was reputed more honorable than those near the king's person. Of these offices the most influential was that of the Major Domus, or Mayor of the Palace, who was a species of prime minister. After Dagobert's death these mayors practically ruled in the place of the Merovingian monarchs, who became mere " do-nothing kings," — *rois fainéants*, as the French call them. The Austrasian Mayor of the Palace, Pippin of Heristal, the great-grandfather of Charlemagne, succeeded in getting, in addition to Austrasia, both Neustria and Burgundy under his control. In this way he laid the foundation of his family's renown. Upon his death, in 714, his task of consolidating and defending the vast territories of the Franks devolved upon his more distinguished son, Charles Martel, i.e., the Hammer.[1]

Foundation of the power of Charlemagne's family, the so-called Carolingians.

1 Reference, Oman, *Dark Ages*, Chapter XV.

15. As one looks back over the German invasions it is natural to ask upon what terms the newcomers lived among the old inhabitants of the Empire, how far they adopted the customs of those among whom they settled, and how far they clung to their old habits? These questions cannot be answered very satisfactorily; so little is known of the confused period of which we have been speaking that it is impossible to follow closely the amalgamation of the two races. *Fusion of the barbarians and the Roman population.*

Yet a few things are tolerably clear. In the first place, we must be on our guard against exaggerating the numbers in the various bodies of invaders. The writers of the time indicate that the West Goths, when they were first admitted to the Empire before the battle of Adrianople, amounted to four or five hundred thousand persons, including men, women, and children. This is the largest band reported, and it must have been greatly reduced before the West Goths, after long wanderings and many battles, finally settled in Spain and southern Gaul. The Burgundians, when they appear for the first time on the banks of the Rhine, are reported to have had eighty thousand warriors among them. When Clovis and his army were baptized the chronicler speaks of " over three thousand " soldiers who became Christians upon that occasion. This would seem to indicate that the Frankish king had no larger force at this time. *The number of the barbarians.*

Undoubtedly these figures are very meager and unreliable. But the readiness with which the Germans appear to have adopted the language and customs of the Romans would tend to prove that the invaders formed but a small minority of the population. Since hundreds of thousands of barbarians had been assimilated during the previous five centuries, the great invasions of the fifth century can hardly have made an abrupt change in the character of the population.

The barbarians within the old empire were soon speaking the same conversational Latin which was everywhere used by *Contrast between spoken and written Latin.*

the Romans about them.[1] This was much simpler than the
elaborate and complicated language used in books, which we
find so much difficulty in learning nowadays. The speech of
the common people was gradually diverging more and more,
in the various countries of southern Europe, from the written
Latin, and finally grew into French, Spanish, Italian, and Portuguese. But the barbarians did not produce this change, for
it had begun before they came and would have gone on without them. They did no more than contribute a few convenient
words to the new languages.

The Germans appear to have had no dislike for the Romans
nor the Romans for them, except as long as the Germans
remained Arian Christians. Where there was no religious
barrier the two races intermarried freely from the first. The
Frankish kings did not hesitate to appoint Romans to important
positions in the government and in the army, just as the
Romans had long been in the habit of employing the barbarians.
In only one respect were the two races distinguished for a
time, — each had its particular law.

The Roman and the German law. The West Goths in the time of Euric were probably the
first to write down their ancient laws, using the Latin language.
Their example was followed by the Franks, the Burgundians, and
later by the Lombards and other peoples. These codes make up
the "Laws of the Barbarians," which form our most important
source of knowledge of the habits and ideas of the Germans
at the time of the invasions.[2] For several centuries following
the conquest, the members of the various German tribes appear
to have been judged by the laws of the particular people to

[1] The northern Franks, who did not penetrate far into the Empire, and the
Germans who remained in Germany proper and in Scandinavia, had of course
no reason for giving up their native tongues ; the Angles and Saxons in Britain
also adhered to theirs. These Germanic languages in time became Dutch, English,
German, Danish, Swedish, etc. Of this matter something will be said later.
See below, § 97.

[2] Extracts from the laws of the Salian Franks may be found in Henderson's
Historical Documents, pp. 176–189.

which they belonged. The older inhabitants of the Empire, on the contrary, continued to have their lawsuits decided according to the Roman law. This survived all through the Middle Ages in southern Europe, where the Germans were few. Elsewhere the Germans' more primitive ideas of law prevailed until the thirteenth or fourteenth century. A good example of these is the picturesque mediæval ordeal by which the guilt or innocence of a suspected person was determined.

The German laws did not provide for the trial, either in the Roman or the modern sense of the word, of a suspected person. There was no attempt to gather and weigh evidence and base the decision upon it. Such a mode of procedure was far too elaborate for the simple-minded Germans. Instead of a regular trial, one of the parties to the case was designated to prove that his assertions were true by one of the following methods: (1) He might solemnly swear that he was telling the truth and get as many other persons of his own class as the court required, to swear that they believed that he was telling the truth. This was called *compurgation*. It was believed that the divine vengeance would be visited upon those who swore falsely. (2) On the other hand, the parties to the case, or persons representing them, might meet in combat, on the supposition that Heaven would grant victory to the right. This was the so-called *wager of battle*. (3) Lastly, one or other of the parties might be required to submit to the *ordeal* in one of its various forms: He might plunge his arm into hot water, or carry a bit of hot iron for some distance, and if at the end of three days he showed no ill effects, the case was decided in his favor. He might be ordered to walk over hot plowshares, and if he was not burned, it was assumed that God had intervened by a miracle to establish the right.[1]

Mediæval trials.

[1] Professor Emerton gives an excellent account of the Germanic ideas of law in his *Introduction*, pp. 73–91; see also Henderson, *Short History of Germany*, pp. 19–21. For examples of the trials, see *Translations and Reprints*, Vol. IV, No. 4. A philosophical account of the character of the Germans and of the effects of the invasions is given by Adams, *Mediæval Civilization*, Chapters IV–V.

This method of trial is but one example of the rude civilization which displaced the refined and elaborate organization of the Romans.

16. The account which has been given of the conditions in the Roman Empire, and of the manner in which the barbarians occupied its western part, makes clear the great problem of the Middle Ages. The Germans, no doubt, varied a good deal in their habits and spirit. The Goths differed from the Lombards, and the Franks from the Vandals; but they all agreed in knowing nothing of the art, literature, and science which had been developed by the Greeks and adopted by the Romans. The invaders were ignorant, simple, vigorous people, with no taste for anything except fighting and bodily comfort. Such was the disorder that their coming produced, that the declining civilization of the Empire was pretty nearly submerged. The libraries, buildings, and works of art were destroyed and there was no one to see that they were restored. So the western world fell back into a condition similar to that in which it had been before the Romans conquered and civilized it.[1]

The loss was, however, temporary. The barbarians did not utterly destroy what they found, but utilized the ruins of the Roman Empire in their gradual construction of a new society. They received suggestions from the Roman methods of agriculture. When they reached a point where they needed them, they used the models offered by Roman roads and buildings. In short, the great heritage of skill and invention which had been slowly accumulated in Egypt, Phœnicia, and Greece, and which formed a part of the culture which the Romans diffused, did not wholly perish.

---

[1] Tacitus' *Germania*, which is our chief source for the German customs, is to be found in *Translations and Reprints*, Vol. VI, No. 3. For the habits of the invading Germans, see Henderson, *Short History of Germany*, pp. 1–11; Hodgkin, *Dynasty of Theodosius*, last half of Chapter II.

It required about a thousand years to educate the new race; but at last Europe, including districts never embraced in the Roman Empire, caught up once more with antiquity. When, in the fourteenth and fifteenth centuries, first Italy, and then the rest of Europe, awoke again to the beauty and truth of the classical literature and began to emulate the ancient art, the process of educating the barbarians may be said to have been completed. Yet the Middle Ages had been by no means a sterile period. They had added their part to the heritage of the West. From the union of two great elements, the ancient civilization, which was completely revived at the opening of the sixteenth century, and the vigor and the political and social ideals of the Germans, a new thing was formed, namely, our modern civilization.

Loss caused by the coming of the barbarians regained during Middle Ages.

General Reading. — By far the most exhaustive work in English upon the German invasions is HODGKIN, *Italy and her Invaders*, — very bulky and costly (8 vols., $36.50). The author has, however, given some of the results of his work in his excellent *Dynasty of Theodosius* (Clarendon Press, $1.50), and his *Theodoric the Goth* (G. P. Putnam's Sons, $1.50). SERGEANT, *The Franks* (G. P. Putnam's Sons, $1.50), gives more than is to be found on the subject in either Emerton or Oman.

CHAPTER IV

THE RISE OF THE PAPACY

The great-ness of the Church.

17. While the Franks were slowly developing the strength which Charlemagne employed to found the most extensive realm that has existed in Europe since the Roman Empire, another government, whose power was far greater, whose organization was far more perfect, and whose vitality was infinitely superior to that of the Frankish empire, namely, the Christian Church, was steadily extending its sway and establishing the foundations of its later supremacy.

We have already seen how marvelously the Christian communities founded by the apostles and their fellow-missionaries multiplied until, by the middle of the third century, writers like Cyprian came to conceive of a "Catholic," or all-embracing, Church. We have seen how Constantine first made Christianity legal, and how his successors worked in the interest of the new religion ; how carefully the Theodosian Code safeguarded the Church and the Christian clergy, and how harshly those were treated who ventured to hold another view of Christianity from that sanctioned by the government.[1]

We must now follow this most powerful and permanent of all the institutions of the later Roman Empire into the Middle Ages. We must stop a moment to consider the sources of its power, and then see how the Western, or Latin, portion of Christendom fell apart from the Eastern, or Greek, region and came to form a separate institution under the longest and mightiest line of rulers that the world has ever seen, the

[1] See above, § 7.

44

Roman bishops. We shall see how a peculiar class of Christians, the monks, developed; how they joined hands with the clergy; how the monks and the clergy met the barbarians, subdued and civilized them, and then ruled them for centuries.

The tremendous power of the Church in the Middle Ages was due, we may be sure, to the way in which it adapted itself to the ideas and needs of the time; for no institution can flourish unless it meets the wants of those who live under it.

Sources of the Church's power.

One great source of the Church's strength lay in the general fear of death and judgment to come, which Christianity had brought with it. The Greeks and Romans of the classical period thought of the next life, when they thought of it at all, as a very uninteresting existence compared with that on this earth. One who committed some signal crime might suffer for it after death with pains similar to those of the hell in which the Christians believed. But the great part of humanity were supposed to lead in the next world a shadowy existence, neither sad nor glad. Religion, even to the devout pagan, was mainly an affair of this life; the gods were to be propitiated with a view to present happiness and success.

Contrast between pagan and Christian ideas.

Since no satisfaction could be expected in the next life, it was naturally deemed wise to make the most of this one. The possibility of pleasure ends — so the poet Horace urges — when we join the shades below, as we all must do soon. Let us, therefore, take advantage of every harmless pleasure and improve our brief opportunity to enjoy the good things of earth. We should, however, be reasonable and temperate, avoiding all excess, for that endangers happiness. Above all, we should not worry uselessly about the future, which is in the hands of the gods and beyond our control. Such were the convictions of the majority of thoughtful pagans.

Christianity opposed this view of life with an entirely different one. It laid persistent emphasis upon man's existence after death, which it declared infinitely more important than

Other-worldliness of mediæval Christianity.

his brief sojourn in the body. Under the influence of the Church this conception of life had gradually supplanted the pagan one in the Roman world, and it was taught to the barbarians. The other-worldliness became so intense that thousands gave up their ordinary occupations and pleasures altogether, and devoted their entire attention to preparation for the next life. They shut themselves in lonely cells; and, not satisfied with giving up most of their natural pleasures, they inflicted bodily suffering upon themselves by hunger, cold, and stripes. They trusted that in this way they might avoid some of the sins into which they were prone to fall, and that, by self-inflicted punishment in this world, they might perchance escape some of that reserved for them in the next. As most of the writers and teachers of the Middle Ages belonged to this class of what may be called professional Christians, i.e., the monks, it was natural that their kind of life should have been regarded, even by those who continued to live in the world, as the ideal one for the earnest Christian.

The Church the one agent of salvation.
The barbarians were taught that their fate in the next world depended largely upon the Church. Its ministers never wearied of presenting the momentous alternative which faced every man so soon as this fleeting earthly existence should be over, — the alternative between eternal bliss and perpetual, unspeakable physical torment. Only those who had been duly baptized could hope to reach heaven; but baptism washed away only past sins and did not prevent constant relapse into new ones. These, unless their guilt was removed through the instrumentality of the Church, would surely drag the soul down to perdition.

Miracles a source of the Church's power.
The divine power of the Church was, furthermore, established in the eyes of the people by the miraculous works which her saints were constantly performing. They healed the sick and succored those in distress. They struck down with speedy and signal disaster those who opposed the Church or treated

her holy rites with contempt. To the reader of to-day the frequency of the miracles recorded in mediæval writings seems astonishing. The chronicles and biographies are filled with accounts of them, and no one appears to have doubted their common occurrence.[1]

18. The chief importance of the Church for the student of mediæval history does not lie, however, in its religious functions, vital as they were, but rather in its remarkable relations to the civil government. At first the Church and the imperial government were on a friendly footing of mutual respect and support. So long as the Roman Empire remained strong and active there was no chance for the clergy to free themselves from the control of the emperor, even if they had been disposed to do so. He made such laws for the Church as he saw fit and the clergy did not complain. The government was, indeed, indispensable to them. It undertook to root out paganism by destroying the heathen shrines and preventing heathen sacrifices, and it harshly punished those who refused to accept the teachings sanctioned by the Church.

The Church and the Roman government

But as the barbarians came in and the great Empire began to fall apart, there was a growing tendency among the churchmen in the West to resent the interference of rulers whom they no longer respected. They managed gradually to free themselves in large part from the control of the civil government. They then proceeded themselves to assume many of the duties of government, which the weak and disorderly states into which the Roman Empire fell were unable to perform properly. In 502, a church council at Rome declared a decree of Odoacer's null and void, on the ground that no layman had a right to interfere in the affairs of the Church. One of the bishops of Rome (Pope Gelasius I, d. 496) briefly stated the principle upon which the Church rested its claims, as follows: " Two powers govern the world, the priestly and the kingly. The first is

The Church begins to seek independence.

[1] For reports of miracles, see *Readings*, especially Chapters V and XVI.

indisputably the superior, for the priest is responsible to God for the conduct of even the emperors themselves." Since no one denied that the eternal interests of mankind, which devolved upon the Church, were infinitely more important than those matters of mere worldly expediency which the state regulated, it was natural for the clergy to hold that, in case of conflict, the Church and its officers, rather than the king, should have the last word.

The Church begins to perform the functions of government. It was one thing, however, for the Church to claim the right to regulate its own affairs; it was quite another for it to assume the functions which the Roman government had previously performed and which our governments perform to-day, such as the maintenance of order, the management of public education, the trial of lawsuits, etc. It did not, however, exactly usurp the prerogatives of the civil power, but rather offered itself as a substitute for it when no efficient civil government any longer existed. For there were no states, in the modern sense of the word, in western Europe for many centuries after the final destruction of the Roman Empire. The authority of the various kings was seldom sufficient to keep their realms in order. There were always many powerful landholders scattered throughout the kingdom who did pretty much what they pleased and settled their grudges against their fellows by neighborhood wars. Fighting was the main business as well as the chief amusement of the noble class. The king was unable to maintain peace and protect the oppressed, however anxious he may have been to do so.

Under these circumstances, it naturally fell to the admirably organized Church to keep order, when it could, by threats or persuasion; to see that sworn contracts were kept, that the wills of the dead were administered, and marriage obligations observed. It took the defenseless widow and orphan under its protection and dispensed charity; it promoted education at a time when few laymen, however rich and noble, pretended even to read. These conditions serve to explain why the Church was finally able greatly to extend the powers which it had enjoyed under the Roman Empire, and why it undertook functions which seem to us to belong to the state rather than to a religious organization.

19. We must now turn to a consideration of the origin and growth of the supremacy of the popes, who, by raising themselves to the head of the Western Church, became in many respects more powerful than any of the kings and princes with whom they frequently found themselves in bitter conflict.

Origin of papal power.

While we cannot discover, either in the Acts of the Council of Nicæa or in the Theodosian Code, compiled more than a century later, any recognition of the supreme headship of the Bishop of Rome, there is little doubt that he and his flock had almost from the very first enjoyed a leading place among the Christian communities. The Roman Church was the only one in the West which could claim the distinction of having been founded by the immediate followers of Christ, — the " two most glorious apostles."

Prestige of the Roman Christian community.

The New Testament speaks repeatedly of Paul's presence in Rome, and Peter's is implied. There had always been, moreover, a persistent tradition, accepted throughout the Christian Church, that Peter was the first Bishop of Rome. While there is no complete documentary proof for this belief, it appears to have been generally accepted at least as early as the middle of the second century. There is, certainly, no conflicting tradition, no rival claimant. The *belief itself*, whether or not it corresponds with actual events, is indubitably a fact, and a fact of the greatest historical importance. Peter enjoyed a certain preëminence among the other apostles and was singled out by Christ upon several occasions. In a passage of the New Testament which has affected political history more profoundly than the edicts of the most powerful monarch, Christ says : " And I say also unto thee, That thou art Peter, and upon this rock I will build

Belief that Peter was the first Bishop of Rome.

my church; and the gates of hell shall not prevail against it. And I will give unto thee the keys of the kingdom of heaven: and whatsoever thou shalt bind on earth shall be bound in heaven: and whatsoever thou shalt loose on earth shall be loosed in heaven." [1]

The Roman Church the mother church.

It was thus natural that the Roman Church should early have been looked upon as the mother church in the West. Its doctrines were considered the purest, since they had been handed down from its exalted founders. When there was a difference of opinion in regard to the truth of a particular teaching, it was natural that all should turn to the Bishop of Rome for his view. Moreover, the majesty of the capital of the world helped to exalt its bishop above his fellows. It was long, however, before all the other bishops, especially those in the large cities, were ready to accept unconditionally the authority of the Bishop of Rome, although they acknowledged his leading position and that of the Roman community.

Obscurity of early bishops of Rome.

We know comparatively little of the bishops of Rome during the first three centuries of the Church's existence. Even as the undisputed heads of their persecuted sect, they could not have begun to exercise the political influence which they later enjoyed, until Christianity had gained the ascendancy and the power of the Empire had become greatly weakened.

Period of the Church fathers.

We are, however, much better instructed in regard to the Church of the fourth and early fifth centuries, because the century following the Council of Nicæa was, in the history of church literature, what the Elizabethan era was in that of England. It was the era of the great "fathers" of Christian theology, to whom all theologians since have looked back as to the foremost interpreters of their religion. Among the chief of these were Athanasius (d. 373), to whom is attributed the

---

[1] Matt. xvi. 18–19. Two other passages in the New Testament were held to substantiate the divinely ordained headship of Peter and his successors: Luke xxii. 32, where Christ says to Peter, "Stablish thy brethren," and John xxi. 15–17, where Jesus said to him, "Feed my sheep." See *Readings*, Chapter IV.

formulation of the creed of the Orthodox Church as opposed to the Arians, against whom he waged unremitting war; Basil (d. 379), the promoter of the monastic life; Ambrose, Bishop of Milan (d. 397); Jerome (d. 420), who prepared a new Latin version of the Scriptures, which became the standard (Vulgate) edition; and, above all, Augustine (354–430), whose voluminous writings have exercised an unrivaled influence upon the minds of Christian thinkers since his day.

Since the church fathers were chiefly interested in matters of doctrine, they say little of the organization of the Church, and it is not clear from their writings that the Bishop of Rome was accorded as yet the supreme and dominating position which the popes later enjoyed. Nevertheless, Augustine calls a contemporaneous Bishop of Rome the "head of the Western Church," and almost immediately after his death one ascended the episcopal chair at Rome whose ambition, energy, and personal bravery were a promise of those qualities which were to render his successors the kings of kings.

With the accession of Leo the Great (440–461) the history of the papacy may, in one sense, be said to have begun. At his instance, Valentinian III, the emperor of the West, issued a decree in 445 declaring the power of the Bishop of Rome supreme, by reason of Peter's merits and apostolic headship, and by reason of the majesty of the city of Rome. He commanded that the bishops throughout the West should receive as law all that the Bishop of Rome sanctioned, and that any bishop refusing to answer a summons to Rome should be forced to obey by the imperial governor. But a council at Chalcedon, six years later, raised new Rome on the Bosphorus (Constantinople) to an ecclesiastical equality with old Rome on the Tiber. The bishops of both cities were to have a co-superiority over all the other prelates. This decree was, however, never accepted in the Western or Latin Church, which was gradually separating from the Eastern or Greek

Leo the Great, 440–461.

Decree of Valentinian III.

Church whose natural head was Constantinople.[1]   Although the powers to which Leo laid claim were not as yet even clearly stated and there were times of adversity to come when for years they appeared an empty boast, still his emphatic assertion of the supremacy of the Roman bishop was a great step toward bringing the Western Church under a single head.

Duties that devolved upon the early popes.

Not long after the death of Leo the Great, Odoacer put an end to the western line of emperors.   Then Theodoric and his East Goths settled in Italy, only to be followed by still less desirable intruders, the Lombards.   During this tumultuous period the people of Rome, and even of all Italy, came to regard the pope as their natural leader.   The emperor was far away, and his officers, who managed to hold a portion of central Italy around Rome and Ravenna, were glad to accept the aid and counsel of the pope.   In Rome the pope watched over the elections of the city officials and directed in what manner the public money should be spent.   He had to manage and defend the great tracts of land in different parts of Italy which from time to time had been given to the bishopric of Rome.   He negotiated with the Germans and even directed the generals sent against them.

Gregory the Great, 590-604.

20. The pontificate of Gregory the Great, one of the half dozen most distinguished heads that the Church has ever had, shows how great a part the papacy could play.   Gregory, who was the son of a rich Roman senator, was appointed by the emperor to the honorable office of prefect.   He began to fear, however, that his proud position and fine clothes were making

---

1 The name *pope* (Latin, *papa* = father) was originally and quite naturally applied to all bishops, and even to priests.   It began to be especially applied to the bishops of Rome perhaps as early as the sixth century, but was not apparently confined to them until two or three hundred years later.   Gregory VII (d. 1085) was the first to declare explicitly that the title should be used only for the Bishop of Rome.   We shall, however, hereafter refer to the Roman bishop as pope, although it must not be forgotten that his headship of the Western Church did not for some centuries imply the absolute power that he came later to exercise over all the other bishops of western Europe.

him vain and worldly. His pious mother and his study of the writings of Augustine, Jerome, and Ambrose led him, upon the death of his father, to spend all his handsome fortune in founding seven monasteries. One of these he established in his own house and subjected himself to such severe discipline and deprivations that his health never entirely recovered from them. He might, in his enthusiasm for monasticism, have brought himself to an early grave if the pope had not commanded him to undertake a difficult mission to Constantinople ; there he had his first opportunity to show his great ability in conducting delicate negotiations.

When Gregory was chosen pope (in 590) and most reluctantly left his monastery, ancient Rome, the capital of the Empire, was already transforming itself into mediæval Rome, the capital of Christendom. The temples of the gods had furnished materials for the many Christian churches. The tombs of the apostles Peter and Paul were soon to become the center of religious attraction and the goal of pilgrimages from every part of western Europe. Just as Gregory assumed office a great plague was raging in the city. In true mediæval fashion, he arranged a solemn procession in order to obtain from heaven a cessation of the pest. Then the archangel Michael was seen over the tomb of Hadrian[1] sheathing his fiery sword as a sign that the wrath of the Lord had been turned away. With Gregory we leave behind us the history of the Rome of Cæsar and Trajan and enter upon that of Innocent III and Leo X. *Ancient Rome becomes mediæval Rome.*

Gregory enjoyed an unrivaled reputation during the Middle Ages as a writer. He is reckoned with Augustine, Ambrose, and Jerome as one of the four great Latin " fathers " of the Church. His works show, however, how much less cultivated his period was than that of his predecessors. His most popular book was his *Dialogues*, a collection of accounts of miracles *Gregory's writings.*

[1] The great circular tomb was later converted into the chief fortress of the popes and called, from the event just mentioned, the Castle of the Angel (San Angelo).

and popular legends. It is hard to believe that it could have been composed by the greatest man of the time and that it was designed for adults. In his commentary on Job, Gregory warns the reader that he need not be surprised to find mistakes in grammar, since in dealing with so high a theme a writer should not stop to make sure whether his cases and tenses are right.[1]

Gregory as a statesman. Gregory's letters show clearly what the papacy was coming to mean for Europe when in the hands of a really great man.

The Castle San Angelo, formerly the Tomb of the Emperor Hadrian

While he assumed the humble title of "Servant of the servants of God," which the popes still use, Gregory was a statesman whose influence extended far and wide. It devolved upon him to govern the city of Rome, — as it did upon his successors down to the year 1870, — for the eastern emperor's control had become merely nominal. He had also to keep the Lombards

[1] For extracts from Gregory's writings, see *Readings*, Chapter IV.

out of central Italy, which they failed to conquer largely on account of the valiant defense of the popes. These duties were functions of the civil power, and in assuming them Gregory may be said to have founded the temporal power of the popes.

Beyond the borders of Italy, Gregory was in constant communication with the emperor, with the rulers of Austrasia, Neustria, and Burgundy. Everywhere he used his influence to have good clergymen chosen as bishops, and everywhere he watched over the interests of the monasteries. But his chief importance in the history of the papacy is attributable to the missionary enterprises which he undertook, through which the great countries which were one day to be called England, France, and Germany were brought under the sway of the Roman Church and its head, the pope.

Gregory's missionary undertakings.

Gregory was, as we have seen, an enthusiastic monk, and he naturally relied chiefly upon the monks in his great work of converting the heathen. Consequently, before considering his missionary achievements, we must glance at the origin and character of the monks, who are so conspicuous throughout the Middle Ages.

General References. — There is no satisfactory history of the mediæval Church in one volume. Perhaps the best short account in English is FISHER, *History of the Christian Church* (Charles Scribner's Sons, $3.50). MOELLER, *History of the Christian Church*, Vols. I–II (Swan Sonnenschein, $4.00 a vol.), is a dry but very reliable manual with full references to the literature of the subject. ALZOG, *Manual of Universal Church History* (Clarke, Cincinnati, 3 vols., $10.00), is a careful presentation by a Catholic scholar. MILMAN, *History of Latin Christianity*, although rather old, is both scholarly and readable, and is to be found in most libraries. GIESELER, *Ecclesiastical History* (5 vols., now out of print, but not difficult to obtain), is really a great collection of the most interesting extracts from the sources, with very little indeed from the author's hand. This and Moeller are invaluable to the advanced student. HATCH, *Growth of Church Institutions* (Whittaker, $1.50), gives an admirably simple account of the most important phases of the organization of the Church.

CHAPTER V

THE MONKS AND THE CONVERSION OF THE GERMANS

Importance of the monks as a class.

21. It would be difficult to overestimate the variety and extent of the influence that the monks exercised for centuries in Europe. The proud annals of the Benedictines, Franciscans, Dominicans, and Jesuits contain many a distinguished name. The most eminent philosophers, scientists, historians, artists, poets, and statesmen may be found among their ranks. Among those whose achievements we shall study later are The Venerable Bede, Boniface, Abelard, Thomas Aquinas, Roger Bacon, Fra Angelico, Savonarola, Luther, Erasmus, — all these, and many others who have been leaders in various branches of human activity, were monks.

Monasticism appealed to many different classes.

The strength of monasticism lay in its appeal to many different classes of persons. The world became a less attractive place as the successive invasions of the barbarians brought ever-increasing disorder. The monastery was the natural refuge not only of the spiritually minded, but of those of a studious or contemplative disposition who disliked the life of a soldier and were disinclined to face the dangers and uncertainties of the times. The monastic life was safe and peaceful, as well as holy. Even the rude and unscrupulous warriors hesitated to destroy the property or disturb the life of those who were believed to enjoy Heaven's special favor. The monastery furnished, too, a refuge for the disconsolate, an asylum for the disgraced, and food and shelter for the indolent who would otherwise have had to earn their living. There were, therefore, many motives which helped to fill the monasteries. Kings and nobles, for the good of their souls, readily gave land upon which to found colonies of monks, and there were plenty of remote spots in the mountains and forests to tempt the recluse.

Monastic communities first developed on a large scale in Egypt in the fourth century. Just as the Germans were winning their first great victory at Adrianople, St. Jerome was engaged in showing the advantages of the ascetic Christian life, which was a new thing in the West. In the sixth century monasteries multiplied so rapidly in western Europe that it became necessary to establish definite rules for the numerous communities which proposed to desert the ordinary ways of the world and lead a peculiar life apart. The monastic regulations which had been drawn up in the East did not answer the purpose, for the climate of the West and the temperament of the Latin peoples differed too much from those of the Orient. Accordingly St. Benedict drew up, about the year 526, a sort of constitution for the monastery of Monte Cassino, in southern Italy, of which he was the head. This was so sagacious, and so well met the needs of the monastic life, that it was rapidly accepted by the other monasteries and gradually became the " rule " according to which all the western monks lived.[1]

Necessity for the regulation of monastic life.

The Rule of St. Benedict is as important as any constitution that was ever drawn up for a state. It is for the most part natural and wholesome. It provides that, since every one is not fitted for the ascetic life, the candidate for admission to the monastery shall pass through a period of probation, called the *novitiate*, before he is permitted to take the solemn and irrevocable vow. The brethren shall elect their head, the

The Rule of St. Benedict.

---

[1] Benedict did not introduce monasticism in the West, as is sometimes supposed, nor did he even found an *order* in the proper sense of the word, under a single head, like the later Franciscans and Dominicans. Nevertheless, the monks who lived under his rule are ordinarily spoken of as belonging to the Benedictine order. A translation of the Benedictine rule may be found in Henderson, *Historical Documents*, pp. 274–314.

abbot, whom they must obey unconditionally in all that is not sinful. Along with prayer and meditation, the monks are to work at manual occupations and cultivate the soil. They shall also read and teach. Those who were incapacitated for outdoor work were assigned lighter tasks, such as copying books. The monk was not permitted to own anything in his own right; he pledged himself to perpetual and absolute poverty, and everything he used was the property of the convent. Along with the vows of obedience and poverty, he also took that of chastity, which bound him never to marry. For not only was the single life considered more holy than the married, but the monastic organization would, of course, have been impossible unless the monks remained single. Aside from these restrictions, the monks were commanded to live rational and natural lives and not to abuse their bodies or sacrifice their physical vigor by undue fasting in the supposed interest of their souls. These sensible provisions were directed against the excesses of asceticism, of which there had been many instances in the East.

The monks copy, and so preserve, the Latin authors.

The influence of the Benedictine monks upon Europe is incalculable. From their numbers no less than twenty-four popes and forty-six hundred bishops and archbishops have been chosen. They boast almost sixteen thousand writers, some of great distinction. Their monasteries furnished retreats where the scholar might study and write in spite of the prevailing disorder of the times. The copying of books, as has been said, was a natural occupation of the monks. Doubtless their work was often done carelessly, with little heart and less understanding. But, with the great loss of manuscripts due to the destruction of libraries and the indifference of individual book-owners, it was most essential that new copies should be made. Even poor and incorrect ones were better than none. It was the monks who prevented the loss of a great part of Latin literature, which, without them, would probably have reached us only in scanty remains.

The monks also helped to rescue honest manual labor, which they believed to be a great aid to salvation, from the disrepute into which slavery had brought it in earlier times. They set the example of careful cultivation on the lands about their monasteries and in this way introduced better methods into the regions where they settled. They entertained travelers at a time when there were few or no inns and so increased the intercourse between the various parts of Europe.[1] *The monks aid in the material development of Europe.*

The Benedictine monks, as well as later monastic orders, were ardent and faithful supporters of the papacy. The Roman Church, which owes much to them, appreciated the aid which they might furnish and extended to them many of the privileges enjoyed by the clergy. Indeed the monks were reckoned as clergymen and were called the " regular " clergy because they lived according to a *regula*, or rule, to distinguish them from the " secular " clergy, who continued to live in the world (*saeculum*) and took no monastic vows. *The regular and secular clergy.*

The Church, ever anxious to maintain as far-reaching a control over its subjects as that of the Roman Empire, whose power it inherited, could hardly expect its busy officers, with their multiform duties and constant relations with men, to represent the ideal of contemplative Christianity which was then held in higher esteem than the active life. The secular clergy performed the ceremonies of the Church, administered its business, and guarded its property, while the regular clergy illustrated the necessity of personal piety and self-denial. Monasticism at its best was a monitor standing beside the Church and constantly warning it against permitting the Christian life to sink into mere mechanical and passive acceptance of its ceremonies as all-sufficient for salvation. It supplied the element of personal responsibility and spiritual ambition upon which Protestantism has laid so much stress. *Monks and secular clergy supplement each other.*

[1] Cunningham, *Western Civilization*, Vol. II, pp. 37–40, gives a brief account of the work of the monks.

22. The first great service of the monks was their mission-ary labors. To these the later strength of the Roman Church is in no small degree due, for the monks made of the unconverted Germans not merely Christians, but also dutiful subjects of the pope. The first people to engage their attention were the heathen Germans who had conquered the once Christian Britain.

The islands which are now known as the kingdom of Great Britain and Ireland were, at the opening of the Christian era, occupied by several Celtic peoples of whose customs and reli-gion we know almost nothing. Julius Cæsar commenced the conquest of the islands (55 B.C.); but the Romans never suc-ceeded in establishing their power beyond the wall which they built, from the Clyde to the Firth of Forth, to keep out the wild Celtic tribes of the North. Even south of the wall the country was not completely Romanized, and the Celtic tongue has actually survived down to the present day in Wales.

At the opening of the fifth century the barbarian invasions forced Rome to withdraw its legions from Britain in order to protect its frontiers on the continent. The island was thus left to be gradually conquered by the Germans, mainly Saxons and Angles, who came across the North Sea from the region south of Denmark. Almost all record of what went on during the two centuries following the departure of the Romans has disappeared. No one knows the fate of the original Celtic inhabitants of England. It is unlikely that they were, as was formerly supposed, all killed or driven to the mountain districts of Wales. More probably they were gradually lost among the dominating Germans with whom they merged into one people. The Saxon and Angle chieftains established petty kingdoms, of which there were seven or eight at the time when Gregory the Great became pope.

Gregory, while still a simple monk, had been struck with the beauty of some Angles whom he saw one day in the slave market of Rome. When he learned who they were he was grieved that such handsome beings should still belong to the kingdom of the Prince of Darkness, and, had he been permitted, he himself would have gone as a missionary to their people. Upon becoming pope he sent forty monks to England from one of the monasteries that he had founded, placing a prior, Augustine, at their head and designating him in advance as Bishop of England. The heathen king of Kent, in whose

Ancient Church of St. Martin's, Canterbury

territory the monks landed with fear and trembling (597), had a Christian wife, the daughter of a Frankish king. Through her influence the monks were kindly received and were assigned an ancient church at Canterbury, dating from the Roman occupation before the German invasions. Here they established a monastery, and from this center the conversion, first of Kent and then of the whole island, was gradually effected. Canterbury has always maintained its early preëminence and may still be considered the religious capital of England.[1]

1 See *Readings*, Chapter V, for Gregory's instructions to his missionaries.

The Irish monks.

Augustine and his monks were not, however, the only Christians in the British Isles. Britain had been converted to Christianity when it was a Roman province, and some of the missionaries, led by St. Patrick (d. about 469), had made their way into Ireland and established a center of Christianity there. When the Germans overran Britain and reheathenized it, the Irish monks and clergy were too far off to be troubled by the barbarians. They knew little of the traditions of the Roman Church and diverged from its customs in some respects. They celebrated Easter upon a different date from that observed by the Roman Church and employed a different style of tonsure. Missionaries from this Irish church were busy converting the northern regions of Britain, when the Roman monks under Augustine began their work in the southern part of the island.

Conflict between the Roman Church and the Irish monks.

There was sure to be trouble between the two parties. The Irish clergy, while they professed great respect for the pope and did not wish to be cut off from the rest of the Christian Church, were unwilling to abandon their peculiar usages and accept those sanctioned by Rome. Nor would they recognize as their superior the Archbishop of Canterbury, whom the pope had made the head of the British church. The pope, on his part, felt that it was all-important that these isolated Christians should become a part of the great organization of which he claimed to be the head. Neither party would make any concessions, and for two generations each went its own way, cherishing a bitter hostility toward the other.

Victory of Roman Church.

At last the Roman Church won the victory, as it so often did in later struggles. In 664, through the influence of the king of Northumbria who did not wish to risk being on bad terms with the pope, the Roman Catholic form of faith was solemnly recognized in an assembly at Whitby, and the leader of the Irish missionaries sadly withdrew to Ireland.

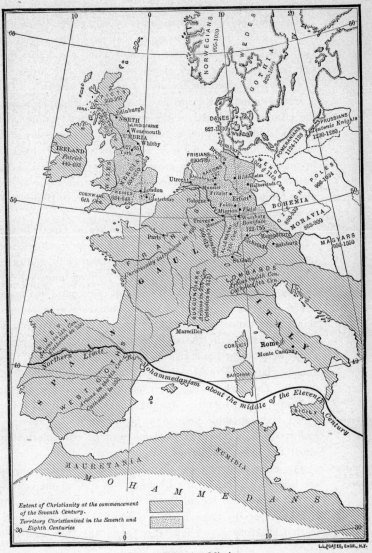

Map of Christian Missions

L.L.POATES, ENGR., N.Y.

Key (bottom left):

Extent of Christianity at the commencement of the Seventh Century.

Territory Christianized in the Seventh and Eighth Centuries

The king of Northumbria, upon opening the Council of Whitby, said " that it was proper that those who served one God should observe one rule of conduct and not depart from one another in the ways of celebrating the holy mysteries, since they all hoped for the same kingdom of heaven." That a remote island of Europe should set up its traditions against the customs sanctioned by the rest of Christendom appeared to him highly unreasonable. This faith in the necessary unity of the Church is one of the secrets of its strength. England became a part of the ever-growing territory embraced in the Catholic Church and remained as faithful to the pope as any other Catholic country, down to the defection of Henry VIII in the early part of the sixteenth century.

Early culture in England. The consolidation of the rival churches in Great Britain was followed by a period of general enthusiasm for Rome and its literature and culture. Lindisfarne, Wearmouth, and other English monasteries became centers of learning unrivaled perhaps in the rest of Europe. A constant intercourse was maintained with Rome. Masons and glassmakers were brought across the Channel to replace the wooden churches of Britain by stone edifices in the style of the Romans. The young clergy were taught Latin and sometimes Greek. Copies of the ancient classics were brought from the continent and reproduced. The most distinguished man of letters of the seventh and early eighth centuries was the English monk Bæda (often **The Venerable Bede.** called The Venerable Bede, 673–735), from whose admirable history of the Church in England most of our information about the period is derived.[1]

Irish missionaries on the continent. **23.** From England missionaries carried the enthusiasm for the Church back across the Channel. In spite of the conversion of Clovis and the wholesale baptism of his soldiers, the Franks, especially those farthest north, had been very imperfectly Christianized. A few years before Augustine landed in

[1] See *Readings*, Chapter V.

Kent, St. Columban, one of the Irish missionaries of whom we have spoken, landed in Gaul. He went from place to place founding monasteries and gaining the respect of the people by his rigid self-denial and by the miracles that he performed. He even penetrated among the still wholly pagan Alemanni about the Lake of Constance. When driven away by their pagan king, he turned his attention to the Lombards in northern Italy, where he died in 615.[1] St. Gall, one of his followers, remained near the Lake of Constance and attracted about him so many disciples and companions that a great monastery grew up which was named after him and became one of the most celebrated in central Europe. Other Irish missionaries penetrated into the forests of Thuringia and Bavaria. The German church looks back, however, to an English missionary as its real founder.

St. Columban and St. Gall.

In 718, about a hundred years after the death of St. Columban, St. Boniface, an English monk, was sent by the pope as an apostle to the Germans. After four years spent in reconnoitering the field of his future labors, he returned to Rome and was made a missionary bishop, taking the same oath of obedience to the pope that the bishops in the immediate vicinity of Rome were accustomed to take. Indeed absolute subordination to the pope was a part of Boniface's religion, and he became a powerful agent in promoting the supremacy of the Roman see.

St. Boniface, the apostle to the Germans.

Under the protection of the powerful Frankish mayor of the palace, Charles Martel, Boniface carried on his missionary work with such zeal that he succeeded in bringing all the older Christian communities which had been established by the Irish missionaries under the papal control, as well as in

---

[1] There is a *Life of St. Columban*, written by one of his companions, which, although short and simple in the extreme, furnishes a better idea of the Christian spirit of the sixth century than the longest treatise by a modern writer. This life may be found in *Translations and Reprints*, Vol. II, No. 7, translated by Professor Munro.

converting many of the more remote German tribes who still clung to their old pagan beliefs. His energetic methods are illustrated by the story of how he cut down the sacred oak of Odin at Fritzlar, in Hesse, and used the wood to build a chapel, around which a monastery soon grew up. In 732 Boniface was raised to the dignity of Archbishop of Mayence and proceeded to establish, in the newly converted region, the German bishoprics of Salzburg, Regensburg, Würzburg, Erfurt, and several others ; this gives us some idea of the geographical extent of his labors.

Boniface reforms the church in Gaul and brings it into subjection to the pope.

After organizing the German church he turned his attention, with the hearty approval of the pope and the support of the Frankish rulers, to a general reformation of the church in Gaul. Here the clergy were sadly demoralized, and the churches and monasteries had been despoiled of much of their property in the constant turmoil of the time. Boniface succeeded, with the help of Charles Martel, in bettering affairs, and through his efforts the venerable church of Gaul, almost as old as that of Rome itself, was brought under the supremacy of the pope. In 748 the assembled bishops of Gaul bound themselves to maintain the Catholic unity of faith and follow strictly the precepts of the vicar of St. Peter, the pope, so that they might be reckoned among Peter's sheep.

General Reading. — The best history of the monks to be had in English is MONTALEMBERT, *The Monks of the West from St. Benedict to St. Bernard* (Longmans, Green & Co., 6 vols., $15.00). The writer's enthusiasm and his excellent style make his work very attractive. The advanced student will gain much from TAYLOR, *Classical Heritage of the Middle Ages* (The Macmillan Company, $1.75), Chapter VII, on the origin and spirit of monasticism. See also HARNACK, *Monasticism* (Scribners, 50 cents). The works on church history referred to at the end of the preceding chapter all contain some account of the monks.

CHAPTER VI

CHARLES MARTEL AND PIPPIN

24. Just as the pope was becoming the acknowledged head of the Western Church, the Frankish realms came successively under the rule of two great statesmen, Charles Martel and his son Pippin the Short, who laid the foundation of Charlemagne's vast empire.

Charles Martel, Frankish mayor of the palace, 714-741.

The difficulties which Charles Martel had to face were much the same as those which for centuries to follow confronted the sovereigns of western Europe. The great problem of the mediæval ruler was to make his power felt throughout his whole territory in spite of the many rich and ambitious officials, bishops, and abbots who eagerly took advantage of all the king's weaknesses and embarrassments to make themselves practically supreme in their respective districts.

Difficulty of holding together a kingdom in the early Middle Ages.

The two classes of officers of which we hear most were the counts (Latin, *comites*) and the dukes (Latin, *duces*). A count ordinarily represented the king within the district comprised in an old municipality of the Empire. Over a number of counts the king might place a duke. Both of these titles were borrowed by the Germans from the names of Roman officials. While the king appointed, and might dismiss, these officers when he pleased, there was a growing tendency for them to hold their positions for life.

Origin of counts and dukes.

We find Charles fighting the dukes of Aquitaine, Bavaria, and Alemannia, each of whom was endeavoring to make the territory which he was deputed to rule in the king's interest a separate and independent country under his own supremacy.

By successive campaigns against these rebellious magnates, Charles succeeded in reuniting all those outlying districts that tended to forget or ignore their connection with the Frankish empire.

Charles and his bishops. The bishops proved almost, if not quite, as troublesome to the mayor of the palace as the dukes, and later the counts. It is true that Charles kept the choice of the bishops in his own hands and refused to give to the clergy and people of the diocese the privilege of electing their head, as the rules of the Church prescribed. But when a bishop had once got possession of the lands attached to the bishopric and exercised the wide powers and influence which fell to him, he was often tempted, especially if he were a nobleman, to use his privileged position to establish a practically independent principality. The same was true of the heads of powerful monasteries. These dangerous bishops and abbots Charles deposed in wholesale fashion. He substituted his own friends for them with little regard to the rules of the Church — for instance, he bestowed on his nephew the three bishoprics of Paris, Rouen, and Bayeux, besides two monasteries. The new incumbents were, however, no better than the old; they were, indeed, in spite of their clerical robes, only laymen, who continued to fight and hunt in their customary manner.

The most famous of Charles' deeds was his decisive defeat of the advancing Mohammedans who were pressing into Gaul from Spain. Before speaking of this a word must be said of the invaders and their religion, for the Saracens, as the followers of Mohammed were commonly called, will come into our story of western Europe now and then, especially during the Crusades.

Mohammed, 571-632. 25. Just as Gregory the Great was dying in Rome, leaving to his successors a great heritage of spiritual and temporal influence, a young Arab in far-off Mecca was meditating upon the mysteries of life and laying the foundation of a religious power rivaling even that of the popes. Before the time of Mohammed the Arabs had played no important part in the world's history. The scattered tribes were at war with one another, and each worshiped its own gods, when it worshiped at all. But when the peoples of the desert accepted Mohammed as their prophet and his religion as theirs, they became an irresistible force for the dissemination of the new teaching and for the subjugation of the world.

Mohammed came of a good family, but was reduced by poverty to enter the employ of a rich widow, named Kadijah, who fell in love with him and became his wife. She was his first convert and kept up his courage when few among his fellow-townsmen in Mecca would believe in his visions or accept the teachings which he claimed to receive direct from the angel Gabriel. Finally he discovered that his many enemies were planning to kill him, so he fled to the neighboring town of Medina, where he had friends. His flight (the Hejira), which took place in the year 622, was taken by his followers as the beginning of a new era, — the year one, as Mohammedans reckon time. A war ensued between the people of Mecca and those in and about Medina who supported Mohammed. It was eight years before he reëntered Mecca, the religious center of Arabia, with a victorious army. Before his death in 632 he had received the adhesion of all the Arab chiefs, and his faith, Islam (which means *submission to God*), was accepted throughout the Arabian peninsula.

The Hejira, 622.

Mohammed was accustomed to fall into a trance from time to time, after which he would recite to his eager listeners the messages which he received from Heaven. These were collected into a volume shortly after his death, and make up the Koran, the Bible of the Mohammedan.[1] This contains all the fundamental beliefs of the new religion, as well as the laws under which the faithful were to live. It proclaims one God, " the

The Koran and the religion of Mohammed.

[1] For extracts from the Koran, see *Readings*, Chapter VI.

Lord of the worlds, the merciful, the compassionate," and Mohammed as his prophet. It announces a day of judgment in which each shall receive his reward for the deeds done in the flesh, and either be admitted to paradise or banished to an eternally burning hell. Those who die fighting for the sacred cause shall find themselves in a high garden, where, "content with their past endeavors," they shall hear no foolish word and shall recline in rich brocades upon soft cushions and rugs and be served by surpassingly beautiful maidens. Islam has much in common with Judaism and Christianity. Jesus even has a place in it, but only as one of the prophets, like Abraham, Moses, and others, who have brought religious truth to mankind.

The religion of Mohammed was simpler than that of the mediæval Christian Church. It provided for no priesthood, nor for any elaborate rites and ceremonies. Five times a day the faithful Mohammedan must pray, always with his face turned toward Mecca. One month in the year he must fast during the daytime. If he is educated, he will know the Koran by heart. The mosque is a house of prayer and the place for the reading of the Koran ; no altars or images are permitted in it.

Mohammedan conquests. Mohammed's successor assumed the title of caliph. Under him the Arabs went forth to conquer the great territories to the north of them, belonging to the Persians and the Roman emperor at Constantinople. They met with marvelous success. Within ten years after Mohammed's death the Arabs had established a great empire with its capital at Damascus, from whence the caliph ruled over Arabia, Persia, Syria, and Egypt. In the following decades new conquests were made all along the coast of Africa, and in 708 Tangier was taken and the Arabs could look across the Straits of Gibraltar to Spain.[1]

[1] An admirable brief description of the culture of the Arabs and their contributions to European civilization will be found in Munro, *Mediæval History*, Chapter IX.

The kingdom of the West Goths was in no condition to defend itself when a few Arabs and a much larger number of Berbers, inhabitants of northern Africa, ventured to cross over. Some of the Spanish towns held out for a time, but the invaders found allies in the numerous Jews who had been shamefully treated by their Christian countrymen. As for the innumerable serfs who worked on the great estates of the aristocracy, a change of landlords made very little difference to

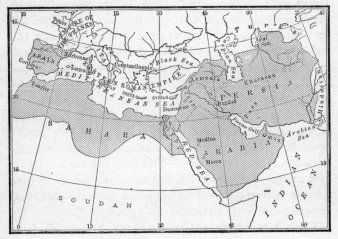

Map of Arabic Conquests

them. In 711 the Arabs and Berbers gained a great battle, and the peninsula was gradually overrun by new immigrants from Africa. In seven years the Mohammedans were masters of almost the whole region south of the Pyrenees. They then began to cross into Gaul and took possession of the district about Narbonne. For some years the duke of Aquitaine kept them in check, but in 732 they collected a large army, defeated the duke near Bordeaux, advanced to Poitiers, where they burned the church, and then set out for Tours.

Charles Martel at once sent out a summons to all who could
bear arms and, in the same year, met and repulsed the Mohammedans near Tours.   We know very little indeed of the details
of the conflict, but it is certain that the followers of Mohammed
retreated and that they never made another attempt to conquer
western Europe.

26. Charles was able, before his death in 741, to secure the
succession to his office of mayor of the palace for his two sons,
Pippin and Carloman.   The brothers left the nominal king on
the throne ; but he had nothing to do, as the chronicler tells
us, " but to be content with his name of king, his flowing hair
and long beard ; to sit on his throne and play the ruler, listening to the ambassadors who came from all directions, and giving them the answers that had been taught him, as if of his
own sovereign will.   In reality, however, he had nothing but
the royal name and a beggarly income at the will of the mayor
of the palace."   The new mayors had succeeded in putting
down all opposition when, to the astonishment of every one,

Carloman abdicated and assumed the gown of a monk.   Pippin
took control of the whole Frankish dominion, and we find the
unusual statement in the Frankish annals that " the whole land
enjoyed peace for two years " (749–750).

Pippin
assumes the
crown with
the approba-
tion of the
pope, 752.

Pippin now felt himself strong enough to get rid of the
" do-nothing " king altogether and assume for himself the
nominal as well as the real kingship of the Franks.   It was,
however, a delicate matter to depose even a quite useless monarch, so he determined to consult the head of the Church.   To
Pippin's query whether it was fitting that the Merovingian king
of the Franks, having no power, should continue to reign, the
pope replied : " It seems better that he who has the power in
the state should be king and be called king, rather than he who
is falsely called king."

It will be noticed that the pope in no sense created Pippin
king, as later writers claimed.   He sanctioned a usurpation

which was practically inevitable and which was carried out with the approbation of the Frankish nation. Raised on the shields of the counts and dukes, anointed by St. Boniface, and blessed by the pope, Pippin became in 752 the first king of the Carolingian family, which had already for several generations ruled the Franks in all but name.

This participation of the pope brought about a very funda- mental change in the theory of kingship. The kings of the Germans up to this time had been military leaders selected, or holding their office, by the will of the people, or at least of the aristocracy. Their rule had had no divine sanction, but only that of general acquiescence backed up by sufficient skill and popularity to frustrate the efforts of rivals. By the anointing of Pippin in accordance with the ancient Jewish custom, first by St. Boniface and then by the pope himself, "a German chieftain was," as Gibbon expresses, it "transformed into the Lord's anointed." The pope uttered a dire anathema of divine vengeance against any one who should attempt to supplant the holy and meritorious race of Pippin. It became a *religious* duty to obey the king. He came to be regarded by the Church, when he had duly received its sanction, as God's representa- tive on earth. Here we have the basis of the later idea of monarchs "by the grace of God," against whom, however bad they might be, it was not merely a political offense, but a sin, to revolt.

A new theory of kingship.

27. The sanction of Pippin's usurpation by the pope was but an indication of the good feeling between the two greatest powers in the West, — the head of the ever-strengthening Frankish state and the head of the Church. This good feeling quickly ripened into an alliance, momentous for the history of Europe. In order to understand this we must glance at the motives which led the popes to throw off their allegiance to their ancient sovereigns, the emperors at Constantinople, and turn for help to Pippin and his successors.

Controversy
over the
veneration of
images and
pictures,—
the so-called
iconoclastic
controversy.

For more than a century after the death of Gregory the Great his successors continued to remain respectful subjects of the emperor. They looked to him for occasional help against the Lombards in northern Italy, who showed a disposition to add Rome to their possessions. In 725, however, the emperor Leo III aroused the bitter opposition of the pope by issuing a decree forbidding the usual veneration of the images of Christ and the saints. The emperor was a thoughtful Christian and felt keenly the taunts of the Mohammedans, who held all images in abhorrence and regarded the Christians as idolaters. He therefore ordered all sacred images throughout his empire to be removed from the churches, and all figures on the church walls to be whitewashed over. This aroused serious opposition even in Constantinople, and the farther west one went, the more obstinate became the resistance. The pope refused to obey the edict, for he held that the emperor had no right to interfere with practices hallowed by the Church. He called a council which declared all persons excommunicated who should "throw down, destroy, profane or blaspheme the holy images." The opposition of the West was successful, and the images kept their places.[1]

The popes
and the
Lombards.

In spite of their abhorrence of the iconoclastic Leo and his successors, the popes did not give up all hope that the emperors might aid them in keeping the Lombards out of Rome. At last a Lombard ruler arose, Aistulf, a " son of iniquity," who refused to consider the prayers or threats of the head of the Church. In 751 Aistulf took Ravenna and threatened Rome. He proposed to substitute his supremacy for that of the eastern emperor and make of Italy a single state, with Rome as its capital. This was a critical moment for the peninsula. Was Italy, like Gaul, to be united under a single German people

---

[1] One of the most conspicuous features of early Protestantism, eight hundred years later, was the revival of Leo's attack upon the statues and frescoes which continued to adorn the churches in Germany, England, and the Netherlands.

and to develop, as France has done, a characteristic civilization? The Lombards had progressed so far that they were not unfitted to organize a state that should grow into a nation. But the head of the Church could not consent to endanger his independence by becoming the subject of an Italian king. It was therefore the pope who prevented the establishment of an Italian kingdom at this time and who continued for the same reason to stand in the way of the unification of Italy for more than a thousand years, until he was dispossessed of his realms not many decades ago by Victor Emmanuel. After vainly turning in his distress to his natural protector, the emperor, the pope had no resource but to appeal to Pippin, upon whose fidelity he had every reason to rely. He crossed the Alps and was received with the greatest cordiality and respect by the Frankish monarch, who returned to Italy with him and relieved Rome (754). *The pope turns to the Franks for aid.*

No sooner had Pippin recrossed the Alps than the Lombard king, ever anxious to add Rome to his possessions, again invested the Eternal City. Pope Stephen's letters to the king of the Franks at this juncture are characteristic of the time. The pope warmly argues that Pippin owes all his victories to St. Peter and should now hasten to the relief of his successor. If the king permits the city of the prince of the apostles to be lacerated and tormented by the Lombards, his own soul will be lacerated and tormented in hell by the devil and his pestilential angels. These arguments proved effective ; Pippin immediately undertook a second expedition to Italy, from which he did not return until the kingdom of the Lombards had become tributary to his own, as Bavaria and Aquitaine already were. *Pippin subdues the Lombards.*

Pippin, instead of restoring to the eastern emperor the lands which the Lombards had recently occupied, handed them over to the pope, — on exactly what terms we do not know, since the deed of cession has disappeared. In consequence of these *Donation of Pippin.*

important additions to the former territories of St. Peter, the popes were thereafter the nominal rulers of a large district in central Italy, extending across the peninsula from Ravenna to a point well south of Rome. If, as many writers have maintained, Pippin recognized the pope as the sovereign of this district, we find here the first state that was destined to endure into the nineteenth century delimited on the map of Europe. A map of Italy as late as the year 1860 shows the same region still marked "States of the Church."

Significance of Pippin's reign.

The reign of Pippin is remarkable in several ways. It witnessed the strengthening of the kingly power in the Frankish state, which was soon to embrace most of western Europe and form the starting point for the development of the modern countries of France, Germany, and Austria. It furnishes the first instance of the interference of a northern prince in the affairs of Italy, which was destined to become the stumbling-block of many a later French and German king. Lastly, the pope had now a state of his own, which, in spite of its small size, proved one of the most important and permanent in Europe.

Pippin and his son Charlemagne saw only the strength and not the disadvantage that accrued to their title from the papal sanction. It is none the less true, as Gibbon says, that "under the sacerdotal monarchy of St. Peter, the nations began to resume the practice of seeking, on the banks of the Tiber, their kings, their laws, and the oracles of their fate." We shall have ample evidence of this as we proceed.

General Reading. — For Mohammed and the Saracens, GILMAN, *The Saracens* (G. P. Putnam's Sons, $1.50). Gibbon has a famous chapter on Mohammed and another upon the conquests of the Arabs. These are the fiftieth and fifty-first of his great work. See also MUIR, *Life of Mohammed* (Smith, Elder & Co., $4.50).

CHAPTER VII

CHARLEMAGNE

28. Charlemagne is the first historical personage among the German peoples of whom we have any satisfactory knowledge.[1] Compared with him, Theodoric, Charles Martel, Pippin, and the rest are but shadowy figures. The chronicles tell us something of their deeds, but we can make only the vaguest inferences in regard to their character and temperament.

The appearance of Charlemagne, as described by his secretary, so exactly corresponds with the character of the king as exhibited in his great reign, that it is worthy of attention. He was tall and stoutly built; his face was round, his eyes were large and keen, his nose somewhat above the common size, his expression bright and cheerful. Whether he stood or sat, his form was full of dignity; for the good proportion and grace of his body prevented the observer from noticing that his neck was rather short and his person somewhat too stout. His step was firm and his aspect manly; his voice was clear, but rather weak for so large a body. He was active in all bodily exercises, delighted in riding and hunting, and was an expert swimmer. His excellent health and his physical alertness and endurance can alone explain the astonishing swiftness with which he moved about his vast realm and conducted innumerable campaigns in widely distant regions in startlingly rapid succession.

Charlemagne's personal appearance

[1] Charlemagne is the French form for the Latin, Carolus Magnus, i.e., Charles the Great. It has been regarded as good English for so long that it seems best to retain it, although some writers, fearful lest one may think of Charles as a Frenchman instead of a German, use the German form, Karl.

His educa-
tion, his atti-
tude toward
learning, and
his public
spirit.

Charles was an educated man and one who knew how to appreciate and encourage scholarship. When at dinner he had some one read to him; he delighted especially in history and in St. Augustine's *City of God*. He could speak Latin well and understood Greek readily. He tried to learn to write, but began too late in life and got no farther than signing his name. He called scholarly men to his court, took advantage of their learning, and did much toward reëstablishing a regular system of public instruction. He was also constantly occupied with buildings and other public works calculated to adorn and benefit his kingdom. He himself planned the remarkable cathedral at Aix-la-Chapelle and showed the greatest interest in its furnishings. He commenced two palaces of beautiful workmanship, one near Mayence and the other at Nimwegen, in Holland, and had a long bridge constructed across the Rhine at Mayence.

The impression which his reign made upon men's minds grew even after his death. He became the hero of a whole cycle of romantic but wholly unhistoric adventures and achievements which were as devoutly believed for centuries as his most authentic deeds. In the fancy of an old monk in the monastery of St. Gall,[1] writing of Charlemagne not long after his death, the king of the Franks swept over Europe surrounded by countless legions of soldiers who formed a very sea of bristling steel. Knights of superhuman valor formed his court and became the models for the chivalrous spirit of the following centuries. Distorted but imposing, the Charlemagne of poetry meets us all through the Middle Ages.

A study of Charlemagne's reign will substantiate our first impression that he was a truly remarkable person, one of the greatest figures in the world's records and deservedly the

[1] Professor Emerton (*Introduction*, pp. 183–185) gives an example of the style and spirit of the monk of St. Gall, who was formerly much relied upon for knowledge of Charlemagne.

hero of the Middle Ages. To few men has it been given to influence so profoundly the course of European progress. We shall consider him first as a conqueror, then as an organizer and creator of governmental institutions, and lastly as a promoter of culture and enlightenment.

29. It was Charlemagne's ideal to bring all the German peoples together into one great Christian empire, and he was wonderfully successful in attaining his end. Only a small portion of what is now called Germany was included in the kingdom ruled over by Pippin. Frisia and Bavaria had been Christianized, and their native rulers had been induced by the efforts of Charlemagne's predecessors and of the missionaries, especially Boniface, to recognize formally the overlordship of the Franks. Between these two half-independent countries lay the unconquered Saxons. They were as yet pagans and appear to have still clung to much the same institutions as those under which they lived when the Roman historian Tacitus described them seven centuries earlier. Charlemagne's idea of a great Christian empire.

The Saxons occupied the region beginning somewhat east of Cologne and extending to the Elbe, and north to where the great cities of Bremen and Hamburg are now situated. The present kingdom of Saxony would hardly have come within their boundaries. The Saxons had no towns or roads and were consequently very difficult to conquer, as they could retreat, with their few possessions, into the forests or swamps as soon as they found themselves unable to meet an invader in the open field. Yet so long as they remained unconquered they constantly threatened the Frankish kingdom, and the incorporation of their country was essential to the rounding out of its boundaries. Charlemagne never undertook, during his long military career, any other task half so serious as the subjugation of the Saxons, and it occupied his attention for many years. Nine successive rebellions had to be put down, and it was finally owing rather to the Church than to Charlemagne's The conquest of the Saxons.

military prowess that the great task was brought to a successful issue.

Conversion of the Saxons. Nowhere do we find a more striking example of the influence of the Church than in the reliance that Charlemagne placed upon it in his dealings with the Saxons. He deemed it quite as essential that after a rebellion they should promise to honor the Church and be baptized as that they should pledge themselves to remain true and faithful vassals of the king. He was in quite as much haste to found bishoprics and abbeys as to build fortresses. The law for the newly conquered Saxon lands, issued sometime between 775 and 790, provides the same death penalty for him who "shall have shown himself unfaithful to the lord king," and him who "shall have wished to hide himself unbaptized and shall have scorned to come to baptism and shall have wished to remain a pagan." Charlemagne believed the Christianizing of the Saxons so important a part of his duty that he decreed that all should suffer death who entered a church by violence and carried off anything by force, or even failed to abstain from meat during Lent.[1] No one, under penalty of heavy fines, was to make vows, in the pagan fashion, at trees or springs, or partake of any heathen feasts in honor of the demons (as the Christians termed the heathen deities), or fail to present infants for baptism before they were a year old.

For the support of the local churches, those who lived in the parish were to give toward three hundred acres of land and a house for the priest. "Likewise, in accordance with the

---

[1] These decrees lose something of their harshness by the provision: "If after secretly committing any one of these mortal crimes any one shall flee of his own accord to the priest and, after confessing, shall wish to do penance, let him be freed, on the testimony of the priest, from death." This is but another illustration of the theory that the Church was in the Middle Ages a governmental institution. It would be quite out of harmony with modern ideas should the courts of law, in dealing with one who had committed a crime, consider in any way the relations of the suspected criminal to his priest or minister, or modify his sentence on account of any religious duties that the criminal might consent to perform.

mandate of God, we command that all shall give a tithe of their property and labor to the churches and the priests; let the nobles as well as the freemen, likewise the serfs, according to that which God shall have given to each Christian, return a part to God."

These provisions are characteristic of the theory of the Middle Ages according to which the civil government and the Church went hand in hand in ordering and governing the life of the people. Defection from the Church was regarded by the state as quite as serious a crime as treason against itself. While the claims of the two institutions sometimes conflicted, there was no question in the minds either of the king's officials or of the clergy that both the civil and ecclesiastical government were absolutely necessary; neither class ever dreamed that they could get along without the other.

Coöperation of the civil government and the Church.

Before the Frankish conquest the Saxons had no towns. Now, around the seat of the bishop, or about a monastery, men began to collect and towns and cities to grow up. Of these the chief was Bremen, which is still one of the most important ports of Germany.

Foundation of towns in northern Germany.

30. Pippin, it will be remembered, had covenanted with the papacy to protect it from its adversaries. The king of the Lombards had taken advantage of Charlemagne's seeming preoccupation with his German affairs to attack the city of Rome again. The pope immediately demanded the aid of Charlemagne, who prepared to carry out his father's pledges. He ordered the Lombard ruler to return the cities that he had taken from the pope. Upon his refusal to do this, Charlemagne invaded Lombardy in 773 with a great army and took Pavia, the capital, after a long siege. The Lombard king was forced to become a monk, and his treasure was divided among the Frankish soldiers. Charlemagne then took the extremely important step, in 774, of having himself recognized by all the Lombard dukes and counts as king of the Lombards.

Charlemagne becomes king of the Lombards.

Aquitaine
and Bavaria
incorporated
in Charle-
magne's
empire.

The considerable provinces of Aquitaine and Bavaria had never formed an integral part of the Frankish realms, but had remained semi-independent under their native dukes up to the time of Charlemagne. Aquitaine, whose dukes had given Pippin much trouble, was incorporated into the Frankish state in 769. As for the Bavarians, Charlemagne felt that so long as they remained under their duke he could not rely upon them to defend the Frankish empire against the Slavs, who were constantly threatening the frontiers. So he compelled the duke of Bavaria to surrender his possessions, shut him up in a monastery, and proceeded to portion out the duchy among his counts. He thus added to his realms the district that lay between his new Saxon conquest and the Lombard kingdom.

Foreign
policy of
Charle-
magne.

31. So far we have spoken only of the relations of Charlemagne with the Germans, for even the Lombard kingdom was established by the Germans. He had, however, other peoples to deal with, especially the Slavs on the east (who were one day to build up the kingdoms of Poland, Bohemia, and the vast Russian empire) and, on the opposite boundary of his dominion, the Arabs in Spain. Against these it was necessary to protect his realms, and the second part of Charlemagne's reign was devoted to what may be called his foreign policy. A single campaign in 789 seems to have sufficed to subdue the Slavs, who lay to the north and east of the Saxons, and to force the Bohemians to acknowledge the supremacy of the Frankish king and pay tribute to him.

The
marches and
margraves.

The necessity of insuring the Frankish realms against any new uprising of these non-German nations led to the establishment, on the confines of the kingdom, of *marches*, i.e., districts under the military control of counts of the march, or *margraves*.[1] Their business was to prevent any hostile

---

[1] The king of Prussia still has, among other titles, that of Margrave of Brandenburg. The German word *Mark* is often used for " march " on maps of Germany.

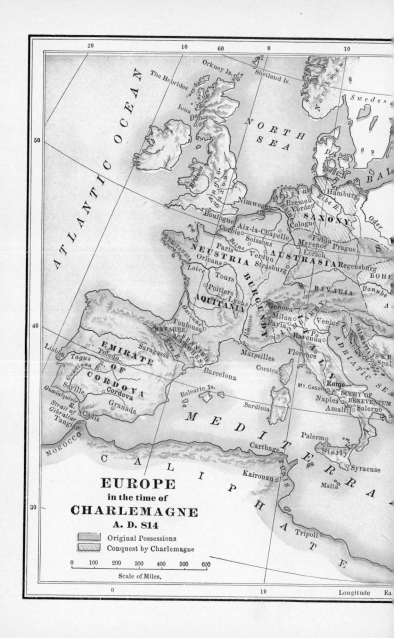

EUROPE
in the time of
CHARLEMAGNE
A. D. 814

Original Possessions
Conquest by Charlemagne

0   100   200   300   400   500   600
Scale of Miles.

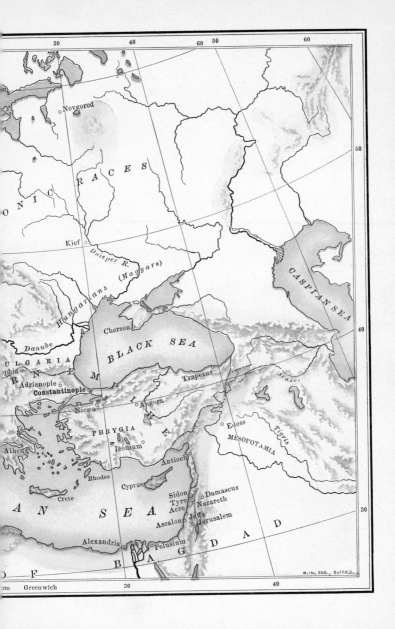

50

Novgorod

R A C E S

ONIC

CASPIAN SEA

Kief

Dnieper R.

(Magyars)

Hungarians

40

Cherson

B L A C K   S E A

Danube

ULGARIA

Araxes

ophia

R   E M

Trapezus

Adrianople

Constantinople

Nicaea

Angora

Edessa

MESOPOTAMIA

Tigris

PHRYGIA

Athens

Iconium

Antioch

Rhodes

Cyprus

Crete

A N   S   E A

Sidon
Tyre   Damascus
Acre Nazareth

Ascalon Jaffa
Jerusalem

Alexandria Pelusium

B A G D A D

30

M.-N. ENG., BUFFALO.

incursions into the interior of the kingdom. Much depended upon the efficiency of these men; in many cases they founded powerful families and later helped to disintegrate the Empire by establishing themselves as practically independent rulers.

At an assembly that Charlemagne held in 777, ambassadors appeared before him from certain disaffected Mohammedans. They had fallen out with the emir of Cordova [1] and now offered to become the faithful subjects of Charlemagne if he would come to their aid. In consequence, he undertook his first expedition to Spain in the following year. The district north of the Ebro was conquered by the Franks after some years of war, and Charlemagne established the Spanish March.[2] In this way he began that gradual expulsion of the Mohammedans from the peninsula which was to be carried on by slowly extending conquests until 1492, when Granada, the last Mohammedan stronghold, fell.[3]

Charlemagne in Spain.

32. But the most famous of all the achievements of Charlemagne was his reëstablishment of the Western Empire in the year 800. It came about in this wise. Charlemagne went to Rome in that year to settle a controversy between Pope Leo III and his enemies. To celebrate the satisfactory adjustment of the dispute, the pope held a solemn service on Christmas day in St. Peter's. As Charlemagne was kneeling before the altar during this service, the pope approached him and set a crown upon his head, saluting him, amid the acclamation of those present, as "Emperor of the Romans."

Charlemagne crowned emperor by the pope.

[1] The Mohammedan state had broken up in the eighth century, and the ruler of Spain first assumed the title of emir (about 756) and later (929) that of caliph. The latter title had originally been enjoyed only by the head of the whole Arab empire, who had his capital at Damascus, and later at Bagdad.

[2] As Charlemagne was crossing the Pyrenees, on his way back from Spain, his rear guard was attacked in the Pass of Roncesvalles. The chronicle simply states that Roland, Count of Brittany, was slain. This episode, however, became the subject of one of the most famous of the epics of the Middle Ages, the *Song of Roland*. See below, § 99.

[3] Reference, for Charlemagne's conquests, Emerton, *Introduction*, Chapter XIII; Oman, *Dark Ages*, Chapters XX–XXI.

Charlemagne
merited the
title of
emperor.

The reasons for this extraordinary act, which Charlemagne afterward persistently asserted took him completely by surprise, are given in one of the Frankish histories, the *Chronicles of Lorsch*, as follows : " The name of Emperor had ceased among the Greeks, for they were enduring the reign of a woman [Irene], wherefore it seemed good both to Leo, the apostolic pope, and to the holy fathers [the bishops] who were in council with him, and to all Christian men, that they should name Charles, king of the Franks, as Emperor. For he held Rome itself, where the ancient Cæsars had always dwelt, in addition to all his other possessions in Italy, Gaul and Germany. Wherefore, as God had granted him all these dominions, it seemed just to all that he should take the title of Emperor, too, when it was offered to him at the wish of all Christendom."

Charlemagne appears to have accepted gracefully the honor thus thrust upon him. Even if he had no right to the imperial title, there was an obvious propriety and expediency in granting it to him under the circumstances. Before his coronation by the pope he was only king of the Franks and the Lombards ; but his conquests seemed to entitle him to a more comprehensive designation which should include his outlying dependencies. Then the imperial power at Constantinople had been in the hands of heretics, from the standpoint of the Western Church, ever since Emperor Leo issued his edict against the veneration of images. What was still worse, the throne had been usurped, shortly before the coronation of Charlemagne, by the wicked Irene, who had deposed and blinded her son, Constantine VI. The coronation of Charlemagne was, therefore, only a recognition of the real political conditions in the West.[1]

Continuity of
the Roman
Empire.

The empire now reëstablished in the West was considered to be a continuation of the Roman Empire founded by Augustus. Charlemagne was reckoned the immediate successor of Constantine VI, whom Irene had deposed. Yet, in

[1] See *Readings*, Chapter VII, and Bryce, *Holy Roman Empire*, Chapter V.

spite of this fancied continuity, it is hardly necessary to say that the position of the new emperor had little in common with that of Marcus Aurelius or Constantine. In the first place, the eastern emperors continued to reign in Constantinople for centuries, quite regardless of Charlemagne and his successors. In the second place, the German kings who wore the imperial crown after Charlemagne were generally too weak really to rule over Germany and northern Italy, to say nothing of the rest of western Europe. Nevertheless, the Western Empire, which in the twelfth century came to be called the Holy Roman Empire, endured for over a thousand years. It came to an end only in 1806, when the last of the emperors, wearied of his empty if venerable title, laid down the crown.

The assumption of the title of emperor was destined to make the German rulers a great deal of trouble. It constantly led them into futile efforts to maintain a supremacy over Italy, which lay without their natural boundaries. Then the circumstances under which Charlemagne was crowned made it possible for the popes to claim, later, that it was they who had transferred the imperial power from the old eastern line of emperors to the Carolingian house, and that this was a proof of their right to dispose of the crown as they pleased. The difficulties which arose necessitated many a weary journey to Rome for the emperors, and many unworthy conflicts between the temporal and spiritual heads of Christendom.

The title of emperor a source of trouble to the German rulers.

33. The task of governing his vast and heterogeneous dominions taxed even the highly gifted and untiring Charlemagne; it quite exceeded the capacity of his successors. The same difficulties continued to exist that had confronted Charles Martel and Pippin,—above all a scanty royal revenue and overpowerful officials who were prone to neglect the interests and commands of their sovereign. Charlemagne's distinguished statesmanship is nowhere so clearly seen as in his measures for extending his control to the very confines of his realms.

Charlemagne's system of government.

**Charle-
magne's
farms.**

His income, like that of all mediæval rulers, came chiefly from his royal estates, as there was no system of general taxation such as had existed under the Roman Empire. He consequently took the greatest care that his numerous plantations should be well cultivated and that not even a turnip or an egg which was due him should be withheld. An elaborate set of regulations for his farms is preserved, which sheds much light upon the times.[1]

**Origin of
titles of
nobility.**

The officials upon whom the Frankish kings were forced to rely chiefly were the counts, the "hand and voice of the king" wherever he could not be in person. They were to maintain order, see that justice was done in their district, and raise troops when the king needed them. On the frontier were the counts of the march, or margraves (marquises), already mentioned. These titles, together with that of duke, still exist as titles of nobility in Europe, although they are no longer associated with governmental duties except where their holders have the right to sit in the upper house of parliament.

**The *missi
dominici*.**

To keep the counts in order, Charlemagne appointed royal commissioners (the *missi dominici*), whom he dispatched to all parts of his realm to investigate and report to him how things were going in the districts assigned to them. They were sent in pairs, a bishop and a layman, so that they might act as a check on one another. Their circuits were changed each year so that they should have no chance to enter into conspiracy with the counts whom it was their special business to watch.[2]

The revival of the Roman Empire in the West made no difference in Charlemagne's system of government, except that he required all his subjects above twelve years of age to take a new oath of fidelity to him as emperor. He held important

[1] See extracts from these regulations, and an account of one of Charlemagne's farms, in *Readings*, Chapter VII.
[2] For the capitulary relating to the duties of the *missi*, see *Readings*, Chapter VII.

assemblies of the nobles and prelates each spring or summer, where the interests of the Empire were considered. With the sanction of his advisers, he issued an extraordinary series of laws, called *capitularies*, a number of which have been preserved. With the bishops and abbots he discussed the needs of the Church, and above all the necessity of better schools for both the clergy and laity. The reforms which he sought to introduce give us an opportunity of learning the condition in which Europe found itself after four hundred years of disorder.

34. Charlemagne was the first important king since Theodoric to pay any attention to book learning, which had fared badly enough since the death of Boethius, three centuries before. About 650 the supply of papyrus had been cut off, owing to the conquest of Egypt by the Arabs, and as paper had not yet been invented there was only the very expensive parchment to write upon. While this had the advantage of being more durable than papyrus, its cost discouraged the multiplication of copies of books. The eighth century, that immediately preceding Charlemagne's coronation, is declared by the learned Benedictine monks, in their great history of French literature, to have been the most ignorant, the darkest, and the most barbarous period ever seen, at least in France. The documents of the Merovingian period often indicate great ignorance and carelessness on the part of those who wrote them out.

The dark century before Charlemagne.

Yet, in spite of this dark picture, there was promise for the future. It was evident, even before Charlemagne's time, that the world was not to continue indefinitely in the path of ignorance. Latin could not be forgotten, for that was the language of the Church and all its official communications were in that tongue. The teachings of the Christian religion had to be gathered from the Bible and other books, and the church services formed a small literature by themselves. Consequently it was absolutely necessary that the Church should maintain

The elements of learning preserved by the Church.

some sort of education in order to perform its complicated services and conduct the extensive duties which devolved upon it. All the really efficient church officers, whatever their nationality, must have been able to read the Latin classics, if they were so inclined. Then there were the compilations of ancient knowledge already mentioned,[1] which, incredibly crude and scanty as they were, kept up the memory of the past. They at least perpetuated the names of the various branches of knowledge and contained, for example, enough about arithmetic and astronomy to help the isolated churchman to calculate each year the date of Easter.

Two letters of Charlemagne's respecting the neglect of education among the clergy.

Charlemagne was the first temporal ruler to realize the serious neglect of education, even among the clergy, and we have two interesting letters from him, written before he was made emperor, relating to this subject. In one to an important bishop, he says : " Letters have been written to us frequently in recent years from various monasteries, stating that the brethren who dwelt therein were offering up holy and pious supplications in our behalf. We observed that the sentiments in these letters were exemplary but that the form of expression was uncouth, because what true devotion faithfully dictated to the mind, the tongue, untrained by reason of neglect of study, was not able to express in a letter without mistakes. So it came about that we began to fear lest, perchance, as the skill in writing was less than it should be, the wisdom necessary to the understanding of the Holy Scriptures was also much less than was needful. We all know well that, although errors of speech are dangerous, errors of understanding are far more dangerous. Therefore, we exhort you not merely not to *neglect* the study of letters, but with a most humble mind, pleasing to God, earnestly to devote yourself to study, in order that you may be able the more easily and correctly to penetrate the mysteries of the Holy Scriptures."

[1] See above, p. 32.

In the other letter he says : " We have striven with watchful zeal to advance the cause of learning which has been almost forgotten through the negligence of our ancestors; and by our own example, we invite all those who can, to master the studies of the liberal arts.   In this spirit, God aiding us, we have already carefully corrected all the books of the Old and New Testaments, corrupted by the ignorance of the copyists."

mereamini; Scit namq; pru
dentia uře . quě terribili
anathematiscensura ferientur:
Qui presumptiose contra statu
te uniuersalice conciliorū
uenire audeunt . Quepropt
&uosdiligentius amonone
ut omni intentione illudor
ribile execratione iudicio

An Example of the Style of Writing used in the Books of
Charlemagne's Time [1]

[1] These lines are taken from a manuscript written in 825.   They form a part of a copy of Charlemagne's admonition to the clergy (789) mentioned below. The part here given is addressed to the bishops and warns them of the terrible results of disobeying the rules of the Church.   Perhaps the scribe did not fully understand what he was doing, for he has made some of those mistakes which Charlemagne was so anxious to avoid.   Then there are some abbreviations which make the lines difficult to read.   They ought probably to have run as follows: . . . *mereamini. Scit namque prudentia vestra, quam terribili anathematis censura feriuntur qui praesumptiose contra statuta universalium conciliorum venire audeant.   Quapropter et vos diligentius ammonemus, ut omni intentione illud horribile execrationis judicium* . . .

It seemed to Charlemagne that it was the duty of the Church not only to look after the education of its own officers but to provide the opportunity of at least an elementary education for the people at large. In accordance with this conviction, he issued (789) an admonition to the clergy to gather together the children both of freemen and serfs in their neighborhood and establish schools "in which the boys may learn to read." [1]

Establishment of monastery schools and the 'school of the palace.' It would be impossible to say how many of the innumerable abbots and bishops established schools in accordance with Charlemagne's recommendations. It is certain that famous centers of learning existed at Tours, Fulda, Corbie, Orleans, and other places during his reign. Charlemagne further promoted the cause of education by the establishment of the famous "school of the palace" for the instruction of the sons of his nobles and of his own children. He placed the Englishman, Alcuin, at the head of the school, and called distinguished men from Italy and elsewhere as teachers. The best known of these was the historian, Paulus Diaconus, who wrote a history of the Lombards, to which we owe most of what we know about them.

Charlemagne appears to have been particularly impressed with the constant danger of mistakes in copying books, a task frequently turned over to ignorant and careless persons. After recommending the founding of schools, he continues : " Correct carefully the Psalms, the signs used in music, the [Latin] grammar, and the religious books used in every monastery or bishopric ; since those who desire to pray to God properly often pray badly because of the incorrect books. And do not let your boys misread or miswrite them. If there is any need to copy the Gospel, Psalter or Missal, let men of maturity do the writing with great diligence." These precautions were amply justified, for a careful transmission of the literature

[1] See *Readings*, Chapter VII.

of the past was as important as the attention to education. It will be noted that Charlemagne made no attempt to revive the learning of Greece and Rome. He deemed it quite sufficient if the churchmen would learn their Latin well enough to read the missal and the Bible intelligently.

The hopeful beginning that was made under Charlemagne in the revival of education and intellectual interest was destined to prove disappointing in its immediate results. It is true that the ninth century produced a few noteworthy men who have left works which indicate acuteness and mental training. But the break-up of Charlemagne's empire, the struggles between his descendants, the coming of new barbarians, and the disorder caused by the unruly feudal lords, who were not inclined to recognize any master, all conspired to keep the world back for at least two centuries more. Indeed, the tenth and the first half of the eleventh centuries seem, at first sight, little better than the seventh and eighth. Yet ignorance and disorder never were quite so prevalent after, as they were before, Charlemagne.

General Reading. — The best life of Charlemagne in English is MOMBERT, *A History of Charles the Great* (D. C. Appleton & Co., $5.00). See also HODGKIN, *Charles the Great* (The Macmillan Company, 75 cents), and WEST, *Alcuin* (Charles Scribner's Sons, $1.00).

CHAPTER VIII

THE DISRUPTION OF CHARLEMAGNE'S EMPIRE

Louis the Pious succeeds Charlemagne.

35. It was a matter of great importance to the world whether Charlemagne's extensive empire was, after his death, to remain one or to fall apart. He himself appears to have had no expectation that it would hold together, for in 806 he divided it up in a very arbitrary manner among his three sons. We do not know whether he was led thus to undo his life's work simply because the older tradition of a division among the king's sons was as yet too strong to permit him to hand down all his possessions to his eldest son, or because he believed it would be impossible to keep together so vast and heterogeneous a realm. However this may have been, the death of his two eldest sons left only Louis, who succeeded his father both as king and emperor.

Partition of Charlemagne's empire among the sons of Louis the Pious.

Louis the Pious had been on the throne but a few years before he took up the all-important problem of determining what share each of his sons should have in the empire after his death. As they were far too ambitious to submit to the will of their father, we find no less than six different partitions between the years 817 and 840. We cannot stop to trace these complicated and transient arrangements, or the rebellions of the undutiful sons, who set the worst possible example to the ambitious and disorderly nobles. On the death of Louis the Pious, in 840, his second son, Louis the German, was in possession of Bavaria and had at various times been recognized as ruler of most of those parts of the empire now included in Germany. The youngest son, Charles the Bald, had all the western portion of the Frankish possessions, while Lothaire, the eldest, had been designated as emperor and ruled over Italy and the district lying between the possessions of the younger brothers. Charles and Louis promptly combined to resist the attempts of Lothaire to assert his superiority as emperor, and defeated him at Fontenay (841). The treaty of Verdun, which followed, is one of the most memorable in the history of western Europe.[1]

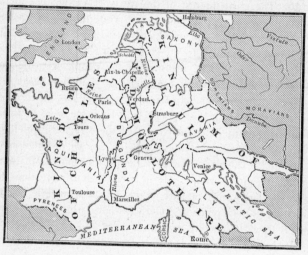

Map of Treaty of Verdun

In the negotiations which led up to the treaty of Verdun there appears to have been entire agreement among the three parties that Italy should go to Lothaire, Aquitaine to Charles the Bald, and Bavaria to Louis the German. The real difficulty lay in the disposal of the rest of the empire. It seemed appropriate that the older brother, as emperor, should have, in addition to Italy, the center of the Frankish dominions,

Treaty of Verdun, 843.

---

[1] References for the reign of Louis the Pious, Henderson, *Germany in the Middle Ages*, Chapter VI; Oman, *Dark Ages*, Chapter XXIII.

including the capital, Aix-la-Chapelle. A state of the most artificial kind, extending from Rome to northern Holland, was thus created, which had no natural unity of language or custom. Louis the German was assigned, in addition to Bavaria, the country north of Lombardy and westward to the Rhine. As for Charles the Bald, his realm included a great part of what is France to-day, as well as the Spanish March and Flanders.

36. The great interest of the treaty of Verdun lies in the tolerably definite appearance of a western and an eastern Frankish kingdom, one of which was to become France and the other Germany. In the kingdom of Charles the Bald the dialects spoken by the majority of the people were derived directly from the spoken Latin, and in time developed into Provençal and French. In the kingdom of Louis the German, on the other hand, both people and language were German. The narrow strip of country between these regions, which fell to Lothaire, came to be called *Lotharii regnum,* or kingdom of Lothaire.[1] This name was perverted in time into Lotharingia and, later, into Lorraine. It is interesting to note that this territory has formed a part of the debatable middle ground over which the French and Germans have struggled so obstinately down to our own day.

The Strasburg oaths.

We have a curious and important evidence of the difference of language just referred to, in the so-called Strasburg oaths (842). Just before the settlement at Verdun, the younger brothers had found it advisable to pledge themselves, in an especially solemn and public manner, to support one another against the pretensions of Lothaire. First, each of the two brothers addressed his soldiers in their own language, absolving them from their allegiance to him should he desert his brother. Louis then took the oath in what the chronicle calls the *lingua romana,* so that his brother's soldiers might understand him, and Charles repeated his oath in the *lingua teudisca* for

[1] Named for Lothaire II.

the benefit of Louis' soldiers.[1] Fortunately the texts of both of these oaths have been preserved. They are exceedingly interesting and important as furnishing our earliest examples, except some lists of words, of the language spoken by the common people, which was only just beginning to be written. Probably German was very rarely written before this time, as all who could write at all wrote in Latin. The same is true of the old

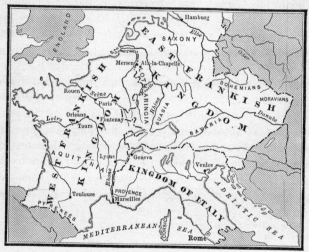

Map of Treaty of Mersen

Romance tongue (from which modern French developed), which had already drifted far from the Latin.

37. When Lothaire died (855) he left Italy and the middle kingdom to his three sons. By 870 two of these had died, and their uncles, Charles the Bald and Louis the German, did not hesitate to appropriate the middle kingdom and divide it

New divisions of the empire corresponding to France, Germany, and Italy.

[1] For the text and translation of the Strasburg oaths, see Emerton, *Mediæval Europe*, pp. 26–27, or Munro, *Mediæval History*, p. 20. A person familiar with Latin and French could puzzle out a part of the oath in the *lingua romana ;* that in the *lingua teudisca* would be almost equally intelligible to one familiar with German.

between them by the treaty of Mersen. Italy was left to Lothaire's only surviving son, together with the imperial crown, which was to mean nothing, however, for a hundred years to come. The result was that, as early as 870, western Europe was divided into three great districts which corresponded with startling exactness to three important states of modern Europe, i.e., France, Germany, and Italy.

The empire temporarily reunited under Charles the Fat. Louis the German was succeeded in the East-Frankish kingdom by his son, Charles the Fat. In 884, owing to the death of the sons and the grandsons of Charles the Bald, there was no one to represent his line except a child of five years. So the aristocracy of the West-Frankish kingdom invited Charles the Fat to become their king. In this way it came about that the whole empire of Charlemagne was reunited for two or three years under a single ruler.[1]

Charles the Fat and the Northmen. Charles the Fat was ill and proved an incompetent emperor, entirely unequal to the serious task of governing and protecting his vast territories. His weakness was especially shown in his pusillanimous treaties with the Northmen. When Paris was making an heroic defense against them under its count, Odo,

[1] The following table will show the relationship of the descendants of Charlemagne:

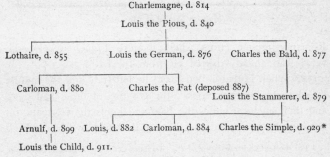

Charlemagne, d. 814

Louis the Pious, d. 840

Lothaire, d. 855   Louis the German, d. 876   Charles the Bald, d. 877

Carloman, d. 880   Charles the Fat (deposed 887)

Louis the Stammerer, d. 879

Arnulf, d. 899   Louis, d. 882   Carloman, d. 884   Charles the Simple, d. 929*

Louis the Child, d. 911.

* Who was too young to be considered in 884, but afterwards became king of France and progenitor of the later Carolingian rulers.

Charles, instead of marching at the head of an army to relieve it, agreed to pay the invaders seven hundred pounds of silver if they would raise the siege. They were then permitted to take up their winter quarters far inland, in Burgundy, where they proceeded to burn and pillage at will.

This degrading agreement so disgusted the West-Frankish nobility that they were glad to join a conspiracy set on foot by Charles' nephew, the brave Arnulf of Carinthia, who had resolved to supplant his inefficient uncle. Charles was deposed and deserted by all his former supporters in 887. No one, except Napoleon, has ever again succeeded in bringing the eastern, western, and southern parts of Charlemagne's empire under his control, even for a brief period. Arnulf, although enjoying the title of emperor, could scarcely hope to be recognized as king in all parts of the Frankish empire. Even nominal unity was no longer possible. As one of the chronicles of the time puts it, " While Arnulf was frittering away his time, many little kingdoms grew up."

Charles the Fat deposed and succeeded by Arnulf.

In the West-Frankish territory the nobility of the northern part chose Odo, the hero of the siege of Paris, as their king; but in the south another enterprising nobleman, Count Boso of Vienne, succeeded in inducing the pope to crown him king of a certain district on the Rhone which included Provence. Immediately after Boso's death a large territory about the Lake of Geneva, which he had hoped to win for himself, became a separate kingdom under its own ruler. This region and that which Boso ruled to the south were later united into the kingdom of Burgundy, or, as it is often called, Arles.

Origin of the kingdom of Burgundy, or Arles.

Even before the deposition of Charles the Fat, many of the counts and other important landowners began to take advantage of the weakness of their king to establish themselves as the rulers of the districts about them, although they did not assume the title of king. In the East-Frankish kingdom the various German peoples whom Charlemagne had managed to control, especially the Bavarians and Saxons, began to revive their old national independence. In Italy the disruption was even more marked than in the north.[1]

Causes of disruption.

38. It is clear, from what has been said, that none of the rulers into whose hands the fragments of Charlemagne's empire fell, showed himself powerful and skillful enough to govern properly a great territory like that embraced in France or Germany to-day. The difficulties in the way of establishing a well-regulated state, in the modern sense of the word, were almost insurmountable. In the first place, it was well-nigh impossible to keep in touch with all parts of a wide realm.

Poor roads.

The wonderful roads which the Romans had built had generally fallen into decay, for there was no longer a corps of engineers maintained by the government to keep them up and repair the bridges. In those parts of Charlemagne's possessions that lay beyond the confines of the old Roman Empire, the impediments to travel must have been still worse than in Gaul and on the Rhine ; there not even the vestiges of Roman roads existed.

Scarcity of money for paying government officers and maintaining armies.

In addition to the difficulty of getting about, the king had to contend with the scarcity of money in the Middle Ages. This prevented him from securing the services of a great corps of paid officials, such as every government finds necessary to-day. Moreover, it made it impossible for him to support the standing army which would have been necessary to suppress the constant insubordination of his officials and of the powerful and restless nobility, whose chief interest in life was fighting.

New invasions, — the Northmen, Slavs, Hungarians, and Saracens.

The disintegration of the Frankish empire was hastened by the continued invasions from all sides. From the north — Denmark, Norway, and Sweden — came the Scandinavian

[1] Reference, Henderson, *Germany in the Middle Ages*, Chapter VII; Oman, *Dark Ages*, Chapter XXV.

pirates, the Northmen.[1] They were skillful and daring sea-men, who not only harassed the coast of the North Sea, but made their way up the rivers, plundering and burning towns inland as far as Paris. On the eastern boundary of the empire the Germans were forced to engage in constant war-fare with the Slavs. Before long the Hungarians, a savage race, began their terrible incursions into central Germany and northern Italy. From the south came the Saracens, who had got possession of Sicily (in 827), and terrorized southern Italy and France, even attacking Rome itself.

39. In the absence of a powerful king with a well-organized army at his back, each district was left to look out for itself. Doubtless many counts, margraves, bishops, and other great landed proprietors who were gradually becoming independent princes, earned the loyalty of the people about them by taking the lead in defending the country against its invaders and by establishing fortresses as places of refuge when the community was hard pressed. These conditions serve to explain why such government as continued to exist during the centuries following the deposition of Charles the Fat was necessarily carried on mainly, not by the king and his officers, but by the great landholders. The grim fortresses of the mediæval lords, which appeared upon almost every point of vantage through-out western Europe during the Middle Ages, would not have been tolerated by the king, had he been powerful enough to destroy them. They plainly indicate that their owners were practically independent rulers.

Growing power and independence of the great landed pro-prietor.

[1] Reference, Munro, *Mediæval History*, pp. 34–39. The Northmen extended their expeditions to Spain, Italy, and even into Russia. In England, under the name of Danes, we find them forcing Alfred the Great to recognize them as the masters of northern England (878). The Norse pirates were often called *vikings*, from their habit of leaving their long boats in the *vik*, i.e., bay or inlet. A goodly number of the Northmen settled in Iceland, and our knowledge of their civilization and customs comes chiefly from the Icelandic *sagas*, or tales. Some of these are of great interest and beauty; perhaps none is finer than *The Story of Burnt Njal*. This and others may be read in English. See *Readings*, Chapter VIII.

When the traveler in France or Germany comes upon the picturesque ruins of a mediæval castle, perched upon some rocky cliff, accessible from one side only, and commanding the surrounding country, he cannot but see that those massive walls, with their towers and battlements, their moat and drawbridge, were never intended as a dwelling place for the peaceful household of a private citizen, but rather as the fortified palace of a ruler. We can picture the great hall crowded with armed retainers, who were ready to fight for the proprietor when he was disposed to attack a neighboring lord, and who knew that below were the dungeons to which the lord might send them if they ventured to rebel against his authority.

Mediæval Fortress, showing Moat and Drawbridges

The landed proprietor and the manor.
In order to understand the position of the mediæval noble and the origin of feudalism we must consider the situation of the great landowners. A large part of western Europe in the time of Charlemagne appears to have been divided up into great estates, resembling the Roman villas. Just how these originated we do not know. These estates, or *manors*, as they were called, were cultivated mainly by serfs, who were bound to the land and were under the control of its proprietor. They

tilled such part of the estate as the owner reserved for his own particular use, and provided for his needs and their own without the necessity of buying much from the outside. When we speak of a mediæval landowner we mean one who held one or more of these manors, which served to support him and left him free to busy himself fighting with other proprietors in the same position as himself.[1]

It had been common even before Charlemagne's time to grant to monasteries and churches, and even to individuals, an extraordinary privilege which exempted their lands from the presence or visits of government officials. No public officer with the power to hear cases, exact fines, obtain lodging or entertainment for the king and his followers when traveling about, or make requisitions of any kind, was to enter the lands or villages belonging to the monastery or person enjoying the *immunity*. These exemptions were evidently sought with a view to getting rid of the exactions of the king's officials and appropriating the various fines and fees, rather than with the purpose of usurping governmental prerogatives. But the result was that the monasteries or individuals who were thus freed from the requisitions of the government were left to perform its functions, — not, however, as yet in their own right, but as representatives of the king.[2] It is not hard to see how those who enjoyed this privilege might, as the central power weakened, become altogether independent. It is certain that a great many landowners who had been granted no exemption from the jurisdiction of the king's officers, and a great many of the officers themselves, especially the counts and margraves, gradually broke away altogether from the control of those above them and became the rulers of the regions in which they lived.

Immunities.

[1] An account of the manor will be given later, Chapter XVIII.

[2] See an example of an immunity granted by Charlemagne to a monastery, in Emerton, *Introduction*, pp. 246–249, also Munro, *Mediæval History*, p. 44. Other examples are given in the *Readings*, Chapter IX.

Tendency to hereditary offices.

The counts were in a particularly favorable position to usurp for their own benefit the powers which they were supposed to exercise for the king. Charlemagne had chosen his counts and margraves in most cases from the wealthy and distinguished families of his realms. As he had little money, he generally rewarded their services by grants of estates, which only served to increase their independence. They gradually came to look upon their office and their land as private property, and they were naturally disposed to hand it on to their sons after them. Charlemagne had been able to keep control of his agents by means of the *missi*. After his death his system fell into disuse and it became increasingly difficult to get rid of inefficient or rebellious officers.

Forces opposed to disruption, viz., partial survival of royal authority and feudalism.

Yet we must not infer that the state ceased to exist altogether during the centuries of confusion that followed the break-up of Charlemagne's empire, or that it fell entirely apart into little local governments independent of each other. In the first place, a king always retained some of his ancient majesty. He might be weak and without the means to enforce his rights and to compel his more powerful subjects to meet their obligations toward him. Yet he was, after all, the *king*, solemnly anointed by the Church as God's representative on earth. He was always something more than a feudal lord. The kings were destined to get the upper hand before many centuries in England, France, and Spain, and finally in Italy and Germany, and to destroy the castles behind whose walls their haughty nobles had long defied the royal power.

Feudalism.

In the second place, the innumerable independent landowners were held together by *feudalism*. One who had land to spare granted a portion of it to another person on condition that the one receiving the land should swear to be true to him and perform certain services, — such as fighting for him, giving him counsel, and lending aid when he was in particular difficulties. In this way the relation of lord and vassal originated.

All lords were vassals either of the king or of other lords, and consequently all were bound together by solemn engagements to be loyal to one another and care for one another's interests. Feudalism served thus as a sort of substitute for the state. Private arrangements between one landowner and another took the place of the weakened bond between the subject and his king.

The feudal form of government and the feudal system of holding land are so different from anything with which we are now familiar that it is difficult for us to understand them. Yet unless we do understand them, a great part of the history of Europe during the past thousand years will be well-nigh meaningless.[1]

[1] Extracts from the chronicles of the ninth century illustrating the disorder of the period will be found in the *Readings*, Chapter VIII.

CHAPTER IX

FEUDALISM

Feudalism
the out-
growth of
prevailing
conditions
and earlier
customs.

40. Feudalism was the natural outcome of the peculiar conditions which prevailed in western Europe during the ninth and tenth centuries. Its chief elements were not, however, newly invented or discovered at that period but were only combined in order to meet the demands of the times. It will be well, therefore, to consider briefly those customs in the later Roman Empire and among the invading Germans which suggest (1) the habit of the mediæval landowner of granting his land to others in such a way that, while he retained the title, they became, to most intents and purposes, the real owners; and (2) the relation of lord and vassal.

Conditions of landholding in the later Roman Empire.

We have seen how, before the barbarian inroads, the small landowners in the Roman Empire had often found it to their advantage to give up the title to their land to more powerful neighboring proprietors.[1] The scarcity of labor was such that the new owner, while extending the protection of his name over the land, was glad to permit the former owner to continue to till it, rent free, much as if it still belonged to him. With the invasions of the barbarians the lot of the defenseless small landholder became worse. He had a new resource, however, in the monasteries. The monks were delighted to accept any real estate which the owner — for the good of his soul and to gain the protection of the saint to whom the monastery church was dedicated — felt moved to turn over to them on the understanding that the abbot should permit the former owner to

[1] See above, p. 16.

continue to cultivate his fields. Though he no longer owned the land, he still enjoyed its products and had only to pay a trifling sum each year in recognition of the monastery's ownership.[1] The use, or *usufruct*, of the land which was thus granted by the monastery to its former owner was called a *beneficium*. The same term was applied to the numerous grants which churches made from their vast possessions for limited periods and upon various conditions. We also find the Frankish kings and other great landowners disposing of their lands in a similar fashion. The *beneficium* forms the first stage in the development of mediæval landowning.

The beneficium.

Side by side with the *beneficium* grew up another institution which helps to explain the relation of lord and vassal in later times. Under the later Roman Empire the freeman who owned no land and found himself unable to gain a living might become the dependent of some rich and powerful neighbor, who agreed to feed, clothe, and protect him on condition that he should engage to be faithful to his patron, " love all that he loved and shun all that he shunned." [2]

The origin of the relationship of lord and vassal.

The invading Germans had a custom that so closely resembled this Roman one that scholars have found it impossible to decide whether we should attribute more influence to the Roman or to the German institution in the development of feudalism. We learn from Tacitus that the young German warriors were in the habit of pledging their fidelity to a popular chieftain, who agreed to support his faithful followers if they would fight at his side. The *comitatus*, as Tacitus named this arrangement, was not regarded by the Germans as a mere

The comitatus.

---

[1] See an example of this form of grant in the seventh century in *Readings*, Chapter IX. The reader will also find there a considerable number of illustrations of feudal contracts, etc.

[2] See formula of " commendation," as this arrangement was called, in *Readings*, Chapter IX. The fact that the Roman imperial government forbade this practice under heavy penalties suggests that the local magnates used their retainers to establish their independence of the imperial taxgatherers and other government officials.

business transaction, but was looked upon as honorable alike to lord and man. Like the later relation of vassal and lord, it was entered upon with a solemn ceremony and the bond of fidelity was sanctioned by an oath. The obligations of mutual aid and support established between the leader and his followers were considered most sacred.

Combination of the *comitatus* and the *beneficium* produces feudal land tenure.

While there was a great difference between the homeless and destitute fellow who became the humble client of a rich Roman landowner, and the noble young German warrior who sat at the board of a distinguished military leader, both of these help to account for the later feudal arrangement by which one person became the " man," or faithful and honorable dependent, of another. When, after the death of Charlemagne, men began to combine the idea of the *comitatus* with the idea of the *beneficium*, and to grant the usufruct of parcels of their land on condition that the grantee should be true, loyal, and helpful to them, that is, become their *vassal*, we may consider that the feudal system of landowning was coming into existence.[1]

Gradual development of feudalism.

41. Feudalism was not established by any decree of a king or in virtue of any general agreement between all the landowners. It grew up gradually and irregularly without any conscious plan on any one's part, simply because it seemed convenient and natural under the circumstances. The owner of vast estates found it to his advantage to parcel them out among vassals who agreed to accompany him to war, attend his court, guard his castle upon occasion, and assist him when he was put to any unusually great expense. Land granted upon the terms

The fief.

mentioned was said to be " infeudated " and was called a *fief*. One who held a fief might himself become a lord by granting a portion of his fief to a vassal upon terms similar to those upon which he held of his lord or suzerain.[2] This was called

[1] See Adams, *Civilization*, pp. 207 *sqq.*

[2] Lord is *dominus*, or *senior*, in mediæval Latin. From the latter word the French *seigneur* is derived. *Suzerain* is used to mean the direct lord and also an *overlord* separated by one or more degrees from a subvassal.

subinfeudation, and the vassal of a vassal was called a *subvassal* or *subtenant*. There was still another way in which the number of vassals was increased. The owners of small estates were usually in a defenseless condition, unable to protect themselves against the insolence of the great nobles. They consequently found it to their advantage to put their land into the hands of a neighboring lord and receive it back from him as a fief. They thus became his vassals and could call upon him for protection.

It is apparent, from what has been said, that, all through the Middle Ages, feudalism continued to grow, as it were, "from the top and bottom and in the middle all at once." (1) Great landowners carved out new fiefs from their domains and granted them to new vassals. (2) Those who held small tracts brought them into the feudal relation by turning them over to a lord or monastery, whose vassals they became. (3) Finally any lord might subinfeudate portions of his estate by granting them as fiefs to those whose fidelity or services he wished to secure. By the thirteenth century it had become the rule in France that there should be "no land without its lord." This corresponded pretty closely to the conditions which existed at that period throughout the whole of western Europe.

It is essential to observe that the fief, unlike the *beneficium*, was not granted for a certain number of years, or for the life of the grantee, to revert at his death to the owner. On the contrary, it became hereditary in the family of the vassal and passed down to the eldest son from one generation to another. So long as the vassal remained faithful to his lord and performed the stipulated services, and his successors did homage and continued to meet the conditions upon which the fief had originally been granted, neither the lord nor his heirs could rightfully regain possession of the land. No precise date can be fixed at which it became customary to make fiefs hereditary; it is safe, however, to say that it was the rule in the tenth century.[1]

The kings and great nobles perceived clearly enough the disadvantage of losing control of their lands by permitting them to become hereditary property in the families of their vassals. But the feeling that what the father had enjoyed should pass to his children, who, otherwise, would ordinarily have been reduced to poverty, was so strong that all opposition on the part of the lord proved vain. The result was that little was left to the original and still nominal owner of the fief except the services and dues to which the practical owner, the vassal, had agreed in receiving it. In short, the fief came really to belong to the vassal, and only a shadow of his former proprietorship remained in the hands of the lord. Nowadays the owner of land either makes some use of it himself or leases it for a definite period at a fixed money rent. But in the Middle Ages most of the land was held by those who neither really owned it nor paid a regular rent for it and yet who could not be deprived of it by the original owner or his successors.

Subvassals of the king not under his control.

Obviously the great vassals who held directly of the king became almost independent of him as soon as their fiefs were granted to them in perpetuity. Their vassals, since they stood in no feudal relation to the king, escaped the royal control altogether. From the ninth to the thirteenth century the king of France or the king of Germany did not rule over a great realm occupied by subjects who owed him obedience as their lawful sovereign, paid him taxes, and were bound to fight under his banner as the head of the state. As a feudal landlord

[1] A relic of the time when fiefs were just becoming hereditary was preserved in the exaction by the lord of a certain due, called the *relief*. This payment was demanded from the vassal when one lord died and a new one succeeded him, and from a new vassal upon the death of his predecessor. It was originally the payment for a new grant of the land at a time when fiefs were not generally held hereditarily. The right did not exist in the case of all fiefs and it varied greatly in amount. It was customarily much heavier when the one succeeding to the fief was not the son of the former holder but a nephew or more distant relative.

himself, he had a right to demand fidelity and certain services from those who were his vassals. But the great mass of the people over whom he nominally ruled, whether they belonged to the nobility or not, owed little to the king directly, because they lived upon the lands of other feudal lords more or less independent of him.

Enough has been said of the gradual and irregular growth of feudalism to make it clear that complete uniformity in feudal customs could hardly exist within the bounds of even a small kingdom, much less throughout the countries of western Europe. Yet there was a remarkable resemblance between the institutions of France, England, and Germany, so that a description of the chief features of feudalism in France, where it was highly developed, will serve as a key to the general situation in all the countries we are studying.

42. The fief (Latin, *feudum*) was the central institution of feudalism and the one from which it derives its name. In the commonest acceptance of the word, the fief was land, the perpetual use of which was granted by its owner, or holder, to another person, on condition that the one receiving it should become his vassal. The one proposing to become a vassal knelt before the lord and rendered him *homage*[1] by placing his hands between those of the lord and declaring himself the lord's " man " for such and such a fief. Thereupon the lord gave his vassal the kiss of peace and raised him from his kneeling posture. Then the vassal took the oath of fidelity upon the Bible, or some holy relic, solemnly binding himself to fulfill all his duties toward his lord. This act of rendering homage by placing the hands in those of the lord and taking the oath of fidelity was the first and most essential obligation of the vassal and constituted the *feudal bond*. For a vassal to refuse to do homage for his fief when it changed hands, was equivalent to a declaration of revolt and independence.

The fief the central institution of feudalism.

Homage.

[1] Homage is derived from the Latin word for man, *homo*.

Obligations of the vassal. Military service.

The obligations of the vassal varied greatly.[1] Sometimes homage meant no more than that the vassal bound himself not to attack or injure his lord in honor or estate, or oppose his interests in any other manner. The vassal was expected to join his lord when there was a military expedition on foot, although it was generally the case that the vassal need not serve at his own expense for more than forty days. The rules, too, in regard to the length of time during which a vassal might be called upon to guard the castle of his lord varied almost infinitely. The shorter periods of military service proved very inconvenient to the lord. Consequently it became common in the thirteenth century for the king and the more important nobles to secure a body of soldiers upon whom they could rely at any time, and for any length of time, by creating money fiefs.

Money fiefs.

A certain income was granted to a knight upon condition that the grantee should not only become a vassal of the lord but should also agree to fight for him whenever it was necessary.

Other feudal obligations.

Besides the military service due from the vassal to his lord, he was expected to attend the lord's court when summoned. There he sat with other vassals to hear and pronounce upon those cases in which his peers — i.e., his fellow-vassals — were involved.[2] Moreover, he had to give the lord the benefit of his counsel when required, and attend him upon solemn

---

[1] The conditions upon which fiefs were granted might be dictated either by interest or by mere fancy. Sometimes the most fantastic and seemingly absurd obligations were imposed. We hear of vassals holding on condition of attending the lord at supper with a tall candle, or furnishing him with a great yule log at Christmas. Perhaps the most extraordinary instance upon record is that of a lord in Guienne who solemnly declared upon oath, when questioned by the commissioners of Edward I, that he held his fief of the king upon the following terms: When the lord king came through his estate he was to accompany him to a certain oak. There he must have waiting a cart loaded with wood and drawn by two cows without any tails. When the oak was reached, fire was to be applied to the cart and the whole burned up "unless mayhap the cows make their escape."

[2] The feudal courts, especially those of the great lords and of the king himself, were destined to develop later into the centers of real government, with regular judicial, financial, and administrative bodies for the performance of political functions.

occasions. Under certain circumstances vassals had to make Money payments. money payments to their lord, as well as serve him in person; as, for instance, when the fief changed hands through the death of the lord or of the vassal, when the fief was alienated, when the lord was put to extra expense by the necessity of knighting his eldest son or providing a dowry for his daughter, or when he was in captivity and was held for a ransom. Lastly, the vassal might have to entertain his lord should the

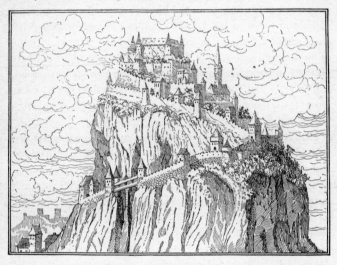

A Mediæval Castle near Klagenfurt, Austria

lord come his way. There are amusingly detailed accounts, in some of the feudal contracts, of exactly how often the lord might come, how many followers he might bring, and what he should have to eat.

There were fiefs of all kinds and of all grades of importance, Different classes of fiefs. from that of a duke or count, who held directly of the king and exercised the powers of a practically independent prince, down to the holding of the simple knight, whose bit of land, cultivated by peasants or serfs, was barely sufficient to enable him to support himself and provide the horse upon which he rode to perform his military service for his lord.

The nobility. In order to rank as a noble in mediæval society it was, in general, necessary to be the holder of land for which only such services were due as were considered honorable, and none of those which it was customary for the peasant or serf to perform. The noble must, moreover, be a free man and have at least sufficient income to maintain himself and his horse **Their privi-** without any sort of labor. The nobles enjoyed certain privi-**leges.** leges which set them off from the non-noble classes. Many of these privileges were perpetuated in France, and elsewhere on the continent, down to the time of the French Revolution, and in Italy and Germany, into the nineteenth century. The most conspicuous privilege was a partial exemption from taxation.

Difficulty of It is natural to wish to classify the nobility and to ask just **classifying** **the nobles.** what was the difference, for example, between a duke, a count, and a marquis. Unfortunately there was no fixed classification, at least before the thirteenth century. A count, for instance, might be a very inconspicuous person, having a fief no larger than the county of Charlemagne's time, or he might possess a great many of the older counties and rank in power with a duke. In general, however, it may be said that the dukes, counts, bishops, and abbots who held directly from the king were of the highest rank. Next to them came an intermediate class of nobles of the second order, generally subvassals of the king, and below these the simple knights.

Feudal 43. The great complexity of the feudal system of land **registers.** tenure made it necessary for the feudal lords to keep careful registers of their possessions. Very few of these registers have been preserved, but we are so fortunate as to have one of the count of Champagne, dating from the early thirteenth century. This gives us an idea of what feudalism really was in practice, and shows how impossible it is to make a satisfactory map of any country during the feudal period.

At the opening of the tenth century we find in the chronicles of the time an account of a certain ambitious count of Troyes, Robert by name, who died in 923 while trying to wrest the crown of France from Charles the Simple. His Growth of the possessions of the counts of Champagne typical of the period.

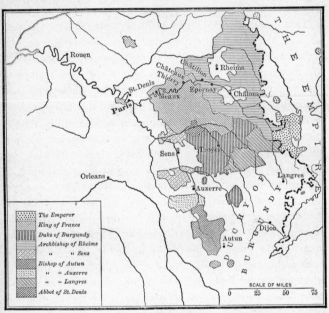

The Emperor

King of France

Duke of Burgundy

Archbishop of Rheims

" " Sens

Bishop of Autun

" " Auxerre

" " Langres

Abbot of St. Denis

SCALE OF MILES

0   25   50   75

Fiefs and Suzerains of the Counts of Champagne

county passed to his son-in-law, who already held, among other possessions, the counties of Château-Thierry and Meaux. His son, in turn, inherited all three counties and increased his dominions by judicious usurpations. This process of gradual aggrandizement went on for generation after generation, until there came to be a compact district under the control of the counts of Champagne, as they began to call themselves at the opening of the twelfth century. It was in this way that the feudal states in France and Germany grew up. Certain lines of feudal lords showed themselves able, partly by craft and violence, and partly, doubtless, by good fortune, to piece together a considerable district, in much the same way as we shall find that the king of France later pieced together France itself.

The register of the counts of Champagne illustrates the complexity of feudal relations. The register referred to above shows that the feudal possessions of the counts of Champagne were divided into twenty-six districts, each of which centered about a strong castle. We may infer that these divisions bore some close relation to the original counties which the counts of Champagne had succeeded in bringing together. All these districts were held as fiefs of other lords. For the greater number of his fiefs the count rendered homage to the king of France, but he was the vassal of no less than nine other lords beside the king. A portion of his lands, including probably his chief town of Troyes, he held of the duke of Burgundy. Châtillon, Épernay, and some other towns, he held as the "man" of the Archbishop of Rheims. He was also the vassal of the Archbishop of Sens, of four other neighboring bishops, and of the abbot of the great monastery of St. Denis. To all of these persons he had pledged himself to be faithful and true, and when his various lords fell out with one another it must have been difficult to see where his duty lay. Yet his situation was similar to that of all important feudal lords.

The chief object, however, of the register was to show not what the count owed to others but what his own numerous vassals owed to him. It appears that he subinfeudated his lands and his various sources of income to no less than two thousand vassal knights. The purpose of the register is to record the terms upon which each of these knights held his fief. Some simply rendered the count homage, some agreed to serve him in war for a certain length of time each year, others to guard his castle for specified periods. A considerable number of the vassals of the count held lands of other lords, there being nothing to prevent a subvassal from accepting a fief directly from the king, or from any other neighboring noble landholder. So it happened that several of the vassals of the counts of Champagne held of the same persons of whom the count himself held.

It is evident that the counts of Champagne were not contented with the number of vassals that they secured by subinfeudating their land. The same homage might be rendered for a fixed income, or for a certain number of bushels of oats to be delivered each year by the lord, as for the use of land. So money, houses, wheat, oats, wine, chickens, were infeudated, and even half the bees which might be found in a particular forest. It would seem to us the simpler way to have hired soldiers outright, but in the thirteenth century the traditions of feudalism were so strong that it seemed natural to make vassals of those whose aid was desired. The mere promise of a money payment would not have been considered sufficiently binding. The feudal bond of homage served to make the contract firmer than it would otherwise have been.

The infeudation of other things than land.

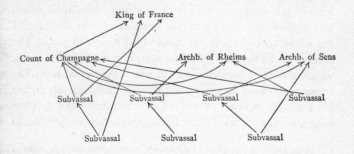

The arrow indicates a lord of whom the vassal held one or more fiefs.

It is clear, then, that no such regular hierarchy existed as some historians have imagined, beginning with the king and ending with the humblest knight included in the feudal aristocracy. The fact that vassals often held of a number of different lords made the feudal relations infinitely complex. The diagram on page 115, while it may not exactly correspond to the situation at any given moment, will serve to illustrate this complexity.

The feudal system maintained only by force.

44. Should one confine one's studies of feudalism to the rules laid down by the feudal lawyers and the careful descriptions of the exact duties of the vassal which are to be found in the contracts of the period, one might conclude that everything had been so minutely and rigorously fixed as to render the feudal bond sufficient to maintain order and liberty. But one has only to read a chronicle of the time to discover that, in reality, brute force governed almost everything outside of the Church. The feudal obligations were not fulfilled except when the lord was sufficiently powerful to enforce them. The bond of vassalage and fidelity, which was the sole principle of order, was constantly broken and faith was violated by both vassal and lord.[1]

The breaking of the feudal bond.

It often happened that a vassal was discontented with his lord and transferred his allegiance to another. This he had a right to do under certain circumstances, as, for instance, when his lord refused to see that justice was done him in his court. But such changes were generally made merely for the sake of the advantages which the faithless vassal hoped to gain. The records of the time are full of accounts of refusal to do homage, which was the commonest way in which the feudal bond was broken. So soon as a vassal felt himself strong enough to face his lord's displeasure, or realized that the lord was a helpless minor, he was apt to declare his independence by refusing to

[1] In the following description of the anarchy of feudalism, I merely condense Luchaire's admirable chapter on the subject in his *Manuel des Institutions Françaises*. The *Readings*, Chapters X, XII, XIII, XIV, furnish many examples of disorder.

recognize the feudal superiority of the one from whom he had received his land.

We may say that war, in all its forms, was the law of the feudal world. War formed the chief occupation of the restless aristocracy who held the land and exercised the governmental control. The inveterate habits of a military race, the discord provoked by ill-defined rights or by self-interest and covetousness, all led to constant bloody struggles in which each lord had for his enemies all those about him. An enterprising vassal was likely to make war at least once, first, upon each of his several lords ; secondly, upon the bishops and abbots with whom he was brought into contact, and whose control he particularly disliked ; thirdly, upon his fellow-vassals ; and lastly, upon his own vassals. The feudal bonds, instead of offering a guarantee of peace and concord, appear to have been a constant cause of violent conflict. Every one was bent upon profiting by the permanent or temporary weakness of his neighbor. This chronic dissension extended even to members of the same family ; the son, anxious to enjoy a part of his heritage immediately, warred against his father, younger brothers against older, and nephews against uncles who might seek to deprive them of their rights.

War the law of the feudal world

In theory, the lord could force his vassals to settle their disputes in an orderly and righteous manner before his court. But often he was neither able nor inclined to bring about a peaceful adjustment, and he would frequently have found it embarrassing to enforce the decisions of his own court. So the vassals were left to fight out their quarrels among themselves and found their chief interest in life in so doing. War was practically sanctioned by law. The great French code of laws of the thirteenth century and the Golden Bull, a most important body of law drawn up for Germany in 1356, did not prohibit neighborhood war, but merely provided that it should be conducted in a decent and gentlemanly way.

Tourneys and jousts.

The jousts, or tourneys, were military exercises—play wars—to fill out the tiresome periods which occasionally intervened between real wars.[1] They were, in fact, diminutive battles in which whole troops of hostile nobles sometimes took part. These rough plays called down the condemnation of the popes and councils, and even of the kings. The latter, however, were too fond of the sport themselves not to forget promptly their own prohibitions.[2]

Disastrous effects of feudal warfare generally recognized.

45. The disastrous nature of the perpetual feudal warfare and the necessity of some degree of peace and order, had already become apparent even as early as the eleventh century. In spite of all the turmoil, mankind was making progress. Commerce and enlightenment were increasing in the older towns and preparing the way for the development of new ones. Those engaged in peaceful pursuits could not but find the prevailing disorder intolerable. The Church was untiring, as it was fitting that it should be, in its efforts to secure peace; and nothing redounds more to the honor of the bishops than the

The 'Truce of God.'

"Truce of God." This prohibited all hostilities from Thursday night until Monday morning, as well as upon all of the numerous fast days.[3] The church councils and the bishops required the feudal lords to take an oath to observe the weekly truce, and, by means of the dreaded penalty of excommunication, met with some success. With the opening of the Crusades in 1096, the popes undertook to effect a general pacification by diverting the prevailing warlike spirit against the Turks.

At the same time the king, in France and England at least, was becoming a power that made for order in the modern

[1] The gorgeous affairs of the fourteenth and fifteenth centuries were but weak and effeminate counterparts of the rude and hazardous encounters of the thirteenth.

[2] References, for the mediæval castle, the jousts, and the life of the nobles, Munro, *Mediæval History*, Chapter XIII, and Henderson, *Short History of Germany*, pp. 111–121.

[3] See the famous "Truce of God" issued by the Archbishop of Cologne in 1083, in *Readings*, Chapter IX.

sense of the word. He endeavored to prevent the customary
resort to arms to settle every sort of difficulty between rival
vassals. By increasing the military force that he had at his
command he compelled the submission of cases of dispute to
his tribunals. But even St. Louis (d. 1270), who made the
greatest efforts to secure peace, did not succeed in accomplishing his end. The gradual bettering of conditions was due
chiefly to general progress and to the development of commerce and industry, which made the bellicose aristocracy
more and more intolerable.

General Reading. — The older accounts of feudalism, such as that
given by Guizot or Hallam, should be avoided as the reader is likely to
be misled by them. The earlier writers appear, from the standpoint
of recent investigations, to have been seriously mistaken upon many
important points. In French, LUCHAIRE, *Manuel des Institutions
Françaises* (Hachette & Co., Paris, $3.00), and ESMEIN, *Cours Élémen-
taire d'Histoire du Droit Français* ($2.00), are excellent.

In English there is EMERTON's Chapter XIV on "Feudal Institutions" in his *Mediæval Europe*, and ADAMS, *Civilization*, Chapter IX,
devoted especially to the origin of feudalism. CHEYNEY gives a selection of documents relating to the subject in *Translations and Reprints*,
Vol. IV, No. 3.

CHAPTER X

THE DEVELOPMENT OF FRANCE

Importance of studying the beginnings of the modern European states.

46. There is no more interesting or important phase of mediæval history than the gradual emergence of the modern national state from the feudal anarchy into which the great empire of Charlemagne fell during the century after his death. No one should flatter himself that he has grasped the elements of the history of western Europe unless he can trace in a clear, if general, way the various stages by which the states which appear now upon the map of Europe — the French republic, the German Empire, Austria-Hungary, and the kingdoms of Italy, Great Britain, and Spain — have grown out of the disorganized Europe of the ninth century.

It might be inferred from what has been said in the preceding chapters that the political history of western Europe during the two or three centuries following the deposition of Charles the Fat was really only the history of innumerable feudal lords. Yet even if the kings of mediæval Europe were sometimes less powerful than some of their mighty subjects, still their history is more important than that of their vassals. It was the kings, and not their rivals, the dukes and counts, who were to win in the long run and to establish national governments in the modern sense of the term. It was about them that the great European states, especially France, Spain, and England, grew up.

Struggle between the Carolingians and the house of Odo.

As we have seen, the aristocracy of the northern part of the West-Frankish kingdom chose (in 888) as their king, in place of the incompetent Charles the Fat, the valiant Odo, Count of

Paris, Blois, and Orleans. He was a powerful lord and held extensive domains besides the regions he ruled as count. But, in spite of his advantageous position, he found it impossible to exert any real power in the southern part of his kingdom. Even in the north he met with constant opposition, for the nobles who elected him had no idea of permitting him to interfere much with their independence. Charles the Simple, the only surviving grandson of Charles the Bald,[1] was eventually elected king by a faction opposed to Odo.

For a hundred years the crown passed back and forth between the family of Odo and that of Charlemagne. The counts of Paris were rich and capable, while the later Carolingians were poor and unfortunate. The latter finally succumbed to their powerful rivals, who definitely took possession of the throne in 987, when Hugh Capet was elected king of the Gauls, Bretons, Normans, Aquitanians, Goths, Spaniards, and Gascons, — in short, of all those peoples who were to be welded, under Hugh's successors, into the great French nation.

Election of Hugh Capet, the first of the Capetians, 987-996.

Hugh inherited from his ancestors the title of Duke of France, which they had enjoyed as the military representatives of the later Carolingian kings in " France," which was originally a district north of the Seine. Gradually the name France came to be applied to all the dominions which the dukes of France ruled as kings. We shall hereafter speak of the West-Frankish kingdom as France.

The West-Frankish kingdom comes to be called France.

It must not be forgotten, however, that it required more than two centuries after Hugh's accession for the French kings to create a real kingdom which should include even half the territory embraced in the France of to-day. For almost two hundred years the Capetians made little or no progress toward real kingly power. In fact, matters went from bad to worse. Even the region which they were supposed to control as counts — their so-called *domain* — melted away in their

Difficulty of establishing the royal power.

1 See genealogical table, above, p. 96.

hands.   Everywhere hereditary lines of usurping rulers sprang up whom it was impossible to exterminate after they had once taken root.   The Capetian territory bristled with hostile castles, permanent obstacles to commerce between the larger towns and intolerable plagues to the country people.   In short, the king of France, in spite of the dignity of his title, no longer dared to move about his own narrow domain.   He to whom the most powerful lords owed homage could not venture out of Paris without encountering fortresses constructed by noble brigands, who were the terror alike of priest, merchant, and laborer.   Without money or soldiers, royalty vegetated within its diminished patrimony.   It retained a certain prestige in distant fiefs situated on the confines of the realm and in foreign lands, but at home it was neither obeyed nor respected.   The enemy's lands began just outside the capital.[1]

Formation of small independent states in France.

47.   The tenth century was the period when the great fiefs of Normandy, Brittany, Flanders, and Burgundy took form. These, and the fiefs into which the older duchy of Aquitaine fell, developed into little nations, each under its line of able rulers.   Each had its own particular customs and culture, some traces of which may still be noted by the traveler in France. These little feudal states were created by certain families of nobles who possessed exceptional energy or statesmanship. By conquest, purchase, or marriage, they increased the number of their fiefs.   By promptly destroying the castles of those who refused to meet their obligations, they secured their control over their vassals.   By granting fiefs of land or money to subvassals, they gained new dependents.

Normandy.

Of these subnations none was more important or interesting than Normandy.   The Northmen had been the scourge of those who lived near the North Sea for many years before one of their leaders, Rollo (or Hrolf), agreed to accept from Charles

[1] Reference, Emerton, *Mediæval Europe*, pp. 405–420.   *Readings*, Chapter X.

the Simple (in 911) a district on the coast, north of Brittany, where he and his followers might peacefully settle. Rollo assumed the title of Duke of the Normans and introduced the Christian religion among his people. For a considerable time the newcomers kept up their Scandinavian traditions and language. Gradually, however, they appropriated such culture as their neighbors possessed, and by the twelfth century their capital, Rouen, was one of the most enlightened cities of Europe. Normandy became a source of infinite perplexity to the French kings when, in 1066, Duke William the Conqueror added England to his possessions; for he thereby became so powerful that his suzerain could hardly hope to control the Norman dukes any longer.

The isolated peninsula of Brittany, inhabited by a Celtic **Brittany.** people of the same race as the early inhabitants of Britain, had been particularly subject to the attacks of the Scandinavian pirates. It seemed at one time as if the district would become an appendage of Normandy. But in 938 a certain valiant Alain of the Twisted Beard arose to deliver it from the oppression of the strangers. The Normans were driven out, and feudalism replaced the older tribal organization in what was hereafter to be called the duchy of Brittany. It was not until the opening of the sixteenth century that this became a part of the French monarchy.

The pressure of the Northmen had an important result in the **Origin of the Flemish towns.** low countries between the Somme and the Scheldt. The inhabitants were driven to repair and seek shelter in the old Roman fortifications. They thus became accustomed to living in close community, and it was in this way that the Flemish towns — Ghent, Bruges, etc. — originated, which became in time famous centers of industry and trade. The founders of the great families of the district first gained their influence in defending the country against the Scandinavian pirates. The counts of Flanders aspired to rule the region, but the lesser counts within their territory were pretty independent of them; so private wars were frequent and bloody.

Burgundy.

Burgundy is a puzzling name because it is applied to several different parts of the territory once included in the kingdom founded by the Burgundians, which Clovis made tributary to his expanding Frankish kingdom. Toward the end of the ninth century we first hear of a *duke* of Burgundy as being appointed military representative of the king (as all dukes originally were) in a large district west of the Saône. The dukes of Burgundy never succeeded in establishing sufficient control over their vassals to render themselves independent, and consequently they always freely recognized the sovereignty of the French kings. We shall meet the name Burgundy later.

Possessions of the duke of Aquitaine and of the counts of Toulouse and Champagne.

The ancient duchy of Aquitaine (later Guienne), including a large part of what is now central and southern France, was abolished in 877, but the title of Duke of Aquitaine was conferred by the king upon a certain family of feudal lords, who gradually extended their power over Gascony and northward. To the southeast, the counts of Toulouse had begun to consolidate a little state which was to be the seat of the extraordinary literature of the troubadours. The county of Champagne has already been considered in the discussion of feudalism.

This completes the survey of the countries over which Hugh Capet and his immediate successors strove to rule. All those districts to the east of the Saône and the Rhone which now form a part of France were amalgamated (in 933) into the kingdom of Arles, or Burgundy,[1] which in 1032 fell into the hands of the German king.

Complicated position of the Capetian kings.

48. The position of the Capetian rulers was a complicated one. As counts of Paris, Orleans, etc., they enjoyed the ordinary rights of a feudal lord; as dukes of France, they might exercise a vague control over the district north of the Seine;

[1] Not to be confounded with the *duchy* of Burgundy just referred to. See p. 97, above.

as suzerains of the great feudal princes, — the duke of Normandy, the counts of Flanders, Champagne, and the rest, — they might require homage and certain feudal services from these great personages. But besides all these rights as feudal lords they had other rights as kings. They were crowned and consecrated by the Church, as Pippin and Charlemagne had been. They thus became, by God's appointment, the protectors of the Church and the true fountain of justice for all who were oppressed or in distress throughout their realms. Therefore they were on a higher plane in the eyes of the people than any of the great vassals. Besides the homage of their vassals, they exacted an oath of fidelity from all whom they could reach.

The great vassals, on the other hand, acted on the theory that the king was simply their feudal lord. As for the king himself, he accepted both views of his position and made use both of the older theory of kingship and of his feudal suzerainty to secure more and more control over his realms. For over three hundred years the direct male line of the Capetians never once failed. It rarely happened, moreover, that the crown was left in the weak hands of a child. By the opening of the fourteenth century there was no doubt that the king, and not the feudal lords, was destined to prevail.

The first of the kings of France to undertake with success the serious task of conquering his own duchy was Louis the Fat (1108–1137). He was an active soldier and strove to keep free the means of communication between the different centers of his somewhat scattered feudal domains and to destroy the power of the usurping castellans in his fortresses. But he made only a beginning; it was reserved for his famous grandson, Philip Augustus (1180–1223), to make the duchy of France into a real kingdom. *Louis the Fat, 1108-1137.*

Philip Augustus, 1180-1223.

49. Philip had a far more difficult problem to face than any of the preceding kings of his house. Before his accession a series of those royal marriages which until recently exercised *The Plantagenets in France. Henry II.*

so great an influence upon political history, had brought most of the great fiefs of central, western, and southern France into the hands of the king of England, Henry II, who now ruled over the most extensive realm in western Europe. Henry II was the son of William the Conqueror's granddaughter Matilda,[1] who had married one of the great vassals of the French kings, the count of Anjou and Maine.[2] Henry, therefore, inherited through his mother all the possessions of the Norman kings of England, — namely, England, the duchy of Normandy, and the suzerainty over Brittany, — and through his father the counties of Maine and Anjou. Lastly, through his own marriage with Eleanor, the heiress of the dukes of Guienne (as Aquitaine was now called), he possessed himself of pretty much all of southern France, including Poitou and Gascony. Henry II, in spite of his great importance in English history, was as much French as English, both by birth and sympathies, and gave more than half his time and attention to his French possessions.

Philip and the Plantagenets.

It thus came about that the king of France suddenly found a new and hostile state, under an able and energetic ruler, erected upon his western borders. It included more than half the territory in which he was recognized as king. The chief business of Philip's life was an incessant war upon the Plantagenets, in which he was constantly aided by the strife among his enemies themselves. Henry II divided his French possessions among his three sons, Geoffrey, Richard, and John, delegating to them such government as existed. Philip took advantage of the constant quarrels of the brothers among themselves and with their father. He espoused, in turn, the cause of Richard the Lion-Hearted against his father, of John Lackland, the youngest brother, against Richard, and so on. Without these family discords the powerful monarchy of the

---

1 See genealogical table and map of the Plantagenet possessions, pp. 140–141, below.

2 Henry's family owes its name, Plantagenet, to the habit that his father, Geoffrey of Anjou, had of wearing a bit of broom (*planta genista*) in his helmet on his crusading expeditions.

Plantagenets might have annihilated the royal house of France, whose narrow dominions it closed in and threatened on all sides.

So long as Henry II lived there was little chance of expelling the Plantagenets or of greatly curtailing their power, but with the accession of his reckless son, Richard I, called the Lion-Hearted,[1] the prospects of the French king brightened wonderfully. Richard left his kingdom to take care of itself, while he went upon a crusade to the Holy Land. He persuaded Philip to join him, but Richard was too overbearing and masterful, and Philip too ambitious, to make it possible for them to agree for long. The king of France, who was physically delicate, was taken ill and was glad of the excuse to return home and brew trouble for his powerful vassal. When Richard himself returned, after several years of romantic but fruitless adventure, he found himself involved in a war with Philip, in the midst of which he died.

Richard the Lion-Hearted.

Richard's younger brother, John, who enjoys the reputation of being the most despicable of English kings, speedily gave Philip a good excuse for seizing a great part of the Plantagenet lands. John was suspected of conniving at the brutal murder of his nephew Arthur (the son of Geoffrey), to whom the nobles of Maine, Anjou, and Touraine had done homage. He was also guilty of the less serious offense of carrying off and marrying a lady betrothed to one of his own vassals. Philip, as John's suzerain, summoned him to appear at the French court to answer the latter charge. Upon John's refusal to appear or to do homage for his continental possessions, Philip caused his court to issue a decree confiscating almost all of the Plantagenet lands, leaving to the English king only the southwest corner of France.

John loses the French possessions of his house.

Philip found little difficulty in possessing himself, not only of the valley of the Loire, but of Normandy itself, which

---

[1] Geoffrey, the eldest of the three sons of Henry II mentioned above, died before his father.

showed no disinclination to accept him in place of the Plantagenets, whom the Normans associated with continual exactions. Six years after Richard's death the English kings had
lost all their continental fiefs except Guienne. The Capetian
domain was, for the first time, the chief among the great feudal
states of France, both in wealth and extent. It should be
observed that Philip, unlike his ancestors, was no longer merely
suzerain of the new conquests, but was himself duke of
Normandy, and count of Anjou, of Maine, etc. The boundaries of his domain, that is, the lands which he himself
controlled directly as feudal lord, now extended to the sea.

Philip strengthens the royal power as well as increases the royal domain.
50. Philip not only greatly increased the extent of the
royal domain, but strengthened his control over all classes of
his subjects as well. He appears, also, to have fully realized
the importance of the towns which had begun to develop a
century earlier. There were several important ones in the districts he annexed, and these he took especial pains to treat
with consideration. He extended his protection, and at the
same time his authority, over them and in this way lessened
the influence and resources of the feudal lords within whose
territories the towns lay.

Appanages.
The chief innovation of Philip's son, Louis VIII, was the
creation of *appanages*. These were fiefs assigned to his
younger sons, one of whom was made count of Artois; another,
count of Anjou and Maine; a third, count of Auvergne. This
has generally been regarded by historians as a most unfortunate reënforcement of the feudal idea. It not only retarded
the consolidation of the kingdom but opened the way to new
strife between the members of the royal family itself.

Louis IX, 1226-1270.
The long reign of Philip's grandson, Louis IX, or St.
Louis (1226–1270), is extremely interesting from many standpoints. St. Louis himself is perhaps the most heroic and
popular figure in the whole procession of French monarchs,
and his virtues and exploits have been far more amply recorded

Legend:

Royal domain at Accession of Philip

Acquired during his Reign from the Plantagenets

Acquired during his Reign from other Vassals

Plantagenet Lands (1223)

Other Vassal Lands

Map of France at the Close of the Reign of Philip Augustus

than those of any of his predecessors. But it is only his part in the consolidation of the French monarchy that immediately concerns us. After a revolt of the barons of central France in alliance with the king of England, which Louis easily put down, he proceeded, in a most fair-minded and Christian spirit, to arrange a definite settlement with the Plantagenets. The king of England was to do him homage for the duchy of Guienne, Gascony, and Poitou and surrender every claim upon the rest of the former possessions of the Plantagenets on the continent.

Settlement of question of the English king's possessions in France, 1258.

Besides these important territorial adjustments, Louis IX did much to better the system of government and strengthen the king's power. Philip Augustus had established a new kind of officer, the *baillis*, who resembled the *missi* of Charlemagne. They were supported by a salary and frequently shifted from place to place so that there should be no danger of their taking root and establishing powerful feudal families, as had happened in the case of the counts, who were originally royal officers. Louis adopted and extended the institution of the *baillis*. In this way he kept his domains under his control and saw that justice was done and his revenue properly collected.

The *baillis* serve to increase the king's power.

Before the thirteenth century there was little government in France in the modern sense of the word. The king relied for advice and aid, in the performance of his simple duties as ruler, upon a council of the great vassals, prelates, and others about his person. This council was scarcely organized into a regular assembly, and it transacted all the various kinds of governmental business without clearly distinguishing one kind from another. In the reign of Louis IX this assembly began to be divided into three bodies with different functions. There was : first, the king's council to aid him in conducting the general affairs of the kingdom ; secondly, a chamber of accounts, a financial body which attended to the revenue ; and

Government of Louis IX.

lastly, the *parlement*, a supreme court made up of those trained in the law, which was becoming ever more complicated as time went on. Instead, as hitherto, of wandering about with the king, the parlement took up its quarters upon the little island in the Seine at Paris, where the great court-house (*Palais de Justice*) still stands. A regular system of appeals from the feudal courts to the royal courts was established. This served greatly to increase the king's power in distant parts of his realms. It was decreed further that the royal coins should alone be used in the domains of the king, and that his money should be accepted everywhere else within the kingdom concurrently with that of those of his vassals who had the privilege of coinage.

The grandson of St. Louis, Philip the Fair, is the first example of a French king who had both the will and the means to play the rôle of an absolute monarch. He had inherited a remarkably well organized government compared with anything that had existed since the time of Charlemagne. He was surrounded by a body of lawyers who had derived their ideas of the powers and rights of a prince from the Roman law. They naturally looked with suspicion upon everything that interfered with the supreme power of the monarch, and encouraged the king to bring the whole government into his own hands regardless of the privileges of his vassals and of the clergy.

Philip the Fair (1285-1314) the first absolute ruler of France.

Philip's attempt to force the clergy to contribute from their wealth to the support of the government led to a remarkable struggle with the pope, of which an account will be given in a later chapter. With the hope of gaining the support of the whole nation in his conflict with the head of the Church, the king summoned a great council of his realm in 1302. He included for the first time the representatives of the towns in addition to the nobles and prelates, whom the king had long been accustomed to consult. At the same period that the

The commons, or third estate, summoned to the Estates General, 1302.

French Estates General,[1] or national assembly, was taking form through the addition of representatives of the commons, England was creating its Parliament. The two bodies were, however, to have a very different history, as will become clear later.

By the sagacious measures that have been mentioned, the French monarchs rescued their realms from feudal disruption and laid the foundation for the most powerful monarchy of western Europe. However, the question of how far the neighboring king across the Channel should extend his power on the continent remained unanswered. The boundary between France and England was not yet definitely determined and became, during the fourteenth and fifteenth centuries, the cause of long and disastrous wars, from which France finally emerged victorious. We must now turn back to trace the development of her English rival.[2]

---

[1] The Estates General were so called to distinguish a general meeting of the representatives of the three estates of the realm from a merely local assembly of the provincial estates of Champagne, Provence, Brittany, Languedoc, etc. There are some vague indications that Philip had called in a few townspeople even earlier than 1302.

[2] For the French monarchy as organized in the thirteenth century, see Emerton, *Mediæval Europe*, pp. 432-433; Adams, *Civilization*, pp. 311-328.

CHAPTER XI

ENGLAND IN THE MIDDLE AGES

51. The country of western Europe whose history is of greatest interest to English-speaking peoples is, of course, England. From England the United States and the vast English colonies have inherited their language and habits of thought, much of their literature, and many peculiarities of their laws and institutions. In this volume it will not, however, be possible to study England except in so far as it has played a part in the general development of Europe. This it has greatly influenced by its commerce, industry, and colonies, as well as by the example it has set of permitting the people to participate with the king in the government. *Importance of England in the history of western Europe.*

The conquest of the island of Britain by the German Angles and Saxons has already been spoken of, as well as the conversion of these pagans to Christianity by the representatives of the Roman Church. The several kingdoms founded by the invaders were brought under the overlordship of the southern kingdom of Wessex [1] by Egbert, a contemporary of Charlemagne. But no sooner had the long-continued invasions of the Germans come to an end and the country been partially unified, than the Northmen (or Danes, as the English called them), who were ravaging France, began to make incursions into England. Before long they had made permanent settlements and conquered a large district north of the Thames. They were defeated, however, in a great battle by Alfred the *Overlordship of Wessex.* *Invasions of the Danes. Their defeat by Alfred the Great, 871-901.*

[1] In spite of the final supremacy of the West Saxons of Wessex, the whole land took its name from the more numerous Angles.

Great, the first English king of whom we have any satisfactory knowledge. He forced the Danes to accept Christianity and established, as the boundary between them and his own kingdom of Wessex, a line running from London across the island to Chester.

Alfred fosters the development of the English language.

Alfred was as much interested in education as Charlemagne had been. He called in learned monks from the continent and from Wales as teachers of the young men. He desired that all those born free, who had the means, should be forced to learn English thoroughly, and that those who proposed to enter the priesthood should learn Latin as well. He himself translated Boethius' *Consolation of Philosophy* and other works from the Latin into English, and doubtless encouraged the composition of the famous *Anglo-Saxon Chronicle*, the first history written in a modern language.[1]

England from the death of Alfred the Great to the Norman Conquest, 901-1066.

The formation of the kingdoms of Denmark, Sweden, and Norway at the end of the ninth century caused many discontented Scandinavian chieftains to go in search of adventure, so that the Danish invasions continued for more than a century after Alfred's death (901), and we hear much of the Danegeld, a tax levied to buy off the invaders when necessary. Finally a Danish king (Cnut) succeeded in making himself king of England in 1017. The Danish dynasty maintained itself only for a few years. Then a last weak Saxon king, Edward the Confessor, held nominal sway for a score of years. Upon his death in 1066, William, Duke of Normandy, claimed the crown and became king of England. The Norman Conquest closes what is called the Saxon period of English history, during which the English nation may be said to have taken form. Before considering the achievements of William the Conqueror we must glance at the condition of England as he found it.

---

[1] References, Green, *Short History of the English People* (revised edition, Harper & Brothers), pp. 48–52 ; extracts from the *Anglo-Saxon Chronicle* may be found in *Readings*, Chapter XI.

The map of Great Britain at the accession of William the Conqueror has the same three great divisions which exist to-day. The little kingdoms had disappeared and England extended north to the Tweed, which separated it, as it now does, from the kingdom of Scotland. On the west was Wales, inhabited then, as it is still, by descendants of the native Britons, of whom only a small remnant had survived the German invasions. The Danes had been absorbed into the mass of the population and all England recognized a single king. The king's power had increased as time went on, although he was bound to act in important matters only with the consent of a council (Witenagemot) made up of high royal officials, bishops, and nobles. The kingdom was divided into shires,[1] as it still is, and each of these had a local assembly, a sort of parliament for the dispatch of local matters.

After the victory of the papal party at the Council of Whitby,[2] the Church had been thoroughly organized and the intercourse of the clergy with the continent served, as we have seen, to keep England from becoming completely isolated. Although the island was much behind some other portions of Europe in civilization, the English had succeeded in laying the foundations for the development of a great nation and an admirable form of government.

England was not, however, to escape feudalism. The Normans naturally brought with them their own feudal institutions, but even before their coming many suggestions of feudalism might have been discovered. Groups of shires had been placed under the government of earls who became dangerous rivals of the kings; and the habit of giving churchmen the right to govern, to a large extent, those who lived upon their vast estates recalls the conditions in the Frankish empire during

---

[1] The shires go back at least as far as Alfred the Great, and many of their names indicate that they had some relation to the earlier little kingdoms, e g., Sussex, Essex, Kent, Northumberland.

[2] See above, p. 62.

the same period. The great landed proprietor in England exercised much the same powers over those about him that the feudal lords enjoyed upon the other side of the Channel.

The struggle for the English crown between Earl Harold and Duke William of Normandy.

52. As has been said, William of Normandy claimed that he was entitled to the English crown; he even assumed that all who refused to acknowledge him in England were traitors. We are, however, somewhat in the dark as to the basis of his claim. There is a story that he had visited the court of Edward the Confessor and had become his vassal on condition that, should Edward die childless, he was to designate William as his successor. But Harold, Earl of Wessex, who had consolidated his power before the death of Edward by securing the appointment of his brothers to three of the other great earldoms, assumed the crown and paid no attention to William's demand that he should surrender it.

The pope favors William's claim.

William thereupon appealed to the pope, promising that if he came into possession of England, he would see that the English clergy submitted to the authority of the Roman bishop. Consequently the pope, Alexander II, condemned Harold and blessed in advance any expedition that William might undertake to assert his rights. The conquest of England therefore took on the character of a sort of holy war, and as the expedition had been well advertised, many adventurers flocked to William's standard. The Norman cavalry and archers proved superior to the English forces, who were on foot and were so armed that they could not fight to advantage except at close range. Harold was killed in the memorable battle of Senlac[1] and his army defeated. In a few weeks a number of influential nobles and several bishops agreed to accept William as their king, and London opened its gates to him. He was crowned on Christmas day, 1066, at Westminster.

Battle of Senlac, 1066. William I crowned at London.

We cannot trace the history of the opposition and the revolts of the great nobles which William had to meet within the

[1] Often called the battle of Hastings from the neighboring town of that name.

next few years. His position was rendered doubly difficult by troubles which he encountered on the continent as duke of Normandy. Suffice it to say that he succeeded in maintaining himself against all his enemies.[1]

William's policy in regard to England exhibited profound statesmanship. He introduced the Norman feudalism to which he was accustomed, but took good care that it should not weaken his power. The English who had refused to join him before the battle of Senlac were declared traitors, but were permitted to keep their lands upon condition of receiving them from the king as his vassals. The lands of those who actually bore arms against him at Senlac, or in later rebellions, including the great estates of Harold's family, were confiscated and distributed among his faithful followers, both Norman and English, though naturally the Normans among them far outnumbered the English.

William's wise policy in England.

William declared that he did not propose to change the English customs but to govern as Edward the Confessor, the last Saxon king whom he acknowledged, had done. He tried to learn English, maintained the Witenagemot, and observed English practices. But he was a man of too much force to submit to the control of his people. While he appointed counts or earls in some of the shires (now come to be called *counties*), he controlled them by means of other royal officers called *sheriffs*. He avoided giving to any one person a great many estates in a single region, so that no one should become inconveniently powerful. Finally, in order to secure the support of the smaller landholders and to prevent combinations against him among the greater ones, he required every landholder in England to take an oath of fidelity directly to him. We read in the *Anglo-Saxon Chronicle* (1086): "After that he went about so that he came, on the first day of August, to Salisbury, and there came to him his wise men

He insures the supremacy of the crown without interfering with English customs.

William requires oath of fidelity from his subvassals.

---

[1] For contemporaneous accounts of William's character and the relations of Normans and English, see Colby, *Sources*, pp. 33–36, 39–41; *Readings*, Ch. XI.

[i.e., counselors], and all the land-owning men of property there were over all England, whosesoever men they were; and all bowed down to him and became his men, and swore oaths of fealty to him that they would be faithful to him against all other men."

Domesday Book.

William's anxiety to have a complete knowledge of his whole kingdom is indicated by a remarkable historical document, the so-called *Domesday Book*. This is a register of the lands throughout England, indicating the value of each parcel, the serfs and stock upon it, the name of its holder and of the person who held it before the Conquest. This government report contained a vast amount of information which was likely to prove useful to William's taxgatherers. It is still valuable to the historian, although unfortunately he is not able in every case to interpret its terms satisfactorily.

William the Conqueror and the Church.

William's policy in regard to the Church indicates a desire to advance its interests in conjunction with his own. He called Lanfranc, an Italian who had been at the head of the famous monastery of Bec in Normandy, to the archbishopric of Canterbury. The king permitted the clergy to manage their own affairs and established bishops' courts to try a variety of cases. But homage was exacted from a bishop as from a lay vassal, and William refused to permit the pope to interfere in English affairs without his permission in each particular case. No papal legate was to enter the land without the king's sanction. No papal decree should be received in the English Church without his consent, nor his servants be excommunicated against his will. When Gregory VII demanded that he should become his vassal for the land that he had conquered under the papal auspices, William promptly refused.

General results of the Norman Conquest.

It is clear that the Norman Conquest was not a simple change of dynasty. A new element was added to the English people. We cannot tell how many Normans actually emigrated across the Channel, but they evidently came in considerable numbers, and their influence upon the English court and government was very great. A century after William's arrival the whole body of the nobility, the bishops, abbots, and government officials, had become practically all Norman. "Besides these, the architects and artisans who built the castles and fortresses, and the cathedrals, abbeys, and parish churches, whose erection throughout the land was such a marked characteristic of the period, were immigrants from Normandy. Merchants from the Norman cities of Rouen and Caen came to settle in London and other English cities, and weavers from Flanders were settled in various towns and even rural districts. For a short time these newcomers remained a separate people, but before the twelfth century was over they had become for the most

Norman Gateway at Bristol, England

part indistinguishable from the great mass of English people amongst whom they had come. They had nevertheless made that people stronger, more vigorous, more active-minded, and more varied in their occupations and interests" (Cheyney).[1]

53. The Conqueror was followed by his sons, William Rufus and Henry I. Upon the death of the latter the country went through a terrible period of civil war, for some

William Rufus, 1087–1100, and Henry I, 1100–1135.

[1] Reference, for the Conqueror and his reign, Green, *Short History*, pp. 74–87, and Gardiner, *Students' History*, pp. 86–114.

Civil war
ending in
the accession
of Henry II,
1154-1189.

of the nobility supported the Conqueror's grandson Stephen, and some his granddaughter Matilda. After the death of Stephen, when Henry II, Matilda's son,[1] was finally recognized in 1154 by all as king, he found the kingdom in a melancholy state. The nobles had taken advantage of the prevalent disorder to erect castles without royal permission and establish themselves as independent rulers. Mercenaries had been called in from the continent by the rivals for the throne, and had become a national plague.

Henry's diffi-
culties and
his success
in meeting
them.

Henry at once adopted vigorous measures. He destroyed the illegally erected fortresses, sent off the mercenaries, and deprived many earls who had been created by Stephen and Matilda of their titles. Henry II's task was a difficult one. He had need of all his indefatigable energy and quickness of mind to restore order in England and at the same time rule the wide realms on the continent which he had either inherited or gained through his marriage with the heiress of the dukes of Guienne.[2] Although he spent the greater part of his reign across the Channel, he still found time to be one of the greatest of all England's rulers.

His reforms
in the
judicial
system.

In order that he might maintain his prerogatives as judge of disputes among his subjects and avoid all excuse for the private warfare, which was such a persistent evil on the continent, he undertook to improve and reform the system of royal courts.

---

[1] William I (1066–1087), m. Matilda, daughter of Baldwin V of Flanders

William II (Rufus) (1087–1100)	Henry I (1100–1135), m. Matilda, daughter of Malcolm, King of Scotland	Adela, m. Stephen, Count of Blois
	Matilda (d. 1167), m. Geoffrey Plantagenet, Count of Anjou	Stephen (1135–1154)
	Henry II (1154–1189), the first Plantagenet king	

[2] See above, p. 126.

The Plantagenet Possessions in England and France

He arranged that his judges should make regular circuits throughout the country, so that they might try cases on the spot at least once a year. He established the famous Court of King's Bench to try all other cases which came under the king's jurisdiction. This was composed of five judges from his council, two clergymen, and three laymen. We find, too, the beginning of our grand jury in a body of men in each neighborhood who were to be duly sworn in, from time to time, and should then bring accusations against such malefactors as had come to their knowledge.

The grand jury.

As for the petty or smaller jury, which actually tried the accused, its origin and history are obscure. It did not originate with Henry II, but he systematized trial by jury and made it a settled law of the land instead of an exceptional favor. The plan of delegating the duty of determining the guilt or innocence of a suspected person to a dozen members of the community who were sworn to form their opinion without partiality was very different from the earlier systems. It resembled neither the Roman trial, where the judges made the decision, nor the mediæval compurgation and ordeals, where God was supposed to pronounce the verdict. In all legal matters the decisions of Henry's judges were so sagacious and consistent that they became the basis of the common law which is still used in all English-speaking countries.

Trial by jury.

The common law.

Henry's reign was embittered by the famous struggle with Thomas à Becket, which illustrates admirably the peculiar dependence of the monarchs of his day upon the churchmen. Becket was born in London. He early entered one of the lower orders of the Church, but grew up in the service of the crown, and was able to aid Henry in gaining the throne. Thereupon the new king made him his chancellor. Becket proved an excellent minister and defended the king's interest even against the Church, of which he was also an officer. He was fond of hunting and of warlike enterprises

Henry II and Thomas à Becket.

Becket as chancellor.

and maintained a brilliant court from the revenues of the numerous church benefices which he held. It appeared to Henry that there could be no better head for the English clergy than his sagacious and worldly chancellor. He therefore determined to make him Archbishop of Canterbury. The kings of that time often chose their most efficient officers from among the prelates. Lanfranc, for example, had been the Conqueror's chief minister. There were several good reasons for this practice. The clergy were not only far better educated than laymen but they were also not ordinarily dangerous as military leaders, nor could their offices become hereditary.

In appointing Becket Archbishop of Canterbury, Henry intended to insure his own complete control of the Church. He proposed to bring clerical criminals before the royal courts and punish them like other offenders, to make the bishops meet all the feudal obligations, and to prevent appeals to the pope. Becket, however, immediately resigned his chancellorship, gave up his gay life, and opposed every effort of the king to reduce the independence of the Church. After a haughty assertion of the supremacy of the spiritual power over the secular government, Thomas fled from the wrathful and disappointed monarch to France and the protection of the pope.

Made Archbishop of Canterbury, Becket defends the cause of the Church against the king.

In spite of a patched-up reconciliation with the king, Becket proceeded to excommunicate or suspend some of the great English prelates and, as Henry believed, was conspiring to rob his son of the crown. In a fit of anger, Henry exclaimed among his followers, "Is there no one to avenge me of this miserable clerk?" Unfortunately certain knights took the rash expression literally, and Becket was murdered in Canterbury cathedral, whither he had returned. The king had really had no wish to resort to violence, and his sorrow and remorse when he heard of the dreadful deed, and his terror at the consequences, were most genuine. The pope proposed to excommunicate the king. Henry, however, made peace with

Murder of Becket and Henry's remorse.

the papal legates by the solemn assertion that he had never wished the death of Thomas and by promising to return to Canterbury all the property which he had confiscated, to send money to aid in the capture of the Holy Sepulcher at Jerusalem, and to undertake a crusade himself.[1]

Richard the Lion-Hearted, 1189-1199.

54. Henry's later years were troubled by the machinations of Philip Augustus of France and by the quarrels and treason of his own sons, of which some account has already been given.[2] He was followed by his son, the picturesque Richard the Lion-Hearted, one of the most romantic figures of the Middle Ages. He was, however, a poor ruler, who spent but a few months of his ten years' reign in England. He died in 1199

John, 1199-1216.

and was succeeded by his brother John, from all accounts one of the most detestable persons who has ever worn a crown. His reign was, nevertheless, a notable one in the annals of England. In the first place, he lost a great part of the possessions of his house upon the continent (Normandy, Brittany, Anjou, etc.); secondly, he was forced by a revolt of his people, who refused to endure his despotism any longer, to grant the Great Charter. The loss of his lands across the Channel has already been described; it remains only to speak of the winning of the Great Charter of English liberties.[3]

The granting of the Great Charter, 1215.

When, in 1213, John proposed to lead his English vassals across the water in order to attempt to reconquer his lost possessions, they refused to accompany him on the ground that their feudal obligations did not bind them to fight outside of their country. Moreover, they showed a lively discontent with John's despotism and his neglect of those limits of the kingly power which several of the earlier Norman kings had solemnly recognized. In 1214 a number of the barons met and took a solemn oath to compel the king, by arms if necessary, to confirm

[1] References, Green, pp. 104-112; Gardiner, pp. 138-158. A contemporaneous account of the murder is given by Colby, *Sources*, pp. 56-59.

[2] See above, p. 126.

[3] For John's reign, see Green, pp. 122-127.

a charter containing the things which, according to English traditions, a king might not do. It proved necessary to march against John, whom the insurgent nobles met at Runnymede, not far from London. Here on the 15th of June, 1215, they forced him to swear to observe the rights of the nation, as they conceived them, which they had carefully written out.

The Great Charter is perhaps the most famous document in the history of government;[1] its provisions furnish a brief and comprehensive statement of the burning governmental questions of the age. It was really the whole nation, not merely the nobles, who concluded this great treaty with a tyrannous ruler. The rights of the commoner are guarded as well as those of the noble. As the king promises to observe the liberties and customs of his vassals and not to abuse his feudal prerogatives, so the vassals agree to observe the rights of their men. The merchant is not to be deprived of his goods for small offenses, nor the farmer of his wagon and implements. The king is to impose no tax, beside the three stated feudal aids,[2] except by the consent of the great council of the nation. This is to include the prelates and greater barons and all who hold directly of the king.

The provisions of the Charter and its importance.

There is no more notable clause in the Charter than that which provides that no one is to be arrested or imprisoned or deprived of his property unless he be immediately sent before a court of his peers for trial. To realize the importance of this, we must recollect that in France, down to 1789, the king exercised such unlimited powers that he could order the arrest of any one he pleased, and could imprison him for any length of time without bringing him to trial, or even informing him of the nature of his offense. The Great Charter provided further that the king should permit merchants to

[1] The text of the Great Charter is given in *Translations and Reprints*, Vol. I, No. 6; extracts, in the *Readings*, Chapter XI.

[2] These were payments made when the lord knighted his eldest son, gave his eldest daughter in marriage, or had been captured and was waiting to be ransomed.

move about freely and should observe the privileges of the various towns; nor were his officers longer to exercise despotic powers over those under them.

"The Great Charter is the first great public act of the nation after it has realized its own identity, the consummation of the work for which unconsciously kings, prelates, and lawyers have been laboring for a century. There is not a word in it that recalls the distinctions of race and blood, or that maintains the differences of English and Norman law. It is in one view the summing up of a period of national life, in another the starting-point of a new period, not less eventful than that which it closes" (Stubbs).

In spite of his solemn confirmation of the Charter, John, with his accustomed treachery, made a futile attempt to abrogate his engagements; but neither he nor his successors ever succeeded in getting rid of the document. Later there were times when the English kings evaded its provisions and tried to rule as absolute monarchs. But the people always sooner or later bethought them of the Charter, which thus continued to form an effective barrier against permanent despotism in England.

Henry III, 1216-1272.

55. During the long reign of John's son, Henry III, England began to construct her Parliament, an institution which has not only played a most important rôle in English history, but has also served as the model for similar bodies in almost every civilized state in the world. Henry's fondness for appointing foreigners to office, his anxiety to enjoy powers which he had not the intelligence or energy to justify by the use he made of them, and his willingness to permit the pope to levy taxes in England, led the nobles to continue their hostility to the crown. The nobles and the people of the towns, who were anxious to check the arbitrary powers of the king, joined forces in what is known as the War of the Barons. They found a leader in the patriotic Simon de Montfort, who proved himself a valiant and unselfish defender of the rights of the nation.

The older Witenagemot of Saxon times, as well as the Great Council of the Norman kings, was a meeting of nobles, bishops, and abbots, which the king summoned from time to time to give him advice and aid, and to sanction important governmental undertakings. During Henry's reign its meetings became more frequent and its discussions more vigorous than before, and the name *Parliament* began to be applied to it.

The English Parliament.

In 1265 a famous Parliament was held, where, through the influence of Simon de Montfort, a most important new class of members — the *commons* — was present, which was destined to give it its future greatness. In addition to the nobles and prelates, the sheriffs were ordered to summon two simple knights from each county and two citizens from each of the more flourishing towns to attend and take part in the discussions.

Simon de Montfort summons the commons to Parliament.

Edward I, the next king, definitely adopted this innovation. He doubtless called in the representatives of the towns because the townspeople were becoming rich and he wished to have an opportunity to ask them to make grants to meet the expenses of the government. He also wished to obtain the approval of all classes when he determined upon important measures affecting the whole realm. Since the Model Parliament of 1295, the commons, or representatives of the people, have always been included along with the clergy and nobility when the national assembly of England has been summoned. We shall see later how the present houses of Lords and Commons came into existence under Edward's son.

The Model Parliament of Edward I, 1295.

From the reign of Edward I we are, as a distinguished English historian has well said, " face to face with modern England. Kings, Lords, Commons, the courts of justice, . . . the relations of Church and State, in a great measure the framework of society itself, have all taken the shape which they still essentially retain " (Green). The English language was, moreover, about to become the speech we use to-day.

England in the fourteenth century.

CHAPTER XII

GERMANY AND ITALY IN THE TENTH AND ELEVENTH CENTURIES

Contrast
between the
development
of Germany
and France.

56. The history of the kingship in the eastern, or German, part of Charlemagne's empire is very different from that in France, which was reviewed in a previous chapter. After a struggle of four hundred years, it had become clear by the thirteenth century that the successors of Louis the German (Charlemagne's grandson) could not make of Germany a kingdom such as St. Louis left to his descendants. From the thirteenth century down to Napoleon's time there was no Germany in a political sense, but only a great number of practically independent states, great and small. It was but a generation ago that, under the leadership of Prussia, — a kingdom unknown until many centuries after Charlemagne's time, — the previously independent kingdoms, principalities, and free towns were formed into the federation now known as the German empire.

Stem
duchies.

The map of the eastern part of Charlemagne's empire a century after his death indicates that the whole region had fallen into certain large divisions ruled over by dukes, who, in Saxony and Bavaria at least, were kings in all but name.[1] Just how these duchies originated is something of a mystery, but two things at least are clear which help to explain their appearance. In the first place, under the weak successors of Louis the German, the old independent spirit of the various peoples, or *stems*, that Charlemagne had been able to hold

[1] See map following p. 152 for the names and position of the several duchies.

together, once more asserted itself and they gladly returned to the leadership of their own chiefs. In the second place, they were driven to do this by the constant attacks from without, first of the Northmen and the Moravians, a Slavic people, then of the terrible Hungarian horsemen who penetrated more than once as far west as France. As there was no competent central power to defend the people, it was natural that they should look to their local leaders for help and guidance.

These *stem duchies*, as the Germans call them, prevented the German kings from getting a firm hold on their realms. The best that they could do was to bring about a sort of confederation. Consequently, when the German aristocracy chose the strong Henry I, of the ducal house of Saxony,[1] as their king in 919, he wisely made no attempt to deprive the several dukes of their power. He needed their assistance in the task of dealing with the invaders who were pressing in on all sides. He prepared the way for the later subjugation of the Slavs and the final repulse of the Hungarians, but he left to his famous son, Otto I, the task of finally disposing of the invaders and attempting to found a real kingdom.

Henry I, 919-936.

The reign of Otto I (936-973), called the Great, is one of the most extraordinary in the history of Germany. He made no attempt to abolish the duchies, but he succeeded in getting all of them into the hands of his sons, brothers, or near relatives, as well as in reducing the power of the dukes. For example, he made his brother Henry duke of Bavaria, after forgiving him for two revolts. His scholarly brother, Archbishop Bruno of Cologne,[2] he made duke of Lorraine in the place of his faithless son-in-law, Conrad, who had rebelled against him.

Otto the Great, 936-973.

---

[1] Arnulf, the grandson of Louis the German, who supplanted Charles the Fat, died in 899 and left a six-year-old son, Louis the Child (d. 911), who was the last of the house of Charlemagne to enjoy the German kingship. The aristocracy then chose Conrad I (d. 918), and, in 919, Henry I of Saxony, as king of the East Franks.

[2] See *Readings*, Chapter XII.

Many of the old ducal families either died out or lost their heritage by unsuccessful revolt. None of them offered a long succession of able rulers. The duchies consequently fell repeatedly into the hands of the king, who then claimed the right to assign them to whom he wished.

In the middle of the tenth century the northern and eastern boundaries of Germany were as yet very ill defined. The Slavic peoples across the Elbe, many of whom were still pagans, were engaged in continual attacks upon the borders of Saxony. Otto I did more than fight these tribes; he established dioceses, such as Brandenburg, Havelberg, etc., in a district which is now the political center of the German empire, and greatly forwarded the Christianizing and colonization of the tract between the Elbe and the Oder.

Final defeat of the Hungarians. Beginnings of Hungary and Austria.

Moreover, he put an end forever to the invasions of the Hungarians. He defeated them in a great battle near Augsburg (955) and pursued them to the confines of Germany. The Hungarians, or Magyars as they are commonly called, then settled down in their own territory and began to lay the foundations of that national development which makes them one of the most important factors in the eastern portion of Europe to-day. A region which had belonged to the Bavarian duchy was organized as a separate district, the Austrian *Mark* (i.e., March), and became the nucleus of the Austrian empire.

Otto interferes in Italian affairs.

57. The most noteworthy, however, of Otto's acts was his interference in Italian affairs, which led to his assuming the imperial crown which Charlemagne had worn. There is no more gloomy chapter in European history than the experiences of Italy and the papacy after the deposition of Charles the Fat in 887. We know little of what went on, but we hear of the duke of Spoleto, the marquis of Friuli, and Burgundian princes from across the Alps, assuming the Italian crown at different times. The Mohammedan invasions added to the confusion, so that Germany and France, in spite of their incessant wars, appear almost tranquil compared with the anarchy in Italy.[1]   Three Italian kings were crowned emperor by the popes during the generation following the deposition of Charles the Fat.   Then for a generation the title of emperor disappeared altogether in the West, until it was again assumed by the German Otto.

Italy was a tempting field of operations for an ambitious ruler.   Otto first crossed the Alps in 951, married the widow of one of the ephemeral Italian kings, and, without being formally crowned, was generally acknowledged as king of Italy.   The revolt of his son compelled him to return to Germany, but a decade later the pope called him to his assistance.   Otto answered the summons promptly, freed the pope from his enemies, and was crowned emperor at Rome in 962.

Otto is crowned emperor, 962.

The coronation of Otto the Great, like that of Charlemagne, was a momentous event in mediæval history.   By assuming the imperial crown he imposed so great a burden on his successors, the German kings, that they finally succumbed beneath it.   For three centuries they strove to keep Germany together and at the same time control Italy and the papacy.   After interminable wars and incalculable sacrifices, they lost all. Italy escaped them, the papacy established its complete independence, and Germany, their rightful patrimony, instead of growing into a strong monarchy, fell apart into weak little states.

Important results for Germany of the coronation of Otto the Great.

Otto's own experiences furnish an example of the melancholy results of his relations with the pope, to whom he owed his crown.   Hardly had he turned his back before the pope began to violate his engagements.   It became necessary for the new emperor to hasten back to Rome and summon a council for the deposition of the pontiff, whose conduct

Example of emperor's trouble in controlling popes and Italian affairs.

---

[1] See Emerton, *Mediæval Europe*, Chapter IV, for a clear account of the condition of the papacy, the struggles between the rival Italian dynasties, and the interference and coronation of Otto the Great.

certainly furnished ample justification. But the Romans refused to accept a pope chosen under Otto's auspices, and he had to return again to Rome and besiege the city before his pope was acknowledged. A few years later, still a third expedition was necessary in order to restore another of the emperor's popes who had been driven out of Rome by the local factions.

The succeeding emperors had usually to make a similar series of costly and troublesome journeys to Rome, — a first one to be crowned, and then others either to depose a hostile pope or to protect a loyal one from the oppression of neighboring lords. These excursions were very distracting, especially to a ruler who left behind him in Germany a rebellious nobility that always took advantage of his absence to revolt.

The Holy Roman Empire. Otto's successors dropped their old title of King of the East Franks as soon as they had been duly crowned by the pope at Rome, and assumed the magnificent and all-embracing designation, "Emperor Ever August of the Romans." [1] Their "Holy Roman Empire," as it came to be called later, which was to endure, in name at least, for more than eight centuries, was obviously even less like that of the ancient Romans than was Charlemagne's. As *kings* of Germany and Italy they had practically all the powers that they enjoyed as *emperors*, except the fatal right that they claimed of taking part in the election of the pope. We shall find that, instead of making themselves feared at home and building up a great state, the German emperors wasted their strength in a long struggle with the popes, who proved themselves in the end incomparably the stronger, and eventually reduced the Empire to a mere shadow.

[1] Henry II (1002–1024) and his successors, not venturing to assume the title of emperor till crowned at Rome, but anxious to claim the sovereignty of Rome as indissolubly attached to the German crown, began to call themselves before their coronation *rex Romanorum*, i.e., King of the Romans. This habit lasted until Luther's time, when Maximilian I got permission from the pope to call himself "Emperor Elect" before his coronation, and this title was thereafter taken by his successors immediately upon their election.

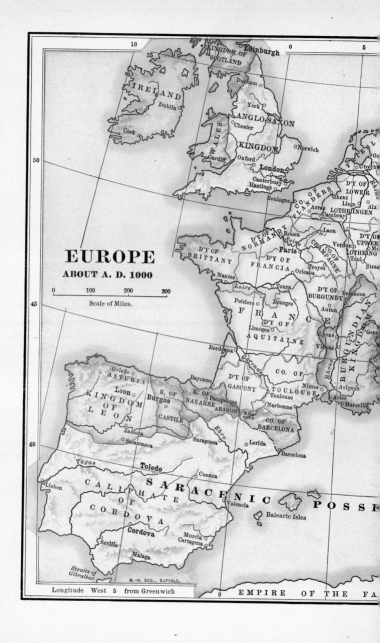

EUROPE

ABOUT A. D. 1000

0   100   200   300

Scale of Miles.

Longitude   West   5   from Greenwich

M.-N. ENG., BUFFALO.

0   EMPIRE   OF   THE   FA

10   55   KINGDOM OF SCOTLAND   Edinburgh   0   5

IRELAND

Dublin

Cork

Durham

York

WALES   ANGLO-SAXON

Chester

KINGDOM

Cardiff   Oxford   Norwich

50   London

Canterbury

Hastings

Boulogne

CO. OF FLANDERS

Ghent   Liege   Aix

Arras   LOTHRINGEN

Cambray

D'Y OF LOWER

Utrecht

Laon

Rouen   D'Y OF UPPER

Paris   Verdun   LOTHRINGEN

D'Y OF NORMANDY   CHAMPAGNE   Toul   Stra

D'Y OF   Troyes

BRITTANY   D'Y OF   Orleans

FRANCIA

Nantes

Loire   Tours   D'Y OF

Poitiers   Bourges   BURGUNDY   Besancon

45   F   R   A   N   C   E   Autun

Limoges   D'Y OF   Lyons   Gene

AQUITAINE   Vienne   BURGUNDIAN

Bordeaux   Garonne

Oviedo   CO. OF   Rhone   KINGDOM

ASTURIA   Bayonne   D'Y OF   TOULOUSE   Avignon

Leon   K. OF   GASCONY   Nimes   Arles

KINGDOM   Burgos   K. OF   Pampelona   Toulouse   Marseille

OF   NAVARRE   Narbonne

L E O N   CASTILE   ARAGON   Rib   CO. OF

Zamora   Ebro   orca   BARCELONA

40   Salamanca   Saragossa   Lerida

Tagus   Barcelona

Toledo

Lisbon   Cuenca

CALIPHATE   S   A   R   A   C   E   N   I   C   POSS

OF   Valencia

CORDOVA   Balearic Isles

Cordova   Murcia

Seville   Cartagena

Malaga

Straits of
Gibraltar

58. We have no space to speak of the immediate successors of Otto the Great.[1] Like him they had to meet opposition at home as well as the attacks of their restless neighbors, especially the Slavs. The Empire is usually considered to have reached its height under Conrad II (1024–1039) and Henry III (1039–1056), the first two representatives of the new Franconian line which succeeded the Saxon house upon its extinction in 1024.

By an amicable arrangement the kingdom of Burgundy came into the hands of Conrad II in 1032. This large and important territory long remained a part of the Empire, serving to render intercourse between Germany and Italy easier, and forming a barrier between Germany and France. On the eastern borders of the Empire the Slavs had organized the kingdom of Poland in the latter half of the tenth century, and its kings, although often at war with the emperor, generally acknowledged his suzerainty. Conrad, following the policy of Otto the Great, endeavored to bring as many of the stem duchies as possible into the hands of his son and successor, Henry III, who was made duke of Franconia, Swabia, and Bavaria. This was the firmest of all foundations for the kingly power.

Conrad II, 1024-1039.

Poland.

Notwithstanding the energy and ability of Conrad II and Henry III, the fact that the Empire stands forth as the great power of western Europe during the first half of the eleventh century is largely due to the absence of any strong rivals. The French kings had not yet overcome the feudal disruption, and although Italy objected to the control of the emperor, it never could agree to combine against him.

Henry III, 1039-1056.

59. The most important question that Henry III had to face was that of a great reform of the Church. This was already under way and it was bound, if carried out, to destroy the

Henry III and the Church.

[1] For Otto II, Otto III, and Henry II, see Emerton, *Mediæval Europe,* Chapter V; and Henderson, *Germany in the Middle Ages,* pp. 145–166.

control of the emperors not only over the papacy but also over the German bishops and abbots, whom they had strengthened by grants of land and authority with the special purpose of making them the chief support of the monarchy. The reform was not directed particularly against the emperor, but he was, as will become apparent, more seriously affected by the changes proposed by the reforming party than any other of the European rulers.

Wealth of the Church.

In order to understand the reform and the long struggle between the emperors and the popes which grew out of it, we must stop a moment to consider the condition of the Church in the time of Henry III. It seemed to be losing all its strength and dignity and to be falling apart, just as Charlemagne's empire had dissolved into feudal bits. This was chiefly due to the vast landed possessions of the clergy. Kings, princes, and rich landowners had long considered it meritorious to make donations to bishoprics and monasteries, so that a very considerable portion of the land in western Europe had come into the hands of churchmen.

The church lands drawn into the feudal system.

When landowners began to give and receive land as fiefs the property of the Church was naturally drawn into the feudal relations. A king, or other proprietor, might grant fiefs to churchmen as well as to laymen. The bishops became the vassals of the king or of other feudal lords by doing homage for a fief and swearing fidelity, just as any other vassal would do. An abbot sometimes placed his monastery under the protection of a neighboring lord by giving up his land and receiving it back again as a fief.

Fiefs held by churchmen not hereditary.

One great difference, however, existed between the church lands and the ordinary fiefs. According to the law of the Church, the bishops and abbots could not marry and so could have no children to whom they might transmit their property. Consequently, when a landholding churchman died, some one had to be chosen in his place who should enjoy his property and perform his duties. The rule of the Church had been, from time immemorial, that the clergy of the diocese should choose the bishop, their choice being ratified by the people. As the church law expresses it, " A bishop is therefore rightly appointed in the church of God when the people acclaim him who has been elected by the common vote of the clergy." As for the abbots, they were, according to the rule of St Benedict, to be chosen by the members of the monastery.

In spite of these rules the bishops and abbots had come, in the tenth and eleventh centuries, to be selected, to all intents and purposes, by the various kings and feudal lords. It is true that the outward forms of a regular (" canonical ") election were usually permitted ; but the feudal lord made it clear whom he wished chosen, and if the wrong person was elected, he simply refused to hand over to him the lands attached to the bishopric or abbey. The lord could in this way control the choice of the prelates, for in order to become a real bishop or abbot one had not only to be elected, he had also to be solemnly " invested " with the appropriate powers of a bishop or abbot and with his lands.

Bishops and abbots practically chosen by the feudal lords.

Since, to the worldly minded, the spiritual powers attached to church offices possessed little attraction if no property went along with them, the feudal lord was really master of the situation. When his appointee was duly chosen he proceeded to the *investiture*. The new bishop or abbot first became the " man " of the feudal lord by doing him homage, and then the lord transferred to him the lands and rights attached to the office. No careful distinction appears to have been made between the property and the spiritual prerogatives. The lord often conferred both by bestowing upon a bishop the ring and the crosier, the emblems of religious authority. It seemed shocking enough that the lord, who was often a rough soldier, should dictate the selection of the bishops, but it was still more shocking that he should audaciously assume to confer spiritual

Investiture.

powers with spiritual emblems. Yet even worse things might happen, since sometimes the lord, for his greater convenience, had himself made bishop.

The Church itself naturally looked at the property attached to a benefice as a mere incident and considered the spiritual prerogatives the main thing. And since the clergy alone could rightly confer these, it was natural that they should claim the right to bestow ecclesiastical offices, including the lands ("temporalities") attached to them, upon whomsoever they pleased without consulting any layman whatever. Against this claim

the king might urge that a simple minister of the Gospel, or a holy monk, was by no means necessarily fitted to manage the interests of a feudal state, such as the great archbishoprics and bishoprics, and even the abbeys, had become in Germany and elsewhere in the eleventh century.

In short, the situation in which the bishops found themselves was a very complicated one. (1) As an officer of the Church, the bishop had certain ecclesiastical and religious duties within the limits of his diocese. He saw that parish priests were properly selected and ordained, he tried certain cases in his court, and performed the church ceremonies. (2) He managed the lands which belonged to the bishopric, which might, or might not, be fiefs. (3) As a vassal of those who had granted lands to the bishopric upon feudal terms, he owed the usual feudal dues, not excluding the duty of furnishing troops to his lord. (4) Lastly, in Germany, the king had found it convenient, from about the beginning of the eleventh century, to confer upon the bishops in many cases the authority of a count in the districts about them. In this way they might have the right to collect tolls, coin money, and perform other important governmental duties.[1] When a prelate was inducted into office he was

---

[1] These grants of the powers of a count to prelates serve to explain the *ecclesiastical* states, — for example, the archbishoprics of Mayence and Salzburg, the bishopric of Bamberg, and so forth, — which continue to appear upon the map of Germany until the opening of the nineteenth century.

invested with all these various functions at once, both spiritual and governmental.

To forbid the king to take part in the investiture was, consequently, to rob him not only of his feudal rights but also of his authority over many of his government officials, since bishops, and sometimes even abbots, were often counts in all but name. Moreover, the monarch relied upon the clergy, both in Germany and France, to counterbalance the influence of his lay vassals, who were always trying to exalt their power at his expense. He therefore found it necessary to take care who got possession of the important church offices.

60. Still another danger threatened the wealth and resources of the Church. During the tenth and eleventh centuries the rule of the Church prohibiting the clergy from marrying[1] appears to have been widely and publicly neglected in Italy, Germany, France, and England. To the stricter critics of the time this appeared a terrible degradation of the clergy, who, they felt, should be unencumbered by family cares and wholly devoted to the service of God. The question, too, had another side. It was obvious that the property of the Church would soon be dispersed if the clergy were allowed to marry, since they would wish to provide for their children. Just as the feudal tenures had become hereditary, so the church lands would become hereditary unless the clergy were forced to remain unmarried.

The marriage of the clergy threatens the wealth of the Church.

[1] From the beginning, single life had appealed to some Christians as more worthy than the married state. Gradually, under the influence of monasticism, the more devout and enthusiastic clergy voluntarily shunned marriage, or, if already married, gave up association with their wives after ordination. Finally the Western Church condemned marriage altogether for the deacon and the ranks above him, and later the subdeacons were included in the prohibition. The records are too incomplete for the historian to form an accurate idea of how far the prohibition of the Church was really observed throughout the countries of the West. There were certainly great numbers of married clergymen in northern Italy, Germany, and elsewhere, in the tenth and eleventh centuries. Of course the Church refused to sanction the marriage of its officials and called the wife of a clergyman, however virtuous and faithful she might be, by the opprobrious name of "concubine."

Buying and
selling of
church
offices.

Besides the feudalizing of its property and the marriage of
the clergy, there was a third great and constant source of
weakness and corruption in the Church, namely, the temptation to buy and sell church offices.　Had the duties and
responsibilities of the bishops, abbots, and priests always been
arduous and exacting, and their recompense barely enough
to maintain them, there would have been little tendency to
bribe those who could bestow the appointments.　But the
incomes of bishoprics and abbeys were usually considerable,
sometimes very great, while the duties attached to the office
of bishop or abbot, however serious in the eyes of the right-
minded, might easily be neglected by the unscrupulous.　The
revenue from a great landed estate, the distinction of high ecclesiastical rank, and the governmental prerogatives that went with
the office, were enough to induce the members of the noblest
families to vie with each other in securing church positions.
The king or prince who possessed the right of investiture was
sure of finding some one willing to pay something for important
benefices.

Origin of the
term simony.

The sin of buying or selling church offices was recognized
as a most heinous one.　It was called *simony*,[1] a name
derived from Simon the Magician, who, according to the
account in the Acts of the Apostles, offered Peter money if
he would give him the power of conferring the Holy Spirit
upon those upon whom he should lay his hands.　As the
apostle denounced this first simonist, so the Church has continued ever since to denounce those who propose to purchase
its sacred powers, — "Thy silver perish with thee, because
thou hast thought to obtain the gift of God with money"
(Acts ix. 20).

Simony not
really the
sale of church
offices.

Doubtless very few bought positions in the Church with the
view of obtaining the "gift of God," that is to say, the
religious office.　It was the revenue and the honor that were

---

1 Pronounced *sĭm'o-ny*.

chiefly coveted. Moreover, when a king or lord accepted a gift from one for whom he procured a benefice, he did not regard himself as selling the office ; he merely shared its advantages. No transaction took place in the Middle Ages without accompanying gifts and fees of various kinds. The church lands were well managed and remunerative. The clergyman who was appointed to a rich bishopric or abbey seemed to have far more revenue than he needed and so was expected to contribute to the king's treasury, which was generally empty.

The evil of simony was, therefore, explicable enough, and perhaps ineradicable under the circumstances. It was, nevertheless, very demoralizing, for it spread downward and infected the whole body of the clergy. A bishop who had made a large outlay in obtaining his office naturally expected something from the priests, whom it was his duty to appoint. The priest in turn was tempted to reimburse himself by improper exactions for the performance of his regular religious duties, for baptizing and marrying his parishioners, and for burying the dead.

Simony corrupts the lower clergy.

So it seemed, at the opening of the eleventh century, as if the Church was to be dragged down by its property into the anarchy of feudalism described in a preceding chapter. There were many indications that its great officers were to become merely the vassals of kings and princes and no longer to represent a great international institution under the headship of the popes. The Bishop of Rome had not only ceased, in the tenth century, to exercise any considerable influence over the churches beyond the Alps, but was himself controlled by the restless nobles of central Italy. He appears much less important, in the chronicles of the time, than the Archbishop of Rheims or Mayence. There is no more extraordinary evolution recorded in history than that which raised the weak and demoralized papacy of the tenth century to a supreme place in European affairs.

Three rival
popes.

61. One of the noble families of Rome had got the selection of the popes into its own hands, and was using the papal authority to secure its control over the city. In the same year (1024) in which Conrad II became emperor, a layman was actually exalted to the headship of the Church, and after him a mere boy of ten or twelve years, Benedict IX, who, in addition to his youth, proved to be thoroughly evil-minded. His powerful family maintained him, however, on the papal throne for a decade, until he proposed to marry. This so scandalized even the not over-sensitive Romans that they drove him out of the city. A rich neighboring bishop then secured his own election. Presently a third claimant appeared in the person of a pious and learned priest who bought out the claims of Benedict IX for a large sum of money and assumed the title of Gregory VI.

The interference of
Henry III
in papal
affairs and
its momentous consequences.

This state of affairs seemed to the emperor, Henry III, to call for his interference. He accordingly went to Italy and summoned a council at Sutri, north of Rome, in 1046, where two of the claimants were deposed. Gregory VI, more conscientious than his rivals, not only resigned his office but tore his pontifical robes in pieces and admitted his monstrous crime in buying the papal dignity, though his motives had been of the purest. The emperor then secured the election of a worthy German bishop as pope, whose first act was to crown Henry and Agnes his wife.[1]

The appearance of Henry III in Italy at this juncture, and the settlement of the question of the three rival popes, are among the most important events of all mediæval history in their results. In lifting the papacy out of the realm of petty Italian politics, Henry unwittingly helped to raise up a rival to the imperial authority which was destined, before the end of the next century, to overshadow it and to become without question the greatest power in western Europe.

[1] Reference, Emerton, *Mediæval Europe*, pp. 201–209.

oversight on the part of the popes was not feasible in the long run, if for no other reason, because they were generally old men who would have found traveling arduous and often danger-

Papal legates.

ous. Leo's successors relied upon legates, to whom they delegated extensive powers and whom they dispatched to all parts of western Europe in something the same way that Charlemagne employed his *missi*. It is supposed that Leo IX was greatly influenced in his energetic policy by a certain subdeacon, Hildebrand by name. Hildebrand was himself destined to become one of the greatest popes, under the title of Gregory VII, and to play a part in the formation of the mediæval Church which justifies us in ranking him, as a statesman, with Cæsar, Charlemagne, Richelieu, and Bismarck.

Pope Nicholas II places the election of the popes in the hands of the cardinals, 1059.

62. The first great step toward the emancipation of the Church from the control of the laity was taken by Nicholas II. In 1059 he issued a remarkable decree which took the election of the head of the Church once for all out of the hands of both the emperor and the people of Rome, and placed it definitely and forever in the hands of the *cardinals*, who represented the Roman clergy.[1] Obviously the object of this decree was to preclude all lay interference, whether of the distant emperor, of the local nobility, or of the Roman mob. The college of cardinals still exists and still elects the pope.[2]

Opposition to further reforms.

The reform party which directed the policy of the popes had, it hoped, freed the head of the Church from the control of worldly men by putting his election in the hands of the

[1] The word *cardinal* (Latin, *cardinalis*, principal) was applied to the priests of the various parishes in Rome, to the several deacons connected with the Lateran, — which was the cathedral church of the Roman bishopric, — and, lastly, to six or seven suburban bishops who officiated in turn in the Lateran. The title became a very distinguished one and was sought by ambitious prelates and ecclesiastical statesmen, like Wolsey, Richelieu, and Mazarin. If their official titles were examined, it would be found that each was nominally a cardinal bishop, priest, or deacon of some Roman church. The number of cardinals varied until fixed, in 1586, at six bishops, fifty priests, and fourteen deacons.

[2] The decree of 1059 is to be found in Henderson, *Historical Documents*, p. 361.

Roman clergy. It now proposed to emancipate the Church as a whole from the base entanglements of earth : first, by strictly forbidding the married clergy to perform religious functions and by exhorting their flocks to refuse to attend their ministrations ; and secondly, by depriving the kings and feudal lords of their influence over the choice of the bishops and abbots, since this influence was deemed the chief cause of worldliness among the prelates. Naturally these last measures met with far more general opposition than the new way of electing the pope. An attempt to expel the married clergy from Milan led to a popular revolt, in which the pope's legate actually found his life in danger. The decrees forbidding clergymen to receive their lands and offices from laymen received little attention from either the clergy or the feudal lords. The magnitude of the task which the popes had undertaken first became fully apparent when Hildebrand himself ascended the papal throne, in 1073, as Gregory VII.

CHAPTER XIII

THE CONFLICT BETWEEN GREGORY VII AND HENRY IV

The *Dictatus* of Gregory VII.

63. Among the writings of Gregory VII there is a very brief statement, called the *Dictatus*, of the powers which he believed the popes to possess. Its chief claims are the following: The pope enjoys a unique title; he is the only universal bishop and may depose and reinstate other bishops or transfer them from place to place. No council of the Church may be regarded as speaking for Christendom without his consent. The Roman Church has never erred, nor will it err to all eternity. No one may be considered a Catholic Christian who does not agree with the Roman Church. No book is authoritative unless it has received the papal sanction.

Gregory does not stop with asserting the pope's complete supremacy over the Church; he goes still further and claims for him the right to restrain the civil government when it seems necessary in the cause of righteousness. He says that "the Pope is the only person whose feet are kissed by all princes"; that he may depose emperors and "absolve subjects from allegiance to an unjust ruler." No one shall dare to condemn one who appeals to the pope. No one may annul a decree of the pope, though the pope may declare null and void the decrees of all other earthly powers; and no one may pass judgment upon his acts.[1]

---

[1] For text of the *Dictatus*, see *Readings*, Chapter XIII. The most complete statement of Gregory's view of the responsibility of the papacy for the civil government is to be found in his famous letter to the Bishop of Metz (1081), *Readings*, Chapter XIII.

These are not the insolent claims of a reckless tyrant, but the expression of a theory of government which has had advocates among some of the most conscientious and learned men of all succeeding ages. Before venturing to criticise Gregory's view of his position we should recollect two important facts. In the first place, what most writers call the *state*, when dealing with the Middle Ages, was no orderly government in our sense of the word; it was represented only by restless feudal lords, to whom disorder was the very breath of life. When, on one occasion, Gregory declared the civil power to be the invention of evil men instigated by the devil, he was making a natural inference from what he observed of the conduct of the princes of his time. In the second place, it should be remembered that Gregory does not claim that the Church should manage the civil government, but that the papacy, which is answerable for the eternal welfare of every Christian, should have the right to restrain a sinful and perverse prince and to refuse to recognize unrighteous laws. Should all else fail, he claimed the right to free a nation which was being led to disaster in this world and to perdition in the next from its allegiance to a wicked monarch.

Inadequacy of civil government in the Middle Ages.

The Church claims the right to interfere only when necessary.

Immediately upon his election as pope, Gregory began to put into practice his high conception of the rôle that the spiritual head of the world should play. He dispatched legates throughout Europe, and from this time on these legates became a powerful instrument of government. He warned the kings of France and England and the youthful German ruler, Henry IV, to forsake their evil ways, to be upright and just, and obey his admonitions. He explains, kindly but firmly, to William the Conqueror that the papal and kingly powers are both established by God as the greatest among the authorities of the world, just as the sun and moon are the greatest of the heavenly bodies.[1] But the papal power

Gregory VII puts his theories of the papal power into practice.

1 For this letter, see Colby, *Sources*, p. 37.

is obviously superior to the kingly, for it is responsible for it; at the Last Day Gregory must render an account of the king as one of the flock intrusted to his care. The king of France was warned to give up his practice of simony, lest he be excommunicated and his subjects freed from their oath of allegiance. All these acts of Gregory appear to have been dictated not by worldly ambition but by a fervent conviction of their righteousness and of his duty toward all men.

Death of Henry III, 1056.

64. Obviously Gregory's plan of reform included all the states of western Europe, but conditions were such that the most striking conflict took place between him and the emperor. The trouble came about in this way. Henry III had died in 1056, leaving only his good wife Agnes and their little son of six years to maintain the hard-fought prerogatives of the German king in the midst of ambitious vassals such as even Otto the Great had found it difficult to control.

Accession of Henry IV, 1065.

In 1065 the fifteen-year-old lad was declared of age, and his lifelong difficulties began with a great rebellion of the Saxons. They accused the young king of having built castles in their land and of filling them with rough soldiers who preyed upon the people. Gregory felt it his duty to interfere. To him the Saxons appeared a people oppressed by a heedless youth under the inspiration of evil counselors.

As one reads of Henry's difficulties and misfortunes it seems miraculous that he was able to maintain himself as king at all. Sick at heart, unable to trust any one, and forced to flee from his own subjects, he writes contritely to the pope: "We have sinned against heaven and before thee and are no longer worthy to be called thy son." But when cheered for a moment by a victory over the rebellious Saxons, he easily forgot his promise of obedience to the pope. He continued to associate with counselors whom the pope had excommunicated and went on filling important bishoprics in Germany and Italy regardless of the pope's prohibitions.

The popes who immediately preceded Gregory had more than once forbidden the churchmen to receive investiture from laymen. Gregory reissued this prohibition in 1075,[1] just as the trouble with Henry had begun. Investiture was, as we have seen, the legal transfer by the king, or other lord, to a newly chosen church official, of the lands and rights attached to the office. In forbidding lay investiture Gregory attempted nothing less than a revolution. The bishops and abbots were often officers of government, exercising in Germany and Italy powers similar in all respects to those of the counts. The king not only relied upon them for advice and assistance in carrying on his government, but they were among his chief allies in his constant struggles with his vassals.

New prohibition of lay investiture.

Gregory dispatched three envoys to Henry (end of 1075) with a fatherly letter[2] in which he reproached the king for his wicked conduct. But he evidently had little expectation that mere expostulation would have any effect upon Henry, for he gave his legates instructions to use threats, if necessary, which were bound to produce either complete subjection or out-and-out revolt. The legates were to tell the king that his crimes were so numerous, so horrible, and so notorious, that he merited not only excommunication but the permanent loss of all his royal honors.

Henry IV angered by the language of the papal legates.

The violence of the legates' language not only kindled the wrath of the king but also gained for him friends among the bishops. A council which Henry summoned at Worms (in 1076) was attended by more than two thirds of the German bishops. Here Gregory was declared deposed owing to the alleged irregularity of his election and the many terrible charges of immorality and ambition brought against him. The bishops renounced their obedience to him and publicly declared

Gregory VII deposed by a council of German bishops at Worms, 1076.

[1] Reissues of this decree in 1078 and 1080 are given in the *Readings*, Chapter XIII.

[2] To be found in the *Readings*, Chapter XIII.

that he had ceased to be their pope. It appears very surprising, at first sight, that the king should have received the prompt support of the German churchmen against the head of the Church. But it must be remembered that the prelates owed their offices to the king and not to the pope.

In a remarkable letter [1] to Gregory, Henry asserts that he has shown himself long-suffering and eager to guard the honor of the papacy, but that the pope has mistaken his humility for fear. "Thou hast not hesitated," the letter concludes, "to rise up against the royal power conferred upon us by God, daring to threaten to deprive us of it, as if we had received our kingdom from thee. As if the kingdom and the Empire were in thine and not in God's hands . . . I, Henry, King by the grace of God, together with all our bishops, say unto thee, come down, come down from thy throne and be accursed of all generations."

Henry IV deposed and excommunicated by the pope. Gregory's reply to Henry and the German bishops who had deposed him was speedy and decisive. "Incline thine ear to us, O Peter, chief of the Apostles. As thy representative and by thy favor has the power been granted especially to me by God of binding and loosing in heaven and earth. On the strength of this, for the honor and glory of thy Church, in the name of Almighty God, Father, Son, and Holy Ghost, I withdraw, through thy power and authority, from Henry the King, son of Henry the Emperor, who has risen against thy Church with unheard-of insolence, the rule over the whole kingdom of the Germans and over Italy. I absolve all Christians from the bonds of the oath which they have sworn, or may swear, to him ; and I forbid anyone to serve him as king." For his intercourse with the excommunicated and his manifold iniquities, the king is furthermore declared accursed and excommunicate.[2]

[1] Henry's letter and one from the German bishops to the pope are both in Henderson, *Historical Documents*, pp. 372–376.

[2] Gregory's deposition and excommunication of Henry may be found in the *Readings*, Chapter XIII.

For a time after the pope had deposed him everything went Attitude of the German princes. against Henry. Even the churchmen now held off. Instead of resenting the pope's interference, the discontented Saxons, and many other of Henry's vassals, believed that there was now an excellent opportunity to get rid of Henry and choose a more agreeable ruler. But after a long conference the great German vassals decided to give Henry another chance. He was to refrain from exercising the functions of government until he had made peace with the pope. If at the end of a year he had failed to do this, he was to be regarded as having forfeited the throne. The pope was, moreover, invited to come to Augsburg to consult with the princes as to whether Henry should be reinstated or another chosen in his stead. It looked as if the pope was, in truth, to control the civil government.

Henry decided to anticipate the arrival of the pope. He Henry submits to the pope at Canossa, 1077. hastened across the Alps in midwinter and appeared as an humble suppliant before the castle of Canossa, whither the pope had come on his way to Augsburg. For three days the German king appeared before the closed door, barefoot and in the coarse garments of a pilgrim and a penitent, and even then Gregory was induced only by the expostulations of his influential companions to admit the humiliated ruler. The spectacle of this mighty prince of distinguished appearance, humiliated and in tears before the nervous little man who humbly styled himself the "servant of the servants of God," has always been regarded as most completely typifying the power of the Church and the potency of her curses, against which even the most exalted of the earth found no weapon of defense except abject penitence.[1]

65. The pardon which Henry received at Canossa did not A new king chosen. satisfy the German princes ; for their main object in demanding that he should reconcile himself with the Church had been to

[1] For Gregory's own account of the affair at Canossa, see *Readings*, Chapter XIII.

cause him additional embarrassment. They therefore proceeded to elect another ruler, and the next three or four years was a period of bloody struggles between the adherents of the rival kings. Gregory remained neutral until 1080, when he again "bound with the chain of anathema" Henry, "the so-called king," and all his followers. He declared him deprived of his royal power and dignity and forbade all Christians to obey him.

Henry again excommunicated.

The new excommunication had precisely the opposite effect from the first one. Henry's friends increased rather than decreased. The German clergy were again aroused, and they again deposed "this same most brazen Hildebrand." Henry's rival fell in battle, and Henry, accompanied by an antipope, betook himself to Italy with the double purpose of putting his pope on the throne and winning the imperial crown. Gregory held out for no less than two years, but at last Rome fell into Henry's hands and Gregory withdrew and soon died. His last words were, "I have loved justice and hated iniquity, therefore I die an exile," and the fair-minded historical student will not question their truth.[1]

Henry triumphs over Gregory.

Death of Gregory.

The death of Gregory did not put an end to Henry's difficulties. He spent the remaining twenty years of his life in trying to maintain his rights as king of Germany and Italy against his rebellious subjects on both sides of the Alps. In Germany his chief enemies were the Saxons and his discontented vassals. In Italy the pope was now actively engaged as a temporal ruler, in building up a little state of his own. He was, moreover, always ready to encourage the Lombard cities — which were growing more and more powerful and less and less willing to submit to the rule of a German — in their opposition to the emperor.

Henry IV's further troubles.

[1] For a fuller account of the troubles between Gregory and Henry, see Henderson, *Germany in the Middle Ages*, pp. 183–210; Emerton, *Mediæval Europe*, pp. 240–259.

A combination of his Italian enemies called Henry again to Italy in 1090, although he was forced to leave Germany but half subdued. He was seriously defeated by the Italians; and the Lombard cities embraced the opportunity to form their first union against their foreign king. In 1093 Milan, Cremona, Lodi, and Piacenza joined in an offensive and defensive alliance for their own protection. After seven years of hopeless lingering in Italy, Henry returned sadly across the Alps, leaving the peninsula in the hands of his enemies. But he found no peace at home. His discontented German vassals induced his son, whom he had had crowned as his successor, to revolt against his father. Thereupon followed more civil war, more treason, and a miserable abdication. In 1106 death put an end to perhaps the saddest reign that history records.

Rebellion at home and in Italy. Treason of Henry's sons.

Death of Henry IV, 1106.

The achievement of the reign of Henry IV's son, Henry V, which chiefly interests us was the adjustment of the question of investitures. Pope Paschal II, while willing to recognize those bishops already chosen by the king, provided they were good men, proposed that thereafter Gregory's decrees against lay investiture should be carried out. The clergy should no longer do homage and lay their hands, consecrated to the service of the altar, in the blood-stained hands of the nobles. Henry V, on the other hand, declared that unless the clergy took the oath of fealty the bishops would not be given the lands, towns, castles, tolls, and privileges attached to the bishoprics.

Henry V, 1106-1125.

After a succession of troubles a compromise was at last reached in the Concordat of Worms (1122), which put an end to the controversy over investitures in Germany.[1] The emperor promised to permit the Church freely to elect the bishops and abbots and renounced his old claim to invest with the spiritual emblems of the ring and the crosier. But the elections were to be held in the presence of the king, and he

Settlement of the question of lay investiture in the Concordat of Worms, 1122.

[1] See *Readings*, Chapter XIII.

was permitted, in a separate ceremony, to invest the new bishop or abbot with his fiefs and secular prerogatives by a touch of the scepter. In this way the spiritual rights of the bishops were obviously conferred by the churchmen who elected him; and although the king might still practically invalidate an election by refusing to invest with the coveted temporal privileges, still the direct appointment of the bishops and abbots was taken out of his hands. As for the emperor's control over the papacy, too many popes, since the advent of Henry IV, had been generally recognized as properly elected without the sanction of the emperor, for any one to believe any longer that his sanction was necessary.

CHAPTER XIV

THE HOHENSTAUFEN EMPERORS AND THE POPES

66. Frederick I, nicknamed Barbarossa, i.e., "Redbeard," who became king of Germany in 1152,[1] is the most interesting of all the German emperors; and the records we have of his reign enable us to gain a pretty good view of Europe in the middle of the twelfth century. With his advent, we feel that we are emerging from that long period which used to be known as the dark ages. Most of our knowledge of European history from the sixth to the twelfth century is derived from meager and unreliable monkish chronicles, whose authors were often ignorant and careless, and usually far away from the scenes of the events they recorded. In the latter half of the twelfth century, however, information grows much more abundant and varied. We begin to have records of the town life and are no longer entirely dependent upon the monks' records. The first historian with a certain philosophic grasp of his theme was Otto of Freising. His *Life of Frederick Barbarossa* and his history of the world form invaluable sources of knowledge of the period we now enter.

Frederick's ambition was to raise the Roman Empire to its old glory and influence. He regarded himself as the successor of the Cæsars, of Justinian, of Charlemagne, and of Otto the Great. He believed his office to be quite as divinely established as the papacy. In announcing his election to the pope, he stated that the Empire had been "bestowed upon him by

Frederick I, Barbarossa, 1152-1190.

The historian, Otto of Freising.

Frederick's ideal of the Empire.

---

[1] For the emperors Lothaire (1125–1137) and Conrad III (1138–1152), the first of the Hohenstaufens, see Emerton, *Mediæval Europe*, pp. 271–282.

God," and he did not ask for the pope's sanction, as his predecessors had done. But in his lifelong attempt to maintain what he assumed to be the rights of the emperor he encountered all the old difficulties. He had to watch his rebellious vassals in Germany and meet the opposition of a series of unflinching popes, ready to defend the most exalted claims of the papacy. He found, moreover, in the Lombard cities unconquerable foes, who finally brought upon him a signal defeat.

The towns begin to play a part in history.

67. One of the most striking differences between the ages before Frederick and the whole period since, lies in the development of town life, with all that that implies. Up to this time we have heard only of emperors, popes, bishops, and feudal lords ; from now on the cities must be reckoned with, as Frederick was to discover to his sorrow.[1]

The government of the Lombard cities becomes partially democratic.

The government of the towns of Lombardy fell, after Charlemagne's time, into the hands of their respective bishops, who exercised the prerogatives of counts. Under the bishops the towns flourished within their walls and also extended their control over the neighboring districts. As industry and commerce increased, the prosperous citizens, and the poorer classes as well, aspired to some control over the government. Cremona very early expelled its bishop, destroyed his castle, and refused to pay him any dues. Later Henry IV stirred up Lucca against its bishop and promised that its liberties should never be interfered with henceforth by bishop, duke, or count. Other towns threw off the episcopal rule, and in practically all of them the government came at last into the hands of municipal officials elected by those citizens who were permitted to have a hand in the government.

The turmoil in the Italian towns; their remarkable civilization.

The more humble artisans were excluded altogether from a voice in city affairs. Their occasional revolts, as well as the feuds between the factions of the nobles, — who took up their residence in the towns instead of remaining on their estates, —

[1] Something will be said of the mediæval towns in Chapter XVIII.

produced a turmoil which we should think intolerable in our modern peaceable cities. This was greatly increased by bitter wars with neighboring towns. Yet, in spite of incredible disorder within and without, the Italian towns became centers of industry, learning, and art, unequaled in history except by the

Italian Towns in the Twelfth Century

famous cities of Greece. They were able, moreover, to maintain their independence for several centuries. Frederick's difficulties in playing the emperor in Italy were naturally greatly increased by the sturdy opposition of the Lombard towns which could always count on a faithful ally in the pope. He and they had a common interest in seeing that the power of the king of Germany remained purely nominal on their side of the mountains.[1]

Frederick's first expedition to Italy, 1154.

68. Milan was the most powerful of the Lombard towns and was heartily detested by her neighbors, over whom she was constantly endeavoring to extend her control. Two refugees from Lodi brought word to the newly elected emperor of Milan's tyranny. When Frederick's representatives reached the offending city they were insulted and the imperial seal was trampled in the dust. Like the other towns, Milan would acknowledge the supremacy of the emperor only so long as he made it no trouble. The wish to gain the imperial crown and to see what this bold conduct of Milan meant, brought Frederick to Italy, in 1154, on the first of six expeditions, which together were to occupy many years of his reign.

Frederick pitched his camp in the plain of Roncaglia and there received representatives from the Lombard towns, who had many and grievous complaints to make of the conduct of their neighbors, especially of the arrogant Milan. We get a hint of the distant commerce of the maritime cities when we read that Genoa sent gifts of ostriches, lions, and parrots. Frederick made a momentary impression by proceeding, upon the complaint of Pavia, to besiege and destroy the town of Tortona. As soon as he moved on to Rome, Milan plucked up courage to punish two or three neighbors who had too enthusiastically supported the emperor; it also lent a hand to Tortona's hapless citizens in rebuilding their city.

Frederick and Pope Hadrian.

When the pope, Hadrian IV, and the emperor first met there was some bitter feeling because Frederick hesitated to hold the pope's stirrup. He made no further objection, however, when he learned that it was the custom. Hadrian was relying upon his assistance, for Rome was in the midst of a remarkable revolution. Under the leadership of the famous

[1] Reference, Emerton, *Mediæval Europe*, pp. 271–291.

Arnold of Brescia,[1] the city was attempting to reëstablish a government similar to that of the times when the Roman senate ruled the civilized world. It is needless to say that the attempt failed, though Frederick gave the pope but little help against Arnold and the rebellious Romans. After receiving his crown, the emperor hastened back to Germany and left the disappointed Hadrian to deal with his refractory people as best he might. This desertion and later misunderstandings produced much ill feeling between the pope and Frederick.

In 1158 Frederick was back in Italy and held another great assembly at Roncaglia. He summoned hither certain teachers of the Roman law from Bologna (where the revived study of the law was actively pursued), as well as representatives of the towns, to decide exactly what his rights as emperor were. There was little danger but that those versed in a law which declared that "whatsoever the prince has willed has the force of law," should give the emperor his due. His *regalia*, or governmental prerogatives, were declared to consist in feudal suzerainty over the various duchies and counties, and in the right to appoint magistrates, collect tolls, impose an extraordinary war tax, coin money, and enjoy the revenue from fisheries and from salt and silver mines. Such persons or towns as could produce proof that any of these privileges had been formally conceded to them might continue to enjoy them ; otherwise the emperor assumed them. As most of the towns had simply succeeded to the rights of the bishops and had no legal proofs of any concessions from the emperor, this decision meant the loss of their independence. The emperor greatly increased his revenue for the moment ; but these extreme measures and the hated governors whom he appointed to represent him were bound to produce ultimate revolt. It became a matter of life and death to the towns to get rid of the imperial officials and taxgatherers.

The assembly at Roncaglia, 1158.

Its decision as to the rights (*regalia*) of the emperor over the Lombard towns.

[1] Reference, Emerton, *Mediæval Europe*, pp. 293–297.

The destruction of Crema and Milan.

The town of Crema refused to level its walls at the command of the emperor. It had to undergo a most terrible siege and finally succumbed. Its citizens were allowed to depart with nothing but their lives, and the place was given over to plunder and destruction. Then Milan drove the emperor's deputies from the gates. A long siege brought even this proud city to terms ; and the emperor did not hesitate to order its destruction, in spite of its commercial and political importance (1162). It is a melancholy commentary upon the relations between the various towns that Milan's neighbors begged to be permitted to carry out her annihilation. Her inhabitants were allowed to settle in the neighborhood of the spot where their prosperous city had stood, and from the rapidity with which they were able to rebuild it later, we may conclude that the demolition was not so thoroughgoing as some of the accounts imply.

The Lombard towns secretly unite to form the Lombard League.

69. The only hope for the Lombard towns was in *union*, which the emperor had explicitly forbidden. Soon after Milan's destruction measures were secretly taken to form the nucleus of what became later the great Lombard League. Cremona, Brescia, Mantua, and Bergamo joined together against the emperor. Encouraged by the pope and aided by the League, Milan was speedily rebuilt. Frederick, who had been engaged in conquering Rome with a view of placing an antipope on the throne of St. Peter, was glad, in 1167, to escape the combined dangers of Roman fever and the wrath of the towns and get back to Germany. The League was extended to include Verona, Piacenza, Parma, and eventually many other towns. It was even deemed best to construct an entirely new town, with a view of harboring forces to oppose the emperor on his return, and Alessandria remains a lasting testimonial to the energy and coöperative spirit of the League. The new town got its name from the League's ally, Pope Alexander III, one of the most conspicuous among the papal opponents of the German kings.

After several years spent in regulating affairs in Germany, Frederick again appeared in Lombardy. He found the new "straw" town, as the imperialists contemptuously called it, too strong for him. The League got its forces together, and a great battle took place at Legnano in 1176, — a really decisive conflict, which was rare enough in the Middle Ages. Frederick had been unable to get the reënforcements he wished from across the Alps, and, under the energetic leadership of Milan, the League so completely and hopelessly defeated him that the question of the mastery in Lombardy was settled for some time.

Frederick completely defeated by the League at Legnano, 1176.

A great congress was thereupon assembled at Venice, and here, under the auspices of Pope Alexander III, a truce was concluded, which was made a perpetual peace at Constance in 1183. The towns received back practically all their regalia and, upon formally acknowledging the emperor's overlordship, were left by him to go their own way. Frederick was forced, moreover, humbly to recognize a pope that he had solemnly sworn should never be obeyed by him. The pope and the towns had made common cause and enjoyed a common victory.

Peace of Constance (1183) establishes independence of Lombard towns.

From this time on we find the name *Guelf* assumed by the party in Italy which was opposed to the emperors.[1] This is but another form of the name of the Welf family, who made most of the trouble for the Hohenstaufens in Germany. A certain Welf had been made duke of Bavaria by Henry IV (in 1070). His son added to the family estates by marrying a rich North-German heiress. His grandson, Henry the Proud, looked still higher and became the son-in-law of the duke of Saxony and the heir to his great duchy. This, added to his other vast possessions, made him the most powerful and dangerous of the vassals of the Hohenstaufen emperors.

Origin of the power of the Guelfs.

---

[1] The origin of the name *Ghibelline*, applied to the adherents of the emperor in Italy, is not known; it may be derived from Waibling, a castle of the Hohenstaufens.

Division of
Saxony and
the other
great German
duchies.

On returning from his disastrous campaign against the
Lombard towns, Frederick Barbarossa found himself at war with
the Guelf leader, Henry the Lion (son of Henry the Proud), who
had refused to come to the emperor's aid before the battle of
Legnano. Henry was banished, and Frederick divided up the
Saxon duchy. His policy was to split up the old duchies, for
he clearly saw the danger of permitting his vassals to control
districts as large as he himself held.

The Hohen-
staufens
extend their
power into
southern
Italy.

70. Before his departure upon the crusading expedition
during which he lost his life, Frederick saw his son, Henry VI,
crowned king of Italy. Moreover, in order to extend the
power of the Hohenstaufens over southern Italy, he arranged a
marriage between the young Henry and Constance, the heiress
to the Norman kingdom of Naples and Sicily.[1] Thus the hopeless attempt to keep both Germany and Italy under the same
head was continued. It brought about new conflicts with the
popes, who were the feudal suzerains of Naples and Sicily, and
ended in the ruin of the house of Hohenstaufen.

Henry VI,
1190-1197.

Henry VI's short reign was beset with difficulties which
he sturdily met and overcame. Henry the Lion, the Guelf
leader, having broken the oath he had sworn to Frederick
to keep away from Germany, returned and organized a rebellion. So soon as this was quelled and the Guelf party was

His troubles
in Italy and
Germany.

under control for a time, Henry VI had to hasten south to
rescue his Sicilian kingdom. There a certain Norman count,
Tancred, was leading a national revolt against the German

---

[1] The attention of the adventurous Normans had been called to southern Italy
early in the eleventh century by some of their people who, in their wanderings,
had been stranded there and had found plenty of opportunities to fight under
agreeable conditions for one or another of the local rival princes. From marauding
mercenaries, they soon became the ruling race. They extended their conquests
from the mainland to Sicily, and by 1140 they had united all southern Italy into
a single kingdom. The popes had naturally taken a lively interest in the new and
strong power upon the confines of their realms. They skillfully arranged to secure
a certain hold upon the growing kingdom by inducing Robert Guiscard, the most
famous of the Norman leaders, to recognize the pope as his feudal lord; in 1059
he became the vassal of Nicholas II.

claimant.   The pope, who regarded Sicily as his fief, had freed the emperor's Norman subjects from their oath of fidelity to him.   Moreover, Richard the Lion-Hearted of England had landed on his way to the Holy Land and allied himself with Tancred.

Henry VI's expedition to Italy proved a complete disaster. His empress was captured by Tancred's people, his army largely perished by sickness, and Henry the Lion's son, whom he held as a hostage, escaped.   To add to his troubles, no sooner had he reached Germany once more than he was confronted by a new and more formidable revolt (1192).   Luckily for him, Richard, stealing home through Germany from his crusade, fell into his hands.   He held the English king, as an ally of the Guelfs, until he obtained an enormous ransom, which supplied him with the means of fighting his enemies in both Germany and Italy.   The death of Tancred enabled him to regain his realms in southern Italy.   But he endeavored in vain to induce the German princes to recognize the permanent union of the southern Italian kingdom with Germany, or to make the imperial crown hereditary in his house.

At the age of thirty-two, and in the midst of plans for a world empire, Henry succumbed to Italian fever, leaving the fate of the Hohenstaufen family in the hands of his infant son, who was to become the famous Frederick II.   Just as Henry VI died, the greatest, perhaps, of all the popes was about to ascend the throne of St. Peter, and for nearly a score of years to dominate the political affairs of western Europe.   For a time the political power of the popes almost overshadows that of a Charlemagne or a Napoleon.   In a later chapter a description will be given of the great institution over which Innocent III presided like a monarch upon his throne.   But first we must follow the history of the struggle between the papacy and the house of Hohenstaufen during the remarkable career of Frederick II.

Pope Innocent III.

Philip of
Hohenstaufen
and Otto of
Brunswick
rival claim-
ants for the
German
throne.

71. No sooner was Henry VI out of the way than Germany became, in the words of Henry's brother Philip, "like a sea lashed by every wind." So wild was the confusion, so torn and so shaken was poor Germany in all its parts, that farsighted men doubted if they would ever see it return to peace and order. Philip first proposed to play the rôle of regent to his little nephew, but before long he assumed the imperial pre-rogatives, after being duly elected king of the Romans. The Archbishop of Cologne, however, summoned an assembly and brought about the election of a rival king, Otto of Brunswick, the youthful son of Henry the Lion.

Innocent III
decides in
favor of Otto.

So the old struggle between Guelf and Hohenstaufen was renewed. Both of the kings bid for the support of Innocent III, who openly proclaimed that the decision of the matter lay with him. Otto was willing to make the most reckless conces-sions to him; and as the pope naturally feared a revival of the power of the Hohenstaufen house should Philip be recognized, he decided in favor of the Guelf claimant in 1201. The grateful Otto wrote to him, "My kingship would have dissolved in dust and ashes had not your hand, or rather the authority of the Apostolic Chair, weighed the scale in my favor." Innocent appears here, as upon other occasions, as the arbiter of Europe.

In the dreary civil wars which followed in Germany, Otto gradually lost all his friends. His rival's promising career was, however, speedily cut short, for he was murdered by a private enemy in 1208. Thereupon the pope threatened to excom-municate any German bishop or prince who failed to support Otto. The following year Otto went to Rome to be crowned, but he promptly made an enemy of the pope by playing the emperor in Italy; he even invaded the Sicilian kingdom of the pope's ward, Frederick, the son of Henry VI.

Innocent III
the arbiter
of western
Europe.

Innocent then repudiated Otto, in whom he claimed to have "been deceived as God himself was once deceived in Saul." He determined that the young Frederick should be made emperor, but he took great precautions to prevent him from becoming a dangerous enemy of the pope, as his father and grandfather had been. When Frederick was elected king in 1212 he made all the promises that Innocent asked.

While the pope had been guiding the affairs of the empire he had by no means neglected to exhibit his power in other quarters, above all in England. The monks of Canterbury had (1205) ventured to choose an archbishop — who was at the same time their abbot — without consulting their king, John. Their appointee hastened off to Rome to gain the pope's confirmation, while the irritated John forced the monks to hold another election and make his treasurer archbishop. Innocent thereupon rejected both of those who had been elected, sent for a new deputation of monks from Canterbury, and bade them choose Stephen Langton, a man of great ability. John then angrily drove the monks of Canterbury out of the kingdom. Innocent replied by placing England under the *interdict*, that is to say, he ordered the clergy to close all the churches and suspend all public services, — a very terrible thing to the people of the time. John was excommunicated, and the pope threatened that unless the king submitted to his wishes he would depose him and give his crown to Philip Augustus of France. As Philip made haste to collect an army for the conquest of England, John humbly submitted to the pope in 1213. He went so far as to hand England over to Innocent III and receive it back as a fief, thus becoming the vassal of the pope. He agreed also to send a yearly tribute to Rome.[1]

John of England becomes a vassal of the pope.

Innocent, in spite of several setbacks, now appeared to have attained all his ambitious ends. The emperor, Frederick II, was his protégé and, as king of Sicily, his acknowledged vassal, as was also the king of England. He not only asserted but also

The fourth Lateran Council, 1215.

[1] For John's cession of England and oath of vassalage, see Henderson, *Historical Documents*, pp. 430-432. For the interdict, see Colby, *Sources*, pp. 72-73.

maintained his right to interfere in all the important political affairs of the various European countries. In 1215 a stately international congress — the fourth Lateran Council — met in his palace. It was attended by hundreds of bishops, abbots, and representatives of kings, princes, and towns. Its decrees were directed against the abuses in the Church and the progress of heresy, both of which were seriously threatening the power of the clergy. It confirmed the election of Frederick II and excommunicated once more the now completely discredited Otto.[1]

Death of Innocent III, 1216. Emperor Frederick II, 1212-1250.

72. Innocent III died during the following year and left a heritage of trouble to his successors in the person of the former papal ward, Frederick II, who was little inclined to obey the pope. He had been brought up in Sicily and was much influenced by the Arabic culture which prevailed there. He appears to have rejected many of the received opinions of the time. His enemies asserted that he was not even a Christian, and that he declared that Moses, Christ, and Mohammed were all alike impostors. He was nearsighted, bald, and wholly insignificant in person ; but he exhibited the most extraordinary energy and ability in the organization of his kingdom of Sicily, in which he was far more interested than in Germany. He drew up an elaborate code of laws for his southern realms and may be said to have founded the first modern well-regulated state, in which the king was indisputably supreme.

His bitter struggle with the papacy.

We cannot stop to relate the romantic and absorbing story of his long struggle with the popes. They speedily discovered that he was bent upon establishing a powerful state to the south of them, and upon extending his control over the Lombard cities in such a manner that the papal possessions would be held as in a vise. This, they felt, should never be permitted. Almost every measure that Frederick adopted aroused their

---

[1] For the career and policy of Innocent III, see Emerton, *Mediæval Europe*, pp. 314-343.

suspicion and opposition, and they made every effort to destroy him and his house.

His chance of success in the conflict with the head of the Church was gravely affected by the promise which he had made before Innocent III's death to undertake a crusade. He was so busily engaged with his endless enterprises that he kept deferring the expedition, in spite of the papal admonitions, until at last the pope lost patience and excommunicated him. While excommunicate, he at last started for the East. He met with signal success and actually brought Jerusalem, the Holy City, once more into Christian hands and was himself recognized as king of Jerusalem.

Frederick recognized as king of Jerusalem.

Frederick's conduct continued, however, to give offense to the popes. The emperor was denounced in solemn councils, and at last the popes began to raise up rival kings in Germany to replace Frederick, whom they deposed. After Frederick died (1250) his sons maintained themselves for a few years in the Sicilian kingdom; but they finally gave way before a French army, led by the brother of St. Louis, Charles of Anjou, upon whom the pope bestowed the southern realms of the Hohenstaufens.[1]

Extinction of the Hohenstaufens' power.

With Frederick's death the mediæval empire may be said to have come to an end. It is true that after a period of " fist law," as the Germans call it, a new king, Rudolf of Hapsburg, was elected in Germany in 1273. The German kings continued to call themselves emperors. Few of them, however, took the trouble to go to Rome to be crowned by the pope. No serious effort was ever made to reconquer the Italian territory for which Otto the Great, Frederick Barbarossa, and his son and grandson had made such serious sacrifices. Germany was hopelessly divided and its king was no real king. He had no capital, no well-organized government.

Frederick's death marks the close of the mediæval empire.

[1] An excellent account of Frederick's life is given by Henderson, *Germany in the Middle Ages*, pp. 349-397.

Division of
Germany and
Italy into
small inde-
pendent
states.

By the middle of the thirteenth century it became apparent that neither Germany nor Italy was to be converted into a strong single kingdom like England and France. The map of Germany shows a confused group of duchies, counties, archbishoprics, bishoprics, abbacies, and free towns, each one of which asserted its practical independence of the weak king and emperor.

In northern Italy each town, including a certain district about its walls, had become an independent state, dealing with its neighbors as with independent powers. The Italian towns were destined to become the birthplace of our modern culture during the fourteenth and fifteenth centuries. Venice and Florence, in spite of their small size, came to be reckoned among the most important states of Europe. In the central part of the peninsula the pope maintained more or less control over his possessions, but he often failed to subdue the towns within his realms. To the south Naples remained for some time under the French dynasty, which the pope had called in, but the island of Sicily drifted into Spanish hands.

CHAPTER XV

THE CRUSADES

73. Of all the events of the Middle Ages, the most romantic and fascinating are the Crusades, the adventurous expeditions to Syria, undertaken by kings and doughty knights with the hope of permanently reclaiming the Holy Land from the infidel Turks. All through the twelfth and thirteenth centuries each generation beheld at least one great army of crusaders gathering from all parts of the West and starting toward the Orient. Each year witnessed the departure of small bands of pilgrims or of solitary soldiers of the cross. For two hundred years there was a continuous stream of Europeans of every rank and station making their way into western Asia. If they escaped the countless hazards of the journey, they either settled in this distant land and devoted themselves to war or commerce, or returned home, bringing with them tales of great cities and new peoples, of skill and luxury unknown in the West.

Our sources of information in regard to the Crusades are so abundant and so rich in picturesque incidents that writers have often yielded to the temptation to give more space to these expeditions than their consequences really justify. They were, after all, only one of the great foreign enterprises which have been undertaken from time to time by the European peoples. While their influence upon the West was doubtless very important, — like that of the later conquest of India by the English and the colonization of America, — the details of the campaigns in the East scarcely belong to the history of western Europe.

Natural temptation to overrate the importance of the Crusades.

187

The Holy
Land con-
quered first
by the Arabs
and then by
the Turks.

Syria had been overrun by the Arabs in the seventh century, shortly after the death of Mohammed, and the Holy City of Jerusalem had fallen into the hands of the infidels. The Arab, however, shared the veneration of the Christian for the places associated with the life of Christ and, in general, permitted the Christian pilgrims who found their way thither to worship unmolested. But with the coming of a new and ruder people, the Seljuk Turks, in the eleventh century, the pilgrims began to bring home news of great hardships. Moreover, the eastern emperor was defeated by the Turks in 1071 and lost Asia Minor. The presence of the Turks in possession of the fortress of Nicæa, just across from Constantinople, was of course a standing menace to the Eastern Empire. When the energetic Emperor Alexius (1081–1118) ascended the throne

Eastern
emperor
appeals to
the pope for
aid against
the infidel
Turks.

he endeavored to expel the infidel. Finding himself unequal to the task, he appealed for assistance to the head of Christendom, Urban II. The first great impetus to the Crusades was the call issued by Urban at the celebrated council which met in 1095 at Clermont in France.

Urban II
issues the
call to the
First Crusade
at the Council
of Clermont,
1095.

In an address, which produced more remarkable immediate results than any other which history records, the pope exhorted knights and foot soldiers of all ranks to give up their usual wicked business of destroying their Christian brethren in private warfare and turn instead to the succor of their fellow-Christians in the East. Otherwise the insolent Turks would, if unchecked, extend their sway still more widely over the faithful servants of the Lord. "Let the Holy Sepulcher of the Lord our Saviour, which is possessed by unclean nations, especially urge you on, and the holy places which they are now treating with ignominy and irreverently polluting." Urban urged besides that France was too poor to support all its people, while the Holy Land flowed with milk and honey. "Enter upon the road to the Holy Sepulcher; wrest the land from the wicked race and subject it to yourselves." When the pope had finished, all who were present exclaimed, with one accord, " It is the will of God." This, the pope declared, should be the rallying cry of the crusaders, who were to wear a cross upon their bosoms as they went forth, and upon their backs as they returned, as a holy sign of their sacred mission.[1]

The Crusades are ordinarily represented as the most striking examples of the simple faith and religious enthusiasm of the Middle Ages. They appealed, however, to many different kinds of men. The devout, the romantic, and the adventurous were by no means the only classes that were attracted. Syria held out inducements to the discontented noble who might hope to gain a principality in the East, to the merchant who was looking for new enterprises, to the merely restless who wished to avoid his responsibilities at home, and even to the criminal who enlisted with a view of escaping the results of his past offenses. It is noteworthy that Urban appeals especially to those who had been " contending against their brethren and relatives," and urges those " who have hitherto been robbers now to become soldiers of Christ." The conduct of many of the crusaders indicates that the pope found a ready hearing among this class. Yet higher motives than a love of adventure and the hope of conquest impelled many who took their way eastward. Great numbers, doubtless, went to Jerusalem "through devotion alone, and not for the sake of honor or gain," with the sole object of freeing the Holy Sepulcher from the hands of the infidel.

The motives of the crusaders.

To such as these the pope promised that the journey itself should take the place of all penance for sin. The faithful crusader, like the faithful Mohammedan, was assured of immediate entrance into heaven if he died repentant in the holy cause. Later the Church exhibited its extraordinary authority by what would seem to us an unjust interference with business contracts. It freed those who, with a pure heart, entered upon

Privileges of the crusaders.

1 For the speech of Urban, see *Readings*, Chapter XV.

the journey from the payment of interest upon their debts, and permitted them to mortgage property against the wishes of their feudal lords. The crusaders' wives and children and property were taken under the immediate protection of the Church, and he who troubled them incurred excommunication.[1] These various considerations help to explain the great popularity of undertakings that, at first sight, would seem to have promised only hardships and disappointment.

Peter the Hermit and his army.

74. The Council of Clermont met in November. Before spring (1096) those who set forth to preach the Crusade, above all the famous Peter the Hermit, who was formerly given credit for having begun the whole crusading movement, had collected, in France and along the Rhine, an extraordinary army of the common folk. Peasants, artisans, vagabonds, and even women and children, answered the summons, all fanatically intent upon rescuing the Holy Sepulcher, two thousand miles away. They were confident that the Lord would sustain them during the weary leagues of the journey, and grant them a prompt victory over the infidel. The host was got under way in several divisions under the leadership of Peter the Hermit,[2] and of Walter the Penniless and other humble knights. Many of the crusaders were slaughtered by the Hungarians, who rose to protect themselves from the depredations of this motley horde. Part of them got as far as Nicæa, only to be slaughtered by the Turks. This is but an example, on a large scale, of what was going on continually for a century or so after this first great catastrophe. Individual pilgrims and adventurers, and sometimes considerable bodies of crusaders, were constantly falling a prey to every form of disaster — starvation, slavery, disease, and death — in their endeavors to reach the Holy Land.

[1] The privileges of the crusaders may be found in *Translations and Reprints*, Vol. I, No. 2.

[2] For Peter the Hermit, see *Translations and Reprints*, Vol. I, No. 2.

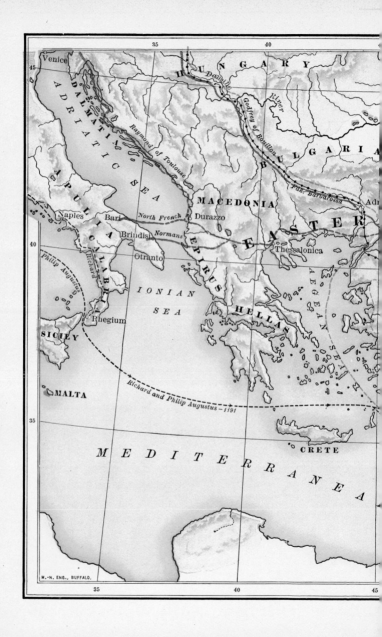

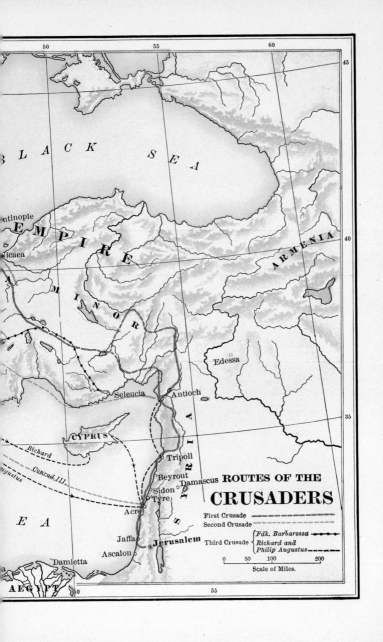

ROUTES OF THE **CRUSADERS**

First Crusade
Second Crusade
Third Crusade { Fdk. Barbarossa
              Richard and
              Philip Augustus

0   50   100   200
Scale of Miles.

The conspicuous figures of the long period of the Crusades The First Crusade, 1096. are not, however, to be found among the lowly followers of Peter the Hermit, but are the knights, in their long coats of mail. A year after the summons issued at Clermont great armies of fighting men had been collected in the West under noble leaders ; — the pope speaks of three hundred thousand soldiers. Of the various divisions which were to meet in Constantinople, the following were the most important :

the volunteers from Provence under the papal legate and Count Raymond of Toulouse ; inhabitants of Germany, particularly of Lorraine, under Godfrey of Bouillon and his brother Baldwin, both destined to be rulers of Jerusalem ; and lastly, an army of French and of the Normans of southern Italy under Bohemond and Tancred.[1]

Knight of the First Crusade

The distinguished knights who have been mentioned were not actually in command of real armies. Each crusader undertook the expedition on his own account and was only obedient to any one's orders so long as he pleased. The knights and men naturally grouped themselves around the more noted leaders, but considered themselves free to change chiefs when they pleased. The leaders themselves reserved the right to look out for their own special interests rather than sacrifice themselves to the good of the expedition.

Upon the arrival of the crusaders at Constantinople it Hostilities between the Greeks and the crusaders quickly became clear that they had little more in common with the Greeks than with the Turks. Emperor Alexius

---

[1] For the routes taken by the different crusading armies, see the accompanying map.

ordered his soldiers to attack Godfrey's army, encamped in the suburbs of his capital, because their chief at first refused to take the oath of feudal homage to him. The emperor's daughter, in her remarkable history of the times, gives a sad picture of the outrageous conduct of the crusaders. They, on the other hand, denounced the "schismatic Greeks" as traitors, cowards, and liars.

The eastern emperor had hoped to use his western allies to reconquer Asia Minor and force back the Turks. The leading knights, on the contrary, dreamed of carving out principalities for themselves in the former dominions of the emperor and proposed to control them by right of conquest. Later we find both Greeks and western Christians shamelessly allying themselves with the Mohammedans against each other. The relations of the eastern and western enemies of the Turks were well illustrated when the crusaders besieged their first town, Nicæa. When it was just ready to surrender, the Greeks arranged with the enemy to have their troops admitted first. They then closed the gates against their western confederates and invited them to move on.

Dissension among the leaders of the crusaders. The first real allies that the crusaders met with were the Christian Armenians, who brought them aid after their terrible march through Asia Minor. With their help Baldwin got possession of Edessa, of which he made himself prince. The chiefs induced the great body of the crusaders to postpone the march on Jerusalem, and a year was spent in taking the rich and important city of Antioch. A bitter strife then broke out, especially between the Norman Bohemond and the count of Toulouse, as to who should have the conquered town. After the most unworthy conduct on both sides, Bohemond won, and Raymond set to work to conquer a principality for himself on the coast about Tripoli.

Capture of Jerusalem. In the spring of 1099 about twenty thousand warriors finally moved upon Jerusalem. They found the city well walled and in the midst of a desolate region where neither food nor water, nor the materials to construct the apparatus necessary for the capture of the town, were to be found. The opportune arrival at Jaffa of galleys from Genoa furnished the besiegers with

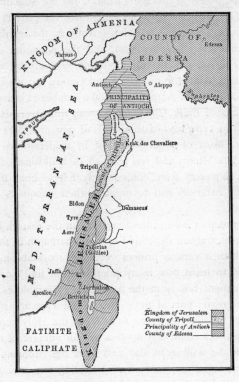

Map of the Crusaders' States in Syria

supplies, and, in spite of all the difficulties, the place was taken in a couple of months. The crusaders, with their customary barbarity, massacred the inhabitants. Godfrey of Bouillon was chosen ruler of Jerusalem and took the modest title of

"Defender of the Holy Sepulcher." He soon died and was succeeded by his brother Baldwin, who left Edessa in 1100 to take up the task of extending the bounds of the Kingdom of Jerusalem.

Founding of Latin kingdoms in Syria.

It will be observed that the "Franks," as the Mohammedans called all the western folk, had established the centers of four principalities. These were Edessa, Antioch, the region about Tripoli conquered by Raymond, and the Kingdom of Jerusalem. The last was speedily increased by Baldwin; with the help of the mariners from Venice and Genoa, he succeeded in getting possession of Acre, Sidon, and a number of coast towns.

The news of these Christian victories quickly reached the West, and in 1101 tens of thousands of new crusaders started eastward. Most of them were lost or dispersed in passing through Asia Minor, and few reached their destination. The original conquerors were consequently left to hold the land against the Saracens and to organize their conquests as best they could.

The permanent hold of the Franks upon the eastern borders of the Mediterranean depended upon the strength of the colonies which their various princes were able to establish. It is impossible to learn how many pilgrims from the West made their permanent homes in the new Latin principalities. Certainly the greater part of those who visited Palestine returned home after fulfilling their vow to kneel at the Holy Sepulcher. Still the princes could rely upon a certain number of soldiers who would be willing to stay and fight the Mohammedans. The Turks, moreover, were so busy fighting one another that they showed less energy than might have been expected in attempting to drive the Franks from the narrow strip of territory — some five hundred miles long and fifty wide — which they had conquered.

The Hospitalers.

75. A noteworthy outcome of the crusading movement was the foundation of several curious orders — the Hospitalers, the

Templars, and the Teutonic Knights — which combined the dominant interests of the time, those of the monk and the soldier. They permitted a man to be both at once; the knight might wear a monkish cowl over his coat of mail. The Hospitalers grew out of a monastic association that was formed before the First Crusade for the succor of the poor and sick among the pilgrims. Later the society admitted noble knights to its membership and became a military order, while continuing its care for the sick. This charitable association, like the earlier monasteries, received generous gifts of land in western Europe and built and controlled many fortified monasteries in the Holy Land itself. After the evacuation of Syria in the thirteenth century, the Hospitalers moved their headquarters to the island of Rhodes, and later to Malta. The order still exists and it is considered a distinction to this day to have the privilege of wearing its emblem, the cross of Malta.

Costume of the Hospitalers, showing the Form of the Cross of Malta

Before the Hospitalers were transformed into a military order, a little group of French knights banded together in 1119 to defend pilgrims on their way to Jerusalem from the attacks of the infidel. They were assigned quarters in the king's palace at Jerusalem on the site of the former Temple of Solomon; hence the name, Templars, which they were destined to render famous. The "poor soldiers of the Temple" were enthusiastically approved by the Church. They wore a white cloak adorned with a red cross, and were under a very strict monastic rule which bound them by the vows of obedience, poverty, and celibacy. The fame of the order spread throughout Europe, and the most

The Templars.

exalted, even dukes and princes, were ready to renounce the world and serve Christ under its black and white banner, with the legend, *Non nobis, Domine.*

The order was aristocratic from the first, and it soon became incredibly rich and independent.   It had its collectors in all parts of Europe, who dispatched the "alms" they received to the Grand Master at Jerusalem.   Towns, churches, and estates were given to the order, as well as vast sums of money.   The king of Aragon proposed to bestow upon it a third of his kingdom.   The pope showered privileges upon the Templars. They were exempted from tithes and taxes, and were brought under his immediate jurisdiction; they were released from feudal obligations, and bishops were forbidden to excommunicate them.

Abolition of the order of Templars.

No wonder they grew insolent and aroused the jealousy and hate of princes and prelates alike.   Even Innocent III violently upbraided them for admitting to their order wicked men, who then enjoyed all the privileges of churchmen.   Early in the fourteenth century, through the combined efforts of the pope and Philip the Fair of France, the order was brought to a terrible end.   Its members were accused of the most abominable practices, — such as heresy, the worship of idols, and the systematic insulting of Christ and his religion.   Many distinguished Templars were burned for heresy, others perished miserably in dungeons.   The order was abolished and its property confiscated.

The Teutonic Knights conquer the Prussians.

As for the third great order, that of the Teutonic Knights, their greatest importance lies in their conquest, after the Crusades were over, of the heathen Prussians.   Through their efforts a new Christian state was formed on the shores of the Baltic, in which the important cities of Königsberg and Dantzig grew up.

The Second Crusade.

76.   Fifty years after the preaching of the First Crusade, the fall of Edessa (1144), an important outpost of the Christians in the East, led to a second great expedition.   This was

forwarded by no less a person than St. Bernard, who went about using his unrivaled eloquence to induce volunteers to take the cross. In a fierce hymn of battle he cried to the Knights Templars: "The Christian who slays the unbeliever in the Holy War is sure of his reward, the more sure if he himself be slain. The Christian glories in the death of the pagan, because Christ is glorified." The king of France readily consented to take the cross, but the emperor, Conrad III, appears to have yielded only after St. Bernard had preached before him and given a vivid picture of the terrors of the Judgment Day.

In regard to the less distinguished recruits, the historian, Otto of Freising, tells us that so many thieves and robbers hastened to take the cross that every one recognized in their enthusiasm the hand of God. St. Bernard himself, the chief promoter of the expedition, gives a most unflattering description of the "soldiers of Christ." "In that countless multitude you will find few except the utterly wicked and impious, the sacrilegious, homicides, and perjurers, whose departure is a double gain. Europe rejoices to lose them and Palestine to gain them; they are useful in both ways, in their absence from here and their presence there." It is quite unnecessary to describe the movements and fate of the crusaders; suffice it to say that, from a military standpoint, the so-called Second Crusade was a miserable failure.

Forty years later, in 1187, Jerusalem was taken by Saladin, the most heroic and distinguished of all the Saracen rulers. The loss of the Holy City led to the most famous of all the military expeditions to the Holy Land, in which Frederick Barbarossa, Richard the Lion-Hearted of England, and his political rival, Philip Augustus of France, all took part. The accounts of the enterprise show that while the several Christian leaders hated one another heartily enough, the Christians and Saracens were coming to respect one another.

The Third Crusade.

We find examples of the most courtly relations between the representatives of the opposing religions. In 1192 Richard concluded a truce with Saladin, by the terms of which the Christian pilgrims were allowed to visit the holy places with safety and comfort.[1]

The Fourth and subsequent Crusades.

In the thirteenth century the crusaders began to direct their expeditions toward Egypt as the center of the Saracen power. The first of these was diverted in an extraordinary manner by the Venetians, who induced the crusaders to conquer Constantinople for their benefit. The further expeditions of Frederick II and St. Louis need not be described. Jerusalem was irrevocably

Ruins of a Fortress of the Hospitalers in the Holy Land

lost in 1244, and although the possibility of recovering the city was long considered, the Crusades may be said to have come to a close before the end of the thirteenth century.

Settlements of the Italian merchants.

77. For one class at least, the Holy Land had great and permanent charms, namely, the Italian merchants, especially those from Genoa, Venice, and Pisa. It was through their early interest and supplies from their ships, that the conquest of the Holy Land had been rendered possible. The merchants were always careful to see that they were well paid for their services. When they aided in the successful siege of a town

[1] For an account of the prowess of Richard the Lion-Hearted, see Colby, *Sources*, pp. 68–70.

they arranged that a definite quarter should be assigned to them in the captured place, where they might have their market, docks, church, and all that was necessary for a permanent center for their commerce. This district belonged to the town to which the merchants belonged. Venice even sent governors to live in the quarters assigned to its citizens in the Kingdom of Jerusalem. Marseilles also had independent quarters in Jerusalem, and Genoa had its share in the county of Tripoli.

This new commerce had a most important influence in bringing the West into permanent relations with the Orient. Eastern products from India and elsewhere — silks, spices, camphor, musk, pearls, and ivory — were brought by the Mohammedans from the East to the commercial towns of Palestine and Syria; then, through the Italian merchants, they found their way into France and Germany, suggesting ideas of luxury hitherto scarcely dreamed of by the still half-barbarous Franks.

Oriental luxury introduced into Europe.

Tomb of a Crusader

Some of the results of the Crusades upon western Europe must already be obvious, even from this very brief account. Thousands and thousands of Frenchmen, Germans, and Englishmen had traveled to the Orient by land and by sea. Most of them came from hamlets or castles where they could never have learned much of the great world beyond the confines of their native village or province. They suddenly found themselves in great cities and in the midst of unfamiliar peoples and customs. This could not fail to make them

Results of the Crusades.

think and give them new ideas to carry home. The Crusade took the place of a liberal education. The crusaders came into contact with those who knew more than they did, above all the Arabs, and brought back with them new notions of comfort and luxury.

Yet in attempting to estimate the debt of the West to the Crusades it should be remembered that many of the new things may well have come from Constantinople, or through the Saracens of Sicily and Spain, quite independently of the armed incursions into Syria.[1] Moreover, during the twelfth and thirteenth centuries towns were rapidly growing up in Europe, trade and manufactures were extending, and the universities were being founded. It would be absurd to suppose that without the Crusades this progress would not have taken place. So we may conclude that the distant expeditions and the contact with strange and more highly civilized peoples did no more than hasten the improvement which was already perceptible before Urban made his ever-memorable address at Clermont.[2]

General Reading. — A somewhat fuller account of the Crusades will be found in EMERTON, *Mediæval Europe*, Chapter XI. Their results are discussed in ADAMS, *Civilization*, Chapter XI. Professor Munro has published a number of very interesting documents in *Translations and Reprints*, Vol. I, Nos. 2, 4 (Letters of the Crusaders), and Vol. III, No. 1 (The Fourth Crusade). See also his *Mediæval History*, Chapter XI, on the Crusades. ARCHER and KINGSFORD, *The Crusades* (G. P. Putnam's Sons, $1.50), is probably the best modern work in English.

[1] Heraldry may be definitely ascribed to the Crusades, for it grew up from the necessity of distinguishing the various groups of knights. Some of its terms, for example, *gules* (red) and *azur*, are of Arabic origin.

[2] References. For the highly developed civilization which the crusaders found in Constantinople, Munro, *Mediæval History*, Chapter X. For the culture of the Saracens, see the same work, Chapter IX.

CHAPTER XVI

THE MEDIÆVAL CHURCH AT ITS HEIGHT

78. In the preceding pages it has been necessary to refer constantly to the Church and the clergy. Indeed, without them mediæval history would become almost a blank, for the Church was incomparably the most important institution of the time and its officers were the soul of nearly every great enterprise. In the earlier chapters, the rise of the Church and of its head, the pope, has been reviewed, as well as the work of the monks as they spread over Europe. We must now consider the mediæval Church as a completed institution at the height of its power in the twelfth and thirteenth centuries.

We have already had abundant proofs that the mediæval Church was very different from modern churches, whether Catholic or Protestant. *Ways in which the mediæval Church differed from modern churches.*

1. In the first place, every one was required to belong to it, just as we all must belong to the state to-day. One was not born into the Church, it is true, but he was ordinarily baptized into it before he had any opinion in the matter. All western Europe formed a single religious association, from which it was a crime to revolt. To refuse allegiance to the Church, or to question its authority or teachings, was reputed treason against God and was punishable with death. *Membership in the mediæval Church compulsory.*

2. The mediæval Church did not rely for its support, as churches usually must to-day, upon the voluntary contributions of its members. It enjoyed, in addition to the revenue from its vast tracts of lands and a great variety of *The wealth of the Church.*

The tithe.

fees, the income from a regular tax, the *tithe*. Those upon whom this fell were forced to pay it, just as we all must now pay taxes imposed by the government.

Resemblance of the Church to a state.

3. It is obvious, moreover, that the mediæval Church was not merely a religious body, as churches are to-day. Of course it maintained places of worship, conducted devotional exercises, and cultivated the spiritual life ; but it did far more. It was, in a way, a state, for it had an elaborate system of law, and its own courts, in which it tried many cases which are now settled in our ordinary tribunals.[1] It had also its prisons, to which it might sentence offenders to lifelong detention.

Unity of organization in the Church.

4. The Church not only performed the functions of a state ; it had the organization of a state. Unlike the Protestant ministers of to-day, all churchmen and religious associations of mediæval Europe were under one supreme head, who made laws for all and controlled every church officer, wherever he might be, whether in Italy or Germany, Spain or Ireland. The whole Church had one official language, Latin, in which all communications were dispatched and in which its services were everywhere conducted.

The mediæval Church a monarchy in its form of government.

79. The mediæval Church may, therefore, properly be called a monarchy in its government. The pope was its all-powerful and absolute head and concentrated in his person its entire spiritual and disciplinary authority. He was the supreme lawgiver. No council of the Church, no matter how large and

---

[1] The law of the Church was known as the *canon law*. It was taught in most of the universities and practiced by a great number of lawyers. It was based upon the acts of the various church councils, from that of Nicæa down, and, above all, upon the decrees and decisions of the popes. See Emerton, *Mediæval Europe*, pp. 582–592.

One may get some idea of the business of the ecclesiastical courts from the fact that the Church claimed the right to try all cases in which a clergyman was involved, or any one connected with the Church or under its special protection, such as monks, students, crusaders, widows, orphans, and the helpless. Then all cases where the rites of the Church, or its prohibitions, were involved came ordinarily before the church courts, as, for example, those concerning marriage, wills, sworn contracts, usury, blasphemy, sorcery, heresy, and so forth.

important, could make laws against his will, for its decrees, to be valid, required his sanction.

The pope might, moreover, set aside or abrogate any law of the Church, no matter how ancient, so long as it was not ordained by the Scriptures or by Nature. He might, for good reasons, make exceptions to all merely human laws; as, for instance, permit cousins to marry, or free a monk from his vows. Such exceptions were known as *dispensations*.

Dispensations.

The pope was not merely the supreme lawgiver; he was the supreme judge. As a distinguished legal writer has said, the whole of western Europe was subject to the jurisdiction of one tribunal of last resort, the pope's court at Rome. Any one, whether clergyman or layman, in any part of Europe, could appeal to him at any stage in the trial of a large class of cases. Obviously this system had serious drawbacks. Grave injustice might be done by carrying to Rome a case which ought to have been settled in Edinburgh or Cologne, where the facts were best known. The rich, moreover, always had the advantage, as they alone could afford to bring suits before so distant a court.

The pope the supreme judge of Christendom.

The control of the pope over the clergy scattered throughout Christendom was secured in several ways. A newly elected archbishop might not venture to perform any of the duties of his office until he had taken an oath of fidelity and obedience to the pope and received from him the *pallium*, the archbishop's badge of office. This was a narrow woolen scarf made by the nuns of the convent of St. Agnes at Rome. Bishops and abbots were also required to have their election duly confirmed by the pope. He claimed, too, the right to settle the very frequent disputed elections of church officials. He might even set aside both of the rival candidates and fill the office himself, as did Innocent III when he forced the monks of Canterbury, after a double election, to choose Stephen Langton.

The control of the pope over the clergy at large.

Since the time of Gregory VII the pope had claimed the right to depose and transfer bishops at will. The control of Rome over all parts of the Christian Church was further increased by the legates. These papal emissaries were intrusted with great powers. Their haughty mien often enough offended the prelates and rulers to whom they brought home the authority of the pope, — as, for instance, when the legate Pandulf grandly absolved all the subjects of King John of England, before his very face, from their oath of fealty to him.

The Roman Curia.

The task assumed by the pope of governing the whole western world naturally made it necessary to create a large body of officials at Rome in order to transact all the multiform business and prepare and transmit the innumerable legal documents.[1] The cardinals and the pope's officials constituted what was called the papal Curia, or court.

Sources of the pope's income.

To carry on his government and meet the expenses of palace and retinue, the pope had need of a vast income. This he secured from various sources. Heavy fees were exacted from those who brought suits to his court for decision. The archbishops were expected to make generous contributions on receiving their palliums, and the bishops and abbots upon their confirmation. In the thirteenth century the pope began to fill many benefices throughout Europe himself, and customarily received half the first year's revenues from those whom he appointed. For several centuries before the Protestants finally threw off their allegiance to the popes, there was widespread complaint on the part of both clergy and laymen that the fees and taxes levied by the Curia were excessive.

The archbishops.

80. Next in order below the head of the Church were the archbishops. An archbishop was a bishop whose power extended beyond the boundaries of his own diocese and who exercised a certain control over all the bishops within his

---

[1] Many of the edicts, decisions, and orders of the popes were called *bulls* from the seal (Latin, *bulla*) attached to them.

province.[1] One of the chief prerogatives of the archbishop was the right to summon the bishops of his province to meet in a provincial council.   His court received appeals from the

Ecclesiastical Map of France in the Middle Ages

bishops' courts. Except, however, for the distinction of his title and the fact that he generally lived in an important city

[1] For an illustration of provinces and bishoprics, see accompanying map of France showing the ecclesiastical divisions.   The seats of the archbishops are indicated by ⛪; those of the bishops by ☦.

and often had vast political influence, the archbishop was not very much more powerful, as an officer of the Church, than the other bishops.

The importance of the bishops.

There is perhaps no class of persons in mediæval times whose position it is so necessary to understand as that of the bishops. They were regarded as the successors of the apostles, whose powers were held to be divinely transmitted to them. They represented the Church Universal in their respective

The Costume of a Bishop, showing Miter and Crosier. From a manuscript of the twelfth century

dioceses, under the supreme headship of their "elder brother," the Bishop of Rome, the successor of the chief of the apostles. Their insignia of office, the miter and crosier, are familiar to every one. Each bishop had his especial church, which was called a cathedral, and usually surpassed the other churches of the diocese in size and beauty.

Duties of a bishop.

Only a bishop could ordain new members of the clergy or degrade the old. He alone could consecrate churches or anoint kings. He alone could perform the sacrament of confirmation, though as priest he might administer any of the other sacraments.[1] Aside from his purely religious duties, he was the overseer of all the churchmen in his diocese, including the monks.[2] He held a court where a great variety of suits were tried. If he were a conscientious prelate, he traveled about his diocese visiting the parish churches and the monasteries to see if the priests did their duty and the monks behaved themselves properly.

In addition to the oversight of his diocese, it was the bishop's business to see to the lands and other possessions which belonged to the bishopric. He had, moreover, to perform those governmental duties which the king, especially in Germany, had thrown upon him, and he was conspicuous among the monarch's counselors. Lastly, the bishop was usually a feudal lord, with the obligations that that implied. He might have vassals and subvassals, and often was himself a vassal, not only of the king but also of some neighboring lord. As one reads through the archives of a bishopric, it is hard to tell whether the bishop should be called, first and foremost, a churchman or a feudal lord. In short, the duties of the bishop were as manifold as those of the mediæval Church itself.

The bishop's temporal duties.

The reforms of Gregory VII had resulted in placing the choice of the bishop in the hands of the cathedral *chapter*,[3] that is, the body of clergy connected with the cathedral church. But this did not prevent the king from suggesting the

Election of the bishops.

---

[1] See below, § 81.

[2] Except those monasteries and orders whose members were especially exempted by the pope from the jurisdiction of the bishops.

[3] Those clergymen who enjoyed the revenue from the endowed offices connected with a cathedral church were called *canons*. The office of canon was an honorable one and much sought after, partly because the duties were light and could often be avoided altogether. A scholar like Petrarch might look to such an office as a means of support without dreaming of performing any of the religious services which the position implied. For an account of the relations between the chapter and the bishop, see Emerton, *Mediæval Europe,* pp. 549–550.

candidate, since the chapter did not venture to proceed to an election without procuring a license from the king. Otherwise he might have refused to invest the person they chose with the lands and political prerogatives attached to the office.

The parish priest and his duties. The lowest division of the Church was the parish. This had definite limits, although the parishioners might vary in number from a few families to a considerable village or an

Canterbury Cathedral

important district of a town. At the head of the parish was the parish priest, who conducted services in the parish church and absolved, baptized, married, and buried his parishioners. The priests were supposed to be supported by the lands belonging to the parish church and by the tithes. But both of these sources of income were often in the hands of laymen, or of a neighboring monastery, while the priest received the merest pittance, scarcely sufficient to keep soul and body together.

The parish church was the center of village life and the priest was the natural guardian of the community. It was his business, for example, to see that no undesirable persons lurked in the village, — heretics, sorcerers, or lepers. It will be observed that the priest, besides attending to the morals of his flock, was expected to see to their bodily welfare by preventing the presence of those afflicted with the only infectious disease against which precautions were taken in the Middle Ages.[1]

81. The unexampled authority of the mediæval Church is, however, only partially explained by its wonderful organization. To understand the hold which it had upon mankind, we must consider the exalted position of the clergy and the teachings of the Church in regard to salvation, of which it claimed to be the exclusive agent.

Other sources of the Church's power.

The clergy were set apart from the laity in several ways. The higher orders — bishop, priest, deacon, and subdeacon — were required to remain unmarried, and in this way were freed from the cares and interests of family life. The Church held, moreover, that the higher clergy, when they had been properly ordained, received through their ordination a mysterious imprint, the "indelible character," so that they could never become simple laymen again, even if they ceased to perform their duties altogether or were cast out of the Church for crime. Above all, the clergy alone could administer the *sacraments* upon which the salvation of every individual soul depended.

The exalted position of the clergy.

[1] It should be remembered that only a part of the priests were intrusted with the care of souls in a parish. There were many priests among the wandering monks, of whom something will be said presently. See below, § 91. There were also many chantry priests whose main function was saying masses for the dead in chapels and churches endowed with revenue or lands by those who in this way provided for the repose of their souls or those of their descendants. See below, p. 213.

Peter Lombard's *Sentences*.

Although the Church believed that all the sacraments were established by Christ, it was not until the middle of the twelfth century that they were clearly described. Peter Lombard (d. 1164), a teacher of theology at Paris, prepared a manual of the doctrines of the Church as he found them in the Scriptures and in the writings of the church fathers, especially Augustine. These *Sentences* (Latin, *sententiæ*, opinions) of Peter Lombard were very influential, for they appeared at a time when there was a new interest in theology, particularly at Paris, where a great university was growing up.[1]

The seven sacraments.

It was Peter Lombard who first distinctly formulated the doctrine of the seven sacraments. His teachings did not claim, of course, to be more than an orderly statement and reconciliation of the various opinions which he found in the Scriptures and the church fathers; but his interpretations and definitions constituted a new basis for mediæval theology. Before his time the word *sacramentum* (that is, something sacred, a mystery) was applied to a variety of sacred things, for example, baptism, the cross, Lent, holy water, etc. But Peter Lombard states that there are seven sacraments, to wit: baptism, confirmation, extreme unction, marriage, penance, ordination, and the Lord's Supper. Through these sacraments all righteousness either has its beginning, or when begun is increased, or if lost is regained. They are essential to salvation, and no one can be saved except through them.[2]

Baptism.

By means of the sacraments the Church accompanied the faithful through life. By baptism all the sin due to Adam's fall was washed away; through that door alone could a soul enter the spiritual life. With the holy oil and the balsam,

---

[1] For several centuries the *Sentences* were used as the text-book in all the divinity schools. Theologians established their reputations by writing commentaries upon them. One of Luther's first acts of revolt was to protest against giving the study of the *Sentences* preference over that of the Bible in the universities.

[2] All the sacraments, — e.g. orders and matrimony, — are not necessary to every one. Moreover, the sincere *wish* suffices if one is so situated that he cannot possibly actually receive the sacraments.

typifying the fragrance of righteousness, which were rubbed upon the forehead of the boy or girl at confirmation by the bishop, the young were strengthened so that they might boldly confess the name of the Lord.   If the believer fell perilously ill, the priest anointed him with oil in the name of the Lord and by this sacrament of extreme unction expelled all vestiges of former sin and refreshed the spirit of the dying.   Through the priest alone might marriage be sanctified ; and when the bonds were once legally contracted they might never be sundered.   If evil desire, which baptism lessened but did not remove, led the Christian into deadly sin, as it constantly did, the Church, through the sacrament of penance, reconciled him once more with God and saved him from the jaws of hell.   For the priest, through the sacrament of ordination, received the most exalted prerogative of forgiving sins.   He enjoyed, too, the awful power and privilege of performing the miracle of the Mass, — of offering up Christ anew for the remission of the sinner's guilt.

Confirmation.

Extreme unction.

Marriage.

Penance.

Ordination.

The Lord's Supper, or Holy Eucharist.

82. The sacrament of penance is, with the Mass, of especial historical importance.   When a bishop ordained a priest, he said to him : " Receive ye the Holy Ghost : whose soever sins ye forgive, they are forgiven them : whose soever sins ye retain, they are retained."   In this way the priest was intrusted with the keys of the kingdom of heaven.   There was no hope of salvation for one who had fallen into mortal sin unless he received — or at least desired and sought — the absolution of the priest. To one who scorned the priest's ministrations the most sincere and prayerful repentance could not by itself bring forgiveness in the eyes of the Church.   Before the priest could utter the solemn " I absolve thee from thy sins," the sinner must have duly confessed his sins and have expressed his vehement detestation of them and his firm resolve never more to offend.   It is clear that the priest could not pronounce judgment unless he had been told the nature of the case.   Nor would he be justified in

The sacrament of penance.

absolving an offender who was not truly sorry for what he had done. Confession and penitence were, therefore, necessary preliminaries to absolution.[1]

Penance and purgatory.

Absolution did not free the contrite sinner from all the results of his sin. It cleared the soul of the deadly guilt which would otherwise have been punished by everlasting suffering, but did not exempt the penitent from temporal penalties. These might be imposed by the priest in this world or suffered after death in the fires of purgatory, which cleansed the soul and prepared it for heaven.

Nature of penance.

The punishment prescribed by the priest was called *penance*. This took a great variety of forms. It might consist in fasting, repeating prayers, visiting holy places, or abstaining from one's ordinary amusements. A journey to the Holy Land was regarded as taking the place of all penance. Instead, however, of requiring the penitent actually to perform the fasts, pilgrimages, or other sacrifices imposed as penance by the priest, the Church early permitted him to change his penance into a contribution, to be applied to some pious enterprise, like building a church or bridge, or caring for the poor and sick.

The Mass.

The priest not only forgave sin; he was also empowered to perform the stupendous miracle of the Mass. The early Christians had celebrated the Lord's Supper or Holy Eucharist in various ways and entertained various conceptions of its nature and significance. Gradually the idea came to be universally accepted that by the consecration of the bread and the wine the whole substance of the bread was converted into the substance of the body of Christ, and the whole substance

Transubstantiation.

of the wine into his blood. This change was termed *transubstantiation*. The Church believed, further, that in this sacrament Christ was offered up anew, as he had been on the cross,

[1] Confession was a very early practice in the Church. Innocent III and the fourth Lateran Council made it obligatory by requiring the faithful to confess at least once a year, at Easter time. For sacraments, see *Readings*, Chapter XVI.

as a sacrifice to God. This sacrifice might be performed for the sins of the absent as well as of the present, and for the dead as well as for the living. Moreover, Christ was to be worshiped under the form of the bread, or *host* (Latin, *hostia*, sacrifice), with the highest form of adoration. The host was to be borne about in solemn procession when God was to be especially propitiated, as in the case of a famine or plague.

This conception of the Mass as a sacrifice had some important practical consequences. It became the most exalted of the functions of the priest and the very center of the Church's services. Besides the public masses for the people, private ones were constantly celebrated for the benefit of individuals, especially of the dead. Foundations were created, the income of which went to support priests for the single purpose of saying daily masses for the repose of the soul of the donor or those of the members of his family. It was also a common practice to bestow gifts upon churches and monasteries on condition that annual or more frequent masses should be said for the giver.

Consequences of conceiving the Mass as a sacrifice.

83. The sublime prerogatives of the Church, together with its unrivaled organization and vast wealth, combined to make its officers, the clergy, the most powerful social class of the Middle Ages. They held the keys of heaven and without their aid no one could hope to enter in. By excommunication they could not only cast an offender out of the Church, but also forbid his fellow-men to associate with him, since he was accursed and consigned to Satan. By means of the *interdict* they could suspend the consolations of religion in a whole city or country by closing the church doors and prohibiting all public services.[1]

The dominant position of the clergy and the sources of their power.

Excommunication and interdict.

The influence of the clergy was greatly enhanced by the fact that they alone were educated. For six or seven centuries after the overthrow of the Roman government in the West,

Their monopoly of the advantages of education.

[1] See above, p. 183, and *Translations and Reprints*, Vol. IV, No. 4, for examples of the interdict and excommunication.

very few outside of the clergy ever dreamed of studying or even of learning to read and write. Even in the thirteenth century an offender who wished to prove that he belonged to the clergy, in order that he might be tried by a church court, had only to show that he could read a single line; for it was assumed by the judges that no one unconnected with the Church could read at all.[1]

It was therefore inevitable that almost all the books should be written by priests and monks and that the clergy should become the ruling power in all intellectual, artistic, and literary matters, — the chief guardians and promoters of civilization. Moreover, the civil government was forced to rely upon churchmen to write out the public documents and proclamations. The priests and monks held the pen for the king. Representatives of the clergy sat in the king's councils and acted as his ministers; in fact, the conduct of the government largely devolved upon them.[2]

Offices in the Church open to all classes.

The offices in the Church were open to all ranks of men, and many of the popes themselves sprang from the humblest classes. The Church thus constantly recruited its ranks with fresh blood. No one held an office simply because his father had held it before him, as was the case in the civil government.

Lea's description of the mediæval Church.

The man who entered the service of the Church "was released from the distraction of family cares and the seduction of family ties. The Church was his country and his home and its interests were his own. The moral, intellectual, and physical forces, which throughout the laity were divided between the claims of patriotism, the selfish struggle for advancement, the provision for wife and children, were in the Church consecrated to a common end, in the success of which all might hope to share,

---

[1] The privilege of being tried by churchmen, which all connected with the Church claimed, was called *benefit of clergy*. See *Readings*, Chapter XVI.

[2] The bishops still constitute an important element in the upper houses of parliament in several European countries.

while all were assured of the necessities of existence, and were relieved of anxiety as to the future." The Church was thus "an army encamped on the soil of Christendom, with its outposts everywhere, subject to the most efficient discipline, animated with a common purpose, every soldier panoplied with inviolability and armed with the tremendous weapons which slew the soul " (Lea).

General Reading. — CUTTS, *Parish Priests and their People* (E. & J. B. Young, $3.00). PRÉVOST, *L'Église et les Campagnes au Moyen Âge* (Paris, $1.50).

For nearly two hundred years the popes had assumed very little responsibility for the welfare of Europe at large. It was a gigantic task to make of the Church a great international monarchy, with its head at the old world-center, Rome ; the difficulties in the way seemed, indeed, well-nigh insurmountable. The great archbishops, who were as jealous of the power of the pope as the great vassals were of the kingly power, must be brought into subjection. National tendencies which made against the unity of the Church must be overcome. The control enjoyed by kings, princes, and other feudal lords in the selection of church officials must be done away with. Simony with its degrading influence must be abolished. The marriage of the clergy must be checked, so that the property of the Church should not be dissipated. The whole body of churchmen, from the priest to the archbishop, must be redeemed from the immorality and worldliness which degraded them in the eyes of the people.

Difficulties to be overcome in establishing the supremacy of the popes in western Europe.

It is true that during the remainder of his life Henry III himself controlled the election of the popes ; but he was sincerely and deeply interested in the betterment of the Church and took care to select able and independent German prelates to fill the papal office. Of these the most important was Leo IX (1049–1054). He was the first to show clearly how the pope might not only become in time the real head and monarch of the Church but might also aspire to rule kings and emperors as well as bishops and abbots. Leo refused to regard himself as pope simply because the emperor had appointed him. He held that the emperor should aid and protect, but might not create, popes. So he entered Rome as an humble barefoot pilgrim and was duly elected by the Roman people according to the rule of the Church.

Pope Leo IX, 1049-1054.

Leo IX undertook to visit France and Germany and even Hungary in person, with the purpose of calling councils to check simony and the marriage of the clergy. But this personal

CHAPTER XVII

HERESY AND THE FRIARS

The question of the character of the mediæval clergy.

84. It is natural to ask whether the commanders of the great army which made up the Church proved valiant leaders in the eternal warfare against evil. Did they, on the whole, resist the temptations which their almost limitless power and wealth constantly placed in their way? Did they use their vast resources to advance the cause of the Great Leader whose humble followers and servants they claimed to be? Or were they, on the contrary, selfish and corrupt, turning the teachings of the Church to their own advantage, and discrediting its doctrines in the eyes of the people by flagrant maladministration and personal wickedness?

The debt of western Europe to the Church.

No simple answer to this question is possible. One who realizes how completely the Church dominated every human interest and influenced every department of life in the Middle Ages must hesitate to attempt to balance the good and evil to be placed to its account. That the Church conferred incalculable benefits upon western Europe, few will question. To say nothing of its chief mission, — the moral uplifting of mankind through the Christian religion, — we have seen how, under its auspices, the barbarians were civilized and brought into the family of nations, how violence was checked by the "Truce of God," and how an educated class was maintained during the centuries when few laymen could either read or write. These are only the more obvious of its achievements; the solace and protection which it afforded to the weak, the wretched, and the heart-sore, no one can assume to estimate.

216

On the other hand, no one can read the sources of our knowledge of the history of the Church without perceiving that there were always bad clergymen who abused their high prerogatives. Many bishops and priests were no more worthy to be intrusted with their extensive powers than the unscrupulous office-seekers to whom high stations in our modern governments sometimes fall.

The corruption of the clergy.

Yet as we read the fiery denunciations of the clergy's evil practices, which may be found in the records of nearly every age, we must not forget that the critic is always prone to take the good for granted and to dwell upon the evil. This is particularly true in dealing with a great religious institution, where corruption is especially shocking. One wicked bishop, or one form of oppression or immorality among the clergy, made a far deeper impression than the humble virtues of a hundred dutiful and God-fearing priests. If, however, we make all due allowance for the good which escaped the writers of the twelfth and thirteenth centuries, it must be admitted by all who read their testimony that they give us a gloomy picture of the life of many prelates, priests, and monks, and of the startling variety of abuses which developed in the Church.

Tendency to exaggerate the evil in the Church.

Gregory VII imagined that the reason for the existence of bad clergymen was that the kings and feudal lords forced their favorites into the offices of the Church. The root of the difficulty lay, however, in the wealth and power of the Church itself. It would have needed saints always to exercise righteously the tremendous powers which the clergy had acquired, and to resist the temptations to which they were subjected. When we consider the position of a rich prelate, it is not surprising that corruption abounded. The offices of the Church offered the same possibilities of money-making that civil offices, especially those in the great American cities, offer to the mere schemer to-day. The descriptions of some of the churchmen of the twelfth and thirteenth centuries remind

Temptations to corruption among the clergy.

us far more of the professional politician than of a modern clergyman, whether Catholic or Protestant.

85. At least a brief description of the more notorious forms of corruption among the clergy will be necessary to an understanding of the various heresies or revolts against the Church. These began seriously to threaten its power in the twelfth century and culminated in the successful Protestant revolt of the sixteenth. The vices of the clergy serve to account also for the appearance of the begging monks, the Franciscans and Dominicans, and to explain the need of the great reform which they undertook in the thirteenth century.

In the first place, there was simony, a disease so deep-seated and persistent that Innocent III declared it incurable. This has already been described in an earlier chapter. Even boys were made bishops and abbots through the influence of their friends and relatives. Wealthy bishoprics and monasteries were considered by feudal lords an admirable means of support for their younger sons, since the eldest born usually inherited the fief. The life led by bishops and abbots was often merely that of a feudal prince. If a prelate had a taste for fighting, he organized military expeditions for conquest or to satisfy a grudge against a neighbor, exactly as if he belonged to the bellicose laity of the period.

Besides simony and the scandalous lives of many of the clergy, there were other evils which brought the Church into disrepute. While the popes themselves, in the twelfth and thirteenth centuries, were usually excellent men and sometimes distinguished statesmen, who honestly endeavored to exalt the vast institution over which they presided, their officials, who tried the innumerable cases which were brought to the papal court, had a reputation for grave corruption.[1] It was generally believed that the decision was always in favor of him who could pay most and

The chief forms of corruption in the Church.

Simony.

The worldly and immoral lives of many bishops and abbots.

Corruption in the ecclesiastical courts.

---

[1] For a satire of the thirteenth century on the papal court, see Emerton, *Mediæval Europe*, p. 475.

that the poor received scant attention. The bishops' courts were notorious for their oppression, since a considerable portion of the bishop's income, like that of the feudal lord, came from the fines imposed upon those condemned by his officials. The same person was sometimes summoned to different courts at the same time and then fined for neglecting to appear at one or the other.

As for the parish priests, they appear often to have followed the demoralizing example set by their superiors. The acts of church councils indicate that the priest sometimes turned his parsonage into a shop and sold wine or other commodities. He further increased his income, as we have seen, by demanding fees for merely doing his duty in baptizing, confessing, absolving, marrying, and burying his parishioners. *The parish priests often no better than their superiors.*

The monks of the twelfth century, with some remarkable exceptions, did little to supply the deficiencies of the secular clergy.[1] Instead of instructing the people and setting before them an example of a pure and holy life, they enjoyed no better reputation than the bishops and priests. Efforts were made, however, by newly founded orders in the eleventh and twelfth centuries — like that of the Cistercians to which St. Bernard belonged — to reform the monks.

The universal impression of selfishness and depravity which the corrupt churchmen made upon all observers is reflected in innumerable writings of the time, — in the letters of the popes, in the exhortations of holy men like St. Bernard, in the acts of the councils, in the satirical poems of the popular troubadours and the sprightly versifiers of the courts.[2] All agree in denouncing the iniquity of the clergy, their greed, and their reckless disregard of their sacred duties. St. Bernard *Corruption and abuses recognized and condemned by the better element in the clergy itself.*

[1] It must not be forgotten that the monks were regarded as belonging to the clergy. For the various new orders of monks and the conditions in the monasteries, see Munro, *Mediæval History*, Chapter XII, and Jessopp, *Coming of the Friars*, Chapter III, " Daily Life in a Mediæval Monastery."

[2] See *Readings*, Chapter XVII.

sadly asks, " Whom can you show me among the prelates who does not seek rather to empty the pockets of his flock than to subdue their vices? "

86. The evils which the churchmen themselves so frankly admitted could not escape the notice and comment of laymen. But while the better element among the clergy vigorously urged a reform of the existing abuses, no churchman dreamed of denying the truth of the Church's doctrines or the efficacy of its ceremonies. Among the laity, however, certain popular leaders arose who declared that the Church was the synagogue of Satan ; that no one ought any longer to rely upon it for his salvation ; that all its elaborate ceremonies were worse than useless ; that its masses, holy water, and relics were mere money-getting devices of a depraved priesthood and helped no one to heaven. These bold rebels against the Church naturally found a hearing among those who felt that the ministrations of a wicked priest could not possibly help a sinner, as well as among those who were exasperated by the tithes and other ecclesiastical dues.

Heresy.

Those who questioned the teachings of the Church and proposed to cast off its authority were, according to the accepted view of the time, guilty of the supreme crime of heresy. To the orthodox believer nothing could exceed the guilt of one who committed treason against God by rejecting the religion which had been handed down in the Roman Church from the immediate followers of his Son. Moreover, doubt and unbelief were not merely sin, they were revolt against the most powerful social institution of the time, which, in spite of the depravity of some of its officials, continued to be venerated by people at large throughout western Europe. The extent and character of the heresies of the twelfth and thirteenth centuries and the efforts of the Church to suppress them by persuasion, by fire and sword, and by the stern court of the Inquisition, form a strange and terrible chapter in mediæval history.

The heretics were of two sorts. One class merely abjured the practices and some of the doctrines of the Roman Catholic Church while they remained Christians and endeavored to imitate as nearly as possible the simple life of Christ and the apostles. On the other hand, there were popular leaders who taught that the Christian religion was false. They held that there were two principles in the universe, the good and the evil, which were forever fighting for the victory. They asserted that the Jehovah of the Old Testament was really the evil power, and that it was, therefore, the evil power whom the Catholic Church worshiped. Two classes of heretics.

This latter heresy was a very old one, by which even St. Augustine had been fascinated in his early years. It was revived in Italy in the eleventh century and became very popular, especially in southern France, in the twelfth. Its adherents called themselves *Cathari* (the pure), but we shall call them *Albigenses*, a name derived from the town of Albi in southern France, where they were very numerous.[1] The Albigenses.

Among those who continued to accept the Christian faith but refused to obey the clergy on account of their wickedness, the most important sect was that of the Waldensians. These were followers of Peter Waldo of Lyons, who gave up all their property and lived a life of apostolic poverty. They went about preaching the Gospel and expounding the Scriptures, which they translated into the language of the people. They made many converts, and before the end of the twelfth century there were great numbers of them scattered throughout western Europe. The Waldensians.

The Church did not wish to condemn the efforts of good and simple men to imitate as exactly as possible the life of Christ and the apostles. Nevertheless these laymen, who claimed the right to preach and hear confession, and who asserted that prayer was quite as efficacious when uttered in

1 See *Readings*, Chapter XVII, for the beliefs of the Albigenses.

bed or in a stable as in a church, seemed clearly to call in question the general belief in the Church as the exclusive agent of salvation, and seriously to threaten its influence among the people.

Before the end of the twelfth century the secular rulers began to take notice of heresy. Henry II of England, in 1166, ordered that no one should harbor heretics in England, and that any house in which they were received should be burned. The king of Aragon decreed (1194) that any one who listened to the preaching of the Waldensians, or even gave them food, should suffer the penalties for treason and should have his property confiscated by the state. These are the beginnings of a series of pitiless decrees which even the most enlightened kings of the thirteenth century issued against all who should be convicted of belonging either to the Albigenses or the Waldensians. The Church and the civil government agreed that heretics were dangerous to the welfare of both, and that they were criminals deserving the terrible death of burning alive.[1]

It is very difficult for us who live in a tolerant age to understand the universal and deep-rooted horror of heresy which prevailed not only in the twelfth and thirteenth centuries, but also down at least to the eighteenth. Too much stress cannot be laid upon the fact that heresy was considered treason against an institution which practically all, both the learned and the unlearned, agreed was not only essential to salvation but was necessary also to order and civilization. Frank criticism of the evil lives of the clergy, not excluding the pope himself, was common enough. But this did not constitute heresy. One might believe that the pope and half the bishops were bad men, and yet in no way question the necessity for the Church's existence or the truth of every one of its dogmas; just as nowadays we might call particular rulers and

[1] Examples of these decrees are given in *Translations and Reprints*, Vol. III, No. 6.

government officials fools or knaves, without being suspected of repudiating government altogether. The heretic was the anarchist of the Middle Ages. He did not simply denounce the immorality of the officers of the Church; he claimed that the Church was worse than useless. He sought to lead people to throw off their allegiance to it and to disregard its laws and commands. The Church and the civil government consequently proceeded against him as against an enemy of society and order. Heresy was, moreover, a contagious disease, and spread rapidly and unobserved, so that to the rulers of the times even the harshest measures appeared justifiable in order to prevent its dissemination.

87. There were several ways of opposing heresy. First, a reform of the character of the clergy and a suppression of the abuses in the Church would have removed a great cause of that discontent to which the writers of the time attributed the rapid growth of heresy. The attempt of Innocent III to improve the conditions in the Church by summoning a great council at Rome in 1215 failed, however, and, according to his successor, matters grew worse rather than better. *Different methods of opposing heresy. Internal reform.*

A second plan was to organize an expedition against the rebels and annihilate them by the sword. This policy was only possible if a large number of heretics could be found in a single district. In southern France there were many adherents of both the Albigenses and the Waldensians, especially in the county of Toulouse. At the beginning of the thirteenth century there was in this region an open contempt for the Church and a bold defense of heretical teachings even among the higher classes. *Extermination by the sword.*

Against the people of this flourishing land Innocent III preached a crusade in 1208. An army under Simon de Montfort[1] marched from northern France into the doomed region *Albigensian crusade.*

---

[1] His son married an English lady, became a leader of the English barons, and was the first to summon the commons to Parliament. See above, pp. 146–147.

and, after one of the most atrocious and bloody wars upon record, suppressed the heresy by wholesale slaughter. At the same time the war checked the civilization and destroyed the prosperity of the most enlightened portion of France.

The third and most permanent defense against heresy was the establishment, under the headship of the pope, of a system of tribunals designed to ferret out secret cases of unbelief and bring the offenders to punishment. These courts of experts, who devoted their whole attention to the discovery and conviction of heresy, constituted the Holy Inquisition, which gradually took form after the Albigensian crusade. We cannot stop to describe these courts, which became especially notorious in Spain some two centuries after their establishment. The unfairness of the trials and the cruel treatment to which those suspected of heresy were subjected, through long imprisonment or torture — inflicted with the hope of forcing them to confess their crime or implicate others — have rendered the name of the Inquisition infamous.

Without by any means attempting to defend the methods employed, it may be remarked that the inquisitors were often earnest and upright men whose feelings were not unlike those of a New England judge presiding at a witch trial in the seventeenth century. The methods of procedure of the Inquisition were not more cruel than those used in the secular courts of the period.

The assertion of the suspected person that he was not a heretic did not receive any attention, for it was assumed that he would naturally deny his guilt, as would any other criminal. A person's belief had, therefore, to be judged by outward acts. Consequently one might fall into the hands of the Inquisition by mere inadvertent conversation with a heretic, by some unintentional neglect to show due respect toward the Church rites, or by the malicious testimony of one's neighbors. This is really the most dreadful aspect of the Inquisition and its procedure. It put a premium on talebearing and resorted to most cruel means to convict those who earnestly denied that their beliefs were different from those of the Church.

If the suspected person confessed his guilt and abjured his heresy, he was forgiven and received back into the Church; but a penance of life imprisonment was imposed upon him as a fitting means of wiping away the unspeakable sin of which he had been guilty. If he remained impenitent, he was "relaxed to the secular arm"[1]; that is to say, the Church, whose law forbade it to shed blood, handed over the convicted person to the civil power, which burned him alive without further trial.

Fate of the convicted heretic.

88. We may now turn to that far more cheerful and effective method of meeting the opponents of the Church, which may be said to have been discovered by St. Francis of Assisi. His teachings and the example of his beautiful life probably did far more to secure continued allegiance to the Church than all the hideous devices of the Inquisition.

Founding of the mendicant orders.

We have seen how the Waldensians tried to better the world by living simple lives and preaching the Gospel. Owing to the disfavor of the church authorities, who declared their teachings erroneous and dangerous, they were prevented from publicly carrying on their missionary work. Yet all conscientious men agreed with the Waldensians that the world was in a sad plight owing to the negligence and the misdeeds of the clergy. St. Francis and St. Dominic strove to meet the needs of their time by inventing a new kind of clergyman, the begging brother, or mendicant friar (Latin, *frater*, brother). He was to do just what the bishops and parish priests ordinarily failed to do, — namely, lead a holy life of self-sacrifice, defend the orthodox beliefs against the reproaches and attacks of the heretics, and awaken the people at large to a new

---

[1] For the form of relaxation and other documents relating to the Inquisition, see *Translations and Reprints*, Vol. III, No. 6.

spiritual life. The founding of the mendicant orders is one of the most important and interesting events of the Middle Ages.

St. Francis of Assisi, 1182-1226.

There is no more lovely and fascinating figure in all history than St. Francis. He was born (probably in 1182) at Assisi, a little town in central Italy. He was the son of a well-to-do merchant, and during his early youth he lived a very gay life, spending his father's money freely. He read the French romances of the time and dreamed of imitating the brave knights whose adventures they described. Although his companions were wild and reckless, there was a delicacy and chivalry in Francis' own make-up which made him hate all things coarse and heartless. When later he voluntarily became a beggar, his ragged coat still covered a true poet and knight.

Francis forsakes his life of luxury and his inheritance and becomes a hermit.

The contrast between his own life of luxury and the sad state of the poor early afflicted him. When he was about twenty, after a long and serious illness which made a break in his gay life and gave him time to think, he suddenly lost his love for the old pleasures and began to consort with the destitute, above all with the lepers. Now Francis, being delicately organized and nurtured, especially loathed these miserable creatures, but he forced himself to kiss their hands, as if they were his friends, and to wash their sores. So he gained a great victory over himself, and that which seemed bitter to him became, as he says, "sweet and easy."

His father does not appear to have had any fondness whatever for beggars, and the relations between him and his son grew more and more strained. When finally he threatened to disinherit the young man, Francis cheerfully agreed to surrender all right to his inheritance. Stripping off his clothes and giving them back to his father, he accepted the worn-out garment of a gardener and became a homeless hermit, busying himself in repairing the dilapidated chapels near Assisi.

One day in February, 1209, as he was listening to Mass, the priest, turning toward him by chance, read : "And as ye go, preach, saying, The kingdom of heaven is at hand. . . . Get you no gold, nor silver, nor brass in your purses, no wallet for your journey, neither two coats, nor shoes, nor staff ; for the laborer is worthy of his food " (Matt. x. 7–10). This seemed to the expectant Francis the answer of Christ himself to his longings for guidance. Here was a complete programme laid out for him. He threw aside his stick, wallet, and shoes and resolved thereafter to lead, literally and absolutely, the life the apostles had led.

He believes he receives a direct message from Heaven.

He began to preach in a simple way, and before long a rich fellow-townsman resolved to sell all and give to the poor, and follow Francis' example. Others soon joined them, and these joyous penitents, free of worldly burdens, calling themselves "God's troubadours," went barefoot and moneyless about central Italy preaching the Gospel. Some of those they met "listened willingly, others scoffed, the greater number overwhelmed them with questions, 'Whence come you? Of what order are you?' and they, though sometimes it was wearisome to answer, said simply, 'We are penitents, natives of the city of Assisi.' "

Francis begins to preach and to attract followers.

When, with a dozen followers, Francis appealed to the pope in 1210 to approve his plan, Innocent III hesitated. He did not believe that any one could lead a life of absolute poverty. Then might not these ragged, ill-kempt vagabonds appear to condemn the Church by adopting a life so different from that of the rich and comfortable clergy? Yet if he disapproved the friars, he would seem to disapprove at the same time Christ's directions to his apostles. He finally decided to give his oral sanction and to authorize the brethren to continue their missions. They were to receive the tonsure, and to come under the spiritual authority of the Roman Church.

Seeks and obtains the approval of the pope.

Missionary
work under-
taken.

89. Seven years later, when Francis' followers had greatly
increased, missionary work was begun on a large scale, and
brethren were dispatched to Germany, Hungary, France, Spain,
and even to Syria.   It was not long before an English chronicler was telling with wonder of the arrival in his country of
these barefoot men, in their patched gowns and with ropes
about their waists, who, with Christian faith, took no thought
for the morrow, believing that their Heavenly Father knew
what things they had need of.

Francis did
not desire
to found a
powerful
order.

The ill treatment which the friars received in their distant
journeys led them to appeal to the pope for a letter which
should request the faithful everywhere to treat them kindly,
since they were good Catholics.   This was the beginning of
numberless privileges from the pope.   It grieved Francis, however, to see his little band of companions converted into a great
and powerful order.   He foresaw that they would soon cease
to lead their simple, holy life, and would become ambitious
and perhaps rich.   " I, little Brother Francis," he writes,
"desire to follow the life and the poverty of Jesus Christ,
persevering therein until the end ; and I beg you all and
exhort you to persevere always in this most holy life of poverty, and take good care never to depart from it upon the
advice and teachings of anyone whomsoever."

Francis
reluctantly
draws up a
new rule for
the guidance
of the friars.

Francis sorrowfully undertook to draw up a new and more
elaborate constitution to take the place of the few Gospel
passages which he had originally brought together as a guide.
After many modifications, to suit the ideas of the pope and
the cardinals, the Franciscan Rule was solemnly ratified
(1228) by Honorius III.   It provides that "The brothers
shall appropriate nothing to themselves, neither a house, nor a
place, nor anything ; but as pilgrims and strangers in this world,
in poverty and humility serving God, they shall confidently
seek alms.   Nor need they be ashamed, for the Lord made
Himself poor for us in this world."   Yet the friars are to

work if they are able and if their charitable and religious duties leave them time to do so. They may be paid for this labor in necessities for themselves or their brethren, but never may they receive coin or money. Those may wear shoes who cannot get along without them. They may repair their garments with sackcloth and other remnants. They must live in absolute obedience to their superior and may not, of course, marry nor may they leave the order.[1]

After the death of St. Francis (1226), many of the order, which now numbered several thousand members, wished to maintain the simple rule of absolute poverty. Others, including the new head of the order, believed that much good might be done with the wealth which people were anxious to give them. They argued that the individual friars might still remain absolutely possessionless, even if the order had beautiful churches and comfortable monasteries. A stately church was immediately constructed at Assisi to receive the remains of their humble founder, who in his lifetime had chosen a deserted hovel for his home; and a great chest was set up in the church to receive offerings.

90. St. Dominic (b. 1170), the founder of the other great St. Dominic. mendicant order, was not a simple layman like Francis. He was a churchman and took a regular course of instruction in theology for ten years in a Spanish university. He then (1208) accompanied his bishop to southern France on the eve of the Albigensian crusade and was deeply shocked to see the prevalence of heresy. His host at Toulouse happened to be an Albigensian, and Dominic spent the night in converting him. He then and there determined to devote his life to the extirpation of heresy. The little we know of him indicates that he was a man of resolute purpose and deep convictions, full of burning zeal for the Christian faith, yet kindly and cheerful, and winning in manner.

1 The whole rule is translated by Henderson, *Historical Documents*, p. 344.

Founding of
the Domini-
can order.

By 1214 a few sympathetic spirits from various parts of
Europe had joined Dominic, and they asked Innocent III to
sanction their new order. The pope again hesitated, but is
said to have dreamed a dream in which he saw the great
Roman Church of the Lateran tottering and ready to fall had
not Dominic supported it on his shoulders. So he inferred that
the new organization might sometime become a great aid to the
papacy and gave it his approval. As soon as possible Dominic
sent forth his followers, of whom there were but sixteen, to
evangelize the world, just as the Franciscans were undertaking
their first missionary journeys. By 1221 the Dominican order
was thoroughly organized and had sixty monasteries scattered
over western Europe. " Wandering on foot over the face of
Europe, under burning suns or chilling blasts, rejecting alms
in money but receiving thankfully whatever coarse food might
be set before the wayfarer, enduring hunger in silent resigna-
tion, taking no thought for the morrow, but busied eternally in
the work of snatching souls from Satan and lifting men up
from the sordid cares of daily life, of ministering to their
infirmities and of bringing to their darkened souls a glimpse
of heavenly light " (Lea), — in this way did the early Franciscans and Dominicans win the love and veneration of the
people.

Contrast
between the
mendicants
and the
older orders.

91. Unlike the Benedictine monks, each of the friars was
under the command not only of the head of his particular monastery, but also of the " general " of the whole order. Like
a soldier, he was liable to be sent by his commander upon any
mission that the work of the order demanded. The friars
indeed regarded themselves as soldiers of Christ. Instead
of devoting themselves to a life of contemplation apart from
the world, like the earlier monks, they were accustomed and
required to mix with all classes of men. They must be ready
to dare and suffer all in the interest of their work of saving not
only themselves but their fellow-men.

The Dominicans were called the "Preaching Friars" and were carefully trained in theology in order the better to refute the arguments of the heretics. The pope delegated to them especially the task of conducting the Inquisition. They early began to extend their influence over the universities, and the two most distinguished theologians and teachers of the thirteenth century, Albertus Magnus and Thomas Aquinas, were Dominicans. Among the Franciscans, on the other hand, there was always a considerable party who were suspicious of learning and who showed far more anxiety to remain absolutely poor than did the Dominicans. Yet as a whole the Franciscans, like the Dominicans, accepted the wealth that came to them, and they, too, contributed distinguished scholars to the universities.

Contrast between the Dominicans and the Franciscans.

The pope quickly recognized the importance of these new orders. He granted them successive privileges which freed them from all control of the bishops, and finally declared that they were to be bound only by their own rules. What was still more important, he gave them the right, if they were priests, to celebrate Mass everywhere, to preach and to perform the ordinary functions of the parish priests, such as hearing confession, granting absolution, and conducting burials. The friars invaded every parish, and appear to have largely replaced the parish priests. The laity believed them to be holier than the secular clergy and therefore regarded their prayers and ministrations as more efficient. Few towns were without a gray friars' (Franciscan) or a black friars' (Dominican) cloister; few princes but had a Dominican or a Franciscan confessor.

Importance and influence of the new orders.

It is hardly necessary to say that the secular clergy took these encroachments very ill. They repeatedly appealed to the pope to abolish the orders, or at least to prevent them from enriching themselves at the expense of the parish priests. But they got little satisfaction. Once the pope quite frankly told a great deputation of cardinals, bishops, and minor clergy

Opposition of the secular clergy.

that it was their own vain and worldly lives which made them hate the mendicant brothers, who spent the bequests they received from the dying for the honor of God, instead of wasting it in pleasure.

The mendicant orders have counted among their numbers men of the greatest ability and distinction, — scholars like Thomas Aquinas, reformers like Savonarola, artists like Fra Angelico and Fra Bartolommeo, and scientists like Roger Bacon. In the busy world of the thirteenth century there was no agency more active for good than the friars. Yet their vagrant lives, free from the ordinary control of the Church, and the great wealth which was showered upon them, afforded many obvious temptations which they did not long withstand. Bonaventura, who was made head of the Franciscan order in 1257, admits the general dislike aroused by the greed, idleness, and vice of its degenerate members, as well as by their importunate begging, which rendered the friar more troublesome to the wayfarer than the robber. Nevertheless the friars were preferred to the ordinary priests by high and low alike; it was they, rather than the secular clergy, who maintained and cultivated the religious life in both city and country.

General Reading. — The opening chapter of Lea's monumental work, *A History of the Inquisition of the Middle Ages* (Harper Bros. & Co., 3 vols., $10.00), gives a remarkable account of the mediæval Church and the abuses which prevailed. The first volume also contains unexcelled chapters upon the origin of both the Franciscan and Dominican orders. For St. Francis, by far the best work is Sabatier's beautiful biography, *St. Francis of Assisi* (Charles Scribner's Sons, $2.50). The earliest and best source for Francis is *The Mirror of Perfection* (Page, Boston, 75 cents), by Brother Leo, which shows the love and admiration in which "Little Brother Francis" was held by one of his companions. See also JESSOPP, *The Coming of the Friars, and Other Historic Essays* (G. P. Putnam's Sons, $1.25), Chapter I.

CHAPTER XVIII

THE PEOPLE IN COUNTRY AND TOWN

92. Since the development of the rather new science of political economy, historical writers have become much interested in the condition and habits of the farmer, tradesman, and artisan in the Middle Ages. Unfortunately no amount of research is likely to make our knowledge very clear or certain regarding the condition of the people at large during the five or six centuries following the barbarian invasions. It rarely occurred to a mediæval chronicler to describe the familiar things about him, such as the way in which the peasant lived and tilled his land. Only the conspicuous personages and the startling events caught his attention. Nevertheless enough is known of the mediæval manor and town to make them very important subjects for the student of general history. *Little known of the life of the people in the Middle Ages.*

There was little town life in western Europe before the twelfth century. The Roman towns were decreasing in population before the German inroads. The confusion which followed the invasions hastened their decline, and a great number of them disappeared altogether. Those which survived and such new towns as sprang up were, to judge from the chronicles, of very little importance during the early Middle Ages. We may assume, therefore, that during the long period from Theodoric to Frederick Barbarossa by far the greater part of the population of England, Germany, and northern and central France were living in the country, on the great estates belonging to the feudal lords, abbots, and bishops.[1] *Unimportance of town life in the early Middle Ages.*

[1] In Italy and southern France town life was doubtless more general.

These mediæval estates were called *vills*, or *manors*, and closely resembled the Roman villas described in an earlier chapter. A portion of the estate was reserved by the lord for his own use; the rest of it was divided up among the peasants,[1] usually in long strips, of which each peasant had several scattered about the manor. The peasants were generally serfs who did not own their fields, but could not, on the other hand, be deprived of them so long as they worked for the lord and paid him certain dues. They were attached to the land and went with it when it changed hands. The serfs

An English Manor House, Thirteenth Century

were required to till those fields which the lord reserved for himself and to gather in his crops. They might not marry without their lord's permission. Their wives and children rendered such assistance as was necessary in the manor house. In the women's buildings the daughters of the serfs engaged in spinning, weaving, sewing, baking, and brewing, thus producing clothes, food, and drink to be used by the whole community.

We get our clearest ideas of the position of the serfs from the ancient descriptions of manors, which give an exact account of what each member of a particular community owed to the lord. For example, we find that the abbot of Peterborough held a manor upon which Hugh Miller and seventeen other serfs, mentioned by name, were required to work for him three days in each week during the whole year, except one

---

[1] The peasants were the tillers of the soil. They were often called *villains*, a word derived from vill.

week at Christmas, one at Easter, and one at Whitsuntide. Each serf was to give the lord abbot one bushel of wheat and eighteen sheaves of oats, three hens and one cock yearly, and five eggs at Easter. If he sold his horse for more than ten shillings, he was to give the said abbot four pence. Five other serfs, mentioned by name, held but half as much land as Hugh and his companions, by paying and doing in all things half as much service.

There were sometimes a few people on the manor who did not belong to the great body of cultivators. The limits of the manor and those of the parish often coincided; in that case there would be a priest who had some scattered acres and whose standing was naturally somewhat superior to that of the people about him. Then the miller, who ground the flour and paid a substantial rent to the lord, was generally somewhat better off than his neighbors, and the same may be said of the blacksmith.

One of the most remarkable characteristics of the manor was its independence of the rest of the world. It produced nearly everything that its members needed and might almost have continued to exist indefinitely without communication with those who lived beyond its bounds. Little or no money was necessary, for the peasants paid what was due to the lord in the form of labor and farm products. They also rendered the needful help to one another and found little occasion for buying and selling. *The manor independent of the outside world.*

There was almost no opportunity to better one's condition, and life, in the greater part of the hamlets, must have gone on for generation after generation in a weary routine. The life was not merely monotonous, it was miserable. The food was coarse and there was little variety, as the peasants did not even take pains to raise fresh vegetables. The houses usually had but one room. This was ill-lighted by a single little window and had no chimney. *The monotony and misery of the peasants' lives.*

Yet the very dependence upon one another can hardly have failed to produce a certain spirit of brotherhood and mutual assistance in the community. It was not only separated from the outside world, but its members were brought together constantly by their intermingled fields, their attendance at one church, and their responsibility to one proprietor. The men were all expected to be present at the "court" which was held in each manor, where the business of the manor was transacted under the supervision of a representative of the lord. Here, for instance, disputes were settled, fines imposed for the violation of the customs of the manor, and redistributions of the strips of land took place.

The manor court.

The serf was ordinarily a bad farmer and workman. He cultivated the soil in a very crude manner, and his crops were accordingly scanty and inferior. Obviously serfdom could exist only as long as land was plentiful. But in the twelfth and thirteenth century western Europe appears to have been gaining steadily in population. Serfdom would, therefore, naturally tend to disappear when the population so increased that the carelessly cultivated fields no longer supplied the food necessary for the growing numbers.

The serf an inferior farmer who could only exist when there was plenty of land.

The increased use of money in the twelfth and thirteenth centuries, which came with the awakening trade and industry, also tended to break up the manor. The old habit of bartering one thing for another without the intervention of money began to disappear. As time went on, neither the lord nor the serf was satisfied with the ancient primitive arrangements, which had answered well enough in the time of Charlemagne. The serfs, on the one hand, began to obtain money by the sale of their products in the markets of neighboring towns. They soon found it more profitable to pay the lord a certain sum instead of working for him, for they could then turn their whole attention to their own farms. The proprietors, on the other hand, found it to their advantage to accept money in place of the services

Barter replaced by money transactions.

of their tenants. With this money the landlord could hire laborers to cultivate his fields and could buy the luxuries which were brought to his notice as commerce increased. So it came about that the lords gradually renounced their control over the peasants, and the serf was no longer easily distinguishable from the freeman who paid a regular rent for his land.[1] A serf might also gain his liberty by fleeing to a town. If he remained undiscovered, or was unclaimed by his lord, for a year and a day, he became a freeman.

The slow extinction of serfdom in western Europe appears to have begun as early as the twelfth century. A very general emancipation had taken place in France by the end of the thirteenth century (and in England somewhat later), though there were still some serfs in France when the revolution came in 1789. Germany was far more backward in this respect. We find the peasants revolting against their hard lot in Luther's time, and it was not until the beginning of the nineteenth century that the serfs were freed in Prussia. *Disappearance of serfdom.*

93. It is hardly necessary to point out that the gradual reappearance of town life in western Europe is of the greatest interest to the student of history. The cities had been the centers of Greek and Roman civilization, and in our own time they dominate the life, culture, and business enterprise of the world. Were they to disappear, our whole life, even in the country, would necessarily undergo a profound change and tend to become primitive again like that of the age of Charlemagne. *Importance of town life.*

A great part of the mediæval towns, of which we begin to have some scanty records about the year 1000, appear to have originated on the manors of feudal lords or about a monastery or castle. The French name for town, *ville*, is derived from vill, the name of the manor. The need of protection was probably the usual reason for establishing a town with a wall about it, so that the neighboring country people might find safety in *Origin of the mediæval towns.*

[1] The manner in which serfs disappeared in England will be described later.

Compactness
of a medi-
æval town.

it when attacked. The way in which a mediæval town was
built seems to justify this conclusion. It was generally crowded
and compact compared with its more luxurious Roman predecessors. Aside from the market place there were few or no
open spaces. There were no amphitheaters or public baths
as in the Roman cities. The streets were often mere alleys
over which the jutting stories of the high houses almost met.
The high, thick wall that surrounded it prevented its extending
easily and rapidly as our cities do nowadays.

Townsmen
originally
serfs.

All towns outside of Italy were evidently small in the
eleventh and twelfth centuries, and, like the manors on which
they had grown up, they had little commerce as yet with the
outside world. They produced almost all that their inhabitants needed except the farm products which came from the
neighboring country. There was likely to be little expansion
so long as the town remained under the absolute control of
the lord or monastery upon whose land it was situated. The
townspeople were scarcely more than serfs, in spite of the fact
that they lived within a wall and engaged in industry instead
of farming. They had to pay irritating dues to their lord, just
as if they had still formed a farming community. The emancipation of the townsmen from their lords and the establishment
of a suitable form of government for their town were necessary
preliminaries to the free development of town life.

Increase of
trade pro-
motes the
growth of
the towns.

With the increase of trade came the longing for this freedom. For when new and attractive commodities began to
be brought from the East and the South, the people of the
towns were encouraged to produce goods with the idea of
exchanging them at some neighboring fair for the products
of distant lands. But no sooner did the townsmen begin to
engage in manufacturing and to enter into relations with the
outside world, than they became conscious that they were
greatly hampered by their half-servile condition and were subject to exactions and restrictions which would render progress

impossible. Consequently during the twelfth century there were many insurrections of the towns against their lords and a general demand that the lords should grant the townsmen *charters* in which the rights of both parties should be definitely stated.

In France the citizens organized themselves into what were called *communes*, or unions for the purpose of gaining their

The communes.

A Castle on the Rhine with a Village below it

independence. This word *commune* appeared a new and detestable one to the lords, for, to their minds, it was merely another name for a company of serfs leagued against their masters. The nobles sometimes put down the insurrections of their townsmen with great cruelty. On the other hand, the lords often realized that they would increase the prosperity of their towns by granting them freedom from arbitrary taxation and the right to govern themselves. In England the towns gained their privileges more gradually by purchasing them from the lords.

Town charters.

The town charters were written contracts between the lord and the commune or the guild of merchants of a town. The charter served at once as the certificate of birth of the town and as its constitution. It contained a promise on the part of the lord or king to recognize the existence of the guild of merchants. It limited the rights of the lord in calling the townsmen before his court and fining them, and enumerated the taxes which he might exact from the townspeople. The old dues and services were either abolished or changed into money payments.

King Henry II of England promised the inhabitants of Wallingford that "wheresoever they shall go on their journeys as merchants through my whole land of England and Normandy, Aquitaine and Anjou, 'by water and by strand, by wood and by land,' they shall be free from toll and passage fees and from all customs and exactions; nor are they to be troubled in this respect by anyone under penalty of ten pounds." In the case of the town of Southampton he concedes "that my men of Hampton shall have and hold their guild and all their liberties and customs, by land and by sea, in as good, peaceable, just, free, quiet, and honorable a manner as they had the same most freely and quietly in the time of King Henry, my grandfather; and let no one upon this do them any injury or insult."

Customs revealed in the charters.

The customs of the times, as revealed in the charters, seem to us very primitive. We find in the charter of the French town of St.-Omer, in 1168, provisions like the following: He who shall commit a murder in the town shall not find an asylum anywhere within the walls. If he shall seek to escape punishment by flight, his buildings shall be torn down and his goods confiscated; nor may he come back into the town unless he be first reconciled with the relations of his victim and pay ten pounds, of which a half shall go to the lord's representatives and the other half to the commune, to be spent on its fortifications. He who strikes another one in the town shall pay one hundred sous; he who pulls out the hair of another shall pay forty sous, etc.

Many of the towns had, as a visible sign of their freedom, a belfry, a high building with a watchtower, where a guard was kept day and night in order that the bell might be rung in

A Mediæval Town, Siegen

case of approaching danger. It contained an assembly hall, where the commune held its meetings, and a prison. In the fourteenth century the wonderful townhalls began to be erected, which, with the exception of the cathedrals and other churches, are usually the most remarkable buildings which the traveler sees to-day in the old commercial cities of Europe.

The tradesmen in the mediæval towns were at once artisans **Craft guilds.** and merchants; they not only made, but offered for sale, the articles which they produced in their shops. In addition to the original guild of merchants which helped the towns to gain and preserve their privileges, many new corporations of tradesmen grew up, the so-called *craft guilds*. The oldest statutes of a guild in Paris are those of the candle makers, which go back to 1061. The number of trades differed greatly in different towns, but the guilds all had the same object, — to prevent every one from practicing a trade who had not been duly admitted to the corporation.

A young man had to spend several years in learning his trade. He lived in the house of a master workman, but received no remuneration. He then became a "journeyman" and could earn wages, although he could still work only for master workmen and not directly for the public. A simple trade might be learned in three years, but to become a goldsmith one must be an apprentice for ten years. The number of apprentices that a master workman might employ was strictly limited, in order that the journeymen might not become too numerous. The way in which each trade was to be practiced was carefully regulated, as well as the time that should be spent in work each day. The system of guilds discouraged enterprise but maintained a uniform efficiency everywhere. Had it not been for these unions, the defenseless, isolated workmen, serfs as they had formerly been, would have found it impossible to secure freedom and municipal independence from the feudal lords who had formerly been their masters.

94. The chief reason for the growth of the towns and their increasing prosperity was a great development of trade throughout western Europe. Commerce had pretty much disappeared with the decline of the Roman roads and the general disorganization produced by the barbarian invasions. There was no one in the Middle Ages to mend the ancient Roman roads. The great network of highways from Persia to Britain fell apart when independent nobles or poor local communities took the place of a world empire. All trade languished, for there was little demand for those articles of luxury which the Roman communities in the North had been accustomed to obtain from the South. There was little money and scarcely any notion of luxury, for the nobility lived a simple life in their dreary and rudely furnished castles.

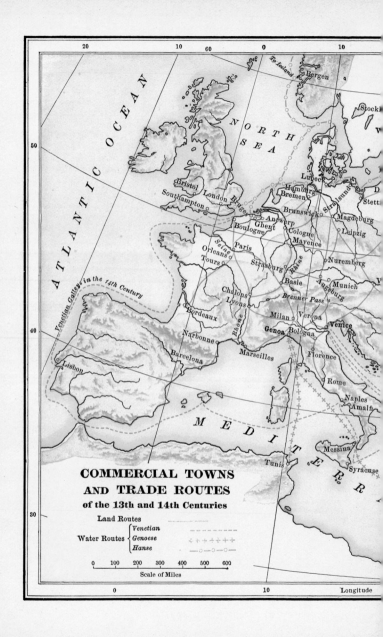

COMMERCIAL TOWNS
AND TRADE ROUTES
of the 13th and 14th Centuries

Land Routes

Water Routes { Venetian
Genoese
Hanse

0   100   200   300   400   500   600
Scale of Miles

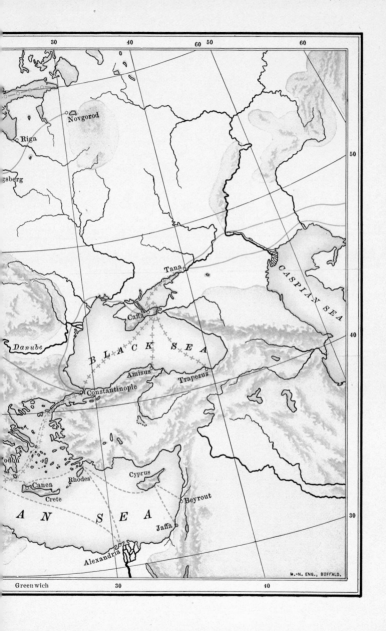

In Italy, however, trade does not seem to have altogether ceased. Venice, Genoa, Amalfi, and other towns appear to have developed a considerable Mediterranean commerce even before the Crusades. Their merchants, as we have seen, supplied the destitute crusaders with the material necessary for the conquest of Jerusalem. The passion for pilgrimages offered inducements to the Italian merchants for expeditions to the Orient, whither they transported the pilgrims and returned with the products of the East. The Italian cities established trading stations in the East and carried on a direct traffic with the caravans which brought to the shores of the Mediterranean the products of Arabia, Persia, India, and the Spice Islands. The southern French towns and Barcelona entered also into commercial relations with the Mohammedans in northern Africa.

Street in Frankfort-on-the-Main

Italian cities trade with the Orient.

This progress in the South could not but stir the lethargy of the rest of Europe. The new commerce encouraged a revolution in industry. So long as the manor system prevailed and each man was occupied in producing only what he and

Commerce stimulates industry.

the other members of his group needed, there was nothing to send abroad and nothing to exchange for luxuries. But when merchants began to come with tempting articles, the members of a community were encouraged to produce a surplus of goods above what they themselves needed, and to sell or exchange this surplus for commodities coming from a distance. Merchants and artisans gradually directed their energies toward the production of what others wished as well as what was needed by the little group to which they belonged.

The luxuries of the East introduced into Europe.

The romances of the twelfth century indicate that the West was astonished and delighted by the luxuries of the East, — the rich fabrics, Oriental carpets, precious stones, perfumes, drugs (like camphor and laudanum), silks and porcelains from China, spices from India, and cotton from Egypt. Venice introduced the silk industry from the East and the manufacture of those glass articles which the traveler may still buy in the Venetian shops. The West learned how to make silk and velvet as well as light and gauzy cotton and linen fabrics. The eastern dyes were introduced, and Paris was soon imitating the tapestries of the Saracens. In exchange for those luxuries which they were unable to produce, the Flemish towns sent their woolen cloths to the East, and Italy its wines. But there was apparently always a considerable cash balance to be paid to the Oriental merchants, since the West could not produce enough to pay by exchange for all that it demanded from the Orient.

Some of the important commercial centers.

The northern merchants dealt mainly with Venice and brought their wares across the Brenner Pass and down the Rhine, or sent them by sea to be exchanged in Flanders. By the thirteenth century important centers of trade had come into being, some of which are still among the great commercial towns of the world. Hamburg, Lübeck, and Bremen carried on active trade with the countries on the Baltic and with England. Augsburg and Nuremberg, in the south of Germany, became important on account of their situation on the line of trade between Italy and the North. Bruges and Ghent sent their manufactures everywhere. English commerce was relatively unimportant as yet compared with that of the great ports of the Mediterranean.

95. A word must be said of the numerous and almost incredible obstacles in the way of commerce in the Middle Ages. There was very little of that freedom which we now regard as essential to successful business. Our wholesale dealers would have been considered an abomination in the Middle Ages. Those who bought up a quantity of a commodity in order to sell it at a high rate were called by the ugly name of *forestallers*. It was universally believed that everything had a "just" price, which was merely enough to cover the cost of the materials used in its manufacture and remunerate the maker for the work he had put upon it. It was considered outrageous to sell a thing for more than the just price, no matter how anxious the purchaser might be to obtain it. Every manufacturer was required to keep a shop in which he offered at retail all that he made. Those who lived near a town were permitted to sell their products in the market place within the walls on condition that they sold directly to the consumers. They might not dispose of their whole stock to one dealer, for fear that if he had all there was of a commodity he might raise the price above a just one.

Akin to these prejudices against wholesale trade was that against interest. Money was believed to be a dead and sterile thing, and no one had a right to demand any return for lending it. Interest was wicked, since it was exacted by those who took advantage of the embarrassments of others. Usury, as the taking of even the most moderate and reasonable rate of interest was then called, was strenuously forbidden by the laws of the Church. We find church councils ordering that impenitent usurers should be refused Christian burial and have their wills annulled. So money-lending, necessary to all great

Restrictions on trade.

Idea of a 'just' price.

Payment of interest on money forbidden.

commercial and industrial undertakings, was left to the Jews, from whom Christian conduct was not expected.

The Jews as money-lenders. This ill-starred people played a most important part in the economic development of Europe, but they were terribly mal-treated by the Christians, who held them guilty of the supreme crime of putting Christ to death. The active persecution of the Jews did not, however, become common before the thirteenth century, when they first began to be required to wear a peculiar cap, or badge, which made them easily recognized and exposed them to constant insult. Later they were sometimes shut up in a particular quarter of the city, called the Jewry. Since they were excluded from the guilds, they not unnaturally turned to the business of money-lending, which no Christian might practice. Undoubtedly their occupation had much to do in causing their unpopularity. The kings permitted them to make loans, often at a most exorbitant rate; Philip Augustus allowed them to exact forty-six per cent, but reserved the right to extort their gains from them when the royal treasury was empty. In England the usual rate was a penny a pound for each week.

The 'Lombards' as bankers. In the thirteenth century the Italians — "Lombards" — began to go into a sort of banking business and greatly extended the employment of bills of exchange. They lent for nothing, but exacted damages for all delay in repayment. This appeared reasonable and right even to those who condemned ordinary interest. Capitalists, moreover, could contribute money towards an enterprise and share the profits as long as no interest was exacted. In these and other ways the obstacles offered by the prejudice against interest were much reduced, and large commercial companies came into existence, especially in Italy.

Tolls, duties, and other annoyances to which merchants were subjected on land. 96. Another serious disadvantage which the mediæval merchant had to face was the payment of an infinite number of tolls and duties which were exacted by the lords through whose domains his way passed. Not only were duties exacted on the highways, bridges, and at the fords, but those barons who were so fortunate as to have castles on a navigable river blocked the stream in such a way that the merchant could not bring his vessel through without a payment for the privilege. The charges were usually small, but the way in which they were exacted and the repeated delays must have been a serious source of irritation and loss to the merchants. For example, a certain monastery lying between Paris and the sea required that those hastening to town with fresh fish should stop and let the monks pick out what they thought worth three pence, with little regard to the condition in which they left the goods. When a boat laden with wine passed up the Seine to Paris, the agent of the lord of Poissy could have three casks broached, and, after trying them all, he could take a measure from the one he liked best. At the markets all sorts of dues had to be paid, such, for example, as payments for using the lord's scales or his measuring rod. Besides this, the great variety of coinage which existed in feudal Europe caused infinite perplexity and delay.

Commerce by sea had its own particular trials, by no means confined to the hazards of wind and wave, rock and shoal. Pirates were numerous in the North Sea. They were often organized and sometimes led by men of high rank, who appear to have regarded the business as no disgrace. Then there were the so-called *strand laws*, according to which a ship with its cargo became the property of the owner of the coast upon which it might be wrecked or driven ashore. Lighthouses and beacons were few and the coasts dangerous. Moreover, natural dangers were increased by false signals which wreckers used to lure ships to shore in order to plunder them. *Dangers by sea.* *Pirates.* *Strand laws.*

With a view to mitigating these manifold perils, the towns early began to form unions for mutual defense. The most famous of these was that of the German cities, called the *Hanseatic League.* Lübeck was always the leader, but among *The Hanseatic League.*

the seventy towns which at one time and another were included in the confederation, we find Cologne, Brunswick, Dantzig, and other centers of great importance. The union purchased and controlled settlements in London, — the so-called *Steelyard* near London Bridge, — at Wisby, Bergen, and the far-off Novgorod in Russia. They managed to monopolize nearly the whole trade on the Baltic and North Sea, either through treaties or the influence that they were able to bring to bear.

The League made war on the pirates and did much to reduce the dangers of traffic. Instead of dispatching separate and defenseless merchantmen, their ships sailed out in fleets under the protection of a man-of-war. On one occasion the League undertook a successful war against the king of Denmark, who had interfered with their interests. At another time it declared war on England and brought her to terms. For two hundred years before the discovery of America, the League played a great part in the commercial affairs of western Europe ; but it had begun to decline even before the discovery of new routes to the East and West Indies revolutionized trade.

Trade regulated by the towns (thirteenth to fifteenth century), not by nations or individuals.

It should be observed that, during the thirteenth, fourteenth, and fifteenth centuries, trade was not carried on between nations, but by the various towns, like Venice, Lübeck, Ghent, Bruges, Cologne. A merchant did not act or trade as an independent individual but as a member of a particular merchant guild, and he enjoyed the protection of his town and of the treaties it arranged. If a merchant from a certain town failed to pay a debt, a fellow-townsman might be seized where the debt was due. At the period of which we have been speaking, an inhabitant of London was considered a foreigner or an alien in Bristol, just as was the merchant from Cologne or Antwerp. Only gradually did the towns merge into the nations to which their people belonged.[1]

1 Reference, Munro, *Mediæval History*, Chapter XIV, where the subject of this chapter is treated in a somewhat different way.

The increasing wealth of the merchants could not fail to raise them to a position of importance in society which they had not hitherto enjoyed.   Their prosperity enabled them to vie with the clergy in education and with the nobility in the luxury of their dwellings and surroundings.   They began to give some attention to reading, and as early as the fourteenth century many of the books appear to have been written with a view of meeting their tastes and needs.   Representatives of the towns were called into the councils of the king, who was obliged to take their advice along with their contributions to the support of the government.   The rise of the burgher class alongside the older orders of the clergy and nobility, which had so long dominated the life of western Europe, is one of the most momentous changes of the thirteenth century.

The burghers, or commons, become an influential class.

General Reading. — GIBBINS, *History of Commerce in Europe* (The Macmillan Company, 90 cents), the best short account of the subject, with good maps of trade routes.   INGRAM, *History of Slavery and Serfdom* (Black, London, $2.00), especially Chapters IV and V.   CUNNINGHAM, *Western Civilization in its Economic Aspects*, Vol. II, Mediæval and Modern Times (The Macmillan Company, $1.25), is very suggestive.   There are several excellent accounts of the economic situation in England in the Middle Ages, which, in many respects, was similar to the conditions on the continent.   CHEYNEY, *Industrial and Social History of England* (The Macmillan Company, $1.40); GIBBINS, *The Industrial History of England* (Methuen, $1.00), and a more elaborate treatise by the same writer, *Industry in England* (Methuen, $3.00); CUNNINGHAM, *Outlines of English Industrial History* (The Macmillan Company, $1.50), and much fuller by the same writer, *Growth of English Industry and Commerce during the Middle Ages* (The Macmillan Company, $4.00).   All these give excellent accounts of the manor, the guilds, the fairs, etc.   See also JESSOPP, *Coming of the Friars*, second essay, " Village Life Six Hundred Years Ago."

CHAPTER XIX

THE CULTURE OF THE MIDDLE AGES

97. The interest of the Middle Ages lies by no means exclusively in the statesmanship of kings and emperors, their victories and defeats; in the policy of popes and bishops; or even in feudalism and Europe's escape from it. Important as all these are, we should have but a very imperfect idea of the period which we have been studying if we left it without considering the intellectual life and the art of the time, the books that were written, the universities that were founded, and the cathedrals that were built.

General use of Latin in the Middle Ages.

To begin with, the Middle Ages differed from our own time in the very general use then made of Latin, both in writing and speaking. In the thirteenth century, and long after, all books that made any claim to learning were written in Latin; [1] the professors in the universities lectured in Latin, friends wrote to one another in Latin, and state papers, treaties, and legal documents were drawn up in the same language. The ability of every educated person to make use of Latin, as well as of his native tongue, was a great advantage at a time when there were many obstacles to intercourse among the various nations. It helps to explain, for example, the remarkable way in which the pope kept in touch with all the clergymen of western Christendom, and the ease with which students, friars, and merchants could wander from one country to another. There is no more interesting or important revolution than that

[1] In Germany the books published annually in the German language did not exceed those in Latin until after 1680.

by which the language of the people in the various European countries gradually pushed aside the ancient tongue and took its place, so that even scholars scarcely ever think now of writing books in Latin.

In order to understand how it came about that two languages, the Latin and the native speech, were both commonly used in all the countries of western Europe all through the Middle Ages, we must glance at the origin of the modern languages. These all fall into two quite distinct groups, the Germanic and the Romance.

Those German peoples who had continued to live outside of the Roman Empire, or who, during the invasions, had not settled far enough within its bounds to be led, like the Franks in Gaul, to adopt the tongue of those they had conquered, naturally adhered to the language they had always used, namely, the particular Germanic dialect which their forefathers had spoken for untold generations. From the various languages spoken by the German barbarians, modern German, English, Dutch, Swedish, Norwegian, Danish, and Icelandic are derived.

The Germanic languages derived from the dialects of the German barbarians.

The second group of languages developed within the territory which had formed a part of the Roman Empire, and includes modern French, Italian, Spanish, and Portuguese. It has now been clearly proved, by a very minute study of the old forms of words, that these Romance languages were one and all derived from the *spoken* Latin, employed by the soldiers, merchants, and people at large. This differed considerably from the elaborate and elegant written Latin which was used, for example, by Cicero and Cæsar. It was undoubtedly much simpler in its grammar and doubtless varied a good deal in different regions ; — a Gaul, for instance, could not pronounce the words like an Italian. Moreover, in conversation people did not always use the same words as those in the books. For example, a horse was commonly spoken of as *caballus*, whereas a writer would use the word *equus*; it is from

The Romance languages derived from the spoken Latin.

caballus that the word for horse is derived in Spanish, Italian, and French (*caballo, cavallo, cheval*).

As time went on the spoken language diverged farther and farther from the written. Latin is a troublesome speech on account of its complicated inflections and grammatical rules, which can be mastered only after a great deal of study. The people of the Roman provinces and the incoming barbarians naturally paid very little attention to the niceties of syntax and found easy ways of saying what they wished.[1] Yet several centuries elapsed after the German invasions before there was anything written in the language of conversation. So long as the uneducated could understand the correct Latin of the books when they heard it read or spoken, there was no necessity of writing anything in their familiar daily speech. But the gulf between the spoken and the written language had become so great by the time Charlemagne came to the throne, that he advised that sermons should be given thereafter in the language of the people, who, apparently, could no longer follow the Latin. The Strasburg oaths[2] are, however, about the first example which has come down to us of the speech which was growing into French.

Earliest examples of the Germanic languages.

98. As for the Germanic languages, one at least was reduced to writing even before the break-up of the Empire. An eastern bishop, Ulfilas (d. 381), had undertaken to convert the Goths while they were still living north of the Danube before the battle of Adrianople. In order to carry on his

Gothic.

work, Ulfilas translated a great part of the Bible into Gothic, using the Greek letters to represent the sounds. With the single exception of the Gothic, there is no example of writing

---

[1] Even the monks and others who wrote Latin in the Middle Ages were unable to follow strictly the rules of the language. Moreover, they introduced many new words to meet the new conditions and the needs of the time, such as *imprisonare*, imprison; *utlagare*, to outlaw; *baptizare*, to baptize; *foresta*, forest; *feudum*, fief, etc.

[2] See above, pp. 94–95.

in any German language before Charlemagne's time. There is no doubt, however, that the Germans possessed an unwritten literature, which was passed down by word of mouth for several centuries before any of it was written out. Charlemagne caused certain ancient poems to be collected, which presumably celebrated the great deeds of the German heroes during the invasions. These invaluable specimens of ancient German are said to have been destroyed by the order of Louis the Pious, who was shocked by their paganism. The great German epic, the *Song of the Niebelungs*, was not reduced to writing until the end of the twelfth century, after it had been transmitted orally for many generations.

The oldest form of English is commonly called Anglo-Saxon and is so different from the language that we use that, in order to read it, it must be learned like a foreign language. We hear of an English poet, Cædmon, as early as Bede's time, a century before Charlemagne. A manuscript of an Anglo-Saxon epic, called *Beowulf*, has been preserved which belongs perhaps to the close of the eighth century. The interest which King Alfred displayed in the mother tongue has already been mentioned. This old form of our language prevailed until after the Norman Conquest; the *Anglo-Saxon Chronicle*, which does not close until 1154, is written in pure Anglo-Saxon. Then changes may be noticed in the language as it appears in the books of the time, and decade by decade it approaches more nearly to that which we speak. Although the first public document in English (1256), which belongs to the reign of Henry III, is scarcely to be understood without study, a poem written in his son's time is tolerably intelligible.[1]

Ancient English, or Anglo-Saxon.

English literature was destined one day to arouse the admiration of the peoples across the Channel and exercise an important

[1] " Bytuene Mershe and Avoril
   When spray beginneth to springe,
   The little foul (bird) hath hire wyl
   On hyre lud (voice) to synge."

influence upon other literatures. In the Middle Ages, however, French, not English, was the most important of the vernacular languages of western Europe. In France a vast literature was produced in the language of the people during the twelfth and thirteenth centuries which profoundly affected the books written in Italy, Spain, Germany, and England.

French and Provençal.

99. Two quite different languages had gradually developed in France from the spoken Latin of the Roman Empire. If a line were drawn on the map from La Rochelle, on the Atlantic, eastward to the Alps, crossing the Rhone a little below Lyons, it would give a general idea of the limits of the two tongues. To the north, French was spoken; to the south, in a region bounded by the Pyrenees and the Alps, Provençal.[1]

Mediæval French romances.

Very little in the ancient French language written before the year 1100 has been preserved. The West Franks undoubtedly began much earlier to sing of their heroes, of the great deeds of Clovis, Dagobert, and Charles Martel. These famous rulers were, however, completely overshadowed later by Charlemagne, who became the unrivaled hero of mediæval poetry and romance. It was believed that he had reigned for a hundred and twenty-five years, and the most marvelous exploits were attributed to him and his knights. He was supposed, for instance, to have led a crusade to Jerusalem. Such themes as these — more legend than history — were woven into long epics, which were the first written literature of the Frankish people. These poems, combined with the stories of adventure, developed a spirit of patriotic enthusiasm among the French which made them regard " fair France" as the especial care of Providence.

The *Song of Roland.*

It is little wonder that the best of these long poems came to be looked upon as the national epic of the French. This

---

[1] Of course there was no sharp line of demarcation between the people who used the one language and the other, nor was Provençal confined to southern France. The language of Catalonia, beyond the Pyrenees, was essentially the same as that of Provence. French was called *langue d'oïl,* and the southern language *langue d'oc,* each after the word used for " yes."

is the *Song of Roland*, probably written just before the First Crusade. It tells the story of Charlemagne's retreat from Spain, during which Roland, one of his commanders, lost his life in a romantic encounter in the defiles of the Pyrenees.

> That death was on him he knew full well;
> Down from his head to his heart it fell.
> On the grass beneath a pine tree's shade,
> With face to earth, his form he laid,
> Beneath him placed he his horn and sword,
> And turned his face to the heathen horde.
> Thus hath he done the sooth to show,
> That Karl and his warriors all may know,
> That the gentle count a conqueror died.[1]

In the latter part of the twelfth century the romances of King Arthur and his Knights of the Round Table begin to appear. These enjoyed great popularity in all western Europe for centuries, and they are by no means forgotten yet. Arthur, of whose historical existence no one can be quite sure, was supposed to have been king of Britain shortly after the Saxons gained a foothold in the island. In other long poems of the time, Alexander the Great, Cæsar, and other ancient worthies appear as heroes. The absolute disregard of historical facts and the tendency to represent the warriors of Troy and Rome as mediæval knights, show the inability of the mediæval mind to understand that the past could have been different from the present. All these romances are full of picturesque adventures and present a vivid picture of the valor and loyalty of the true knight, as well as of his ruthlessness and contempt for human life.[2]

Romances of King Arthur and the Knights of the Round Table.

[1] The *Song of Roland* is translated into spirited English verse by O'Hagan, London, 1880.

[2] The reader will find a beautiful example of a French romance of the twelfth century in an English translation of *Aucassin and Nicolette* (Mosher, Portland, Me.). Mr. Steele gives charming stories of the twelfth and thirteenth centuries in *Huon of Bordeaux*, *Renaud of Montauban*, and *The Story of Alexander* (Allen, London). Malory's *Mort d'Arthur*, a collection of the stories of the Round Table made in the fifteenth century for English readers, is the best place to turn for these famous stories.

The *fabliaux* and the fables.

Besides the long and elaborate epics, like *Roland*, and the romances in verse and prose, there were numberless short stories in verse (the *fabliaux*), which usually dealt with the incidents of everyday life, especially with the comical ones. Then there were the fables, the most famous of which are the stories of Reynard the Fox, which were satires upon the customs of the time, particularly the weaknesses of the priests and monks.

The troubadours.

100. Turning now to southern France, the beautiful songs of the troubadours, which were the glory of the Provençal tongue, reveal a gay and polished society at the courts of the numerous feudal princes. The rulers not merely protected and encouraged the poets; they aspired to be poets themselves and to enter the ranks of the troubadours, as the composers of these elegant verses were called. These songs were always sung to an accompaniment on some instrument, usually the lute. Those who merely sang them, without being themselves poets, were called *jongleurs*. The troubadours and jongleurs traveled from court to court, not only in France, but north into Germany and south into Italy, carrying with them the southern French poetry and customs. We have few examples of Provençal before the year 1100, but from that time on, for two centuries, countless songs were written, and many of the troubadours enjoyed an international reputation. The terrible Albigensian crusade brought misery and death into the sprightly circles which had gathered about the count of Toulouse and others who had treated the heretics too leniently. But the literary critic traces signs of decline in the Provençal verse even before this disaster.[1]

Chivalry.

For the student of history, the chief interest of the epics of northern France and the songs of the South lies in the insight that they give into the life and aspirations of this feudal

[1] An excellent idea of the spirit and character of the troubadours and of their songs may be got from Justin H. Smith, *Troubadours at Home* (G. P. Putnam's Sons, New York). See *Readings*, Chapter XIX.

period. These are usually summed up in the term *chivalry*, or *knighthood*, of which a word may properly be said here, since we should know little of it were it not for the literature of which we have been speaking. The knights play the chief rôle in all the mediæval romances; and, as many of the troubadours belonged to the knightly class, they naturally have much to say of it in their songs.

Chivalry was not a formal institution established at any particular moment. Like feudalism, with which it was closely connected, it had no founder, but appeared spontaneously throughout western Europe to meet the needs and desires of the period. We learn from Tacitus that even in his time the Germans considered the moment a solemn one when the young warrior was first invested with the arms of a soldier. "This was the sign that the youth had reached manhood; this was his first honor." It is probably a survival of this feeling which we find in the idea of knighthood. When the youth of good family had been carefully trained to ride his horse, use his sword, and manage his hawk in the hunt, he was made a *knight* by a ceremony in which the Church took part, although the knighthood was actually conferred by an older knight.

The knight was a Christian soldier, and he and his fellows were supposed to form, in a way, a separate order with high ideals of the conduct befitting their class. Knighthood was not, however, membership in an association with officers and a written constitution. It was an ideal, half-imaginary society, — a society to which even those who enjoyed the title of king or duke were proud to belong. One was not born a knight as he might be born a duke or count, and could become one only through the ceremony mentioned above. One might be a noble and still not belong to the knightly order, and, on the other hand, one baseborn might be raised to knighthood on account of some valorous deed.

Nature of the knightly order.

The ideals of the knight.

The knight must, in the first place, be a Christian and must obey and defend the Church on all occasions. He must respect all forms of weakness and defend the helpless wherever he might find them. He must fight the infidel ceaselessly, pitilessly, and never give way before the enemy. He must perform all his feudal duties, be faithful in all things to his lord, never lie or violate his plighted word. He must be generous and give freely and ungrudgingly to the needy. He must be faithful to his lady and be ready to defend her person and her honor at all costs. Everywhere he must be the champion of the right against injustice and oppression. In short, chivalry was the Christianized profession of arms.

In the stories of King Arthur and his Knights of the Round Table there is a beautiful picture of the ideal knight. The dead Lancelot is addressed by one of his sorrowing companions as follows : " Thou wert the courtliest knight that ever bare shield, and thou wert the truest friend to thy lover that ever bestrode horse, and thou wert the truest lover of a sinful man [i.e., among sinful men] that ever loved woman, and thou wert the kindest man that ever struck with sword, and thou wert the goodliest person that ever came among the press of knights, and thou wert the meekest man and the gentlest that ever ate in hall among ladies, and thou wert the sternest knight to thy mortal foe that ever put spear in breast."

The German minne-singers.

The Germans also made their contribution to the literature of chivalry. The German poets of the thirteenth century are called *minnesingers*. Like the troubadours, whom they greatly admired, they usually sang of love (German, *Minne*). The

Walther von der Vogelweide.

most famous of the minnesingers was Walther von der Vogelweide (d. about 1228), whose songs are full of charm and of enthusiasm for his German fatherland. Wolfram von Eschenbach (d. about 1225) in his story of *Parsifal* gives the long and sad adventures of a knight in search of the Holy Grail, — the sacred vessel which had held the blood of Christ. Only those perfectly pure in thought, word, and deed could hope to behold it.   Parsifal failed to speak a word of sympathy to a *Parsifal.* suffering man and was forced to undergo a long atonement. At last he learned that only through pity and humility and faith in God could he hope to find the Grail.

The chivalry depicted in the *Song of Roland* and the more Difference between the serious poems of northern France is of a severe type, in earlier and later ideals which the service of the Church, especially against the infidel, of chivalry. and the obligations to the feudal suzerain have the predominant place.   On the other hand, in the Arthurian legends, and, above all, in the songs of the troubadours, the ideal conduct of a polished and valorous gentleman, especially toward the lady of his choice, finds expression.   The later romances of chivalry (in the thirteenth and following centuries) deal very largely with knighthood in the latter sense of the word.   No one, indeed, any longer thought of fighting the infidel; for the Crusades were over and the knight was forced to seek adventures nearer home.[1]

101.   So long as all books had to be copied by hand, there were, of course, but few of them compared with modern times. The literature of which we have been speaking was not in general read, but was listened to, as it was sung or recited by those who made it their profession.   Wherever the wandering jongleur appeared he was sure of a delighted audience for his songs and stories, both serious and light.   Those unfamiliar with Latin General ignorance could, however, learn little of the past; there were no trans- of the past. lations of the great classics of Greece and Rome, of Homer, Plato, Cicero, or Livy.   All that they could know of ancient history was derived from the fantastic romances referred to above, which had for their theme the quite preposterous deeds ascribed to Alexander the Great, Æneas, and Cæsar.   As for their own history, the epics relating to the earlier course of events in France and the rest of Europe were hopelessly confused.

[1] Reference, Henderson, *Short History of Germany*, Vol. I, pp. 111–121.

The writers attributed a great part of the acts of the Frankish kings, from Clovis to Pippin, to Charlemagne. The first real history written in French is Villehardouin's account of the capture of Constantinople by the crusaders (in 1204), which he witnessed.

Mediæval popular science. What we should call scientific literature was practically wanting. It is true that there was a kind of encyclopedia in verse which gave a great deal of misinformation about things in general. Every one believed in strange animals like the unicorn, the dragon, and the phenix, and in still stranger habits of real animals. A single example will suffice to show what passed for zoölogy in the thirteenth century.

"There is a little beast made like a lizard and such is its nature that it will extinguish fire should it fall into it. The beast is so cold and of such a quality that fire is not able to burn it, nor will trouble happen in the place where it shall be." This beast signifies the holy man who lives by faith, who "will never have hurt from fire nor will hell burn him. . . . This beast we name also by another name, — it is called salamander, as you find written, — it is accustomed to mount into apple-trees, poisons the apples, and in a well where it shall fall it will poison the water."

It will be noticed that the habits of the animals were supposed to have some spiritual meaning and carry with them a lesson for mankind. It may be added that this and similar stories were centuries old. The most improbable things were repeated from generation to generation without its occurring to any one to inquire if there was any truth in them. Even the most learned men of the time believed in astrology and in the miraculous virtues of herbs and gems. For instance, Albertus Magnus, one of the most distinguished scientists of the thirteenth century, agrees that a sapphire will drive away boils and that the diamond can be softened in the blood of a stag, which will work best if the stag has been fed on wine and parsley.[1]

102. It is not only in the literature of the Middle Ages that we find the thought and life of the people reflected, but in the art as well, for painters, sculptors, and builders were at work in every country of western Europe.

The paintings were altogether different from those of to-day, and consisted chiefly of illustrations in the books, called *illuminations*. Just as the books had all to be laboriously written out by hand, so each picture was painted on the parchment page with tiny brushes and usually in brilliant colors with a generous use of gold. And as the monks wrote out the books, so it was, in general, the monks who painted the pictures. The books that they adorned were chiefly those used in the church services, especially the breviary, the psalter, and the book of hours. Naturally these pictures usually dealt with religious subjects and illustrated the lives of the saints or the events of biblical history. Virtue was encouraged by representations of the joys of heaven and also stimulated by spirited portrayals of the devil and his fiends, and of the sufferings of the lost.

Illuminations done by the monks.

In religious works.

Secular works, too, were sometimes provided with pictures drawn from a wide variety of subjects. We find in their pages such homely and familiar figures as the farmer with his plow, the butcher at his block, the glass blower at his furnace ; then, again, we are transported to an imaginary world, peopled with strange and uncouth beasts and adorned with fantastic architecture.

In secular books.

The mediæval love of symbols and of fixed rules for doing things is strikingly illustrated in these illuminations. Each color had its especial significance. There were certain established attitudes and ways of depicting various characters and emotions which were adhered to by generation after generation

The artist governed by fixed rules.

[1] See Steele's *Mediæval Lore* for examples of the science of the Middle Ages. For the curious notions of the world and its inhabitants, see the *Travels*, attributed to Sir John Mandeville. The best edition is published by The Macmillan Company, 1900. See *Readings*, Chapter XIX.

of artists and left comparatively little opportunity for individual talent or lifelike presentation. On the other hand, these little pictures — for of course they were always small[1] — were often executed with exquisite care and skill and sometimes in the smaller details with great truth to nature.

Beside the pictures of which we have been speaking, it was a common practice to adorn the books with gay illuminated initials or page borders, which were sometimes very beautiful in both design and color. In these rather more freedom was allowed to the caprice of the individual artist, and they

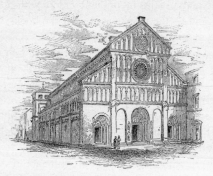

A Romanesque Church

were frequently enlivened with very charming and lifelike flowers, birds, squirrels, and other small animals.

The art of sculpture was more widely and successfully cultivated during the Middle Ages than painting. Mediæval sculpture did not, however, concern itself

Sculpture subservient to architecture. chiefly with the representation of the human figure, but with what we may call *decorative carving;* it was almost wholly subservient to the dominant art of the Middle Ages, namely, architecture.

Architecture the dominant art of the Middle Ages. It is in the great cathedrals and other churches scattered throughout England, France, Spain, Holland, Belgium, and Germany, that we find the noblest and most lasting achievements of mediæval art, which all the resources of modern skill have

[1] The word *miniature*, which is often applied to them, is derived from *minium*, i.e., vermilion, which was one of the favorite colors. Later the word came to be applied to anything small. See the frontispiece for an example of an illuminated page from a book of hours.

been unable to equal. Everybody belonged to the Church, but the Church, too, belonged to each individual. The building and beautifying of a new church was a matter of interest to the whole community, — to men of every rank. It gratified at once their religious sentiments, their local pride, and their artistic cravings. All the arts and crafts ministered to the con-

Durham Cathedral (Romanesque)

struction and adornment of the new edifice, and, in addition to its religious significance, it took the place of our modern art museum.

Up to the beginning of the thirteenth century the churches were built in the Romanesque style.[1] They were, generally speaking, in the form of a cross, with a main aisle, and two side aisles which were both narrower and lower than the main aisle. The aisles were divided from each other by massive round pillars which supported the round vaulting of the roof and were connected by round arches. The round-arched windows were usually small for the size of the building, so that the interior was not very light. The whole effect was one of massive simplicity. There was, however,

The Romanesque style.

[1] So called because it was derived from the old Roman basilicas, or buildings in which the courts were held.

especially in the later churches of this style, a profusion of carved ornament, usually in geometric designs.

Introduction of the Gothic style. The *pointed* form of arch was used occasionally in windows during the eleventh and twelfth centuries. But about the beginning of the thirteenth century [1] it began to be employed

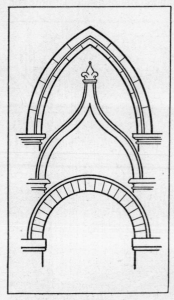

The pointed arch.

much more extensively, and in an incredibly short time practically superseded the round arch and became the characteristic feature of a new style, called *Gothic*. The adoption of the pointed arch had very important results. It enabled the builder to make arches of the same height but various widths, and of varying height and the same width. A round arch of a given span can be only half as high as it is wide, but the pointed arch may have a great diversity of proportions. The development of the Gothic style was greatly forwarded by the invention of the "flying buttress."

Round and Pointed Arches

Flying buttresses. By means of this graceful outside prop it became possible to lighten the masonry of the hitherto massive walls and pierce them with great windows which let a flood of light into the hitherto dark churches. [2]

Stained glass. The light from all these great windows might even have been too glaring had it not been for the wonderful stained

---

[1] In France as early as the twelfth century.

[2] Notice flying buttresses shown in the picture of Canterbury cathedral, p. 208.

FAÇADE OF RHEIMS CATHEDRAL

glass set in exquisite stone tracery with which they were filled. The stained glass of the mediæval cathedral, especially in France, where the glass workers brought their art to the greatest perfection, was one of its chief glories. By far the greater part of this old glass has of course been destroyed, but it is still so highly prized that every bit of it is now carefully preserved, for it has never since been equaled. A window set with odd bits of it pieced together like crazy patchwork is more beautiful, in its rich and jewel-like coloring, than the finest modern work.

As the Gothic style developed and the builders grew all the time more skillful and daring, the churches became marvels of lightness and delicacy of detail and finish, while still retaining

Flying Buttresses of Notre Dame, Paris

their dignity and beauty of proportion. Sculptors enriched them with the most beautiful creations of their art. Moldings and capitals, pulpits, altars, and choir screens, the wooden seats for the clergy and choristers, are sometimes literally covered with carving representing graceful leaf and flower forms, familiar animals or grotesque monsters, biblical incidents or homely scenes from everyday life. In the cathedral of Wells,

Sculptured ornament.

in England, one capital shows us among its vines and leaves a boy whose face is screwed up with pain from the thorn he is extracting from his foot; another depicts a whole story of sin found out, thieves stealing grapes pursued by an angry farmer with a pitchfork. One characteristic of the mediæval imagination is its fondness for the grotesque. It loved queer beasts, half eagle, half lion, hideous batlike creatures, monsters like nothing on land or sea. They lurk among the foliage on choir screens, leer at you from wall or column, or squat upon the gutters high on roof and steeple.

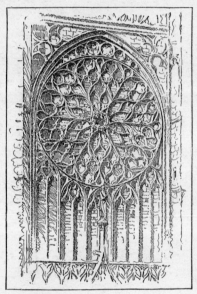

Window in the Cathedral of Sens, France

A striking peculiarity of the Gothic structure is the great number of statues of apostles, saints, and rulers which adorn the façades and especially the main portal of the churches. These figures are cut from the same kind of stone of which the

Gothic sculpture. building is made and appear to be almost a part of it. While, compared with later sculpture, they seem somewhat stiff and unlifelike, they harmonize wonderfully with the whole building, and the best of them are full of charm and dignity.

Secular buildings. So far we have spoken only of the church architecture, and that was by far the most important during the period with which we have been dealing. Later, in the fourteenth

INTERIOR OF EXETER CATHEDRAL

century, many beautiful secular buildings were constructed in the Gothic style. The most striking and important of these were the guildhalls built by the rich merchant guilds, and the townhalls of some of the important cities. But the Gothic style has always been especially dedicated to, and seems peculiarly fitted for, ecclesiastical architecture. Its lofty aisles and open floor spaces, its soaring arches leading the eye toward heaven, and its glowing windows suggesting the glories of paradise, may well have fostered the ardent faith of the mediæval Christian.

We have already touched upon some of the characteristics of domestic architecture in referring to the mediæval castle. This was rather a stronghold than a home,—strength and inaccessibility were its main requirements. The walls were many feet thick and the tiny windows, often

Figures (gargoyles) on Notre Dame, Paris

hardly more than slits in the massive walls, the stone floors, the great bare halls warmed only by large fireplaces, suggest nothing of the comfort of a modern household. At the same time they imply a simplicity of taste and manners and a hardihood of body which we may well envy.

The mediæval castle.

103. On turning from the language and books of the people and the art of the period to the occupations of the learned class, who carried on their studies and discussions in Latin, we naturally inquire where such persons obtained their education. During the long centuries which elapsed between the time when Justinian closed the government schools and the advent of Frederick Barbarossa, there appears to have been nothing

The schools before the eleventh century.

in western Europe, outside of Italy and Spain, corresponding to our universities and colleges. Some of the schools which the bishops and abbots had established in accordance with Charlemagne's commands were, it is true, maintained all through the dark and disorderly times which followed his death. But the little that we know of the instruction offered in them would indicate that it was very elementary, although there were sometimes noted men at their head.

Abelard, d. 1142.

About the year 1100 an ardent young man named Abelard started out from his home in Brittany to visit all the places where he might hope to receive instruction in logic and philosophy, in which, like all his learned contemporaries, he was especially interested. He reports that he found teachers in several of the French towns, particularly in Paris, who were attracting large numbers of students to listen to their lectures upon logic, rhetoric, and theology. Abelard soon showed his superiority to his teachers by defeating them several times in debate. Before long he began lecturing on his own account, and such was his success that thousands of students flocked to hear him.

Abelard's *Yea and Nay.*

He prepared a remarkable little text-book, called *Yea and Nay*, containing seemingly contradictory opinions of the church fathers upon particular questions. The student was left to reconcile the contradictions, if he could, by careful reasoning; for Abelard held that a constant questioning was the only path to real knowledge. His free way of dealing with the authorities upon which men based their religious beliefs seemed wicked to many of his contemporaries, especially to St. Bernard, who made him a great deal of trouble. Nevertheless it soon became the fashion to discuss the various doctrines of Christianity with great freedom and to try to make a well-reasoned system of theology by following the rules of Aristotle's logic. It was just after Abelard's death (1142) that Peter Lombard published his *Sentences*, already described.

Abelard did not found the University of Paris, as has sometimes been supposed, but he did a great deal to make the discussions of theological problems popular, and by his attractive method of teaching he greatly increased the number of those who wished to learn. The sad story of his life, which he wrote when he was worn out with the calamities that had overtaken him, is the best and almost the only account which exists of the remarkable interest in learning which explains the origin of the University of Paris.[1]

Before the end of the twelfth century the teachers had become so numerous in Paris that they formed a union, or guild, for the advancement of their interests. This union of professors was called by the usual name for corporations in the Middle Ages, *universitas;* hence our word "university." The king and pope both favored the university and granted the teachers and students many of the privileges of the clergy, a class to which they were regarded as belonging, because learning had for so many centuries been confined to the clergy. *Origin of the University of Paris.*

About the time that we find the beginnings of a university or guild of professors at Paris, a great institution of learning was growing up at Bologna. Here the chief attention was given, not to theology, as at Paris, but to the study of the law, both Roman and canon. Very early in the twelfth century a new interest in the Roman law became apparent in Italy, where the old jurisprudence of Rome had never been completely forgotten. Then, in 1142 or thereabouts, a monk, Gratian, published a great work in which he aimed to reconcile all the conflicting legislation of the councils and popes and to provide a convenient text-book for the study of the church or canon law. Students then began to stream to Bologna in greater numbers than ever before. In order to protect themselves in a town where they were regarded as strangers, they organized themselves into associations, which became so *Study of the Roman and canon law in Bologna.* *The De-cretum of Gratian.*

[1] See *Readings*, Chapter XIX.

powerful that they were able to force the professors to obey the rules which they laid down.

Other universities founded.

The University of Oxford was founded in the time of Henry II, probably by English students and masters who had become discontented at Paris for some reason. The University of Cambridge, as well as numerous universities in France, Italy, and Spain, appeared in the thirteenth century. The German universities, which are still so famous, were established somewhat later, most of them in the latter half of the fourteenth and in the fifteenth centuries. The northern institutions generally took the great mother university on the Seine as their model, while those in southern Europe usually adopted the habits of Bologna.

The academic degree.

When, after some years of study, a student was examined by the professors, he was, if successful, admitted to the corporation of teachers and became a master himself. What we call a degree to-day was originally, in the mediæval universities, nothing more than the qualification to teach. But in the thirteenth century many began to desire the honorable title of master or doctor (which is only the Latin word for *teacher*) who did not care to become professors in our sense of the word.[1]

Simple methods of instruction.

The students in the mediæval universities were of all ages, from thirteen to forty, and even older. There were no university buildings, and in Paris the lectures were given in the Latin quarter, in Straw Street, so called from the straw strewn on the floors of the hired rooms where the lecturer explained the text-book, with the students squatting on the floor before him. There

---

[1] The origin of the bachelor's degree, which comes at the end of our college course nowadays, may be explained as follows: The bachelor in the thirteenth century was a student who had passed part of his examinations in the course in "arts," as the college course was then called, and was permitted to teach certain elementary subjects before he became a full-fledged master. So the A.B. was inferior to the A.M. then as now. After finishing his college course and obtaining his A.M., the young teacher often became a student in one of the professional schools of law, theology, or medicine, and in time became a master in one of these sciences. The words *master*, *doctor*, and *professor* meant pretty much the same thing in the thirteenth century.

were no laboratories, for there was no experimentation. All that was required was a copy of the text-book, — Gratian's *Decretum*, the *Sentences*, a treatise of Aristotle, or a medical book. This the lecturer explained sentence by sentence, and the students listened and sometimes took notes.

The fact that the masters and students were not bound to any particular spot by buildings and apparatus left them free to wander about. If they believed themselves ill-treated in one town they moved to another, greatly to the disgust of the tradespeople of the place which they deserted, who of course profited by the presence of the university. The universities of Oxford and of Leipsic, among others, were founded by professors and students who had deserted their former home.

The universities could move freely from one town to another.

The course in arts, which corresponded to our college course and led to the degree of Master of Arts, occupied six years at Paris. The studies were logic, various sciences, — physics, astronomy, etc., — studied in Aristotle's treatises, and some philosophy and ethics. There was no history, no Greek. Latin had to be learned in order to carry on the work at all, but little attention was given to the Roman classics. The new modern languages were considered entirely unworthy of the learned. It must of course be remembered that none of the books which we consider the great classics in English, French, Italian, or Spanish had as yet been written.

Course of study.

104. The most striking peculiarity of the instruction in the mediæval university was the supreme deference paid to Aristotle. Most of the courses of lectures were devoted to the explanation of some one of his numerous treatises, — his *Physics*, his *Metaphysics*, his various treatises on logic, his *Ethics*, his minor works upon the soul, heaven and earth, etc. Only his *Logic* had been known to Abelard, as all his other works had been forgotten. But early in the thirteenth century all his comprehensive contributions to science reached the West, either from Constantinople or through the Arabs who had brought

Aristotle's works become known in the West.

them to Spain. The Latin translations were bad and obscure, and the lecturer had enough to do to give some meaning to them, to explain what the Arab philosophers had said of them, and, finally, to reconcile them to the teachings of Christianity.

Veneration for Aristotle. Aristotle was, of course, a pagan. He was uncertain whether the soul continued to exist after death; he had never heard of the Bible and knew nothing of the salvation of man through Christ. One would have supposed that he would have been promptly rejected with horror by those who never questioned the doctrines of Christianity. But the teachers of the thirteenth century were fascinated by his logic and astonished at his learning. The great theologians of the time, Albertus Magnus (d. 1280) and Thomas Aquinas (d. 1274), did not hesitate to prepare elaborate commentaries upon all his works. He was called "The Philosopher"; and so fully were scholars convinced that it had pleased God to permit Aristotle to say the last word upon each and every branch of knowledge that they humbly accepted him, along with the Bible, the church fathers, and the canon and Roman law, as one of the unquestioned authorities which together formed a complete guide for humanity in conduct and in every branch of science.

Scholasticism. The term *scholasticism* is commonly given to the philosophy, theology, and method of discussion of the mediæval professors. To those who later outgrew the fondness for logic and the supreme respect for Aristotle, scholasticism, with its neglect of Greek and Roman literature, came to seem an arid and profitless plan of education. Yet if we turn over the pages of the wonderful works of Thomas Aquinas, we see that the scholastic philosopher might be a person of extraordinary insight and erudition, ready to recognize all the objections to his position, and able to express himself with great clearness and cogency.[1] The training in logic, if it did not increase the

---

[1] An example of the scholastic method of reasoning of Thomas Aquinas may be found in *Translations and Reprints*, Vol. III, No. 6.

sum of human knowledge, accustomed the student to make careful distinctions and present his material in an orderly way.

Even in the thirteenth century there were a few scholars who criticised the habit of relying upon Aristotle for all knowledge. The most distinguished fault-finder was Roger Bacon, an English Franciscan monk (d. about 1290), who declared that even if Aristotle were very wise he had only planted the tree of knowledge and that this had " not as yet put forth all its branches nor produced all its fruits." " If we could continue to live for endless centuries we mortals could never hope to reach full and complete knowledge of all the things which are to be known. No one knows enough of nature completely to describe the peculiarities of a single fly and give the reason for its color and why it has just so many feet, no more and no less." Bacon held that truth could be reached a hundred thousand times better by experiments with real things than by poring over the bad Latin translations of Aristotle. " If I had my way," he declared, " I should burn all the books of Aristotle, for the study of them can only lead to a loss of time, produce error and increase ignorance."

Roger Bacon's attack on scholasticism.

So we find that even when scholasticism was most popular in the universities, there were keen-sighted scientists who recommended the modern scientific method of discovering truth. This does not consist in discussing, according to the rules of logic, what a Greek philosopher said hundreds of years ago, but in the patient observation of things about us.

———

We have now traversed somewhat over one half of the long period of fifteen hundred years which separates Europe of to-day from the disintegrating Roman Empire of the fifth century. The eight hundred years which lie between the century of Alaric, Attila, Leo the Great, and Clovis, and that of Innocent III, St. Louis, and Edward I, witnessed momentous changes, quite as important as any that have occurred since.

Review of the great changes between the break-up of the Roman Empire in the west and the end of the thirteenth century.

It is true that it seemed at first as if the barbarous Goths, Franks, Vandals, and Burgundians were bringing nothing but turmoil and distraction. Even the strong hand of Charlemagne curbed the unruly elements for only a moment; then the discord of his grandsons and the incursions of Northmen, Hungarians, Slavs, and Saracens plunged western Europe once more into the same anarchy and ignorance through which it had passed in the seventh and eighth centuries.

Two hundred years and more elapsed after Charlemagne's death before we can begin once more to note signs of progress. While we know little of the eleventh century, and while even its most distinguished writers are forgotten by all save the student of the period, it was undoubtedly a time of preparation for the brilliant twelfth century — for Abelard and St. Bernard, for the lawyers, poets, architects, and philosophers who seem to come suddenly upon the scene.

The Middle Ages may therefore be divided into two fairly distinct and quite different periods. The centuries prior to the age of Gregory VII and of William the Conqueror may, on account of their disorder and ignorance, be properly called the "dark ages," although they beheld some important stages in the transformation of Europe. The later Middle Ages, on the contrary, were a time of rapid and unmistakable progress in almost every line of human endeavor. Indeed by the end of the thirteenth century a great part of those changes were well under way which serve to make modern Europe so different from the condition of western Europe under the Roman Empire. The most striking of these are the following.

(1) A group of national states in which a distinct feeling of nationality was developing had taken the place of the Roman Empire, which made no allowance in its government for the differences between Italians, Gauls, Germans, and Britons. The makeshift feudal government which had grown up

during the dark ages was yielding to the kingly power (except in Germany and Italy) and there was no hope of ever reuniting western Europe into a single empire.

(2) The Church had, in a way, taken the place of the Roman Empire by holding the various peoples of western Europe together under the headship of the pope and by assuming the powers of government during the period when the feudal lords were too weak to secure order and justice. Organized like an absolute monarchy, the Church was in a certain sense far the most powerful state of the Middle Ages. But it attained the zenith of its political influence under Innocent III, at the opening of the thirteenth century; before its close the national states had so grown in strength that it was clear that they would gradually reassume the powers of government temporarily exercised by the Church and confine the pope and clergy more and more to their strictly religious functions.

The national states begin to deprive the Church of its governmental powers.

(3) A new social class had come into prominence alongside the clergy and the knightly aristocracy. The emancipation of the serfs, the founding of towns, and the growth of commerce made it possible for merchants and successful artisans to rise to importance and become influential through their wealth. From these beginnings the great intelligent and educated public of modern times has sprung.

Appearance of the commons or third estate.

(4) The various modern languages began to be used in writing books. For five or six hundred years after the invasions of the Germans, Latin was used by all writers, but in the eleventh and following centuries the language of the people began to replace the ancient tongue. This enabled the laymen who had not mastered the intricacies of the old Roman speech to enjoy the stories and poems which were being composed in French, Provençal, German, English, and Spanish, and, somewhat later, in Italian.

Books begin to be written in the language of the people.

The clergy lose the monopoly of learning.

Although the clergy still directed education, laymen were beginning to write books as well as to read them, and gradually the churchmen ceased to enjoy the monopoly of learning which they had possessed during the early Middle Ages.

Study of law, theology, and philosophy. The universities.

(5) Scholars began as early as the year 1100 to gather eagerly about masters who lectured upon the Roman and canon law or upon logic, philosophy, or theology. The works of Aristotle, the most learned of the ancients, were sought out, and students followed him enthusiastically into all fields of knowledge. The universities grew up which are now so conspicuous a feature of our modern civilization.

Beginnings of experimental science.

(6) Scholars could not satisfy themselves permanently with the works of Aristotle but began themselves to add to the fund of human knowledge. In Roger Bacon and his sympathizers we find a group of scientific investigators who were preparing the way for the unprecedented achievements in natural science which are the glory of recent times.

Artistic progress.

(7) The developing appreciation of the beautiful is attested by the skill and taste expressed in the magnificent churches of the twelfth and thirteenth centuries, which were not a revival of any ancient style but the original production of the architects and sculptors of the period.

General Reading. — The most convenient and readable account of mediæval literature is perhaps that of SAINTSBURY, *The Flourishing of Romance* (Charles Scribner's Sons, $1.50). For chivalry, see CORNISH, *Chivalry* (The Macmillan Company, $1.75). For Gothic architecture, see C. H. MOORE, *Development and Character of Gothic Architecture* (The Macmillan Company, $4.50). For the art in general, LÜBKE, *Outlines of the History of Art* (Dodd, Mead & Co., 2 vols., $7.50). For the universities, RASHDALL, *History of the Universities of the Middle Ages* (Clarendon Press, 3 vols., $14.00).

CHAPTER XX

THE HUNDRED YEARS' WAR

105. In dealing with the history of Europe during the four- Plan of the following four chapters.
teenth and fifteenth centuries the following order has been
adopted. (1) England and France are treated together, since
the claims of the English kings to the French crown, and the
long Hundred Years' War between the two countries, bring
them into the same tale of disorder and final reorganization. (2) Next the history of the papal power and the
remarkable efforts to better the Church at the great Council
of Constance (1414) are considered. (3) Then the progress
of enlightenment is taken up, particularly in the Italian towns,
which were the leaders in culture during this period. This
leads to an account of the invention of printing and the
extraordinary geographical discoveries of the latter part of
the fifteenth century. (4) In a fourth chapter the situation
of western Europe at the opening of the sixteenth century
is described, in order that the reader may be prepared to
understand the great revolt against the Church under the
leadership of Martin Luther.

We turn first to England. The English kings who pre- Extent of the king of England's realms before Edward I (1272-1307).
ceded Edward I had ruled over only a portion of the island of
Great Britain. To the west of their kingdom lay the mountainous district of Wales, inhabited by that remnant of the
original Britons which the German invaders had been unable
to conquer. To the north of England was the kingdom of
Scotland, which was quite independent except for an occasional vague recognition on the part of its rulers of the English

kings as their feudal superiors. Edward I, however, succeeded in conquering Wales permanently and Scotland temporarily.

The Welsh and their bards.

For centuries a border warfare had been carried on between the English and the Welsh. William the Conqueror had found it necessary to establish a chain of earldoms on the Welsh frontier, and Chester, Shrewsbury, and Monmouth became the outposts of the Normans. While the raids of the Welsh constantly provoked the English kings to invade Wales, no permanent conquest was possible, for the enemy retreated into the mountains about Snowdon and the English soldiers were left to starve in the wild regions into which they had ventured. The long and successful resistance which the Welsh made against the English must be attributed not only to their inaccessible retreats but also to the patriotic inspiration of their bards. These fondly believed that their people would sometime reconquer the whole of England, which they had possessed before the coming of the Angles and Saxons.[1]

Edward I conquers Wales.

When Edward I came to the throne he demanded that Llewelyn, Prince of Wales, as the head of the Welsh clans was called, should do him homage. Llewelyn, who was a man of ability and energy, refused the king's summons, and Edward marched into Wales. Two campaigns were necessary before the Welsh finally succumbed. Llewelyn was killed (1282), and with him expired the independence of the Welsh people. Edward divided the country into shires and introduced English laws and customs, and his policy of conciliation was so successful that there was but a single rising in the country for a whole century. He later presented his son to the Welsh as

The title of ' Prince of Wales.'

their prince, and from that time down to the present the title of " Prince of Wales " has usually been conferred upon the heir to the English throne.

Scotland before Edward I.

The conquest of Scotland proved a far more difficult matter than that of Wales. The early history of the kingdom of

[1] Reference, Green, *Short History of the English People*, pp. 161–169.

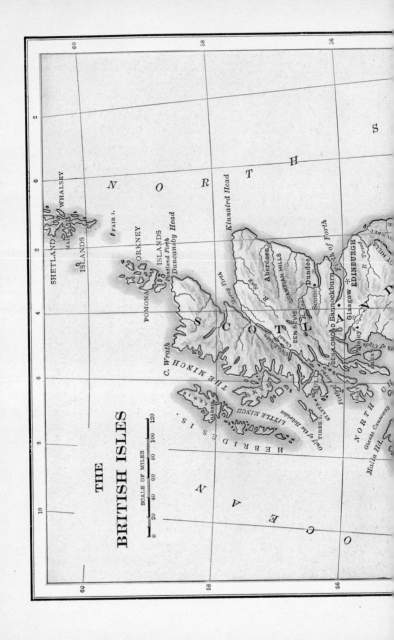

THE
BRITISH ISLES

SCALE OF MILES

0   20   40   60   80   100   120

Scotland is a complicated one. When the Angles and Saxons
landed in Britain, a great part of the mountainous region north
of the Firth of Forth was inhabited by a Celtic tribe, the Picts.
There was, however, on the west coast a little kingdom of the
Irish Celts, who were then called Scots. By the opening of
the tenth century the Picts had accepted the king of the Scots
as their ruler, and the annalists begin to refer to the highland
region as the land of the Scots. As time went on the English
kings found it to their advantage to grant to the Scottish
rulers certain border districts, including the Lowlands, between
the river Tweed and the Firth of Forth. This region was
English in race and speech, while the Celts in the Highlands
spoke, and still speak, Gaelic.

The Highlands and Lowlands.

It was very important in the history of Scotland that its
kings chose to dwell in the Lowlands rather than in the
Highlands, and made Edinburgh, with its fortress, their chief
town. With the coming of William the Conqueror many Englishmen, and also a number of discontented Norman nobles, fled
across the border to the Lowlands of Scotland, and founded
some of the great families, like those of Balliol and Bruce, who
later fought for Scottish liberty. During the twelfth and thirteenth centuries the country, especially in the south, developed
rapidly under the influence of the neighboring Anglo-Norman
civilization, and the towns increased in size and importance.

Character of the inhabitants of the Lowlands.

It was not until the time of Edward I that the long series
of troubles between England and Scotland began. The death
of the last representative of the old line of Scotch kings in
1290 was followed by the appearance of a number of claimants
to the crown. In order to avoid civil war, Edward was asked
to decide who should be king. He agreed to make the decision on condition that the one whom he selected should hold
Scotland as a fief from the English king. This arrangement
was adopted, and the crown was given to Robert Balliol. But
Edward unwisely made demands upon the Scots which aroused

Edward intervenes in Scotch affairs.

their anger, and their king renounced his homage to the king

of England. The Scotch, moreover, formed an alliance with Edward's enemy, Philip the Fair of France; thenceforth, in all the difficulties between England and France, the English kings had always to reckon with the disaffected Scotch, who were glad to aid England's enemies.

Edward
attempts to
incorporate
Scotland
with
England.

Edward marched in person against the Scotch (1296) and speedily put down what he regarded as a rebellion. He declared that Balliol had forfeited his fief through treason, and that consequently the English king had become the immediate lord of the Scotch nobles, whom he forced to do him homage. He emphasized his claim by carrying off the famous Stone of Scone, upon which the kings of Scotland had been crowned for ages. Continued resistance led Edward to attempt to incorporate Scotland with England in the same way that he had treated Wales. This was the beginning of three hundred years of intermittent war between England and Scotland, which ended only when a Scotch king, James VI, succeeded to the English throne in 1603 as James I.

That Scotland was able to maintain her independence was mainly due to Robert Bruce, a national hero who succeeded in bringing both the nobility and the people under his leadership. Edward I died, old and worn out, in 1307, when on his way north to put down a rising under Bruce, and left the task of dealing with the Scotch to his incompetent son, Edward II. The Scotch acknowledged Bruce as their king and decisively

defeated Edward II in the great battle of Bannockburn, the most famous conflict in Scottish history. Nevertheless, the English refused to acknowledge the independence of Scotland until forced to do so in 1328.

In the course of their struggles with England the Scotch people of the Lowlands had become more closely welded together, and the independence of Scotland, although it caused much bloodshed, first and last, served to develop certain permanent differences between the little Scotch nation and the rest of the English race. The peculiarities of the people north of the Tweed have been made familiar by the writings of gifted Scotchmen like Burns, Scott, and Stevenson.

Edward II's numerous enemies took advantage of his weakness to bring about his downfall, but it is noteworthy that they worked through Parliament and in that way strengthened that fundamental national institution. We have seen how Edward I called representatives of the townspeople, as well as the nobles and prelates, to the Model Parliament of 1295.[1] This important innovation was formally ratified by his son, who solemnly promised that all questions relating to his realm and its people should be settled in parliaments in which the commons should be included. Thereafter no statute could be legally passed without their consent. In 1327 Parliament showed its power by forcing Edward II to abdicate in favor of his son, and thereby established the principle that the representatives of the nation might even go so far as to depose their ruler, should he show himself clearly unfit for his high duties. About this time Parliament began to meet in two distinct divisions, which later became the House of Lords and the House of Commons. In modern times this form of legislative assembly has been imitated by most of the countries of Europe.

Growth of the power of Parliament.

106. The so-called Hundred Years' War, which we must now review, was a long but frequently interrupted series of conflicts between the English and the French kings. It began in the following manner. The king of England, through John's misconduct, had lost Normandy and other portions of the great Plantagenet realm on the continent.[2] He still retained, however, the extensive duchy of Guienne, for which he did homage to the king of France, whose most powerful vassal

Cause of the Hundred Years' War.

---

1 See above, p. 147.
2 See above, pp. 127–128 and 130.

he was. This arrangement was bound to produce constant
difficulty, especially as the French kings were, as we have
discovered, bent upon destroying as fast as possible the
influence of their vassals, so that the royal power should
everywhere take the place of that of the feudal lords. It
was obviously out of the question for the king of England
meekly to permit the French monarch to extend his control
directly over the people of Guienne, and yet this was the
constant aim of Philip the Fair [1] and his successors.

THE FRENCH KINGS DURING THE FOURTEENTH AND
FIFTEENTH CENTURIES

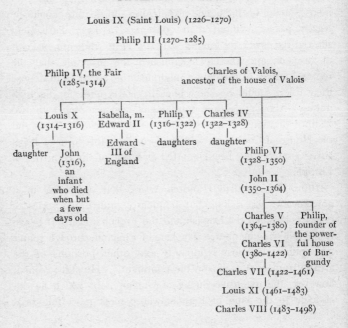

[1] See above, pp. 131–132.

The inevitable struggle between England and France was rendered the more serious by the claim made by Edward III that he was himself the rightful king of France. He based his pretensions upon the fact that his mother Isabella was the daughter of Philip the Fair. Philip, who died in 1314, had been followed by his three sons in succession, none of whom had left a male heir, so that the direct male line of the Capetians was extinguished in 1328. The lawyers thereupon declared that it was a venerable law in France that no woman should succeed to the throne. The principle was also asserted that a woman could not even transmit the crown to her son. Consequently Edward III appeared to be definitely excluded, and Philip VI of Valois, a nephew of Philip the Fair, became king.

The French succession in 1328.

At first Edward III, who was a mere boy in 1328, appeared to recognize the propriety of this settlement and did qualified homage to Philip VI for Guienne. But when it became apparent later that Philip was not only encroaching upon Edward's prerogatives in Guienne but had sent French troops to aid the Scotch, the English king bethought him of his neglected claim to the French crown.

Edward III claims the French crown.

The advantage of publicly declaring himself the rightful king of France was increased by the attitude of the flourishing towns of Flanders. Philip VI had assisted the count of Flanders in a bitter struggle to prevent the towns from establishing their independence. Consequently the Flemish burghers now announced their willingness to desert Philip and acknowledge and aid Edward as their king.

The Flemish towns.

Flanders at this period was the most important trading and manufacturing country in western Europe. Ghent was a great manufacturing town, like Manchester to-day, and Bruges a busy port, like modern Antwerp or Liverpool. All this prosperity was largely dependent upon England, for it was from there that the Flemish manufacturers procured the fine, long wool which they wove on their looms into cloth and spun into

Commercial relations between the Flemish towns and England.

English wool.

yarn. In 1336 the count of Flanders, perhaps at Philip's suggestion, ordered the imprisonment of all the Englishmen in Flanders. Edward promptly retaliated by prohibiting the export of wool from England and the importation of cloth.

Royal Arms of Edward III

At the same time he protected and encouraged the Flemish artisans who had emigrated across the Channel and were carrying on their industry in the county of Norfolk.

It is clear, then, that the Flemish burghers had good reason for wishing Edward to become their king, so that their relations with England might not be broken off. They did their part in inducing him to undertake the conquest of France, and (in 1340) we find him adding the *fleur de lis* of France to the lions of the English royal arms.

Edward III invades France, 1346. Edward did not invade France for some years, but his sailors destroyed the French fleet and began to show themselves able to maintain their king's claim to be lord of the English seas upon every side. In 1346 Edward himself landed in Normandy, devastated the country, and marched up the Seine almost to Paris, but was then obliged to retreat northward before a large army which Philip had collected. Edward

The English victory at the battle of Crécy, 1346. made a halt at Crécy, and here one of the most celebrated battles of history took place. It taught the world a great lesson in warfare by proving once more, as the battle of Bannockburn had already done, that foot soldiers, properly armed and trained to act in concert, could defeat the feudal cavaliers in spite of their lances and heavy armor. The proud mounted knights of France performed prodigies of valor, each for himself, but they did not act together and could not hold their ground against the deadly shower of arrows poured into their midst from the long bows of the English archers. The flower of French chivalry was routed with terrible slaughter by the serried ranks of the humble English foot soldiers.[1] It was at Crécy that Edward's son, the Black Prince, — so named from his black armor, — won his spurs.[2]

After this great victory the English king proceeded to lay siege to Calais, the French coast town nearest England. This he took, drove out a great part of the inhabitants, and substituted Englishmen for them. The town remained subject to England for two centuries. When the war was renewed the Black Prince, now at the height of his fame, was able to deal the enemy a still more crushing blow than at Crécy. He again put the French knights to flight in the battle of Poitiers; he even captured the French king, John, and carried him off to London.

The English take Calais.

The Black Prince wins a second great victory at Poitiers, 1356.

107. The French quite properly attributed the signal disasters of Crécy and Poitiers to the inefficiency of their king and his advisers. Accordingly, after the second defeat, the Estates General, which had been summoned to approve the raising of more money, attempted to take matters into their own hands. The representatives of the towns, whom Philip the Fair had first called in,[3] were on this occasion more numerous than the members of the clergy and nobility. A great list of reforms was drawn up, which provided, among other things, that the Estates should meet regularly whether summoned by

The Estates General attempt to control the king and reform the government.

---

[1] Formerly it was supposed that gunpowder helped to decide the battle in favor of the English, but if siege guns, which were already beginning to be used, were employed at all they were too crude and the charges too light to do much damage. For some generations to come the bow and arrow held its own; it was not until the sixteenth century that gunpowder came to be commonly and effectively used in battles.

[2] For the account of Crécy by Froissart, the celebrated historian of the fourteenth century, see *Readings*, Chapter XX.

[3] See above, pp. 131–132.

the king or not, and that the collection and expenditure of the public revenue should be no longer entirely under the control of the king but should be supervised by the representatives of the people. The city of Paris rose in support of the revolutionary Estates, but the violence of its allies discredited rather than helped the movement, and France was soon glad to accept the unrestricted rule of its king once more.[1]

Contrast between the position of the Estates General and the English Parliament.

This unsuccessful attempt to reform the French government is interesting in two ways. In the first place, there was much in the aims of the reformers and in the conduct of the Paris mob that suggests the great successful French revolution of 1789, which at last fundamentally modified the organization of the state. In the second place, the history of the Estates forms a curious contrast to that of the English Parliament, which was laying the foundation of its later power during this very period. While the French king occasionally summoned the Estates when he needed money, he did so only in order that their approbation of new taxes might make it easier to collect them. He never admitted that he had not the right to levy taxes if he wished without consulting his subjects. In England, on the other hand, the kings ever since the time of Edward I had repeatedly agreed that no new taxes should be imposed without the consent of Parliament. Edward II had gone farther and accepted the representatives of the people as his advisers in all important matters touching the welfare of the realm. While the French Estates gradually sank into insignificance, the English Parliament soon learned to grant no money until the king had redressed the grievances which it pointed out, and thus it insured its influence over the king's policy.

Treaty of Bretigny, 1360.

Edward III found it impossible to conquer France in spite of the victories of the Black Prince and the capture of John. He was glad in 1360 to sign the treaty of Bretigny, in which he not only renounced his pretensions to the French crown

[1] Reference, Adams, *Growth of the French Nation*, pp 116-123.

but agreed to say no more of the old claims of his family to Normandy and the Plantagenet provinces north of the Loire. In return for these concessions he received, in full sovereignty and without any feudal obligations to the king of France, Poitou, Guienne, Gascony, and the town of Calais, amounting to about one third of the territory of France.

French Territory ceded to England by the Treaty of Bretigny, 1360

The promising peace of Bretigny was however soon broken. The Black Prince, to whom the government of Guienne was delegated by his father, levied such heavy taxes that he quickly alienated the hearts of a people naturally drawn to France rather than to England. When the sagacious Charles V of France (1364–1380) undertook to reconquer the territory which his father had ceded to England, he met with no

England loses most of its French territory before the death of Edward III, 1377.

determined opposition; Edward III was getting old and his warlike son, the Black Prince, had fallen mortally ill. So when Edward died in 1377 nothing remained to the English king except Calais and a strip of land from Bordeaux southward.

Miserable condition of France.

For a generation after the death of Edward III the war with France was almost discontinued. France had suffered a great deal more than England. In the first place, all the fighting had been done on her side of the Channel, and in the second place, the soldiers who found themselves without occupation after the treaty of Bretigny had wandered about in bands maltreating and plundering the people. Petrarch, who visited France at this period, tells us that he could not believe that this was the same kingdom which he had once seen so rich and flourishing. "Nothing presented itself to my eyes but fearful solitude and extreme poverty, uncultivated land and houses in ruins. Even about Paris there were everywhere signs of fire and destruction. The streets were deserted; the roads overgrown with weeds."

The bubonic plague of 1348-1349, commonly called the 'black death.'

The horrors of war had been increased by the deadly bubonic plague which appeared in Europe early in 1348. In April it had reached Florence; by August it was devastating France and Germany; it then spread over England from the southwest northward, attacking every part of the country during the year 1349. This disease, like other terrible epidemics, such as smallpox and cholera, came from Asia. Those who were stricken with it usually died in two or three days. It is impossible to tell what proportion of the population perished. Reports of the time say that in one part of France but one tenth of the people survived, in another but one sixteenth; and that for a long time five hundred bodies were carried from the great hospital of Paris every day. A careful estimate shows that in England toward one half of the population died. At the Abbey of Newenham only the abbot and two monks were left alive out of twenty-six. There were constant complaints that certain lands were no longer of any value to their lords because the tenants were all dead.

108. In England the growing discontent among the agricultural classes may be ascribed partly to the results of the great pestilence and partly to the new taxes which were levied in order to prolong the disastrous war with France. Up to this time the majority of those who cultivated the land belonged to some particular manor, paid stated dues to their lord, and performed definite services for him. Hitherto there had been relatively few farm hands who might be hired and who sought employment anywhere that they could get it. The black death, by greatly decreasing the number of laborers, raised wages and served to increase the importance of the unattached laborer. Consequently he not only demanded higher wages than ever before, but readily deserted one employer when another offered him more money.

Conditions of English labor.

This appeared very shocking to those who were accustomed to the traditional rates of payment ; and the government undertook to keep down wages by prohibiting laborers from asking more than had been customary during the years that preceded the pestilence. Every laborer, when offered work at the established wages, was ordered to accept it on pain of imprisonment. The first "Statute of Laborers"[1] was issued in 1351 ; but apparently it was not obeyed and similar laws were enacted from time to time for a century. Nevertheless complaints continued that serfs and laborers persisted in demanding "outrageous and excessive hire." This seems to indicate that the efforts of Parliament to interfere with the law of supply and demand were unsuccessful.

The Statutes of Laborers issued in 1351 and following years.

The old manor system was breaking up. Many of the laboring class in the country no longer held land as serfs but moved

Breaking up of the mediæval manors in England.

---

[1] For an example of the Statutes of Laborers, see *Translations and Reprints*, Vol. II, No. 5, and Lee, *Source-book of English History*, pp. 206–208.

from place to place and made a living by working for wages. The *villain*, as the serf was called in England, began to regard the dues which he had been accustomed to pay to his lord as unjust. A petition to Parliament in 1377 asserts that the villains are refusing to pay their customary services to their lords or to acknowledge the obligations which they owe as serfs.

Causes of discontent among the English peasants.

'The Vision of Piers Ploughman.'

The discontent was becoming general. We see it reflected in a remarkable poem of the time, "The Vision of Piers Ploughman," in which the unfortunate position of the peasant is vividly portrayed.[1] This is only the most notable example of a great number of pamphlets, some in prose and some in bad verse, which were calculated to make the people more discontented than ever. The efforts to enforce the provisions of the Statutes of Laborers had undoubtedly produced much friction between the landlords and their employees. A new form of taxation also caused much irritation. A general poll tax, which was to be paid by every one above sixteen years of age, was established in 1379 and another one in the following year to meet the expenses of the hopeless French war which was now being conducted by incapable and highly unpopular ministers.

The peasant revolt of 1381.

In 1381 rioting began among the peasants in Kent and Essex, and several bodies of the insurgents determined to march upon London. As they passed along the road their ranks were swelled by discontented villagers and by many of the poorer workingmen from the towns. Soon the revolt spread all through southern and eastern England. The peasants burned some of the houses of the gentry and of the rich ecclesiastics, and took particular pains to see that the lists for the collection of the hated poll tax were destroyed, as well as the registers kept by the various lords enumerating the obligations of their serfs. The gates of London were opened to the insurgents by sympathizers within the walls, and several of the king's

[1] For extracts, see *Readings*, Chapter XX.

officers were seized and put to death. Some of the simple people imagined that they might induce the boy king, Richard II, to become their leader. He had no idea of aiding them; he went out, however, to meet them and induced them to disperse by promising that he would abolish serfdom.

Although the king did not keep his promise, serfdom decayed rapidly. It became more and more common for the serf to pay his dues to the lord in money instead of working for him, and in this way he lost one of the chief characteristics of a serf. The landlord then either hired men to cultivate the fields which he reserved for his own use [1] or rented the land to tenants. These tenants were not in a position to force their fellow-tenants on the manor to pay the full dues which had formerly been exacted by the lord. Sixty or seventy years after the Peasants' War the English rural population had in one way or another become free men, and serfs had practically disappeared.

Final disappearance of serfdom in England.

109. The war with France had, as we have seen, almost ceased for a generation after the death of Edward III. The young son of the Black Prince, Richard II, who succeeded his grandfather on the throne, was controlled by the great noblemen whose rivalries fill much space in the annals of England. He was finally forced to abdicate in 1399. Henry IV, of the powerful house of Lancaster,[2] was recognized as king in spite of the fact that he had less claim than another descendant of Edward III, who was, however, a mere boy. Henry IV's uncertain title may have made him less enterprising than Edward III; at any rate, it was left for his son, Henry V (1413–1422), to continue the French war. The conditions in France were such as to encourage the new claim which Henry V made to the French crown in 1414.

Deposition of Richard II and accession of Henry IV of Lancaster, 1399–1413.

Henry V claims the French crown, 1414.

---

1 See description of manor, see above, pp. 234–235.
2 For this younger line of the descendants of Edward I, see genealogical table below, p. 297.

Civil war
in France
between the
houses of
Burgundy
and Orleans.

The able French king, Charles V, who had delivered his country for a time from the English invaders,[1] had been followed in 1380 by Charles VI, who soon lost his mind. The right to govern France consequently became a matter of dispute among the insane king's uncles and other relations. The country was divided between two great factions, one of which was headed by the powerful duke of Burgundy, who was building up a new state between France and Germany, and the other by the duke of Orleans. In 1407 the duke of Orleans was brutally murdered by order of the duke of Burgundy, — a by no means uncommon way at that time of disposing of one's enemies in both France and England. This led to a prolonged civil war between the two parties, and saved England from an attack which the duke of Orleans had been planning.

Position of
Henry V.

Henry V had no real basis for his claim to the French crown. Edward III had gone to war because France was encroaching upon Guienne and aiding Scotland, and because he was encouraged by the Flemish towns. Henry V, on the other hand, was merely anxious to make himself and his house popular by deeds of valor. Nevertheless his very first victory, the battle of Agincourt, was as brilliant as that of Crécy or Poitiers. Once more the English bowmen slaughtered great numbers of French knights. The English then proceeded to conquer Normandy and march upon Paris.

Agincourt,
1415.

Treaty of
Troyes,
1420.

Burgundians and Orleanists were upon the point of forgetting their animosities in their common fear of the English, when the duke of Burgundy, as he was kneeling to kiss the hand of his future sovereign, the Dauphin,[2] was treacherously attacked and killed by a band of his enemies. His son, the new duke of Burgundy, Philip the Good, immediately joined

---

[1] See above, p. 287.

[2] The title of Dauphin, originally belonging to the ruler of Dauphiny, was enjoyed by the eldest son of the French king after Dauphiny became a part of France in 1349, in the same way that the eldest son of the English king was called Prince of Wales.

the English against the Dauphin, whom he believed to be responsible for his father's murder. Henry then forced the French to sign the treaty of Troyes (1420), which provided that he was to become king of France upon the death of the mad Charles VI.

Both Henry V and Charles VI died two years later. Henry V's son, Henry VI, was but nine months old; nevertheless according to the terms of the treaty of Troyes he succeeded to the throne in France as well as in England. The child was recognized only in a portion of northern France. Through the ability of his uncle, the duke of Bedford, his interests were defended with such good effect that the English succeeded in a few years in conquering all of France north of the Loire, although the south continued to be held by Charles VII, the son of Charles VI. *Henry VI recognized as king in northern France.*

Charles VII had not yet been crowned and so was still called the Dauphin even by his supporters. Weak and indolent, he did nothing to stem the tide of English victories or restore the courage and arouse the patriotism of his distressed subjects. This great task was reserved for a young peasant girl from a remote village on the eastern border of France. To her family and her companions Joan of Arc seemed only "a good girl, simple and pleasant in her ways," but she brooded much over the disasters that had overtaken her country, and a "great pity on the fair realm of France" filled her heart. She saw visions and heard voices that bade her go forth to the help of the king and lead him to Rheims to be crowned. *Joan of Arc.*

It was with the greatest difficulty that she got anybody to believe in her mission or to help her to get an audience with the Dauphin. But her own firm faith in her divine guidance triumphed over all doubts and obstacles. She was at last accepted as a God-sent champion and placed at the head of some troops despatched to the relief of Orleans. This city, which was the key to southern France, had been besieged by *Relief of Orleans by Joan, 1429.*

the English for some months and was on the point of surrender. Joan, who rode on horseback at the head of her
troops, clothed in armor like a man, had now become the
idol of the soldiers and of the people. Under the guidance
and inspiration of her indomitable courage, sound sense, and
burning enthusiasm, Orleans was relieved and the English

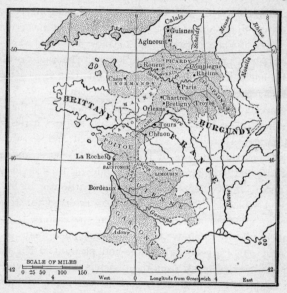

Possessions of the English King in France upon the Accession
of Henry VI, 1424

completely routed. The Maid of Orleans, as she was henceforth called, was now free to conduct the Dauphin to Rheims,
where he was crowned in the cathedral (July 17, 1429).

The Maid now felt that her mission was accomplished and
begged permission to return to her home and her brothers
and sisters. To this the king would not consent, and she
continued to fight his battles with undiminished loyalty. But

the other leaders were jealous of her, and even her friends, the soldiers, were sensitive to the taunt of being led by a woman. During the defense of Compiègne in May, 1430, she was allowed to fall into the hands of the duke of Burgundy, who sold her to the English. They were not satisfied with simply holding as prisoner that strange maiden who had so discomfited them; they wished to discredit everything that she had done, and so declared, and undoubtedly believed, that she was a witch who had been helped by the Evil One. She was tried by a court of ecclesiastics, found guilty of heresy, and burned at Rouen in 1431. Her bravery and noble constancy affected even her executioners, and an English soldier who had come to triumph over her death was heard to exclaim: " We are lost — we have burned a saint." The English cause in France was indeed lost, for her spirit and example had given new courage and vigor to the French armies.[1]

Execution of Joan, 1431.

The English Parliament became more and more reluctant to grant funds when there were no more victories gained. Bedford, through whose ability the English cause had hitherto been maintained, died in 1435, and Philip the Good, Duke of Burgundy, renounced his alliance with the English and joined Charles VII. Owing to his acquisition of the Netherlands, the possessions of Philip were now so great that he might well be regarded as a European potentate whose alliance with France rendered further efforts on England's part hopeless. From this time on the English lost ground steadily. They were expelled from Normandy in 1450. Three years later, the last vestige of their long domination in southern France passed into the hands of the French king. The Hundred Years' War was over, and although England still retained Calais, the great question whether she should extend her sway upon the continent was finally settled.

England loses her French possessions.

End of the Hundred Years' War, 1453.

[1] Reference, Green, *Short History*, pp. 274–281. For official account of the trial of Joan, see Colby, *Sources*, pp. 113–117.

The Wars of
the Roses
between the
houses of
Lancaster
and York,
1455-1485.

110. The close of the Hundred Years' War was followed in England by the Wars of the Roses, between the rival houses which were struggling for the crown. The badge of the house of Lancaster, to which Henry VI belonged, was a red rose, and that of the duke of York, who proposed to push him off his throne, was a white one. Each party was supported by a group of the wealthy and powerful nobles whose rivalries, conspiracies, treasons, murders, and executions fill the annals of England during the period which we have been discussing. Vast estates had come into the hands of the higher nobility by inheritance, and marriages with wealthy heiresses. Many of the dukes and earls were related to the royal family and consequently were inevitably drawn into the dynastic struggles.

The nobles no longer owed their power to vassals who were bound to follow them to war. Like the king, they relied upon hired soldiers. It was easy to find plenty of restless fellows who were willing to become the retainers of a nobleman if he would agree to clothe them with his livery and keep open house, where they might eat and drink their fill. Their master was to help them when they got into trouble, and they on their part were expected to intimidate, misuse, and even murder at need those who opposed the interests of their chief. When the French war was over, the unruly elements of society poured back across the Channel and, as retainers of the rival lords, became the terror of the country. They bullied judges and juries, and helped the nobles to control the selection of those who were sent to Parliament.

It is needless to speak of the several battles and the many skirmishes of the miserable Wars of the Roses. These lasted from 1455, when the duke of York set seriously to work to displace the weak-minded Lancastrian king, Henry VI, until the accession of Henry VII, of the house of Tudor, thirty years later. After several battles the Yorkist leader, Edward IV, assumed the crown in 1461 and was recognized by Parliament, which declared Henry VI and the two preceding Lancastrian kings usurpers.[1] Edward was a vigorous monarch and maintained his own until his death in 1483.

Edward's son, Edward V, was only a little boy, so that the government fell into the hands of the young king's uncle, Richard, Duke of Gloucester. The temptation to make himself king was too great to be resisted, and Richard soon seized the crown. Both the sons of Edward IV were killed in the Tower of London, and with the knowledge of their uncle, as it was commonly believed. This murder made Richard unpopular even at a time when one could kill one's political rivals without incurring general opprobrium. A new aspirant to the throne organized a conspiracy. Richard III was defeated and slain in the battle of Bosworth Field in 1485, and the crown which had fallen from his head was placed upon that of the first Tudor king, Henry VII. The latter had no particular right to it, although he was descended from Edward III through his mother. He hastened to procure the recognition of

Edward V, 1483; Richard III, 1483-1485.

Death of Richard in the battle of Bosworth Field. Accession of Henry VII of the house of Tudor, 1485.

[1] DESCENT OF THE RIVAL HOUSES OF LANCASTER AND YORK

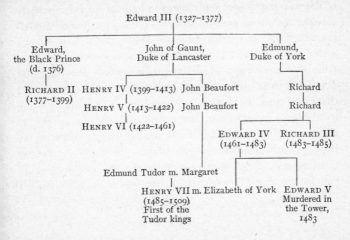

End of the
Wars of the
Roses.

Parliament, and married Edward IV's daughter, thus blending
the red and white roses in the Tudor badge.[1]

The Wars of the Roses had important results. Nearly all
the powerful families of England had been drawn into the
fierce struggles, and a great part of the nobility, whom the
kings had formerly feared, had perished on the battlefield or
lost their heads in the ruthless executions carried out by each
party after it gained a victory. This left the king far more
powerful than ever before. He could now dominate Parliament, if he could not dispense with it. For a century and more
the Tudor kings enjoyed almost despotic power. England
ceased for a time to enjoy the free government for which
the foundations had been laid under the Edwards and the
Lancastrian kings, whose embarrassments at home and abroad
had made them constantly dependent upon the aid of the
nation.[2]

III. In France the closing years of the Hundred Years' War
had witnessed a great increase of the king's power through the
establishment of a well-organized standing army. The feudal
army had long since disappeared. Even before the opening
of the war the nobles had begun to be paid for their military
services and no longer furnished troops as a condition of holding fiefs. But the companies of soldiers, although nominally
under the command of royal officers, were often really independent of the king. They found their pay very uncertain, and
plundered their countrymen as well as the enemy. As the war
drew to a close, the lawless troopers became a terrible scourge
to the country and were known as *flayers*, on account of
the horrible way in which they tortured the peasants in the
hope of extracting money from them. In 1439 the Estates
General approved a plan devised by the king, for putting an
end to this evil. Thereafter no one was to raise a company

[1] References, Green, *Short History*, pp. 281–293, 299–303.
[2] See *Readings*, Chapter XX.

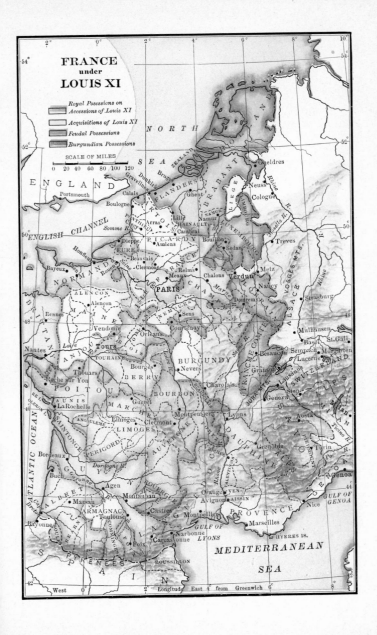

FRANCE
under
LOUIS XI

Royal Possessions on
Accessions of Louis XI
Acquisitions of Louis XI
Feudal Possessions
Burgundian Possessions

SCALE OF MILES
0 20 40 60 80 100 120

without the permission of the king, who was to name the captains and fix the number of the soldiers and the character of their arms.[1]

The Estates agreed that the king should use a certain tax, called the *taille*, to support the troops necessary for the protection of the frontier. This was a fatal concession, for the king now had an army and the right to collect what he chose to consider a permanent tax, the amount of which he later greatly increased; he was not dependent, as was the English king, upon the grants made for brief periods by the representatives of the nation.

The permanent tax fatal to the powers of the Estates General.

Before the king of France could hope to establish a compact, well-organized state it was necessary for him to reduce the power of his vassals, some of whom were almost his equals in strength. The older feudal dynasties, as we have seen, had many of them succumbed to the attacks and the diplomacy of the kings of the thirteenth century, especially of St. Louis. But he and his successors had raised up fresh rivals by granting whole provinces, called *appanages*,[2] to their younger sons. In this way new and powerful lines of feudal nobles were established, such, for example, as the houses of Orleans, Anjou, Bourbon, and, above all, of Burgundy. The accompanying map shows the region immediately subject to the king — the royal domain — at the time of the expulsion of the English. It clearly indicates what still remained to be done in order to free France from feudalism and make it a great nation. The process of reducing the prerogatives of the nobles had been begun. They had been forbidden to coin money, to maintain armies, and to tax their subjects, and the powers of the king's judges had been extended over all the realm. But the task of consolidating France was reserved for the son of Charles VII, the shrewd and treacherous Louis XI (1461–1483).

The new feudalism.

[1] Reference, Adams, *Growth of the French Nation*, pp. 121–123, 134–135.
[2] See above, p. 128.

Extent of the
Burgundian
possessions
in the
fifteenth
century.

By far the most dangerous of Louis' vassals were Philip the Good, Duke of Burgundy (1419–1467), and his impetuous son, Charles the Bold (1467–1477). Just a century before Louis XI came to the throne, the old line of Burgundian dukes had died out, and in 1363 the same King John whom the English captured and carried off to

Louis XI

England, presented Burgundy to his younger son Philip.[1] By fortunate marriages and lucky windfalls the dukes of Burgundy had added a number of important fiefs to their original possessions, and Philip the Good ruled over Franche-Comté, Luxembourg, Flanders, Artois, Brabant, and other provinces and towns which lie in what is now Holland and Belgium.

Ambition of
Charles the
Bold, 1467-
1477.

Charles the Bold busied himself for some years before his father's death in forming alliances with the other powerful French vassals and conspiring against Louis. Upon becoming duke himself he set his heart upon two things. He resolved, first, to conquer Lorraine, which divided his territories into two parts and made it difficult to pass from Franche-Comté to Luxembourg. In the second place, he proposed to have himself crowned king of the territories which his forefathers had accumulated and in this way establish a strong new state between France and Germany.

Charles
defeated by
the Swiss at
Granson and
Murten,
1476.

Naturally neither the king of France nor the emperor sympathized with Charles' ambitions. Louis taxed his exceptional ingenuity in frustrating his aspiring vassal; and the emperor refused to crown Charles as king when he appeared at Trier

[1] See geneological table above, p. 282.

BRONZE STATUES OF PHILIP THE GOOD AND CHARLES THE BOLD.
AT INNSBRUCK

eager for the ceremony. The most humiliating, however, of the defeats which Charles encountered came from an unexpected quarter. He attempted to chastise his neighbors the Swiss for siding with his enemies and was soundly beaten by that brave people in two memorable battles.

The next year Charles fell ingloriously in an attempt to take the town of Nancy. His lands went to his daughter Mary, who was immediately married to the emperor's son, Maximilian, much to the disgust of Louis, who had already seized the duchy of Burgundy and hoped to gain still more. The great importance of this marriage, which resulted in bringing the Netherlands into the hands of Austria, will be seen when we come to consider Charles V (the grandson of Mary and Maximilian) and his vast empire.[1]

Death of Charles, 1477.

Marriage of Mary of Burgundy to Maximilian of Austria.

Louis XI did far more for the French monarchy than check his chief vassal and reclaim a part of the Burgundian territory. He had himself made heir to a number of provinces in central and southern France, — Anjou, Maine, Provence, etc., — which by the death of their possessors came under the king's immediate control (1481). He humiliated in various ways the vassals who in his early days had combined with Charles the Bold against him. The duke of Alençon he imprisoned; the rebellious duke of Nemours he caused to be executed in the most cruel manner. Louis' political aims were worthy, but his means were generally despicable. It sometimes seemed as if he gloried in being the most rascally among rascals, the most treacherous among the traitors whom he so artfully circumvented in the interests of the French monarchy.[2]

Work of Louis XI.

Both England and France emerged from the troubles and desolations of the Hundred Years' War stronger than ever before. In both countries the kings had overcome the menace of feudalism by destroying the power of the great families.

England and France establish strong national governments.

---

[1] See below, Chapter XXIII.
[2] Reference, Adams, *French Nation*, pp. 136–142.

The royal government was becoming constantly more powerful. Commerce and industry increased the national wealth and supplied the monarchs with the revenue necessary to maintain government officials and a sufficient armed force to execute the laws and keep order throughout their realms. They were no longer forced to rely upon the uncertain pledges of their vassals. In short, the French and the English were both becoming nations, each with a strong national feeling and a king whom every one, both high and low, recognized and obeyed as the head of the government.

Influence of the development of modern states upon the position of the mediæval Church. It is obvious that the strengthening of the royal power could hardly fail to alter the position of the mediæval Church. This was, as we have seen, not simply a religious institution but a sort of international state which performed a number of important governmental duties. We must, therefore, now turn back and review the history of the Church from the time of Edward I and Philip the Fair to the opening of the sixteenth century.

General Reading. — For the political history of this period, LODGE, *Close of the Middle Ages* (The Macmillan Company, $1.75), is the best work, although rather dry and cumbered with names which might have been omitted. For the general history of France, see in addition to ADAMS, *Growth of the French Nation* (The Macmillan Company, $1.25), DURUY, *A History of France* (T. Y. Crowell, $2.00). The economic history of England is to be found in the works mentioned at the end of Chapter XVIII. The following collections of documents furnish illustrative material in abundance: LEE, *Source-book of English History* (Holt, $2.00); COLBY, *Selections from the Sources of English History*, (Longmans, Green & Co., $1.50); ADAMS & STEPHENS, *Select Documents of English Constitutional History* (The Macmillan Company, $2.25); KENDALL, *Source Book of English History* (The Macmillan Company, 80 cents).

CHAPTER XXI

THE POPES AND THE COUNCILS

112. The influence which the Church and its head exercised over the civil government in the Middle Ages was due largely to the absence of strong, efficient rulers who could count upon the support of a large body of prosperous and loyal subjects. So long as the feudal anarchy continued, the Church endeavored to supply the deficiencies of the restless and ignorant princes by striving to maintain order, administer justice, protect the weak, and encourage learning. So soon, however, as the modern state began to develop, difficulties arose. The clergy naturally clung to the powers and privileges which they had long enjoyed, and which they believed to be rightly theirs. On the other hand, the state, so soon as it felt itself able to manage its own affairs, protect its subjects, and provide for their worldly interests, was less and less inclined to tolerate the interference of the clergy and their head, the pope. Educated laymen were becoming more and more common, and the king was no longer obliged to rely upon the assistance of the clergy in conducting his government. It was natural that he should look with disfavor upon their privileges, which put them upon a different footing from the great mass of his subjects, and upon their wealth, which he would deem excessive and dangerous to his power. This situation raised the fundamental problem of the proper relation of church and state, upon which Europe has been working ever since the fourteenth century and has not completely solved yet.

Edward I and
Philip the
Fair attempt
to tax the
clergy.

The difficulty which the Church experienced in maintaining its power against the kings is excellently shown by the famous struggle between Philip the Fair, the grandson of St. Louis, and Boniface VIII, an old man of boundless ambition and inexhaustible energy who came to the papal throne in 1294. The first serious trouble arose over the habit into which the kings of England and France had fallen, of taxing the property of the churchmen like that of other subjects. It was natural after a monarch had squeezed all that he could out of the Jews and the towns, and had exacted every possible feudal due, that he should turn to the rich estates of the clergy, in spite of their claim that their property was dedicated to God and owed the king nothing. The extensive enterprises of Edward I led him in 1296 to demand one fifth of the personal property of the clergy. Philip the Fair exacted one hundredth and then one fiftieth of the possessions of clergy and laity alike.

The bull
Clericis laicos
of Boniface
VIII, 1296.

Against this impartial system Boniface protested in the famous bull *Clericis laicos* (1296). He claimed that the laity had always been exceedingly hostile to the clergy, and that the rulers were now exhibiting this hostility by imposing heavy burdens upon the Church, forgetting that they had no control over the clergy and their possessions. The pope, therefore, forbade all churchmen, including the monks, to pay, without his consent, to a king or ruler any part of the Church's revenue or possessions upon any pretext whatsoever. He likewise forbade the kings and princes under pain of excommunication to presume to exact any such payments.

Boniface
concedes a
limited right
to tax
churchmen.

It happened that just as the pope was prohibiting the clergy from contributing to the taxes, Philip the Fair had forbidden the exportation of all gold and silver from the country. In that way he cut off an important source of the pope's revenue, for the church of France could obviously no longer send anything to Rome. The pope was forced to give up his extreme claims. He explained the following year that he had not meant to interfere with the payment on the clergy's part of customary feudal dues nor with their loans of money to the king.[1]

In spite of this setback, the pope never seemed more completely the recognized head of the western world than during the first great jubilee, in the year 1300, when Boniface called together all Christendom to celebrate the opening of the new century by a great religious festival at Rome. It is reported that two millions of people, coming from all parts of Europe, visited the churches of Rome, and that in spite of widening the streets many were crushed in the crowd. So great was the influx of money into the papal treasury that two assistants were kept busy with rakes collecting the offerings which were deposited at the tomb of St. Peter.

The jubilee of 1300.

Boniface was, however, very soon to realize that even if Christendom regarded Rome as its religious center, the nations would not accept him as their political head. When he dispatched an obnoxious prelate to Philip the Fair, ordering him to free the count of Flanders whom he was holding prisoner, the king declared the harsh language of the papal envoy to be high treason and sent one of his lawyers to the pope to demand that the messenger be degraded and punished.

Philip was surrounded by a body of lawyers, and it would seem that they, rather than the king, were the real rulers of France. They had, through their study of Roman law, learned to admire the absolute power exercised by the Roman emperor. To them the civil government was supreme, and they urged the king to punish what they regarded as the insolent conduct of the pope. Before taking any action against the head of the Church, Philip called together the representatives of his people, including not only the clergy and the nobility but the people of the towns as well. The

The Estates General of 1302.

[1] See *Readings*, Chapter XXI.

Estates General, after hearing a statement of the case from one of Philip's lawyers, agreed to support their monarch.

Nogaret insults Boniface VIII.

Nogaret, one of the chief legal advisers of the king, undertook to face the pope. He collected a little troop of soldiers in Italy and marched against Boniface, who was sojourning at Anagni, where his predecessors had excommunicated two emperors, Frederick Barbarossa and Frederick II. As Boniface, in his turn, was preparing solemnly to proclaim the king of France an outcast from the Church, Nogaret penetrated into the papal palace with his soldiers and heaped insults upon the helpless but defiant old man. The townspeople forced Nogaret to leave the next day, but Boniface's spirit was broken and he soon died at Rome.

Death of Boniface, 1303.

Clement V, 1305-1314, and his subservience to Philip the Fair.

King Philip now proposed to have no more trouble with popes. He arranged in 1305 to have the Archbishop of Bordeaux chosen head of the Church, with the understanding that he should transfer the papacy to France. The new pope accordingly summoned the cardinals to meet him at Lyons, where he was crowned under the title of Clement V. He remained in France during his whole pontificate, moving from one rich abbey to another. At Philip's command he reluctantly undertook a sort of trial of the deceased Boniface VIII, who was accused by the king's lawyers of all sorts of abominable crimes. A great part of Boniface's decrees were revoked, and those who had attacked him were exculpated. Then, to please the king, Clement brought the Templars to trial; the order was abolished and its possessions in France, for which the king had longed, were confiscated. Obviously it proved very advantageous to the king to have a pope within his realm. Clement V died in 1314. His successors took up their residence in the town of Avignon, just outside the French frontier of those days. There they built a sumptuous palace in which successive popes lived in great splendor for sixty years.

The popes take up their residence at Avignon.

113. The prolonged exile of the popes from Rome, lasting from 1305 to 1377, is commonly called the Babylonian Captivity[1] of the Church, on account of the woes attributed to it. The popes of this period were for the most part good and earnest men ; but they were all Frenchmen, and the proximity of their court to France led to the natural suspicion that they were controlled by the French kings. This, together with their luxurious court, brought them into discredit with the other nations.[2]

The Babylonian Captivity of the Church.

At Avignon the popes were naturally deprived of some of the revenue which they had enjoyed from their Italian possessions when they lived at Rome. This deficiency had to be made up by increased taxation, especially as the expenses of the splendid papal court were very heavy. The papacy was, consequently, rendered still more unpopular by the methods employed to raise money, particularly by the granting of benefices throughout Europe to the pope's courtiers, by the heavy contributions which were demanded for dispensations, for the confirmation of bishops, and for granting the pallium to archbishops, as well as the high fees for the trial of law suits.

The papal taxation.

Many of the church offices, such as those of the bishops and abbots, insured a more than ample revenue to their holders. It was natural, therefore, that the pope, in his endeavor to increase his income, should have tried to bring as many of these appointments as he could into his own hands. He did this by reserving to himself the filling of certain benefices so soon as they should become vacant. He then chose some one to whom he wished to do a favor and promised him the benefice upon the death of the one then holding it. Men appointed in this way were called *provisors* and were extremely unpopular. They were very often foreigners, and it was suspected that they had obtained these positions from the pope simply

Pope's control of church benefices.

---

[1] The name recalled of course the long exile of the Jews from their land.
[2] See *Readings*, Chapter XXI.

for the sake of the revenue, and had no intention whatever of performing the duties connected with them.

Statute of provisors, 1352.

The papal exactions met with the greatest opposition in England because the popes were thought to favor France, with which country the English were at war. A law was passed by Parliament in 1352 ordering that all who procured appointments from the pope should be outlawed, that any one might injure such offenders at will, and that the injured should have no redress, since they were enemies of the king and his realm.[1] This and similar laws failed, however, to prevent the pope from filling English benefices to the advantage of himself and his courtiers. The English king was unable to keep the money of his realm from flowing to Avignon on one pretext or another. It was declared by the Good Parliament, held in 1376, that the taxes levied by the pope in England were five times those raised by the king.

John Wycliffe.

The most famous and conspicuous critic of the pope and of the policy of the Roman Church at this time was John Wycliffe, a teacher at Oxford. He was born about 1320 ; but we know little of him before 1366, when Urban V demanded that England should pay the tribute promised by King John when he became the pope's vassal.[2] Parliament declared that John had no right to bind the people without their consent, and Wycliffe began his career of opposition to the papacy by trying to prove that John's compact was void. About ten years later we find the pope issuing bulls against the teachings of Wycliffe, who had begun to assert that the state might appropriate the property of the Church if it was misused, and that the pope had no authority except as he acted according to the Gospels. Soon Wycliffe went further and boldly attacked the papacy itself, as well as indulgences, pilgrimages, and the

[1] For statutes, see *Translations and Reprints*, Vol. II, No. 5, and Lee, *Source-book*, pp. 198–202.

[2] See above, p. 183.

worship of the saints; finally he even denied the truth of the doctrine of transubstantiation.

He did not, however, confine his work to a denunciation of what he considered wrong in the teaching and conduct of the churchmen. He established an order of "simple priests" who were to go about doing good and reprove by their example the worldly habits of the general run of priests and monks.

Wycliffe's 'simple priests.'

Wycliffe's anxiety to reach the people and foster a higher spiritual life among them led him to have the Bible translated into English. He also prepared a great number of sermons and tracts in English. He is the father of English prose, and it has been well said that "the exquisite pathos, the keen, delicate irony, and the manly passion of his short, nervous sentences, fairly overmaster the weakness of the unformed language and give us English which cannot be read without a feeling of its beauty to this hour."

Wycliffe the father of English prose.

Wycliffe and his "simple priests" were charged with fomenting the discontent and disorder which culminated in the Peasants' War. Whether this charge was true or not, it caused many of his more aristocratic followers to fall away from him. But in spite of this and the denunciations of the Church, Wycliffe was not seriously interfered with and died peaceably in 1384. While his followers appear to have yielded pretty readily to the persecution which soon overtook them, his doctrines were spread abroad in Bohemia by another ardent reformer, John Huss, who was destined to give the Church a great deal of trouble. Wycliffe is remarkable as being the first distinguished scholar and reformer to repudiate the headship of the pope and those practices of the Church of Rome which a hundred and fifty years after his death were attacked by Luther in his successful revolt against the mediæval Church.[1]

Influence of Wycliffe's teaching.

[1] Reference, Green, *Short History*, pp. 235-244. For extracts, see *Readings*, Chapter XXI; *Translations and Reprints*, Vol. II, No. 5; Lee, *Source-book*, for the treatment of the Lollards, as the followers of Wycliffe were called, pp. 209-223.

The papal
court moves
back to
Rome, 1377.

114. In 1377 Pope Gregory XI moved back again to Rome after the popes had been exiles for seventy years, during which much had happened to undermine the papal power and supremacy. Yet the discredit into which the papacy had fallen during its stay at Avignon was as nothing compared with the disasters which befell it after the return to Rome.

Election of
Urban VI,
1378.

Gregory died the year after his return and the cardinals assembled to choose his successor. A great part of them were French. They had found Rome in a sad state of ruin and disorder and heartily regretted the gay life and the comforts and luxuries of Avignon. They determined therefore to select a pope who would take them back to the banks of the Rhone. While they were deliberating, the Roman populace was yelling outside the conclave and demanding that a Roman be chosen, or at least an Italian. A simple Italian monk was accordingly selected, Urban VI, who it was supposed would agree to the wishes of the cardinals.

Election of an
anti-pope,
Clement VII.

The new pope, however, soon showed that he had no idea of returning to Avignon. He treated the cardinals with harshness and proposed a stern reformation of their habits. The cardinals speedily wearied of this treatment; they retired to the neighboring Anagni and declared that they had been frightened by the Roman mob into selecting the obnoxious Urban. They then elected a new pope, who took the title of Clement VII, returned to Avignon, and established his court there. Urban, although deserted by his cardinals, had no intention of yielding and proceeded to create twenty-eight new cardinals.

The Great
Schism.

This double election was the beginning of the *Great Schism*, which was to last for forty years and expose the papacy to new attacks on every side. There had been many anti-popes in earlier centuries, set up usually by the emperors; but there had ordinarily been little question as to who was really the legitimate pope. In the present case Europe was seriously in doubt, for it was difficult to decide whether the election of Urban had really been forced and was consequently invalid as the cardinals claimed. No one, therefore, could be perfectly sure which of the rival popes was the real successor of St. Peter. There were now two colleges of cardinals whose very existence depended upon the exercise of their right of choosing the pope. It was natural that Italy should support Urban VI, while France as naturally obeyed Clement VII; England, hostile to France, accepted Urban; Scotland, hostile to England, supported Clement.

Each of two men, with seemingly equal right, now claimed to be Christ's vicar on earth; each proposed to enjoy to the full the vast prerogatives of the head of Christendom, and each denounced, and attempted to depose, the other. The schism in the headship of the Church naturally extended to the bishoprics and abbeys, and everywhere there were rival prelates, each of whom could claim that he had been duly confirmed by one pope or the other. All this produced an unprecedented scandal in the Church. It emphasized all the abuses among the clergy and gave free rein to those who were inclined to denounce the many evils which had been pointed out by Wycliffe and his followers. The condition was, in fact, intolerable and gave rise to widespread discussion, not only of the means by which the schism might be healed, but of the nature and justification of the papacy itself. The discussion which arose during these forty years of uncertainty did much to prepare the mind of western Europe for the Protestant revolt in the sixteenth century.

The Church divided within itself and the consequences.

The selfish and futile negotiations between the colleges of cardinals and the popes justified the notion that there might perhaps be a power in Christendom superior even to that of the pope. Might not a council, representing all Christendom, and inspired by the Holy Ghost, judge even a pope? Such councils had been held in the East during the later Roman

Idea of the supremacy of a general council.

Empire, beginning with the first general or ecumenical council of Nicæa under Constantine.   They had established the teachings of the Church and had legislated for all Christian people and clergy.[1]

As early as 1381 the University of Paris advocated the summoning of a general council which should adjust the claims of the rival popes and give Christendom once more a single head.   This raised the question whether a council was really superior to the pope or not.   Those who believed that it was, maintained that the Church at large had deputed the election of the pope to the cardinals and that it might, therefore, interfere when the cardinals had brought the papacy into disrepute; that a general assembly of all Christendom, speaking under the inspiration of the Holy Spirit, was a higher authority than even the successor of St. Peter.   Others strenuously denied this.   They claimed that the pope received his authority over the Church immediately from Christ, and that he had always possessed supreme power from the very first, although he had not always exercised it and had permitted the earlier councils a certain freedom.   No council, they urged, could be considered a general one which was called against the will of the pope, because, without the bishop of the Roman or mother church, the council obviously could not lay claim to represent all Christendom.   The defenders of the papal power maintained, moreover, that the pope was the supreme legislator, that he might change or annul the act of any council or of a previous pope, that he might judge others but might not himself be judged by any one.[2]

---

[1] The eighth and last of these eastern councils, which were regarded by the Roman Church as having represented all Christendom, occurred in Constantinople in 869.   In 1123 the first Council of the Lateran assembled, and since that five or six Christian congresses had been convoked in the West.   But these, unlike the earlier ones, were regarded as merely ratifying the wishes of the pope, who completely dominated the assembly and published its decrees in his own name.

[2] See above, pp. 202–203.

After years of discussion and fruitless negotiations between the rival popes and their cardinals, members of both of the colleges decided in 1409 to summon a council at Pisa which should put an end to the schism. While large numbers of churchmen answered the summons and the various monarchs took an active interest in the council, its action was hasty and ill-advised. Gregory XII, the Roman pope, elected in 1406, and Benedict XIII, the Avignon pope, elected in 1394, were solemnly summoned from the doors of the cathedral at Pisa. As they failed to appear they were condemned for contumacy and deposed. A new pope was then elected, and on his death a year later, he was succeeded by the notorious John XXIII, who had been a soldier of fortune in his earlier days. John was selected on account of his supposed military prowess. This was considered essential in order to guard the papal territory against the king of Naples, who had announced his intention of getting possession of Rome. Neither of the deposed popes yielded, and as they each continued to enjoy a certain support, the Council of Pisa, instead of healing the schism, added a third person who claimed to be the supreme ruler of Christendom.[1]

The Council of Pisa, 1409, adds a third rival pope.

[1] THE POPES DURING THE GREAT SCHISM

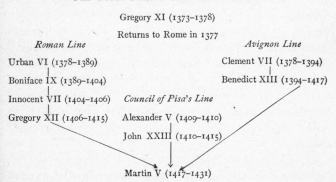

Gregory XI (1373–1378)

Returns to Rome in 1377

Roman Line

Urban VI (1378–1389)

Boniface IX (1389–1404)

Innocent VII (1404–1406)

Gregory XII (1406–1415)

Avignon Line

Clement VII (1378–1394)

Benedict XIII (1394–1417)

Council of Pisa's Line

Alexander V (1409–1410)

John XXIII (1410–1415)

Martin V (1417–1431)

115. The failure of the Council of Pisa made it necessary to summon another congress of Christendom. Through the influence of the emperor Sigismund, John XXIII reluctantly agreed that the council should be held in Germany, in the imperial town of Constance. The Council of Constance, which began to assemble in the fall of 1414, is one of the most noteworthy international assemblies ever held. It lasted for over three years and excited the deepest interest throughout Europe. There were in attendance, besides the pope and the emperor-elect, twenty-three cardinals, thirty-three archbishops and bishops, one hundred and fifty abbots, and one hundred dukes and earls, as well as hundreds of lesser persons.

Three great tasks confronted the council : (1) the healing of the schism, which involved the disposal of the three existing popes and the selection of a single universally acknowledged head of the Church; (2) the extirpation of heresy, which, under the influence of Huss, was threatening the authority of the Church in Bohemia; (3) a general reformation of the Church "in head and members."

1. The healing of the long schism was the most important of the council's achievements. John XXIII was very uncomfortable in Constance. He feared not only that he would be forced to resign but that there might be an investigation of his very dubious past. In March he fled in disguise from Constance, leaving his cardinals behind him. The council was dismayed at the pope's departure, as it feared that he would dissolve it as soon as he was out of its control. It thereupon issued a

famous decree (April 6, 1415) declaring its superiority to the pope. It claimed that a general council had its power immediately from Christ. Every one, even the pope, who should refuse to obey its decrees or instructions should be suitably punished.

A long list of terrible crimes of which John was suspected, was drawn up and he was formally deposed. He received but little encouragement in his opposition to the council and soon surrendered unconditionally. Gregory XII, the Roman pope, showed himself amenable to reason and relieved the perplexity of the council by resigning in July. The third pope, the obstinate Benedict XIII, flatly refused to resign. But the council induced the Spaniards, who were his only remaining supporters, to desert him and send envoys to Constance. Benedict was then deposed (July, 1417) and in the following November the cardinals who were at the council were permitted to elect a new pope, Martin V, and so the Great Schism was brought to an end.

2. During the first year of its sessions the Council of Con- John Huss stance was attempting to stamp out heresy as well as to heal the schism. The marriage of an English king, Richard II, to a Bohemian princess shortly before Wycliffe's death, had encouraged some intercourse between Bohemia and England and had brought the works of the English reformer to the attention of those in Bohemia who were intent upon the improvement of the Church. Among these the most conspicuous was John Huss (b. about 1369), whose ardent devotion to the interests of the Bohemian nation and enthusiasm for reform secured for him great influence in the University of Prague, with which he was connected.

Huss reached the conclusion that Christians should not be forced to obey those who were living in mortal sin and were apparently destined never to reach heaven themselves. This view was naturally denounced by the Church as a most dangerous error, destructive of all order and authority. As his opponents urged, the regularly appointed authorities must be obeyed, not because they are good men but because they govern in virtue of the law. In short, Huss appeared not only to defend the heresies of Wycliffe, but at the same time to preach a doctrine dangerous alike to the power of the civil government and of the Church.

The ' safe-
conduct.'

Huss felt confident that he could convince the council of the truth of his views and willingly appeared at Constance. He was provided with a " safe-conduct," a document in which Emperor Sigismund ordered that no one should do him any violence and which permitted the bearer to leave Constance whenever he wished. In spite of this he was speedily arrested and imprisoned, in December, 1414. His treatment well illustrates the mediæval attitude towards heresy. When Sigismund indignantly protested against the violation of his safe-conduct, he was informed that the law did not recognize faith pledged to suspected heretics, for they were out of the king's jurisdiction. The council declared that no pledge which was prejudicial to the Catholic faith was to be observed. In judging Sigismund's failure to enforce his promise of protection to Huss it must be remembered that heresy was at that time considered a far more terrible crime than murder, and that it was the opinion of the most authoritative body in Christendom that Sigismund would do a great wrong if he prevented the trial of Huss.

Trial of
Huss.

Huss was treated in what would seem to us a very harsh way; but from the standpoint of the council he was given every advantage. By special favor he was granted a public hearing. The council was anxious that Huss should retract; but no form of retraction could be arranged to which he would agree. The council, in accordance with the usages of the time, demanded that he should recognize the error of all the propositions which they had selected from his writings, that he should retract them and never again preach them, and that he should agree to preach the contrary. The council did not consider it its business to decide whether Huss was right or wrong, but simply whether his doctrines, which they gathered from his books, were in accordance with the traditional views of the Church.

Conviction
and execution
of Huss,
July, 1415.

Finally, the council condemned Huss as a convicted and impenitent heretic. On July 6, 1415, he was taken out before the gates of the city and given one more chance to retract. As he refused, he was degraded from the priesthood and handed over to the civil government to be executed for heresy, which, as we have seen, the state regarded as a crime and undertook to punish.[1] The civil authorities made no further investigation but accepted the verdict of the council and burned Huss upon the spot. His ashes were thrown into the Rhine lest they should become an object of veneration among his followers.

The death of Huss rather promoted than checked the spread of heresy in Bohemia. A few years later the Germans undertook a series of crusades against the Bohemians. This embittered the national animosity between the two races, which has even yet by no means died out. The heretics proved valiant fighters and after several bloody wars succeeded in repulsing the enemy and even invaded Germany.

The Hussite wars, 1419–1431.

3. The third great task of the Council of Constance was the general reformation of the Church. After John's flight it had claimed the right (in the decree *Sacrosancta*) to reform even the papacy. This was a splendid opportunity at least to mitigate the abuses in the Church. The council was a great representative body, and every one was looking to it to remedy the old evils which had become more pronounced than ever during the Great Schism. Many pamphlets were published at the time by earnest men denouncing the corrupt practices of the clergy. The evils were of long standing and have all been described in earlier chapters.[2]

Opportunity of the council to reform the Church.

Although every one recognized the abuses, the council found itself unable to remedy them or to accomplish the hoped-for reformation. After three years of fruitless deliberations the members of the assembly became weary and hopeless. They finally contented themselves with passing a decree (Oct. 9, 1417) declaring that the neglect to summon general

The failure of the council to effect any definite reforms.

[1] See above, pp. 222–223.
[2] For examples of the general criticism of the abuses in the Church, see *Translations and Reprints*, Vol. III, No. 6.

councils in the past had fostered all the evils in the Church and that thereafter councils should be regularly summoned at least every ten years.[1] In this way it was hoped that the absolute power of the popes might be checked in somewhat the same way that the Parliament in England and the Estates General in France controlled the monarch.

Abuses enumerated by the council

After the passing of this decree the council drew up a list of abuses demanding reform, which the new pope was to consider with certain of its members after the main body of the council had returned home. Chief among the questions which the council enumerated for consideration were the number, character, and nationality of the cardinals, the benefices to which the pope had a right to appoint, what cases might be brought before his court, for what reason and in what manner the pope might be corrected or deposed, how heresy might be extirpated, and the matter of dispensations, indulgences, etc.

Aside from the healing of the schism, the results of the Council of Constance were slight. It had burned Huss but had by no means checked heresy. It had considered for three years the reformation of the Church but had at last confessed its inability to carry it out. The pope later issued a few reform decrees, but the state of the Church was not materially bettered.

Council of Basel, 1431–1449.

116. The sturdy resistance of the Bohemians to those who proposed to bring them back to the orthodox faith by arms finally attracted the attention of Europe and called forth considerable sympathy. In 1431 the last of the crusades against them came to an ignominious end, and Martin V was forced to summon a new council in order to consider the policy which should be adopted toward the heretics. The Council of Basel lasted for no less than eighteen years. At first its prestige was sufficient to enable it to dominate the

---

[1] This decree, *Frequens*, may be found in *Translations and Reprints*, Vol. III, No. 6.

pope, and it reached its greatest authority in 1434 after it had arranged a peace with the moderate party of the Bohemian heretics. The council, however, continued its hostility towards Pope Eugene IV (elected in 1431), and in 1437 he declared the council dissolved and summoned a new one to meet at Ferrara. The Council of Basel thereupon deposed Eugene and chose an anti-pope. This conduct did much to discredit the idea of a general council in the eyes of Europe. The assembly gradually dwindled away and finally in 1449 acknowledged the legitimate pope once more.

Meanwhile the Council of Ferrara [1] had taken up the momentous question of consolidating the Eastern and Western Churches. The empire of the East was seriously threatened by the on-coming Ottoman Turks, who had made conquests even west of Constantinople. The Eastern emperor's advisers urged that if a reconciliation could be arranged with the Western Church, the pope might use his influence to supply arms and soldiers to be used against the Mohammedans. When the representatives of the Eastern Church met with the Council of Ferrara the differences in doctrine were found to be few, but the question of the headship of the Church was a most difficult one. A form of union was, nevertheless, agreed upon in which the Eastern Church accepted the headship of the pope, " saving the privileges and rights of the patriarchs of the East."

While Eugene received the credit for healing the breach between the East and the West, the Greek prelates, upon returning home, were hailed with indignation and branded as robbers and matricides for the concessions which they had made. The chief results of the council were (1) the advantage gained by the pope in once more becoming the recognized head of Christendom in spite of the opposition of the Council of Basel, and (2) the fact that certain learned Greeks remained

Council of Ferrara-Florence, 1438–1439.

Union of Eastern and Western Churches.

Results of the Council of Ferrara.

[1] On account of an outbreak of sickness the council was transferred to Florence.

in Italy, and helped to stimulate the growing enthusiasm for Greek literature.

No more councils were held during the fifteenth century, and the popes were left to the task of reorganizing their dominions in Italy. They began to turn their attention very largely to their interests as Italian princes, and some of them, beginning with Nicholas V (1447–1455), became the patrons of artists and men of letters. There is probably no period in the history of the papacy when the head of the Church was more completely absorbed in forwarding his political interests and those of his relatives, and in decorating his capital, than in the seventy years which elapsed between 1450 and the beginning of the German revolt against the Church.

General Reading. — CREIGHTON, *History of the Papacy* (Longmans, Green & Co., 6 vols., $2.00 each), Vol. I, is perhaps the best treatment of the Great Schism and the Council of Constance. PASTOR, *History of the Popes* (Herder, 6 vols., $18.00), Vol. I, Book 1, gives the most recent and scholarly account from the standpoint of a Roman Catholic.

CHAPTER XXII

THE ITALIAN CITIES AND THE RENAISSANCE

117. While England and France were settling their differences in the wretched period of the Hundred Years' War, and the little German principalities, left without a leader,[1] were busied with their petty concerns, Italy was the center of European culture. Its cities, — Florence, Venice, Milan, and the rest, — reached a degree of prosperity and refinement undreamed of beyond the Alps. Within their walls learning and art made such extraordinary progress that this period has received a special name, — the *Renaissance*,[2] or new birth. The Italian towns, like those of ancient Greece, were really little states, each with its own peculiar life and institutions. Of these city-states a word must be said before considering the new enthusiasm for the works of the Romans and Greeks and the increasing skill which the Italian artists displayed in painting, sculpture, and architecture.

Italy the center of European culture in the fourteenth and fifteenth centuries.

The map of Italy at the beginning of the fourteenth century was still divided into three zones, as it had been in the time of the Hohenstaufens. To the south lay the kingdom of Naples. Then came the states of the Church, extending diagonally across the peninsula. To the north and west lay the group of city-states to which we now turn our attention.

Map of Italy in the fourteenth century.

Of these none was more celebrated than Venice, which in the history of Europe ranks in importance with Paris and London. This singular town was built upon a group of sandy islets lying in

Venice and its relations with the East.

---

[1] See above, p. 186.

[2] This word, although originally French, has come into such common use that it is quite permissible to pronounce it as if it were English, — *rĕ-nā′sens*.

the Adriatic Sea about two miles from the mainland. It was
protected from the waves by a long, narrow sand bar, similar to
those which fringe the Atlantic coast from New Jersey southward. Such a situation would not ordinarily have been delib-
erately chosen as the site of a great city ; but its very desolation
and inaccessibility had recommended it to its first settlers, who,
in the middle of the fifth century, had fled from their homes

A Scene in Venice

on the mainland to escape the savage Huns.[1] As time went
on the location proved to have its advantages commercially,
and even before the Crusades Venice had begun to engage in
foreign trade. Its enterprises carried it eastward, and it early
acquired possessions across the Adriatic and in the Orient.[2]
The influence of this intercourse with the East is plainly shown

[1] See above, p. 27.
[2] See above, pp. 198–199 and 243.

in the celebrated church of St. Mark, whose domes and decorations suggest Constantinople rather than Italy.

It was not until early in the fifteenth century that Venice found it to her interest to extend her sway upon the Italian mainland. She doubtless believed it dangerous to permit her rival, Milan, to get possession of the Alpine passes through which her goods found their way north. It may be, too, that

Venice extends her sway on the Italian mainland.

St. Mark's, Venice

she preferred to draw her food supplies from the neighborhood instead of transporting them across the Adriatic from her eastern possessions. Moreover, all the Italian cities except Venice already controlled a larger or smaller area of country about them. Although Venice was called a republic, there was a strong tendency toward a government of the few. About the year 1300 all the townsmen except the members of certain noble families were excluded from the Grand Council, which was supposed to represent the people at large.

The aristocratic government of Venice.

In 1311 the famous Council of Ten was created, whose members were elected by the Grand Council for one year. The whole government, domestic and foreign, was placed in the hands of this smaller council, in conjunction with the doge (i.e., duke), the nominal head of the republic; but they were both held strictly accountable to the Grand Council for all that they did. The government was thus concentrated in the hands of a very few. Its proceedings were carried on with great secrecy, so that public discussion, such as prevailed in Florence and led to innumerable revolutions there, was unheard of in Venice. The Venetian merchant was a busy person who was quite willing that the state should exercise its functions without his interference. In spite of the aristocratic measures of the council, there was little tendency to rebellion, so common in the other Italian towns. The republic of Venice maintained pretty much the same form of government from 1300 until its destruction by Napoleon in 1797.

Milan and the despotically governed towns of northern Italy.

118. Milan was the most conspicuous example of the large class of Italian cities which were governed by an absolute and despotic ruler, who secured control of a town either by force or guile, and then managed its affairs for his own personal advantage. At the opening of the fourteenth century a great part of the towns which had leagued themselves against Frederick Barbarossa [1] had become little despotisms. Their rulers were constantly fighting among themselves, conquering, or being conquered by, their neighbors. The practices of the Visconti, the family who seized the government of Milan, offer a fair example of the policy of the Italian tyrants.

The power of the Visconti was first established by the archbishop of Milan. He imprisoned (1277) in three iron cages the leading members of the family who were in control of the city government at the moment, and had his nephew, Matteo Visconti, appointed by the emperor as the imperial

[1] See above, pp. 174 *sqq.*

representative. Before long Matteo was generally recognized as the ruler of Milan, and was followed by his son. For over a century and a half some one of the family always showed himself skillful enough to hold his precarious position.

The most distinguished of the Visconti despots was Gian Galeazzo. He began his reign by capturing and poisoning his uncle, who was ruling over a portion of the already exten- sive territory of the Visconti.[1] It seemed for a time that he might conquer all of northern Italy; but his progress was checked by the republic of Florence and then cut short by premature death. Gian Galeazzo exhibited all the characteristic traits of the Ital- ian despots. He showed himself a skillful and suc- cessful ruler, able to organize his government admirably. He gathered literary

Gian Galeazzo Visconti, 1385-1402.

Tomb of Gian Galeazzo Visconti

[1] In the year 1300 Milan occupied a territory scarcely larger than that of the neighboring states, but under the Visconti it conquered a number of towns, Pavia, Cremona, etc., and became, next to Venice, the most considerable state of northern Italy.

men about him ; and the beautiful buildings which were begun by him indicate his enthusiasm for art. Yet he was utterly unprincipled, and resorted to the most hideous methods in order to gain possession of coveted towns which he could not conquer or buy outright.

Position and character of the Italian despots.

There are many stories of the incredible ferocity exhibited by the Italian despots.[1] It must be remembered that they were very rarely legitimate rulers, but usurpers, who could only hope to retain their power so long as they could keep their subjects in check and defend themselves against equally illegitimate usurpers in the neighboring cities. This situation developed a high degree of sagacity, and many of the despots found it to their interest to govern well and even to give dignity to their rule by patronizing artists and men of letters. But the despot usually made many bitter enemies and was almost necessarily suspicious of treason on the part of those about him. He was ever conscious that at any moment he might fall a victim to the dagger or the poison cup.

The *condottieri.*

The Italian towns carried on their wars among themselves largely by means of hired troops. When a military expedition was proposed, a bargain was made with one of the leaders (*condottieri*), who provided the necessary force. As the soldiers had no more interest in the conflict than did those whom they opposed, who were likewise hired for the occasion, the fight was not usually very bloody ; for the object of each side was to capture the other without unnecessarily rough treatment.

It sometimes happened that the leader who had conquered a town for his employer appropriated the fruits of the victory for himself. This occurred in the case of Milan in 1450.

---

[1] A single example will suffice. Through intrigue and misrepresentation on the part of Gian Galeazzo Visconti, the Marquis of Ferrara became so wildly jealous of his nephew that he beheaded the young man and his mother, then burned his own wife and hung a fourth member of the family.

The Visconti family having died out, the citizens hired a certain captain, named Francesco Sforza, to assist them in a war against Venice, whose possessions now extended almost to those of Milan. When Sforza had repelled the Venetians, the Milanese found it impossible to get rid of him, and he and his successors became rulers over the town.

An excellent notion of the position and policy of the Italian despots may be derived from a little treatise called *The Prince*, written by the distinguished Florentine historian, Machiavelli. The writer appears to have intended his book as a practical manual for the despots of his time. It is a cold-blooded discussion of the ways in which a usurper may best retain his control over a town after he has once got possession of it. The author even takes up the questions as to how far princes should consider their promises when it is inconvenient to keep them, and how many of the inhabitants the despot may wisely kill. Machiavelli concludes that the Italian princes who have not observed their engagements over-scrupulously, and who have boldly put their political adversaries out of the way, have fared better than their more conscientious rivals.

Machiavelli's Prince.

119. The history of Florence, perhaps the most important of the Italian cities, differs in many ways from that of Venice and of the despotisms of which Milan is an example. In Florence all classes claimed the right to interest themselves in the government. This led to constant changes in the constitution and to frequent struggles between the different political parties. When one party got the upper hand it generally expelled its chief opponents from the city. Exile was a terrible punishment to a Florentine, for Florence was not merely his native city,—it was his *country*, and loved and honored as such.

Florence.

By the middle of the fifteenth century Florence had come under the control of the great family of the Medici, whose

The Medici.

members played the rôle of very enlightened political bosses. By quietly watching the elections and secretly controlling the selection of city officials, they governed without letting it be suspected that the people had lost their power. The most

distinguished member of the house of Medici was Lorenzo the Magnificent (d. 1492); under his rule Florence reached the height of its glory in art and literature.

The Palace of the Medici in Florence

As one wanders about Florence today, he is impressed with the contradictions of the Renaissance period. The streets are lined with the palaces of the noble families to whose rivalries

much of the continual disturbance was due. The lower stories of these buildings are constructed of great stones, like fortresses, and their windows are barred like those of a prison; yet within they were often furnished with the greatest taste and luxury. For in spite of the disorder, against which the rich protected themselves by making their houses half strongholds, the beautiful churches, noble public buildings, and works of art which now fill the museums indicate that mankind has never, perhaps, reached a higher degree of perfection in the arts of peace than amidst the turmoil of this restless town.

" Florence was essentially the city of intelligence in modern times. Other nations have surpassed the Italians in their genius ... But nowhere else except at Athens has the whole population of a city been so permeated with ideas, so highly intellectual by nature, so keen in perception, so witty and so subtle, as at Florence. The fine and delicate spirit of the Italians existed in quintessence among the Florentines. And of this superiority not only they, but the inhabitants also of Rome and Lombardy and Naples were conscious. ... The primacy of the Florentines in literature, the fine arts, law, scholarship, philosophy, and science was acknowledged throughout Italy " (Symonds).

120. The thirteenth century had been, as we have seen, a period of great enthusiasm for learning. The new universities attracted students from all parts of Europe, and famous thinkers like Albertus Magnus, Thomas Aquinas, and Roger Bacon wrote great treatises on religion, science, and philosophy. The public delighted in the songs and romances composed and recited in the language of the people. The builders contrived a new and beautiful style of architecture, and, with the aid of the sculptors, produced buildings which have never since been surpassed and rarely equaled. Why, then, are the two succeeding centuries called the period of the *new birth*, — the Renaissance, — as if there was a sudden reawakening after a long sleep, as if Europe first began in the fourteenth century to turn to books and art?

The word *renaissance* was originally used by writers who had very little appreciation of the achievements of the thirteenth century. They imagined that there could have been no high degree of culture during a period when the Latin and

The Renaissance, or new birth.

Greek classics, which seemed so all-important to them, were not carefully studied. But it is now coming to be generally recognized that the thirteenth century had worthy intellectual and artistic ambitions, although they were different both from those of Greece and Rome and from our own.

We cannot, therefore, conceive the "new birth" of the fourteenth and fifteenth centuries quite as it was viewed by writers of a century ago, who failed to do justice to the preceding period. Nevertheless, about the middle of the fourteenth century, a very great and fundamental change did begin in thought and taste, in books, buildings, and pictures, and this change we may very well continue to call the *Renaissance*. We can best judge of its nature by considering the work of the two greatest men of the fourteenth century, Dante and Petrarch.

Dante, 1264-1321. Dante was first and foremost a poet, and is often ranked with Homer, Virgil, and Shakespeare. He is, however, interesting to the historian for other things than his flights of fancy and the music of his verse. He had mastered all the learning of his day; he was a scientist and a scholar as well as a poet. His writings show us how the world appeared about the year 1300 to a very acute mind, and what was the range of knowledge available to the most thoughtful men of that day.

Dante's use of Italian. Dante was not a churchman, as were all the scholars whom we have hitherto considered. He was the first literary layman of renown since Boethius,[1] and he was interested in helping other laymen who knew only their mother tongue to the knowledge heretofore open only to those who could read Latin. In spite of his ability to write Latin, he chose the mother tongue for his great poem, *The Divine Comedy*. Italian was the last of the important modern languages to develop, perhaps because in Italy Latin remained longest intelligible to the mass of the people. But Dante believed

[1] See above, pp. 31-32.

that the exclusive use of Latin for literary purposes had already in his time become an affectation. He was confident that there were many people, both men and women, who knew only Italian, who would gladly read not only his verses but his treatise on science, — *The Banquet*,[1] as he poetically calls it.

Dante's writings indicate that mediæval scholars were by no means so ignorant of the universe as they are popularly supposed to have been. Although they believed, like the ancients, that the earth was the center around which the sun and stars revolved, they were familiar with some important astronomical phenomena. They knew that the earth was a sphere and guessed very nearly its real size. They knew that everything that had weight was attracted towards its center, and that there would be no danger of falling off should one get on the opposite side of the globe ; they realized also that when it was day on one side of the earth it was night on the other.

Extent of Dante's knowledge.

While Dante shows a keen interest in the theological studies so popular in his time and still speaks of Aristotle as "the Philosopher," he exhibits a profound admiration for the other great authors of Rome and Greece. When in a vision he visits the lower world, Virgil is his guide. He is permitted to behold the region inhabited by the spirits of virtuous pagans, and there he finds Horace and Ovid, and Homer, the sovereign poet. As he reclines upon the green turf he sees a goodly company of ancient worthies, — Socrates, Plato, and other Greek philosophers, Cæsar, Cicero, Livy, Seneca, and many others. He is so overcome by the honor of sitting among such great men that he finds no words to report what passed between them. He feels no horror for their paganism, and while he believes

Dante's veneration for the ancient writers.

[1] The translation of *The Banquet* in Morley's "Universal Library" is very poor, but that of Miss Hillard (London, 1889) is good and is supplied with helpful notes.

that they are not admitted to the beatific joys of heaven, he assigns them a comfortable abode, where they hold dignified converse with "faces neither sad nor glad."[1]

Petrarch,
1304-1374.

121. The veneration for the ancient writers felt by Dante becomes a burning enthusiasm with Petrarch, who has been well called "the first modern man."   He was the first scholar

and man of letters to desert entirely the mediæval learning and lead his contemporaries back to a realization of the beauty and value of Greek and Roman literature.   In the mediæval universities, logic, theology, and the interpretation of Aristotle were the chief subjects of study.   While scholars in the twelfth and thirteenth centuries possessed and read most of the Latin

Petrarch

writers who have come down to us, they failed to appreciate their beauty and would never have dreamed of making them the basis of a liberal education.[2]

Petrarch declares that when a boy he delighted in the sonorous language of Cicero even before he could understand its meaning.   As the years went on he became convinced that he could have no higher aim in life than that of collecting copies of all the Latin classics upon which he could lay hands. He was not only an indefatigable scholar himself, but he possessed the power of stimulating, by his example, the intellectual ambition of those with whom he came in contact.   He rendered the study of the Latin classics popular among cultivated persons; and by his own untiring efforts to discover the lost

---

[1] See the close of the fourth canto of the *Inferno*.
[2] See above, pp. 271-272.

or forgotten works of the great writers of antiquity he roused a new enthusiasm for the formation of libraries.[1]

It is hard for us to imagine the obstacles which confronted Petrarch and the scholars of the early Renaissance. They possessed no good editions of the Roman and Greek authors, in which the correct wording had been determined by a careful comparison of all the known ancient copies. They considered themselves fortunate to secure a single manuscript of even the best known authors, and they could have no assurance that it was not full of mistakes. Indeed, the texts were so corrupted by the carelessness of the copyists that Petrarch declares that if Cicero or Livy should return and stumblingly read his own writings, he would promptly pronounce them the work of another, perhaps a barbarian.

Obstacles to the study of the classics.

Petrarch enjoyed an unrivaled influence throughout western Europe, akin to that of Erasmus and Voltaire in later times. He was in constant communication with scholars, not only in Italy, but in the countries beyond the Alps. From his numerous letters which have been preserved, a great deal may be learned of the intellectual life of the time.[2]

Petrarch's European reputation and influence.

It is clear that he not only promoted the new study of the Roman writers, but that he also did much to discredit the learning which was popular in the universities. He refused to

Petrarch has no sympathy with the popular studies of his time.

[1] Copies of the *Æneid*, of Horace's *Satires*, of certain of Cicero's *Orations*, of Ovid, Seneca, and a few other authors, were apparently by no means uncommon during the twelfth and thirteenth centuries. It seemed, however, to Petrarch, who had learned through the references of Cicero, St. Augustine, and others, something of the original extent of Latin literature, that treasures of inestimable value had been lost by the shameful indifference of the Middle Ages. "Each famous author of antiquity whom I recall," he indignantly exclaims, "places a new offense and another cause of dishonor to the charge of later generations, who, not satisfied with their own disgraceful barrenness, permitted the fruit of other minds and the writings that their ancestors had produced by toil and application, to perish through shameful neglect. Although they had nothing of their own to hand down to those who were to come after, they robbed posterity of its ancestral heritage."

[2] Petrarch's own remarkable account of his life and studies, which he gives in his famous "Letter to Posterity," may be found in Robinson and Rolfe, *Petrarch*, pp. 59–76.

include the works of the great scholastic writers of the thirteenth century in his library.   Like Roger Bacon he was disgusted by the reverence in which the bad translations of Aristotle were held. As for the popular study of logic, Petrarch declared that it was good enough for boys, but that nothing irritated him more than to find a person of mature years devoting himself to the subject.

Contrast between Petrarch's and Dante's attitude toward their mother tongue.

While Petrarch is far better known for his beautiful Italian verses than for his long Latin poems, histories, and essays, he did not share Dante's confidence in the dignity of their mother tongue.   He even depreciates his Italian sonnets as mere popular trifles written in his youth.   It was not unnatural that he and those in whom he aroused an enthusiasm for Latin literature should look scornfully upon Italian.   It seemed to them a crude form of speech, good enough perhaps for the common people and for the transaction of the daily business of life, but immeasurably inferior to the language in which their predecessors, the Roman poets and prose writers, had written. The Italians, it must be remembered, felt the same pride in Latin literature that we feel in the works of Chaucer and Shakespeare.   The Italian scholars of the fourteenth and fifteenth centuries merely turned back to their own earlier national literature for their models, and tried their best to imitate the language and style of its masters.

The humanists.

122. Those who devoted themselves to the study and imitation first of Roman, and later of Greek literature, are commonly called *humanists*, a name derived from the Latin word *humanitas;* that is, culture, especially in the sense of literary appreciation.   They no longer paid much attention to Peter Lombard's *Sentences.*   They had, indeed, little taste for theology, but looked to Cicero for all those accomplishments which go to the making of a man of refinement.

Reason for the enthusiastic study of the classics.

The *humanities*, as Greek and Latin are still called, became almost a new religion among the Italian scholars during the century following Petrarch's death.   In order to understand their exclusive attention to ancient literature we must remember that they did not have a great many of the books that we prize most highly nowadays. Now, every nation of Europe has an extensive literature in its own particular tongue, which all can read. Besides admirable translations of all the works of antiquity, there are innumerable masterpieces, like those of Shakespeare, Voltaire, and Goethe, which were unheard of four centuries ago. Consequently we can now acquaint ourselves with a great part of the best that has been written in all ages without knowing either Latin or Greek. The Middle Ages enjoyed no such advantage. So when men began to tire of theology, logic, and Aristotle's scientific treatises, they naturally turned back with single-hearted enthusiasm to the age of Augustus, and, later, to that of Pericles, for their models of literary style and for their ideals of life and conduct.

A sympathetic study of the pagan authors led many of the humanists to reject the mediæval view of the relation of this life to the next.[1] They reverted to the teachings of Horace and ridiculed the self-sacrifice of the monk. They declared that it was right to make the most of life's pleasures and needless to worry about the world to come. In some cases the humanists openly attacked the teachings of the Church, but generally they remained outwardly loyal to it and many of them even found positions among the officers of the papal curia. *Pagan tendencies of the Italian humanists.*

Humanism produced a revolution in the idea of a liberal education. In the sixteenth century, through the influence of those who visited Italy, the schools of Germany, England, and France began to make Latin and Greek literature, rather than logic and other mediæval subjects, the basis of their college course. It is only within the last generation that Latin and Greek have begun to be replaced in our colleges by a variety of scientific and historical studies; and many would still *The classics become the basis of a liberal education.*

[1] See above, pp. 45–46.

maintain, with the humanists of the fifteenth century, that Latin and Greek are better worth studying than any other subjects.

Ignorance of Greek in the Middle Ages. The humanists of the fourteenth century ordinarily knew no Greek. Some knowledge of that language lingered in the West all through the Middle Ages, but we hear of no one attempting to read Plato, Demosthenes, Æschylus, or even Homer, and these authors were scarcely ever found in the libraries. Petrarch and his followers were naturally much interested in the constant references to Greek literature which occur in Cicero and Horace, both of whom freely recognized their debt to Athens. Shortly after Petrarch's death the city of Florence called to its university a professor of Greek, Chrysoloras from Constantinople.

Revival of Greek studies in Italy. Chrysoloras in Florence. A young Florentine law student, Leonardo Bruni, tells us of a dialogue which he had with himself when he heard of the coming of Chrysoloras. "Art thou not neglecting thy best interests if thou failest now to get an insight into Homer, Plato, Demosthenes, and the other great poets, philosophers, and orators of whom they are telling such wonderful things? Thou, too, mightest commune with them and imbue thyself with their wisdom. Wouldst thou let the golden opportunity slip? For seven hundred years no one in Italy has known Greek literature, and yet we agree that all language comes from the Greeks. How greatly would familiarity with that language advantage thee in promoting thy knowledge and in the mere increase of thy pleasure? There are teachers of Roman law to be found everywhere, and thou wilt never want an opportunity to continue that study, but there is but one teacher of Greek, and if he escapes thee there will be no one from whom thou canst learn."

The knowledge of Greek becomes common in Europe. Many students took advantage of the opportunity to study Greek, and Chrysoloras prepared the first modern Greek grammar for their use. Before long the Greek classics became as well known as the Latin. Italians even went to Constantinople to learn the language; and the diplomatic negotiations which the Eastern Church carried on with the Western, with the hope of gaining help against the Turks, brought some Greek scholars to Italy. In 1423 an Italian scholar arrived at Venice with no less than two hundred and thirty-eight Greek books, thus transplanting a whole literature to a new and fruitful soil.[1] Greek as well as Latin books were carefully copied and edited, and beautiful libraries were established by the Medici, the duke of Urbino, and Pope Nicholas V, who founded the great library of the Vatican,[2] still one of the most important collections of books in the world.

123. It was the glory of the Italian humanists to revive the knowledge and appreciation of the ancient literatures, but it remained for patient experimenters in Germany and Holland to perfect a system by which books could be multiplied rapidly and cheaply. The laborious copying of books by hand[3] had several serious disadvantages. The best copyists were, it is true, incredibly dexterous with their quills, and made their letters as clear and small as if they had been printed. But the work was necessarily very slow. When Cosimo, the father of Lorenzo the Magnificent, wished to form a library, he applied to a book contractor, who procured forty-five copyists. By working hard for nearly two years these men were able to produce only two hundred volumes.

Advantages of printing with movable types.

Moreover, it was impossible before the invention of printing to have two books exactly alike. Even with the greatest care a scribe could not hope to avoid all mistakes, and a careless

[1] Historians formerly supposed that it was only after Constantinople was captured by the Turks in 1453 that Greek scholars fled west and took with them the knowledge of their language and literature. The facts given above serve as a sufficient refutation of this oft-repeated error.

[2] In Whitcomb, *Source Book of the Italian Renaissance*, pp. 70 *sqq.*, interesting accounts of these libraries may be found, written by Vespasiano, the most important book dealer of the time.

[3] Manuscript, *manu scriptum*, means simply written by hand.

copyist was sure to make a great many. The universities required their students to report immediately any mistakes discovered in their text-books, in order that the error might be promptly rectified and not lead to a misunderstanding of the author. With the invention of printing it became possible to produce in a short time a great many copies of a given book which were exactly alike. Consequently, if great care were taken to see that the types were properly set, the whole edition, not simply a single copy, might be relied upon as correct.

The earliest printed books.

The earliest book of any considerable size to be printed was the Bible, which appears to have been completed at Mayence in the year 1456. A year later the famous Mayence Psalter was finished, the first dated book. There are, however, earlier examples of little books printed with engraved blocks and even with movable types. In the German towns, where

Closing Lines of the Psalter of 1459 (much reduced) [1]

the art spread rapidly, the printers adhered to the style of letters which the scribe had found it convenient to make with his

[1] The closing lines (i.e., the so-called *colophon*) of the second edition of the Psalter which are here reproduced, are substantially the same as those of the first edition. They may be translated as follows: "The present volume of the Psalms, which is adorned with handsome capitals and is clearly divided by means of rubrics, was produced not by writing with a pen but by an ingenious invention of printed characters; and was completed to the glory of God and the honor of St. James by John Fust, a citizen of Mayence, and Peter Schoifher of Gernsheim, in the year of our Lord 1459, on the 29th of August."

quill— the so-called *Gothic*, or black letter.[1] In Italy, where Black letter. the first printing press was set up in 1466, a type was soon adopted which resembled the letters used in ancient Roman Roman letters. inscriptions. This was quite similar to the style of letter commonly used to-day. The Italians also invented the compressed *italic* type, which enabled them to get a great many Italics. words on a page. The early printers generally did their work conscientiously, and the very first book printed is in most respects as well done as any later book.

124. The stimulus of the antique ideals of beauty and the Importance of Italian art renewed interest in man and nature is nowhere more apparent in the than in the art of the Renaissance period in Italy. The bonds Renaissance period. of tradition, which had hampered mediæval art,[2] were broken. The painters and sculptors continued, it is true, to depict the same religious subjects which their mediæval predecessors had chosen. But in the fourteenth century the Italian artists began to draw their inspiration from the fragments of antique art which they found about them and from the world full of life and beauty in which they lived. Above all, they gave freer rein to their own imagination. The tastes and ideals of the individual artist were no longer repressed but became the dominant element in his work. The history of art becomes, during the Renaissance, a history of artists.

The Gothic style in architecture had never taken root in Italian architecture. Italy. The Italians had continued to build their churches in a more or less modified Romanesque [3] form. While the soaring arches and delicate tracery of the Gothic cathedral had become the ideal of the North, in Italy the curving lines and harmonious proportions of the dome inspired the best efforts

---

[1] Note the similarity in form of the letters in the accompanying illustration and those in the illuminated page which serves as the frontispiece of this volume. It is not easy at first sight to tell some early printed books from the best manuscripts. It may be observed that the Germans still adhere to a type something like that used by the first printers.

[2] See above, pp. 261–262.   [3] See above, p. 263.

of the Renaissance builders. They borrowed many fine details, such as capitals and cornices, from the antique, and also — what was far more important — the simplicity and beauty of proportion which characterized classical architecture. Just as Italy had inherited, in a special sense, the traditions of classical literature, so it was natural that it should be more directly affected than the rest of Europe by the remains of Greek and Roman art. It is in harmony of proportion and beauty of detail that the great charm of the best Renaissance buildings consists.

Italy inherits the art of Greece and Rome.

It is, perhaps, in sculpture that the influence of the antique models was earliest and most obviously shown. The sculptor, Niccola of Pisa (Niccola Pisano), stands out as the first distinguished leader in the forward movement. It is evident that he studied certain fragments of antique sculpture — a sarcophagus and a marble vase that had been found in Pisa — with the greatest care and enthusiasm. He frankly copied from them many details, and even several whole figures, in the reliefs on his most famous work, the pulpit in the baptistery at Pisa.[1] But while sculpture was the first of the arts to feel the new impetus, its progress was slow; it was not until the fifteenth century that it began, in Italy, to develop on wholly independent and original lines.

Niccola of Pisa, 1206-1280.

The paintings of the period of the early Renaissance were usually frescoes; that is, they were painted directly upon the plaster walls of churches and sometimes of palaces. A few pictures, chiefly altar pieces, were executed on wooden panels, but it was not until the sixteenth century that easel paintings, that is, detached pictures on canvas, wood, or other material, became common.

Frescoes and easel pictures.

---

[1] With the appearance of the mendicant orders, preaching again became an important part of the church service, and pulpits were erected in the body of the church, where the people could gather around them. These pulpits offered a fine opportunity to the sculptor and were often very elaborate and beautiful.

In the fourteenth century there was an extraordinary development in the art of painting under the guidance and inspiration of the first great Italian painter, Giotto. Before his time the frescoes, like the illuminations in the manuscripts of which we have spoken in a previous chapter, were exceedingly stiff and unlifelike. With Giotto there comes a change. Antique art did not furnish him with any models to

Relief by Niccola of Pisa from Pulpit at Pisa, showing
Influence of Antique Models

copy, for whatever the ancients had accomplished in painting had been destroyed.[1] He had therefore to deal with the problems of his art unaided, and of course he could only begin their solution. His trees and landscapes look like caricatures, his faces are all much alike, the garments hang in stiff straight

[1] The frescoes in Pompeii and other slight remnants of ancient painting were not discovered till much later.

folds. But he aimed to do what the earlier painters apparently did not dream of doing — that is, paint living, thinking, feeling men and women. He was not even satisfied to confine himself to the old biblical subjects. Among his most famous frescoes are the scenes from the life of St. Francis,[1] a theme which appealed very strongly to the imagination of people and artists alike all through the fourteenth century.

Renaissance artists often practiced several arts. Giotto's dominating influence upon the art of his century is due partly to the fact that he was a builder as well as a painter, and also designed reliefs for sculpture. This practicing of several different arts by the same artist was one of the striking features of the Renaissance period.

Italian art in the fifteenth century. **125.** During the fifteenth century, which is known as the period of the Early Renaissance, art in Italy developed and progressed steadily, surely, and with comparative rapidity, toward the glorious heights of achievement which it reached in the following century. The traditions of the Middle Ages were wholly thrown aside, the lessons of ancient art thoroughly learned. As the artists became more complete masters of their tools and of all the technical processes of their art, they found themselves ever freer to express in their work what they saw and felt.

Florence the art center of Italy. Florence was the great center of artistic activity during the fifteenth century. The greatest sculptors and almost all of the most famous painters and architects of the time either were natives of Florence or did their best work there. During the first half of the century sculpture again took the lead. The bronze doors of the baptistery at Florence by Ghiberti, which were completed about 1450, are among the very best products of Renaissance sculpture. Michael Angelo declared them worthy to be the doors of paradise. A comparison of them with the doors of the cathedral of Pisa, which date from the end of the twelfth century, furnishes a striking illustration

[1] In the church of Santa Croce in Florence and in that of St. Francis at Assisi.

of the change that had taken place. A contemporary of Ghiberti, Luca della Robbia (1400–1482), is celebrated for his beautiful reliefs in glazed baked clay and in marble, of which many may be seen in Florence.

One of the best known painters of the first half of the fifteenth century, Fra[1] Angelico, was a monk.   His frescoes on

Relief by Luca della Robbia

the walls of the monastery of San Marco (and elsewhere) reflect a love of beauty and a cheerful piety, in striking contrast to the fiery zeal of Savonarola,[2] who, later in the century,

1 Fra is an abbreviation of *frate*, brother.   2 See below, pp. 361, 363, 364.

went forth from this same monastery to denounce the vanities of the art-loving Florentines.[1]

Rome becomes the center of artistic activity.

126. Florence reached the height of its preëminence as an art center during the reign of Lorenzo the Magnificent, who was an ardent patron of all the arts. With his death (1492), and the subsequent brief but overwhelming influence of Savonarola, this preëminence passed to Rome, which was fast becoming one of the great capitals of Europe. The art-loving popes, Julius II and Leo X,[2] took pains to secure the services of the most distinguished artists and architects of the time in the building and adornment of St. Peter's and the Vatican, i.e., the papal church and palace.

The church of St. Peter.

The idea of the dome as the central feature of a church, which appealed so strongly to the architects of the Renaissance, reached its highest realization in rebuilding the ancient church of St. Peter. The task was begun in the fifteenth century; in 1506 it was taken up by Pope Julius II with his usual energy, and it was continued all through the sixteenth century and well into the seventeenth, under the direction of a succession of the most famous artist-architects of the time, including Raphael and Michael Angelo. The plan was changed repeatedly, but in its final form the building is a Latin cross surmounted by a great dome, one hundred and thirty-eight feet in diameter. The dimensions and proportions of this greatest of all churches never fail to impress the beholder with something like awe.

Height of Renaissance art. Da Vinci, Michael Angelo, Raphael.

During the sixteenth century the art of the Renaissance reached its highest development. Among all the great artists of this period three stand out in heroic proportions — Leonardo da Vinci, Michael Angelo, and Raphael. The first two not only

---

[1] One of the most celebrated among the other Florentine painters of the period was Botticelli. He differs from most of his contemporaries in being at his best in easel pictures. His poetic conceptions, the graceful lines of his draperies, and the pensive charm of his faces have especially inspired a famous school of English painters in our own day — the Preraphaelites.   [2] See below, pp. 364, 365.

practiced, but achieved almost equal distinction in, the three
arts of architecture, sculpture, and painting.[1] It is impossible
to give in a few lines any idea of the beauty and significance
of the work of these great geniuses. Both Raphael and
Michael Angelo left behind them so many and such magnificent frescoes and paintings, and in the case of Michael
Angelo statues as well, that it is easy to appreciate their

St. Peter's and the Vatican, Rome

importance. Leonardo, on the other hand, left but little completed work. His influence on the art of his time, which
was probably greater than that of either of the others, came
from his many-sidedness, his originality, and his unflagging
interest in the discovery and application of new methods.
He was almost more experimenter than artist.

While Florence could no longer boast of being the art
center of Italy, it still produced great artists, among whom

The Venetian
school.

[1] Leonardo was engineer and inventor as well.

Andrea del Sarto may be especially mentioned.[1]   But the most important center of artistic activity outside of Rome in the sixteenth century was Venice.   The distinguishing characteristic of the Venetian pictures is their glowing color.   This is strikingly exemplified in the paintings of Titian, the most famous of all the Venetian painters.

Titian, 1477-1576.

It was natural that artists from the northern countries should be attracted by the renown of the Italian masters and, after learning all that Italy could teach them, should return home to practice their art in their own particular fashion. About a century after Giotto's time two Flemish brothers, Van Eyck by name, showed that they were not only able to paint quite as excellent pictures as the Italians of their day, but they also discovered a new way of mixing their colors superior to that employed in Italy.   Later, when painting had reached its height in Italy, Albrecht Dürer and Hans Holbein the Younger [2] in Germany vied with even Raphael and Michael Angelo in the mastery of their art.   Dürer is especially celebrated for his wonderful woodcuts and copperplate engravings, in which field he has perhaps never been excelled.[3]

Painting in northern Europe.

Dürer, 1471-1528.

When, in the seventeenth century, painting had declined south of the Alps, Dutch and Flemish masters, — above all, Rubens and Rembrandt, — developed a new and admirable school of painting.   To Van Dyck, another Flemish master, we owe many noble portraits of historically important persons.[4] Spain gave to the world in the seventeenth century a painter whom some would rank higher than even the greatest artists of Italy, namely, Velasquez (1599–1660).   His genius, like that of Van Dyck, is especially conspicuous in his marvellous portraits.

Rubens, 1577-1640, and Rembrandt, 1607-1669.

Van Dyck, 1599-1641, and his portraits.

Velasquez.

---

[1] Compare his Holy Family with the reproduction of one of Giotto's paintings, in order to realize the great change in art between the fourteenth and sixteenth centuries.   [2] See his portrait of Erasmus below, p. 382.

[3] For an example of the magnificent bronze work produced in Germany in the early sixteenth century, see the statues of Philip the Good and Charles the Bold, pp. 300, 301, above.   [4] See his portrait of Charles I below, p. 480.

HOLY FAMILY BY ANDREA DEL SARTO

GIOTTO'S MADONNA

127. Shortly after the invention of printing, which promised so much for the diffusion of knowledge, the horizon of western Europe was further enlarged by a series of remarkable sea voyages which led to the exploration of the whole globe. The Greeks and Romans knew little about the world beyond southern Europe, northern Africa, and western Asia; and much that they knew was forgotten during the Middle Ages. The Crusades took many Europeans as far east as Egypt and Syria. As early as Dante's time two Venetian merchants, the Polo brothers, visited China and were kindly received at Pekin by the emperor of the Mongols. On a second journey they were accompanied by Marco Polo, the son of one of the brothers. When they got safely back to Venice in 1295, after a journey of twenty years, Marco gave an account of his experiences which filled his readers with wonder. Nothing stimulated the interest of the West more than his fabulous description of the golden island of Zipangu (Japan) and of the spice markets of the Moluccas and Ceylon.[1]

Geographical knowledge in the Middle Ages.

Marco Polo.

About the year 1318 Venice and Genoa opened up direct communication by sea with the towns of the Netherlands.[2] Their fleets, which touched at the port of Lisbon, aroused the commercial enterprise of the Portuguese, who soon began to undertake extended maritime expeditions. By the middle of the fourteenth century they had discovered the Canary Islands, Madeira, and the Azores. Before this time no one had ventured along the coast of Africa beyond the arid region of Sahara. The country was forbidding, there were no ports, and mariners were, moreover, hindered in their progress by the

The discoveries of the Portuguese in the fourteenth and fifteenth centuries.

---

[1] Marco Polo's travels can easily be had in English; for example, in *The Story of Marco Polo*, by Noah Brooks, Century Company, 1898. A certain Franciscan monk, William of Rubruk, visited the far East somewhat earlier than the Polo brothers. The account of his journey, as well as the experiences of other mediæval travelers, may be found in *The Travels of Sir John Mandeville*, published by The Macmillan Company, 1900.

[2] See map above, pp. 242–243.

general belief that the torrid region was uninhabitable. In 1445, however, some adventurous sailors came within sight of a headland beyond the desert and, struck by its luxuriant growth of tropical trees, they called it Cape Verde (the green cape). Its discovery put an end once for all to the idea that there were only parched deserts to the south.

For a generation longer the Portuguese continued to venture farther and farther along the coast, in the hope of finding it coming to an end, so that they might make their way by sea to India. At last, in 1486, Diaz rounded the Cape of Good Hope. Twelve years later (1498) Vasco da Gama, spurred on by Columbus' great discovery, after sailing around the Cape of Good Hope and northward beyond Zanzibar, steered straight across the Indian Ocean and reached Calicut, in Hindustan, by sea.

The spice trade. These adventurers were looked upon with natural suspicion by the Mohammedan spice merchants, who knew very well that their object was to establish a direct trade between the spice islands and western Europe. Hitherto the Mohammedans had had the monopoly of the spice trade between the Moluccas and the eastern ports of the Mediterranean, where the products were handed over to Italian merchants. The Mohammedans were unable, however, to prevent the Portuguese from concluding treaties with the Indian princes and establishing trading stations at Goa and elsewhere. In 1512 a successor of Vasco da Gama reached Java and the Moluccas, where the Portuguese speedily built a fortress. By 1515 Portugal had become the greatest among maritime powers; and spices reached Lisbon regularly without the intervention of the Italian towns, which were mortally afflicted by the change.

Importance of spices in encouraging navigation. There is no doubt that the desire to obtain spices was the main reason for the exploration of the globe. This motive led European navigators to try in succession every possible way to reach the East — by going around Africa, by sailing west in the

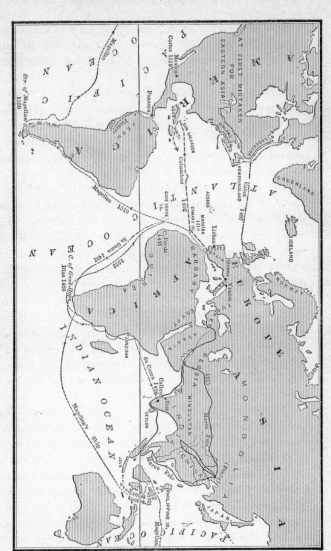

The Voyages of Discovery

hope of reaching the Indies, before they knew of the existence of America; then, after America was discovered, by sailing around it to the north or south, and even sailing around Europe to the north. It is hard for us to understand this enthusiasm for spices, for which we care much less nowadays. One former use of spices was to preserve food, which could not then as now be carried rapidly, while still fresh, from place to place; nor did our conveniences then exist for keeping it by the use of ice. Moreover, spice served to make even spoiled food more palatable than it would otherwise have been.

Idea of reaching the spice islands by sailing westward.

It inevitably occurred to thoughtful men that the East Indies could be reached by sailing westward. The chief authority upon the form and size of the earth was still the ancient astronomer, Ptolemy, who lived about A.D. 150. He had reckoned the earth to be about one sixth smaller than it is; and as Marco Polo had given an exaggerated idea of the distance which he and his companions had traveled eastward, it was supposed that it could not be a very long journey from Europe across the Atlantic to Japan.

Columbus discovers America, 1492.

The first plan for sailing west was, perhaps, submitted to the Portuguese king in 1474, by Toscanelli, a Florentine physician. In 1492, as we all know, a Genoese navigator, Columbus (b. 1451), who had had much experience on the sea, got together three little ships and undertook the journey westward to Zipangu, which he hoped to reach in five weeks. After thirty-two days from the time he left the Canary Islands he came upon land, the island of San Salvador, and believed himself to be in the East Indies. Going on from there he discovered the island of Cuba, which he believed to be the mainland of Asia, and then Haiti, which he mistook for the longed-for Zipangu. Although he made three later expeditions and sailed down the coast of South America as far as the Orinoco, he died without realizing that he had not been exploring the coast of Asia.[1]

[1] Reference, *Cambridge Modern History*, Chapter I.

After the bold enterprises of Vasco da Gama and Colum-
bus, an expedition headed by Magellan succeeded in circum-
navigating the globe. There was now no reason why the new
lands should not become more and more familiar to the Euro-
pean nations. The coast of North America was explored
principally by English navigators, who for over a century
pressed north, still in the vain hope of finding a northwest
passage to the spice islands.

Magellan's
expedition
around the
world.

Cortez began the Spanish conquests in the western world by
undertaking the subjugation of the Aztec empire in Mexico
in 1519. A few years later Pizarro established the Spanish
power in Peru. It is hardly necessary to say that Europeans
exhibited an utter disregard for the rights of the people with
whom they came in contact, and treated them with con-
temptuous cruelty. Spain now superseded Portugal as a
maritime power and her importance in the sixteenth century
is to be attributed largely to the wealth which came to her
from her possessions in the New World.

The Spanish
conquests in
America.

By the end of the century the Spanish main — i.e., the
northern coast of South America — was much frequented by
adventurous seamen, who combined in about equal parts the
occupations of merchant, slaver, and pirate. Many of these
hailed from English ports, and it is to them that England owes
the beginning of her commercial greatness.[1]

The Spanish
main.

128. While Columbus and the Portuguese navigators were
bringing hitherto unknown regions of the earth to the knowl-
edge of Europe, a Polish astronomer, Kopernik (commonly
known by his Latinized name, Copernicus), was reaching the
conclusion that the ancient writers had been misled in sup-
posing that the earth was the center of the universe. He

Copernicus
(1473-1543)
discovers
that the
earth is not
the center
of the
universe.

---

[1] Reference, *Cambridge Modern History*, Chapter II. Kingsley has described these mariners in his *Westward Ho*. He derives his notions of them from the collection of voyages made by an English geographer, Hakluyt (died 1616). Some of these are published by Payne, *Voyages of Elizabethan Seamen* (Clarendon Press, 2 vols., $1.25 each).

discovered that, with the other planets, the earth revolved about the sun. This opened the way to an entirely new conception of the heavenly bodies and their motions, which has formed the basis of modern astronomy.

It was naturally a great shock to men to have it suggested that their dwelling place, instead of being God's greatest work to which He had subordinated everything, was but a tiny speck in comparison to the whole universe, and its sun but one of an innumerable host of similar bodies, each of which might have its particular family of planets revolving about it. Theologians, both Protestant and Catholic, declared the statements of Copernicus foolish and wicked and contrary to the teachings of the Bible. He was prudent enough to defer the publication of his great work until just before his death ; he thus escaped any persecution to which his discovery might have subjected him.

Miscellaneous inventions.

In addition to the various forms of progress of which we have spoken, the fourteenth and fifteenth centuries witnessed the invention or wide application of a considerable number of practical devices which were unknown to the Greeks and Romans. Examples of these are, besides printing, the compass, gunpowder, spectacles, and a method of not merely softening but of thoroughly melting iron so that it could be cast.

The fourteenth and fifteenth centuries not merely a period of revival.

The period of which we have been speaking was, in short, by no means merely distinguished for the revival of classical learning. It was not simply a re-birth of the ancient knowledge and art, but a time during which Europe laid the foundations for a development essentially different from that of the ancient world and for achievements undreamed of by Aristotle or Pliny.

General Reading. — The culture of Italy during the fourteenth and fifteenth centuries is best treated by BURCKHARDT, *The Civilization of the Renaissance in Italy* (The Macmillan Company, $4.00). This is especially adapted for the rather advanced student. The towns are interestingly described in SYMONDS, *Age of Despots* (Scribner's Sons, $2.00). For Florence and the Medici, see ARMSTRONG, *Lorenzo de'*

Medici and Florence in the Fifteenth Century (G. P. Putnam's Sons, $1 50). MACHIAVELLI'S *Prince* may be had in translation (Clarendon Press, $1.10). The best prose translation of DANTE'S *Divine Comedy* is that of Charles Eliot Norton (Houghton, Mifflin & Co., 3 vols., $4.50). In ROBINSON and ROLFE, *Petrarch the First Modern Scholar and Man of Letters* (G. P. Putnam's Sons, $2.00), the reader will find much material to illustrate the beginnings of humanism. The volume consists mainly of Petrarch's own letters to his friends. The introduction gives a much fuller account of his work than it was possible to include in the present volume. For similar material from other writers of the time, see WHIT-COMB, *A Literary Source Book of the Italian Renaissance* (Philadelphia, $1.00). The autobiography of Benvenuto Cellini is a very amusing and instructive book by one of the well-known artists of the sixteenth century. Roscoe's translation in the Bohn series (The Macmillan Company, $1.00) is to be recommended for school libraries.

The greatest of the sources for the lives of the artists is VASARI, *Lives of Seventy of the Most Eminent Painters, Sculptors, and Architects*. This may be had in the Temple Classics (The Macmillan Company, 8 vols., 50 cents each) or a selection of the more important lives admirably edited in Blashfield and Hopkins' carefully annotated edition (Scribner's Sons, 4 vols., $8.00). Vasari was a contemporary of Michael Angelo and Cellini, and writes in a simple and charming style. The outlines of the history of the various branches of art, with ample bibliographies, are given in the "College Histories of Art," edited by John C. Van Dyke; viz., VAN DYKE, *The History of Painting*, HAMLIN, *The History of Architecture*, and MARQUAND and FROTHING-HAM, *The History of Sculpture* (Longmans, Green & Co., each $2.00). Larger works with more illustrations, which might be found in any good town library are : FERGUSSON, *History of Modern Architecture*, LÜBKE, *History of Sculpture*, WOLTMANN and WOERMANN, *History of Painting*, and FLETCHER, *A History of Architecture*. Two companies publish very inexpensive reproductions of works of art : the so-called Perry pictures at a cent apiece, and the still better Cosmos pictures (Cosmos Picture Company, New York), costing somewhat more.

For the invention of printing see DE VINNE, *The Invention of Printing*, unfortunately out of print, and BLADES, *Pentateuch of Printing* (London, $4.75). Also PUTNAM, *Books and their Makers during the Middle Ages*, Vol. I (G. P. Putnam's Sons, $2.50).

CHAPTER XXIII

EUROPE AT THE OPENING OF THE SIXTEENTH CENTURY

129. Two events took place in the early sixteenth century which fundamentally influenced the history of Europe. (1) By a series of royal marriages a great part of western Europe was brought under the control of a single ruler, Emperor Charles V. He inherited Burgundy, Spain, portions of Italy, and the Austrian territories; and, in 1519, he was chosen emperor. There had been no such dominion as his in Europe since the time of Charlemagne. Within its bounds lay Vienna, Brussels, Madrid, Palermo, Naples, Milan, even the city of Mexico. Its creation and the struggles which accompanied its dissolution form one of the most important chapters in the history of modern Europe. (2) Just at the time that Charles was assuming the responsibilities that his vast domains brought with them, the first successful revolt against the mediæval Church was beginning. This was to result in the disruption of the Church and the establishment of two great religious parties, the Catholic and the Protestant, which have endured down to the present time. The purpose of the present chapter is to describe the origin, extent, and character of the empire of Charles V, and to prepare the reader to grasp the *political* import of the Protestant revolt.

Before mentioning the family alliances which led to the consolidation of such tremendous political power in the hands of one person, it will be necessary, first, to note the rise of the house of Hapsburg to which Charles belonged, and secondly, to account for the appearance in European affairs of Spain, which has hitherto scarcely come into our story.

The German kings had failed to create a strong kingdom such as those over which Louis XI of France and Henry VII of England ruled. Their fine title of "emperor" had made them a great deal of trouble, as we have seen.[1] Their attempts to keep Italy as well as Germany under their rule, and the alliance of the mighty Bishop of Rome with their enemies had well-nigh ruined them. Their position was further weakened by their failure to render their office strictly hereditary. Although the emperors were often succeeded by their sons, each new emperor had to be *elected*, and those great vassals who controlled the election naturally took care to bind the candidate by solemn promises not to interfere with their privileges and independence. The result was that, after the downfall of the Hohenstaufens, Germany fell apart into a great number of practically independent states, of which none were very large and some were extremely small.

Reasons why the German kings failed to establish a strong state.

After an interregnum, Rudolf of Hapsburg had been chosen emperor in 1273.[2] The original seat of the Hapsburgs, who were destined to play a great part in European affairs, was in northern Switzerland, where the vestiges of their original castle may still be seen. Rudolf was the first prominent member of the family; he established its position and influence by seizing the duchies of Austria and Styria, which were to become, under his successors, the nucleus of the extensive Austrian possessions.

Rudolf of Hapsburg gets possession of Austria.

About a century and a half after the death of Rudolf the electors began regularly to choose as emperor the ruler of the Austrian possessions, so that the imperial title became, to all intents and purposes, hereditary in the Hapsburg line.[3] The Hapsburgs were, however, far more interested in adding to

The imperial title becomes practically hereditary in the house of Austria.

[1] See above, pp. 85, 151 *sq.*, and Chapters XIII–XIV.
[2] Rudolf, like many of his successors, was strictly speaking only king of the Romans, since he was never crowned emperor at Rome. See above, pp. 152 n., 185.
[3] From 1438 to 1806 only two emperors belonged to another family than the Hapsburgs.

their family domains than in advancing the interests of the now almost defunct Holy Roman Empire. This, in the memorable words of Voltaire, had ceased to be either holy, or Roman, or an empire.

Maximilian I, 1493-1519, extends the power of the Hapsburgs over the Netherlands and Spain.

Maximilian I, who was emperor at the opening of the sixteenth century, was absorbed in his foreign enterprises rather than in the improvement of the German government. Like so many of his predecessors, he was especially anxious to get possession of northern Italy. By his marriage with the daughter of Charles the Bold he brought the Netherlands into what proved a fateful union with Austria.[1] Still more important was the extension of the power of the Hapsburgs over Spain, a country which had hitherto had almost no connection with Germany.

Arab civilization in Spain.

130. The Mohammedan conquest served to make the history of Spain very different from that of the other states of Europe. One of its first and most important results was the conversion of a great part of the inhabitants to Mohammedanism.[2] During the tenth century, which was so dark a period in the rest of Europe, the Arab civilization in Spain reached its highest development. The various elements in the population, Roman, Gothic, Arab, and Berber, appear to have been thoroughly amalgamated. Agriculture, industry, commerce, art, and the sciences made rapid progress. Cordova, with its half million of inhabitants, its stately palaces, its university, its three thousand mosques and three hundred public baths, was perhaps unrivaled at that period in the whole world. There were thousands of students at the university of Cordova at a time when, in the North, only clergymen had mastered even the simple arts of reading and writing. This brilliant civilization lasted, however, for hardly more than a hundred years. By the middle of the eleventh century the caliphate of Cordova had fallen to pieces, and shortly afterwards the country was overrun by new invaders from Africa.

[1] See above, p. 301.   [2] See above, p. 71.

Meanwhile the vestiges of the earlier Christian rule continued to exist in the mountain fastnesses of northern Spain. Even as early as the year 1000,[1] several small Christian kingdoms — Castile, Aragon, and Navarre — had come into existence. Castile, in particular, began to push back the demoralized Arabs and, in 1085, reconquered Toledo from them. Aragon also widened its bounds by incorporating Barcelona and conquering the territory watered by the Ebro. By 1250, the long war of the Christians against the Mohammedans, which fills the mediæval annals of Spain, had been so successfully prosecuted that Castile extended to the south coast and included the great towns of Cordova and Seville. The kingdom of Portugal was already as large as it is to-day.

The rise of new Christian kingdoms in Spain.

The Moors, as the Spanish Mohammedans were called, maintained themselves for two centuries more in the mountainous kingdom of Granada, in the southern part of the peninsula. During this period, Castile, which was the largest of the Spanish kingdoms and embraced all the central part of the peninsula, was too much occupied by internal feuds and struggles over the crown to wage successful war against the Moorish kingdom to the south.

Granada and Castile.

The first Spanish monarch whose name need be mentioned here was Queen Isabella of Castile, who, in 1469, concluded an all-important marriage with Ferdinand, the heir of the crown of Aragon. It is with the resulting union of Castile and Aragon that the great importance of Spain in European history begins. For the next hundred years Spain was to enjoy more military power than any other European state. Ferdinand and Isabella undertook to complete the conquest of the peninsula, and in 1492, after a long siege, the city of Granada fell into their hands, and therewith the last vestige of Moorish domination disappeared.[2]

Marriage of Isabella of Castile and Ferdinand of Aragon.

Granada, the last Moorish stronghold, falls.

---

1 See map above, following p. 152.
2 No one can gaze upon the great castle and palace of the Alhambra, which was built for the Moorish kings, without realizing what a high degree of culture

Spain's
income from
the New
World enables
her to become
a European
power.

In the same year that the conquest of the peninsula was completed, the discoveries of Columbus, made under the auspices of Queen Isabella, opened up the sources of undreamed-of wealth beyond the seas. The transient greatness of Spain in the sixteenth century is largely to be attributed to the riches which poured in from her American possessions. The shameless and cruel looting of the Mexican and Peruvian cities by Cortez and Pizarro, and the products of the silver mines of the New World, enabled Spain to assume, for a time, a position in Europe which her internal strength and normal resources would never have permitted.

Persecution
of the Jews
and Moors.

Unfortunately, the most industrious, skillful, and thrifty among the inhabitants of Spain, i.e., the Moors and the Jews, who well-nigh supported the whole kingdom with the products of their toil, were bitterly persecuted by the Christians. So anxious was Isabella to rid her kingdom of the infidels that she

The revival
of the Inqui-
sition.

revived the court of the Inquisition.[1] For several decades its tribunals arrested and condemned innumerable persons who were suspected of heresy, and thousands were burned at the stake during this period. These wholesale executions have served to associate Spain especially with the horrors of the Inquisition. Finally, in 1609, the Moors were driven out of the country altogether. The persecution diminished or disheartened the most useful and enterprising portion of the Spanish people, and speedily and permanently crippled a country which in the sixteenth century was granted an unrivaled opportunity to become a flourishing and powerful monarchy.

Heritage of
Charles V.

Maximilian, the German emperor, was not satisfied with securing Burgundy for his house by his marriage with the daughter of Charles the Bold. He also arranged a marriage between their son, Philip, and Joanna, the daughter of Ferdinand

---

the Moors had attained. Its beautiful and impressive arcades, its magnificent courts, and the delicate tracery of its arches represent the highest achievement of Arabic architecture.   [1] See above, pp. 224–225.

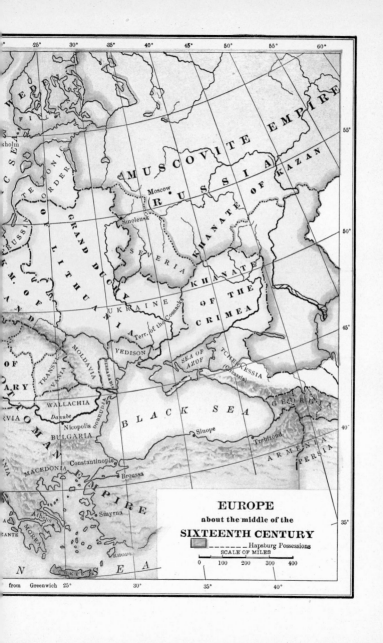

EUROPE

about the middle of the

SIXTEENTH CENTURY

---- Hapsburg Possessions

SCALE OF MILES

0   100   200   300   400

and Isabella. Philip died in 1506, and his poor wife, Joanna, became insane with grief and was thus incapacitated for ruling. So their eldest son, Charles, could look forward to an unprecedented accumulation of glorious titles as soon as his grandfathers, Maximilian and Ferdinand, should pass away.[1] He was soon to be duke of Brabant, margrave of Antwerp, count of Holland, archduke of Austria, count of Tyrol, king of Castile, Aragon, and Naples, and of the vast Spanish possessions in America, — to mention a few of his more important titles.

Ferdinand died in 1516, and Charles, now a lad of sixteen, who had been born and reared in the Netherlands, was much bewildered when he landed in his Spanish dominions. His Flemish advisers were distasteful to the haughty Spaniards; suspicion and opposition awaited him in each of his several Spanish kingdoms, for he found by no means a united Spain. Each kingdom demanded special recognition of its rights and suggested important reforms before it would acknowledge Charles as its king.

Charles and his Spanish possessions.

It seemed as if the boy would have his hands full in asserting his authority as "king of Spain"; nevertheless, a still more imposing title and still more perplexing responsibilities were to fall upon his shoulders before he was twenty years old. It had long been Maximilian's ambition that his grandson should succeed him upon the imperial throne. After his death in 1519 the electors finally chose Charles instead of the rival

Charles elected emperor, 1519.

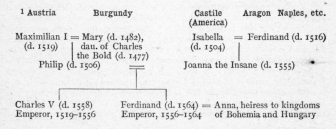

[1] Austria   Burgundy   Castile (America)   Aragon   Naples, etc.

Maximilian I = Mary (d. 1482),   Isabella   = Ferdinand (d. 1516)
(d. 1519)   dau. of Charles   (d. 1504)
    the Bold (d. 1477)
Philip (d. 1506)   Joanna the Insane (d. 1555)

Charles V (d. 1558)   Ferdinand (d. 1564) = Anna, heiress to kingdoms
Emperor, 1519–1556   Emperor, 1556–1564   of Bohemia and Hungary

candidate, Francis I of France.   By this election the king of
Spain, who had not yet been in Germany and who never
learned its language, became its ruler at a critical juncture,

Charles V

when the teachings of Luther were
producing unprecedented dissension and political distraction.   We
shall hereafter refer to him by his
imperial title of Charles V.

131.   In order to understand the
Europe of Charles V and the constant wars which occupied him all
his life, we must turn back and
review the questions which had
been engaging the attention of his
fellow-kings before he came to the
throne.   It is particularly necessary

to see clearly how Italy had suddenly become the center of
commotion, — the battlefield for Spain, France, and Germany.

**Charles VIII
of France
invades
Italy.**

Charles VIII of France (1483–1498) possessed little of the
practical sagacity of his father, Louis XI.   He dreamed of a
mighty expedition against the Turks and of the conquest of
Constantinople.   As the first step he determined to lead an
army into Italy and assert his claim, inherited from his father,
to the kingdom of Naples, which was in the hands of the
house of Aragon.[1]   While Italy had everything to lose by permitting a powerful monarch to get a foothold in the South, there

---

[1] It will be remembered that the popes, in their long struggle with Frederick II
and the Hohenstaufens, finally called in Charles of Anjou, the brother of St. Louis,
and gave to him both Naples and Sicily.   See above, p. 185.   Sicily revolted in
1282 and was united with the kingdom of Aragon, which still held it when
Charles V came to the Spanish throne.   The older branch of the house of Anjou
died out in 1435 and Naples was conquered by the king of Aragon, and was still in
his family when Charles VIII undertook his Italian expedition.   The younger
branch of the house of Anjou had never reigned in Naples, but its members were
careful to retain their asserted title to it, and, upon the death of their last representative, this title was transferred to Louis XI.   He, however, prudently refused
to attempt to oust the Aragonese usurpers, as he had quite enough to do at home.

was no probability that the various little states into which the peninsula was divided would lay aside their perpetual animosities and combine against the invader. On the contrary, Charles VIII was urged by some of the Italians themselves to come.

Had Lorenzo the Magnificent still been alive, he might have organized a league to oppose the French king, but he had died in 1492, two years before Charles started. Lorenzo's sons failed to maintain the influence over the people of Florence which their father had enjoyed ; and the leadership of the city fell into the hands of the Dominican friar, Savonarola, whose fervid preaching attracted and held for a time the attention of the fickle Florentine populace. He believed himself to be a prophet, and proclaimed that God was about to scourge Italy for its iniquities, and that men should flee before His wrath by renouncing their lives of sin and pleasure.

Savonarola and Charles VIII.

When Savonarola heard of the French invasion, it appeared to him that this was indeed the looked-for scourge of God, which might afflict, but would also purify, the Church. His prophecies seemed to be fulfilled, and his listeners were stricken with terror. As Charles approached Florence, the people rose in revolt against the Medici, sacked their palaces, and drove out the three sons of Lorenzo. Savonarola became the chief figure in the new republic which was established. Charles was admitted into Florence, but his ugly, insignificant figure disappointed the Florentines. They soon made it clear to him that they would not regard him in any sense as a conqueror, and would oppose a prolonged occupation by the French. Savonarola said to him : " The people are afflicted by your stay in Florence, and you waste your time. God has called you to renew His Church. Go forth to your high calling lest God visit you in His wrath and choose another instrument in your stead to carry out His designs." So, after a week's stay, the French army left Florence and proceeded on its southward journey.

The popes
since the
Great Schism. The next power with which Charles VIII had to deal was represented by a person in every way the opposite of the Dominican monk — Pope Alexander VI. After the troubles of the Great Schism and the councils, the popes had set to work to organize their possessions in central Italy into a compact principality. For a time they seemed to be little more than Italian princes. But they did not make rapid progress in their political enterprises because, in the first place, they were usually advanced in years before they came to power and so had little time to carry out their projects ; and, in the second place, they showed too much anxiety to promote the interests of their relatives. The selfish, unscrupulous means employed by these worldly prelates naturally brought great discredit upon the Church.

Pope Alexander VI
and Cæsar
Borgia. There was probably never a more openly profligate Italian despot than Alexander VI (1493–1503) of the notorious Spanish house of Borgia. He frankly set to work to advance the interests of his children, as if he were merely a secular ruler. For one of his sons, Cæsar Borgia, he proposed to form a duchy east of Florence. Cæsar outdid his father in crime. He not only entrapped and mercilessly slaughtered his enemies, but had his brother assassinated and thrown into the Tiber. Both he and his father were accused of constant recourse to poisoning, in which art they were popularly supposed to have gained extraordinary proficiency. It is noteworthy that when Machiavelli prepared his *Prince*,[1] he chose for his hero Cæsar Borgia, as possessing in the highest degree those qualities which went to make up a successful Italian ruler.

The pope was greatly perturbed by the French invasion, and in spite of the fact that he was the head of Christendom, he entered into negotiations with the Turkish sultan in the hope of gaining aid against the French king. He could not, however, prevent Charles from entering Rome and later continuing on his way to Naples.

[1] See above, p. 327.

The success of the French king seemed marvelous, for even Naples speedily fell into his hands. But he and his troops were demoralized by the wines and other pleasures of the South, and meanwhile his enemies at last began to form a combination against him. Ferdinand of Aragon was fearful lest he might lose Sicily, and Maximilian objected to having the French control Italy. Charles' situation became so precarious that he may well have thought himself fortunate, at the close of 1495, to escape, with the loss of only a single battle, from the country he had hoped to conquer. Charles VIII leaves Italy unconquered.

The results of Charles' expedition appear at first sight trivial; in reality they were momentous. In the first place, it was now clear to Europe that the Italians had no real national feeling, however much they might despise the "barbarians" who lived north of the Alps. From this time down to the latter half of the nineteenth century, Italy was dominated by foreign nations, especially Spain and Austria. In the second place, the French learned to admire the art and culture of Italy. The nobles began to change their feudal castles, which since the invention of gunpowder were no longer impregnable, into luxurious country houses. The new scholarship of Italy took root and flourished not only in France, but in England and Germany as well. Consequently, just as Italy was becoming, politically, the victim of foreign aggressions, it was also losing, never to regain, that intellectual preëminence which it had enjoyed since the revival of interest in classical literature. Results of Charles' expedition.

After Charles VIII's departure, Savonarola continued his reformation with the hope of making Florence a model state which should lead to the regeneration of the world. At first he carried all before him, and at the Carnival of 1496 there were no more of the gorgeous exhibitions and reckless gayety which had pleased the people under Lorenzo the Magnificent. The next year the people were induced to make a great bonfire, in the spacious square before the City Hall, of all the Savonarola's reforms in Florence.

"vanities" which stood in the way of a godly life — frivolous and immoral books, pictures, jewels, and trinkets.

Savonarola
condemned
and exe-
cuted, 1498.

Savonarola had enemies, however, even in his own Dominican order, while the Franciscans were naturally jealous of his renown and maintained that he was no real prophet. What was more serious, Alexander VI was bitterly hostile to the reforming friar because he urged the Florentines to remain in alliance with France. Before long even the people began to lose confidence in him. He was arrested by the pope's order in 1497 and condemned as a heretic and despiser of the Holy See. He was hanged, and his body burned, in the same square where the "vanities" had been sacrificed hardly more than a twelvemonth before.

Louis XII's
Italian
policy.

In the same year (1498), the romantic Charles VIII died without leaving any male heirs and was succeeded by a distant relative, Louis XII, who renewed the Italian adventures of his predecessor. As his grandmother was a member of the Milanese house of the Visconti, Louis laid claim to Milan as well as to Naples. He quickly conquered Milan, and then arranged a secret treaty with Ferdinand of Aragon (1500) for the division of the kingdom of Naples between them. It was not hard for the combined French and Spanish troops to conquer the country, but the two allies soon disagreed, and four years later Louis sold his title to Naples for a large sum to Ferdinand.

Pope
Julius II.

132. Pope Julius II, who succeeded the unspeakable Alexander VI (1503), was hardly more spiritual than his predecessor. He was a warlike and intrepid old man, who did not hesitate on at least one occasion to put on a soldier's armor and lead his troops in person. Julius was a Genoese, and harbored an inveterate hatred against Genoa's great commercial rival, Venice. The Venetians especially enraged the pope by taking possession of some of the towns on the northern border of his dominions, and he threatened to reduce their city to a fishing village. The Venetian ambassador replied, "As for you, Holy Father, if you are not more reasonable, we shall reduce you to a village priest."

With the pope's encouragement, the League of Cambray was formed in 1508 for the express purpose of destroying one of the most important Italian states. The Empire, France, Spain, and the pope were to divide among them Venice's possessions on the mainland. Maximilian was anxious to gain the districts bordering upon Austria, Louis XII to extend the boundaries of his new duchy of Milan, while the pope and Ferdinand were also to have their appropriate shares.

League of Cambray against Venice, 1508.

Venice was quickly reduced to a few remnants of its Italian domains, but the Venetians hastened to make their peace with the pope, who, after receiving their humble submission, gave them his forgiveness. In spite of his previous pledges to his allies, the pope now swore to exterminate the "barbarians" whom he had so recklessly called in. He formed an alliance with Venice and induced the new king of England, Henry VIII, to attack the French king. As for Maximilian, the pope declared him as "harmless as a newborn babe." This "Holy League" against the French led to their loss of Milan and their expulsion from the Italian peninsula in 1512, but it in no way put an end to the troubles in Italy.

The bellicose Julius was followed in 1513 by Leo X, a son of Lorenzo the Magnificent. Like his father, he loved art and literature, but he was apparently utterly without religious feelings. He was willing that the war should continue, in the hope that he might be able to gain a couple of duchies for his nephews.

Pope Leo X 1513-1521.

Louis XII died and left his brilliant cousin and successor, Francis I, to attempt once more to regain Milan. The new king was but twenty years old, gracious in manner, and chivalrous in his ideals of conduct. His proudest title was "the gentleman king." Like his contemporaries, Leo X, and Henry VIII of England, he patronized the arts, and literature flourished

Francis I of France, 1515-1547.

during his reign. He was not, however, a wise statesman; he was unable to pursue a consistent policy, but, as Voltaire says, "did everything by fits and starts."

Francis I in Italy.

He opened his reign by a very astonishing victory. He led his troops into Italy over a pass which had hitherto been regarded as impracticable for cavalry, and defeated the Swiss — who were in the pope's pay — at Marignano. He then occupied Milan and opened negotiations with Leo X, who was glad to make terms with the victorious young king. The pope agreed that Francis should retain Milan, and Francis on his part acceded to Leo's plan for turning over Florence once more to the Medici. This was done, and some years later

The republic of Florence becomes the grand duchy of Tuscany.

this wonderful republic became the grand duchy of Tuscany, governed by a line of petty princes under whom its former glories were never renewed.[1]

Sources of discord between France and the Hapsburgs.

Friendly relations existed at first between the two young sovereigns, Francis I and Charles V, but there were several circumstances which led to an almost incessant series of wars between them. France was clamped in between the northern and southern possessions of Charles, and had at that time no natural boundaries. Moreover, there was a standing dispute over portions of the Burgundian realms, for both Charles and Francis claimed the *duchy* of Burgundy and the neighboring *county* of Burgundy—commonly called Franche-Comté. Charles also believed that, through his grandfather, Maximilian, he was entitled to Milan, which the French kings had set their hearts

---

[1] More important for France than the arrangements mentioned above was the so-called *Concordat*, or agreement, between Francis and the pope in regard to the selection of the French prelates. Francis was given the privilege of appointing the archbishops, bishops, and abbots, and in this way it came about that he and his successors had many rich offices to grant to their courtiers and favorites. He agreed in return that the pope should receive a part of the first year's revenue from the more important offices in the Church of France. The pope was, moreover, thereafter to be regarded as superior to a council, a doctrine which had been denied by the French monarchs since the Council of Basel. The arrangements of the Concordat of 1516 were maintained down to the French Revolution.

upon acquiring. For a generation the rivals fought over these and other matters, and the wars between Charles and Francis were but the prelude to a conflict lasting over two centuries between France and the overgrown power of the house of Hapsburg.

In the impending struggle it was natural that both monarchs should try to gain the aid of the king of England, whose friendship was of the greatest importance to each of them, and who was by no means loath to take a hand in European affairs. Henry VIII had succeeded his father (Henry VII) in 1509 at the age of eighteen. Like Francis, he was good-looking and graceful, and in his early years made a very happy impression upon those who came in contact with him. He gained much popularity by condemning to death the two men who had been most active in extorting the "benevolences" which his father had been wont to require of unwilling givers. With a small but important class, his learning brought him credit. He married, for his first wife, an aunt of Charles V, Catherine of Aragon, and chose as his chief adviser Thomas Wolsey, whose career and sudden downfall were to be strangely associated with the fate of the unfortunate Spanish princess.[1]

Henry VIII of England, 1509-1547.

In 1520 Charles V started for Germany to receive the imperial crown at Aix-la-Chapelle. On his way he landed in England with the purpose of keeping Henry from forming an alliance with Francis. He judged the best means to be that of freely bribing Wolsey, who had been made a cardinal by Leo X, and who was all-powerful with Henry. Charles therefore bestowed on the cardinal a large annuity in addition to one which he had granted him somewhat earlier. He then set sail for the Netherlands, where he was duly crowned king of the Romans. From there he proceeded, for the first time, to Germany, where he summoned his first diet at Worms. The most important business of the assembly proved to be the

Charles V goes to Germany.

[1] See below, p. 428-429.

consideration of the case of a university professor, Martin Luther, who was accused of writing heretical books, and who had in reality begun what proved to be the first successful revolt against the seemingly all-powerful mediæval Church.

General Reading. — For the Italian wars of Charles VIII and Louis XII, *Cambridge Modern History* (The Macmillan Company, $3.75 per vol.), Vol. I, Chapter IV; JOHNSON, *Europe in the Sixteenth Century* (The Macmillan Company, $1.75), Chapter I; DYER and HASSALL, *Modern Europe* (The Macmillan Company, 6 vols., $2.00 each), Vol. I; CREIGHTON, *History of the Papacy* (see above, p. 320), Vols. IV, V. For Savonarola, *Cambridge Modern History*, Vol. I, Chapter V; CREIGHTON, Vol. IV, Chapter VIII; LEA, *History of the Inquisition* (see above, p. 232), Vol. III, pp. 209–237; SYMONDS, *Age of Despots* (see above, p. 352), Chapter IX; PASTOR, *History of the Popes* (see above, p. 320), Vol. V. For Spain, *Cambridge Modern History*, Vol. I, Chapter XI.

CHAPTER XXIV

GERMANY BEFORE THE PROTESTANT REVOLT

133. By far the most important event in the sixteenth century and one of the most momentous in the history of the western world, was the revolt of a considerable portion of northern and western Europe from the mediæval Church. There had been but two serious rebellions earlier. The first of these was that of the Albigenses in southern France in the thirteenth century; this had been fearfully punished, and the Inquisition had been established to ferret out and bring to trial those who were disloyal to the Church. Then, some two centuries later, the Bohemians, under the inspiration of Wycliffe's writings, had attempted to introduce customs different from those which prevailed elsewhere in the Church. They, too, had been forced, after a terrific series of conflicts, once more to accept the old system.

Two unsuccessful revolts preceded the Protestant revolution.

Finally, however, in spite of the great strength and the wonderful organization of the Church, it became apparent that it was no longer possible to keep all of western Europe under the sway of the pope. In the autumn of 1520, Professor Martin Luther called together the students of the University of Wittenberg, led them outside the town walls, and there burned the constitution and statutes of the mediæval Church, i.e., the canon law. In this way he publicly proclaimed and illustrated his purpose to repudiate the existing Church with many of its doctrines and practices. Its head he defied by destroying the papal bull directed against his teachings.

Luther secedes from the Church, 1520.

369

Origin of the two great religious parties in western Europe,— the Catholics and Protestants.

Other leaders, in Germany, Switzerland, England, and elsewhere, organized separate revolts; rulers decided to accept the teachings of the reformers, and used their power to promote the establishment of churches independent of the pope. In this way western Europe came to be divided into two great religious parties. The majority of its people continued to regard the pope as their religious head and to accept the institutions under which their forefathers had lived since the times of Theodosius. In general, those regions (except England) which had formed a part of the Roman empire remained Roman Catholic in their belief. On the other hand, northern Germany, a part of Switzerland, England, Scotland, and the Scandinavian countries sooner or later rejected the headship of the pope and many of the institutions and doctrines of the mediæval Church, and organized new religious institutions. The Protestants, as those who seceded from the Church of Rome were called, by no means agreed among themselves what particular system should replace the old one. They were at one, however, in ceasing to obey the pope and in proposing to revert to the early Church as their model and accepting the Bible as their sole guide.[1]

Revolt against the mediæval Church implied a general revolution.

To revolt against the Church was to inaugurate a fundamental revolution in many of the habits and customs of the people. It was not merely a change of religious belief, for the Church permeated every occupation and dominated every social interest. For centuries it had directed and largely controlled education, high and low. Each and every important act in the home, in the guild, in the town, was accompanied by religious ceremonies. The clergy of the Roman Catholic Church had hitherto written most of the books; they sat in

[1] The Catholic Church, on the other hand, held that certain important teachings, institutions, and ceremonies, although not expressly mentioned in the Bible, were nevertheless sanctioned by "tradition." That is, they had been handed down orally from Christ and his apostles as a sacred heritage to the Church, and like the Bible were to be received as from God. See *Readings*, Chapter XXIV.

the government assemblies, acted as the rulers' most trusted ministers, constituted, in short, outside of Italy, the only really educated class. Their rôle and the rôle of the Church were incomparably more important than that of any church which exists to-day.

Just as the mediæval Church was by no means an exclusively religious institution, so the Protestant revolt was by no means simply a religious change, but a social and political one as well. The conflicts which the attempt to overthrow this institution, or rather social order, brought about were necessarily terrific. They lasted for more than two centuries and left no interest, public or private, social or individual, earthly or heavenly, unaffected. Nation rose against nation, kingdom against kingdom; households were divided among themselves; wars and commotion, wrath and desolation, treachery and cruelty filled the states of western Europe.

The wars of religion.

Our present object is to learn how this successful revolt came about, what was its real nature, and why the results were what they were. In order to do this, it is necessary to turn to the Germany in which Luther lived and see how the nation had been prepared to sympathize with his attack on the Church.

134. To us to-day, Germany means the German Empire, one of the three or four best organized and most powerful of the European states. It is a compact federation, somewhat like that of the United States, made up of twenty-two monarchies and three little city republics. Each member of the union manages its local affairs, but leaves all questions of national importance to be settled by the central government at Berlin. This federation is, however, of very recent date, being scarcely more than thirty years old.

Germany of to-day.

In the time of Charles V there was no such Germany as this, but only what the French called " the Germanies "; i.e., two or three hundred states, which differed greatly from one another

The 'Germanies' of the sixteenth century.

in size and character. One had a duke, another a count at its head, while some were ruled over by archbishops, bishops, or abbots. There were many cities, like Nuremberg, Augsburg, Frankfort, and Cologne, which were just as independent as the great duchies of Bavaria, Würtemberg, and Saxony. Lastly there were the knights, whose possessions might consist of no more than a single strong castle with a wretched village lying at its foot. Their trifling territories must, however, be called states; for some of the knights were at that time as sovereign and independent as the elector of Brandenburg, who was one day to become the king of Prussia, and long after, the emperor of Germany.

The seven electors and the other greater German princes. As for the emperor, he no longer had any power to control his vassals. He could boast of unlimited pretensions and a great past, but he had neither money nor soldiers. At the time of Luther's birth the poverty-stricken Frederick III might have been seen picking up a free meal at a monastery, or riding behind a slow but economical ox team. The real power in Germany lay in the hands of the more important vassals. First and foremost among these were the seven electors, so called because, since the thirteenth century, they had enjoyed the right to elect the emperor. Three of them were archbishops — kings in all but name of considerable territories on the Rhine, namely, of the electorates of Mayence, Treves, and Cologne.[1] Near them, to the south, was the region ruled over by the elector of the Palatinate; to the northeast were the territories of the electors of Brandenburg and of Saxony; the king of Bohemia made the seventh of the group. Beside these states, the dominions of other rulers scarcely less important than the electors appear on the map. Some of these territories, like Würtemberg, Bavaria, Hesse, and Baden, are familiar to us to-day as members of the present German empire, but

[1] For the origin of these and of the other ecclesiastical states of Germany, see above, p. 156.

GERMANY

ABOUT 1550

Boundary of Empire
Habsburg Territories
Hohenzollern Territories
Ecclesiastical Territories
Imperial Cities

0 10 20 30 40 50   100

Scale of Miles.

M.-N. ENG., BUFFALO.

all of them have been much enlarged since the sixteenth century by the absorption of the little states that formerly lay within and about them.[1]

The towns, which had grown up since the great economic **The towns.** revolution that had brought in commerce and the use of money in the thirteenth century, were centers of culture in the north of Europe, just as those of Italy were in the south. Nuremberg, the most beautiful of the German cities, still possesses a great part of the extraordinary buildings and works of art which it produced in the sixteenth century. Some of the towns held directly of the emperor, and were consequently independent of the particular prince within whose territory they were situated. These were called *free*, or *imperial*, cities and must be reckoned among the states of Germany.

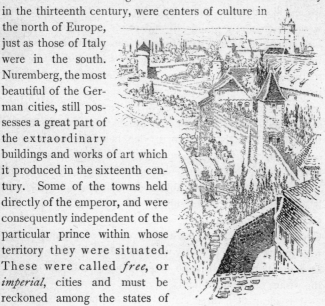

Wall of the formerly Free Town of Rothenburg

The knights, who ruled over the smallest of the German territories, had once formed an important military class, but the **The knights.** invention of gunpowder and of new methods of fighting had made their individual prowess of little avail. As their tiny realms were often too small to support them, they frequently turned to out-and-out robbery for a living. They hated the

---

[1] The manner in which the numerous and often important ecclesiastical states all disappeared in Napoleon's time will become clear later. See below, § 244.

cities because the prosperous burghers were able to live in a luxurious comfort which the poor knights envied but could not imitate. They hated the princes because these were anxious to incorporate into their own territories the inconvenient little districts controlled by the knights, many of whom, like the free cities, held directly of the emperor, and were consequently practically independent.

Complexity of the map of Germany. It would be no easy task to make a map of Germany in the time of Charles V sufficiently detailed to show all the states and scattered fragments of states. If, for example, the accompanying map were much larger and indicated all the divisions, it would be seen that the territory of the city of Ulm completely surrounded the microscopic possessions of a certain knight, the lord of Eybach, and two districts belonging to the abbot of Elchingen. On its borders lay the territories of four knights, — the lords of Rechberg, Stotzingen, Erbach, and Wiesensteig, — and of the abbots of Söflingen and Wiblingen, besides portions of Würtemberg and outlying Austrian possessions. The main cause of this bewildering subdivision of Germany was the habit of dealing with a principality as if it were merely private property which might be divided up among several children, or disposed of piecemeal, quite regardless of the wishes of the inhabitants.

No central power to maintain order. It is clear that these states, little and big, all tangled up with one another, would be sure to have disputes among themselves which would have to be settled in some way. It would appear to have been absolutely necessary under the circumstances that there should be some superior court or judge to adjust differences between the many members of the empire, as well as a military or police force to carry out the will of the tribunal, should one of the parties concerned resist its decrees. But although there was an imperial court, it followed the emperor about and was therefore hard to get at. Moreover, even if a decision was obtained from it, there was no way for the aggrieved party to secure the execution of the judgment, for the emperor had no force sufficient to coerce the larger states. The natural result was a resort to self-help. Neighborhood war was permitted by law if only some courteous preliminaries were observed. For instance, a prince or town was required to give warning three days in advance before attacking another member of the empire.[1]

Neighborhood war.

Toward the end of the fifteenth century the terrible disorder and uncertainty which resulted from the absence of a strong central government led to serious efforts upon the part of the *diet*, or national assembly, to remedy the evils. It was proposed to establish a court to settle all disputes which should arise among the rulers of the various states. This was to be held permanently in some convenient place. The empire was also to be divided into districts, or "circles," in each of which a military force was to be organized and maintained to carry out the law and the decisions of the court. Little was accomplished, however, for some years, although the diet met more frequently and regularly, and this gave an opportunity to discuss public questions. The towns began to send delegates to the diet in 1487, but the restless knights and some of the other minor nobles had no part in the deliberations and did not always feel that the decisions of the assembly were binding upon them. Of the diets which met almost every year during the Lutheran period in some one of the great German cities, we shall hear more later.

The German diet.

Effort to better the German government.

135. It is natural that Protestant and Catholic writers should differ in their views of Germany at this period. Among Protestants there has always been a tendency to see the dark side of affairs, for this exalted the work of Luther and made him

Contradiction between Catholic and Protestant writers.

[1] See above, pp. 117 *sqq.* For the German law permitting feuds, see Henderson, *Historical Documents*, p. 246. In 1467, the German diet ventured to forbid neighborhood war for five years. It was not, however, permanently prohibited until a generation later.

appear the savior of his people. On the other hand, the Catholic historians have devoted years of research to an attempt to prove that conditions were, on the whole, happy and serene and full of hope for the future before Luther and the other revolutionary leaders brought division and ruin upon the fatherland by attacking the Church.

Corresponding contradictions in the conditions in Germany. As a matter of fact, the life and thought of Germany during the fifty years preceding the opening of the Protestant revolt present all sorts of contradictions and anomalies. The period was one of marked progress. The people were eager to learn, and they rejoiced in the recent invention of printing which brought them the new learning from Italy and hints of another world beyond the seas. Foreigners who visited Germany were astonished at the prosperity, wealth, and luxury of the rich merchants, who often spent their money in the encouragement of art and literature and in the founding of schools and libraries.

On the other hand, there was great ill feeling between the various classes — the petty princes, the townspeople, the knights, and the peasants. It was generally believed by the other classes that the wealth of the merchants could only be accounted for by deceit, usury, and sharp dealing. Never was begging more prevalent, superstition more rife, vulgarity and coarseness more apparent. Attempts to reform the government and stop neighborhood war met with little success. Moreover, the Turks were advancing steadily upon Christendom. The people were commanded by the pope to send up a prayer each day as the noon bell rang, that God might deliver them from the on-coming infidel.

Yet we need not be astonished by these contradictions, for history teaches that all periods of progress are full of them. Any newspaper will show how true this is to-day : we are, as a nation, good and bad, rich and poor, peaceful and warlike, learned and ignorant, satisfied and discontented, civilized and barbarous, all at once.

In considering the condition of the Church and of religion in Germany, four things are particularly important as explaining the origin and character of the Protestant revolt. First, there was an extraordinary enthusiasm for all the pomp and ceremony of the old religion, and a great confidence in pilgrimages, relics, miracles, and all those things which the Protestants were soon to discard. Secondly, there was a tendency to read the Bible and to dwell upon the attitude of the sinner toward God, rather than upon the external acts of religion. Thirdly, there was a conviction, especially among scholars, that the theologians had made religion needlessly complicated with their fine-spun logical distinctions. And lastly, there was the old and very general belief that the Italian prelates, including the pope, were always inventing new plans for getting money out of the Germans, whom they regarded as a stupid people, easily hoodwinked. These four matters we shall consider in turn.

Four important characteristics of the time which serve to explain the Protestant revolt.

136. Never had the many ceremonies and observances of the mediæval Church attracted more attention or been carried out on a more prodigious scale than during the latter part of the fifteenth, and the opening years of the sixteenth century. It seemed as if all Germany agreed to join in one last celebration of the old religion, unprecedented in magnificence, before its people parted into two irreconcilable parties. Great numbers of new churches were erected, and adorned with the richest productions of German art. Tens of thousands of pilgrims flocked to the various sacred places, and gorgeous ecclesiastical processions moved through the streets of the prosperous imperial towns.

Enthusiasm for religious ceremonies and observances.

The princes rivaled each other in collecting the relics of saints, which were venerated as an aid to salvation. The elector of Saxony, Frederick the Wise, who was later to become Luther's protector, had accumulated no less than five thousand of these sacred objects. In a catalogue of them

Relics.

we find the rod of Moses, a bit of the burning bush, thread spun by the Virgin, etc. The elector of Mayence possessed even a larger collection, which included forty-two whole bodies of saints and some of the earth from a field near Damascus out of which God was supposed to have created man.

The treasury of ' good works.'

It was the teaching of the Church that prayers, fasts, masses, pilgrimages, and other " good works " might be accumulated and form a treasury of spiritual goods. Those who were wanting in good deeds might, therefore, have their deficiencies offset by the inexhaustible surplus of righteous deeds which had been created by Christ and the saints.

The idea was certainly a beautiful one, that Christians should thus be able to help one another by their good works, and that the strong and faithful worshiper could aid the weak and indifferent. Yet the thoughtful teachers in the Church realized that the doctrine of the treasury of good works might be gravely

Popular reliance upon outward religious acts.

misunderstood ; and there was certainly a strong inclination among the people to believe that God might be propitiated by various outward acts — attendance at church ceremonies, giving of alms, the veneration of relics, the making of pilgrimages, etc. It was clear that the hope of profiting by the good works of others might lead to the neglect of the true welfare of the soul.

Demand for more spiritual religion.

137. In spite, however, of the popular confidence in outward acts and ceremonies, from which the heart was often absent, there were many signs of a general longing for deeper and more spiritual religion than that of which we have been speaking. The new art of printing was used to increase the number of religious manuals. These all emphasized the uselessness of outward acts without true contrition and sorrow for sin, and urged the sinner to rely upon the love and forgiveness of God.

The Bible in German before Luther.

All good Christians were urged, moreover, to read the Bible, of which there were a number of editions in German, besides little books in which portions of the New Testament were given. There are many indications that the Bible was commonly read before Luther's time.[1]

It was natural, therefore, that the German people should take a great interest in the new and better translation of the Scriptures which Luther prepared. Preaching had also become common — as common perhaps as it is now — before the Protestants appeared. Some towns even engaged special preachers of known eloquence to address their citizens regularly.

These facts would seem to justify the conclusion that there were many before Luther appeared who were approaching the ideas of religion which later appealed especially to the Protestants. The insistence of the Protestants upon salvation through faith alone in God, their suspicion of ceremonies and "good works," their reliance upon the Bible, and the stress they laid upon preaching, — all these were to be found in Germany and elsewhere before Luther began to preach.

138. Among the critics of the churchmen, monks, and theologians, none were more conspicuous than the humanists. The Renaissance in Italy, which may be said to have begun with Petrarch and his library, has already been described. The Petrarch of Germany was Rudolph Agricola, who, while not absolutely the first German to dedicate himself to classical studies, was the first who by his charming personality and varied accomplishments stimulated others, as Petrarch had done, to carry on the pursuits which he himself so much enjoyed. Unlike most of the Italian humanists, however, Agricola and his followers were interested in the language of the people as well as in Latin and Greek; and proposed that the works of antiquity should be translated

The German humanists.

Rudolph Agricola, 1442-1485.

---

[1] For example, in one of the books of instruction for the priest we find that he is warned, when he quotes the Bible, to say to the people that he is not translating it word for word from the Latin, for otherwise they are likely to go home and find a different wording from his in their particular version and then declare that the priest had made a mistake.

into German. Moreover, the German humanists were generally far more serious and devout than the Italian scholars.

The humanists desire to reform the German universities.

As the humanists increased in numbers and confidence they began to criticise the excessive attention given in the German universities [1] to logic and the scholastic theology. These studies had lost their earlier vitality [2] and had degenerated into fruitless disputations. The bad Latin which the professors used themselves and taught their students, and the preference still given to Aristotle over all other ancient writers, disgusted the humanists. They therefore undertook to prepare new and better text-books, and proposed that the study of the Greek and Roman poets and orators should be introduced into the schools and colleges. Some of the classical scholars were for doing away with theology altogether, as a vain, monkish study which only obscured the great truths of religion. The old-fashioned professors, on their part, naturally denounced the new learning, which they declared made pagans of those who became enamored of it. Sometimes the humanists were permitted to teach their favorite subjects in the universities, but as time went on it became clear that the old and the new teachers could not work amicably side by side.

The humanist satire on the monks and theologians, the so-called *Letters of Obscure Men.*

At last, a little before Luther's public appearance, a conflict occurred between the " poets," as the humanists were fond of calling themselves, and the " barbarians," as they called the theologians and monkish writers. An eminent Hebrew scholar, Reuchlin, had become involved in a bitter controversy with the Dominican professors of the University of Cologne. His cause was championed by the humanists, who prepared an extraordinary satire upon their opponents. They wrote a series of letters, which were addressed to one of the Cologne

[1] Some seventeen universities had been established by German rulers and towns in a little over one hundred years. The oldest of them was founded in 1348 at Prague. Several of these institutions, for example, Leipsic, Vienna, and Heidelberg, are still ranked among the leading universities of the world.

[2] See above, § 104.

professors and purported to be from his former students and admirers. In these letters the writers take pains to exhibit the most shocking ignorance and stupidity. They narrate their scandalous doings with the ostensible purpose of obtaining advice as to the best way to get out of their scrapes. They vituperate the humanists in comically bad Latin, which is perhaps the best part of the joke.[1] In this way those who later opposed Luther and his reforms were held up to ridicule in these letters and their opposition to progress seemed clearly made out.

139. The acknowledged prince of the humanists was Erasmus. No other man of letters, unless it be Voltaire, has ever enjoyed such a European reputation during his lifetime. He was venerated by scholars far and wide, even in Spain and Italy. Although he was born in Rotterdam he was not a Dutchman, but a citizen of the world ; he is, in fact, claimed by England, France, and Germany. He lived in each of these countries for a considerable period and in each he left his mark on the thought of the time. Erasmus, like most of the northern humanists, was deeply interested in religious reform, and he aspired to give the world a higher conception of religion and the Church than that which generally prevailed. He clearly perceived, as did all the other intelligent people of the time,

Erasmus of Rotterdam, 1467?-1536.

---

[1] For examples of these *Letters of Obscure Men*, see Whitcomb, *Source Book of the German Renaissance*, pp. 67 *sq.*, and *Translations and Reprints*, Vol. II, No. 6. The peculiar name of the satire is due to the fact that Reuchlin's sympathizers wrote him many letters of encouragement, which he published under the title, *Letters of Celebrated Men to John Reuchlin*. The humanists then pitched upon the modest title, *Letters of Obscure Men*, for the supposed correspondence of the admirers of the monks. The following is an example of the " obscure men's " poetry. One of them goes to Hagenau and meets a certain humanist, Wolfgang Angst, who, the writer complains, struck him in the eye with his staff.

> Et ivi hinc ad Hagenau
> Da wurden mir die Augen blau
> Per te, Wolfgang Angst,
> Gott gib das du hangst,
> Quia me cum baculo
> Percusseras in oculo.

the vices of the prelates, priests, and especially of the monks. Against the latter he had a personal grudge, for he had been forced into a monastery when he was a boy, and always looked back to the life there with disgust. Erasmus reached the height of his fame just before the public appearance of Luther; consequently his writings afford an admirable means of determining how he and his innumerable admirers felt about the Church and the clergy before the opening of the great revolt.

Erasmus'
edition of
the New
Testament. Erasmus spent some time in England between the years 1498 and 1506, and made friends of the scholars there. He was especially fond of Sir Thomas More, who wrote the famous *Utopia*, and of a young man, John Colet, who was lectur-

ing at Oxford upon the Epistles of St. Paul.[1] Colet's enthusiasm for Paul appears to have led Erasmus to direct his vast knowledge of the ancient languages to the explanation of the New Testament. This was only known in the common Latin version (the Vulgate), into which many mistakes and misapprehensions had crept. Erasmus felt that the first thing to do, in order to promote higher ideas of Christianity, was

Portrait of Erasmus by Holbein

to purify the sources of the faith by preparing a correct edition of the New Testament. Accordingly, in 1516, he published the original Greek text with a new Latin translation and explanations which mercilessly exposed the mistakes of the great body of theologians.

Erasmus would have had the Bible in the hands of every one. In the introduction to his edition of the New Testament he says that women should read the Gospels and the Epistles of

[1] See below, pp. 426–7.

Paul as well as the men. The peasant in the field, the artisan in his shop, and the traveler on the highroad should while away the time with passages from the Bible.

Erasmus believed that the two arch enemies of true religion were (1) paganism, — into which many of the more enthusiastic Italian humanists fell in their admiration for the ancient literatures, — and (2) the popular confidence in mere outward acts and ceremonies, like visiting the graves of saints, the mechanical repetition of prayers, and so forth. He claimed that the Church had become careless and had permitted the simple teachings of Christ to be buried under myriads of dogmas introduced by the theologians. "The essence of our religion," he says, "is peace and harmony. These can only exist where there are few dogmas and each individual is left to form his own opinion upon many matters."

Erasmus' idea of true religion.

In his celebrated *Praise of Folly*,[1] Erasmus has much to say of the weaknesses of the monks and theologians, and of the foolish people who thought that religion consisted simply in pilgrimages, the worship of relics, and the procuring of indulgences. Scarcely one of the abuses which Luther later attacked escaped Erasmus' satirical pen. The book is a mixture of the lightest humor and the bitterest earnestness. As one turns its pages one is sometimes tempted to think Luther half right when he declared Erasmus "a regular jester who makes sport of everything, even of religion and Christ himself." Yet there was in this humorist a deep seriousness that cannot be ignored. Erasmus was really directing his extraordinary industry, knowledge, and insight, not toward a revival of classical literature, but to *a renaissance of Christianity*. He believed, however, that revolt from the pope and the Church would produce a great disturbance and result in more harm than good. He preferred to trust in the slower but surer effects of enlightenment

In his Praise of Folly Erasmus attacks the evils in the Church.

[1] This may be had in English, published by Scribner's Sons ($1.25) or Brentano ($1.25).

and knowledge. Popular superstitions and any undue regard for the outward forms of religion would, he argued, be outgrown and quietly disappear as mankind became more cultivated.

To Erasmus and his many sympathizers, culture, promoted especially by classical studies, should be the chief agency in religious reform. Nevertheless, just as Erasmus thought that his dreams of a peaceful reform were to be realized, as he saw the friends and patrons of literature, — Maximilian, Henry VIII, Francis I, — on the thrones of Europe, and a humanist pope, Leo X, at the head of the Church, a very different revolution from that which he had planned, had begun and was to embitter his declining years.

Sources of discontent in Germany with the policy of the papal court.

140. The grudge of Germany against the papal court never found a more eloquent expression than in the verses of its greatest minnesinger, Walther von der Vogelweide. Three hundred years before Luther's time he declared that the pope was making merry over the stupid Germans. " All their goods will be mine, their silver is flowing into my far-away chest ; their priests are living on poultry and wine and leaving the silly layman to fast." Similar sentiments may be found in the German writers of all the following generations. Every one of the sources of discontent with the financial administration of the Church which the councils had tried to correct[1] was particularly apparent in Germany. The great German prelates, like the archbishops of Mayence, Treves, Cologne, and Salzburg, were each required to contribute no less than ten thousand gold guldens to the papal treasury upon having their election duly confirmed by the pope ; and many thousands more were expected from them when they received the pallium.[2] The pope enjoyed the right to fill many important benefices in Germany, and frequently appointed Italians, who drew the revenue without dreaming of performing any of the duties attached to the office. A single person frequently held

[1] See above, pp. 317–318.   [2] See above, p. 203.

several church offices. For example, early in the sixteenth century, the Archbishop of Mayence was at the same time Archbishop of Magdeburg and Bishop of Halberstadt. In some instances a single person had accumulated over a score of benefices.

It is impossible to exaggerate the impression of deep and widespread discontent with the condition of the Church which one meets in the writings of the early sixteenth century. The whole German people, from the rulers down to the humblest tiller of the fields, felt themselves unjustly used. The clergy were denounced as both immoral and inefficient. One devout writer exclaims that young men are considered quite good enough to be priests to whom one would not intrust the care of a cow. While the begging friars — the Franciscans, Dominicans, and Augustinians[1] — were scorned by many, they, rather than the secular clergy, appear to have carried on the real religious work. It was an Augustinian monk, we shall find, who preached the new gospel of justification by faith.

Very few indeed thought of withdrawing from the Church or of attempting to destroy the power of the pope. All that most of the Germans wished was that the money which, on one pretense or another, flowed toward Rome should be kept at home, and that the clergy should be upright, earnest men who should conscientiously perform their religious duties. One patriotic writer, however, Ulrich von Hutten, was preaching something very like revolution at the same time that Luther began his attack on the pope.

Hutten was the son of a poor knight, but early tired of the monotonous life of the castle and determined to seek the universities and acquaint himself with the ancient literatures, of which so much was being said. In order to carry on his

Ulrich von Hutten, 1488-1523.

---

[1] The Augustinian order, to which Luther belonged, was organized in the thirteenth century, a little later than the Dominican and the Franciscan.

studies he visited Italy and there formed a most unfavorable impression of the papal court and of the Italian churchmen, whom he believed to be oppressing his beloved fatherland. When the *Letters of Obscure Men* appeared, he was so delighted with them that he prepared a supplementary series in which he freely satirized the theologians. Soon he began to write in German as well as in Latin, in order the more readily to reach the ears of the people. In one of his pamphlets attacking the popes he explains that he has himself seen how Leo X spends the money which the Germans send him. A part goes to his relatives, a part to maintain the luxurious papal court, and a part to worthless companions and attendants, whose lives would shock any honest Christian.

In Germany, of all the countries of Europe, conditions were such that Luther's appearance wrought like an electric shock throughout the nation, leaving no class unaffected. Throughout the land there was discontent and a yearning for betterment. Very various, to be sure, were the particular longings of the prince and the scholar, of knight, burgher, and peasant; but almost all were ready to consider, at least, the teachings of one who presented to them a new conception of salvation which made the old Church superfluous.

General Reading. — The most complete account of the conditions in Germany before Luther is to be found in JANSSEN, *History of the German People* (Herder, Vols. I and II, $6.25). *Cambridge Modern History* (The Macmillan Company, $3.75 per vol.), Vol. I, Chapters IX and XIX; CREIGHTON, *History of the Papacy* (see Vol. I, p. 320), Vol. VI, Chapters I and II; and BEARD, *Martin Luther* (P. Green, London, $1.60), Chapters I and III, are excellent treatments of the subject. For Erasmus, see EMERTON'S charming *Desiderius Erasmus* (G. P. Putnam's Sons, $1.50), which gives a considerable number of his letters.

CHAPTER XXV

MARTIN LUTHER AND HIS REVOLT AGAINST THE CHURCH

141. Martin Luther was of peasant origin. His father was very poor, and was trying his fortune as a miner near the Harz Mountains when his eldest son, Martin, was born in 1483. Martin sometimes spoke, in later life, of the poverty and superstition which surrounded him in his childhood; of how his mother carried on her back the wood for the household and told him stories of a witch who had made away with the village priest. The boy was sent early to school, for his father was determined that his eldest son should be a lawyer. At eighteen, Martin entered the greatest of the north-German universities, at Erfurt, where he spent four years. There he became acquainted with some of the young humanists, for example, the one who is supposed to have written a great part of the *Letters of Obscure Men*. He was interested in the various classical writers, but devoted the usual attention to logic and Aristotle. *Luther's birth and education.*

Suddenly, when he had completed his college course and was ready to enter the law school, he called his friends together for one last hour of pleasure, and the next morning he led them to the gate of an Augustinian monastery, where he bade them farewell and turning his back on the world became a mendicant friar. That day, July 17, 1505, when the young master of arts, regardless of his father's anger and disappointment, sought salvation within the walls of a monastery, was the beginning of a religious experiment which had momentous consequences for the world. *Luther decides to become a monk.*

387

Luther later declared that "if ever a monk got to heaven through monkery," he was assuredly among those who merited salvation. So great was his ardor, so nervously anxious was he to save his soul by the commonly recognized means of fasts, vigils, prolonged prayers, and a constant disregard of the usual rules of health, that he soon could no longer sleep. He fell into despondency, and finally into despair. The ordinary observance of the rules of the monastery, which satisfied most of the monks, failed to give him peace. He felt that even if he outwardly did right he could never purify all his thoughts and desires. His experience led him to conclude that neither the Church nor the monastery provided any device which enabled him to keep his affections always centered on what he knew to be holy and right. Therefore they seemed to him to fail and to leave him, at heart, a hopelessly corrupt sinner, justly under God's condemnation.

Gradually a new view of Christianity came to him. The head of the monastery bade him trust in God's goodness and mercy and not to rely upon his own "good works." He began to study the writings of St. Paul and of Augustine, and from them was led to conclude that man was incapable, in the sight of God, of any good works whatsoever, and could only be saved by faith in God's promises. This gave him much comfort, but it took him years to clarify his ideas and to reach the conclusion that the existing Church was opposed to the idea of justification by faith, because it fostered what seemed to him a delusive confidence in "good works." He was thirty-seven years old before he finally became convinced that it was his duty to become the leader in the destruction of the old order.

It was no new thing for a young monk, suddenly cut off from the sunshine and hoping for speedy spiritual peace, to suffer disappointment and fall into gloomy forebodings, as did Brother Martin. He, however, having fought the battle through to victory, was soon placed in a position to bring comfort to others similarly afflicted with doubts as to their power to please God. In 1508 he was called to the new university which Frederick the Wise, elector of Saxony, had established at Wittenberg. We know little of his early years as a professor, but he soon began to lecture on the epistles of Paul and to teach his students the doctrine of justification by faith.

Luther had as yet no idea of attacking the Church. When, about 1511, he journeyed to Rome on business of his order, he devoutly visited all the holy places for the good of his soul, and was almost tempted to wish that his father and mother were dead, so that he might free them from purgatory by his pious observances. Yet he was shocked by the impiety of the Italian churchmen and the scandalous stories about popes Alexander VI and Julius II, the latter of whom was just then engaged in his warlike expeditions into northern Italy. The evidences of immorality on the part of the popes may well have made it easier for him later to reach the conclusion that the head of the Church was the chief enemy of religion.

Luther's visit to Rome.

Luther

Before long he began to encourage his students to defend his favorite beliefs in the debates in which they took part. For instance, one of the candidates for a degree, under Luther's inspiration, attacked the old theology against which the humanists had been fighting. "It is an error," he says, "to declare that no one can become a theologian without Aristotle; on the contrary, no one can become a theologian except it be without him." Luther desired the students to

Luther teaches a new kind of theology.

rely upon the Bible, Paul's writings above all, and upon the church fathers, especially Augustine.[1]

142. In October, 1517, Tetzel, a Dominican monk, began granting indulgences in the neighborhood of Wittenberg, and making claims for them which appeared to Luther wholly irreconcilable with the deepest truths of Christianity as he understood and taught them. He therefore, in accordance with the custom of the time, wrote out a series of ninety-five statements in regard to indulgences. These he posted on the church door and invited any one interested in the matter to enter into a discussion with him on the subject, which he believed was very ill understood. In posting these *theses*, as they were called, Luther did not intend to attack the Church, and had no expectation of creating a sensation. The theses were in Latin and addressed only to scholars. It turned out, however, that every one, high and low, learned and unlearned, was ready to discuss the perplexing theme of the nature of indulgences. The theses were promptly translated into German, printed, and scattered throughout the land.

In order to understand the indulgence, it must be remembered that the priest had the right to forgive the sin of the truly contrite sinner who had duly confessed his evil deeds.[2] Absolution freed the sinner from the deadly guilt which would otherwise have dragged him down to hell, but it did not free him from the penalties which God, or his representative, the priest, might choose to impose upon him. Serious penances had earlier been imposed by the Church for wrongdoing, but in Luther's time the sinner who had been absolved was chiefly afraid of the sufferings reserved for him in purgatory. It was

---

[1] He writes exultingly to a friend: "Our kind of theology reigns supreme in the university; only one who lectures on the Bible, Augustine, or some real Church father, can reckon on any listeners; and Aristotle sinks lower and lower every day." In this way he sought to discredit Peter Lombard, Aquinas, and all the writers who were then most popular in the theological schools. Walker, *The Reformation*, pp. 77–91.　　　[2] See above, p. 211–212.

there that his soul would be purified by suffering and prepared for heaven. The indulgence was a pardon, usually granted by the pope, through which the contrite sinner escaped a part, or all, of the punishment which remained even after he had been absolved. The pardon did not therefore forgive the guilt of the sinner, for that had necessarily to be removed before the indulgence was granted; it only removed or mitigated the penalties which even the forgiven sinner would, without the indulgence, have expected to undergo in purgatory.[1]

The first indulgences for the *dead* had been granted shortly before the time of Luther's birth. By securing one of these, the relatives or friends of those in purgatory might reduce the period of torment which the sufferers had to undergo before they could be admitted to heaven. Those who were in purgatory had, of course, been duly absolved of the guilt of their sins before their death; otherwise their souls would have been lost and the indulgence could not advantage them in any way.

With a view of obtaining funds from the Germans to continue the reconstruction of the great church of St. Peter,[2] Leo X had arranged for the extensive grant of indulgences, both for the living and for the dead. The contribution for them varied greatly; the rich were required to pay a considerable sum, while the *very* poor were to receive these pardons gratis. The representatives of the pope were naturally anxious to collect all the money possible, and did their best to induce every one to secure an indulgence, either for himself or for his deceased friends in purgatory. In their zeal they made many reckless claims for the indulgences, to which no thoughtful churchman or even layman could listen without misgivings.

Leo X issues indulgences in connection with the rebuilding of St. Peter's.

[1] It is a common mistake of Protestants to suppose that the indulgence was forgiveness granted beforehand for sins to be committed in the future. There is absolutely no foundation for this idea. A person proposing to sin could not possibly be contrite in the eyes of the Church, and even if he secured an indulgence it would, according to the theologians, have been quite worthless.

[2] See above, p. 344.

Luther was not the first to criticise the current notions of indulgences, but his theses, owing to the vigor of their language and the existing irritation of the Germans against the administration of the Church, first brought the subject into prominence. He declared that the indulgence was very unimportant and that the poor man would better spend his money for the needs of his household. The truly repentant, he argued, do not flee punishment, but bear it willingly in sign of their sorrow. Faith in God, not the procuring of pardons, brings forgiveness, and every Christian who feels true contrition for his sins will receive full remission of the punishment as well as of the guilt. Could the pope know how his agents misled the people, he would rather have St. Peter's burn to ashes than build it up with money gained under false pretenses. Then, Luther adds, there is danger that the common man will ask awkward questions. For example, "If the pope releases souls from purgatory for money, why not for charity's sake?" or, "Since the pope is rich as Crœsus, why does he not build St. Peter's with his own money, instead of taking that of the poor man?"[1]

143. The theses were soon forwarded to Rome, and a few months after they were posted Luther received a summons to appear at the papal court to answer for his heretical assertions. Luther still respected the pope as the head of the Church, but he had no wish to risk his safety by going to Rome. As Leo X was anxious not to offend so important a person as the elector of Saxony, who intervened for Luther, he did not press the matter, and agreed that Luther should confer with the papal emissaries in Germany.

Brother Martin was induced to keep silence for a time, but was aroused again by a great debate arranged at Leipsic in the summer of 1519. Here Eck, a German theologian noted

[1] The complete text of the theses may be found in *Translations and Reprints*, Vol. II, No. 6.

for his devotion to the pope and his great skill in debate, challenged one of Luther's colleagues, Carlstadt, to discuss publicly some of the matters in which Luther himself was especially interested. Luther therefore asked to be permitted to take part.

The discussion turned upon the powers of the pope. Luther, who had been reading church history, declared that the pope had not enjoyed his supremacy for more than four hundred years. This statement was inaccurate, but, nevertheless, he had hit upon an argument against the customs of the Roman Catholic Church which has ever since been constantly urged by Protestants. They assert that the mediæval Church and the papacy developed slowly, and that the apostles knew nothing of masses, indulgences, purgatory, and the headship of the Bishop of Rome. *The debate at Leipsic, 1519.*

Eck promptly pointed out that Luther's views resembled those of Wycliffe and Huss, which had been condemned by the Council of Constance. Luther was forced reluctantly to admit that the council had condemned some thoroughly Christian teachings. This was a decisive admission. Like other Germans, Luther had been accustomed to abhor Huss and the Bohemians, and to regard with pride the great general Council of Constance, which had been held in Germany and under the auspices of its emperor. He now admitted that even a general council could err, and was soon convinced " that we are all Hussites, without knowing it ; yes, Paul and St. Augustine were good Hussites." Luther's public encounter with a disputant of European reputation, and the startling admissions which he was compelled to make, first made him realize that he might become the leader in an attack on the Church. He began to see that a great change and upheaval was unavoidable. *Eck forces Luther to admit that the Council of Constance was wrong and Huss right.*

144. As Luther became a confessed revolutionist he began to find friends among other revolutionists and reformers. He had some ardent admirers even before the disputation at Leipsic, *Luther and the humanists natural allies.*

especially at Wittenberg and in the great city of Nuremberg. To the humanists, Luther seemed a natural ally. They might not understand his religious beliefs, but they clearly saw that he was beginning to attack a class of people that they disliked, particularly the old-fashioned theologians who venerated Aristotle. He felt, moreover, as they did in regard to the many vices in the Church, and was becoming suspicious of the begging monks, although he was himself at the head of the Wittenberg monastery. So those who had defended Reuchlin were now ready to support Luther, to whom they wrote encouraging letters. Luther's works were published by Erasmus' printer at Basel, and sent to Italy, France, England, and Spain.

Erasmus' attitude toward the Lutheran movement.

But Erasmus, the mighty sovereign of the men of letters, refused to take sides in the controversy. He asserted that he had not read more than a dozen pages of Luther's writings. Although he admitted that " the monarchy of the Roman high priest was, in its existing condition, the pest of Christendom," he believed that a direct attack upon it would do no good. Luther, he urged, would better be discreet and trust that mankind would become more intelligent and outgrow their false ideas.

Contrast between Luther and Erasmus.

To Erasmus, man was capable of progress ; cultivate him and extend his knowledge, and he would grow better and better. He was a free agent, with, on the whole, upright tendencies. To Luther, on the other hand, man was utterly corrupt, and incapable of a single righteous wish or deed. His will was enslaved to evil, and his only hope lay in the recognition of his absolute inability to better himself, and in a humble reliance upon God's mercy. By faith only, not by conduct, could he be saved. Erasmus was willing to wait until every one agreed that the Church should be reformed. Luther had no patience with an institution which seemed to him to be leading souls to destruction by inducing men to rely upon their good works. Both men realized that they could not agree. For a time they expressed respect for each other, but at last they became involved in a bitter controversy in which they gave up all pretense to friendship. Erasmus declared that Luther, by scorning good works and declaring that no one could do right, had made his followers indifferent to their conduct, and that those who accepted Luther's teachings straightway became pert, rude fellows, who would not take off their hats to him on the street.

Ulrich von Hutten, on the other hand, warmly espoused Luther's cause as that of a German patriot and an opponent of Roman tyranny, intrigue, and oppression. " Let us defend our freedom," he wrote, " and liberate the long enslaved fatherland. We have God on our side, and if God be with us, who can be against us ? " Hutten enlisted the interest of some of the other knights, who offered to defend Luther should the churchmen attack him, and invited him to take refuge in their castles.

Ulrich von Hutten espouses Luther's cause.

145. Thus encouraged, Luther, who gave way at times to his naturally violent disposition, became threatening, and suggested that the civil power should punish the churchmen and force them to reform their conduct. " We punish thieves with the gallows, bandits with the sword, heretics with fire ; why should we not, with far greater propriety, attack with every kind of weapon these very masters of perdition, the cardinals, popes, and the whole mob in the Roman Sodom ? " " The die is cast," he writes to a friend ; " I despise Rome's wrath as I do her favor ; I will have no reconciliation or intercourse with her in all time to come. Let her condemn and burn my writings. I will, if fire can be found, publicly condemn and burn the whole papal law."

Luther begins to use violent language.

Hutten and Luther vied with one another during the year 1520 in attacking the pope and his representatives. They both possessed a fine command of the German language, and they were fired by a common hatred of Rome. Hutten had little or none of Luther's religious fervor, but he could not find colors

Luther's and Hutten's appeal to the German people.

too dark in which to picture to his countrymen the greed of
the papal curia, which he described as a vast den, to which
everything was dragged which could be filched from the
Germans. Of Luther's popular pamphlets, the first really

**Luther's
Address to
the German
Nobility.**

famous one was his *Address to the German Nobility*, in which
he calls upon the rulers of Germany, especially the knights,
to reform the abuses themselves, since he believed that it was
vain to wait for the Church to do so.

He explains that there are three walls behind which the
papacy had been wont to take refuge when any one proposed
to remedy its abuses. There was, first, the claim that the
clergy formed a separate class, superior even to the civil
rulers, who might not punish a churchman, no matter how
bad he was. Secondly, the pope claimed to be superior to
a council, so that even the representatives of the Church
might not correct him. And, lastly, the pope assumed the
sole right to interpret the meaning of the Scriptures; consequently he could not be refuted by arguments from the Bible.
Thus the pope had stolen the three rods with which he might
have been punished. Luther claimed to cast down these
defenses by denying, to begin with, that there was anything
especially sacred about a clergyman except the duties which
he had been designated to perform. If he did not attend to
his work he might be deprived of his office at any moment,
just as one would turn off an incompetent tailor or farmer,
and in that case he became a simple layman again. Luther
claimed that it was the right and duty of the civil government to punish a churchman who does wrong just as if
he were the humblest layman. When this first wall was
destroyed the others would fall easily enough, for the dominant position of the clergy was the very corner stone of
the mediæval Church.[1]

---

[1] See above, p. 209, for the Church's doctrine of the "indelible character"
which the priest received at ordination.

The pamphlet closes with a long list of evils which must be done away with before Germany can become prosperous. Luther saw that his view of religion really implied a social revolution. He advocated reducing the monasteries to a tenth of their number and permitting those who were disappointed in the good they got from living in them freely to leave. He would not have them prisons, but hospitals and refuges for the soul-sick. He points out the evils of pilgrimages and of the numerous church holidays, which interfere with daily work. The clergy, he urged, should be permitted to marry and have families like other citizens. The universities should be reformed, and " the accursed heathen, Aristotle," should be cast out from them.

Luther advocates social as well as religious reforms.

It should be noted that Luther appeals to the authorities not in the name of religion chiefly, but in that of public order and prosperity. He says that the money of the Germans flies feather-light over the Alps to Italy, but it suddenly becomes like lead when there is a question of its coming back. He showed himself a master of vigorous language, and his denunciations of the clergy and the Church resounded like a trumpet call in the ears of his countrymen.

Luther had said little of the doctrines of the Church in his *Address to the German Nobility*, but within three or four months he issued a second work, in which he sought to overthrow the whole system of the sacraments, as it had been taught by Peter Lombard and the theologians of the thirteenth century.[1] Four of the seven sacraments — ordination, marriage, confirmation, and extreme unction — he rejected altogether. He completely revised the conception of the Mass, or the Lord's Supper. He stripped the priest of his singular powers by denying that he performed the miracle of transub-

Luther attacks the sacramental system in his Babylonian Captivity of the Church, 1520.

---

[1] See above, §§ 81–82. The two great works of Luther, here mentioned, as well as his *Freedom of the Christian*, in which he explains his own doctrine very simply, may be found translated in Wace and Buchheim, *Luther's Primary Works*.

stantiation or offered a sacrifice for the living and the dead when he officiated at the Lord's Supper. The priest was, in his eyes, only a minister, in the Protestant sense of the word, one of whose chief functions was preaching.

Luther excommunicated.

146. Luther had long expected to be excommunicated. But it was not until late in 1520 that his adversary, Eck, arrived in Germany with a papal bull condemning many of Luther's assertions as heretical and giving him sixty days in which to recant. Should he fail to come to himself within that time, he and all who adhered to or favored him were to be excommunicated, and any place which harbored him should fall under the interdict. Now, since the highest power in Christendom had pronounced Luther a heretic, he should unhesitatingly have been delivered up by the German authorities. But no one thought of arresting him.

The German authorities reluctant to publish the bull against Luther.

The bull irritated the German princes; whether they liked Luther or not, they decidedly disliked to have the pope issuing commands to them. Then it appeared to them very unfair that Luther's personal enemy should have been intrusted with the publication of the bull. Even the princes and universities that were most friendly to the pope published the bull with great reluctance. The students of Erfurt and Leipsic pursued Eck with pointed allusions to Pharisees and devil's emissaries. In many cases the bull was ignored altogether. Luther's own sovereign, the elector of Saxony, while no convert to the new views, was anxious that Luther's case should be fairly considered, and continued to protect him. One mighty prince, however, the young emperor Charles V, promptly and willingly published the bull; not, however, as emperor, but as ruler of the Austrian dominions and of the Netherlands. Luther's works were burned at Louvain, Mayence, and Cologne, the strongholds of the old theology.

Luther defies pope and emperor.

" Hard it is," Luther exclaimed, " to be forced to contradict all the prelates and princes, but there is no other way to escape hell and God's anger." Never had one man so unreservedly declared war upon pretty much the whole consecrated order of things. As one power arrayed against an equal, the Wittenberg professor opposed himself to pope and emperor, giving back curse for curse and fagot for fagot. His students were summoned to witness " the pious, religious spectacle," when he cast Leo's bull on the fire, along with the canon law and one of the books of scholastic theology which he most disliked.

Never was the temptation so great for Luther to encourage a violent demolition of the old structure of the Church as at this time. Hutten was bent upon the speedy carrying out of the revolution which both he and Luther were forwarding by their powerful writings. Hutten had taken refuge in the castle of the leader of the German knights, Franz von Sickingen, who he believed would be an admirable military commander in the coming contest for truth and liberty. Hutten frankly proposed to the young emperor that the papacy should be abolished, that the property of the Church should be confiscated, and that ninety-nine out of a hundred of the clergy should be dispensed with as superfluous. In this way Germany would be freed, he argued, from the control of the " parsons " and from their corruption. From the vast proceeds of the confiscation the state might be strengthened and an army of knights might be maintained for the defense of the empire.

Hutten's plan for an immediate destruction of the old Church.

Public opinion appeared ready for a revolution. " I am pretty familiar with the history of this German nation," Leo's representative, Aleander, remarked ; " I know their past heresies, councils, and schisms, but never were affairs so serious before. Compared with present conditions, the struggle between Henry IV and Gregory VII was as violets and roses. . . . These mad dogs are now well equipped with knowledge and arms ; they boast that they are no longer ignorant brutes like their predecessors ; they claim that Italy has lost

Views of the papal representative on public opinion in Germany.

the monopoly of the sciences and that the Tiber now flows
into the Rhine." "Nine-tenths of the Germans," he calculated, "are shouting 'Luther,' and the other tenth goes so far
at least as ' Death to the Roman curia.' "

Luther's
attitude
toward a
violent reali-
zation of his
reforms.
Luther was too frequently reckless and violent in his writings. He often said that bloodshed could not be avoided when
it should please God to visit his judgments upon the stiff-
necked and perverse generation of " Romanists," as the Germans contemptuously called the supporters of the pope. Yet
he always discouraged precipitate reform. He was reluctant
to make changes, except in belief. He held that so long as
an institution did not mislead, it did no harm. He was, in
short, no fanatic at heart. The pope had established himself
without force, so would he be crushed by God's word without
force. This, we may assume, was Luther's most profound conviction, even in the first period of enthusiasm and confidence.
He perhaps never fully realized how different Hutten's ideas
were from his own, for the poet knight died while still a young
man. And as for Franz von Sickingen, Luther soon learned
to execrate the ruthless, worldly soldier who brought discredit
by his violence upon the cause of reform.

Charles V's
want of sym-
pathy with
the German
reformers.
147. Among the enemies of the German reformers none
was more important than the young emperor. It was toward
the end of the year 1520 that Charles came to Germany for
the first time. After being crowned king of the Romans at
Aix-la-Chapelle, he assumed, with the pope's consent, the title
of emperor elect, as his grandfather Maximilian had done. He
then moved on to the town of Worms, where he was to hold
his first diet and face the German situation.

Although scarcely more than a boy in years, Charles had
already begun to take life very seriously. He had decided
that Spain, not Germany, was to be the bulwark and citadel of
all his realms. Like the more enlightened of his Spanish subjects, he realized the need of reforming the Church, but he had

no sympathy whatever with any change of doctrine. He proposed to live and die a devout Catholic of the old type, such as his orthodox ancestors had been. He felt, moreover, that he must maintain the same religion in all parts of his heterogeneous dominions. If he should permit the Germans to declare their independence of the Church, the next step would be for them to claim that they had a right to regulate their government regardless of their emperor.

Upon arriving at Worms the case of Luther was at once forced upon Charles' attention by the assiduous papal representative, Aleander, who was indefatigable in urging him to outlaw the heretic without further delay. While Charles seemed convinced of Luther's guilt, he could not proceed against him without serious danger. The monk had become a national hero and had the support of the powerful elector of Saxony. Other princes, who had ordinarily no wish to protect a heretic, felt that Luther's denunciation of the evils in the Church and of the actions of the pope was very gratifying. After much discussion it was finally arranged, to the great disgust of the zealous Aleander, that Luther should be summoned to Worms and be given an opportunity to face the German nation and the emperor, and to declare plainly whether he was the author of the heretical books ascribed to him, and whether he still adhered to the doctrines which the pope had declared wrong.

Luther summoned to the diet at Worms.

The emperor accordingly wrote the "honorable and respected" Luther a very polite letter, ordering him to appear at Worms and granting him a safe-conduct thither. Luther said, on receiving the summons, that if he was going to Worms merely to retract, he might better stay in Wittenberg, where he could, if he would, abjure his errors quite as well as on the Rhine. If, on the other hand, the emperor wished him to come to Worms in order that he might be put to death, he was quite ready to go, "for, with Christ's help, I will not flee and leave the Word in the lurch. My revocation will be

in this wise : 'Earlier I said that the pope was God's vicar ;
now I revoke and say, the pope is Christ's enemy and an
envoy of the devil.' "

148. Luther accordingly set out for Worms accompanied
by the imperial herald. He enjoyed a triumphal progress
through the various places on his way and preached repeatedly, in spite of the fact that he was an excommunicated
heretic. He found the diet in a great state of commotion.
The papal representative was the object of daily insults, and
Hutten and Sickingen talked of scattering Luther's enemies
by a sally from the neighboring castle of Ebernburg.

Luther before
the diet.

It was not proposed to give Luther an opportunity to defend
his beliefs before the diet. When he appeared before "emperor and empire," he was simply asked if a pile of his Latin
and German works were really his, and, if so, whether he
revoked what he had said in them. To the first question the
monk replied in a low voice that he had written these and
more. As to the second question, which involved the welfare
of the soul and the Word of God, he asked that he might have
a little while to consider.

The following day, in a Latin address which he repeated in
German, he admitted that he had been overviolent in his
attacks upon his opponents; but he said that no one could
deny that, through the popes' decrees, the consciences of
faithful Christians had been miserably ensnared and tormented, and their goods and possessions, especially in Germany, devoured. Should he recant those things which he had
said against the pope's conduct he would only strengthen the
papal tyranny and give an opportunity for new usurpations.
If, however, adequate arguments against his position could be
found in the Scriptures, he would gladly and willingly recant.
He could not, however, accept the decision either of pope or
of council, since both, he believed, had made mistakes and
contradicted themselves. " I must," he concluded, " allow my

conscience to be controlled by God's Word. Recant I can not and will not, for it is hazardous and dishonorable to act against one's conscience."

There was now nothing for the emperor to do but to outlaw Luther, who had denied the binding character of the commands of the head of the Church and of the highest Christian tribunal, a general council. His argument that the Scriptures sustained him in his revolt could not be considered by the diet.[1]

The emperor forced by the law to outlaw Luther.

Aleander was accordingly assigned the agreeable duty of drafting the famous Edict of Worms. This document declared Luther an outlaw on the following grounds : that he disturbed the recognized number and celebration of the sacraments, impeached the regulations in regard to marriage, scorned and vilified the pope, despised the priesthood and stirred up the laity to dip their hands in the blood of the clergy, denied free will, taught licentiousness, despised authority, advocated a brutish existence, and was a menace to Church and State alike. Every one was forbidden to give the heretic food, drink, or shelter, and required to seize him and deliver him to the emperor.

The Edict of Worms, 1521.

Moreover, the decree provides that " no one shall dare to buy, sell, read, preserve, copy, print, or cause to be copied or printed any books of the aforesaid Martin Luther, condemned by our holy father the pope, as aforesaid, or any other writings in German or Latin hitherto composed by him, since they are foul, noxious, suspected, and published by a notorious and stiff-necked heretic. Neither shall any one dare to affirm his opinions, or proclaim, defend, or advance them in any other

---

[1] It must be remembered that it was the emperor's business to execute the law, not to discuss its propriety with the accused. In the same way nowadays, should a man convicted, for example, of bigamy urge that he believed it Scriptural to have two wives, the court would refuse to listen to his arguments and would sentence him to the penalty imposed by law, in spite of the fact that the prisoner believed that he had committed no wrong.

way that human ingenuity can invent,— notwithstanding that he may have put some good into his writings in order to deceive the simple man." [1]

For the last time the empire had recognized its obligation to carry out the decrees of the Bishop of Rome. "I am becoming ashamed of my fatherland," Hutten cried. So general was the disapproval of the edict that few were willing to pay any attention to it. Charles immediately left Germany, and for nearly ten years was occupied outside it with the government of Spain and a succession of wars.

General Reading. — BEARD, *Martin Luther* (see above, p. 386), is probably the best account in English of Luther before his retirement to the Wartburg; KÖSTLIN, *Life of Luther* (Scribner's Sons, $2.50), is excellent. An account of Luther and Hutten by a learned Roman Catholic writer may be found in JANSSEN, *History of the German People* (see above, p. 386), Vol. III; CREIGHTON, *History of the Papacy* (see above, p. 320), Vol. VI; Chapters III and V are devoted to Luther and the diet of Worms.

[1] The text of the Edict of Worms is published in English in the *Historical Leaflets* issued by the Crozer Theological Seminary, Chester, Pa.

CHAPTER XXVI

COURSE OF THE PROTESTANT REVOLT IN GERMANY
1521–1555

149. As Luther neared Eisenach upon his way home from Worms he was seized by a band of men and conducted to the Wartburg, a castle belonging to the elector of Saxony. Here he was concealed until any danger from the action of the emperor or diet should pass by. His chief occupation during several months of hiding was to begin a new translation of the Bible into German. He had finished the New Testament before he left the Wartburg in March, 1522.

Luther begins a new translation of the Bible in the Wartburg.

Up to this time, German editions of the Scriptures, while not uncommon, were poor and obscure. Luther's task was a difficult one. He said with truth that "translation is not an art to be practiced by every one; it demands a right pious, true, industrious, reverent, Christian, scholarly, experienced, and well-trained mind." He had studied Greek for only two or three years, and he knew far less Hebrew than Greek. Moreover, there was no generally accepted form of the German language of which he could make use. Each region had its peculiar dialect which seemed outlandish to the neighboring district.

He was anxious above all that the Bible should be put into language that would seem perfectly clear and natural to the common folk. So he went about asking the mothers and children and the laborers questions which might draw out the expression that he was looking for. It sometimes took him two or three weeks to find the right word. But so well did

Luther's Bible the first important book in modern German.

he do his work that his Bible may be regarded as a great land-mark in the history of the German language. It was the first book of any importance written in modern German, and it has furnished an imperishable standard for the language.

General discussion of public questions in pamphlets and satires.

Previous to 1518 there had been very few books or pamphlets printed in German. The translation of the Bible into language so simple that even the unlearned might profit by it was only one of the signs of a general effort to awaken the minds of the common people. Luther's friends and enemies also commenced to write for the great German public in its own language. The common man began to raise his voice, to the scandal of the learned.

Hundreds of pamphlets, satires, and pictorial caricatures have come down to us which indicate that the religious and other questions of the day were often treated in somewhat the same spirit in which our comic papers deal with political problems and discussions now. We find, for instance, a correspondence between Leo X and the devil, and a witty dialogue between Franz von Sickingen and St. Peter at the gate of heaven. In the latter Peter confesses that he has never heard of the right "to loose and to bind," of which his successors say so much. He refuses to discuss military matters with Sickingen, but calls in St. George, who is supposed to be conversant with the art of war. In another satire, a vacation visit of St. Peter to the earth is described. He is roughly treated, especially by the soldiers at an inn, and hastens back to heaven with a sad tale of the evil plight of Germany, of how badly children are brought up, and how unreliable the servants are.[1]

Divergent notions of how the Church should actually be reformed.

150. Hitherto there had been a great deal of talk of reform, but as yet nothing had actually been done. There was no sharp line drawn between the different classes of reformers. All agreed that something should be done to better the Church, few realized how divergent were the real ends in view. The

[1] See *Readings*, Chapter XXVI.

princes listened to Luther because they hoped to control the churchmen and their property and check the outflow of money to Rome. The knights, under Sickingen, hated the princes, of whose increasing power they were jealous. Their idea of "righteousness" involved the destruction of the existing rulers and the exaltation of their own class. The peasants heard Luther gladly because he seemed to furnish new proofs of the injustice of the dues which they paid to their lords. The higher clergy were bent upon escaping the papal control, and the lower clergy wished to have their marriages sanctioned. It is clear that religious motives must have been often subordinated to other interests.

Disappointment and chagrin awaited Luther when each of the various parties began to carry out its particular notions of reform. His doctrines were misunderstood, distorted, and dishonored. He sometimes was driven to doubt if his belief in justification by faith were not after all a terrible mistake. His first shock came from Wittenberg.

While Luther was still at the Wartburg, Carlstadt, one of his colleagues in the university, became convinced that the monks and nuns ought to leave their cloisters and marry like other people. This was a serious proposition for two reasons. In the first place, those who deserted the cloister were violating an oath which they had voluntarily taken; in the second place, if the monasteries were broken up the problem would present itself of the disposal of the property, which had been given to them by pious persons for the good of their souls, and with the expectation that the monks would give the donors the benefit of their prayers. Nevertheless, the monks began to leave Luther's own monastery, and the students and citizens to tear down the images of the saints in the churches. The Lord's Supper was no longer celebrated in the form of the Mass, since that was declared to be an idolatrous worshiping of the bread and wine. Then Carlstadt reached the conclusion

Carlstadt advocates breaking up the monasteries.

that all learning was superfluous, for the Scriptures said plainly that God had concealed himself from the wise and revealed the truth unto babes. He astonished the trades-people by consulting them in regard to obscure passages in the Bible. The school at Wittenberg was turned into a bake-shop. The students, who had been attracted to the university from all parts of Germany, began to return home, and the professors prepared to emigrate.

Luther returns to Wittenberg and explains his plan of reform, 1522.

When the news of these events reached Luther, he left his concealment, regardless of the danger, and returned to Witten-berg. Here he preached a series of vigorous sermons in which he pleaded for moderation and reason. With some of the changes advocated by Carlstadt he sympathized. He would, for instance, have done away with the adoration of the host and the celebration of private masses. On the other hand, he disapproved of the disorderly breaking up of the monasteries, although he held that those who had accepted the doctrine of justification by faith might lay aside their cowls, since they had taken their vows when they were under the misapprehension that they could save themselves by good works. Those who remained in the monasteries were not, moreover, to beg any longer, but should earn an honest livelihood.

Luther advocates patience and moderation.

Luther felt that all changes in religious practices should be made by the government; it should not be left to "Mr. Every-body" (*Herr Omnes*) to determine what should be rejected and what retained. If the authorities refused to act, then there was nothing to do but to be patient and use one's influence for good. "Teach, speak, write, and preach that the ordinances of man are naught. Advise that no one shall any more become a priest, monk, or nun, and that those who occupy such posi-tions shall leave them. Give no more money for papal privi-leges, candles, bells, votive tablets, and churches, but say that a Christian life consists in faith and love. Let us keep this up for two years and you will see where pope, bishop, monks, nuns, and all the hocus-pocus of the papal government will be; it will vanish away like smoke." God, Luther urged, has left us free to choose whether we shall marry, become monks, fast, confess, or place images in the churches. These things are not vital to salvation, and each may do what seems to him to be helpful in his particular case.

Luther's plan of moderation was, however, wholly imprac- ticable. The enthusiasm of those who rejected the old views led to a whole-hearted repudiation of everything which sug- gested their former beliefs. Few could look with forbearance upon the symbols and practices of a form of religion which they had learned to despise. Moreover, many who had no deep religious feelings delighted in joining in the destruction of the paintings, stained glass, and statues in the churches, simply from a love of disorder.

Impossibility of peaceful reform.

151. Luther was soon to realize that a peaceful revolution was out of the question. His knightly adherents, Hutten and Franz von Sickingen, were the first to bring discredit upon the religious movement by their violence. In the autumn of 1522 Sickingen declared war upon his neighbor, the Archbishop of Treves, in order to make a beginning in the knights' proposed attack upon the princes in general. He promised the people of Treves " to free them from the heavy, unchristian yoke of the parsons and to lead them into evangelical liberty." He had already abolished the Mass in his castle and given shelter to some of Luther's followers. But Franz, in undertaking to put the gospel, as he understood it, in practice by arms, had other than religious motives. His admiration of Luther probably had but little to do with his anxiety to put down a hated ecclesiastical prince and seize his property.

Franz von Sickingen attacks the Archbishop of Treves.

The Archbishop of Treves proved himself a sagacious mili- tary commander and gained the support of his subjects. Franz was forced to retire to his castle, where he was besieged by the neighboring elector of the Palatinate and the landgrave of

Confedera- tion of knights broken up by the princes.

Hesse, a friend of Luther's. The walls of the stronghold were battered down by the "unchristian cannonading," and the "executor of righteousness," as Franz was called, was fatally

injured by a falling beam. A few months later, Hutten died, a miserable fugitive in Switzerland. A confederation of the knights, of which Sickingen had been the head, aroused the apprehension of the princes, who gathered sufficient forces to destroy more than twenty of the knights' castles. So Hutten's great plan for restoring the knights to their former influence came to a sad and sudden end. It is clear that these men had little in common with Luther; yet they talked much of evangelical reform, and he was naturally blamed for their misdeeds. Those who adhered to the old Church now felt that they had conclusive proof that heresy led to anarchy; and since it threatened the civil government as well as the Church, they urged that it should be put down with fire and sword.

152. While Luther was in the Wartburg, the cultured and worldly Leo X had died and had been succeeded by a devout professor of theology, who had once been Charles V's tutor. The new pope, Hadrian VI, was honest and simple, and a well-known advocate of reform without change of belief. He believed that the German revolt was a divine judgment called down by the wickedness of men, especially of the priests and prelates. He freely confessed, through his legate, in a meeting of the German diet at Nuremberg, that the popes had been perhaps the most conspicuous sinners. " We well know that for many years the most scandalous things have happened in this holy see [of Rome], — abuses in spiritual matters, violations of the canons,— that, in short, everything has been just the opposite of what it should have been. What wonder, then, if the disease has spread from the head to the members, from the popes to the lower clergy. We clergymen have all strayed from the right path, and for a long time there has been no one of us righteous, no, not one."

In spite of this honest confession, Hadrian was unwilling to listen to the grievances of the Germans until they had put down Luther and his heresies. He was, the pope declared, a worse foe to Christendom than the Turk. There could be nothing fouler or more disgraceful than Luther's teachings. He sought to overthrow the very basis of religion and morality. He was like Mohammed, but worse, for he would have the consecrated monks and nuns marry. Nothing would be securely established among men if every presumptuous upstart should insist that he had the right to overturn everything which had been firmly established for centuries and by saints and sages.

Hadrian's denunciation of Luther.

The diet was much gratified by the pope's frank avowal of the sins of his predecessors, in which it heartily concurred. It was glad that the pope was going to begin his reform at home, but it strenuously refused to order the enforcement of the Edict of Worms for fear of stirring up new troubles. The Germans were too generally convinced that they were suffering from the oppression of the Roman curia to permit Luther to be injured. His arrest would seem an attack upon the freedom of gospel teaching and a defence of the old system ; it might even lead to civil war. So the diet advised that a Christian council be summoned in Germany to be made up of laymen as well as clergymen, who should be charged to speak their opinions freely and say, not what was pleasant, but what was true. In the meantime, only the pure gospel should be preached according to the teaching of the Christian Church. As to the complaint of the pope that the monks had deserted their monasteries and the priests taken wives, these were not matters with which the civil authority had anything to do. As the elector of Saxony observed, he paid no attention to the monks when they ran into the monastery, and he saw no reason for noticing when they ran out. Luther's books were, however, to be no longer published, and learned men were to admonish the erring preachers. Luther, himself, was to hold his peace.

The action of the diet of Nuremberg, 1522.

This doubtless gives a fair idea of public opinion in Germany. It is noteworthy that Luther did not seem to the diet to be a very discreet person and it showed no particular respect for him.

153. Poor Hadrian speedily died, worn out with the vain effort to correct the abuses close at home. He was followed by Clement VII, a member of the house of Medici, less gifted but not less worldly than Leo X. A new diet, called in 1524, adhered to the policy of its predecessor. It was far from approving of Luther, but it placed no effective barrier in the way of his work.

The papal legate, realizing the hopelessness of inducing all the members of the diet to coöperate with him in bringing the country once more under the pope's control, called together at Regensburg a certain number of rulers whom he believed to be rather more favorably disposed toward the pope than their fellows. Among these were Charles V's brother, Ferdinand, Duke of Austria, the two dukes of Bavaria, the archbishops of Salzburg and of Trent, and the bishops of Bamberg, Speyer, Strasburg, etc. By means of certain concessions on the part of the pope, he induced all these to unite in opposing the Lutheran heresy. The chief concession was a reform decree which provided that only authorized preachers should be tolerated, and that these should base their teaching on the works of the four great church fathers, Ambrose, Jerome, Augustine, and Gregory the Great. The clergy were to be subjected to careful discipline ; there was to be no more financial oppression and no unseemly payments demanded for performing the church services. Abuses arising from the granting of indulgences were to be remedied and the excessive number of holidays reduced.

This agreement of Regensburg is of great importance, for it served to separate Germany into two camps. Austria, Bavaria, and the great ecclesiastical states in the south definitely took sides with the pope against Luther, and to this day they still remain Catholic countries. In the north, on the other hand, it became more and more apparent that the princes proposed to secede from the Catholic Church. Moreover, the skillful diplomacy of the papal legate was really the beginning of a reformation of the old Church in Germany. Many of the abuses were done away with, and the demand for reform, without revolution in doctrine and institutions, was thereby gratified.[1] A German Bible for Catholic readers was soon issued, and a new religious literature grew up designed to prove the truth of the beliefs sanctioned by the Roman Catholic Church and to spiritualize its institutions and rites.

Beginning of a reform within the Catholic Church.

154. In 1525 the conservative party, who were frankly afraid of Luther, received a new and terrible proof, as it seemed to them, of the noxious influence of his teachings. The peasants rose, in the name of "God's justice," to avenge their wrongs and establish their rights. Luther was not responsible for the civil war which ensued, but he had certainly helped to stir up discontent. He had asserted that, owing to the habit of foreclosing small mortgages, "any one with a hundred guldens could gobble up a peasant a year." The German feudal lords he had declared to be hangmen, who knew only how to swindle the poor man. "Such fellows were formerly called rascals, but now must we call them 'Christian and revered princes.'" Wise rulers are rare indeed: "they are usually either great fools or the worst rogues on earth." Yet in spite of his harsh talk about the princes, Luther really relied upon them to forward his movement, and he justly claimed that he had greatly increased their power by destroying the authority of the pope and subjecting the clergy in all things to the government.

Luther's rash talk about the princes and nobles serves to encourage the revolt of the peasants.

Some of the demands of the peasants were perfectly reasonable. The most popular expression of their needs was the dignified "Twelve Articles."[2] In these they claimed that the

The demands of the peasants in the 'Twelve Articles.'

---

[1] See below, § 167.

[2] The "Twelve Articles" may be found in *Translations and Reprints*, Vol. II, No. 6.

Bible did not sanction many of the dues which the lords demanded of them, and that as Christians they should no longer be held as serfs. They were willing to pay all the old and well-established dues, but they asked to be properly remunerated for extra services demanded by the lord. They thought too that each community should have the right freely to choose its own pastor and to dismiss him if he proved negligent or inefficient.

Demands of the working classes of the towns.

Much more radical demands came from the working classes in the towns, who in some cases joined the country people in their revolt. The articles drawn up in the town of Heilbronn, for example, give a good idea of the sources of discontent. The church property was to be confiscated and used for the good of the community, except in so far as it was necessary to support the pastors chosen by the people. The clergy and nobility were to be deprived of all their privileges and powers, so that they could no longer oppress the poor man.

Luther urges the government to suppress the revolt.

There were, moreover, leaders who were still more violent, who proposed to kill the " godless " priests and nobles. Hundreds of castles and monasteries were destroyed by the frantic peasantry, and some of the nobility were murdered with shocking cruelty. Luther tried to induce the peasants, with whom, as the son of a peasant, he was at first inclined to sympathize, to remain quiet; but when his warnings proved vain, he attacked the rebels violently. He declared that they were guilty of the most fearful crimes, for which they deserved death of both body and soul many times over. They had broken their allegiance, they had wantonly plundered and robbed castles and monasteries, and lastly, they had tried to cloak their dreadful sins with excuses from the Gospel. He therefore urged the government to put down the insurrection. " Have no pity on the poor folk ; stab, smite, throttle, who can ! "

The peasant revolt put down with great cruelty.

Luther's advice was followed with terrible literalness by the German rulers, and the nobility took fearful revenge for the depredations of the peasants. In the summer of 1525 the chief leader of the peasants was defeated and killed, and it is estimated that ten thousand peasants were put to death, many with the utmost cruelty. Few rulers or lords introduced any reforms, and the misfortunes due to the destruction of property and to the despair of the peasants cannot be imagined. The people concluded that the new gospel was not for them, and talked of Luther as "Dr. Lügner," i.e., liar. The old exactions of the lords of the manors were in no way lightened, and the situation of the peasants for centuries following the great revolt was worse rather than better.

155. The terror inspired by the peasant war led to new measures against further attempts to change the religious beliefs of the land. The League of Dessau was formed among some of the leading rulers of central and northern Germany, to stamp out "the accursed Lutheran sect." The union included Luther's arch enemy, Duke George of Saxony, the electors of Brandenburg and Mayence, and two princes of Brunswick. The rumor that the emperor, who had been kept busy for some years by his wars with Francis I, was planning to come to Germany in order to root out the growing heresy, led the few princes who openly favored Luther to unite also. Among these the chief were the new elector of Saxony, John Frederick, and Philip, landgrave of Hesse. These two proved themselves the most ardent and conspicuous defenders of the Protestant faith in Germany. *Catholic and Protestant unions of the German princes.*

A new war, in which Francis and the pope sided against the emperor, prevented Charles from turning his attention to Germany, and he accordingly gave up the idea of enforcing the Edict of Worms against the Lutherans. Since there was no one who could decide the religious question for all the rulers, the diet of Speyer (1526) determined that, pending the meeting of a general council, each ruler, and each knight and town owing immediate allegiance to the emperor, should decide individually what particular form of religion should *The diet of Speyer gives to the individual rulers the right to determine the religion of their subjects, 1526.*

prevail in his realm. Each prince was "so to live, reign, and conduct himself as he would be willing to answer before God and His Imperial Majesty." For the moment, then, the various German governments were left to determine the religion of their subjects.

Yet all still hoped that one religion might ultimately be agreed upon. Luther trusted that all Christians would sometime accept the new gospel. He was willing that the bishops should be retained, and even that the pope should still be regarded as a sort of presiding officer in the Church. As for his enemies, they were equally confident that the heretics would in time be suppressed as they had always been in the past, and that harmony would thus be restored. Neither party was right; for the decision of the diet of Speyer was destined to become a permanent arrangement, and Germany remained divided between different religious faiths.

Charles V again intervenes in the religious controversy in Germany.

New sects opposed to the old Church had begun to appear. Zwingli, a Swiss reformer, was gaining many followers, and the Anabaptists were rousing Luther's apprehensions by their radical plans for doing away with the Catholic religion. As the emperor found himself able for a moment to attend to German affairs he bade the diet, again meeting at Speyer in 1529, to order the enforcement of the edict against the heretics. No one was to preach against the Mass and no one was to be prevented from attending it freely.

Origin of the term 'Protestant.'

This meant that the "Evangelical" princes would be forced to restore the most characteristic Catholic ceremony. As they formed only a minority in the diet, all that they could do was to draw up a *protest*, signed by John Frederick, Philip of Hesse, and fourteen of the imperial towns (Strasburg, Nuremberg, Ulm, etc.). In this they claimed that the majority had no right to abrogate the edict of the former diet of Speyer for that had passed unanimously and all had solemnly pledged themselves to observe the agreement. They therefore appealed to the emperor and a future council against the tyranny of the majority.[1] Those who signed this appeal were called from their action *Protestants*. Thus originated the name which came to be generally applied to those who do not accept the rule and teachings of the Roman Catholic Church.

156. Since the diet at Worms the emperor had resided in Spain, busied with a succession of wars carried on with the king of France. It will be remembered that both Charles and Francis claimed Milan and the duchy of Burgundy, and they sometimes drew the pope into their conflicts.[2] But in 1530 the emperor found himself at peace for the moment and held a brilliant diet of his German subjects at Augsburg in the hope of settling the religious problem, which, however, he understood very imperfectly. He ordered the Protestants to draw up a statement of exactly what they believed, which should serve as a basis for discussion. Melanchthon, Luther's most famous friend and colleague, who was noted for his great learning and moderation, was intrusted with the delicate task.

Preparations for the diet of Augsburg.

The Augsburg Confession, as his declaration was called, is an historical document of great importance for the student of the Protestant revolt.[3] Melanchthon's gentle and conciliatory disposition led him to make the differences between his belief and that of the old Church seem as few and slight as possible. He showed that both parties held the same fundamental views of Christianity. The Protestants, however, defended their rejection of a number of the practices of the Roman Catholics, such as the celibacy of the clergy and the observance of

The Augsburg Confession.

[1] The Protest of Speyer is to be had in English in the *Historical Leaflets* published by the Crozer Theological Seminary, Chester, Pa.

[2] For the successive wars between Charles and Francis and the terrible sack of Rome in 1527, see Johnson, *Europe in the Sixteenth Century*, pp. 172–175 and 181–195.

[3] It is still accepted as the creed of the Lutheran Church. Copies of it in English may be procured from the Lutheran Publication Society, Philadelphia, for ten cents each.

fast days. There was little or nothing in the Augsburg Confession concerning the organization of the Church.

Charles V's attempt at pacification.

Certain theologians, some of whom, like Eck, had been loud in their denunciations of Luther, were ordered by the emperor to prepare a refutation of the Protestant views. The statement of the Catholics admitted that a number of Melanchthon's positions were perfectly orthodox; but the portion of the Augsburg Confession which dealt with the practical reforms introduced by the Protestants was rejected altogether. Charles declared the Catholic statement to be "Christian and judicious" and commanded the Protestants to accept it. They were to cease troubling the Catholics and were to give back all the monasteries and church property which they had seized. The emperor agreed to urge the pope to call a council to meet within a year. This, he hoped, would be able to settle all differences and reform the Church according to the views of the Catholics.

Progress of Protestantism up to the Peace of Augsburg, 1555.

157. It is unnecessary to follow in detail the progress of Protestantism in Germany during the quarter of a century succeeding the diet of Augsburg. Enough has been said to show the character of the revolt and the divergent views taken by the German princes and people. For ten years after the emperor left Augsburg he was kept busy in southern Europe by new wars; and in order to secure the assistance of the Protestants, he was forced to let them go their own way. Meanwhile the number of rulers who accepted Luther's teachings gradually increased. Finally there was a brief war between Charles and the Protestant princes, but the origin of the conflict was mainly political rather than religious. It occurred to the youthful Maurice, Duke of Saxony, that by aiding the emperor against the Protestants he might find a good excuse for dispossessing his Protestant relative, John Frederick, of his electorate. There was but little fighting done. Charles V brought his Spanish soldiers into Germany and captured both John Frederick and

his ally, Philip of Hesse, the chief leaders of the Lutheran cause, whom he kept prisoners for several years.[1]

This episode did not check the progress of Protestantism. Maurice, who had been granted John Frederick's electorate, soon turned about and allied himself with the Protestants. The king of France promised them help against his enemy, the emperor, and Charles was forced to agree to a preliminary peace with the Protestants. Three years later, in 1555, the religious Peace of Augsburg was ratified. Its provisions are memorable. Each German prince and each town and knight immediately under the emperor was to be at liberty to make a choice between the beliefs of the venerable Catholic Church and those embodied in the Augsburg Confession. If, however, an ecclesiastical prince — an archbishop, bishop, or abbot — declared himself a Protestant, he must surrender his possessions to the Church. Every one was either to conform to the religious practices of his particular state, or emigrate.

The Peace of Augsburg.

This religious peace in no way established freedom of conscience, except for the rulers. Their power, it must be noted, was greatly increased, inasmuch as they were given the control of religious as well as of secular matters. This arrangement which permitted the ruler to determine the religion of his realm was natural, and perhaps inevitable, in those days. The Church and the civil government had been closely associated with one another for centuries. No one as yet dreamed that every individual, so long as he did not violate the law of the land, might safely be left quite free to believe what he would and to practice any religious rites which afforded him help and comfort.

The principle that the government should determine the religion of its subjects.

There were two noteworthy weaknesses in the Peace of Augsburg which were destined to make trouble. In the first place, only one group of Protestants was included in it. The

Weaknesses of the Peace of Augsburg.

[1] Reference, Johnson, *Europe in the Sixteenth Century*, Chapter V ; Walker, *The Reformation*, pp. 188–216.

now numerous followers of the French reformer, Calvin, and of the Swiss reformer, Zwingli, who were hated alike by Catholic and Lutheran, were not recognized. Every German had to be either a Catholic or a Lutheran in order to be tolerated. In the second place, the clause which decreed that ecclesiastical princes converted to Protestantism should surrender their property could not be enforced, for there was no one to see to its execution.

CHAPTER XXVII

THE PROTESTANT REVOLT IN SWITZERLAND AND ENGLAND

158. For at least a century after Luther's death the great issue between Catholics and Protestants dominates the history of all the countries with which we have to do, except Italy and Spain, where Protestantism never took permanent root. In Switzerland, England, France, and Holland the revolt against the mediæval Church produced profound changes, which must be understood in order to follow the later development of these countries.

We turn first to Switzerland, lying in the midst of the great chain of the Alps which extends from the Mediterranean to Vienna. During the Middle Ages, the region destined to be included in the Swiss Confederation formed a part of the empire, and was scarcely distinguishable from the rest of southern Germany. As early as the thirteenth century the three "forest" cantons on the shores of the winding lake of Lucerne had formed a union to protect their liberties against the encroachments of their neighbors, the Hapsburgs. It was about this tiny nucleus that Switzerland gradually consolidated. In 1315 the cantons gained their first great victory over the Hapsburgs at Morgarten and thereupon solemnly renewed their league. This was soon joined by Lucerne and the free imperial towns of Zurich and Berne. By brave fighting the Swiss were able to frustrate the renewed efforts of the Hapsburgs to subjugate them. Later, when a still more formidable

Origin of the Swiss Confederation.

enemy, Charles the Bold, undertook to conquer them they put his armies to rout at Granson and Murten (1476).[1]

Various districts in the neighborhood successively joined the Swiss union, and even the region lying on the Italian slopes of the Alps was brought under its control. Gradually the bonds between the members of the union and the empire were

Switzerland becomes a separate country; mixed nationality of its people.

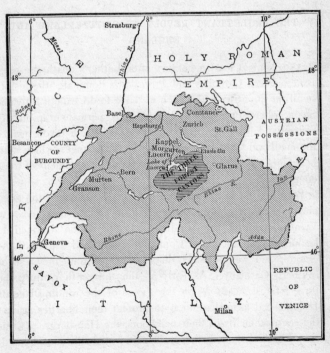

The Swiss Confederation

broken. They were recognized as being no more than "relatives" of the empire; in 1499 they were finally freed from the jurisdiction of the emperor, and Switzerland became a

[1] See above, p. 300.

practically independent country. Although the original union had been made up of German-speaking people, considerable districts had been annexed in which Italian or French was spoken.[1] The Swiss did not, therefore, form a compact, well-defined nation, and for some centuries their confederation was weak and ill-organized.

159. In Switzerland the leader of the revolt against the Church was Zwingli, who was a year younger than Luther and like him was the son of peasant parents. Zwingli's father was prosperous, however, and the boy had the best education which could be obtained, at Basel and Vienna. His later discontent with the old Church came not through spiritual wrestlings in the monastery, but from the study of the classics and of the Greek New Testament. Zwingli had become a priest and settled at the famous monastery of Einsiedeln near the lake of Zurich. This was the center of pilgrimages on account of a wonder-working image in the cell of St. Meinrad. "Here," he says, "I began to preach the Gospel of Christ in the year 1516, before any one in my locality had so much as heard the name of Luther."

Zwingli (1484-1531) leads the revolt in Switzerland against the Church.

Three years later he was called to an influential position as preacher in the cathedral of Zurich, and there his great work began. Through his efforts a Dominican who was preaching indulgences was expelled from the country. He then began to denounce the abuses in the Church as well as the shameless traffic in soldiers, which he had long regarded as a blot upon his country's honor.[2] The pope had found the help of the Swiss troops indispensable, and had granted annuities and

Zwingli denounces the abuses in the Church and the traffic in soldiers.

[1] This condition has not changed; all Swiss laws are still proclaimed in three languages.

[2] Switzerland had made a business, ever since the time when Charles VIII of France invaded Italy, of supplying troops of mercenaries to fight for others, especially for France and the pope. It was the Swiss who gained the battle of Marignano for Francis I, and Swiss guards may still be seen in the pope's palace.

lucrative positions in the Church to influential Swiss, who were expected to work in his interest. So, from the first, Zwingli was led to combine with his religious reform a political reform which should put the cantons on better terms with one another and prevent the destruction of their young men in wars in which they had no possible interest. A new demand of the pope for troops in 1521 led Zwingli to attack him and his commissioners. "How appropriate," he exclaims, "that they should have red hats and cloaks! If we shake them, crowns and ducats fall out. If we wring them, out runs the blood of your sons and brothers and fathers and good friends." [1]

Zurich, under the influence of Zwingli, begins a reform.

Such talk soon began to arouse comment, and the old forest cantons were for a violent suppression of the new teacher, but the town council of Zurich stanchly supported their priest. Zwingli then began to attack fasts and the celibacy of the clergy. In 1523 he prepared a complete statement of his belief, in the form of sixty-seven theses. In these he maintained that Christ was the only high priest and that the Gospel did not gain its sanction from the authority of the Church. He denied the existence of purgatory and rejected those practices of the Church which Luther had already set aside. Since no one presented himself to refute Zwingli, the town council ratified his conclusions and so withdrew from the Roman Catholic Church. The next year the Mass, processions, and the images of the saints were abolished; the shrines were opened and the relics buried.

Other towns follow Zurich's example.

Some other towns followed Zurich's example; but the original cantons about the lake of Lucerne, which feared that they might lose the great influence that, in spite of their small size, they had hitherto enjoyed, were ready to fight for the old faith. The first armed collision, half political and half religious, between the Swiss Protestants and Catholics took

[1] So eloquent was the new preacher that one of his auditors reports that after a sermon he felt as if "he had been taken by the hair and turned inside out."

place at Kappel in 1531, and Zwingli fell in the battle. The various cantons and towns never came to an agreement in religious matters, and Switzerland is still part Catholic and part Protestant.

The chief importance for the rest of Europe of Zwingli's revolt was the influence of his conception of the Lord's Supper. He not only denied transubstantiation,[1] but also the "real presence" of Christ in the elements (in which Luther believed), and conceived the bread and wine to be mere symbols. Those in Germany and England who accepted Zwingli's idea added one more to the Protestant parties, and consequently increased the difficulty of reaching a general agreement among those who had revolted from the Church.[2]

160. Far more important than Zwingli's teachings, especially for England and America, was the work of Calvin, which was carried on in the ancient city of Geneva on the very outskirts of the Swiss confederation. It was Calvin who organized the Presbyterian Church and formulated its beliefs. He was born in northern France in 1509; he belonged, therefore, to the second generation of Protestants. He was early influenced by the Lutheran teachings, which had already found their way into France. A persecution of the Protestants under Francis I drove him out of the country and he settled for a time in Basel.[3]

Calvin (1509-1564) and the Presbyterian Church.

Here he issued the first edition of his great work, *The Institutes of Christianity*, which has been more widely discussed than any other Protestant theological treatise. It was the first orderly exposition of the principles of Christianity from a Protestant standpoint. Like Peter Lombard's *Sentences*, it formed a convenient manual for study and discussion. The *Institutes* are based upon the infallibility of the Bible and reject

Calvin's *Institutes of Christianity*.

[1] See above, pp. 212–213.

[2] For Zwingli's life and work see the scholarly biography by Samuel Macauley Jackson, *Huldreich Zwingli* (G. P. Putnam's Sons, 1901).

[3] See below, p. 452.

the infallibility of the Church and the pope. Calvin possessed a remarkably logical mind and a clear and admirable style. The French version of his great work is the first example of the successful use of that language in an argumentative treatise.

Calvin was called to Geneva about 1540 and intrusted with the task of reforming the town, which had secured its independence of the duke of Savoy. He drew up a constitution and established an extraordinary government, in which the church and the civil government were as closely associated as they had ever been in any Catholic country.[1] The Protestantism which found its way into France was that of Calvin, not that of Luther, and the same may be said of Scotland.

161. The revolt of England from the mediæval Church was very gradual and halting. Although there were some signs that Protestantism was gaining a foothold in the island not long after Luther's burning of the canon law, a generation at least passed away before the country definitely committed itself, upon the accession of Queen Elizabeth in 1558, to the change in religion. It seems at first sight as if the revolution were due mainly to the irritation of Henry VIII against the pope, who refused to grant the king a divorce from his first wife in order that he might marry a younger and prettier woman. But a permanent change in the religious convictions of a whole people cannot fairly be attributed to the whim of even so despotic a ruler as Henry. There were changes taking place in England before the revolt similar to those which prepared the way in Germany for Luther's success.

English scholars began, in the latter part of the fifteenth century, to be affected by the new learning which came to them from Italy. Colet,[2] among others, strove to introduce the study of Greek in Oxford. Like Luther he found himself

---

[1] Calvin intrusted the management of church affairs to the ministers and the elders, or *presbyters*, hence the name Presbyterian. For Calvin's work, see Johnson, *Europe in the Sixteenth Century*, pp. 272–276.

[2] See above, p. 382.

especially attracted by St. Paul, and had begun to teach the doctrine of justification by faith long before the German reformer was heard of.

The most distinguished writer of the period was, perhaps, Sir Thomas More. The title of his famous little book, *Utopia,* i.e. "Nowhere," published about 1515, has become synonymous with ideal and impracticable schemes for bettering the world. He pictures the happy conditions in an undiscovered land where a perfect form of government has done away with all the evils which he observes about him in the England of his day. The Utopians, unlike the English, fought only to keep out invaders or to free others from tyranny, and never undertook wars of aggression such as Henry VIII was constantly contemplating. In Utopia no one was persecuted for his religion so long as he treated others fairly.[1]

Sir Thomas More and his 'Utopia.'

When Erasmus came to England about 1500 he was delighted with the society which he found, and we may assume that his views, which we have before described,[2] represented those of a considerable number of intelligent Englishmen. It was at the house of More that he finished the *Praise of Folly*, and he carried on his studies with such success in England and found such congenial companions there that it seemed to him that it was hardly worth while to go to Italy for intellectual inspiration. There is every reason to suppose that there were, in England, many who were quite conscious of the vices of the churchmen and who were ready to accept a system which would abolish those practices that had come to seem useless and pernicious.

The English admirers of Erasmus.

162. Henry VIII's minister, Cardinal Wolsey, deserves great credit for having constantly striven to discourage his sovereign's ambition to take part in the wars on the continent. The cardinal's argument that England could become great by

Wolsey's policy of peace and his idea of the balance of power.

---

[1] An English translation of the *Utopia* is published by the Macmillan Company at 50 cents.

[2] See above, § 139.

peace better than by war was a momentous discovery. Peace he felt would be best secured by maintaining the *balance of power* on the continent so that no ruler should become dan-

Henry VIII of England

gerous by unduly extending his sway. For example, he thought it good policy to side with Charles when Francis was successful, and then with Francis after his terrible defeat at Pavia (1525) when he fell into the hands of Charles. This idea of the balance of power came to be recognized later by the European countries as a very important consideration in determining their policy. But Wolsey was not long to be permitted to put his enlightened ideas in practice. His fall and the progress of Protestantism in England are both closely associated with the notorious divorce case of Henry VIII.

Henry VIII's divorce case. It will be remembered that Henry had married Catherine of Aragon, the aunt of Charles V. Only one of their children, Mary, had survived to grow up. Henry was very anxious to have a son and heir, for he was fearful lest a woman might not be permitted to succeed to the throne. Moreover, Catherine, who was older than he, had become distasteful to him.

Catherine had first married Henry's older brother, who had died almost immediately after the marriage. Since it was a violation of the rule of the Church to marry a deceased brother's wife, Henry professed to fear that he was committing a sin by retaining Catherine as his wife and demanded to be divorced from her on the ground that his marriage had never been legal. His anxiety to rid himself of Catherine was greatly increased by the appearance at court of a black-eyed girl of sixteen, named Anne Boleyn, with whom the king fell in love.

Unfortunately for his case, his marriage with Catherine had been authorized by a dispensation from the pope, so that Clement VII, to whom the king appealed to annul the marriage, could not, even if he had been willing to alienate the queen's nephew, Charles V, have granted Henry's request. Wolsey's failure to induce the pope to permit the divorce excited the king's anger, and with rank ingratitude for his minister's great services, Henry drove him from office (1529) and seized his property. From a life of wealth which was fairly regal, Wolsey was precipitated into extreme poverty. An imprudent but innocent act of his soon gave his enemies a pretext for charging him with treason ; but the unhappy man died on his way to London before his head could be brought to the block.

Clement VII refuses to divorce Henry.

Fall of Wolsey.

163. The king's next move was to bring a preposterous charge against the whole English clergy by declaring that, in submitting to Wolsey's authority as papal legate, they had violated an ancient law forbidding papal representatives to appear in England without the king's permission. Yet Henry had approved Wolsey's appointment as papal legate. The clergy met at Canterbury and offered to buy pardon for their alleged offense by an enormous grant of money. But Henry refused to forgive them unless they would solemnly acknowledge him to be the supreme head of the English Church. This they accordingly did ;[1] they agreed, moreover, to hold no general meetings or pass any rules without the king's sanction. The submission of the clergy ensured Henry against any future criticism on their part of the measures he proposed to take in the matter of his divorce.

Henry forces the English clergy to recognize him as the supreme head of the Church of England.

---

[1] The clergy only recognized the king as " Head of the Church and Clergy so far as the law of Christ will allow." They did not abjure the headship of the pope over the whole Church.

He now induced Parliament to threaten to cut off the income which the pope had been accustomed to receive from newly appointed bishops. The king hoped in this way to bring Clement VII to terms. He failed, however, in this design and, losing patience, married Anne Boleyn secretly without waiting for the divorce. Parliament was then persuaded to pass the Act of Appeals, declaring that lawsuits of all kinds should be finally and definitely decided within the realm, and that no appeal might be made to any one outside the kingdom.

An English
court de-
clares
Henry's mar-
riage with
Catherine
void.

Catherine's appeal to the pope was thus rendered illegal. When, shortly after, her marriage was declared void by a Church court summoned by Henry, she had no remedy. Parliament also declared Henry's marriage with Catherine unlawful and that with Anne legal. Consequently it was decreed that Elizabeth, Anne's daughter, who was born in 1533, was to succeed her father on the throne, instead of Mary, the daughter of Catherine.

The Act of
Supremacy
and the
denial of
the pope's
authority
over England.

In 1534 the English Parliament completed the revolt of the English Church from the pope by assigning to the king the right to appoint all the English prelates and to enjoy all the income which had formerly found its way to Rome. In the Act of Supremacy, Parliament declared the king to be " the only supreme head in earth of the Church of England," and that he should enjoy all the powers which the title naturally carried with it. Two years later every officer in the kingdom, whether lay or ecclesiastical, was required to swear to renounce the authority of the Bishop of Rome. Refusal to take this oath was to be adjudged high treason. Many were unwilling to deny the pope's headship merely because king and Parliament renounced it, and this legislation led to a persecution in the name of treason which was even more horrible than that which had been carried on in the supposed interest of religion.

It must be carefully noted that Henry VIII was not a Protestant in the Lutheran sense of the word. He was led, it is true, by Clement VII's refusal to declare his first marriage illegal, to break the bond between the English and the Roman Church, and to induce the English clergy and Parliament to acknowledge him as supreme head in the religious as well as in the temporal interests of the country. No earlier English sovereign had ever ventured to go so far as this in the previous conflicts with Rome. He was ready, too, as we shall see, to appropriate the property of the monasteries on the ground that these institutions were so demoralized as to be worse than useless. Important as these acts were, they did not lead Henry to accept the teachings of Protestant leaders, like Luther, Zwingli, or Calvin. He shared the popular distrust of the new doctrines, and showed himself anxious to explain the old ones and free them from the objections which were beginning to be urged against them. A proclamation was made, under the authority of the king, in which the sacraments of baptism, penance, and the Mass were explained. Henry also authorized a new translation of the Bible into English. A fine edition of this was printed (1539), and every parish was ordered to obtain a copy and place it in the parish church, where all the people could readily make use of it.

The English Bible

Henry was anxious to prove that he was orthodox, especially after he had seized the property of the monasteries and the gold and jewels which adorned the receptacles in which the relics of the saints were kept. He presided in person over the trial of one who accepted the opinion of Zwingli, that the body and blood of Christ were not present in the sacrament. He quoted Scripture to prove the contrary, and the prisoner was condemned and burned as a heretic.

Henry's anxiety to prove himself a good Catholic.

In 1539 Parliament passed a statute called the "Six Articles." These declared first that the body and blood of Christ were actually present in the bread and the wine of the Lord's Supper; whoever ventured publicly to question this was to be burned. For speaking against five other

The 'Six Articles.'

tenets [1] of the old Church, offenders were to suffer imprisonment and loss of goods for the first offense, and to be hanged for the second. Two bishops, who had ventured to go farther in the direction of Protestantism than Henry himself had done, were driven from office and some offenders were put to death under this act.

Henry's tyranny.

Execution of Sir Thomas More.

164. Henry was heartless and despotic. With a barbarity not uncommon in those days, he allowed his old friend and adviser, Sir Thomas More, to be beheaded for refusing to pronounce the marriage with Catherine void. He caused numbers of monks to be executed for refusing to swear that his first marriage was illegal and for denying his title to supremacy in the Church. Others he permitted to die of starvation and disease in the filthy prisons of the time. Many Englishmen would doubtless have agreed with one of the friars who said humbly: " I profess that it is not out of obstinate malice or a mind of rebellion that I do disobey the king, but only for the fear of God, that I offend not the Supreme Majesty ; because our Holy Mother, the Church, hath decreed and appointed otherwise than the king and Parliament hath ordained."

Dissolution of the English monasteries.

Henry wanted money ; some of the English abbeys were rich, and the monks were quite unable to defend themselves against the charges which were brought against them. The king sent commissioners about to inquire into the moral state of the monasteries. A large number of scandalous tales were easily collected, some of which were undoubtedly true. The monks were doubtless often indolent and sometimes wicked.

---

[1] These were the sufficiency of the bread without the wine for the laity in partaking of the communion ;* the celibacy of the clergy ; the perpetual obligation of vows to remain unmarried; the propriety of private masses ; and, lastly, of confession. The act was popularly known as " the whip with six strings."

* The custom of the Church had long been that the priest alone should partake of the wine at communion. The Hussites, and later the Protestants, demanded that the laity should receive both the bread and the wine.

Nevertheless, they were kind landlords, hospitable to the stranger, and good to the poor. The plundering of the smaller monasteries, with which the king began, led to a revolt, due to a rumor that the king would next proceed to despoil the parish churches as well. This gave Henry an excuse for attacking the larger monasteries. The abbots and priors who had taken part in the revolt were hanged and their monasteries confiscated. Other abbots, panic-stricken, confessed that they and their monks had been committing the most loathsome sins and asked to be permitted to give up their monasteries to the king. The royal commissioners then took possession, sold every article upon which they could lay hands, including the bells and the lead on the roofs. The picturesque remains of the great abbey churches are still among the chief objects of interest to the sight-seer in England. The monastery lands were, of course, appropriated by the king. They were sold for the benefit of the government or given to nobles whose favor the king wished to secure.

Along with the destruction of the monasteries went an attack upon the shrines and images in the churches, which were adorned with gold and jewels. The shrine of St. Thomas of Canterbury was destroyed and the bones of the saint were burned. An old wooden figure revered in Wales was used to make a fire to burn an unfortunate friar who maintained that in things spiritual the pope rather than the king should be obeyed. These acts suggest the Protestant attacks on images which occurred in Germany, Switzerland, and the Netherlands. The object of the king and his party was probably in the main a mercenary one, although the reason urged for the destruction was the superstitious veneration in which the relics and images were popularly held.

Henry's domestic troubles by no means came to an end with his marriage with Anne Boleyn. Of her, too, he soon tired, and three years after their marriage he had her executed

Destruction of shrines and images for the benefit of the king's treasury.

Henry's third marriage and the birth of Edward VI.

on a series of monstrous charges. The next day he married
his third wife, Jane Seymour, who was the mother of his son
and successor, Edward VI. Jane died a few days after her
son's birth, and later Henry married in succession three
other women who are historically unimportant since they left
no children as claimants for the crown. Henry took care that
his three children, all of whom were destined to reign, should
be given their due place by act of Parliament in the line of
inheritance.[1] His death in 1547 left the great problem of
Protestantism and Catholicism to be settled by his son and
daughters.

Edward VI's ministers introduce Protestant practices. 165. While the revolt of England against the ancient Church
was carried through by the government at a time when the
greater part of the nation was still Catholic, there was
undoubtedly, under Henry VIII, an ever-increasing number
of aggressive and ardent Protestants who applauded the
change. During the six years of the boy Edward's reign —
he died in 1553 at the age of sixteen — those in charge of
the government favored the Protestant party and did what they
could to change the faith of all the people by bringing Protestant teachers from the Continent.

A general demolition of all the sacred images was ordered;
even the beautiful stained glass, the glory of the cathedrals,
was destroyed, because it often represented saints and angels.
The king was to appoint bishops without troubling to observe
the old forms of election, and Protestants began to be put
into the high offices of the Church. Parliament turned over
to the king the funds which had been established for the purpose of having masses chanted for the dead, and decreed that
thereafter the clergy should be free to marry.

[1] Henry VIII, m. (1) Catherine,   m. (2) Anne Boleyn,   m. (3) Jane Seymour
     | | |
  Mary (1553-1558)   Elizabeth (1558-1603)   Edward VI (1547-1553)

It was arranged that the son was to succeed to the throne. In case he died
without heirs, Mary and then Elizabeth were to follow.

A prayer-book in English was prepared under the auspices of Parliament not very unlike that used in the Church of England to-day. Moreover, forty-two articles of faith were drawn up by the government, which were to be the standard of belief for the country. These, in the time of Queen Elizabeth, were revised and reduced to the famous "Thirty-Nine Articles," which still constitute the creed of the Church of England.[1]

The prayer-book and the 'Thirty-Nine Articles.'

The changes in the church services must have sadly shocked a great part of the English people, who had been accustomed to watch with awe and expectancy the various acts associated with the many church ceremonies and festivals.[2] Earnest men who watched the misrule of those who conducted Edward's government in the name of Protestantism, must have concluded that the reformers were chiefly intent upon advancing their own interests by plundering the Church. We get some idea of the desecrations of the time from the fact that Edward was forced to forbid "quarreling and shooting in churches" and "the bringing of horses and mules through the same, making God's house like a stable or common inn." Although many were heartily in favor of the recent changes it is no wonder that after Edward's death there was a revulsion in favor of the old religion.

Protestantism partially discredited by Edward's ministers.

166. Edward VI was succeeded in 1553 by his half-sister Mary, who had been brought up in the Catholic faith and held firmly to it. Her ardent hope of bringing her kingdom back once more to her religion did not seem altogether ill-founded, for the majority of the people were still Catholics at heart, and many who were not disapproved of the policy of Edward's ministers, who had removed abuses "in the devil's own way, by breaking in pieces."

Queen Mary, 1553-1558, and the Catholic reaction.

---

[1] These may be found in any Book of Common Prayer of the English Church or of the Protestant Episcopal Church in the United States.

[2] For an extract from the Bishop of Worcester's diary, recording these changes, see *Readings*, Chapter XXVII.

The Catholic cause appeared, moreover, to be strengthened by Mary's marriage with the Spanish prince, Philip II, the son of the orthodox Charles V. But although Philip later distinguished himself, as we shall see, by the merciless way in which he strove to put down heresy within his realms, he never gained any great influence in England. By his marriage with Mary he acquired the title of king, but the English took care that he should have no hand in the government, nor be permitted to succeed his wife on the English throne.

Mary succeeded in bringing about a nominal reconciliation between England and the Roman Church. In 1554 the papal legate restored to the communion of the Catholic Church the "Kneeling Parliament," which theoretically, of course, represented the nation.

During the last four years of Mary's reign the most serious religious persecution in English history occurred. No less than 277 persons were put to death for denying the teachings of the Roman Church. The majority of the victims were humble artisans and husbandmen. The two most notable sufferers were Bishops Latimer and Ridley, who were burned in Oxford. Latimer cried to his fellow-martyr in the flames: "Be of good cheer and play the man; we shall this day light such a candle in England as shall never be put out!"

Mary's
failure to
restore the
Catholic
religion in
England.
It was Mary's hope and belief that the heretics sent to the stake would furnish a terrible warning to the Protestants and check the spread of the new teachings, but it fell out as Latimer had prophesied. Catholicism was not promoted; on the contrary, doubters were only convinced of the earnestness of the Protestants who could die with such constancy.[1]

[1] The Catholics in their turn, it should be noted, suffered serious persecution under Elizabeth and James I, the Protestant successors of Mary. Death was the penalty fixed in many cases for those who obstinately refused to recognize the monarch as the rightful head of the English Church, and heavy fines were imposed for the failure to attend Protestant worship. Two hundred Catholic priests are said to have been executed under Elizabeth; others were tortured or perished miserably in prison. See below, p. 462, and Green, *Short History*, pp. 407-410.

CHAPTER XXVIII

THE CATHOLIC REFORMATION — PHILIP II

167. There had been many attempts, as we have seen, before Luther's appearance, to better the clergy and remedy the evils in the Church without altering its organization or teachings. Hopeful progress toward such a conservative reform had been made even before the Protestants threw off their allegiance to the pope.[1] Their revolt inevitably hastened and stimulated the reform of the ancient Church, to which the greater part of western Europe still remained faithful. The Roman Catholic churchmen were aroused to great activity by the realization that they could no longer rely upon the general acceptance of their teachings. They were forced to defend the beliefs and ceremonies of their Church from the attacks of the Protestants, to whose ranks whole countries were deserting. If the clergy were to make head against the dreaded heresy which threatened their position and power, they must secure the loyalty of the people to them and to the great institution which they represented, by leading upright lives, giving up the old abuses, and thus regaining the confidence of those intrusted to their spiritual care.

The conservative or Catholic reformation.

A general council was accordingly summoned at Trent to consider once more the remedying of the long recognized evils, and to settle authoritatively numerous questions of belief upon which theologians had differed for centuries. New religious orders sprang up, whose object was better to prepare the

---

[1] There is an admirable account of the spirit of the conservative reformers in the *Cambridge Modern History*, Vol. I, Chapter XVIII.

priests for their work and to bring home religion to the hearts of the people. Energetic measures were taken to repress the growth of heresy in countries which were still Roman Catholic and to prevent the dissemination of Protestant doctrines in books and pamphlets. Above all, better men were placed in office, from the pope down. The cardinals, for example, were no longer merely humanists and courtiers, but among them might be found the leaders of religious thought in Italy. Many practices which had formerly irritated the people were permanently abolished. These measures resulted in a remarkable reformation of the ancient Church, such as the Council of Constance had striven in vain to bring about.[1] Before turning to the terrible struggles between the two religious parties in the Netherlands and France during the latter half of the sixteenth century, a word must be said of the Council of Trent and of an extraordinarily powerful new religious order, the Jesuits.

Charles V's confidence in the settlement of the religious differences by a council. Charles V, who did not fully grasp the irreconcilable differences between Protestant and Catholic beliefs, made repeated efforts to bring the two parties together by ordering the Protestants to accept what seemed to him a simple statement of the Christian faith. He had great confidence that if representatives of the old and the new beliefs could meet one another in a church council all points of disagreement might be amicably settled. The pope was, however, reluctant to see a council summoned in Germany, for he had by no means forgotten the conduct of the Council of Basel. To call the German Protestants into Italy, on the other hand, would have been useless, for none of them would have responded or

---

[1] Protestant writers commonly call the reformation of the mediæval Catholic Church the "counter-reformation" or "Catholic reaction," as if Protestantism were entirely responsible for it. It is clear, however, that the conservative reform began some time before the Protestants revolted. Their secession from the Church only stimulated a movement already well under way. See Maurenbrecher, *Geschichte der Katholischen Reformation.*

have paid any attention to the decisions of a body which would appear to them to be under the pope's immediate control. It was only after years of delay that in 1545, just before Luther's death, a general council finally met in the city of Trent, on the border between Germany and Italy.

As the German Protestants were preoccupied at the moment by an approaching conflict with the emperor and, moreover, hoped for nothing from the council's action, they did not attend its sessions. Consequently the papal representatives and the Roman Catholic prelates were masters of the situation. The council immediately took up just those matters in which the Protestants had departed farthest from the old beliefs. In its early sessions it proclaimed all those accursed who taught that the sinner was saved by faith alone, or who questioned man's power, with God's aid, to forward his salvation by good works. Moreover, it declared that if any one should say — as did the Protestants — that the sacraments were not all instituted by Christ; "or that they are more or less than seven, to wit, Baptism, Confirmation, the Eucharist, Penance, Extreme Unction, Ordination, and Matrimony; or even that any one of these is not truly and properly a sacrament, let him be accursed." The ancient Latin translation of the Bible — the Vulgate — was fixed as the standard. No one should presume to question its accuracy so far as doctrine was concerned, or be permitted to publish any interpretation of the Bible differing from that of the Church.

The Council of Trent, 1545-1563, sanctions the teaching of the Roman Catholic Church.

While the council thus finally rejected any possibility of compromise with the Protestants, it took measures to do away with the abuses of which the Protestants complained. The bishops were ordered to reside in their respective dioceses, to preach regularly, and to see that those who were appointed to church benefices should fulfill the duties of their offices and not merely enjoy the revenue. Measures were also taken to

Reform measures of the council.

improve education and secure the regular reading of the Bible in churches, monasteries, and schools.

Final sessions of the Council of Trent, 1562-1563. When the council had been in session for something more than a year, its meetings were interrupted by various unfavorable conditions. Little was accomplished for a number of years, but in 1562 the members once more reassembled to prosecute their work with renewed vigor. Many more of the doctrines of the Roman Church in regard to which there had been some uncertainty, were carefully defined, and the teachings of the heretics explicitly rejected. A large number of decrees directed against existing abuses were also ratified. *The Canons and Decrees of the Council of Trent*, which fill a stout volume, provided a new and solid foundation for the law and doctrine of the Roman Catholic Church, and they constitute an historical source of the utmost importance.[1] They furnish, in fact, our most complete and authentic statement of the Roman Catholic form of Christianity. They, however, only restate long-accepted beliefs and sanction the organization of the Church briefly described in an earlier chapter (XVI).

Importance of the council's work.

Ignatius Loyola, 1491-1556, the founder of the Jesuits. 168. Among those who, during the final sessions of the council, sturdily opposed every attempt to reduce in any way the exalted powers of the pope, was the head of a new religious society, which was becoming the most powerful organization in Europe. The Jesuit order, or Society of Jesus, was founded by a Spaniard, Ignatius Loyola. He had been a soldier in his younger days, and while bravely fighting for his king, Charles V, had been wounded by a cannon ball (1521). Obliged to lie inactive for weeks, he occupied his time in reading the lives of the saints, and became filled with a burning ambition to emulate their deeds. Upon recovering he dedicated himself to the service of the Lord, donned a beggar's

[1] They may be had in English, *Decrees and Canons of the Council of Trent*, translated by Rev. J. Waterworth, London and New York. See extracts from the acts of the council in *Translations and Reprints*, Vol. II, No. 6.

gown, and started on a pilgrimage to Jerusalem. When there he began to realize that he could do little without an education. So he returned to Spain and, although already thirty-three years old, took his place beside the boys who were learning the elements of Latin grammar. After two years he entered a Spanish university, and later went to Paris to carry on his theological studies.

In Paris he sought to influence his fellow-students at the university, and finally, in 1534, seven of his companions agreed to follow him to Palestine, or, if they were prevented from that, to devote themselves to the service of the pope. On arriving in Venice they found that war had broken out between that republic and the Turks. They accordingly gave up their plan for converting the infidels in the Orient and, with the pope's permission, began to preach in the neighboring towns, explaining the Scriptures and bringing comfort to those in the hospitals. When asked to what order they belonged, they replied, " to the Society of Jesus."

In 1538 Loyola summoned his disciples to Rome, and there they worked out the principles of their order. The pope then incorporated these in a bull in which he gave his sanction to the new society.[1] The organization was to be under the absolute control of a *general*, who was to be chosen for life by the general assembly of the order. Loyola had been a soldier, and he laid great and constant stress upon the source of all efficient military discipline, namely, absolute and unquestioning obedience. This he declared to be the mother of all virtue and happiness. Not only were all the members to obey the pope as Christ's representative on earth, and undertake without hesitation any journey, no matter how distant or perilous, which he might command, but each was to obey his superiors in the order as if he were receiving directions from Christ in person. He must have no will or preference of his

Rigid organization and discipline of the Jesuits.

1 See *Readings*, Chapter XXVIII.

own, but must be as the staff which supports and aids its bearer in any way in which he sees fit to use it. This admirable organization and incomparable discipline were the great secret of the later influence of the Jesuits.

The object of the society was to cultivate piety and the love of God, especially through example. The members were to pledge themselves to lead a pure life of poverty and devotion. Their humility was to show itself in face and attitude, so that their very appearance should attract those with whom they came in contact to the service of God. The methods adopted by the society for reaching its ends are of the utmost importance. A great number of its members were priests, who went about preaching, hearing confession, and encouraging devotional exercises. But the Jesuits were teachers as well as preachers and confessors. They clearly perceived the advantage of bringing young people under their influence, and they became the schoolmasters of Catholic Europe. So successful were their methods of instruction that even Protestants sometimes sent their children to them.

It was originally proposed that the number of persons admitted to the order should not exceed sixty, but this limit was speedily removed, and before the death of Loyola over a thousand persons had joined the society. Under his successor the number was trebled, and it went on increasing for two centuries. The founder of the order had been, as we have seen, attracted to missionary work from the first, and the

Jesuits rapidly spread not only over Europe, but throughout the whole world. Francis Xavier, one of Loyola's original little band, went to Hindustan, the Moluccas, and Japan. Brazil, Florida, Mexico, and Peru were soon fields of active missionary work at a time when Protestants scarcely dreamed as yet of carrying Christianity to the heathen. We owe to the Jesuits' reports much of our knowledge of the condition of America when white men first began to explore Canada and the Mississippi valley, for the followers of Loyola boldly penetrated into regions unknown to Europeans, and settled among the natives with the purpose of bringing the Gospel to them.[1]

Dedicated as they were to the service of the pope, the Jesuits early directed their energies against Protestantism. They sent their members into Germany and the Netherlands, and even made strenuous efforts to reclaim England. Their success was most apparent in southern Germany and Austria, where they became the confessors and confidential advisers of the rulers. They not only succeeded in checking the progress of Protestantism, but were able to reconquer for the pope districts in which the old faith had been abandoned.

Their fight against the Protestants.

Protestants soon realized that the new order was their most powerful and dangerous enemy. Their apprehensions produced a bitter hatred which blinded them to the high purposes of the founders of the order and led them to attribute an evil purpose to every act of the Jesuits. The Jesuits' air of humility the Protestants declared to be mere hypocrisy under which they carried on their intrigues. The Jesuits' readiness to adjust themselves to circumstances and the variety of the tasks that they undertook seemed to their enemies a willingness to resort to any means in order to reach their ends. They were popularly supposed to justify the most deceitful and immoral measures on the ground that the result would be "for the greater glory of God." The very obedience of which the Jesuits said so much was viewed by the hostile Protestant as one of their worst offenses, for he believed that the members of the order were the blind tools of their superiors and that they would not hesitate even to commit a crime if so ordered.

Accusations brought against the Jesuits.

Doubtless there have been many unscrupulous Jesuits and some wicked ones, and as time went on the order degenerated

Decline and abolition of the Jesuits, 1773.

[1] Reference, Parkman's *Jesuits in North America*, Vol. I, Chapters II and X.

just as the earlier ones had done. In the eighteenth century it undertook great commercial enterprises, and for this and other reasons lost the confidence and respect of even the Catholics. The king of Portugal was the first to banish the Jesuits from his kingdom, and then France, where they had long been very unpopular with an influential party of the Catholics, expelled them in 1764. Convinced that the order had outgrown its usefulness, the pope abolished it in 1773. It was, however, restored in 1814, and now again has thousands of members.

Reëstablishment of the order, 1814.

169. The chief ally of the pope and the Jesuits in their efforts to check Protestantism in the latter half of the sixteenth century was the son of Charles V, Philip II. Like the Jesuits he enjoys a most unenviable reputation among Protestants. Certain it is that they had no more terrible enemy

Philip II, the chief enemy of Protestantism among the rulers of Europe.

among the rulers of the day than he. He closely watched the course of affairs in France and Germany with the hope of promoting the cause of the Catholics. He eagerly forwarded every conspiracy against England's Protestant queen, Elizabeth, and finally manned a mighty fleet with the purpose of overthrowing her. He resorted, morever, to incredible cruelty in his attempts to bring back his possessions in the Netherlands

Philip II of Spain

to what he considered the true faith.

Charles V, crippled with the gout and old before his time, laid down the cares of government in 1555–1556. To his brother Ferdinand, who had acquired by marriage the kingdoms of Bohemia and Hungary, Charles had earlier

Division of the Hapsburg possessions between the German and Spanish branches.

transferred the German possessions of the Hapsburgs. To his son, Philip II (1556–1598), he gave Spain with its great American colonies, Milan, the kingdom of the Two Sicilies, and the Netherlands.[1]

Charles had constantly striven to maintain the old religion within his dominions. He had never hesitated to use the Inquisition in Spain and the Netherlands, and it was the great disappointment of his life that a part of his empire had become Protestant. He was, nevertheless, no fanatic. Like many of the princes of the time, he was forced to take sides on the religious question without, perhaps, himself having any deep religious sentiments. The maintenance of the Catholic faith he believed to be necessary in order that he should keep his hold upon his scattered and diverse dominions. On the other hand, the whole life and policy of his son Philip were guided by a fervent attachment to the old religion. He was willing to sacrifice both himself and his country in his long fight against the detested Protestants within and without his realms. And he had vast resources at his disposal, for Spain was a strong power, not only on account of her income from America, but also because her soldiers and their commanders were the best in Europe at this period.

Philip II's fervent desire to stamp out Protestantism.

[1] Division of the Hapsburg Possessions between the Spanish and the German Branches

Maximilian I (d. 1519), m. Mary of Burgundy (d. 1482)
      |
    Philip (d. 1506), m. Joanna the Insane (d. 1555)
         |

| Charles V (d. 1558) | Ferdinand (d. 1564), m. Anna, heiress to kingdoms |
| Emperor, 1519–1556 | Emperor, 1556–1564   of Bohemia and Hungary |

Philip II (d. 1598)   Maximilian II (d. 1576)
inherits Spain, the Netherlands,   Emperor, and inherits Bohemia,
and the Italian possessions of   Hungary, and the Austrian pos-
the Hapsburgs   sessions of the Hapsburgs

The map of Europe in the sixteenth century (see above, p. 372) indicates the vast extent of the combined possessions of the Spanish and German Hapsburgs.

The Netherlands.

170. The Netherlands,[1] which were to cause Philip his first and greatest trouble, included seventeen provinces which Charles V had inherited from his grandmother, Mary of Burgundy. They occupied the position on the map where we now find the kingdoms of Holland and Belgium. Each of the provinces had its own government, but Charles had grouped them together and arranged that the German empire should protect them. In the north the hardy Germanic population had been able, by means of dikes which kept out the sea, to reclaim large tracts of lowlands. Here considerable cities had grown up, — Harlem, Leyden, Amsterdam, and Rotterdam. To the south were the flourishing towns of Ghent, Bruges, Brussels, and Antwerp, which had for hundreds of years been centers of manufacture and trade.

Philip II's harsh attitude toward the Netherlands.

Charles, in spite of some very harsh measures, had retained the loyalty of the people of the Netherlands, for he was himself one of them and they felt a patriotic pride in his achievements. Toward Philip their attitude was very different. His sour face and haughty manner made a disagreeable impression upon the people at Brussels when Charles V first introduced him to them as their future ruler. He was to them a Spaniard and a foreigner, and he ruled them as such after he returned to Spain. Instead of attempting to win them by meeting their legitimate demands, he did everything to alienate all classes in his Burgundian realm and increase their natural hatred and suspicion of the Spaniards. The people were forced to house Spanish soldiers whose insolence drove them nearly to desperation. A half-sister of the king, the duchess of Parma, who did not even know their language, was given to them as their regent. Philip put his trust in a group of upstarts rather than in the nobility of the provinces, who naturally felt that they should be given some part in the direction of affairs.

[1] Reference, Johnson, *Europe in the Sixteenth Century*, Chapter VIII.

What was still worse, Philip proposed that the Inquisition should carry on its work far more actively than hitherto and put an end to the heresy which appeared to him to defile his fair realms. The Inquisition was no new thing to the provinces. Charles V had issued the most cruel edicts against the followers of Luther, Zwingli, and Calvin. According to a law of 1550, heretics who persistently refused to recant were to be burned alive. Even those who confessed their errors and abjured their heresy were, if men, to lose their heads, if women, to be buried alive. In both cases their property was to be confiscated. The lowest estimate of those who were executed in the Netherlands during Charles' reign is fifty thousand. Although these terrible laws had not checked the growth of Protestantism, all of Charles' decrees were solemnly reënacted by Philip in the first month of his reign.

The Inquisition in the Netherlands.

For ten years the people suffered Philip's rule; but their king, instead of listening to the protests of their leaders who were quite as earnest Catholics as himself, appeared to be bent on the destruction of the land. So in 1566 some five hundred of the nobles, who were later joined by many of the citizens, pledged themselves to make a common stand against Spanish tyranny and the Inquisition. Although they had no idea as yet of a revolt, they planned a great demonstration during which they presented a petition to the duchess of Parma requesting the suspension of the king's edicts. The story is that one of the duchess' councilors assured her that she had no reason to fear these "beggars." This name was voluntarily assumed by the petitioners and an important group of the insurgents in the later troubles were known as "Beggars."

Protest against Philip's policy.

The 'Beggars.'

The Protestant preachers now took courage, and large congregations gathered in the fields to hear them. Excited by their exhortations, those who were converted to the new religion rushed into the Catholic churches, tore down the

The image-breaking Protestants.

images, broke the stained glass windows, and wrecked the altars. The duchess of Parma was just succeeding in quieting the tumult when Philip took a step which led finally to the revolt of the Netherlands. He decided to dispatch to the low countries the remorseless duke of Alva, whose conduct has made his name synonymous with blind and unmeasured cruelty.

Philip sends the duke of Alva to the Netherlands.

171. The report that Alva was coming caused the flight of many of those who especially feared his approach. William of Orange, who was to be the leader in the approaching war against Spain, went to Germany. Thousands of Flemish weavers fled across the North Sea, and the products of their looms became before long an important article of export from England.

Alva brought with him a fine army of Spanish soldiers, ten thousand in number and superbly equipped. He judged that the wisest and quickest way of pacifying the discontented provinces was to kill all those who ventured to criticise "the best of kings," of whom he had the honor to be the faithful servant. He accordingly established a special court for the speedy trial and condemnation of all those whose fidelity to Philip was suspected. This was popularly known as the Council of Blood, for its aim was not justice but butchery. Alva's administration from 1567 to 1573 was a veritable reign of terror. He afterwards boasted that he had slain eighteen thousand, but probably not more than a third of that number were really executed.

Alva's cruel administration, 1567-1573.

The Council of Blood.

The Netherlands found a leader in William, Prince of Orange and Count of Nassau. He is a national hero whose career bears a striking resemblance to that of Washington. Like the American patriot, he undertook the seemingly hopeless task of freeing his people from the oppressive rule of a distant king. To the Spaniards he appeared to be only an impoverished nobleman at the head of a handful of armed

William of Orange, called the Silent, 1533-1584.

peasants and fishermen, contending against the sovereign of the richest realm in the world.

William had been a faithful servant of Charles V and would gladly have continued to serve his son after him had the oppression and injustice of the Spanish dominion not become intolerable. But Alva's policy convinced him that it was useless to send any more complaints to Philip. He accordingly collected a little army in 1568 and opened the long struggle with Spain.

William the Silent collects an army.

William found his main support in the northern provinces, of which Holland was the chief. The Dutch, who had very generally accepted Protestant teachings, were purely German in blood, while the people of the southern provinces, who adhered (as they still do) to the Roman Catholic faith, were more akin to the population of northern France.

Differences between the northern i.e., Dutch, provinces and the southern.

The Spanish soldiers found little trouble in defeating the troops which William collected. Like Washington again, he seemed to lose almost every battle and yet was never conquered. The first successes of the Dutch were gained by the " sea beggars," — freebooters who captured Spanish ships and sold them in Protestant England. Finally they seized the town of Brille and made it their headquarters. Encouraged by this, many of the towns in the northern provinces of Holland and Zealand ventured to choose William as their governor, although they did not throw off their allegiance to Philip. In this way these two provinces became the nucleus of the United Netherlands.

William chosen governor of Holland and Zealand, 1572.

Alva recaptured a number of the revolted towns and treated their inhabitants with his customary cruelty; even women and children were slaughtered in cold blood. But instead of quenching the rebellion, he aroused even the Catholic southern provinces to revolt. He introduced an unwise system of taxation which required that ten per cent of the proceeds of every sale should be paid to the government.

Both the northern and southern provinces combine against Spain, 1576.

This caused the thrifty Catholic merchants of the southern towns to close their shops in despair.

After six years of this tyrannical and mistaken policy, Alva was recalled. His successor soon died and left matters worse than ever. The leaderless soldiers, trained in Alva's school, indulged in wild orgies of robbery and murder; they plundered and partially reduced to ashes the rich city of Antwerp. The "Spanish fury," as this outbreak was called, together with the hated taxes, created such general indignation that representatives from all of Philip's Burgundian provinces met at Ghent in 1576 with the purpose of combining to put an end to the Spanish tyranny.

This union was, however, only temporary. Wiser and more moderate governors were sent by Philip to the Netherlands, and they soon succeeded in again winning the confidence of the southern provinces. So the northern provinces went their own way. Guided by William the Silent, they refused to consider the idea of again recognizing Philip as their king. In 1579 seven provinces (Holland, Zealand, Utrecht, Gelderland, Overyssel, Groningen, and Friesland, all lying north of the mouths of the Rhine and the Scheldt) formed the new and firmer Union of Utrecht. The articles of this union served as a constitution for the United Provinces which, two years later, at last formally declared themselves independent of Spain.

Philip realized that William was the soul of the revolt and that without him it might not improbably have been put down. The king therefore offered a patent of nobility and a large sum of money to any one who should make way with the Dutch patriot. After several unsuccessful attempts, William, who had been chosen hereditary governor of the United Provinces, was shot in his house at Delft, 1584. He died praying the Lord to have pity upon his soul and "on this poor people."

The Dutch had long hoped for aid from Queen Elizabeth or from the French, but had heretofore been disappointed. At last the English queen decided to send troops to their assistance. While the English rendered but little actual help, Elizabeth's policy so enraged Philip that he at last decided to attempt the conquest of England. The destruction of the great fleet which he equipped for that purpose interfered with further attempts to subjugate the United Provinces, which might otherwise have failed to preserve their liberty in spite of their heroic resistance. Moreover, Spain's resources were being rapidly exhausted and the state was on the verge of bankruptcy in spite of the wealth which it had been drawing from across the sea. But even when Spain had to surrender the hope of winning back the lost provinces, which now became a small but important European power, she refused formally to acknowledge their independence until 1648 [1] (Peace of Westphalia).

Reasons why the Dutch finally won their independence.

Independence of the United Provinces acknowledged by Spain, 1648.

172. The history of France during the latter part of the sixteenth century is little more than a chronicle of a long and bloody series of civil wars between the Catholics and Protestants. Each party, however, had political as well as religious objects, and the religious issues were often almost altogether obscured by the worldly ambition of the leaders.

Protestantism began in France [2] in much the same way as in England. Those who had learned from the Italians to love the Greek language, turned to the New Testament in the original and commenced to study it with new insight.

Beginnings of Protestantism in France.

---

[1] It is impossible in so brief an account to relate the heroic deeds of the Dutch, such, for example, as the famous defence of Leyden. The American historian Motley gives a vivid description of this in his well-known *Rise of the Dutch Republic*, Part IV, Chapter II. The most recent and authoritative account of the manner in which the Dutch won their independence is to be found in the third volume of *A History of the People of the Netherlands*, by the Dutch scholar Blok, translated by Ruth Putnam (G. P. Putnam's Sons, 3 vols., $7.50). Miss Putnam's own charming *William the Silent* (G. P. Putnam's Sons, 2 vols., with many fine illustrations, $3.75) gives an impressive picture of the tremendous odds which he faced and of his marvellous patience and perseverance.

[2] Reference, Johnson, *Europe in the Sixteenth Century*, pp. 386–389.

Lefèvre,
1450-1537.

Lefèvre, the most conspicuous of these Erasmus-like reformers, translated the Bible into French and began to preach justification by faith before he had ever heard of Luther. He and his followers won the favor of Margaret, the sister of Francis I and queen of the little kingdom of Navarre, and under her protection they were left unmolested for some years.

Persecution of the Protestants under Francis I.

The Sorbonne, the famous theological school at Paris, finally stirred up the suspicions of the king against the new ideas. While, like his fellow-monarchs, Francis had no special interest in religious matters, he was shocked by an act of desecration ascribed to the Protestants, and in consequence forbade the circulation of Protestant books. About 1535 several adherents of the new faith were burned, and Calvin was forced to flee to Basel, where he prepared a defense of his beliefs in his *Institutes of Christianity*. This is prefaced by a letter to Francis in which he pleads with him to protect the Protestants.[1] Francis,

Massacre of the Waldensians, 1545.

before his death, became so intolerant that he ordered the massacre of three thousand defenseless peasants who dwelt on the slopes of the Alps, and whose only offense was adherence to the simple teachings of the Waldensians.[2]

Persecution under Henry II, 1547-1559.

Francis' son, Henry II (1547-1559), swore to extirpate the Protestants, and hundreds of them were burned. Nevertheless, Henry's religious convictions did not prevent him from willingly aiding the German Protestants against his enemy Charles V, especially when they agreed to hand over to him three bishoprics which lay on the French boundary, — Metz, Verdun, and Toul.

Francis II, 1559-1560, Mary, Queen of Scots, and the Guises.

Henry II was accidentally killed in a tourney and left his kingdom to three weak sons, the last scions of the house of Valois, who succeeded in turn to the throne during a period of unprecedented civil war and public calamity. The eldest son, Francis II, a boy of sixteen, succeeded his father. His chief importance for France arose from his marriage with the

[1] See *Readings*, Chapter XXVIII.   [2] See above, p. 221.

RELATIONS OF THE GUISES, MARY STUART, THE VALOIS, AND THE BOURBONS

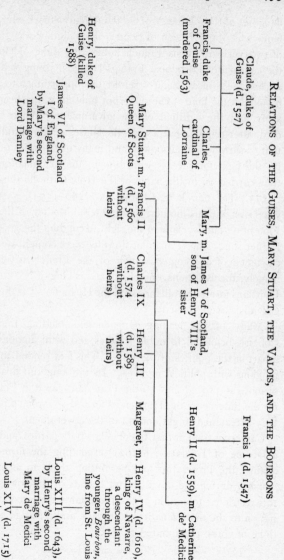

Claude, duke of Guise (d. 1527)

Francis, duke of Guise (murdered 1563)

Charles, cardinal of Lorraine

Mary, m. James V of Scotland, son of Henry VIII's sister

Henry, duke of Guise (killed 1588)

Mary Stuart, m. Francis II (d. 1560 without heirs), Queen of Scots

James VI of Scotland I of England, by Mary's second marriage with Lord Darnley

Charles IX (d. 1574 without heirs)

Henry III (d. 1589 without heirs)

Margaret, m. Henry IV (d. 1610), king of Navarre, a descendant through the younger, *Bourbon*, line from St. Louis

Henry II (d. 1559), m. Catherine de' Medici

Francis I (d. 1547)

Louis XIII (d. 1643), by Henry's second marriage with Mary de' Medici

Louis XIV (d. 1715)

Louis XV (d. 1774) great grandson of Louis XIV

daughter of King James V of Scotland, Mary Stuart, who became famous as Mary, Queen of Scots. Her mother was the sister of two very ambitious French nobles, the duke of Guise and the cardinal of Lorraine. Francis II was so young that Mary's uncles, the Guises, eagerly seized the opportunity to manage his affairs for him. The duke put himself at the head of the army, and the cardinal of the government. When the king died, after reigning but a year, the Guises were naturally reluctant to surrender their power, and many of the woes of France for the next forty years were due to the machinations which they carried on in the name of the Holy Catholic religion.

The queen mother, Catherine de' Medici.

173. The new king, Charles IX (1560–1574), was but ten years old, and his mother, Catherine de' Medici, of the famous Florentine family, claimed the right to conduct the government for her son. The rivalries of the time were complicated by the existence of a younger branch of the French royal family,

The Bourbons.

namely, the Bourbons, one of whom was king of Navarre. The Bourbons formed an alliance with the Huguenots,[1] as the French Calvinists were called.

The Huguenots and their political ambition.

Many of the leading Huguenots, including their chief Coligny, belonged to noble families and were anxious to play a part in the politics of the time. This fact tended to confuse religious with political motives. In the long run this mixture of motives proved fatal to the Protestant cause in France, but for the time being the Huguenots formed so strong a party that they threatened to get control of the government.

Catherine grants conditional toleration to the Protestants, 1562.

Catherine tried at first to conciliate both parties, and granted a Decree of Toleration (1562) suspending the former edicts against the Protestants and permitting them to assemble for worship during the daytime and outside of the towns. Even this restricted toleration of the Protestants appeared an abomination to the more fanatical Catholics, and a savage act of the duke of Guise precipitated civil war.

---

1 The origin of this name is uncertain.

As he was passing through the town of Vassy on a Sunday he found a thousand Huguenots assembled in a barn for worship. The duke's followers rudely interrupted the service, and a tumult arose in which the troops killed a considerable number of the defenseless multitude. The news of this massacre aroused the Huguenots and was the beginning of a war which continued, broken only by short truces, until the last weak descendant of the house of Valois ceased to reign. As in the other religious wars of the time, both sides exhibited the most inhuman cruelty. France was filled for a generation with burnings, pillage, and every form of barbarity. The leaders of both the Catholic and the Protestant party, as well as two of the French kings themselves, fell by the hands of assassins, and France renewed in civil war all the horrors of the English invasion in the fourteenth and fifteenth centuries.

The massacres of Vassy and the opening of the wars of religion.

In 1570 a brief peace was concluded. The Huguenots were to be tolerated, and certain towns were assigned to them, including La Rochelle, where they might defend themselves in case of renewed attacks from the Catholics. For a time both the king and the queen mother were on the friendliest terms with the Huguenot leader Coligny, who became a sort of prime minister. He was anxious that Catholics and Protestants should join in a great national war against Spain. In this way the people of France would combine, regardless of their differences in religion, in a patriotic effort to win the county of Burgundy and a line of fortresses to the north and east, which seemed naturally to belong to France rather than to Spain. Coligny did not, of course, overlook the consideration that in this way he could aid the Protestant cause in the Netherlands.

Coligny's influence and plan for a national war against Philip II.

The strict Catholic party of the Guises frustrated this plan by a most fearful expedient. They easily induced Catherine de' Medici to believe that she was being deceived by Coligny, and an assassin was engaged to put him out of the way; but the scoundrel missed his aim and only wounded his victim.

The massacre of St. Bartholomew's Day, 1572.

Fearful lest the young king, who was faithful to Coligny, should discover her part in the attempted murder, the queen mother invented a story of a great Huguenot conspiracy. The credulous king was deceived, and the Catholic leaders at Paris arranged that at a given signal not only Coligny, but all the Huguenots, who had gathered in great numbers in the city to witness the marriage of the Protestant Henry of Navarre with the king's sister, should be massacred on the eve of St. Bartholomew's Day (August 23, 1572).

The signal was duly given, and no less than two thousand persons were ruthlessly murdered in Paris before the end of the next day. The news of this attack spread into the provinces and it is probable that, at the very least, ten thousand more Protestants were put to death outside of the capital. Both the pope and Philip II expressed their gratification at this signal example of French loyalty to the Church. Civil war again broke out, and the Catholics formed the famous **The Holy League.** Holy League, under the leadership of Henry of Guise, for the advancement of their interests and the extirpation of heresy.

Question of the succession to the French throne. Henry III (1574–1589), the last of the sons of Henry II, who succeeded Charles IX, had no heirs, and the great question of succession arose. The Huguenot, Henry of Navarre, was the nearest male relative, but the League could never consent to permit the throne of France to be sullied by heresy, especially as their leader, Henry of Guise, was himself anxious to become king.

War of the Three Henrys, 1585-1589. Henry III was driven weakly from one party to the other, and it finally came to a war between the three Henrys, — Henry III, Henry of Navarre, and Henry of Guise (1585–1589). It ended in a characteristic way. Henry the king had Henry of Guise assassinated. The sympathizers of the League then assassinated Henry the king, which left the field to Henry of Navarre. He ascended the throne as Henry IV [1] in 1589, and is an heroic figure in the line of French kings.

1 Reference for Henry IV, Wakeman, *Europe from 1598–1715*, Chapter I.

174. The new king had many enemies, and his kingdom was devastated and demoralized by years of war. He soon saw that he must accept the religion of the majority of his people if he wished to reign over them. He accordingly asked to be readmitted to the Catholic Church (1593), excusing himself on the ground that "Paris was worth a mass." He did not forget his old friends, however, and in 1598 he issued the Edict of Nantes.

Henry IV, 1589-1610, becomes a Catholic.

By this edict of toleration the Calvinists were permitted to hold services in all the towns and villages where they had previously held them, but in Paris and a number of other towns all Protestant services were prohibited. The Protestants were to enjoy the same political rights as Catholics, and to be eligible to public office. A number of fortified towns were to remain in the hands of the Huguenots, particularly La Rochelle, Montauban, and Nîmes. Henry's only mistake lay in granting the Huguenots the exceptional privilege of holding and governing fortified towns. In the next generation, this privilege aroused the suspicion of the king's minister, Richelieu, who attacked the Huguenots, not so much on religious grounds, as on account of their independent position in the state, which suggested that of the older feudal nobles.

The Edict of Nantes, 1598.

Henry IV chose Sully, an upright and able Calvinist, for his chief minister. Sully set to work to reëstablish the kingly power, which had suffered greatly under the last three brothers of the house of Valois. He undertook to lighten the tremendous burden of debt which weighed upon the country. He laid out new roads and canals, and encouraged agriculture and commerce ; he dismissed the useless noblemen and officers whom the government was supporting without any advantage to itself. Had his administration not been prematurely interrupted, France might have reached unprecedented power and prosperity ; but religious fanaticism put an end to his reforms.

Ministry of Sully.

In 1610 Henry IV, like William the Silent, was assassinated just in the midst of his greatest usefulness to his country. Sully could not agree with the regent, Henry's widow, and retired to his castle, where he dictated his memoirs, which give a remarkable account of the stirring times in which he had played so important a part. Before many years, Richelieu, perhaps the greatest minister France has ever had, rose to power, and from 1624 to his death in 1642 he governed France for Henry's son, Louis XIII (1610–1643). Something will be said of his policy in connection with the Thirty Years' War.[1]

175. The long and disastrous civil war between Catholics and Protestants, which desolated France in the sixteenth century, had happily no counterpart in England. During her long and wise reign Queen Elizabeth[2] succeeded not only in maintaining peace at home, but in frustrating the conspiracies and attacks of Philip II, which threatened her realm from without. Moreover, by her interference in the Netherlands, she did much to secure their independence of Spain.

Upon the death of Catholic Mary and the accession of her sister Elizabeth in 1558, the English government became once more Protestant. Undoubtedly a great majority of Elizabeth's subjects would have been satisfied to have had her return to the policy of her father, Henry VIII. They still venerated the Mass and the other ancient ceremonies, although they had no desire to acknowledge the supremacy of the pope over their country. Elizabeth believed, however, that Protestantism would finally prevail. She therefore reintroduced the Book of Prayer of Edward VI, with some modifications, and proposed that all her subjects should conform in public to the form of worship sanctioned by the state. Elizabeth did not adopt the Presbyterian organization, which had a good many

---

[1] Reference, Schwill, *History of Modern Europe*, Chapter VI, or a somewhat fuller account in Johnson, *Europe in the Sixteenth Century*, Chapter IX.

[2] Reference, Green, *Short History*, pp. 370–376, 392–405.

advocates, but retained the old system of church government with its archbishops, bishops, deans, etc.   Naturally, however, Protestant clergymen were substituted for the Catholics who had held office under Mary.   Elizabeth's first Parliament gave to the queen the power though not the title of supreme head of the English church.

Elizabeth's position in regard to the religious question was first threatened by events in Scotland.   There, shortly after her accession, the ancient Church was abolished, largely in the interest of the nobles, who were anxious to get the lands of the bishops into their own hands and enjoy the revenue from them.   John Knox, a veritable second Calvin in his stern energy, secured the introduction of the Presbyterian form of faith and church government which still prevail in Scotland.

Presbyterian Church established in Scotland.

In 1561 the Scotch queen, Mary Stuart, whose French husband, Francis II, had just died, landed at Leith.   She was but nineteen years old, of great beauty, and, by reason of her Catholic faith and French training, almost a foreigner to her subjects.   Her grandmother was a sister of Henry VIII, and Mary claimed to be the rightful heiress to the English throne should Elizabeth die childless.   Consequently the beautiful Queen of Scots became the hope of all those, including Philip II and Mary's relatives, the Guises, who wished to bring back England and Scotland to the Roman Catholic faith.

Mary Stuart the Scotch queen, becomes the hope of the Catholics.

Mary made no effort to undo the work of John Knox, but she quickly discredited herself with both Protestants and Catholics by her conduct.   After marrying her second cousin, Lord Darnley, she discovered that he was a dissolute scapegrace, and came to despise him.   She then formed an attachment for a reckless nobleman named Bothwell.   The house near Edinburgh in which the wretched Darnley was lying ill was blown up one night with gunpowder, and he was killed.   The public suspected that both Bothwell and the queen were implicated.   How far Mary was responsible for her husband's

Mary's suspicious conduct.

death no one can be sure. It is certain that she later married Bothwell and that her indignant subjects thereupon deposed her as a murderess. After fruitless attempts to regain her power, she abdicated in favor of her infant son, James VI, and then fled to England to appeal to Elizabeth. While the prudent Elizabeth denied the right of the Scotch to depose their queen, she took good care to keep her rival practically a prisoner.

The rising in the north, 1569, and Catholic plans for deposing Elizabeth.

176. As time went on it became increasingly difficult for Elizabeth to adhere to her policy of moderation in the treatment of the Catholics. A rising in the north of England (1569) showed that there were many who would gladly reëstablish the Catholic faith by freeing Mary and placing her on the English throne. This was followed by the excommunication of Elizabeth by the pope, who at the same time absolved her subjects from their allegiance to their heretical ruler. Happily for Elizabeth the rebels could look for no help either from Alva or the French king. The Spaniards had their hands full, for the war in the Netherlands had just begun; and Charles IX, who had accepted Coligny as his adviser, was at that moment in hearty accord with the Huguenots. The rising in the north was suppressed, but the English Catholics continued to harbor treasonable designs and to look to Philip for help. They opened correspondence with Alva and invited him to come with six thousand Spanish troops to dethrone Elizabeth and make Mary Stuart queen of England in her stead. Alva hesitated, for he characteristically thought that it would be better to kill Elizabeth, or at least capture her. Meanwhile the plot was discovered and came to naught.

English mariners capture Spanish ships.

Although Philip found himself unable to harm England, the English mariners, like the Dutch "sea beggars," caused great loss to Spain. In spite of the fact that Spain and England were not openly at war, the English seamen extended their operations as far as the West Indies, and seized Spanish treasure ships, with the firm conviction that in robbing Philip they were serving God.

The daring Sir Francis Drake even ventured into the Pacific, where only the Spaniards had gone heretofore, and carried off much booty on his little vessel, the *Pelican*. At last he took "a great vessel with jewels in plenty, thirteen chests of silver coin, eighty pounds weight of gold, and twenty-six tons of silver." He then sailed around the world, and on his return presented his jewels to Elizabeth, who paid little attention to the expostulations of the king of Spain.[1]

One hope of the Catholics has not yet been mentioned, namely, Ireland, whose relations with England from very early times down to the present day form one of the most cheerless pages in the history of Europe. Ireland was no longer, as it had been in the time of Gregory the Great, a center of culture.[2] The population was divided into numerous clans and their chieftains fought constantly with one another as well as with the English, who were vainly endeavoring to subjugate the island. Under Henry II and later kings England had conquered a district in the eastern part of Ireland, and here the English managed to maintain a foothold in spite of the anarchy outside. Henry VIII had suppressed a revolt of the Irish and assumed the title of King of Ireland. Mary had hoped to promote better relations by colonizing Kings County and Queens County with Englishmen. This led, however, to a long struggle which only ended when the colonists had killed all the natives in the district they occupied.

Elizabeth's interest in the perennial Irish question was stimulated by the probability that Ireland might become a basis for Catholic operations, since Protestantism had made little progress among its simple and half-barbarous people. Her fears were

Relations between England and Catholic Ireland.

[1] For English mariners and their voyages and conflicts with Spain, see Froude's *English Seamen in the Fifteenth Century*. The account of Drake's voyage is on pp. 75–103. See also "The Famous Voyage of Sir Francis Drake," by one of Drake's gentlemen at arms, in E. J. Payne's *Voyages of Elizabethan Seamen to America*, Vol. I, pp. 196–229, Oxford, 1893.

[2] See above, p. 62.

realized. Several attempts were made by Catholic leaders to land troops in Ireland with the purpose of making the island the base for an attack on England. Elizabeth's officers were able to frustrate these enterprises, but the resulting disturbances greatly increased the misery of the Irish. In 1582 no less than thirty thousand people are said to have perished, chiefly from starvation.

Persecution of the English Catholics.

As Philip's troops began to get the better of the opposition in the southern Netherlands, the prospect of sending a Spanish army to England grew brighter. Two Jesuits were sent to England in 1580 to strengthen the adherents of their faith and urge them to assist the foreign force against their queen when it should come. Parliament now grew more intolerant and ordered fines and imprisonment to be inflicted on those who said or heard mass, or who refused to attend the English services. One of the Jesuits was cruelly tortured and executed for treason, the other escaped to the continent and from there directed a conspiracy aimed at Elizabeth's life.

Plans to assassinate Elizabeth.

In the spring of 1582 the first attempt to assassinate the heretical queen was made at Philip's instigation. It was proposed that, when Elizabeth was out of the way, the duke of Guise should see that an army was sent to England in the interest of the Catholics. But Guise was kept busy at home by the War of the Three Henrys, and Philip was left to undertake the invasion of England by himself.

Execution of Mary Queen of Scots, 1587.

Mary did not live to witness the attempt. She became implicated in another plot for the assassination of Elizabeth. Parliament now realized that as long as Mary lived Elizabeth's life was in constant danger ; whereas, if Mary were out of the way, Philip would have no interest in the death of Elizabeth, since Mary's son, James VI of Scotland, was a Protestant. Elizabeth was therefore reluctantly persuaded by her advisers to sign a warrant for Mary's execution in 1587.[1]

---

[1] Reference for life and death of Mary Stuart, Green, *Short History*, pp. 379–392, 416–417.

Philip by no means gave up his project of reclaiming Protestant England. In 1588 he brought together a great fleet, including his best and largest warships, which was proudly called by the Spaniards the "Invincible Armada" (i.e., fleet). This was to sail up the Channel to Flanders and bring over the duke of Parma and his veterans, who, it was expected, would soon make an end of Elizabeth's raw militia. The English ships were inferior to those of Spain in size although not in number, but they had trained commanders, such as Drake and Hawkins. These famous captains had long sailed the Spanish Main and knew how to use their cannon without getting near enough to the Spaniards to suffer from their short-range weapons. When the Armada approached, it was permitted by the English fleet to pass up the Channel before a strong wind which later became a storm. The English ships then followed and both fleets were driven past the coast of Flanders. Of the hundred and twenty Spanish ships, only fifty-four returned home ; the rest had been destroyed by English valor, or by the gale to which Elizabeth herself ascribed the victory.[1] The defeat of the Armada put an end to the danger from Spain.

177. As we look back over the period covered by the reign of Philip II, it is clear that it was a most notable one in the history of the Catholic Church. When he ascended the throne Germany, as well as Switzerland and the Netherlands, had become largely Protestant. England, however, under his Catholic wife, Mary, seemed to be turning back to the old religion, while the French monarchs showed no inclination to tolerate the heretical Calvinists. Moreover, the new and enthusiastic order of the Jesuits promised to be a potent agency in inducing the disaffected people to accept once more the supremacy of the pope and the doctrines of the ancient church as formulated by the Council of Trent. The

Destruction of Philip's Armada, 1588.

Prospects of the Catholic cause at the opening of the reign of Philip II.

---

[1] References, Green, *Short History of the English People*, pp. 418–420 ; Froude, *English Seamen*, pp. 176–228.

tremendous power and apparently boundless resources of Spain itself, — which were viewed by the rest of Europe with the gravest apprehension, not to say terror, — Philip was willing to dedicate to the extirpation of heresy in his own dominions and the destruction of Protestantism throughout western Europe.

Outcome of Philip's policy.

When Philip died all was changed. England was hopelessly Protestant : the " Invincible Armada " had been miserably wrecked, and Philip's plan for bringing England once more within the fold of the Roman Catholic Church was forever frustrated. In France the terrible wars of religion were over, and a powerful king, lately a Protestant himself, was on the throne, who not only tolerated the Protestants but chose one of them for his chief minister, and would brook no more meddling of Spain in French affairs. A new Protestant state, the United Netherlands, had actually appeared within the bounds of the realm bequeathed to Philip by his father. In spite of its small size this state was destined to play, from that time on, quite as important a part in European affairs as the harsh Spanish stepmother from whose control it had escaped.

Decline of Spain after the sixteenth century.

Spain itself had suffered most of all from Philip's reign.[1] His domestic policy and his expensive wars had weakened a country which had never been intrinsically strong. The income from across the sea was bound to decrease as the mines were exhausted. The final expulsion of the industrious Moors, shortly after Philip's death, left the indolent Spaniards to till their own fields, which rapidly declined in fertility under their careless cultivation. Poverty was deemed no disgrace but manual labor was. Some one once ventured to tell a Spanish king that " not gold and silver but sweat is the most precious metal, a coin which is always current and never depreciates " ; but it was a rare form of currency in the Spanish peninsula. After Philip II's death Spain sinks to the rank of a secondary European power.

[1] Reference, Johnson, *Europe in the Sixteenth Century*, Chapter VII, §§ 1 and 3.

CHAPTER XXIX

THE THIRTY YEARS' WAR

178. The last great conflict caused by the differences between the Catholics and Protestants was fought out in Germany during the first half of the seventeenth century. It is generally known as the Thirty Years' War (1618-1648), but there was in reality a series of wars; and although the fighting was done upon German territory, Sweden, France, and Spain played quite as important a part as Germany.

The Thirty Years' War really a series of wars.

Just before the abdication of Charles V, the Lutheran princes had forced the emperor to acknowledge their right to their own religion and to the church property which they had appropriated. The religious Peace of Augsburg had, however, as we have seen,[1] two great weaknesses. In the first place, only those Protestants who held the Lutheran faith were to be tolerated. The Calvinists, who were increasing in numbers, were not included in the peace. In the second place, the peace did not put a stop to the seizure of church property by the Protestant princes.

Weaknesses of the Peace of Augsburg.

During the last years of Ferdinand I's reign and that of his successor there was little trouble. Protestantism, however, made rapid progress and invaded Bavaria, the Austrian possessions, and above all, Bohemia, where the doctrines of Huss had never died out. So it looked for a time as if even the German Hapsburgs were to see large portions of their territory falling away from the old Church. But the Catholics had in the Jesuits a band of active and efficient missionaries. They

Spread of Protestantism.

---

[1] See above, pp. 419-420.

not only preached and founded schools, but also succeeded in gaining the confidence of some of the German princes, whose chief advisers they became. Conditions were very favorable, at the opening of the seventeenth century, for a renewal of the religious struggle.

Formation of the Protestant Union and the Catholic League.

The Lutheran town of Donauwörth permitted the existence of a monastery within its limits. In 1607 a Protestant mob attacked the monks as they were passing in procession through the streets. Duke Maximilian of Bavaria, an ardent Catholic, on the border of whose possessions the town lay, gladly undertook to punish this outrage. His army entered Donauwörth, reëstablished the Catholic worship, and drove out the Lutheran pastor. This event led to the formation of the Protestant Union under the leadership of Frederick, elector of the Palatinate. The Union included by no means all the Protestant princes; for example, the Lutheran elector of Saxony refused to have anything to do with the Calvinistic Frederick. The next year the Catholics, on their part, formed the Catholic League under a far more efficient head, namely, Maximilian of Bavaria.[1]

Bohemia revolts from the Hapsburg rule, 1618.

These were the preliminaries of the Thirty Years' War. Hostilities began in Bohemia, which had been added to the Hapsburg possessions through the marriage of Ferdinand I. The Protestants were so strong in that country that they had forced the emperor in 1609 to grant them privileges greater even than those enjoyed by the Huguenots in France. The government, however, failed to observe this agreement, and the destruction of two Protestant churches resulted in a revolution at Prague in 1618. Three representatives of the emperor were seized by the irritated Bohemian leaders and thrown out of the window of the palace. After this emphatic protest against the oppressive measures of the government, Bohemia endeavored to establish itself once more as an independent kingdom. It renounced the rule of the Hapsburgs and chose Frederick,

[1] Reference, Wakeman, *Europe from 1598–1715,* Chapter III.

the elector of the Palatinate, as its new king. He appeared to the Bohemians to possess a double advantage; in the first place, he was the head of the Protestant Union, and in the second, he was the son-in-law of the king of England, James I, to whom they looked for help.

Frederick, elector of the Palatinate, chosen king of Bohemia.

The Bohemian venture proved a most disastrous one for Germany and for Protestantism. The new emperor, Ferdinand II (1619–1637), who was at once an uncompromising Catholic and a person of considerable ability, appealed to the League for assistance. Frederick, the new king of Bohemia, showed himself entirely unequal to the occasion. He and his English wife, the Princess Elizabeth, made a bad impression on the Bohemians, and they failed to gain the support of the neighboring Lutheran elector of Saxony. A single battle, which the army of the League under Maximilian won in 1620, put to flight the poor "winter king," as he was derisively called on account of his reign of a single season. The emperor and the duke of Bavaria set vigorously to work to suppress Protestantism within their borders. The emperor arbitrarily granted the eastern portion of the Palatinate to Maximilian and gave him the title of Elector, without consulting the diet.

Failure of the Bohemian revolt.

Battle on the White Hill, 1620.

179. Matters were becoming serious for the Protestant party, and England might have intervened had it not been that James I believed that he could by his personal influence restore peace to Europe and induce the emperor and Maximilian of Bavaria to give back the Palatinate to the " winter king." Even France might have taken a hand, for although Richelieu, then at the head of affairs, had no love for the Protestants, he was still more bitterly opposed to the Hapsburgs. However, his hands were tied for the moment, for he was just undertaking to deprive the Huguenots of their strong towns.

England and France unable to assist the Protestants.

A diversion came, nevertheless, from without. Christian IV, king of Denmark, invaded northern Germany in 1625 with a

Christian IV of Denmark invades Germany, but is defeated.

view of relieving his fellow Protestants. In addition to the army of the League which was dispatched against him, a new **Wallenstein.** army was organized by the notorious commander, Wallenstein. The emperor was poor and gladly accepted the offer of this ambitious Bohemian nobleman[1] to collect an army which should support itself upon the proceeds of the war, to wit, confiscation and robbery. Christian met with two serious defeats in northern Germany; even his peninsula was invaded by the imperial forces, and in 1629 he agreed to retire from the conflict.

The Edict of Restitution, 1629. The emperor was encouraged by the successes of the Catholic armies to issue that same year an Edict of Restitution. In this he ordered the Protestants throughout Germany to give back all the church possessions which they had seized since the religious Peace of Augsburg (1555). These included two archbishoprics (Magdeburg and Bremen), nine bishoprics, about one hundred and twenty monasteries, and other church foundations. Moreover, he decreed that only the Lutherans might enjoy the practice of their religion; the other "sects" were to be broken up. As Wallenstein was preparing to execute this decree in his usual merciless fashion, the war took a new turn. The League had become jealous of a general who threatened to become too powerful, and it accordingly joined in the complaints, which came from every side, of the terrible extortions and incredible cruelty practiced by Wallenstein's **Dismissal of Wallenstein. Appearance of Gustavus Adolphus of Sweden, 1594-1632.** troops. The emperor consented, therefore, to dismiss this most competent commander and lose a large part of his army. Just as the Catholics were thus weakened, a new enemy arrived upon the scene who was far more dangerous than any they had yet had to face, Gustavus Adolphus, king of Sweden.[2]

The kingdom of Sweden. 180. We have had no occasion hitherto to speak of the Scandinavian kingdoms of Norway, Sweden, and Denmark,

---

[1] Wallenstein (b. 1583) had been educated in the Catholic faith, although he came of a family with Hussite sympathies.

[2] Reference, Wakeman, *Europe from 1598-1715*, Chapter IV.

which the northern German peoples had established about Charlemagne's time; but from now on they begin to take part in the affairs of central Europe. The Union of Calmar (1397) had brought these three kingdoms, previously separate, under a single ruler. About the time that the Protestant revolt began in Germany the union was broken by the withdrawal of Sweden. Gustavus Vasa, a Swedish noble, led the movement and was subsequently chosen king of Sweden (1523). In the same year Protestantism was introduced. Vasa confiscated the church lands, got the better of the aristocracy, and started Sweden on its way toward national greatness. Under his successor the eastern shores of the Baltic were conquered and the Russians cut off from the sea.

Gustavus Vasa, 1523–1560.

Gustavus Adolphus (1594–1632) was induced to invade Germany for two reasons. In the first place, he was a sincere and enthusiastic Protestant and by far the most generous and attractive figure of his time. He was genuinely afflicted by the misfortunes of his Protestant brethren and anxious to devote himself to their welfare. Secondly, he dreamed of extending his domains so that one day the Baltic might perhaps become a Swedish lake. He undoubtedly hoped by his invasion not only to free his co-religionists from the oppression of the emperor and of the League, but to gain a strip of territory for Sweden.

Motives of Gustavus Adolphus in invading Germany, 1630.

Gustavus was not received with much cordiality at first by the Protestant princes of the north; but they were brought to their senses by the awful destruction of Magdeburg by the troops of the League under General Tilly. Magdeburg was the most important town of northern Germany. When it finally succumbed after an obstinate and difficult siege, twenty thousand of its inhabitants were killed and the town burned to the ground. Although Tilly's reputation for cruelty is quite equal to that of Wallenstein, he was probably not responsible for the fire. After Gustavus Adolphus had met

Destruction of Magdeburg, 1631.

Gustavus
Adolphus
victorious at
Breitenfeld,
1631.

Tilly near Leipsic and victoriously routed the army of the League, the Protestant princes began to look with more favor on the foreigner. Gustavus then moved westward and took up his winter quarters on the Rhine.

Wallenstein
recalled.

The next spring he entered Bavaria and once more defeated Tilly (who was mortally wounded in the battle), and forced Munich to surrender. There seemed now to be no reason why he should not continue his way to Vienna. At this juncture the emperor recalled Wallenstein, who collected a new army over which the emperor gave him absolute command.

Gustavus
Adolphus
killed at
Lützen, 1632.

After some delay Gustavus met Wallenstein on the field of Lützen, in November, 1632, where, after a fierce struggle, the Swedes gained the victory. But they lost their leader and Protestantism its hero, for the Swedish king ventured too far into the lines of the enemy and was surrounded and killed.

Murder of
Wallenstein.

The Swedes did not, however, retire from Germany, but continued to participate in the war, which now degenerated into a series of raids by leaders whose soldiers depopulated the land by their unspeakable atrocities. Wallenstein roused the suspicions of the Catholics by entering into mysterious negotiations with Richelieu and with the German Protestants. This treasonable correspondence quickly reached the ears of the emperor. Wallenstein, who had long been detested by · even the Catholics, was deserted by his soldiers and murdered (in 1634), to the great relief of all parties. In the same year

Battle of
Nördlingen,
1634.

the imperial army won the important battle of Nördlingen, one of the most bloody and at the same time decisive engagements of the war. Shortly after, the elector of Saxony withdrew from his alliance with the Swedes and made peace with the emperor. It looked as if the war were about to come to an end, for many others among the German princes were quite ready to lay down their arms.[1]

[1] Reference, Wakeman, *Europe from 1598–1715*, Chapter V.

181. Just at this critical moment Richelieu decided that it would be to the interest of France to renew the old struggle with the Hapsburgs by sending troops against the emperor. France was still shut in, as she had been since the time of Charles V, by the Hapsburg lands. Except on the side toward the ocean her boundaries were in the main artificial ones, and not those established by great rivers and mountains. She therefore longed to weaken her enemy and strengthen herself by winning Roussillon on the south, and so make the crest of the Pyrenees the line of demarcation between France and Spain. She dreamed, too, of extending her sway toward the Rhine by adding the county of Burgundy (i.e., Franche-Comté) and a number of fortified towns which would afford protection against the Spanish Netherlands.

Richelieu renews the struggle of France against the Hapsburgs.

Richelieu had been by no means indifferent to the Thirty Years' War. He had encouraged the Swedish king to intervene, and had supplied him with funds if not with troops. Moreover, he himself had checked Spanish progress in northern Italy. In 1624 Spanish troops had invaded the valley of the Adda, a Protestant region, with the evident purpose of conquest. This appeared a most serious aggression to Richelieu, for if the Spanish won the valley of the Adda, the last barrier between the Hapsburg possessions in Italy and in Germany would be removed. French troops were dispatched to drive out the Spaniards, but it was in the interest of France rather than in that of the oppressed Calvinists, for whom Richelieu could hardly have harbored a deep affection. A few years later it became a question whether a Spanish or a French candidate should obtain the vacant duchy of Mantua, and Richelieu led another French army in person to see that Spain was again discomfited. It was, then, not strange that he should decide to deal a blow at the emperor when the war appeared to be coming to a close that was tolerably satisfactory from the standpoint of the Hapsburgs.

Richelieu checks Spanish aggression in Italy.

Richelieu's
intervention
prolongs
the war.

Richelieu declared war against Spain in May, 1635. He had already concluded an alliance with the chief enemies of the house of Austria. Sweden agreed not to negotiate for peace until France was ready for it. The United Provinces joined France, as did some of the German princes. So the war was renewed, and French, Swedish, Spanish, and German soldiers ravaged an already exhausted country for a decade longer. The dearth of provisions was so great that the armies had to move quickly from place to place in order to avoid starvation. After a serious defeat by the Swedes, the emperor (Ferdinand III, 1637–1657) sent a Dominican monk to expostulate with Cardinal Richelieu for his crime in aiding the German and Swedish heretics against the unimpeachably orthodox Austria.

France suc-
ceeds Spain
in the
military
supremacy
of western
Europe.

The cardinal had, however, just died (December, 1642), well content with the results of his diplomacy. The French were in possession of Roussillon and of Artois, Lorraine, and Alsace. The military exploits of the French generals, especially Turenne and Condé, during the opening years of the reign of Louis XIV (1643–1715) showed that a new period had begun in which the military and political supremacy of Spain was to give way to that of France.

Close of the
Thirty Years'
War, 1648.

182. The participants in the war were now so numerous and their objects so various and conflicting, that it is not strange that it required some years to arrange the conditions of peace even when every one was ready for it. It was agreed (1644) that France and the empire should negotiate at Münster, and the emperor and the Swedes at Osnabrück, — both of which towns lie in Westphalia. For four years the representatives of the several powers worked upon the difficult problem of satisfying every one, but at last the treaties of Westphalia were signed late in 1648. Their provisions continued to be the basis of the international law of Europe down to the French Revolution.

The religious troubles in Germany were settled by extending the toleration of the Peace of Augsburg so as to include the Calvinists as well as the Lutherans. The Protestant princes were, regardless of the Edict of Restitution, to retain the lands which they had in their possession in the year 1624, and each ruler was still to have the right to determine the religion of his state. The dissolution of the German empire was practically acknowledged by permitting the individual states to make treaties among themselves and with foreign powers; this was equivalent to recognizing the practical independence which they had, as a matter of fact, already long enjoyed. A part of Pomerania and the districts at the mouth of the Oder, the Elbe, and the Weser were ceded to Sweden. This territory did not, however, cease to form a part of the empire, for Sweden was thereafter to have three votes in the German diet.

Provisions of the treaties of Westphalia.

As for France, it was definitely given the three bishoprics of Metz, Verdun, and Toul, which Henry II had bargained for when he allied himself with the Protestants a century earlier.[1] The emperor also ceded to France all his rights in Alsace, although the city of Strasburg was to remain with the empire. Lastly, the independence both of the United Netherlands and of Switzerland was acknowledged.[2]

The accounts of the misery and depopulation of Germany caused by the Thirty Years' War are well-nigh incredible. Thousands of villages were wiped out altogether; in some regions the population was reduced by one half, in others to a third, or even less, of what it had been at the opening of the conflict. The flourishing city of Augsburg was left with but sixteen thousand souls instead of eighty thousand. The people were fearfully barbarized by privation and suffering and

Disastrous results of the war in Germany.

---

[1] See above, p. 452.

[2] Reference, Wakeman, *Europe from 1598–1715*, Chapter VI. For a brief and excellent review of the whole war, see Schwill, *Modern Europe*, pp. 141–160.

by the atrocities of the soldiers of all the various nations. Until the end of the eighteenth century Germany was too exhausted and impoverished to make any considerable contribution to the culture of Europe. Only one hopeful circumstance may be noted as we leave this dreary subject. After the Peace of Westphalia the elector of Brandenburg was the most powerful of the German princes next to the emperor. As king of Prussia he was destined to create another European power, and at last to humble the house of Hapsburg and create a new German empire in which Austria should have no part.

General Reading. — The most complete and scholarly account of the Thirty Years' War to be had in English is GINDELY, *History of the Thirty Years' War* (G. P. Putnam's Sons, 2 vols., $3.50).

CHAPTER XXX

STRUGGLE IN ENGLAND FOR CONSTITUTIONAL GOVERNMENT

183. The great question which confronted England in the seventeenth century was whether the king should be permitted to rule the people, as God's representative, or should submit to the constant control of the nation's representatives, i.e., Parliament. In France the Estates General met for the last time in 1614, and thereafter the French king made laws and executed them without asking the advice of any one except his immediate counselors. In general, the rulers on the continent exercised despotic powers, and James I of England and his son Charles I would gladly have made themselves absolute rulers, for they entertained the same exalted notions of the divine right of kings which prevailed across the English Channel. England finally succeeded, however, in adjusting the relations between king and Parliament in a very happy way, so as to produce a limited, or constitutional, monarchy. The long and bitter struggle between the house of Stuart and the English Parliament plays an important rôle in the history of Europe at large, as well as in that of England. After the French Revolution, at the end of the eighteenth century, the English system began to become popular on the continent, and it has now replaced the older absolute monarchy in all the kingdoms of western Europe.

On the death of Elizabeth in 1603, James I, the first of the Stuarts, ascended the English throne. He was, it will be remembered, the son of Mary Queen of Scots, and was known

475

in Scotland as James VI; consequently England and Scotland now came under the same ruler. This did not, however, make the relations between the two countries much happier, for a century to come at least.

The chief interest of James' reign lay in his tendency to exalt the royal prerogative, and in the systematic manner in which he extolled absolute monarchy in his writings and speeches and discredited it by his conduct. James was an unusually learned man, for a king, but his learning did not enlighten him in matters of common sense. As a man and a ruler, he was far inferior to his unschooled and light-hearted contemporary, Henry IV of France. Henry VIII had been a heartless despot, and Elizabeth had ruled the nation in a high-handed manner; but both of them had known how to make themselves popular and had had the good sense to say as little as possible about their rights. James, on the contrary, had a fancy for discussing his high position.

"As for the absolute prerogative of the crown," he declares, "that is no subject for the tongue of a lawyer, nor is it lawful to be disputed. It is atheism and blasphemy to dispute what God can do : . . . so it is presumption and high contempt in a subject to dispute what a king can do, or say that a king cannot do this or that." The king, James claimed, could make any kind of law or statute that he thought meet, without any advice from Parliament, although he might, if he chose, accept its suggestions. "He is overlord of the whole land, so is he master over every person who inhabiteth the same, having power over the life and death of every one of them : for although a just prince will not take the life of one of his subjects without a clear law, yet the same laws whereby he taketh them are made by himself and his predecessors ; so the power flows always from himself." A good king will act according to law, but he is above the law and is not bound thereby except voluntarily and for good-example giving to his subjects.

These theories, taken from James' work on *The Law of Free Monarchies*, seem strange and unreasonable to us. But he was really only claiming the rights which his predecessors had enjoyed, and such as were conceded to the kings of France until the French Revolution. According to the theory of "divine right," the king did not owe his power to the nation but to God, who had appointed him to be the father of his people. From God he derived all the prerogatives necessary to maintain order and promote justice; consequently he was responsible to God alone, and not to the people, for the exercise of his powers. It is unnecessary to follow in detail the troubles between James and his Parliament and the various methods which he invented for raising money without the sanction of Parliament, for all this forms only the preliminary to the fatal experience of James' son, Charles I.

The theory of 'divine right.'

In his foreign policy James showed as little sense as in his relations with his own people. He refused to help his son-in-law when he became king of Bohemia.[1] But when the Palatinate was given by the emperor to Maximilian of Bavaria, James struck upon the extraordinary plan of forming an alliance with the hated Spain and inducing its king to persuade the emperor to reinstate the "winter king" in his former possessions. In order to conciliate Spain, Charles, Prince of Wales, was to marry a Spanish princess. Naturally this proposal was very unpopular among the English Protestants, and it finally came to nothing.

James I's foreign policy.

Although England under James I failed to influence deeply the course of affairs in Europe at large, his reign is distinguished by the work of unrivaled writers who gave England a literature which outshone that of any other of the European countries. Shakespeare is generally admitted to have been the greatest dramatist the world has ever produced. While he wrote many of his plays before the death of Elizabeth,

Literature in the time of Elizabeth and James I.

Shakespeare, 1564-1616.

[1] See above, p. 467.

Othello, *King Lear*, and *The Tempest* belong to the reign
of James. Francis Bacon, philosopher and statesman, did
much for the advancement of scientific research by advocating
new methods of reasoning based upon a careful observation
of natural phenomena instead of upon Aristotle's logic. He
urged investigators to take the path already indicated over
three centuries earlier by his namesake, Roger Bacon.[1] The
most worthy monument of the strong and beautiful English
of the period is to be found in the translation of the Bible,
prepared in James' reign and still generally used in all the
countries where English is spoken.[2]

184. Charles I was somewhat more dignified than his father,
but he was quite as obstinately set upon having his own way
and showed no more skill in winning the confidence of his
subjects. He did nothing to remove the disagreeable impres-
sions of his father's reign and began immediately to quarrel
with Parliament. When that body refused to grant him any
money, mainly because they thought that it was likely to be
wasted by his favorite, the duke of Buckingham, Charles
formed the plan of winning their favor by a great military
victory.

After James I had reluctantly given up his cherished Spanish alliance, Charles had married a French princess, Henrietta
Maria, the daughter of Henry IV. In spite of this marriage
Charles now proposed to aid the Huguenots whom Richelieu
was besieging in their town of La Rochelle. He also hoped
to gain popularity by prosecuting a war against Spain, whose
king was energetically supporting the Catholic League in Germany. Accordingly, in spite of Parliament's refusal to grant

Marginal notes:
Francis Bacon, 1561-1626.

The King James translation of the Bible.

Charles I, 1625-1649.

---

[1] See above, p. 273.

[2] See the translators' dedication to James I in the authorized version of the
Bible. Only recently has it been deemed necessary to revise the remarkable work
of the translators of the early seventeenth century. Modern scholars discovered
very few serious mistakes in this authorized version, but found it expedient for
the sake of clearness to modernize a number of words and expressions.

him the necessary funds, he embarked in war. With only the money which he could raise by irregular means, Charles arranged an expedition to take Cadiz and the Spanish treasure ships which arrived there once a year from America, laden with gold and silver. The expedition failed, as well as Charles' attempt to help the Huguenots.

In his attempts to raise money without a regular grant from Parliament, Charles had resorted to vexatious exactions. The law prohibited him from asking for *gifts* from his people, but it did not forbid his asking them to *lend* him money, however little prospect there might be of his ever repaying it. Five gentlemen who refused to pay such a forced loan were imprisoned by the mere order of the king. This raised the question of whether the king had the right to send to prison those whom he wished without showing legal cause for their arrest.

Charles' exactions and arbitrary acts.

This and other attacks upon the rights of his subjects roused Parliament. In 1628 that body drew up the celebrated Petition of Right,[1] which is one of the most important documents in the history of the English Constitution. In it Parliament called the king's attention to his illegal exactions, and to the acts of his agents who had in sundry ways molested and disquieted the people of the realm. Parliament therefore " humbly prayed " the king that no man need thereafter " make or yield any gift, loan, benevolence, tax, or such like charge " without consent of Parliament; that no free man should be imprisoned or suffer any punishment except according to the laws and statutes of the realm as presented in the Great Charter; and that soldiers should not be quartered upon the people on any pretext whatever. Very reluctantly Charles consented to this restatement of the limitations which the English had always, in theory at least, placed upon the arbitrary power of their king.

The Petition of Right

[1] See Lee, *Source-book of English History*, pp. 348–352.

The disagreement between Charles and Parliament was rendered much more serious by religious differences. The king had married a Catholic princess, and the Catholic cause seemed to be gaining on the continent. The king of Denmark had

just been defeated by Wallenstein and Tilly, and Richelieu had succeeded in depriving the Huguenots of their cities of refuge. Both James and Charles had shown their readiness to enter into engagements with France and Spain to protect English Catholics, and there was evidently a growing inclination in England to revert to the older ceremonies of the Church, which shocked the more strongly Protestant members of the House of Commons. The communion table was again placed by many clergymen at the eastern end of the church and became fixed there as an altar, and portions of the service were once more chanted.

These "popish practices," with which the king was supposed to sympathize, served to widen the breach between him and the

Charles I

(After a painting by Vandyke)

Commons which had been opened by the king's attempt to raise taxes on his own account. The Parliament of 1629, after a stormy session, was dissolved by the king, who determined to rule thereafter by himself. For eleven years no new Parliament was summoned.

185. Charles was not well fitted by nature to try the experiment of personal government. Moreover, the methods resorted to by his ministers to raise money without recourse to Parliament rendered the king more and more unpopular and prepared the way for the triumphant return of Parliament.

According to an ancient law of England, those who had a certain amount of land must become knights; but since the decay of the feudal system, landowners had given up the meaningless form of qualifying themselves as knights. It now occurred to the king's government that a large amount of money might be raised by fining these delinquents. Other unfortunates who had settled within the boundaries of the royal forests were either heavily fined or required to pay enormous arrears of rent.

Charles' financial exactions.

In addition to these sources of income, Charles applied to his subjects for *ship money*.[1] He was anxious to equip a fleet, but instead of requiring the various ports to furnish ships, as was the ancient custom, he permitted them to buy themselves off by contributing to the fitting out of large ships owned by himself. Even those living inland were asked for ship money. The king maintained that this was not a tax but simply a payment by which his subjects freed themselves from the duty of defending their country. John Hampden, a squire of Buckinghamshire, made a bold stand against this illegal demand by refusing to pay twenty shillings of ship money which was levied upon him. The case was tried before the king's judges, a bare majority of whom decided against Hampden. But the trial made it tolerably clear that the country would not put up long with the king's despotic policy.

In 1633 Charles made William Laud Archbishop of Canterbury. Laud believed that the English Church would strengthen both itself and the government by following a middle course

William Laud made Archbishop of Canterbury.

[1] See Lee, *Source-book of English History*, pp. 352–355, for the first writ of ship money.

which should lie between that of the Church of Rome and that of Calvinistic Geneva. He declared that it was the part of good citizenship to conform outwardly to the services of the state church, but that the state should not undertake to oppress the individual conscience, and that every one should be at liberty to make up his own mind in regard to the interpretation to be given to the Bible and to the church fathers. As soon as he became archbishop he began a series of visitations through his province. Every clergyman who refused to conform to the Prayer Book, or opposed the placing of the communion table at the east end of the church, or declined to bow at the name of Jesus, was, if obstinate, to be brought before the king's special Court of High Commission to be tried and if convicted to be deprived of his benefice.

The different sects of Protestants. Laud's conduct was no doubt gratifying to the High Church party among the Protestants, that is, those who still clung to some of the ancient practices of the Roman Church, although they rejected the doctrine of the Mass and refused to regard the pope as their head. The Low Church party, or *Puritans*, on the contrary, regarded Laud and his policy with aversion. While, unlike the Presbyterians, they did not urge the abolition of the bishops, they disliked all " superstitious usages," as they called the wearing of the surplice by the clergy, the use of the sign of the cross at baptism, the kneeling posture in partaking of the communion. The Presbyterians, who are often confused with the Puritans, agreed with them in many respects, but went farther and demanded the introduction of Calvin's system of church government.[1]

The Independents. Lastly, there was an ever-increasing number of Separatists, or Independents. These rejected both the organization of the Church of England and that of the Presbyterians, and desired that each religious community should organize itself independently. The government had forbidden these Separatists

[1] See above, p. 426, n. 1.

to hold their little meetings, which they called *conventicles*, and about 1600 some of them fled to Holland. The community of them which established itself at Leyden dispatched the *Mayflower*, in 1620, with colonists — since known as the Pilgrim Fathers — to the New World across the sea.[1] It was these colonists who laid the foundations of a *New England* which has proved a worthy offspring of the mother country. The form of worship which they established in their new home is still known as Congregational.[2]

The Pilgrim Fathers.

186. In 1640 Charles found himself forced to resort to Parliament, for he was involved in a war with Scotland which he could not carry on without money. There the Presbyterian system had been pretty generally introduced by John Knox in Queen Mary's time, but the bishops had been permitted to maintain a precarious existence in the interest of the nobles who enjoyed their revenues. James I had always had a strong dislike for Presbyterianism. He once said, " A Scottish presbytery agreeth as well with the monarchy as God with the devil. Then Jack and Tom and Will and Dick shall meet and at their pleasure censure me and my council." He much preferred a few bishops appointed by himself to hundreds of presbyteries over whose sharp eyes and sharper tongues he could have little control. So bishops were reappointed in Scotland in the early years of his reign and got back some of their powers. The Presbyterians, however, were still in the majority, and they continued to regard the bishops as the tools of the king.

Charles summons Parliament once more, to aid him in fighting the Scotch Presbyterians, 1640.

An attempt on the part of Charles to force the Scots to accept a modified form of the English Prayer Book led to the signing of the National Covenant in 1638. This pledged those

The National Covenant, 1638.

[1] The name Puritan, it should be noted, was applied loosely to the English Protestants, whether Low Churchmen, Presbyterians, or Independents, who aroused the antagonism of their neighbors by advocating a godly life and opposing popular pastimes, especially on Sunday.

[2] Reference, Green, *Short History*, pp. 595–514. For a contemporary account of Puritans, see *Readings*, Chapter XXX.

who attached their names to it to reëstablish the purity and liberty of the Gospel, which, to most of the Covenanters, meant Presbyterianism. Charles thereupon undertook to coerce the Scots. Having no money, he bought on credit a large cargo of pepper, which had just arrived in the ships of the East India Company, and sold it cheap for ready cash. The soldiers, however, whom he got together showed little inclination to fight the Scots, with whom they were in tolerable agreement on religious matters. Charles was therefore at last obliged to summon a Parliament, which, owing to the length of time it remained in session, is known as the Long Parliament.

The measures of the Long Parliament against the king's tyranny. The Long Parliament began by imprisoning Strafford, the king's most conspicuous minister, and Archbishop Laud in the Tower of London. The help that Strafford had given to the king in ruling without Parliament had mortally offended the House of Commons. They declared him guilty of treason, and he was executed in 1641, in spite of Charles' efforts to save him. Laud met the same fate four years later. Parliament also tried to strengthen its position by passing the Triennial Bill, which provided that it should meet at least once in three years, even if not summoned by the king. The courts of Star Chamber and High Commission, which had arbitrarily condemned a number of the king's opponents, were abolished, and ship money declared illegal.[1] In short, Charles' whole system of government was abrogated. The efforts of the queen to obtain money and soldiers from the pope, and a visit of Charles to Scotland, which Parliament suspected was for the purpose of forcing the Scots to lend him an army to use against themselves, led to the Grand Remonstrance. In this all of Charles' errors were enumerated and a demand was made that the king's ministers should thereafter be responsible to Parliament. This document Parliament ordered to be printed and circulated throughout the country.

[1] Reference, Lee, *Source-book of English History*, pp. 355-357.

Exasperated at the conduct of the Commons, Charles attempted to intimidate the opposition by undertaking the arrest of five of its most active leaders, whom he declared to be traitors. But when he entered the House of Commons and looked around for his enemies, he found that they had taken shelter in London, whose citizens later brought them back in triumph to Westminster.

Charles' attempts to arrest five members of the House of Commons

187. Both Charles and Parliament now began to gather troops for the inevitable conflict, and England was plunged into civil war. Those who supported Charles were called *Cavaliers.* They included not only most of the aristocracy and the papal party, but also a number of members of the House of Commons who were fearful lest Presbyterianism should succeed in doing away with the English Church. The parliamentary party was popularly known as the *Roundheads,* since some of them cropped their hair close because of their dislike for the long locks of their more aristocratic and worldly opponents.

The beginning of civil war, 1642. Cavaliers and Roundheads.

Oliver Cromwell

The Roundheads soon found a distinguished leader in Oliver Cromwell[1] (b. 1599), a country gentleman and member of Parliament, who was later to become the most powerful ruler of his time. Cromwell organized a compact army of God-fearing men, who indulged in no profane words or light talk, as is the wont of soldiers, but advanced upon their enemies singing psalms. The king enjoyed the support of northern

Oliver Cromwell

[1] Reference for Cromwell's early career and his generalship, Green, *Short History*, pp. 554–559.

England, and also looked for help from Ireland, where the royal and Catholic causes were popular.

Battles of Marston Moor and Naseby.

The war continued for several years, and a number of battles were fought which, after the first year, went in general against the Cavaliers. The most important of these were the battle of Marston Moor in 1644, and that of Naseby the next year, in which the king was disastrously defeated. The enemy

The losing cause of the king.

came into possession of his correspondence, which showed them how their king had been endeavoring to bring armies from France and Ireland into England. This encouraged Parliament to prosecute the war with more energy than ever. The king, defeated on every hand, put himself in the hands of the Scotch army which had come to the aid of Parliament (1646), and the Scotch soon turned him over to Parliament. During the next two years Charles, while held in captivity, entered into negotiations with the various parties in turn, but played fast and loose with them all.

Pride's Purge.

There were many in the House of Commons who still sided with the king, and in December, 1648, that body declared for a reconciliation with the monarch, whom they had safely imprisoned in the Isle of Wight. The next day Colonel Pride, representing the army, — which constituted a party in itself and was opposed to all negotiations between the king and the Commons, — stood at the door of the House with a body of soldiers and excluded all the members who took the side of the king. This outrageous act is known in history as Pride's Purge.

Execution of Charles, 1649.

In this way the House was brought completely under the control of those most bitterly hostile to Charles, whom they now proposed to bring to trial. They declared that the House of Commons, since it was chosen by the people, was supreme in England and the source of all just power, and that consequently neither king nor House of Lords was necessary. The mutilated House appointed a special High Court of Justice made up of Charles' sternest opponents, who alone would consent to sit in judgment on him. They passed sentence upon him, and on January 30, 1649, Charles was beheaded in front of his palace of Whitehall, London. It must be clear from the above account that it was not the nation at large which demanded Charles' death, but a very small group of extremists who claimed to be the representatives of the nation.[1]

188. The Rump Parliament, as the remnant of the House of Commons was contemptuously called, proclaimed England to be thereafter a commonwealth, that is, a republic, without a king or House of Lords. Cromwell, the head of the army, was the real ruler of England. He derived his main support from the Independents; and it is very surprising that he was able to maintain himself so long, considering what a small portion of the English people was in sympathy with the religious ideas of that sect and with the abolition of kingship. Even the Presbyterians were on the side of Charles II, the legal heir to the throne. Yet Cromwell represented the principles for which the opponents of tyranny had been contending. He was, moreover, a vigorous and skillful administrator, and had a well-organized army of fifty thousand men at his command; otherwise the republic could scarcely have lasted more than a few months.

England becomes a commonwealth or republic. Cromwell at the head of the government.

Cromwell found himself confronted by every variety of difficulty. The three kingdoms had fallen apart. The nobles and Catholics in Ireland proclaimed Charles II as king, and Ormond, a Protestant leader, formed an army of Irish Catholics and English royalist Protestants with a view of overthrowing the Commonwealth. Cromwell accordingly set out for Ireland, where he took an important fortified town and put two thousand men to the sword. Town after town surrendered to the forces of the Commonwealth, and in

Ireland and Scotland subdued.

---

[1] For charge against the king, etc., see Lee, *Source-book of English History*, pp. 364–372.

1652, after much cruelty, the island was once more conquered. A large part of it was confiscated for the benefit of the English, and the Catholic landowners were driven into the mountains. In the meantime (1650) Charles II had landed in Scotland, and upon his agreeing to be a Presbyterian king, the whole Scotch nation was ready to support him. But Scotland was subdued even more promptly than Ireland had been. So completely was the Scottish army destroyed that Cromwell found no need to draw the sword again in the British Isles.

The Navigation Act, 1651.

Although it would seem that Cromwell had enough to keep him busy at home, he had already engaged in a victorious foreign war against the Dutch, who had become dangerous commercial rivals of England. The ships which went out from Amsterdam and Rotterdam were the best merchant vessels in the world, and had got control of the carrying trade between Europe and the colonies. In order to put an end to this, the English Parliament passed the Navigation Act (1651), which permitted only English vessels to bring goods to England, unless the goods came in vessels belonging to the country which had produced them. This led to a commercial war between Holland and England, and a series of battles was fought between the English and Dutch fleets, in which sometimes one and sometimes the other gained the upper hand. This war is notable as the first example of the commercial struggles which were thereafter to take the place of the religious conflicts of the preceding period.

Commercial war between Holland and England.

Cromwell dissolves the Long Parliament (1653), and is made Lord Protector by his own Parliament.

Cromwell failed to get along with Parliament any better than Charles had done. The Rump Parliament had become very unpopular, for its members, in spite of their boasted piety, accepted bribes and were zealous in the promotion of their relatives in the public service. At last Cromwell upbraided them angrily for their injustice and self-interest, which were injuring the public cause. On being interrupted by a member, he cried out, " Come, come, we have had enough of this.

I'll put an end to this. It's not fit that you should sit here any longer," and calling in his soldiers he turned the members out of the House and sent them home. Having thus made an end of the Long Parliament (April, 1653), he summoned a Parliament of his own, made up of God-fearing men whom he and the officers of his army chose. This extraordinary body is known as Barebone's Parliament, from a distinguished member, a London merchant, with the characteristically Puritan name of Praisegod Barebone. Many of these godly men were unpractical and hard to deal with. A minority of the more sensible ones got up early one winter morning (December, 1653) and, before their opponents had a chance to protest, declared Parliament dissolved and placed the supreme authority in the hands of Cromwell.

For nearly five years Cromwell was, as Lord Protector, — a title equivalent to that of regent, — practically king of England, although he refused actually to accept the royal insignia. He did not succeed in permanently organizing the government at home but showed remarkable ability in his foreign negotiations. He formed an alliance with France, and English troops aided the French in winning a great victory over Spain. England gained thereby Dunkirk, and the West Indian island of Jamaica. The French king, Louis XIV, at first hesitated to address Cromwell, in the usual courteous way of monarchs, as "my cousin," but soon admitted that he would have to call Cromwell "father" should he wish it, as the Protector was undoubtedly the most powerful person in Europe. *The Protector's foreign policy.*

In May, 1658, Cromwell fell ill, and as a great storm passed over England at that time, the Cavaliers asserted that the devil had come to fetch home the soul of the usurper. Cromwell was dying, it is true, but he was no instrument of the devil. He closed a life of honest effort for his fellow-beings with a last touching prayer to God, whom he had consistently sought to serve: "Thou hast made me, though very unworthy, a *Death of Cromwell, September, 1658.*

mean instrument to do Thy people some good and Thee service : and many of them have set too high a value upon me, though others wish and would be glad of my death. Pardon such as desire to trample upon the dust of a poor worm, for they are Thy people too ; and pardon the folly of this short prayer, even for Jesus Christ's sake, and give us a good night, if it be Thy pleasure. Amen." [1]

The Restoration.

189. After Cromwell's death his son Richard, who succeeded him, found himself unable to carry on the government. He soon abdicated, and the remnants of the Long Parliament met once more. But the power was really in the hands of the soldiers. In 1660 George Monk, who was in command of the forces in Scotland, came to London with a view of putting an end to the anarchy. He soon concluded that no one cared to support the Rump, and that body peacefully disbanded of its own accord. Resistance would have been vain in any case with the army against it. The nation was glad to acknowledge

Charles II welcomed back as king, 1660.

Charles II, whom every one preferred to a government by soldiers. A new Parliament, composed of both houses, was assembled, which welcomed a messenger from the king and solemnly resolved that, " according to the ancient and fundamental laws of this kingdom, the government is, and ought to be, by king, lords, and commons." Thus the Puritan revolution and the ephemeral republic was followed by the *Restoration* of the Stuarts.

Character of Charles II.

Charles II was quite as fond as his father of having his own way, but he was a man of more ability. He disliked to be ruled by Parliament ; but, unlike his father, he was unwilling to arouse the nation against him. He did not propose to let anything happen which would send him on his travels again. He and his courtiers were fond of pleasure of a light-minded and immoral kind. The licentious dramas of the Restoration seem to indicate that those who had been forced by the

[1] Reference, Green, *Short History*, pp. 580–588, 594–600.

Puritans to give up their legitimate pleasures now welcomed the opportunity to indulge in reckless gayety without regard to the bounds imposed by custom and decency.

Charles' first Parliament was a moderate body, but his second was made up almost wholly of Cavaliers, and it got along, on the whole, so well with the king that he did not dissolve it for eighteen years. It did not take up the old question, which was still unsettled, as to whether Parliament or the king was really supreme. It showed its hostility, however, to the Puritans by a series of intolerant acts, which are very important in English history. It ordered that no one should hold a municipal office who had not received the Eucharist according to the rites of the Church of England. This was aimed at both the Presbyterians and the Independents. By the Act of Uniformity (1662), every clergyman who refused to accept everything contained in the Book of Common Prayer was to be excluded from holding his benefice. Two thousand clergymen thereupon resigned their positions for conscience' sake. These laws tended to throw all those Protestants who refused to conform to the Church of England into a single class, still known as Dissenters. It included the Independents, the Presbyterians, and the newer bodies of the Baptists, and the Society of Friends, commonly known as Quakers. These sects abandoned any idea of controlling the religion or politics of the country, and asked only that they might be permitted to worship in their own way outside of the English Church.

Toleration found an unexpected ally in the king, who, in spite of his dissolute habits, had interest enough in religion to have secret leanings toward Catholicism. He asked Parliament to permit him to moderate the rigor of the Act of Uniformity by making some exceptions. He even issued a declaration in the interest of toleration, with a view of bettering the position of the Catholics and nonconformists. Suspicion was, however, aroused lest this toleration might lead to the restoration of

Religious measures adopted by Parliament.

The Act of Uniformity.

The Dissenters.

Toleration favored by the king.

The Conventicle Act.

"popery," and Parliament passed the harsh Conventicle Act (1664). Any adult attending a conventicle — that is to say, any religious meeting not held in accordance with the practice of the English Church — was liable to penalties which culminated in transportation to some distant colony. Samuel Pepys, who saw some of the victims of this law upon their way to a terrible exile, notes in his famous diary : "They go like lambs without any resistance. I would to God that they would conform or be more wise and not be caught." A few years later Charles issued a declaration giving complete religious liberty to Roman Catholics as well as to Dissenters. Parliament not only forced him to withdraw this enlightened measure but passed the Test Act, which excluded every one from public office who did not accept the Anglican views.

The Test Act.

War with Holland.

The old war with Holland, begun by Cromwell, was renewed under Charles II, who was earnestly desirous to increase English commerce and to found new colonies. The two nations were very evenly matched on the sea, but in 1664 the English seized some of the West Indian Islands from the Dutch and also their colony on Manhattan Island, which was renamed New York in honor of the king's brother. In 1667 a treaty was signed by England and Holland which confirmed these conquests. Three years later Charles was induced by Louis XIV to conclude a secret treaty, by which he engaged to aid Louis in a fresh war upon Holland. Louis cherished a grudge against Holland for preventing him from seizing the Spanish Netherlands, to which he asserted a claim on behalf of his Spanish wife.[1] In return for Charles' promised aid, Louis was to support him with money and troops whenever Charles thought fit publicly to declare himself a Catholic — he had already acknowledged his conversion to a select circle. But Charles' nephew, William of Orange, — the great-grandson of William the Silent, — who was later to become king

1 See below, p. 502.

'of England, encouraged the Dutch to withstand, and Louis was forced to relinquish his purpose of conquering this stubborn people. Peace was concluded in 1674, and England and Holland soon became allies against Louis, who was now recognized as the greatest danger which Europe had to face.

190. Upon Charles' death he was succeeded by his brother James, who was an avowed Catholic and had married, as his second wife, a Catholic, Mary of Modena. He was ready to reëstablish Catholicism in England regardless of what it might cost him. Mary, James' daughter by his first wife, had married William, Prince of Orange, the head of the United Netherlands. The nation might have tolerated James so long as they could look forward to the accession of his Protestant daughter. But when a son was born to his Catholic second wife, and James showed unmistakably his purpose of favoring the Catholics, messengers were dispatched by a group of Protestants to William of Orange, asking him to come and rule over them.

James II,
1685-1688.

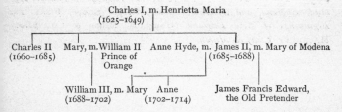

Charles I, m. Henrietta Maria
(1625–1649)

Charles II   Mary, m. William II   Anne Hyde, m. James II, m. Mary of Modena
(1660–1685)   Prince of   (1685–1688)
                Orange

William III, m. Mary   Anne   James Francis Edward,
(1688–1702)   (1702–1714)   the Old Pretender

William landed in November, 1688, and marched upon London, where he received general support from all the English Protestants, regardless of party. James started to oppose William, but his army refused to fight, and his courtiers deserted him. William was glad to forward James' flight to France, as he would hardly have known what to do with him had James insisted on remaining in the country. A new Parliament declared the throne vacant, on the ground that King

The revolu-
tion of 1688
and the
accession of
William III,
1688-1702.

James II, "by the advice of the Jesuits and other wicked persons, having violated the fundamental laws and withdrawn himself out of the kingdom, had abdicated the government."

The Declaration of Right.

A Declaration of Rights was then drawn up, condemning James' violation of the constitution and appointing William and Mary joint sovereigns. The Declaration of Rights, which is an important monument in English constitutional history, once more stated the fundamental rights of the English nation and the limitations which the Petition of Right and Magna Charta had placed upon the king. By this peaceful revolution of 1688 the English rid themselves of the Stuarts and their claims to rule by divine right, and once more declared themselves against the domination of the Church of Rome.

General Reading. — GARDINER, *The First Two Stuarts and the Puritan Revolution* (Charles Scribner's Sons, $1.00). GARDINER, *Constitutional Documents of the Puritan Revolution* (Clarendon Press, $2.25). For Cromwell, CARLYLE, "The Hero as King" in *Heroes and Hero Worship*. MORLEY, *Oliver Cromwell* (The Century Company, $3.50). For the Puritans, CAMPBELL, *The Puritans in Europe, Holland, England, and America* (2 vols., Harper, $5.00). FISKE, *The Beginnings of New England* (Houghton, Mifflin & Co., $2.00). MACAULAY, *Essay on Milton.*

CHAPTER XXXI

THE ASCENDENCY OF FRANCE UNDER LOUIS XIV

191. Under the despotic rule of Louis XIV (1643–1715) France enjoyed a commanding influence in European affairs. After the wars of religion were over, the royal authority had been reëstablished by the wise conduct of Henry IV. Richelieu had solidified the monarchy by depriving the Huguenots of the exceptional privileges granted to them for their protection by Henry IV; he had also destroyed the fortified castles of the nobles, whose power had greatly increased during the turmoil of the Huguenot wars. His successor, Cardinal Mazarin, who conducted the government during Louis XIV's boyhood, was able to put down a last rising of the discontented nobility.[1]

France at the accession of Louis XIV, 1643–1715.

When Mazarin died in 1661, he left to the young monarch a kingdom such as no previous French king had enjoyed. The nobles, who for centuries had disputed the power with Hugh Capet and his successors, were no longer feudal lords but only courtiers. The Huguenots, whose claim to a place in the state beside the Catholics had led to the terrible civil wars of the sixteenth century, were reduced in numbers and no longer held fortified towns from which they could defy the king's agents. Richelieu and Mazarin had successfully taken a hand in the Thirty Years' War, and France had come out of it with enlarged territory and increased importance in European affairs.

What Richelieu and Mazarin had done for the French monarchy.

Louis XIV carried the work of these great ministers still farther. He gave that form to the French monarchy which

The government of Louis XIV.

[1] Reference, Wakeman, *Europe from 1598–1715*, Chapter VII.

it retained until the French Revolution. He made himself the very mirror of kingship. His marvelous court at Versailles became the model and the despair of other less opulent and powerful princes, who accepted his theory of the absolute power of kings but could not afford to imitate his luxury. By his incessant wars of aggression he kept Europe in turmoil for over half a century. The distinguished generals who led his newly organized troops, and the wily diplomats who arranged his alliances and negotiated his treaties, made France feared and respected by even the most powerful of the other European states.

The theory of the 'divine right' of kings in France.

192. Louis XIV had the same idea of kingship that James I had tried in vain to induce the English people to accept. God had given kings to men, and it was His will that monarchs should be regarded as His lieutenants and that all those subject to them should obey them absolutely, without asking any questions or making any criticisms; for in yielding to their prince they were really yielding to God Himself. If the king were good and wise, his subjects should thank the Lord; if he proved foolish, cruel, or perverse, they must accept their evil ruler as a punishment which God had sent them for their sins. But in no case might they limit his power or rise against him.[1]

Different attitude of the English and French nations toward absolute monarchy.

Louis had two great advantages over James. In the first place the English nation has always shown itself far more reluctant than France to place absolute power in the hands of its rulers. By its Parliament, its courts, and its various declarations of the nation's rights, it had built up traditions which made it impossible for the Stuarts to establish their claim to be absolute rulers. In France, on the other hand, there was no Great Charter or Bill of Rights; the Estates General did not hold the purse strings,

---

[1] Louis does not appear to have himself used the famous expression, "*I* am the *state*," usually attributed to him, but it exactly corresponds to his idea of the relation of the king and the state.

and the king was permitted to raise money without asking their permission or previously redressing the grievances which they chose to point out. They were therefore only summoned at irregular intervals. When Louis XIV took charge of the government, forty-seven years had passed without a meeting of the Estates General, and a century and a quarter was still to elapse before another call to the representatives of the nation was issued in 1789. Moreover, the French people placed far more reliance upon a powerful king than the English, perhaps because they were not protected by the sea from their neighbors, as England was. On every side France had enemies ready to take advantage of any weakness or hesitation which might arise from dissension between a parliament

Louis XIV

and the king. So the French felt it best, on the whole, to leave all in the king's hands, even if they suffered at times from his tyranny.

Louis had another great advantage over James. He was a handsome man, of elegant and courtly mien and the most exquisite perfection of manner; even when playing billiards he retained an air of world mastery. The first of the Stuarts, on the contrary, was a very awkward man, whose slouching gait, intolerable manners, and pedantic conversation were

Personal characteristics of Louis XIV.

utterly at variance with his lofty pretensions. Louis added
to his graceful exterior a sound judgment and quick apprehension. He said neither too much nor too little. He was,
for a king, a hard worker and spent several hours a day
attending to the business of government. It requires, in fact, a
great deal of energy and application to be a real despot. In
order really to understand and to solve the problems which
constantly face the ruler of a great state, a monarch must, like
Frederick the Great or Napoleon, rise early and toil late.
Louis was greatly aided by the able ministers who sat in his
council, but he always retained for himself the place of first
minister. He would never have consented to be dominated
by an adviser, as his father had been by Richelieu. "The
profession of the king," he declared, "is great, noble, and
delightful if one but feels equal to performing the duties which
it involves,"— and he never harbored a doubt that he himself was born for the business.

The king's palace at Versailles. **193.** Louis XIV was careful that his surroundings should
suit the grandeur of his office. His court was magnificent
beyond anything that had been dreamed of in the West. He
had an enormous palace constructed at Versailles, just outside
of Paris, with interminable halls and apartments and a vast
garden stretching away behind it. About this a town was laid
out, where those who were privileged to be near his majesty or
supply the wants of the royal court lived. This palace and
its outlying buildings, including two or three less gorgeous
residences for the king when he occasionally tired of the
ceremony of Versailles, probably cost the nation about a
hundred million dollars, in spite of the fact that thousands
of peasants and soldiers were forced to turn to and work without remuneration. The furnishings and decorations were as
rich and costly as the palace was splendid. For over a
century Versailles continued to be the home of the French
kings and the seat of their government.

This splendor and luxury helped to attract the nobility, who no longer lived on their estates in well-fortified castles, planning how they might escape the royal control. They now dwelt in the effulgence of the king's countenance. They saw him to bed at night and in stately procession they greeted him in the morning. It was deemed a high honor to hand him his shirt as he was being dressed, or, at dinner, to provide him

Life at Louis XIV's court.

The King's Bedroom in the Palace of Versailles

with a fresh napkin. Only by living close to the king could the courtiers hope to gain favors, pensions, and lucrative offices for themselves and their friends, and perhaps occasionally to exercise some little influence upon the policy of the government. For they were now entirely dependent upon the good will of their monarch.[1]

The reforms which Louis carried out in the earlier part of his reign were largely the work of the great financier,

The reforms of Colbert.

[1] Reference, Perkins, *France under the Regency*, pp. 129-141.

Colbert, to whom France still looks back with gratitude. He early discovered that Louis' officials were stealing and wasting vast sums. The offenders were arrested and forced to disgorge, and a new system of bookkeeping was introduced similar to that employed by business men. He then turned his attention to increasing the manufactures of France by establishing new industries and seeing that the older ones kept to a high standard, which would make French goods sell readily in foreign markets. He argued justly that if foreigners could be induced to buy French goods, these sales would bring gold and silver into the country and so enrich it. He made rigid rules as to the width and quality of cloths which the manufacturers might produce and the dyes which they might use. He even reorganized the old mediæval guilds ; for through them the government could keep its eye on all the manufacturing that was done, and this would have been far more difficult if every one had been free to carry on any trade which he might choose. There were serious drawbacks to this kind of government regulation, but France accepted it, nevertheless, for many years.[1]

Art and literature in the reign of Louis XIV.

It was, however, as a patron of art and literature that Louis XIV gained much of his celebrity. Molière, who was at once a playwright and an actor, delighted the court with comedies in which he delicately satirized the foibles of his time. Corneille, who had gained renown by the great tragedy of *The Cid* in Richelieu's time, found a worthy successor in Racine, the most distinguished perhaps of French tragic poets. The charming letters of Madame de Sévigné are models of prose style and serve at the same time to give us a glimpse into the more refined life of the court. In the famous memoirs of Saint-Simon, the weaknesses of the king, as well as the numberless intrigues of the courtiers, are freely exposed with inimitable skill and wit.

[1] Reference, Perkins, *France under the Regency*, Chapter IV.

Men of letters were generously aided by the king with pensions. Colbert encouraged the French Academy, which had been created by Richelieu. This body gave special attention to making the French tongue more eloquent and expressive by determining what words should be used. It is now the greatest honor that a Frenchman can obtain to be made one of the forty members of this association. A magazine which still exists, the *Journal des Savants*, was founded for the promotion of science. Colbert had an astronomical observatory built at Paris; and the Royal Library, which only possessed about sixteen thousand volumes, began to grow into that great collection of two and a half million volumes — by far the largest in existence — which to-day attracts scholars to Paris from all parts of the world. In short, Louis and his ministers believed one of the chief objects of any government to be the promotion of art, literature, and science, and the example they set has been followed by almost every modern state.[1]

The government fosters the development of the French language and literature.

194. Unfortunately for France, the king's ambitions were by no means altogether peaceful. Indeed, he regarded his wars as his chief glory. He employed a carefully reorganized army and the skill of his generals in a series of inexcusable attacks on his neighbors, in which he finally squandered all that Colbert's economies had accumulated and led France to the edge of financial ruin.

Louis XIV's warlike enterprises.

Louis XIV's predecessors had had, on the whole, little time to think of conquest. They had first to consolidate their realms and gain the mastery of their feudal dependents, who shared the power with them; then the claims of the English Edwards and Henrys had to be met, and the French provinces freed from their clutches; lastly, the great religious dispute was only settled after many years of disintegrating civil war. But Louis was now at liberty to look about him

He aims to restore the 'natural boundaries' of France.

[1] Reference, Perkins, *France under the Regency*, pp. 141-147.

and consider how he might best realize the dream of his ancestors and perhaps reëstablish the ancient boundaries which Cæsar reported that the Gauls had occupied. The "natural limits" of France appeared to be the Rhine on the north and east, the Jura Mountains and the Alps on the southeast, and to the south the Mediterranean and the Pyrenees. Richelieu had believed that it was the chief end of his ministry to restore to France the boundaries determined for it by nature. Mazarin had labored hard to win Savoy and Nice, and to reach the Rhine on the north. Before his death France at least gained Alsace and reached the Pyrenees, "which," as the treaty with Spain says (1659), "formerly divided the Gauls from Spain."

Louis lays claim to the Spanish Netherlands. Louis first turned his attention to the conquest of the Spanish Netherlands, to which he laid claim through his wife, the elder sister of the Spanish king, Charles II (1665–1700). In 1667 he surprised Europe by publishing a little treatise in which he set forth his claims not only to the Spanish Netherlands, but even to the whole Spanish monarchy. By confounding the kingdom of France with the old empire of the Franks he could maintain that the people of the Netherlands were his subjects.

The invasion of the Netherlands, 1667. Louis placed himself at the head of the army which he had reformed and reorganized, and announced that he was to undertake a "journey," as if his invasion was only an expedition into another part of his undisputed realms. He easily took a number of towns on the border, and completely conquered Franche-Comté. This was an outlying province of Spain, isolated from her other lands, and a most tempting morsel for the hungry king of France. These conquests alarmed Europe, and especially Holland, which could not afford to have the barrier between it and France removed, for Louis would be an uncomfortable neighbor. A Triple Alliance, composed of Holland, England, and Sweden, was accordingly organized to induce France to make peace with Spain. Louis contented himself for the moment with the dozen border towns that he had taken and which Spain ceded to him on condition that he would return Franche-Comté (Peace of Aix-la-Chapelle, 1668).

The success with which Holland had held her own against the navy of England [1] and brought the proud king of France to a halt, produced an elation on the part of that tiny country which was very aggravating to Louis. He was thoroughly vexed that he should have been blocked by so trifling an obstacle as Dutch intervention. He consequently conceived a strong dislike for the United Provinces, which was increased by the protection that they afforded to political writers who annoyed him with their attacks. He broke up the Triple Alliance by inducing Charles II of England to conclude a treaty which arranged that England should help France in a new war against the Dutch.

Louis breaks up the Triple Alliance and allies himself with Charles II of England.

Louis then startled Europe again by seizing the duchy of Lorraine, which brought him to the border of Holland. At the head of a hundred thousand men he crossed the Rhine (1672) and easily conquered southern Holland. For the moment the Dutch cause appeared to be lost. But William of Orange showed the spirit of his great ancestor, William the Silent; the sluices in the dikes were opened and the country flooded, so the French army was checked before it could take Amsterdam and advance into the north. Holland found an ally in the elector of Brandenburg, and the war became general. The emperor sent an army against Louis, and England deserted him and made peace with Holland.

Louis' invasion of Holland, 1672.

When a general peace was concluded at Nimwegen, at the end of six years, the chief provisions were that Holland should be left intact, and that France should retain Franche-Comté, which had been conquered by Louis in person. This bit of the Burgundian heritage thus became at last a part of France, after France and Spain had quarreled over it for a century

Peace of Nimwegen, 1678.

[1] See above, pp. 488 and 492, 493.

Louis' en-
croachments
on German
territory.

and a half. For the ten years following there was no open
war, but Louis busied himself in the interval by instituting
courts in the debatable region between France and Germany,
to decide what neighboring districts belonged to the various
territories and towns which had been ceded to France by the
treaties of Westphalia and later ones. The vestiges of the old
feudal entanglements gave ample scope for claims, which were
reënforced by Louis' troops. Louis, moreover, seized the
important free city of Strasburg, and made many other less
conspicuous but equally unwarranted additions to his territory.
The emperor was unable to do more than protest against these
outrageous encroachments, for he was fully occupied with the
Turks, who had just laid siege to Vienna.[1]

Situation of
the Hugue-
nots at the
beginning of
Louis XIV's
reign.

195. Louis XIV exhibited as woeful a want of statesmanship in the treatment of his Protestant subjects as in the prose-
cution of disastrous wars. The Huguenots, deprived of their
former military and political power, had turned to manufacture,
trade, and banking; " as rich as a Huguenot " had become
a proverb in France. There were perhaps a million of them
among fifteen million Frenchmen, and they undoubtedly formed
by far the most thrifty and enterprising part of the nation.
The Catholic clergy, however, did not cease to urge the
complete suppression of heresy.

Louis' policy
of suppres-
sion.

Louis XIV had scarcely taken the reins of government into
his own hands before the perpetual nagging and injustice to
which the Protestants had been subjected at all times took a
more serious form. Upon one pretense or another their churches
were demolished. Children were authorized to renounce Protestantism when they reached the age of seven. If they were
induced by the offer of a toy or a sweetmeat to say, for example, the words "Ave Maria" (Hail, Mary), they might be taken
from their parents to be brought up in a Catholic school. In
this way Protestant families were pitilessly broken up. Rough

[1] See below, pp. 517–518.

and licentious dragoons were quartered upon the Huguenots with the hope that the insulting behavior of the soldiers might drive the heretics to accept the religion of the king.

At last Louis was led by his officials to believe that practically all the Huguenots had been converted by these drastic measures. In 1685, therefore, he revoked the Edict of Nantes, and the Protestants thereby became outlaws and their ministers subject to the death penalty. Even liberal-minded Catholics, like the kindly writer of fables, La Fontaine, and the charming letter writer, Madame de Sévigné, hailed the reëstablishment of "religious unity" with delight. They believed that only an insignificant and seditious remnant still clung to the beliefs of Calvin. But there could have been no more serious mistake. Thousands of the Huguenots succeeded in eluding the vigilance of the royal officials and fled, some to England, some to Prussia, some to America, carrying with them their skill and industry to strengthen France's rivals. This was the last great and terrible example of that fierce religious intolerance which had produced the Albigensian Crusade, the Spanish Inquisition, and the Massacre of St. Bartholomew.[1]

Revocation of the Edict of Nantes and its results.

Louis now set his heart upon conquering the Rhenish Palatinate, to which he easily discovered that he had a claim. The rumor of his intention and the indignation occasioned in Protestant countries by the revocation of the Edict of Nantes, resulted in an alliance against the French king headed by William of Orange. Louis speedily justified the suspicions of Europe by a frightful devastation of the Palatinate, burning whole towns and destroying many castles, including the exceptionally beautiful one of the elector at Heidelberg. Ten years later, however, Louis agreed to a peace which put things back as they were before the struggle began. He was preparing for the final and most ambitious undertaking of his life, which precipitated the longest and bloodiest war of all his warlike reign.

Louis' operations in the Rhenish Palatinate.

[1] Reference, Perkins, *France under the Regency*, Chapter VI.

The question
of the Span-
ish succes-
sion.

196. The king of Spain, Charles II, was childless and brotherless, and Europe had long been discussing what would become of his vast realms when his sickly existence should come to an end. Louis had married one of his sisters, and the emperor, Leopold I, another, and these two ambitious rulers had been considering for some time how they might divide the Spanish possessions between the Bourbons and the Hapsburgs. But when Charles II died, in 1700, it was discovered that he had left a will in which he made Louis' younger grandson, Philip, the heir to his twenty-two crowns, but on the condition that France and Spain should never be united.

Louis' grand-
son, Philip,
becomes
king of
Spain.

It was a weighty question whether Louis should permit his grandson to accept this hazardous honor. Should Philip become king of Spain, Louis and his family would control all of southwestern Europe from Holland to Sicily, as well as a great part of North and South America. This would mean the establishment of an empire more powerful than that of Charles V. It was clear that the disinherited emperor and the ever watchful William of Orange, now king of England, would never permit this unprecedented extension of French influence. They had already shown themselves ready to make great sacrifices in order to check far less serious aggressions on the part of the French king. Nevertheless, family pride and personal ambition led Louis criminally to risk the welfare of his country. He accepted the will and informed the Spanish ambassador at the French court that he might salute Philip V as his new king. The leading French newspaper of the time boldly proclaimed that the Pyrenees were no more.

The War of
the Spanish
Succession.

King William soon succeeded in forming a new Grand Alliance (1701) in which Louis' old enemies, England, Holland, and the emperor, were the most important members. William himself died just as hostilities were beginning, but the long War of the Spanish Succession was carried on vigorously by the great English general, the duke of Marlborough, and the

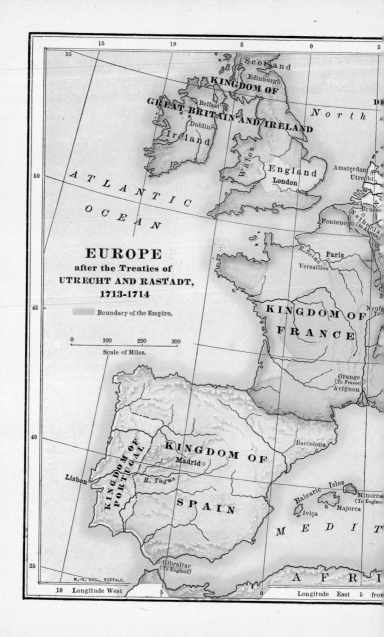

EUROPE
after the Treaties of
UTRECHT AND RASTADT,
1713-1714

Boundary of the Empire.

0   100   200   300
Scale of Miles.

ATLANTIC OCEAN

North

KINGDOM OF GREAT BRITAIN AND IRELAND

Scotland
Edinburgh
Belfast
Dublin
Ireland
England
London
Wales

D

Amsterdam
Utrecht

Brusse
Netherla
Fontenoy (to Austr

KINGDOM OF FRANCE

R. Seine
Paris
Versailles

Neuf
(To

Orange
(To France)
Avignon

KINGDOM OF SPAIN

KINGDOM OF PORTUGAL

Madrid

Lisbon
R. Tagus

Barcelona

Balearic Isles
Minorca
(To England)
Iviça
Majorca

M E D I T

Gibraltar
(To England)

A F R I

M. N. ENG., BUFFALO.

10   Longitude West   5   0   Longitude East   5   from

KINGDOM OF
SWEDEN
Copenhagen

RWAY

Stralsund
Swedish
Pomerania

Baltic Sea

Königsberg
Prussia

en
rden
Berlin

Hanover

P r u s s i a

R. Vistula

P O L A N D

Saxony

Silesia

55

50

Bohemia
Prague

EMPIRE

Electorate
of
Bavaria
Munich

Moravia

Arch. Duchy
of
Austria

Vienna

Buda Pesth
Kingdom of Hungary

Transylvania

Tyrol

45

Temesvar

R. Danube

V
e
n
i
c
e

Venice

1728
Dy. of
Parma
1708
Dy. of
Modena
Lucca
Florence

Gr. Dy.
of
Tuscany

Rome

States of the Church

O T T O M A N

D O M I N I O N S

Ragusa

Cattaro

N
a
p
l
e
s
(To Austria)

y

Naples

40

Palermo

Messina

Sicily
(To Savoy)
(later, 1720, to Austria)

R
A
N
E

Morea

A
N

S E A

Candia

35

15   20   25   30

10   15   20   25

Austrian commander, Eugene of Savoy. The conflict was even more general than the Thirty Years' War; even in America there was fighting between French and English colonists, which passes in American histories under the name of Queen Anne's War. All the more important battles went against the French, and after ten years of war, which was rapidly ruining the country by the destruction of its people and its wealth, Louis was willing to consider some compromise, and after long discussion a peace was arranged in 1713.

The Treaty of Utrecht changed the map of Europe as no previous treaty had done, not even that of Westphalia. Each of the chief combatants got its share of the Spanish booty over which they had been fighting. The Bourbon Philip V was permitted to retain Spain and its colonies on condition that the Spanish and French crowns should never rest on the same head. To Austria fell the Spanish Netherlands, hereafter called the Austrian Netherlands, which continued to form a barrier between Holland and France. Holland received certain fortresses to make its position still more secure. The Spanish possessions in Italy, i.e., Naples and Milan, were also given to Austria, and in this way Austria got the hold on Italy which it retained until 1866. England acquired from France, Nova Scotia, Newfoundland, and the Hudson Bay region, and so began the expulsion of the French from North America. Besides these American provinces she received the island of Minorca with its fortress, and the rock and fortress of Gibraltar, which still gives her command of the narrow entrance to the Mediterranean.

The period of Louis XIV is remarkable for the development of international law. The incessant wars, the great alliances embracing several powers, and the prolonged peace negotiations, such as those which preceded the treaties of Westphalia and Utrecht, made increasingly clear the need of well-defined rules governing independent states in their relations with one

The Treaty of Utrecht, 1713.

The development of international law.

another both in peace and in war. It was of the utmost importance to determine, for instance, the rights of ambassadors and of the vessels of neutral powers not engaged in the war, and what should be considered fair conduct in warfare and in the treatment of prisoners.

Grotius' *War and Peace.*

The first great systematic treatise on international law was published by Grotius in 1625, when the horrors of the Thirty Years' War were impressing men's minds with the necessity of finding some other means than war of settling disputes between nations. Grotius' *War and Peace* was followed, in Louis XIV's time, by Pufendorf's *On the Law of Nature and Nations* (1672). While the rules laid down by these and later writers on international law have by no means put an end to war, they have prevented many conflicts by settling certain questions and by increasing the ways in which nations may come to an understanding with one another through their ambassadors without recourse to arms.

Louis XIV outlived his son and grandson, and left a sadly demoralized kingdom to his five-year-old great-grandson, Louis XV (1715-1774). The national treasury was depleted, the people were reduced in numbers and were in a miserable state, and the army, once the finest in Europe, was in no condition to gain further victories. Later we must study the conditions in France which led to the great Revolution. Now, however, we turn to the rise of two new European powers, Prussia and Russia, which began in the eighteenth century to play a prominent rôle in European affairs.

CHAPTER XXXII

RISE OF RUSSIA AND PRUSSIA

197. We have had little occasion hitherto, in dealing with the history of western Europe, to speak of the Slavic peoples, to whom the Russians, Poles, Bohemians, and many other nations of eastern Europe belong. Together they form the most numerous race in Europe, but, as has been well said, "they occupy a greater place on the map than in history." In the eighteenth century, however, Russia began to take an increasingly important part in European affairs, and it is now a great force in the politics of the world. The realms of the Tsar which lie in Europe exceed in extent those of all the other rulers of the continent put together, and yet they are scarcely more than a quarter of his whole dominion, which embraces northern and central Asia, and forms together an empire occupying toward three times the area of the United States.

The Slavs were settled along the Dnieper, Don, and Vistula long before the Christian era. After the East Goths had penetrated into the Roman empire, the Slavs followed their example and invaded, ravaged, and conquered the Balkan Peninsula, which they held for some time. When the German Lombards went south into Italy, about 569, the Slavs pressed behind them into Styria, Carinthia, and Carniola, where they still live within the bounds of the Austrian empire. Other Slavic hordes had driven the Germans across the Oder and upper Elbe. Later the German emperors, beginning with Charlemagne, began to push them back, but the Bohemians and Moravians still hold an advanced position on the borders of Bavaria and Saxony.

Movements of the Slavs during the period of the German invasions.

Beginnings of Russia.

In the ninth century some of the Northmen invaded the districts to the east of the Baltic, while their relatives were causing grievous trouble in France and England. It is generally supposed that one of their leaders, Rurik, was the first to consolidate the Slavic tribes about Novgorod into a sort of state in 862. Rurik's successor extended the bounds of the new empire so as to include the important town of Kiev on the Dnieper. The word *Russia* is probably derived from *Rous*, the name given by the neighboring Finns to the Norman adventurers. Before the end of the tenth century the Greek form of Christianity was introduced and the Russian ruler was baptized. The frequent intercourse with Constantinople might have led to rapid advance in civilization had it not been for a great disaster which put Russia back for centuries.

The Tartar invasion in the thirteenth century.

Russia is geographically nothing more than an extension of the vast plain of northern Asia, which the Russians were destined finally to conquer. It was therefore exposed to the great invasion of the Tartars or Mongols, who swept in from the east in the thirteenth century. The powerful Tartar ruler, Genghiz Khan (1162–1227), conquered northern China and central Asia, and the mounted hordes of his successors crossed into Europe and overran Russia, which had fallen apart into numerous principalities. The Russian princes became the dependents of the Great Khan, and had frequently to seek his far distant court, some three thousand miles away, where he freely disposed of both their crowns and their heads. The Tartars exacted tribute of the Russians, but left them undisturbed in their laws and religion.

Influence of the Tartar occupation on manners and customs.

Of the Russian princes who went to prostrate themselves at the foot of the Great Khan's throne, none made a more favorable impression upon him than the prince of Moscow, in whose favor the Khan was wont to decide all cases of dispute between the prince and his rivals. When the Mongol power had begun to decline in strength and the princes of Moscow had grown stronger, they ventured to kill the Mongol ambassadors sent to demand tribute in 1480, and thus freed themselves from the Mongol yoke. But the Tartar occupation had left its mark, for the princes of Moscow imitated the Khans rather than the western rulers, of whom, in fact, they knew nothing. In 1547 Ivan the Terrible assumed the Asiatic title of Tsar,[1] which appeared to him more worthy than that of king or emperor. The costumes and etiquette of the court were also Asiatic. The Russian armor suggested that of the Chinese, and their headdress was a turban. It was the task of Peter the Great to Europeanize Russia.

Ivan the Terrible assumes the title of Tsar.

198. At the time of Peter's accession, Russia, which had grown greatly under Ivan the Terrible and other enterprising rulers, still had no outlet to the sea. In manners and customs the kingdom was Asiatic, and its government was that of a Tartar prince. Peter had no quarrel with the despotic power which fell to him and which the Russian monarchs still exercise, since there is no parliament or constitution in that country down to the present day. But he knew that Russia was very much behind the rest of Europe, and that his crudely equipped soldiers could never make head against the well armed and disciplined troops of the West. He had no seaport and no ships, without which Russia could never hope to take part in the world's affairs. His two great tasks were, therefore, to introduce western habits and to " make a window," as he expressed it, through which Russia might look abroad.

Peter the Great, 1672-1725.

In 1697–1698 Peter himself visited Germany, Holland, and England with a view to investigating every art and science of the West, as well as the most approved methods of manufacture, from the making of a man-of-war to the etching of an engraving. Nothing escaped the keen eyes of this rude, half-savage northern giant. For a week he put on the wide

Peter's travels in Europe.

[1] The title Tsar, or Czar, was formerly supposed to be connected with Cæsar (German, *Kaiser*), i.e., emperor, but this appears to have been a mistake.

breeches of a Dutch laborer and worked in the shipyard at Saardam near Amsterdam. In England, Holland, and Germany he engaged artisans, scientific men, architects, ship captains, and those versed in artillery and the training of troops, all of whom he took back with him to aid in the reform and development of Russia.

Suppression of revolt against foreign ideas.

He was called home by the revolt of the royal guard, who had allied themselves with the very large party of nobles and churchmen who were horrified at Peter's desertion of the habits and customs of his forefathers. They hated what they called "German ideas," such as short coats, tobacco smoking, and beardless faces. The clergy even suggested that Peter was perhaps Antichrist. Peter took a fearful revenge upon the rebels, and is said to have himself cut off the heads of many of them. Like the barbarian that he was at heart, he left their heads and bodies lying about all winter, unburied, in order to make the terrible results of revolt against his power quite plain to all.

Peter's reform measures.

Peter's reforms extended through his whole reign. He made his people give up their cherished oriental beards and long flowing garments. He forced the women of the better class, who had been kept in a sort of oriental harem, to come out and meet the men in social assemblies, such as were common in the West. He invited foreigners to settle in Russia, and insured them protection, privileges, and the free exercise of their religion. He sent young Russians abroad to study. He reorganized the government officials on the model of a western kingdom, and made over his army in the same way.

Founding of a new capital, St. Petersburg.

Finding that the old capital of Moscow clung persistently to its ancient habits, he prepared to found a new capital for his new Russia. He selected for this purpose a bit of territory on the Baltic which he had conquered from Sweden, — very marshy, it is true, but where he might hope to construct

Russia's first real port. Here he built St. Petersburg at enormous expense and colonized it with Russians and foreigners. Russia was at last becoming a European power.

In his ambition to get to the sea, Peter naturally collided with Sweden, to which the provinces between Russia and the Baltic belonged. Never had Sweden, or any other country,

The military prowess of Charles XII of Sweden.

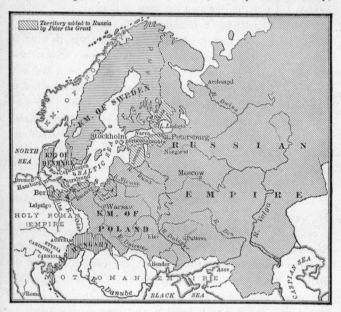

Northeastern Europe at the Opening of the Eighteenth Century

had a more warlike king than the one with whom Peter had to contend, the youthful prodigy, Charles XII. When Charles came to the throne in 1697 he was only fifteen years old, and it seemed to the natural enemies of Sweden an auspicious time to profit by the supposed weakness of the boy ruler. So a union was formed between Denmark, Poland, and Russia, with the object of increasing their territories at Sweden's expense.

But Charles turned out to be a second Alexander the Great in military prowess. He astonished Europe by promptly besieging Copenhagen and forcing the king of Denmark to sign a treaty of peace. He then turned like lightning against Peter, who was industriously besieging Narva, and with eight thousand Swedes wiped out an army of fifty thousand Russians (1700). Lastly he defeated the king of Poland.

Though Charles was a remarkable military leader, he was a foolish ruler. He undertook to wrest Poland from its king, to whom he attributed the formation of the league against him. He had a new king crowned at Warsaw, whom he at last succeeded in getting recognized. He then turned his attention to Peter, who had meanwhile been conquering the Baltic provinces. This time fortune turned against the Swedes. The long march to Moscow proved as fatal to them as to Napoleon a century later. Charles XII was totally defeated in the battle of Pultowa (1709). He fled to Turkey and spent some years there in vainly urging the Sultan to attack Peter. At last he returned to his own kingdom, which he had utterly neglected for years. He was killed in 1718 while besieging a town.

Defeat and death of Charles XII.

Russia acquires the Baltic provinces and attempts to get a footing on the Black Sea.

Soon after Charles' death a treaty was concluded between Sweden and Russia by which Russia gained Livonia, Esthonia, and the other Swedish provinces at the eastern end of the Baltic. Peter had made less successful attempts to get a footing on the Black Sea. He had first taken Azof, which he soon lost during the war with Sweden, and then several towns on the Caspian. It had become evident that if the Turks should be driven out of Europe, Russia would be a mighty rival of the western powers in the division of the spoils.[1]

For a generation after the death of Peter the Great, Russia fell into the hands of incompetent rulers. It only appears again as a European state when the great Catherine II came

[1] References, Schwill, *Modern Europe*, pp. 215–230; Wakeman, *European History from 1598–1715*, pp. 300–308.

to the throne in 1762.   From that time on, the western powers
had always to consider the vast Slavic empire in all their great
struggles.   They had also to consider a new kingdom in northern Germany, which was just growing into a great power as
Peter began his work.   This was Prussia, whose beginnings we
must now consider.

199.   The electorate of Brandenburg had figured on the map *Brandenburg*
of Germany for centuries, and there was no particular reason *and the*
Hohenzol-
to suppose that it was to become one day the dominant state *lerns.*
in Germany.   At the time of the Council of Constance the old
line of electors had died out, and the impecunious Emperor
Sigismund had sold it to a hitherto inconspicuous house, the
Hohenzollerns, which is known to us now through such names
as those of Frederick the Great, William I, the first German
emperor, and his grandson, the present emperor.   Beginning
with a strip of territory extending some ninety or a hundred
miles to the east and to the west of the little town of Berlin, the
successive representatives of the line have gradually extended
their boundaries until the present kingdom of Prussia embraces
nearly two thirds of Germany.   Of the earlier little annexa-
tions nothing need be said.   While it has always been the
pride of the Hohenzollern family that practically every one of
its reigning members has added something to what his ancestors handed down to him, no great extension took place until
just before the Thirty Years' War.   About that time the elector
of Brandenburg inherited Cleves, and thus got his first hold on
the Rhine district.

What was quite as important, he won, far to the east, the duchy *Prussia*
of Prussia, which was separated from Brandenburg by Polish *acquired by*
the elector of
territory.   Prussia was originally the name of a region on the *Brandenburg.*
Baltic inhabited by heathen Slavs.   These had been conquered
in the thirteenth century by one of the orders of crusading
knights, who, when the conquest of the Holy Land was abandoned, looked about for other occupation.   The region filled

up with German colonists, but it came under the sovereignty of the neighboring kingdom of Poland, whose king annexed the western half of the territory of the Teutonic Order, as the German knights were called.[1] In Luther's day the Grand Master of the Teutonic Knights, who happened to be a relative of the electors of Brandenburg, concluded to abolish the order and

The elector of Brandenburg assumes the title of King of Prussia, 1701.

become duke of Prussia. In good time his family died out, and the duchy fell to the electors of Brandenburg. When one of them was permitted by the emperor, in the year 1701, to assume the title of king, he chose to be called King of Prussia.[2]

The Great Elector, 1640-1688.

Brandenburg accepted the Protestant religion before Luther's death, but played a pitiful part in the Thirty Years' War. Its real greatness dates from the Great Elector (1640–1688). In the treaties of Westphalia he acquired a goodly strip on the Baltic, and he succeeded in creating an absolute monarchy on the model furnished by his contemporary, Louis XIV. He joined England and Holland in their alliances against Louis, and the army of Brandenburg began to be known and feared.

Frederick William I, 1713-1740.

While it was reserved for Frederick the Great to stir Europe to its depths and establish the right of the new kingdom of Prussia to be considered one of the great European powers, he owed to his father, Frederick William I, the resources which made his victories possible. Frederick William strengthened the government and collected an army nearly as large as that maintained by France or Austria. He had, moreover, by miserly thrift and entire indifference to the amenities and luxuries of life, treasured up a large sum of money. Consequently Frederick, upon his accession, had an admirable army ready for use and an ample supply of gold.[3]

---

[1] See above, p. 196.

[2] The title King of Prussia appeared preferable to the more natural King of Brandenburg, because Prussia lay wholly without the empire, and consequently its king was not in any sense subject to the emperor but was wholly independent. Since western Prussia still belonged to Poland in 1701 the new king satisfied himself at first with the title, King *in* Prussia.

[3] Reference, Schwill, *Modern Europe*, pp. 230–238.

200. Prussia's aspiration to become a great European power made it necessary for her to extend her territory. This inevitably brought her into rivalry with Austria. It will be remembered that Charles V, shortly after his accession, ceded to his brother, Ferdinand I, the German or Austrian possessions of the house of Hapsburg, while he himself retained the Spanish, Burgundian, and Italian dominions. Ferdinand, by a fortunate marriage with the heiress of the kingdoms of Bohemia and Hungary, greatly augmented his territory. Hungary was, however, almost completely occupied by the Turks at that time, and till the end of the seventeenth century the energies of the Austrian rulers were largely absorbed in a long struggle against the Mohammedans.

The Hapsburgs in Austria.

A Turkish tribe from western Asia had, at the opening of the fourteenth century, established themselves in western Asia Minor under their leader Othman (d. 1326). It was from him that they derived their name of Ottoman Turks, to distinguish them from the Seljuk Turks, with whom the crusaders had come into contact. The leaders of the Ottoman Turks showed great energy. They not only extended their Asiatic territory far toward the east, and later into Africa, but they gained a footing in Europe as early as 1353. They gradually conquered the Slavic peoples in Macedonia and occupied the territory about Constantinople, although it was a hundred years before they succeeded in capturing the ancient capital of the Eastern Empire.

Conquests of the Turks in Europe.

This advance of the Turks naturally aroused grave apprehensions in the states of western Europe lest they too might be deprived of their independence. The brunt of the defense against the common foe devolved upon Venice and the German Hapsburgs, who carried on an almost continuous war with the Turks for nearly two centuries. As late as 1683 the Mohammedans collected a large force and besieged Vienna, which might very well have fallen into their hands had it

The defense of Europe against the Turks.

not been for the timely assistance which the city received from the king of Poland. From this time on, the power of the Turks in Europe rapidly decreased, and the Hapsburgs were able to regain the whole territory of Hungary and Transylvania, their possession of which was formally recognized by the Sultan in 1699.

The question of the Austrian succession.

In 1740, a few months before the accession of Frederick II of Prussia, the emperor Charles VI, who was the last representative of the direct line of the Hapsburgs, died. Foreseeing the difficulties which would arise at his death in regard to the inheritance of his possessions, he had spent a great part of his life in trying to induce the European powers to promise that his daughter, Maria Theresa, should be recognized as his successor. England, Holland, and even Prussia were ready to bid Godspeed to the new archduchess of Austria and queen of Hungary and Bohemia, but France, Spain, and the neighboring Bavaria held back in the hope of gaining some portion of the scattered Austrian dominions for themselves. The duke of Bavaria insisted that he was the rightful heir and managed to have himself elected emperor under the title of Charles VII.

Accession of Frederick II of Prussia, called 'the Great,' 1740–1786.

201. In his early years Frederick II grieved and disgusted his boorish but energetic old father by his dislike for military life and his interest in books and music. He was a particular admirer of the French and preferred their language to his own. No sooner had he become king, however, than he suddenly developed marvelous energy and skill in warlike enterprises. He realized that Prussia must widen its boundaries, and he saw no better way of accomplishing this than by robbing the seemingly defenseless Maria Theresa of Silesia, a strip of territory lying to the southeast of Brandenburg. He accordingly marched his army into the coveted district, and occupied the important city of Breslau without declaring war or offering any excuse except a vague claim to a portion of the land.

Frederick's attack upon Silesia.

France, stimulated by Frederick's example, joined with Bavaria in the attack upon Maria Theresa. It seemed for a time as if her struggle to maintain the integrity of her realm would be vain ; but the loyalty of all the various peoples under her scepter was roused by her extraordinary courage and energy. The French were driven back, but Maria Theresa was forced to grant Silesia to Frederick in order to induce him to retire from the war. Finally, England and Holland joined in an alliance for maintaining the balance of power, for they had no desire to see France annex the Austrian Netherlands. On the death of the emperor Charles VII (1745), Maria Theresa's husband, Francis, duke of Lorraine, was chosen emperor. A few years later (1748) all the powers, tired of the war, laid down their arms and agreed to what is called in diplomacy the *status quo ante bellum*, which simply means that things were to be restored to the condition in which they had been before the opening of hostilities.

The War of the Austrian Succession.

Frederick was, however, permitted to keep Silesia, which increased his dominions by about one third of their former extent. He now turned his attention to making his subjects happier and more prosperous, by draining the swamps, promoting industry, and drawing up a new code of laws. He found time, also, to gratify his interest in men of letters, and invited Voltaire, the most distinguished writer of the eighteenth century, to make his home at Berlin. It will not seem strange to any one who knows anything of the character of these two men, that they quarreled after two or three years, and that Voltaire left the Prussian king with very bitter feelings.[1]

Frederick promotes the material development of Prussia.

Frederick and Voltaire.

202. Maria Theresa was by no means reconciled to the loss of Silesia, and she began to lay her plans for expelling the perfidious Frederick and regaining her lost territory. This led to one of the most important wars in modern history, in which not only almost every European power joined, but which

The Seven Years' War.

[1] Reference, Schwill, *Modern Europe*, pp. 238–247.

involved the whole world, from the Indian rajahs of Hindustan to the colonists of Virginia and New England. This Seven Years' War (1756–1763) will be considered in its broader aspects in the next chapter. We note here only the part played in it by the king of Prussia.

The alliance against Prussia. Maria Theresa's ambassador at Paris was so skillful in his negotiations with the French court that in 1756 he induced it, in spite of its two hundred years of hostility to the house of Hapsburg, to enter into an alliance with Austria against Prussia. Russia, Sweden, and Saxony also agreed to join in a concerted attack on Prussia. Their armies, coming as they did from every point of the compass, threatened the complete annihilation of Austria's rival. It seemed as if the new kingdom of Prussia might disappear altogether from the map of Europe.

Frederick's victorious defense. However, it was in this war that Frederick earned his title of "the Great" and showed himself the equal of the ablest generals the world has seen, from Alexander to Napoleon. Learning the object of the allies, he did not wait for them to declare war against him, but occupied Saxony at once and then moved on into Bohemia, where he nearly succeeded in taking the capital, Prague. Here he was forced to retire, but in 1757 he defeated the French and his German enemies in the most famous, perhaps, of his battles, at Rossbach. A month later he routed the Austrians at Leuthen, not far from Breslau. Thereupon the Swedes and Russians retired from the field and left Frederick for the moment master of the situation.

Frederick finally triumphs over Austria. England now engaged the French and left Frederick at liberty to deal with his other enemies. While he exhibited marvelous military skill, he was by no means able to gain all the battles in which he engaged. For a time, indeed, it looked as if he might after all be vanquished. But the accession of a new Tsar, who was an ardent admirer of Frederick, led Russia to conclude peace with Prussia, whereupon Maria Theresa reluctantly agreed to give up once more her struggle with her inveterate enemy.

Frederick was able during his reign greatly to strengthen his kingdom by adding to it the Polish regions which had hitherto divided his possessions in Brandenburg from those which lay across the Vistula. The kingdom of Poland, which in its declining years was to cause western Europe much trouble, was shut in between Russia, Austria, and Prussia. The Slavic population of this region had come under an able ruler about the year 1000, and the Polish kings had succeeded for a time in extending their power over a large portion of Russia, Moravia, and the Baltic regions. They had never been able, however, to establish a successful form of government. This was largely due to the fact that the kings were elected by the nobles, the crown not passing from father to son, as in the neighboring kingdoms. The elections were tumultuous affairs, and foreigners were frequently chosen. Moreover, each noble had the right to veto any law proposed in the diet, and consequently a single person might prevent the passage of even the most important measure. The anarchy which prevailed in Poland had become proverbial.

The kingdom of Poland and its defective constitution.

On the pretense that this disorderly country was a menace to their welfare, the neighboring powers, Russia, Austria, and Prussia, agreed to reduce the danger by each helping itself to a slice of the unfortunate kingdom. This amicable arrangement resulted in what is known as the first partition of Poland. It was succeeded by two others (1793 and 1795), by the last of which this ancient state was wiped from the map altogether.[1]

The first partition of Poland, 1772.

When Frederick died (1786) he left the state which had been intrusted to him by his father nearly doubled in size. He had rendered it illustrious by his military glory, and had

Achievements of Frederick the Great.

---

[1] Reference, Hassall, *The Balance of Power*, pp. 18, 19, 303-317. See map below, p. 584.

vastly increased its resources by improving the condition of the people in the older portions of his territory and by establishing German colonies in the desolate regions of West Prussia, which he strove in this way to bind closely to the rest of the kingdom.

General Reading. — TUTTLE, *History of Prussia* (4 vols., Houghton, Mifflin & Co., $8.25). CARLYLE, *Frederick the Great* (3 vols., Chapman, $2.25). LONGMAN, F. W., *Frederick the Great* (Charles Scribner's Sons, $1.00). RAMBAUD, *History of Russia* (2 vols., Coryell & Co., $2.00). For Peter the Great and his Age, WALISZEWSKI, *Life of Peter the Great* (D. Appleton & Co., $2.00). For the Seven Years' War and France, PERKINS, *France under Louis XV* (2 vols., Houghton, Mifflin & Co., $4.00).

CHAPTER XXXIII

THE EXPANSION OF ENGLAND

203. In the last chapter we reviewed the progress of affairs in eastern Europe and noted the appearance of two new and important powers, Prussia and Russia, which, together with Austria, were engaged during the eighteenth century in extending their bounds at the expense of their weak neighbors, Poland and Turkey.

In the west, England was rapidly becoming a dominant power. While she did not play a very important part in the wars on the continent, she was making herself mistress of the seas. At the close of the War of the Spanish Succession her navy was superior to that of any other European power, for both France and Holland had been greatly weakened by the long conflict. Fifty years after the Treaty of Utrecht, England had succeeded in driving the French from both North America and India and in laying the foundation of her vast colonial empire, which still gives her the commercial supremacy among the European countries.

In the eighteenth century England lays the foundation of her commercial greatness.

With the accession of William and Mary, England may be regarded as having practically settled the two great questions which had produced such serious dissensions during the previous fifty years. In the first place, the nation had clearly shown that it proposed to remain Protestant ; and the relations beween the Church of England and the dissenters were gradually being satisfactorily adjusted. In the second place, the powers of the king had been carefully defined, and from the

Questions settled by the accession of William and Mary.

opening of the eighteenth century to the present time no English monarch has ventured to veto an act of Parliament.[1]

Queen Anne, 1702-1714.

William III was succeeded in 1702 by his sister-in-law, Anne, a younger daughter of James II. Far more important than the war which her generals carried on against Spain was the final union of England and Scotland. As we have seen, the difficulties between the two countries had led to much

The union of England and Scotland, 1707.

bloodshed and suffering ever since Edward I's futile attempt to conquer Scotland.[2] The two countries had, it is true, been under the same ruler since the accession of James I, but each had maintained its own independent parliament and system of government. Finally, in 1707, both nations agreed to unite their governments into one. Forty-five members of the British House of Commons were to be chosen thereafter in Scotland, and sixteen Scotch lords were to be added to the British House of Lords. In this way the whole island of Great Britain was placed under a single government, and the occasions for strife were thereby greatly reduced.

Accession of George I (1714-1727), the first of the house of Hanover.

Since none of Anne's children survived her, she was succeeded, according to an arrangement made before her accession, by the nearest Protestant heir. This was the son of James I's granddaughter Sophia. She had married the elector of Hanover[3]; consequently the new king of England, George I, was also elector of Hanover and a member of the Holy Roman Empire.

The king ceases to attend the meetings of the cabinet, which comes to be regarded as the real governing body.

The new king was a German who could not speak English and was forced to communicate with his ministers in bad Latin. The king's leading ministers had come to form a little body by themselves, called the *cabinet*. As George could not understand the discussions he did not attend the meetings of his

---

[1] The last instance in which an English ruler vetoed a measure passed by Parliament was in 1707.   [2] See above, pp. 278-280.

[3] Originally there had been but seven electors (see above, p. 372), but the duke of Bavaria had been made an elector during the Thirty Years' War, and in 1692 the father of George I had been permitted to assume the title of Elector of Hanover.

ministers, and thereby set an example which has been followed by his successors. In this way the cabinet came to hold its meetings and transact its business independently of the king. Before long it became a recognized principle in England that it was the cabinet that really governed rather than the king; and that its members, whether the king liked them or not, might retain their offices so long as they continued to enjoy the confidence and support of Parliament.

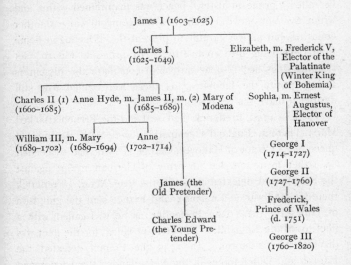

James I (1603–1625)

Charles I (1625–1649) — Elizabeth, m. Frederick V, Elector of the Palatinate (Winter King of Bohemia)

Charles II (1) Anne Hyde, m. James II, m. (2) Mary of Modena (1660–1685) (1685–1689)

Sophia, m. Ernest Augustus, Elector of Hanover

William III, m. Mary (1689–1702) (1689–1694) Anne (1702–1714)

George I (1714–1727)

George II (1727–1760)

James (the Old Pretender)

Frederick, Prince of Wales (d. 1751)

Charles Edward (the Young Pretender)

George III (1760–1820)

204. William of Orange had been a continental statesman before he became king of England, and his chief aim had always been to prevent France from becoming overpowerful. He had joined in the War of the Spanish Succession in order to maintain the "balance of power" between the various European countries.[1] During the eighteenth century England continued, for the same reason, to engage in the struggles between the

England and the 'balance of power.'

---

[1] Wolsey, it will be remembered, had advanced the same reason in Henry VIII's time for England's intervention in continental wars. See above, p. 428.

continental powers, although she had no expectation of attempting to extend her sway across the Channel. The wars which she waged in order to increase her own power and territory were carried on in distant parts of the world, and more often on sea than on land.

Peace under Walpole as prime minister, 1721-1742.

For a quarter of a century after the Treaty of Utrecht, England enjoyed peace.[1] Under the influence of Walpole, who for twenty-one years was the head of the cabinet and the first to be called " prime minister," peace was maintained within and without. Not only did Walpole avoid going to war with other countries, but he was careful to prevent the ill-feeling at home from developing into civil strife. His principle was to " let sleeping dogs lie "; so he strove to conciliate the dissenters and to pacify the Jacobites,[2] as those were called who still desired to have the Stuarts return.

England in the War of the Austrian Succession.

When, in 1740, Frederick the Great and the French attacked Maria Theresa, England's sympathies were with the injured queen. As elector of Hanover, George II (who had succeeded his father in 1727), led an army of German troops against the French and defeated them on the river Main. Frederick then declared war on England ; and France sent the grandson of James II,[3] the Young Pretender, as he was called, with a fleet to invade England. The attempt failed, for the fleet was dispersed by a storm. In 1745 the French defeated the English and Dutch forces in the Netherlands ; this encouraged the Young Pretender to make another attempt to gain the English crown. He landed in Scotland, where he found support among the Highland chiefs, and even Edinburgh welcomed

' Prince Charlie,' the Young Pretender, in Scotland.

---

[1] Except in 1718–1720, when she joined an alliance against Spain, and her admiral, Byng, destroyed the Spanish fleet.

[2] Derived from *Jacobus*, the Latin for James. The name was applied to the adherents of James II and of his son and grandson, the elder and younger pretenders to the throne.

[3] It will be remembered that the children of James II by his second and Catholic wife, Mary of Modena, were excluded from the throne at the accession of William and Mary. See genealogical table on preceding page.

"Prince Charlie." He was able to collect an army of six thousand men, with which he marched into England. He was quickly forced back into Scotland, however, and after a disastrous defeat on Culloden Moor (1746) and many romantic adventures, he was glad to reach France once more in safety.

205. Soon after the close of the War of the Austrian Succession in 1748, England entered upon a series of wars which were destined profoundly to affect not only her position, but also the fate of distant portions of the globe. In order to follow these changes intelligently we must briefly review the steps by which the various European states had extended their sway over regions separated from them by the ocean.

The voyages which had brought America and India within the ken of Europe during the fifteenth and early sixteenth centuries were, as we know, mainly undertaken by the Portuguese and Spaniards. Portugal was the first to realize the advantage of extending her commerce by establishing stations in India and on the Brazilian coast of South America; then Spain laid claim to Mexico, the West Indies, and a great part of South America. These two powers found their first rival in the Dutch; for when Philip II was able to add Portugal to the realms of the Spanish monarchs for a few decades (1580–1640), he immediately closed the port of Lisbon to the Dutch ships. Thereupon the United Provinces, whose merchants could no longer procure the spices which the Portuguese brought from the East, resolved to take possession of the source of supplies. They accordingly expelled the Portuguese from a number of their settlements in India and the Spice Islands and brought Java, Sumatra, and other tropical regions under Dutch control.[1]

Colonial policy of Portugal, Spain, and Holland in the sixteenth and seventeenth centuries.

In North America the chief rivals were England and France, both of which succeeded in establishing colonies in the early part of the seventeenth century. Englishmen successively

Settlements of the French and English in North America.

---

[1] The Dutch occupation of a portion of the coast of North America was brought to an end, as has been mentioned, by the English. See above, p. 492.

settled at Jamestown in Virginia (1607), then in New England, Maryland, Pennsylvania, and elsewhere. The colonies owed their growth to the influx of refugees, — Puritans, Catholics, and Quakers, — who exiled themselves in the hope of gaining the right freely to enjoy their particular forms of religion.[1]

Just as Jamestown was being founded by the English the French were making their first successful settlement in Nova Scotia and at Quebec. Although England made no attempt to oppose the French occupation of Canada, it progressed but slowly. In 1673 Marquette, a Jesuit missionary, and Joliet, a merchant, discovered the Mississippi River. La Salle sailed down the great stream and named the new country which he entered Louisiana, after his king. The city of New Orleans was founded near the mouth of the river in 1718, and the French established a chain of forts between it and Montreal.

England was able, however, by the Treaty of Utrecht, to establish herself in the northern regions, for France thereby ceded to her Newfoundland, Nova Scotia, and the borders of Hudson Bay. While the number of English in North America at the beginning of the Seven Years' War is supposed to have been over a million, the French scarcely exceeded a twentieth of that number. Yet careful observers at the time were by no means sure that France was not destined to dominate the new country, rather than England.

Extent of India.

The rivalry of England and France was not confined to the wildernesses of North America, occupied by half a million of savage red men. At the opening of the eighteenth century both countries had gained a foothold on the borders of the vast Indian empire, inhabited by two hundred millions of people and the seat of an ancient and highly developed civilization. One may gain some idea of the extent of India by

[1] For the settlement of the English and French in North America, see Morris, *The History of Colonization*, Vol. I, Chapter X, and Vol. II, Chapter XVII; also Parkman, *Montcalm and Wolfe*, Vol. I, pp. 20–35.

laying the map of Hindustan upon that of the United States. If the southernmost point, Cape Comorin, be placed over New Orleans, Calcutta will lie nearly over New York City and Bombay in the neighborhood of Des Moines, Iowa.

A generation after Vasco da Gama landed in Calicut,[1] a Mongolian conqueror, Baber,[2] had established his empire in India. The dynasty of Mongolian rulers which he founded had been able to keep the whole country under its control for toward two centuries; then their empire had fallen apart in much the same way as that of Charlemagne had done. Like the counts and dukes of the Carolingian period, the emperor's officials, the subahdars and nawabs (nabobs), and the rajahs — i.e., Hindu princes temporarily subjugated by the Mongols — had gradually got the power in their respective districts into their own hands. Although the emperor, or Great Mogul, as the English called him, continued to maintain himself in his capital of Delhi, he could no longer be said to rule the country at the opening of the eighteenth century when the French and English were seriously beginning to turn their attention to his coasts.

The Mongolian emperors of Hindustan.

In the time of Charles I (1639), a village had been purchased by the English East India Company on the southeastern coast of Hindustan, which grew into the important English station of Madras. About a generation later the district of Bengal was occupied and Calcutta founded. Bombay was already an English station. The Mongolian emperor of India at first scarcely deigned to notice the presence of a few foreigners on the fringe of his vast realms. But before the end of the seventeenth century hostilities began between the English

English and French settlements in India.

---

[1] See above, p. 348.

[2] Baber claimed to be descended from an earlier invader, the famous Timur (or Tamerlane), who died in 1405. The so-called Mongol (or Mogul) emperors were really Turkish rather than Mongolian in origin. A very interesting account of them and their enlightenment may be found in Holden, *The Mogul Emperors of Hindustan* (Charles Scribner's Sons, $2.00).

East India Company and the native rulers which made it plain
that the foreigners would be forced to defend themselves.

The English had not only to face the opposition of the
natives, but that of a European power as well. France also
had an East India Company; and Pondicherry, at the opening
of the eighteenth century, was its chief center with a population of sixty thousand, of which two hundred only were Europeans. It soon became apparent that there was little danger
from the Great Mogul; moreover, the Portuguese and Dutch
were out of the race. So the native princes and the French
and English were left to fight among themselves for the
supremacy.

England victorious in the struggle for suprem-acy in America.

206. Just before the general clash of European rulers
known as the Seven Years' War came in 1756, the French and
English had begun their struggle for control in both America
and India. In America the so-called French and Indian War
began in 1754 between the English and French colonists.
General Braddock was sent from England to capture Fort
Duquesne, which the French had established to keep their
rivals out of the Ohio valley. Braddock knew nothing of
border warfare, and he was killed and his troops routed. Fortunately for England, France, as the ally of Austria, was soon
engaged in a war with Prussia that prevented her from giving
proper attention to her American possessions. A famous
statesman, the elder Pitt, was now at the head of the English
ministry. He was able not only to succor the hard-pressed
king of Prussia with money and men, but also to support the
militia of the thirteen American colonies. The French forts
at Ticonderoga and Niagara were taken in 1759. Quebec
was won in Wolfe's heroic attack, and the following year all
Canada submitted to the English. England's supremacy on
the sea was demonstrated by three admirals, each of whom
destroyed a French fleet in the same year that Quebec was
lost to France.

In India conflicts between the French and the English had occurred during the War of the Austrian Succession. The governor of the French station of Pondicherry was Dupleix, a soldier of great energy, who proposed to drive out the English and firmly establish the power of France over Hindustan. His chances of success were greatly increased by the quarrels among the native rulers, some of whom belonged to the earlier Hindu inhabitants and some to the Mohammedan Mongolians who had conquered India in 1526. Dupleix had very few French soldiers, but he began the enlistment of the natives, a custom eagerly adopted by the English. These native soldiers, whom the English called Sepoys, were taught to fight in the manner of Europeans.[1]

Dupleix and Clive in India.

But the English colonists, in spite of the fact that they were mainly traders, discovered among the clerks in Madras a leader equal in military skill and energy to Dupleix himself. Robert Clive, who was but twenty-five years old at this time, organized a large force of Sepoys and gained a remarkable ascendency over them by his astonishing bravery. Dupleix paid no attention to the fact that peace had been declared in Europe at Aix-la-Chapelle, but continued to carry on his operations against the English. But Clive proved more than his equal and in two years had established English supremacy in the southeastern part of India.

Clive defeats Dupleix.

At the moment that the Seven Years' War was beginning, bad news reached Clive from the English settlement of Calcutta, about a thousand miles to the northeast of Madras. The subahdar of Bengal had seized the property of some English merchants and imprisoned one hundred and forty-five Englishmen in a little room, where most of them died of suffocation before morning. Clive hastened to Bengal, and with a little army of nine hundred Europeans and fifteen hundred Sepoys he gained a great victory at Plassey over the subahdar's

Clive renders English influence supreme in India.

The 'Black Hole' of Calcutta.

Battle of Plassey, 1757.

[1] Reference, Perkins, *France under Louis XV*, Vol. I, Chapter XI.

army of fifty thousand men. Clive then replaced the subahdar of Bengal by a man whom he believed to be friendly to the English. Before the Seven Years' War was over the English had won Pondicherry and deprived the French of all their former influence in the region of Madras.

England's gains in the Seven Years' War.

When the Seven Years' War was brought to an end in 1763 by the Treaty of Paris, it was clear that England had gained far more than any other power. She was to retain her two forts commanding the Mediterranean, Gibraltar, and Port Mahon on the island of Minorca; in America, France ceded to her the vast region of Canada and Nova Scotia, as well as several of the islands in the West Indies. The region beyond the Mississippi was ceded to Spain by France, who thus gave up all her claims to North America. In India, France, it is true, received back the towns which the English had taken from her, but she had permanently lost her influence over the native rulers, for Clive had made the English name greatly feared among them.

Beginning of trouble with the American colonies.

207. England, with the help of her colonists, had thus succeeded in driving the French from North America and in securing the continent, with the exception of Mexico, for the English race. She was not, however, long to enjoy her victory, for no sooner had the Peace of Paris been signed than she and her American colonies became involved in a dispute over taxation, which led to a new war and the creation of an independent English-speaking nation, the United States of America.

The Stamp Act and its repeal.

It seemed right to England that the colonies should help pay the expenses of the late war, which were very heavy, and also support a small standing army of English soldiers. Parliament therefore passed the Stamp Act in 1765, which required the colonists to pay for stamps to be used on legal documents. The Americans declared that Parliament had no right to tax them, since they were not represented in that body. The opposition to the stamp tax was so great that Parliament repealed the act, but with the explicit assertion that it nevertheless had the right to tax the colonies as well as to make laws for them.

The effort to make the Americans pay a very moderate import duty on tea produced further trouble in 1773. The young men of Boston seditiously boarded a tea ship in the harbor and threw the cargo into the water. Burke, perhaps the most able member of the House of Commons, urged the ministry to leave the Americans to tax themselves, but George III (1760–1820) and Parliament as a whole could not forgive the colonists their opposition. They believed that the trouble was largely confined to New England and could be easily overcome. In 1774 acts were passed prohibiting the landing and shipping of goods at Boston, and the colony of Massachusetts was deprived of its former right to choose its judges and the members of the upper house of its legislature. These appointments were now placed in the hands of the king.

Opposition to 'taxation without representation.'

Such measures, instead of bringing Massachusetts to terms, so roused the apprehension of the rest of the colonists that a congress was summoned, and met at Philadelphia. This decided that all trade with Great Britain should cease until the grievances of the colonies had been redressed. The following year the Americans attacked the British troops at Lexington and defeated them in the battle of Bunker Hill. The new Congress decided to prepare for war and raised an army which was put under the command of George Washington, a Virginia planter who had gained some distinction in the late French and Indian War. Up to this time the colonies had not intended to secede from the mother country, but the proposed compromises came to nothing, and in July, 1776, Congress declared that "these United States are, and of right ought to be, free and independent."

The Continental Congress.

Outbreak of war.

Declaration of Independence, July 4, 1776.

This occurrence naturally excited great interest in France. The outcome of the Seven Years' War had been most lamentable for that country, and any trouble which came to her old

The United States seeks and receives aid from France.

enemy England could not but be a source of congratulation to the French. The United States regarded France as her natural ally and immediately sent Benjamin Franklin to Versailles with the hope of obtaining the aid of the new French king, Louis XVI. The king's ministers were doubtful whether the colonies could long maintain their resistance against the overwhelming strength of the mother country. It was only after the Americans had defeated Burgoyne at Saratoga in 1777, that France concluded a treaty with the United States in which the independence of the new republic was recognized. This was tantamount to declaring war upon England. The enthusiasm for the Americans was so great in France that a number of the younger nobles, the most conspicuous of whom was Lafayette, crossed the Atlantic to fight in the American army.[1]

Close of the war, 1783.

In spite of the skill and heroic self-sacrifice of Washington, the Americans lost more battles than they gained. It is extremely doubtful if they would have succeeded in bringing the war to a favorable close, by forcing the English general, Cornwallis, to capitulate at Yorktown (1781), had it not been for the aid of the French fleet. Before the war was terminated by the Peace of Paris (1783), Spain had joined in the hostilities, and the Spanish and French fleets laid siege to Gibraltar. Their floating batteries were finally destroyed by the red-hot shot of the British, and the enemies of England gave up further

England acknowledges the independence of the United States.

attempts to dislodge her from this important station. The chief result of the war was the recognition by England of the United States, whose territory was to extend to the Mississippi River. To the west of the Mississippi, the vast territory of Louisiana still remained in the hands of Spain.

Results in Europe of wars between Treaty of Utrecht and Peace of Paris.

208. The results of the European wars during the sixty years which elapsed between the Treaty of Utrecht and the Peace of Paris may be summarized as follows. In the northeast two new powers, Russia and Prussia, had come into the

[1] Reference, Green, *Short History of the English People*, pp. 776–786.

European family of nations. Prussia had greatly extended her territory by gaining Silesia and West Poland. She and Austria were, in the nineteenth century, to engage in a struggle for supremacy in Germany, which was to result in substituting the present German empire under the headship of the Hohenzollerns for the Holy Roman Empire, of which the house of Hapsburg had so long been the nominal chief.

The power of the Sultan was declining so rapidly that Austria and Russia were already considering the seizure of his European possessions. This presented a new problem to the European powers, which came to be known in the nineteenth century as the "eastern question." Were Austria and Russia permitted to aggrandize themselves by adding the Turkish territory to their possessions, it would gravely disturb the balance of power which England had so much at heart. So it came about that, from this time on, Turkey was admitted in a way to the family of western European nations, for it soon appeared that some of the states of western Europe were willing to form alliances with the Sultan, and even aid him directly in defending himself against his neighbors. *Origin of the 'eastern question.'*

England had lost her American colonies, and by her perverse policy had led to the creation of a sister state speaking her own language and destined to occupy the central part of the North American continent from the Atlantic to the Pacific. She still retained Canada, however, and in the nineteenth century added a new continent in the southern hemisphere, Australia, to her vast colonial empire. In India she had no further rivals among European nations, and gradually extended her influence over the whole region south of the Himalayas. In 1877 Queen Victoria was proclaimed Empress of India as the successor of the Grand Mogul. *England's colonial possessions.*

As for France, she had played a rather pitiful rôle during the long reign of Louis XIV's great grandson, Louis XV (1715–1774). She had, however, been able to increase her *France under Louis XV, 1715–1774.*

territory by the addition of Lorraine (1766) and, in 1768, of the island of Corsica.   A year later a child was born in the Corsican town of Ajaccio, who one day, by his genius, was to make France the center for a time of an empire rivaling that of Charlemagne in extent.   When the nineteenth century opened France was no longer a monarchy, but a republic; and her armies were to occupy in turn every European capital, from Madrid to Moscow.   In order to understand the marvelous transformations produced by the French Revolution and the wars of Napoleon, we must consider somewhat carefully the conditions in France which led to a great reform of her institutions in 1789, and to the founding of a republic four years later.

General Reading. — For the French in America, PARKMAN, *The Pioneers of France in the New World* (Little, Brown & Co., $2.00), also *A Half Century of Conflict* (same publisher, 2 vols., $6.00).   For India, MALLESON, *Clive* (Oxford, University Press, 60 cents), and Macaulay's Essay on Clive.   For the growth of the British Empire, H. DE B. GIBBINS, *History of Commerce in Europe* (The Macmillan Company, 90 cents), and SEELEY, *The Expansion of England* (Little, Brown & Co., $1.75).

CHAPTER XXXIV

THE EVE OF THE FRENCH REVOLUTION

209. When we meet the words "French Revolution," they are pretty sure to call up before our mind's eye the guillotine and its hundreds of victims, the storming of the Bastile, the Paris mob shouting the Marseillaise hymn as they parade the streets with heads of unfortunate "aristocrats" on their pikes. Every one knows something of this terrible episode in French history. Indeed, it has made so deep an impression on posterity that we sometimes forget that the Reign of Terror was *not* the French Revolution. Mere disorder and bloodshed never helped mankind along; and the Revolution must assuredly have produced some great and lasting alteration in France and in Europe to deserve to be ranked — as it properly is — with the Renaissance and the Protestant Revolt, as one of the three most momentous changes of the last six hundred years. The Reign of Terror was, in fact, only a sequel to the *real* Revolution.

The French Revolution, in the truest sense of the term, was a great and permanent reform, which did away with many absurd and vexatious laws and customs, and with abuses of which the whole nation was heartily tired, from the king down to the humblest peasant. Whenever a Frenchman, in the eighteenth century, seriously considered the condition of his country, most of the institutions in the midst of which he lived appeared to him to be *abuses*, contrary to reason and humanity. These vicious institutions, — relics of bygone times and outlived conditions, — which the Revolution destroyed

The Ancien Régime.

forever, are known by the general name *Ancien Régime*, that is, "the old system." Whole volumes have been written about the causes of the French Revolution. The real cause is, however, easily stated; the old system was bad, and almost every one, both high and low, had come to realize that it was bad, and consequently the French did away with it and substituted a modern and more rational order for the long-standing disorder.

France not a well-organized state in the eighteenth century.

Of the evils which the Revolution abolished, none was more important than the confusion due to the fact that France was not in the eighteenth century a well-organized, homogeneous state whose citizens all enjoyed the same rights and privileges. A long line of kings had patched it together, adding bit by bit as they could. By conquest and bargain, by marrying heiresses, and through the extinction of the feudal dynasties, the original restricted domains of Hugh Capet about Paris and Orleans had been gradually increased by his descendants until, when Louis XVI came to the throne in 1774, he found himself ruler of practically the whole territory which makes up France to-day.

Some of the districts which the kings of France brought under their sway, like Languedoc, Provence, Brittany, and Navarre, were considerable states in themselves, each with its own laws, customs, and system of government. When these provinces had come, at different times, into the possession of the king of France, he had not changed their laws so as to make them correspond with those of his other domains. He was satisfied if his new provinces paid their due share of the taxes and treated his officials with respect. In some cases the provinces retained their local assemblies, and controlled, to a certain extent, their own affairs. The provinces into which France was divided before the Revolution were not, therefore, merely artificial divisions created for the purposes of administrative convenience, like the modern French departments,[1] but represented real historical differences.

[1] See below, p. 568.

While in a considerable portion of southern France the Roman law still prevailed, in the central parts and in the west and north there were no less than two hundred and eighty-five different local codes of law in force; so that one who *Various systems of law.*

The Provinces of France in the Eighteenth Century

moved from his own to a neighboring town might find a wholly unfamiliar legal system.

Neither was France commercially a single state. The chief customs duties were not collected upon goods as they entered French territory from a foreign country; for the customs lines lay within France itself, so that the central provinces about Paris were cut off from the outlying ones as from a foreign *Interior customs lines.*

land.[1] A merchant of Bordeaux sending goods to Paris would have to see that the duties were paid on them as they passed the customs line, and, conversely, a merchant of Paris would have to pay a like duty on commodities sent to places without the line.

Inequalities of taxation illustrated by the salt tax. The monstrous inequalities in levying one of the oldest and heaviest of the taxes, i.e., the salt tax, still better illustrates the strange disorder that existed in France in the eighteenth century. The government raised this tax by monopolizing the sale of salt and then charging a high price for it. There would have been nothing remarkable in this had the same price been charged everywhere, but as it was, the people in one town might be forced to pay thirty times as much as their neighbors in an adjacent district. The accompanying map shows how France was arbitrarily divided. To take a single example : at Dijon, a certain amount of salt cost seven francs ; a few miles to the east, on entering Franche-Comté, one had to pay, for the same amount, twenty-five francs ; to the north, in Burgundy, fifty-eight francs ; to the south, in the region of the little salt tax, twenty-eight francs ; while still farther off, in Gex, there was no tax whatever. The government had to go to great expense to guard the boundary lines between the various districts, for there was every inducement to smugglers to carry salt from those parts of the country where it was cheap into the land of the great salt tax.

The privi-leged classes. **210.** Besides these unfortunate local differences, there were class differences which caused great discontent. All Frenchmen did not enjoy the same rights as citizens. Two small but very important classes, the nobility and the clergy, were treated differently by the state from the rest of the people. They did not have to pay one of the heaviest of the taxes, the notorious *taille*, and on one ground or another they escaped other

[1] The interior customs lines roughly coincided with the boundaries of the region of the great salt tax. See accompanying map.

burdens which the rest of the citizens bore. For instance, they were not required to serve in the militia or help build the roads.

We have seen how great and powerful the mediæval Church The Church. was. In France, as in other Catholic countries of Europe, it

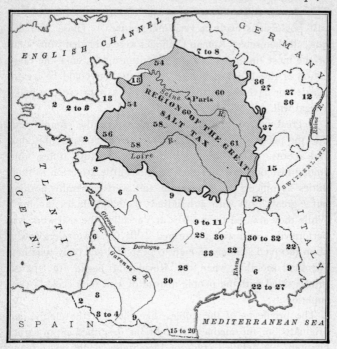

Map showing the Amount paid in the Eighteenth Century for Salt in Various Parts of France [1]

still retained in the eighteenth century a considerable part of the power that it had possessed in the thirteenth, and it still performed important public functions. It took charge of education and of the relief of the sick and the poor. It was very wealthy and is supposed to have owned one fifth of all the

[1] The figures indicate the various prices of a given amount of salt.

land in France. The clergy still claimed, as Boniface VIII
had done, that their property, being dedicated to God, was
not subject to taxation. They consented, however, to help
the king from time to time by a " free gift," as they called it.
The church still collected the tithes from the people, and its
vast possessions made it very independent. Those who did
not call themselves Roman Catholics were excluded from some
of the most important rights of citizenship. Since the revocation of the Edict of Nantes no Protestant could be legally
married or have the births of his children registered, or make
a legal will.

The clergy.   A great part of the enormous income of the church went
into the pockets of the higher clergy, the bishops, archbishops,
and abbots. These were appointed by the king,[1] often from
among his courtiers, and they paid but little attention to their
duties as officers of the church and were generally nothing
but " great lords with a hundred thousand francs income."
While they amused themselves at Versailles, the real work was
performed — and well performed — by the lower clergy, who
often received scarcely enough to keep soul and body together.
We shall see that, when the Revolution began, the parish
priests sided with the people instead of with their ecclesiastical
superiors.[2]

**The privi-
leges of the
nobility.**   The privileges of the nobles, like those of the clergy, had
originated in the mediæval conditions described in an earlier
chapter.[3] A detailed study of their rights would reveal many
survivals of the conditions which prevailed in the eleventh
and twelfth centuries, when the great majority of the people
were serfs living upon the manors. While serfdom had largely
disappeared in France long before the eighteenth century, and
the peasants were generally free men who owned or rented

---

[1] See above, p. 366.
[2] Reference, Lowell, *Eve of the French Revolution*, Chapter III.
[3] See above, Chapter XVIII.

their land, the lords still enjoyed the right to collect a variety of time-honored dues from the inhabitants living within the limits of the former manors.

The privileges and dues enjoyed by the nobles varied greatly in different parts of France. It was quite common for the noble landowner to have a right to a certain portion of the peasants' crops; occasionally he could collect a toll on sheep and cattle driven past his house. In some cases the lord maintained, as he had done in the Middle Ages, the only mill, wine press, or oven within a certain district, and could require every one to make use of these and pay him a share of the product. Even when a peasant owned his land, the neighboring lord usually had the right to exact one fifth of its value every time it was sold. The nobles, too, enjoyed the aristocratic privilege of the hunt. The game which they preserved for their amusement often did great damage to the crops of the peasants, who were forbidden to interfere with hares, deer, pigeons, etc.

All these privileges were vestiges of the powers which the nobles had enjoyed when they ruled their estates as feudal lords. Louis XIV had, as we know, induced them to leave their domains and gather round him at Versailles, where all who could afford it lived for at least part of the year. The higher offices in the army were reserved for the nobles, as well as the easiest and most lucrative places in the church and about the king's person.[1]

211. Everybody who did not belong to either the clergy or nobility was regarded as being of the *third estate*. The third estate was therefore nothing more than the nation at large, which was made up in 1789 of about twenty-five million souls.

The third estate.

---

[1] Only a very small portion of the nobility were descendants of the ancient and illustrious families of France. The king could grant nobility to whom he would; moreover, many of the government offices, especially those of the higher judges, carried the privileges of nobility with them.

The privileged classes can scarcely have counted altogether more than two hundred and seventy thousand individuals. A great part of the third estate lived in the country and tilled the soil. Most historians have been inclined to make out their condition as very bad indeed. They were certainly oppressed by an abominable system of taxation and were irritated by the dues which they had to pay to the lords. They also suffered frequently from local famines. Yet there is no doubt that the evils of their situation have been greatly exaggerated. When Thomas Jefferson traveled through France in 1787 he reports that the country people appeared to be comfortable and that they had plenty to eat. Arthur Young, a famous English traveler who has left us an admirable account of his journeys in France during the years 1787–1789, found much prosperity and contentment, although he gives, too, some forlorn pictures of destitution.

Favorable situation of the peasant in France compared with other countries. The latter have often been unduly emphasized by historical writers; for it has commonly been thought that the Revolution was to be explained by the misery and despair of the people who could tolerate the old system no longer. If, however, instead of comparing the situation of the French peasant under the old régime with that of an English or American farmer to-day, we contrast his position with that of his fellow-peasant in Prussia, Austria, or Italy, it will be clear that in France the agricultural classes were really much better off than elsewhere on the continent. In Prussia, for example, the peasants were still serfs: they had to work three whole days in each week for their lord; they could not marry or dispose of their land with-**Rapid increase of population in the eighteenth century.** out his permission. Moreover, the fact that the population of France had steadily increased from seventeen million after the close of the wars of Louis XIV to about twenty-five million at the opening of the Revolution, indicates that the general condition of the people was improving rather than growing worse.

The real reason why France was the first among the European countries to carry out a great reform and do away with the irritating survivals of feudalism was not that the nation was miserable and oppressed above all others, but that it was sufficiently free and enlightened to realize the evils and absurdities of the old régime. Mere oppression and misery does not account for a revolution, there must also be active *discontent;* and of that there was a great abundance in France, as we shall see. The French peasant no longer looked up to his lord as his ruler and protector, but viewed him as a sort of legalized robber who demanded a share of his precious harvest, whose officers awaited the farmer at the crossing of the river to claim a toll, who would not let him sell his produce when he wished, or permit him to protect his fields from the ravages of the pigeons which it pleased the lord to keep.[1]

Popular discontent, not the exceptionally miserable condition of the French people, accounts for the Revolution.

212. In the eighteenth century France was still the despotism that Louis XIV had made it.[2] Louis XVI once described it very well in the following words : " The sovereign authority resides exclusively in my person. To me solely belongs the power of making the laws, and without dependence or coöperation. The entire public order emanates from me, and I am its supreme protector. My people are one with me. The rights and interests of the nation are necessarily identical with mine and rest solely in my hands." In short, the king still ruled " by the grace of God," as Louis XIV had done. He needed to render account to no man for his governmental acts ; he was responsible to God alone. The following illustrations will make clear the dangerous extent of the king's power.

France still a despotism in the eighteenth century.

In the first place, it was he who levied each year the heaviest of the taxes, the hated *taille*, from which the privileged classes were exempted. This tax brought in about one sixth

The king's control of the government funds.

[1] Reference, Lowell, *Eve of the French Revolution*, Chapter XIII.
[2] See above, § 192.

of the whole revenue of the state. The amount collected was kept secret, and no report was made to the nation of what was done with it or with any other part of the king's income. Indeed, no distinction was made between the king's private funds and the state treasury, whereas in England the monarch was given a stated allowance. The king of France could issue as many drafts payable to bearer as he wished; the royal officials must pay all such orders and ask no questions. Louis XV is said to have spent no less than seventy million dollars in this fashion in a single year.

Lettres de cachet.

But the king not only controlled his subjects' purses ; he had a terrible authority over their persons as well. He could issue orders for the arrest and arbitrary imprisonment of any one he pleased. Without trial or formality of any sort, a person might be cast into a dungeon for an indefinite period, until the king happened to remember him again or was reminded of him by the poor man's friends. These notorious orders of arrest were called *lettres de cachet*, i.e., sealed letters. They were not difficult to obtain for any one who had influence with the king or his favorites, and they furnished a particularly easy and efficacious way of disposing of an enemy. These arbitrary orders lead one to appreciate the importance of the provision of Magna Carta which establishes that "no freeman shall be taken or imprisoned except by the lawful sentence of his peers and in accordance with the law of the land." Some of the most distinguished men of the time were shut up by the king's order, often on account of books or pamphlets written by them which displeased the king or those about him. The distinguished statesman, Mirabeau, was imprisoned several times through *lettres de cachet* obtained by his father as a means of checking his reckless dissipation.[1]

213. Yet, notwithstanding the seemingly unlimited powers of the French king, and in spite of the fact that France had no

[1] See Lowell, *Eve of the French Revolution*, pp. 116–118.

written constitution and no legislative body to which the nation sent representatives, the monarch was by no means absolutely free to do just as he pleased. He had not the time nor inclination to carry on personally the government of twenty-five million subjects, and he necessarily and willingly left much of the work to his ministers and the numerous public officials, who were bound to obey the laws and regulations established for their control and guidance.

Limitations placed upon the power of the French king.

Next to the king's council the most important governmental bodies were the higher courts of law, the *parlements*. These resembled the English Parliament in almost nothing but name. The French *parlements* — of which the most important one was at Paris and a dozen more were scattered about the provinces — did not, however, confine themselves strictly to the business of trying lawsuits. They claimed, and quite properly, that when the king decided to make a new law he must send it to them to be registered, else they would have no means of knowing just what the law was of which they were to be the guardians. Now, although they acknowledged that the right to make the laws belonged to the monarch, they nevertheless often sent a " protest " to the king instead of registering a law of which they disapproved. They would urge that the ministers had abused His Majesty's confidence. They would see, too, that their protest was printed and sold on the streets at a penny or two a copy, so that people should get the idea that the *parlement* was defending the nation against the oppressive measures of the king's ministers.

The *parlements* and their protests.

When the king received one of these protests two alternatives were open to him. He might recall the distasteful decree altogether or modify it so as to suit the court; or he could summon the *parlement* before him and in a solemn session (called a *lit de justice*) command it with his own mouth to register the law in its books. The *parlement* would then reluctantly obey, but as the Revolution approached it began to claim that a decree registered against its will was not valid.

The *parlements* help to prepare the way for the Revolution.

Struggles between the *parlements* and the ministers were very frequent in the eighteenth century. They prepared the way for the Revolution, first, by bringing important questions to the attention of the people ; for there were no newspapers and no parliamentary or congressional debates to enable the public to understand the policy of the government. Secondly, the *parlements* not only frankly criticised the proposed measures of the king and his ministers, but they familiarized the nation with the idea that the king was not really at liberty to alter what they called " the fundamental laws " of the state. By this they meant that there was an unwritten constitution, of which they were the guardians and which limited the king's power. In this way they promoted the growing discontent with a government which was carried on in secret, and which left the nation at the mercy of the men in whom the king might for the moment repose confidence.

Public opinion.

It is a great mistake to suppose that public opinion did not exercise a powerful check upon the king, even under the autocratic old régime. It was, as one of Louis XVI's ministers declared, " an invisible power which, without treasury, guards, or an army, ruled Paris and the court, — yes, the very palace of the king." The latter half of the eighteenth century was a period of outspoken and acrid criticism of the whole existing social and governmental system. Reformers, among whom many of the king's ministers were counted, loudly and eloquently discussed the numerous abuses and the vicious character of the government, which gradually came to seem just as bad to the people of that day as it would to us now.

Discussion of public questions.

Although there were no daily newspapers to discuss public questions, large numbers of pamphlets were written and circulated by individuals whenever there was an important crisis, and they answered much the same purpose as the editorials in a modern newspaper. These pamphlets and the books of the time sometimes treated the government, the clergy, or the

Catholic religion, with such open contempt, that the king, the clergy, or the courts felt it necessary to prevent their circulation. The *parlement* of Paris now and then ordered some offensive writing to be burned by the common hangman. Several distinguished writers were even imprisoned for expressing themselves too freely, and some booksellers and printers banished. But the attempted suppression of free discussion seemed an outrage to the more thoughtful among the public, and rather promoted than prevented the consideration of the weaknesses of the church and of the king's government.

214. By far the most conspicuous and important reformer of the eighteenth century was Voltaire (1694–1778), who was born twenty years before Louis XIV died, and yet lived to see Louis XVI mount the throne. "When the right sense of historical proportion is more fully developed in men's minds, the name of Voltaire will stand out like the names of the great decisive movements in the European advance, like the Revival of Learning or the Reformation. The existence, character, and career of this extraordinary person constituted in themselves a new and prodigious era" (Morley). To understand Voltaire and the secret of his fame would be to understand France before the Revolution. His mission was to exalt and popularize reason; and since a great part of the institutions of his day were not based upon reason, but upon mere tradition, and were utterly opposed to common sense, "the touch of reason was fatal to the whole structure, which instantly began to crumble."

Voltaire, 1694-1778.

Voltaire

Voltaire's
wide influ-
ence and
popularity.

Voltaire had little respect for the past which had bequeathed to France her disorderly government and, above all, her church. His keen eye was continually discovering some new absurdity in the existing order, which, with incomparable wit and literary skill, he would expose to his eager readers. He was interested in almost everything; he wrote histories, dramas, philosophic treatises, romances, epics, and innumerable letters to his innumerable admirers. He was a sort of intellectual arbiter of Europe, such as Petrarch and Erasmus had been. The vast range of his writings enabled him to bring his bold questionings to the attention of all sorts and conditions of men, — not only to the general reader, but even to the careless playgoer.

Voltaire's
attack upon
the church.

While Voltaire was successfully inculcating free criticism in general, he led in a relentless attack upon the most venerable, probably the most powerful, institution in France, the Roman Catholic church. The absolute power of the king did not greatly trouble him, but the church, with, as he deemed, its deep-seated opposition to a free exercise of reason and its hostility to reform, seemed to him fatally to block all human progress. He was wont to close his letters with the exhortation, "Crush the infamous thing." The church, as it fully realized, had never encountered a more deadly enemy. Not only was Voltaire supremely skillful in his varied methods of attack, but there were thousands of both the thoughtful and the thoughtless ready to applaud him; for many had reached the same conclusions, although they might not be able to express their thoughts so persuasively as he. Voltaire repudiated the beliefs of the Protestant churches as well as of the Roman church. He was, however, no atheist, as his enemies — and they have been many and bitter — have so often asserted. He believed in God, and at his country home near Geneva he dedicated a temple to Him. Like many of his contemporaries he was a deist, and held that God had revealed Himself in nature and in our hearts, not in Bible or church.

Were there space at command a great many good things and plenty of bad ones might be told of this extraordinary man. He was often superficial in his judgments, and sometimes jumped to unwarranted conclusions. He saw only the evil in the church, and seemed incapable of understanding all that it had done for mankind during the bygone ages. He maliciously attributed to evil motives teachings which were accepted by the best and loftiest of men. He bitterly ridiculed even the holiest and purest aspirations, along with the alleged deceptions of the Jesuits and the quarrels of the theologians. He could, however, fight bravely against wrong and oppression.[1] The abuses against which he fought were in large part abolished by the Revolution. It is extremely unfair to notice only his mistakes and exaggerations, as many writers, both Catholic and Protestant, have done, for he certainly did more than any one else to prepare the way for the great and permanent reform of the church, as a political and social institution, in 1789–1790.

Next to Voltaire the writer who did most to cultivate discontent was Jean Jacques Rousseau (1712–1778). His famous little treatise, *The Social Contract*, takes up the great question, By what right does one man rule over others? The book opens with the words : " Man is born free and yet is now everywhere in chains. One man believes himself the master of others and yet is after all more of a slave than they. How did this change come about? I do not know. What can render it legitimate? I believe that I can answer that question." It is, Rousseau declares, the will of the people that renders government legitimate. The real sovereign is the people. Although they may appoint a single person, a king, to manage the government for them, they should make the laws, since it is they who must obey them. We shall find that the first French constitution

Rousseau,
1712–1778.

---

[1] See the account of Voltaire's defense of Calas in Perkins, *Louis XV*, Vol. II, pp. 198 *sqq.*

accepts Rousseau's doctrine and defines law as " the expression of the general will," — not the will of a king reigning by the grace of God.

Montesquieu. Montesquieu, the most profound of the political writers of the eighteenth century, did his part in opening the eyes of thoughtful Frenchmen to the disadvantages of their government by his eulogy of the limited monarchy of England. He pointed out that the freedom which Englishmen enjoyed was due to the fact that the three powers of government — legislative, executive, and judicial — were not as in France in the same hands. Parliament made the laws, the king executed them, and the courts, independent of both, saw that they were observed. He believed that the English would lose their liberties so soon as these powers fell under the control of one person or body of persons. This principle of " the separation of powers " is now recognized in many modern governments, notably in that of the United States.

The new science of political economy. 215. About the middle of the eighteenth century the science of political economy was born. Scholars began to investigate far more thoroughly than ever before the sources and distribution of the wealth of the nation. The unjust system of taxation, which tended to exempt the richer classes from their just share of the public burdens; the wasteful and irritating methods of collecting the taxes; the interior customs lines, preventing the easy passage of goods from one part of France to another; the extravagance of the king's household; the pensions granted to undeserving persons; every evil of the bungling, iniquitous old régime was brought under the scrutiny of the new thinkers, who tested the existing system by the light of reason and the welfare of the great mass of the people.

Economists argue against government restrictions on trade and manufacture. The economists wrote treatises on taxation, scattered pamphlets about, and conducted a magazine or two. They not only brought the existing economic evils home to the intelligent reader, but suggested remedies for them.

The French government had been in the habit of regulating well-nigh everything. In order that the goods that were produced in France might find a ready sale abroad, the government fixed the quality and width of the cloth which might be manufactured and the character of the dyes which should be used.[1] The king's ministers kept a constant eye upon the dealers in grain and breadstuffs, forbidding the storing up of these products or their sale outside a market. In this way they had hoped to prevent speculators from accumulating grain in times of scarcity in order to sell it at a high rate.

It was now pointed out that these government restrictions produced some very bad results. They failed to prevent famine, and in the case of industry they discouraged new inventions and the adoption of better methods. The economists claimed that it would be far better to leave the manufacturer to carry on his business in his own way. They urged the king to adopt the motto, *laissez faire*, "Let things alone," if he would see his realms prosper.[2]

216. In 1774 the old king, Louis XV, died after a long and disgraceful reign. His unsuccessful wars had brought France to the verge of bankruptcy, and his ministers had been unable to meet the obligations of the government. The taxes were already so oppressive as to arouse great discontent, and yet the government was running behind seventy million dollars a year. His grandson and successor, Louis XVI (1774-1793), was a young man of excellent intentions. He was only twenty,

Accession of Louis XVI.

---

[1] See above, p. 500.

[2] Turgot, the leading economist of the time, argues that it would be quite sufficient if "the government should always protect the natural liberty of the buyer to buy, and of the seller to sell. For the buyer being always the master to buy or not to buy, it is certain that he will select among the sellers the man who will give him at the best bargain the goods that suit him best. It is not less certain that every seller, it being his chief interest to merit preference over his competitors, will sell in general the best goods and at the lowest price at which he can make a profit in order to attract customers. The merchant or manufacturer who cheats will be quickly discredited and lose his custom without the interference of government."

and his wife, the beautiful Marie Antoinette, daughter of Maria Theresa, was still younger. The new king almost immediately summoned Turgot, the ablest of the economists, and placed him in the most important of the government offices, that of controller general.

Turgot controller general, 1774-1776.

Turgot was an experienced government official as well as a scholar. For thirteen years he had been the king's representative in Limoges, one of the least prosperous portions of France. There he had had ample opportunity to see the vices of the prevailing system of taxation. He had made every effort to induce the government to better its methods, and had tried to familiarize the people with the principles of political economy. Consequently, when he was put in charge of the nation's finances, it seemed as if he and the conscientious young king might find some remedy for the long-standing abuses.

Turgot advocates economy.

The first and most natural measure was economy, for only in that way could the government be saved from bankruptcy, and the burden of taxation be lightened. Turgot felt that the vast amount spent in maintaining the luxury of the royal court at Versailles should be reduced. The establishments of the king, the queen, and the princes of the blood royal cost the state annually toward twelve million dollars. Then the French king had long been accustomed to grant "pensions" in a reckless manner to his courtiers, and this required nearly twelve million dollars more. Any attempt, however, to reduce this amount would arouse the immediate opposition of the courtiers, and it was the courtiers who really governed France. They had every opportunity to influence the king's mind against a man whose economies they disliked. They were constantly about the monarch from the moment when he awoke in the morning until he went to bed at night; therefore they had an obvious advantage over the controller general, who only saw him in business hours.[1]

[1] Reference, Lowell, *Eve of the French Revolution*, Chapter II.

Although the privileged class so stoutly opposed Turgot's reforms that he did not succeed in abolishing the abuses himself,[1] he did a great deal to forward their destruction not many years after his retirement. Immediately after coming into power he removed a great part of the restrictions on the grain trade. He prefaced the edict with a very frank denunciation of the government's traditional policy of preventing persons from buying and selling their grain when and where they wished. He showed that this did not obviate famines, as the government hoped that it might, and that it caused great loss and hardship. If the government would only let matters alone the grain would always go to those provinces where it was most needed, for there it would bring the best price. Turgot seized this and every similar opportunity to impress important economic truths upon the minds of the people.[2]

An Italian economist, when he heard of Turgot's appointment, wrote to a friend in France as follows: "So Turgot is controller general! He will not remain in office long enough to carry out his plans. He will punish some scoundrels; he will bluster about and lose his temper; he will be anxious to do good, but will run against obstacles and rogues at every turn. Public credit will fall; he will be detested; it will be said that he is not fitted for his task. Enthusiasm will cool; he will retire or be sent off, and we shall have a new proof of the mistake of filling a position like his in a monarchy like yours with an upright man and a philosopher."

Turgot's position.

The Italian could not have made a more accurate statement of the case had he waited until after the dismissal of Turgot, which took place in May, 1776, much to the satisfaction of the court. The king, although upright and well-intentioned,

Turgot dismissed, May, 1776.

---

[1] Turgot succeeded in inducing the king to abolish the guilds and the forced labor on the roads, but the decrees were revoked after Turgot's dismissal. For an admirable short account of Turgot's life, ideas, and reforms, see Say, *Turgot* (McClurg, 75 cents).

[2] See *Readings*, Chapter XXIV.

was not fond of the governmental duties to which Turgot was always calling his attention. It was much the easiest way to let things go along in the old way; for reforms not only required much extra work, but they also forced him to refuse the customary favors to those around him. The discontent of his young queen or of an intimate companion outweighed the woes of the distant peasant.

Necker succeeds Turgot.

217. Necker, who after a brief interval succeeded Turgot, contributed to the progress of the coming revolution in two ways. He borrowed vast sums of money in order to carry on the war which France, as the ally of the United States, had undertaken against England. This greatly embarrassed the treasury later and helped to produce the financial crisis which was the immediate cause of the Revolution. Secondly, he gave the nation its first opportunity of learning what was done with the public funds, by presenting to the king (February, 1781) a

Necker's financial report.

report on the financial condition of the kingdom; this was publicly printed and eagerly read. There the people could see for the first time how much the *taille* and the salt tax actually took from them, and how much the king spent on himself and his favorites.[1]

Calonne, controller general, 1783-1787.

Necker was soon followed by Calonne, who may be said to have precipitated the momentous reform which constitutes the French Revolution. He was very popular at first with king and courtiers, for he spent the public funds far more recklessly than his predecessors. But, naturally, he soon found himself in a position where he could obtain no more money. The *parlements* would consent to no more loans in a period of peace, and the taxes were as high as it was deemed possible to make them. At last Calonne, finding himself desperately put to it,

Calonne informs the king that France is on the verge of bankruptcy, August, 1786.

informed the astonished king that the state was on the verge of bankruptcy and that in order to save it a radical reformation of the whole public order was necessary. This report of

[1] Reference, Lowell, *Eve of the French Revolution*, pp. 238-242.

Calonne's may be taken as the beginning of the French Revolution, for it was the first of the series of events that led to the calling of a representative assembly which abolished the old régime and gave France a written constitution.

General Reading. — For general conditions in France before the Revolution, LOWELL, *Eve of the French Revolution* (Houghton, Mifflin & Co., $2.00). MACLEHOSE, *The Last Days of the French Monarchy* (The Macmillan Company, $2.25). DE TOCQUEVILLE, *State of Society in France before the Revolution of 1789* (John Murray, $3.00), a very remarkable work. TAINE, *The Ancient Régime* (Henry Holt & Co., $2.50) contains excellent chapters on the life at the king's court and upon the literature of the period. ARTHUR YOUNG, *Travels in France in 1787–1789* (The Macmillan Company, $1.00), very interesting and valuable. For Turgot's reforms, STEPHENS, *Life and Writings of Turgot* (Longmans, Green & Co., $4.50), containing translations from Turgot's writings. MONTESQUIEU, *The Spirit of Laws* (The Macmillan Company, 2 vols., $2.00). ROUSSEAU, *The Social Contract* (G. P. Putnam's Sons, $1.25, or Charles Scribner's Sons, $1.00). *Translations and Reprints*, Vol. VI, No. 1, gives short extracts from some of the most noted writers of the eighteenth century. In Vol. V, No. 2, of the same series, may be found a " Protest of the Cour des Aides," one of the higher courts of France, issued in 1775, which casts a great deal of light upon the evils of the old régime. John Morley has written a number of works upon France before the Revolution : *Voltaire, Rousseau,* 2 vols., *Diderot and the Encyclopædists,* 2 vols. (The Macmillan Company, $1.50 a volume).

CHAPTER XXXV

THE FRENCH REVOLUTION

Reforms proposed by Calonne.

218. It was necessary, in order to avoid ruin, Calonne claimed, "to reform everything vicious in the state." He proposed, therefore, to reduce the *taille*, reform the salt tax, do away with the interior customs lines, correct the abuses of the guilds, etc. But the chief reform, and by far the most difficult one, was to force the privileged classes to surrender their important exemptions from taxation. He hoped, however, that if certain concessions were made to them they might be brought to consent to a land tax to be paid by all alike. So he proposed to the king that he should summon an assembly of persons prominent in church and state, called *Notables*, to ratify certain changes which would increase the prosperity of the country and give the treasury money enough to meet the necessary expenses.

Summoning of the Notables, 1786.

The summoning of the Notables in 1786 was really a revolution in itself. It was a confession on the part of the king that he found himself in a predicament from which he could not escape without the aid of his people. The Notables whom he selected— bishops, archbishops, dukes, judges, high government officials— were practically all members of the privileged classes; but they still represented the nation, after a fashion, as distinguished from the king's immediate circle of courtiers. At any rate it proved an easy step from calling the Notables to summoning the ancient Estates General, and that, in its turn, speedily became a modern representative body.

In his opening address Calonne gave the Notables an idea of the sad financial condition of the country. The government was running behind some forty million dollars a year. He could not continue to borrow, and economy, however strict, would not suffice to cover the deficit. "What, then," he asked, "remains to fill this frightful void and enable us to raise the revenue to the desired level? *The Abuses!* Yes, gentlemen, the abuses offer a source of wealth which the state should appropriate, and which should serve to rëestablish order in the finances. . . . The abuses which must now be destroyed for the welfare of the people are the most important and the best guarded of all, the very ones which have the deepest roots and the most spreading branches. For example, those which weigh on the laboring classes, the pecuniary privileges, exceptions to the law which should be common to all, and many an unjust exemption which can only relieve certain taxpayers by embittering the condition of others; the general want of uniformity in the assessment of the taxes and the enormous difference which exists between the contributions of different provinces and of the subjects of the same sovereign; the severity and arbitrariness in the collection of the *taille;* the apprehensions, embarrassment, almost dishonor, associated with the trade in breadstuffs; the interior custom-houses and barriers which make the various parts of the kingdom like foreign countries to one another . . . ," — all these evils, which public-spirited citizens had long deprecated, Calonne proposed to do away with forthwith.

The Notables, however, had no confidence in Calonne, and refused to ratify his programme of reform. The king then dismissed him and soon sent them home, too (May, 1787). Louis XVI then attempted to carry through some of the more pressing financial reforms in the usual way by sending them to the *parlements* to be registered.

219. The *parlement* of Paris resolved, as usual, to make the king's ministry trouble and gain popularity for itself. This time

The *parle-
ment* of Paris
refuses to
register new
taxes and
calls for the
Estates
General.

it resorted to a truly extraordinary measure. It not only refused to register two new taxes which the king desired, but asserted that " *Only the nation assembled in the Estates General can give the consent necessary to the establishment of a permanent tax.*" "Only the nation," the *parlement* continued, "after it has learned the true state of the finances can destroy the great abuses and open up important resources." This declaration was followed in a few days by the humble request that the king assemble the Estates General of his kingdom.

The refusal of the *parlement* to register the new taxes led to one of the old struggles between it and the king's ministers. A compromise was arranged in the autumn of 1787; the *parlement* agreed to register a great loan, and the king pledged himself to assemble the Estates General within five years. In the early months of 1788 many pamphlets appeared, criticising the system of taxation and the unjust privileges and exemptions enjoyed by a few of the citizens to the detriment of the great mass of the nation.

The *parle-
ment* of Paris
protests
against the
' reform ' of
the judicial
system.

Suddenly the *parlement* of Paris learned that the king's ministers were planning to put an end to its troublesome habit of opposing their measures. The ministers proposed to remodel the whole judicial system and take from the courts the right to register new decrees and consequently the right to protest. This the *parlement* loudly proclaimed was in reality a blow at the nation itself. The ministers were attacking the court simply because it had acknowledged its lack of power to grant new taxes and had requested the king to assemble the representatives of the nation. The ministers, it claimed, were bent upon establishing an out-and-out despotism in which there should no longer be any check whatever on the arbitrary power of the king.

Some of the provinces became very apprehensive when they learned that the king proposed to take from the local *parlements* the right to examine edicts before registering them.

Might not the tyrannically inclined ministers proceed to make new laws for the whole realm and ignore the special privileges which the king had pledged himself to maintain when Brittany, Dauphiny, Bearn, and other important provinces were originally added to France? The cause of the *parlements* became in this way the cause of the people.

Meanwhile the ministers were becoming very hard pressed for funds to meet the regular expenses of the government. The *parlements* had not only refused to register taxes but had done everything that they could to embarrass the ministers and destroy the confidence of those who might otherwise have lent money to the government. There seemed no other resort except to call the representatives of the people together. The Estates General were accordingly summoned to meet on May 1, 1789.

The Estates General summoned.

220. It was now discovered that no one knew much about this body of which every one was talking, for it had not met since 1614. The king accordingly issued a general invitation to scholars to find out all they could about the customs observed in the former meetings of the Estates. The public naturally became very much interested in a matter which touched them so closely, and there were plenty of readers for the pamphlets which now began to appear in greater numbers than ever before. The old Estates General had been organized in a way appropriate enough to the feudal conditions under which they originated.[1] All three of the estates of the realm— clergy, nobility, and third estate—each sent an equal number of representatives, who were expected to consider not the interests of the nation but the special interests of the particular social class to which they respectively belonged. Accordingly, the deputies of the three estates did not sit together, or vote as a single body. The members of each group first came to an agreement among themselves and then a single vote was cast for the whole order.

General ignorance in regard to the Estates General.

The old system of voting by classes in the Estates General.

[1] See above, pp. 131–132.

Objections to this system.　　It was natural that this system should seem preposterous to the average Frenchman in 1788. If the estates should be convoked according to the ancient forms, the two privileged classes would be entitled to twice the number of representatives allotted to the other twenty-five million inhabitants of France. What was much worse, it seemed impossible that any important reforms could be adopted in an assembly where those who had every selfish reason for opposing the most necessary changes were given two votes out of three. Necker, whom the king had recalled in the hope that he might succeed in adjusting the finances, agreed that the third estate might have as many deputies as both the other orders put together, namely six hundred, but he would not consent to having the three orders sit and vote together like a modern representative body.

The *cahiers*.　　Besides the great question as to whether the deputies should vote by head or by order, the pamphlets discussed what reforms the Estates should undertake.[1] We have, however, a still more interesting and important expression of public opinion in France at this time, in the *cahiers*,[2] or lists of grievances and suggestions for reform which, in pursuance of an old custom, the king asked the nation to prepare. Each village and town throughout France had an opportunity to tell quite frankly exactly what it suffered from the existing system, and what reforms it wished that the Estates General might bring about. These *cahiers*[3] were the " last will and testament " of the old régime, and they constitute a unique historical document, of unparalleled completeness and authenticity. No one can read the *cahiers* without seeing that the whole nation was ready for the great transformation which within a year was to

---

[1] Reference, H. Morse Stephens, *The French Revolution*, Vol. I, pp. 13–15, 20–24.　　[2] Pronounced kä-yä′.

[3] Examples of the *cahiers* may be found in *Translations and Reprints*, Vol. IV, No. 5.

destroy a great part of the social and political system under which the French had lived for centuries.

Almost all the *cahiers* agreed that the prevailing disorder and the vast and ill-defined powers of the king and his ministers were perhaps the fundamental evils. One of the *cahiers* says : "Since arbitrary power has been the source of all the evils which afflict the state, our first desire is the establishment of a really national constitution, which shall define the rights of all and provide the laws to maintain them." No one dreamed at this time of displacing the king or of taking the government out of his hands. The people only wished to change an absolute monarchy into a limited, or constitutional, one. All that was necessary was that the things which the government might *not* do should be solemnly and irrevocably determined and put upon record, and that the Estates General should meet periodically to grant the taxes, give the king advice in national crises, and expostulate, if necessary, against any violations of the proposed charter of liberties.[1]

Desire of the nation for a constitutional, instead of an absolute, monarchy.

221. With these ideas in mind, the Estates assembled in Versailles and held their first session on May 5, 1789. The king had ordered the deputies to wear the same costumes that had been worn at the last meeting of the Estates in 1614 ; but no royal edict could call back the spirit of earlier centuries. In spite of the king's commands the representatives of the third estate refused to organize themselves in the old way as a separate order. They sent invitation after invitation to the deputies of the clergy and nobility, requesting them to join the people's representatives and deliberate in common on the great interests of the nation. Some of the more liberal of the nobles — Lafayette, for example — and a large minority of the clergy wished to meet with the deputies of the third estate. But they were outvoted, and the deputies of the third estate, losing patience, finally declared themselves, on June 17, a

The Estates General meet May 5, 1789.

[1] Reference, Lowell, *Eve of the French Revolution*, Chapter XXI.

The representatives of the third estate declare themselves a 'National Assembly.'

"National Assembly." They argued that, since they represented at least ninety-six per cent of the nation, the deputies of the privileged orders might be neglected altogether. This usurpation of power on the part of the third estate transformed the old feudal Estates, voting by orders, into the first modern national representative assembly on the continent of Europe.

The 'Tennis-Court' oath.

Under the influence of his courtiers the king tried to restore the old system by arranging a solemn joint session of the three orders, at which he presided in person. He presented a long programme of excellent reforms, and then bade the Estates sit apart, according to the old custom. But it was like bidding water to run up hill. Three days before, when the commons had found themselves excluded from their regular place of meeting on account of the preparations for the royal session, they had betaken themselves to a neighboring building called the "Tennis Court." Here, on June 20, they took the famous "Tennis-Court" oath, "to come together wherever circumstances may dictate, until the constitution of the kingdom shall be established." They were emboldened in their purpose to resist all schemes to frustrate a general reform by the support of over half of the deputies of the clergy, who joined them the day before the royal session.

The nobility and clergy forced to join the third estate.

Consequently, when the king finished his address and commanded the three orders to disperse immediately in order to resume their separate sessions, most of the bishops, some of the parish priests, and a great part of the nobility obeyed; the rest sat still, uncertain what they should do. When the master of ceremonies ordered them to comply with the king's commands, Mirabeau, the most distinguished statesman among the deputies, told him bluntly that they would not leave their places except at the point of the bayonet. The weak king almost immediately gave in and a few days later ordered all the deputies of the privileged orders who had not already done so to join the commons.

222. The National Assembly now began in earnest the great task of preparing a constitution and regenerating France. It was soon interrupted, however, by events at Paris. The king had been advised by those about him to gather together the Swiss and German troops who formed the royal guard, so that if he decided to send the insolent deputies home he would be able to put down any disorder which might result. He was also induced to dismiss Necker, who enjoyed a popularity that he had done little to merit. When the people of Paris saw the troops gathering and when they heard of the dismissal of Necker, there was general excitement and some disorder.

The fall of
the Bastile,
July 14, 1789

On July 14 crowds of people assembled, determined to procure arms to protect themselves and mayhap to perform some daring "deed of patriotism." One of the bands, led by the old Parisian guards, turned to the ancient fortress of the Bastile, on the parapets of which guns had been mounted which made the inhabitants of that

Mirabeau

part of the city very nervous. The castle had long had a bad reputation as a place of confinement for prisoners of state and for those imprisoned by *lettres de cachet*. When the mob demanded admission, it was naturally denied them, and they were fired upon and nearly a hundred were killed. After a brief, courageous attack the place was surrendered, and the mob rushed into the gloomy pile. They found only seven prisoners, but one poor fellow had lost his wits and another had no idea why he had been kept there for years. The captives were freed amidst great enthusiasm, and the people soon set to work to demolish the walls.

Formation of the 'national guard.'

The actual occurrences of this celebrated day were soon "disfigured and transfigured by legends," and the anniversary of the fall of the Bastile is still celebrated as the great national holiday of France.[1] The rising of the people to protect themselves against the machinations of the king's associates who, it was believed, wished to block reform, and the successful attack on a monument of ancient tyranny appeared to be the opening of a new era of freedom. The disorders of these July days led to the formation of the "national guard." This was made up of volunteers from among the more prosperous citizens, who organized themselves to maintain order and so took from the king every excuse for calling in the regular troops for that purpose. Lafayette was put in command of this body.

Establishment of communes in Paris and other cities.

The government of Paris was reorganized, and a mayor, chosen from among the members of the National Assembly, was put at the head of the new *commune*, as the municipal government was called. The other cities of France also began with one accord, after the dismissal of Necker and the fall of the Bastile, to promote the Revolution by displacing or supplementing their old royal or aristocratic governments by committees of their citizens. These improvised communes, or city governments, established national guards, as Paris had done, and thus maintained order. The news that the king had approved the Paris revolution confirmed the opinion that the citizens of other cities had done right in taking the control into their own hands. We shall hear a good deal of the commune of Paris later, as it played a very important rôle in the Reign of Terror.

Disorder in the country districts.

By the end of the month of July the commotion reached the country districts. A curious panic swept over the land, which the peasants long remembered as "the great fear." A mysterious rumor arose that the "brigands" were coming! The terrified people did what they could to prepare for the danger;

[1] Reference, Stephens, *The French Revolution*, Vol. I, pp. 128–145.

neighboring communities combined with one another for mutual protection. When the panic was over and people saw that there were no brigands after all, they turned their attention to an enemy by no means imaginary, i.e., the old régime. The peasants assembled on the village common or in the parish church and voted to pay the feudal dues no longer. The next step was to burn the castles of the nobles in order to destroy the records of the peasants' obligations to their feudal lords.[1]

223. About the first of August news began to reach the National Assembly of the serious disorders in the provinces. This led to the first important reforms of the Assembly. A momentous decree abolishing the survivals of serfdom and feudalism was passed in a night session (August 4–5) amid great excitement, the representatives of the privileged orders vying with each other in surrendering their ancient privileges. The exclusive right of the nobility to hunt and to maintain pigeon houses was abolished, and the peasant was permitted to kill game which he found on his land. The president of the Assembly was "commissioned to ask the king to recall those persons who had been sent to the galleys or exiled simply for the violation of the hunting regulations." The tithes of the church were done away with. Exemptions from the payment of taxes were abolished forever. It was decreed that "taxes shall be collected from all citizens and from all property in the same manner and in the same form," and that "all citizens, without distinction of birth, are eligible to any office or dignity." Moreover, inasmuch as a national constitution would be of more advantage to the provinces than the privileges which some of these enjoyed, and, — so the decree continues, — "inasmuch as the surrender of such privileges is essential to the intimate union of all parts of the realm, it is decreed that all the peculiar privileges, pecuniary or otherwise, of the provinces, principalities, districts, cantons, cities and communes,

The decree abolishing the survivals of serfdom and feudalism, August, 1789.

[1] Reference, Stephens, *The French Revolution*, Vol. I, Chapter VI.

are once for all abolished and are absorbed into the law common to all Frenchmen."[1]

Unification of France through the abolition of the ancient provinces and the creation of the present departments.

This decree established the equality and uniformity for which the French people had sighed so long. The injustice of the former system of taxation could never be reintroduced. All France was to have the same laws, and its citizens were henceforth to be treated in the same way by the state, whether they lived in Brittany or Dauphiny. The Assembly soon went a step farther in consolidating and unifying France. It wiped out the old provinces altogether, by dividing the whole country into districts of convenient size, called *departments*. These were much more numerous than the ancient divisions, and were named after rivers and mountains. This obliterated from the map all reminiscences of the feudal disunion.

The Declaration of the Rights of Man.

224. Many of the *cahiers* had suggested that the Estates should draw up a clear statement of the rights of the individual citizen. It was urged that the recurrence of abuses and the insidious encroachments of despotism might in this way be forever prevented. The National Assembly consequently determined to prepare such a declaration in order to gratify and reassure the people and to form a basis for the new constitution.

This Declaration (completed August 26) is one of the most notable documents in the history of Europe. It not only aroused general enthusiasm when it was first published, but it appeared over and over again, in a modified form, in the succeeding French constitutions down to 1848, and has been the model for similar declarations in many of the other continental states. It was a dignified repudiation of the abuses described in the preceding chapter. Behind each article there was some crying evil of long standing against which the people wished to be forever protected.

Contents of the Declaration.

The Declaration sets forth that " Men are born and remain equal in rights. Social distinctions can only be founded upon

[1] This decree may be found in *Translations and Reprints*, Vol. I, No. 5.

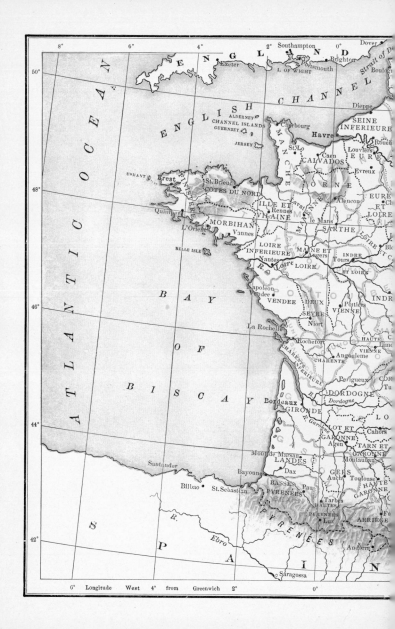

FRANCE
showing the
ANCIENT PROVINCES
and the
MODERN DEPARTMENTS

SCALE OF MILES
0 10 25   50   100   150

the general good." "Law is the expression of the general will. Every citizen has a right to participate, personally or through his representative, in its formation. It must be the same for all." "No person shall be accused, arrested, or imprisoned except in the cases and according to the forms prescribed by law." "No one shall be disquieted on account of his opinions, including his religious views, provided that their manifestation does not disturb the public order established by law." "The free communication of ideas and opinions is one of the most precious of the rights of man. Every citizen may, accord-ingly, speak, write, and print with freedom, being responsible, how-ever, for such abuses of this free-dom as shall be defined by law." "All citizens have a right to decide, either personally or by their repre-sentative, as to the necessity of the public contribution, to grant this freely, to know to what uses it is

Louis XVI

put, and to fix the proportion, the mode of assessment and of collection, and the duration of the taxes." "Society has the right to require of every public agent an account of his administration." Well might the Assembly claim, in its address to the people, that "the rights of man had been mis-conceived and insulted for centuries," and boast that they were "reëstablished for all humanity in this declaration, which shall serve as an everlasting war cry against oppressors."

225. The king hesitated to ratify the Declaration of the Rights of Man, and about the first of October rumors became current that, under the influence of the courtiers, he was calling together troops and preparing for another attempt to put an end to the Revolution, similar to that which the attack on the

Suspicion aroused against the court.

Bastile had frustrated. It was said that the new national colors —red, white, and blue—had been insulted at a banquet at Versailles. These things, along with the scarcity of food due to the poor crops of the year, aroused the excitable Paris populace.

A Paris mob invades the king's palace and carries him off to Paris.

On October 5 several thousand women and a number of armed men marched out to Versailles to ask bread of the king, in whom they had great confidence personally, however suspicious they might be of his friends and advisers. Lafayette marched after the mob with the national guard, but did not prevent some of the rabble from invading the king's palace the next morning and nearly murdering the queen, who had become very unpopular. She was believed to be still an Austrian at heart and to be in league with the counter-revolutionary party.

The mob declared that the king must accompany them to Paris, and he was obliged to consent. Far from being disloyal, they assumed that the presence of the royal family would insure plenty and prosperity. So they gayly escorted the "baker and the baker's wife and the baker's boy," as they jocularly termed the king and queen and the little dauphin, to the Palace of the Tuilleries, where the king took up his residence, practically a prisoner, as it proved. The National Assembly soon followed him and resumed its sittings in a riding school near the Tuilleries.

This transfer of the king and the Assembly to the capital was the first great misfortune of the Revolution. At a serious crisis the government was placed at the mercy of the leaders of the disorderly elements of Paris. We shall see how the municipal council of Paris finally usurped the powers of the national government.[1]

Unjust apportionment of the revenue of the church.

226. As we have seen, the church in France was very rich and retained many of its mediæval prerogatives and privileges.

[1] Reference, Stephens, *French Revolution*, Vol. I, Chapter VII.

Its higher officials, the bishops and abbots, received very large revenues and often a single prelate held a number of rich benefices, the duties of which he utterly neglected. The parish priests, on the other hand, who really performed the manifold and important functions of the church, were scarcely able to live on their incomes. This unjust apportionment of the vast revenue of the church naturally suggested the idea that, if the state confiscated the ecclesiastical possessions, it could see that those who did the work were properly paid for it, and might, at the same time, secure a handsome sum which would help the government out of its financial troubles. Those who sympathized with Voltaire's views were naturally delighted to see their old enemy deprived of its independence and made subservient to the state, and even many good Catholics could not but hope that the new system would be an improvement upon the old.

The tithes had been abolished in August along with the feudal dues. That deprived the church of perhaps thirty million dollars a year. On November 2 a decree was passed providing that " All the ecclesiastical possessions are at the disposal of the nation on condition that it provides properly for the expenses of maintaining religious services, for the support of those who conduct them and for the succor of the poor." This decree deprived the bishops and priests of their benefices and made them dependent on salaries paid by the state. The monks, monasteries, and convents, too, lost their property.

The property of the church confiscated by the government.

The National Assembly resolved to issue a paper currency for which the newly acquired lands should serve as security. Of these *assignats*, as this paper money was called, we hear a great deal during the revolutionary period. They soon began to depreciate, and ultimately a great part of the forty billions of francs issued during the next seven years was repudiated.

The assignats, or paper currency.

The Assembly set to work completely to reorganize the church. The anxiety for simplification and complete uniformity shows itself in the reckless way that it dealt with this

The Civil Constitution of the Clergy.

most venerable institution of France, the customs of which were hallowed not only by age, but by religious veneration. The one hundred and thirty-four ancient bishoprics, some of which dated back to the Roman Empire, were replaced by the eighty-three new departments into which France had already been divided.[1] Each of these became the diocese of a bishop, who was looked upon as an officer of the state and was to be elected by the people. The priests, too, were to be chosen by the people, and their salaries were much increased, so that even in the smallest villages they received over twice the minimum amount paid under the old régime.

This Civil Constitution of the Clergy[2] was the first serious mistake on the part of the National Assembly. While the half-feudalized church had sadly needed reform, the worst abuses might have been remedied without shocking and alienating thousands of those who had hitherto enthusiastically applauded the great reforms which the Assembly had effected. The king gave his assent to the changes, but with the feeling that he might be losing his soul by so doing. From that time on, he became at heart an enemy of the Revolution.

Harsh treatment of the 'non-juring' clergy. The discontent with the new system on the part of the clergy led to another serious error on the part of the Assembly. It required the clergy to take an oath to be faithful to the law and "to maintain with all their might the constitution decreed by the assembly." Only six of the bishops consented to this and but a third of the lower clergy, although they were much better off under the new system. Forty-six thousand parish priests refused to sacrifice their religious scruples, and before long the pope forbade them to take the required oath to the Constitution. As time went on, the "non-juring" clergy were dealt with more and more harshly by the government,

---

[1] See above, p. 568.

[2] The text of the Civil Constitution of the Clergy may be found in *Translations and Reprints*, Vol. I, No. 5.

and the way was prepared for the horrors of the Reign of Terror. The Revolution ceased to stand for liberty, order, and the abolition of ancient abuses, and came to mean, in the minds of many besides those who had lost their former privileges, irreligion, violence, and a new kind of oppression worse than the old.

General Reading. — There are a great many histories of the French Revolution. The best and most modern account is STEPHENS, *The French Revolution* (Charles Scribner's Sons, 3 vols., $2.50 each). SHAILER MATHEWS, *The French Revolution* (Longmans, Green & Co., $1.25), is an excellent short account. See also the brief but admirable chapters in ROSE, *The Revolutionary and Napoleonic Era* (The Macmillan Company, $1.25). CARLYLE's famous *French Revolution* is hardly a history but rather a series of vivid pictures, valuable only to those who already have some knowledge of the course of events. For Mirabeau see WILLERT, *Mirabeau* (The Macmillan Company, 75 cents).

CHAPTER XXXVI

THE FIRST FRENCH REPUBLIC

The permanent reforms of 1789.

227. We have now studied the progress and nature of the revolution which destroyed the old régime and created modern France. Through it the unjust privileges, the perplexing irregularities, and the local differences were abolished, and the people admitted to a share in the government. This vast reform had been accomplished without serious disturbance and, with the exception of some of the changes in the church, it had been welcomed with enthusiasm by the French nation.

The second revolution.

This permanent, peaceful revolution, or reformation, was followed by a second revolution of unprecedented violence, which for a time destroyed the French monarchy. It also introduced a series of further changes many of which were absurd and unnecessary and could not endure since they were approved by only a few fanatical leaders. France, moreover, became involved in a war with most of the powers of western Europe. The weakness of her government which permitted the forces of disorder and fanaticism to prevail, combined with the imminent danger of an invasion by the united powers of Europe, produced the Reign of Terror. After a period of national excitement and disorder, France gladly accepted the rule of a foreigner, who proved himself far more despotic than its former kings had been. Napoleon did not, however, undo the great work of 1789; his colossal ambition was, indeed, the means of extending, directly or indirectly, many of the benefits of the Revolution to other parts of western Europe. When, after Napoleon's fall, the brother of Louis XVI came to the throne, the first thing that he did was solemnly to assure the people that all the great gains of the first revolution should be maintained.

228. While practically the whole of the nation heartily rejoiced in the earlier reforms introduced by the National Assembly and celebrated the general satisfaction and harmony by a great national festival held at Paris on the first anniversary of the fall of the Bastile, some of the higher nobility refused to remain in France. The king's youngest brother, the count of Artois, set the example by leaving the country. He was followed by others who were terrified or disgusted by the burning of the châteaux, the loss of their privileges, and the unwise abolition of hereditary nobility by the National Assembly in June, 1790. Before long these emigrant nobles (*émigrés*), among whom were many military officers, organized a little army across the Rhine, and the count of Artois began to plan an invasion of France. He was ready to ally himself with Austria, Prussia, or any other foreign government which he could induce to help undo the Revolution and give back to the French king his former absolute power and to the nobles their old privileges.

The emigration of the nobles.

The threats and insolence of the emigrant nobles and their shameful negotiations with foreign powers discredited the members of their class who still remained in France. The people suspected that the plans of the runaways met with the secret approval of the king, and more especially of the queen, whose brother was now emperor and ruler of the Austrian dominions. This, added to the opposition of the non-juring clergy, produced a bitter hostility between the so-called "patriots" and those who, on the other hand, were supposed to be secretly hoping for a counter revolution which would reëstablish the old régime.

The conduct of the emigrant nobles discredits the king and queen.

The worst fears of the people appeared to be justified by the secret flight of the royal family from Paris, in June, 1791. Ever since the king had reluctantly signed the Civil Constitution

The flight to Varennes, June 21, 1791.

of the Clergy, flight had seemed to him his only resource. There was a body of regular troops on the northeastern boundary; if he could escape from Paris and join them he hoped that, aided by a demonstration on the part of the queen's brother, he might march back and check the further progress of the revolutionary movement with which he could no longer sympathize. He had, it is true, no liking for the emigrants and heartily disapproved of their policy, nor did he believe that the old régime could ever be restored. But, unfortunately, his plans led him to attempt to reach the boundary just at that point where the emigrants were collected. He and the queen were, however, arrested on the way, at Varennes, and speedily brought back to Paris.

Effect of the king's flight. The desertion of the king appears to have terrified rather than angered the nation. The grief of the people at the thought of losing, and their joy at regaining, a poor weak ruler like Louis XVI clearly shows that France was still profoundly royalist in its sympathies. The National Assembly pretended that the king had not fled, but that he had been carried off. This gratified France at large; still in Paris there were some who advocated the deposition of the king, and for the first time a *republican* party appeared, though it was still small.

The National Assembly at last put the finishing touches to the new constitution upon which it had been working for two years, and the king readily swore to observe it faithfully. A general amnesty was then proclaimed. All the discord and suspicion of the past months were to be forgotten. The **The constitution completed, 1791.** National Assembly had completed its appointed task, perhaps the greatest that a single body of men ever undertook. It had made France over and had given her an elaborate constitution. It was now ready to give way to the regular Legislative Assembly provided for in the constitution. This held its first session October 1, 1791.[1]

[1] Reference, Mathews, *The French Revolution*, Chapter XII.

229. In spite of the great achievements of the National Assembly it left France in a critical situation. Besides the emigrant nobles abroad, there were the non-juring clergy at home, and a king who was secretly corresponding with foreign powers with the hope of securing their aid. When the news of the arrest of the king and queen at Varennes reached the ears of Marie Antoinette's brother, the Austrian ruler, Leopold II, he declared that the violent arrest of the king sealed with unlawfulness all that had been done in France and "compromised directly the honor of all the sovereigns and the security of every government." He therefore proposed to the rulers of Russia, England, Prussia, Spain, Naples, and Sardinia that they should come to some understanding between themselves as to how they might "reëstablish the liberty and honor of the most Christian king and his family, and place a check upon the dangerous excesses of the French Revolution, the fatal example of which it behooves every government to repress."

Sources of danger at the opening of the Legislative Assembly, October, 1791.

On August 27 Leopold had issued, in conjunction with the king of Prussia, the famous Declaration of Pillnitz. In this the two sovereigns state that, in accordance with the wishes of the king's brothers (the leaders of the emigrant nobles), they are ready to join the other European rulers in an attempt to place the king of France in a position to establish a form of government "that shall be once more in harmony with the rights of sovereigns and shall promote the welfare of the French nation." In the meantime they promised to prepare their troops for active service.

The Declaration of Pillnitz, August 27, 1791.

The Declaration was little more than an empty threat; but it seemed to the French people a sufficient proof that the monarchs were ready to help the seditious French nobles to reëstablish the old régime against the wishes of the nation and at the cost of infinite bloodshed. The idea of foreign rulers intermeddling with their internal affairs would in itself

Effect of the Declaration.

have been intolerable to a proud people like the French, even if the permanence of the new reforms had not been endangered. Had it been the object of the allied monarchs to hasten instead of to prevent the deposition of Louis XVI, they could hardly have chosen a more efficient means than the Declaration of Pillnitz.

The newspapers.

230. The political excitement and the enthusiasm for the Revolution were kept up by the newspapers which had been established, especially in Paris, since the meeting of the Estates General. The people did not need

Caricature representing Louis XVI as a Constitutional Monarch [1]

longer to rely upon an occasional pamphlet, as was the case before 1789. Many journals of the most divergent kinds and representing the most diverse opinions were published. Some were no more than a periodical editorial written by one man; for example, the notorious "Friend of the People," by the insane Marat. Others, like the famous "Moniteur," were much like our papers of to-day and contained news, reports of the debates in the assembly, announcements of theaters, etc. Some of the papers were illustrated, and the representations of contemporaneous events, especially the numerous caricatures, are highly diverting.

The Jacobins.

Of the numerous political clubs, by far the most famous was that of the *Jacobins*. When the Assembly moved into Paris, some of the provincial representatives of the third estate rented

---

[1] The formerly despotic king is represented as safely caged by the National Assembly. When asked by Marie Antoinette's brother what he is about, Louis XVI replies, "I am signing my name," — that is, he had nothing to do except meekly to ratify the measures which the Assembly chose to pass.

a large room in the monastery of the Jacobin monks, not far from the building where the National Assembly itself met. A hundred deputies perhaps were present at the first meeting. The next day the number had doubled. The aim of this society was to discuss questions which were about to come before the National Assembly. The club decided beforehand what should be the policy of its members and how they should vote; and in this way they successfully combined to counteract the schemes of the aristocratic party in the assembly. The club rapidly grew and soon admitted some who were not deputies to its sessions. In October, 1791, it decided to permit the public to attend its discussions.

Gradually similar societies were formed in the provinces.[1] These affiliated themselves with the "mother" society at Paris and kept in constant communication with it. In this way the Jacobins of Paris stimulated and controlled public opinion throughout France, and kept the opponents of the old régime alert. When the Legislative Assembly met, the Jacobins had not as yet become republicans, but they believed that the king should have hardly more power than the president of a republic. They were even ready to promote his deposition if he failed to stand by the Revolution.

231. The growing discord in the nation was increased by the severe edicts that the Legislative Assembly directed against the emigrant nobles and the non-juring clergy. "The Frenchmen assembled on the frontier" were declared under suspicion of conspiring against their country. If they did not return to France by January 1, 1792, they were to be regarded as convicted traitors, to be punished, if caught, with death; their property was to be confiscated. *The emigrant nobles declared traitors.*

The harsh treatment of the emigrant nobles was perhaps justified by their desertion and treasonable intrigues; but the conduct of the Assembly toward the clergy was both unstatesmanlike *Harsh measures of the Assembly toward non-juring clergy.*

[1] By June, 1791, there were four hundred and six of these affiliated clubs.

and iniquitous. Those who had refused to take the oath to support a system which was in conflict with their religious convictions and which had been condemned by the pope, were commanded to do so within a week on penalty of losing their income from the state and being put under surveillance as suspects. As this failed to bring the clergy to terms, the Assembly later (May, 1792) ordered the deportation from the country of those who steadily persisted in their refusal to accept the Civil Constitution of the Clergy. In this way the Assembly aroused the active hostility of a great part of the most conscientious among the lower clergy, who had loyally supported the commons in their fight against the privileged orders. It also lost the confidence of the great mass of faithful Catholics, — merchants, artisans, and peasants, — who had gladly accepted the abolition of the old abuses, but who would not consent to desert their religious leaders.

The Legislative Assembly precipitate a war with Europe.

232. By far the most important act of the Legislative Assembly during the one year of its existence was its precipitation of a war between France and Austria. It little dreamed that this was the beginning of a war between revolutionary France and the rest of western Europe, which was to last, with slight interruptions, for over twenty years.

To many of the leaders in the Assembly it seemed that the existing conditions were intolerable. The emigrant nobles were forming little armies on the boundaries of France and had, as we have seen, induced Austria and Prussia to consider interfering in French affairs. The Assembly suspected that Louis was negotiating with foreign rulers and would be glad to have them intervene and reëstablish him in his old despotic power. The deputies argued, therefore, that a war against the hated Austria would unite the sympathies of the nation and force the king to show his true character; for he would be obliged either to become the nation's leader or show himself the traitor they suspected him to be.

It was with a heavy heart that the king, urged on by the clamors of the Assembly, declared war upon Austria in April, 1792. The unpopularity of the king only increased, however. He refused to ratify certain popular measures of the Assembly and dismissed the ministers who had been forced upon him. In June a mob of Parisians invaded the Palace of the Tuilleries, and the king might have been killed had he not consented to don the "cap of liberty," the badge of the "citizen patriots."

France declares war upon Austria, April, 1792.

The king suspected and his life threatened.

When France declared war, Prussia immediately allied itself with Austria. Both powers collected their forces and, to the great joy of the emigrant nobles, who joined them, prepared to march upon France. The early attempts of the French to get a footing in the Austrian Netherlands were not successful, and the troops and people accused the nobles, who were in command of the French troops, of treason. As the allies approached the boundaries it became clearer and clearer that the king was utterly incapable of defending France, and the Assembly began to consider the question of deposing him. The duke of Brunswick, who was at the head of the Prussian forces, took the very worst means of helping the king, by issuing a manifesto in which he threatened utterly to destroy Paris should the king suffer any harm.

Growth of republican feeling.

Angered by this declaration and aroused by the danger, the populace of Paris again invaded the Tuilleries, August 10, 1792, and the king was obliged to take refuge in the building in which the Assembly was in session. Those who instigated the attack were men who had set their heart upon doing away with the king altogether and establishing a republic. A group of them had taken possession of the city hall, pushed the old members of the municipal council off from their seats, and taken the government in their own hands. In this way the members of the Paris commune became the leaders in the revolution which established the first French republic.

Insurrection of August 10, 1792.

France proclaimed a republic, September 22, 1792.

233. The Assembly agreed with the commune in desiring a republic. If, as was proposed, France was henceforth to do without a king, it was obviously necessary that the monarchical constitution so recently completed should be replaced by a republican one. Consequently, the Assembly arranged that the people should elect delegates to a constitutional *Convention*, which should draw up a new system of government. The Convention met on the 21st of September, and its first act was to abolish the ancient monarchy and proclaim France a republic. It seemed to the enthusiasts of the time that a new era of liberty had dawned, now that the long oppression by "despots" was ended forever. The twenty-second day of September, 1792, was reckoned as the first day of the Year One of French liberty.[1]

The September massacres, 1792.

Meanwhile the usurping Paris commune had taken matters into its own hands and had brought discredit upon the cause of liberty by one of the most atrocious acts in history. On the pretext that Paris was full of traitors, who sympathized with the Austrians and the emigrant nobles, they had filled the prisons with three thousand innocent citizens. On September 2 and 3 hundreds of these were executed with scarcely a pretense of a trial. The members of the commune who perpetrated this deed probably hoped to terrify those who might still dream of returning to the old system of government.

Progress of the war with Austria and Prussia.

Late in August the Prussians crossed the French boundary and on September 2 took the fortress of Verdun. It now seemed as if there was nothing to prevent their marching upon Paris. The French general, Dumouriez, blocked their advance, however, and without a pitched battle caused the enemy to

---

[1] A committee of the Convention was appointed to draw up a new republican calendar. The year was divided into twelve months of thirty days each. The five days preceding September 22, at the end of the year, were holidays. Each month was divided into three *decades*, and each "tenth day" (*décadi*) was a holiday. The days were no longer dedicated to saints, but to agricultural implements, vegetables, domestic animals, etc.

retreat. Notwithstanding the fears of the French, the king of Prussia had but little interest in the war; the Austrian troops were lagging far behind, and both powers were far more absorbed in a second partition of Poland, which was approaching, than in the fate of the French king. The French now invaded Germany and took several important towns on the Rhine, including Mayence, which gladly opened its gates to them. They also occupied the Spanish Netherlands and Savoy.

Meanwhile the new Convention was puzzled to determine what would best be done with the king. A considerable party felt that he was guilty of treason in secretly encouraging the foreign powers to come to his aid. He was therefore brought to trial, and when it came to a final vote, he was, by a small majority, condemned to death. He mounted the scaffold on January 21, 1793, with the fortitude of a martyr. Nevertheless, one cannot but feel that through his earlier weakness and indecision he brought untold misery upon his own kingdom and upon Europe at large. The French people had not dreamed of a republic until his absolute incompetence forced them, in self-defense, to abolish the monarchy in the hope of securing a more efficient government.

Trial and execution of the king, January, 1793

234. The exultation of the Convention over the conquests which their armies were making, encouraged them to offer the assistance of the new republic to any country that wished to establish its freedom by throwing off the yoke of monarchy. They even proposed a republic to the English people. One of the French ministers declared, "We will hurl thither fifty thousand caps of liberty, we will plant there the sacred tree of liberty." February 1, 1793, France greatly added to her embarrassments by declaring war on England, a country which proved her most inveterate enemy.

The Convention proposes to aid other countries to rid themselves of their monarchs.

France declares war on England, February 1, 1793.

The war now began to go against the French. The allies had hitherto been suspicious of one another and fearful lest Russia should take advantage of their preoccupation with France to

The allies settle their differences and renew the war against France.

seize more than her share of Poland. They now came to an agreement. It was arranged that Prussia and Russia should each take another piece of Poland, while Austria agreed to go without her share if the powers would aid her in inducing the elector of Bavaria to exchange his possessions for the Spanish Netherlands.

The Partitions of Poland

French driven from the Netherlands; desertion of Dumouriez.

This adjustment of the differences between the allies gave a wholly new aspect to the war with France. When in March, 1793, Spain and the Holy Roman Empire joined the coalition, France was at war with all her neighbors. The Austrians defeated Dumouriez at Neerwinden and drove the French out of the Netherlands. Thereupon Dumouriez, disgusted by the failure of the Convention to support him and by their execution of the king, deserted to the enemy with a few hundred soldiers who consented to follow him.

The loss of the Netherlands and the treason of their best general made a deep impression upon the members of the Convention. If the new French republic was to defend itself against the "tyrants" without and its many enemies within, it could not wait for the Convention to draw up an elaborate, permanent constitution. An efficient government must be devised immediately to maintain the loyalty of the nation to the republic, and to raise and equip armies and direct their commanders. The Convention accordingly put the government into the hands of a small committee, consisting originally of nine, later of twelve, of its members. This famous Committee of Public Safety was given practically unlimited powers. "We must," one of the leaders exclaimed, "establish the despotism of liberty in order to crush the despotism of kings."

French government put in the hands of the Committee of Public Safety, April, 1793.

235. Within the Convention itself there were two groups of active men who came into bitter conflict over the policy to be pursued. There was, first, the party of the Girondists, so called because their leaders came from the department of Gironde, in which the great city of Bordeaux lay. They were moderate republicans and counted among their numbers some speakers of remarkable eloquence. The Girondists had enjoyed the control of the Legislative Assembly in 1792 and had been active in bringing on the war with Austria and Prussia. They hoped in that way to complete the Revolution by exposing the bad faith of the king and his sympathy with the emigrant nobles. They were not, however, men of sufficient decision to direct affairs in the terrible difficulties in which France found herself after the execution of the king. They consequently lost their influence, and a new party, called the "Mountain" from the high seats that they occupied in the Convention, gained the ascendency.

The Girondists.

This was composed of the most vigorous and uncompromising republicans. They believed that the French people had been depraved by the slavery to which their kings had subjected

The extreme republicans, called the 'Mountain.'

them. Everything, they argued, which suggested the former rule of kings must be wiped out. A new France should be created, in which liberty, equality, and fraternity should take the place of the tyranny of princes, the insolence of nobles, and the impostures of the priests. The leaders of the Mountain held that the mass of the people were by nature good and upright, but that there were a number of adherents of the old system who would, if they could, undo the great work of the Revolution and lead the people back to slavery under king and church. All who were suspected by the Mountain of having the least sympathy with the nobles or persecuted priests were branded as counter-revolutionary. The Mountain was willing to resort to any measures, however shocking, to rid the nation of those suspected of counter-revolutionary tendencies, and its leaders relied upon the populace of Paris to aid them in reaching their ends.

Girondist leaders expelled from the Convention, June 2, 1793.

The Girondists, on the other hand, abhorred the furious Paris mob and the cruel fanatics who composed the commune of the capital. They argued that Paris was not France, and that it had no right to assume a despotic rule over the nation. They proposed that the commune should be dissolved and that the Convention should remove to another town where they would not be subject to the intimidation of the Paris mob. The Mountain thereupon accused the Girondists of an attempt to break up the republic, " one and indivisible," by questioning the supremacy of Paris and the duty of the provinces to follow the lead of the capital. The mob, thus encouraged, rose against the Girondists. On June 2 it surrounded the meeting place of the Convention, and deputies of the commune demanded the expulsion from the Convention of the Girondist leaders, who were placed under arrest.

France threatened with civil war.

The conduct of the Mountain and its ally, the Paris commune, now began to arouse opposition in various parts of France, and the country was threatened with civil war at a time when it was absolutely necessary that all Frenchmen should combine in the loyal defense of their country against the invaders who were again approaching its boundaries. The first and most serious opposition came from the peasants of Brittany, especially in the department of La Vendée. There the people still loved the monarchy and their priests and even the nobles; they refused to send their sons to fight for a republic which had killed their king and was persecuting the clergymen who declined to take an oath which their conscience forbade. The Vendean royalists defeated several corps of the national guard which the Convention sent against them, and it was not until autumn that the distinguished general, Kléber, was able to put down the insurrection.

The revolt of the peasants of Brittany against the Convention.

The great cities of Marseilles and Bordeaux were indignant at the treatment to which the Girondist deputies were subjected in Paris, and organized a revolt against the Convention. In the manufacturing city of Lyons the merchants hated the Jacobins and their republic, since the demand for silk and other luxuries produced at Lyons had come from the nobility and clergy, who were now no longer in a position to buy. The prosperous classes were therefore exasperated when the commissioners of the Convention demanded money and troops. The citizens gathered an army of ten thousand men and placed it under a royalist leader. The Convention, however, called in troops from the armies on the frontier, bombarded and captured the city, and wreaked a terrible vengeance upon those who had dared to revolt against the Mountain. Frightened by the experience of Lyons, Bordeaux and Marseilles decided that resistance was futile and admitted the troops of the Convention. Some of the Girondist deputies had escaped from Paris and attempted to gather an army in Normandy; but they failed, too. The Convention's Committee of Public Safety showed itself far more efficient than the scattered and disunited opponents who questioned its right to govern France.

Revolt of the cities against the Convention.

The French
repulse the
English and
Austrians.

While the Committee of Public Safety had been suppressing the revolts within the country, it had taken active measures to meet its foreign enemies. The distinguished military organizer, Carnot, had become a member of the Committee in August and immediately called for a general levy of troops. He soon had five hundred and fifty thousand men; these he divided into thirteen armies and dispatched them against the allies. The English and Hanoverians, who were besieging Dunkirk, were driven off and the Austrians were defeated, so that by the close of the year 1793 all danger from invasion was past, for the time being at least.

The Reign
of Terror.

236. In spite of the marvelous success with which the Committee of Public Safety had crushed its opponents at home and repelled the forces of the coalition, it continued its policy of stifling all opposition by terror. Even before the fall of the Girondists a special court had been established in Paris, known The Revolutionary
Tribunal. as the Revolutionary Tribunal. Its duty was to try all those who were suspected of treasonable acts. At first the cases were very carefully considered and few persons were condemned. In September, after the revolt of the cities, two new men, who had been implicated in the September massacres, were added to the Committee of Public Safety. They were selected with the particular purpose of intimidating the counter-revolutionary party by bringing all the disaffected to the guillotine.[1] A terrible law was passed, declaring all those to be suspects who by their conduct or remarks had shown themselves enemies of liberty. The former nobles, including the wives, fathers, mothers, and children of the "emigrants," unless they had constantly manifested their attachment to the Revolution, were ordered to be imprisoned.

---

[1] In former times it had been customary to inflict capital punishment by decapitating the victim with the sword. At the opening of the Revolution a certain Dr. Guillotin recommended a new device, which consisted of a heavy knife sliding downward between two uprights. This instrument, called after him, the guillotine, which is still used in France, was more speedy and certain in its action than the sword in the hands of the executioner.

In October, the queen, Marie Antoinette, after a trial in which the most false and atrocious charges were brought against her, was executed in Paris, and a number of high-minded and distinguished persons suffered a like fate. But the most horrible acts of the Reign of Terror were perpetrated in the provinces. A representative of the Convention had thousands of the people of Nantes shot down or drowned. The convention proposed to destroy the great city of Lyons altogether, and though this decree was only partially carried out, thousands of its citizens were executed.[1]

Execution of Marie Antoinette, October, 1793.

Soon the radical party which was conducting the government began to disagree among themselves. Danton, a man of fiery zeal for the republic, who had hitherto enjoyed great popularity with the Jacobins, became tired of bloodshed, and believed that the system of terror was no longer necessary. On the other hand, Hébert the leader of the commune felt that the revolution was not yet complete. He proposed, for example, that the worship of Reason should be substituted for the worship of God, and arranged a service in the great church of Notre Dame, where Reason, in the person of a handsome actress, took her place on the altar. The most powerful member of the Committee of Public Safety was Robespierre, who, although he was insignificant in person and a tiresome speaker, enjoyed a great reputation for republican virtue. He disapproved alike of Danton's moderation and of the worship of Reason advocated by the commune. Through his influence the leaders of both the moderate and the extreme party were arrested and executed (March and April, 1794).

Schism in the party of the Mountain.

Robespierre as dictator.

[1] Reference, for the conduct of the terrorists and the executions at Paris, Nantes, and Lyons: Mathews, *The French Revolution*, Chapter XVII.

It should not be forgotten that very few of the people at Paris stood in any fear of the guillotine. The city during the Reign of Terror was not the gloomy place that we might imagine. Never did the inhabitants appear happier, never were the theaters and restaurants more crowded. The guillotine was making away with the enemies of liberty, so the women wore tiny guillotines as ornaments, and the children were given toy guillotines and amused themselves decapitating the figures of "aristocrats." See Stephens, *French Revolution*, Vol. II, pp. 343-361.

Fall of Robespierre, July 27, 1794. It was, of course, impossible for Robespierre to maintain his dictatorship permanently. He had the revolutionary tribunal divided into sections, and greatly increased the rapidity of the executions with a view of destroying all his enemies; but his colleagues in the Convention began to fear that he would demand their heads next. A coalition was formed against him, and the Convention ordered his arrest.[1] He called upon the commune to defend him, but the Convention roused Paris against the commune, which was no longer powerful enough to intimidate the whole city, and he and his supporters were sent to the guillotine.

Reaction after the overthrow of Robespierre. 237. In successfully overthrowing Robespierre the Convention and Committee of Public Safety had rid the country of the only man, who, owing to his popularity and his reputation for uprightness, could have prolonged the Reign of Terror. There was an immediate reaction after his death, for the country was weary of executions. The Revolutionary Tribunal henceforth convicted very few indeed of those who were brought before it. It made an exception, however, of those who had themselves been the leaders in the worst atrocities, for example, as the public prosecutor, who had brought hundreds of victims to the guillotine in Paris, and the brutes who had ordered the massacres at Nantes and Lyons. Within a few months the Jacobin Club at Paris was closed by the Convention, and the commune abolished.

Constitution of the year III. The Convention now at last turned its attention to the great work for which it had originally been summoned, and drew up a constitution for the republic. This provided that the lawmaking power should be vested in a legislative assembly consisting of two houses. The lower house was called the Council of the Five Hundred, and the upper chamber the Council of the Elders. Members of the latter were required to be at least

[1] The date of Robespierre's fall is generally known as the 9th Thermidor, the day and month of the republican calendar.

forty years of age.   The executive powers were put in the hands of a *Directory* of five persons to be chosen by the two chambers.

In October, 1795, the Convention finally dissolved itself, having governed the country during three years of unprecedented excitement, danger, and disorder.   While it was responsible for the horrors of the Reign of Terror, its committees had carried France through the terrible crisis of 1793. The civil war had been brought to a speedy end, and the coalition of foreign powers had been defeated.   Meanwhile other committees appointed by the Convention had been quietly working upon the problem of bettering the system of education, which had been taken by the state out of the hands of the clergy.   Progress had also been made toward establishing a single system of law for the whole country to replace the old confusion.   The new republican calendar was not destined to survive many years, but the metric system of weights and measures introduced by the Convention has now been adopted by most European countries, and is used by men of science in England and America.

On the other hand, the Reign of Terror, the depreciated paper currency,[1] and many hasty and unwise laws passed by the Convention had produced all sorts of disorder and uncertainty.   The Directory did little to better conditions, and it was not until Napoleon's strong hand grasped the helm of government in the year 1800 that order was really restored.

The dissolution of the Convention, October, 1795; its achievements.

General Reading. — In addition to the references given at the end of the preceding chapter, BELLOC, *Danton* (Charles Scribner's Sons, $2.50) and *Robespierre* by the same author (same publisher, $2.00).

[1] There were about forty billions of francs in assignats in circulation at the opening of 1796.   At that time it required nearly three hundred francs in paper money to procure one in specie.

CHAPTER XXXVII

NAPOLEON BONAPARTE

The Napoleonic Period.

238. The aristocratic military leaders of old France had either run away or been discredited along with the noble class to which they belonged. Among the commanders who, through exceptional ability, arose in their stead, one was soon to dominate the history of Europe as no man before him had ever done. For fifteen years, his biography and the political history of Europe are so nearly synonomous that the period that we are now entering upon may properly be called after him, the Napoleonic Period.

Napoleon Bonaparte (b. 1769), a Corsican by birth, an Italian by descent.

Napoleon Bonaparte was hardly a Frenchman in origin. It is true that the island of Corsica, where he was born August 15, 1769, had at that time belonged to France for a year. But Napoleon's native language was Italian, he was descended from Italian ancestors who had come to the island in the sixteenth century, and his career revives, on a magnificent scale, the ambitions and the policy of a *condottiere* despot of the fifteenth century.[1]

The young Bonaparte in a French military school.

When he was ten years old he was taken to France by his father. After learning a little of the French language, which he is said never to have mastered perfectly, he was put into a military school where he remained for six years. He soon came to hate the young French aristocrats with whom he was associated. He wrote to his father, " I am tired of exposing my poverty and seeing these shameless boys laughing over it, who are superior to me only in their wealth, but infinitely beneath me in noble sentiments." Gradually the ambition

[1] See above, pp. 326–327.

to free his little island country from French control developed in him.

On completing his course in the military school he was made second lieutenant. Poor and without influence, he had little hope of any considerable advance in the French army, and he was drawn to his own country both by a desire to play a political rôle there and to help his family, which had been left in straitened circumstances by his father's death. He therefore absented himself from his command as often and as long as he could, and engaged in a series of intrigues in Corsica with a hope of getting control of the forces of the island. He fell out, however, with the authorities, and he and his family were banished in 1793, and fled to France. *His political intrigues in Corsica.*

The Bonapartes banished from Corsica, 1793.

The following three years were for Bonaparte a period of great uncertainty. He had lost his love for Corsica and as yet he had no foothold in France. He managed, however, to demonstrate his military skill and decision on two occasions and gained thereby the friendship of the Directory. In the spring of 1796 he was made by the Directory commander-in-chief of the army of Italy. This important appointment at the age of twenty-seven forms the opening of a military career which in extent and grandeur hardly finds a parallel in history, except that of Alexander the Great. And of all Bonaparte's campaigns, none is more interesting perhaps than his first, that in Italy in 1796–1797. *Napoleon made commander-in-chief of the army of Italy, 1796.*

239. After the armies raised by the Committee of Public Safety had driven back their enemies in the autumn of 1793, the French occupied the Austrian Netherlands, Holland, and that portion of Germany which lies on the left, or west, bank of the Rhine. Austria and Prussia were again busy with a new, and this time final, partition of Poland. As Prussia had little real interest in the war with France, she soon concluded peace with the new republic, April, 1795. Spain followed her example and left Austria, England, and Sardinia to carry on *Prussia and Spain conclude peace with the French republic, 1795.*

the war.   General Bonaparte had to face the combined armies of Austria and of the king of Sardinia.   By marching north from Savona he skillfully separated his two enemies, forced the Sardinian troops back toward Turin, and compelled the king of Sardinia to conclude a truce with France.

This left him free to advance against the Austrians.   These he outflanked and forced to retreat.   On May 15, 1796, he entered Milan.   The Austrian commander then shut himself

Napoleon Bonaparte during the Italian Campaign

up in the impregnable fortress of Mantua, where Bonaparte promptly besieged him. There is no more fascinating chapter in the history of warfare than the story of the audacious maneuvers by which Bonaparte successfully repulsed four attempts on the part of the Austrians to relieve Mantua, which was finally forced to capitulate at the beginning of February of the following year. As soon as he had removed all danger of an attack in the rear, the young French general led his army toward Vienna, and by April, 1797, the Austrian court was glad to sign a preliminary peace.

The provisions of the definitive peace which was concluded at Campo-Formio, October 17, 1797, illustrate the unscrupulous manner in which Austria and the French republic disposed of the helpless lesser states.   It inaugurated the bewilderingly rapid territorial redistribution of Europe, which was so characteristic of the Napoleonic period. Austria ceded to France the Austrian Netherlands and secretly agreed to use its good offices to secure for France a great part of the left bank of the Rhine. Austria also recognized the Cisalpine republic which Bonaparte had created out of the smaller states of northern Italy, and which was under the "protection" of France. This new state included Milan, Modena, some of the papal dominions, and, lastly, a part of the possessions of the venerable and renowned but defenseless republic of Venice which Napoleon had iniquitously destroyed. Austria received as a partial indemnity the rest of the possessions of the Venetian republic, including Venice itself.

Creation of the Cisalpine republic.

240. While the negotiations were going on at Campo-Formio, the young general had established a brilliant court. "His salons," an observer informs us, "were filled with a throng of generals, officials, and purveyors, as well as the highest nobility and the most distinguished men of Italy, who came to solicit the favor of a glance or a moment's conversation." He appears already to have conceived the rôle that he was to play later. We have a report of a most extraordinary conversation which occurred at this time.

General Bonaparte holds court; his analysis of the French character and of his own aims.

"What I have done so far," he declared, "is nothing. I am but at the opening of the career that I am to run. Do you suppose that I have gained my victories in Italy in order to advance the lawyers of the Directory? . . . Do you think either that my object is to establish a republic? What a notion! . . . What the French want is Glory and the satisfaction of their vanity; as for Liberty, of that they have no conception. Look at the army! The victories that we have just gained have given the French soldier his true character. I am everything to him. Let the Directory attempt to deprive me of my command and they will see who is the master. The nation must have a head, a head who is rendered illustrious by glory and not by theories of government, fine phrases, or the talk of idealists, of which the French understand not a whit."

There is no doubt whom General Bonaparte had in mind when he spoke of the needed head of the French nation who should be "rendered illustrious by glory." This son of a poor Corsican lawyer, but yesterday a mere unlucky adventurer, had arranged his programme; two years and a half later he was the master of the French republic.

Personal characteristics.

We naturally ask what manner of person this was who could frame such audacious schemes at twenty-eight and realize them at thirty years of age. He was a little man, less than five feet two inches in height. At this time he was extremely thin, but his striking features, quick, searching eye, abrupt, animated gestures and rapid speech, incorrect as it was, made a deep impression upon those who came in contact with him. He possessed in a supreme degree two qualities that are ordinarily incompatible. He was a dreamer, and at the same time a man whose practical skill and mastery of detail amounted to genius. He once told a friend that he was wont, when a poor lieutenant, to allow his imagination full play and fancy things just as he would have them. Then he would coolly consider the exact steps to be taken if he were to try to make his dream come true.

Sources of power in Napoleon's character.

In order to explain Bonaparte's success it must be remembered that he was not hampered or held back by the fear of doing wrong. He was utterly unscrupulous, whether dealing with an individual or a nation, and appears to have been absolutely without any sense of moral responsibility. Affection for his friends and relatives never stood in the way of his personal aggrandizement. To these traits must be added unrivaled military genius and the power of intense and almost uninterrupted work.

But even Bonaparte, unexampled as were his abilities, could never have extended his power over all of western Europe, had it not been for the peculiar political weakness of most of the states with which he had to deal. There was no strong German empire in his day, no united Italy, no Belgium whose neutrality was guaranteed — as it now is — by the other powers of Europe. The French republic was surrounded by petty independent, or practically independent, principalities which were defenseless against an unscrupulous invader. Prussia, much smaller than it now is, offered, as we shall see, no efficient opposition to the extension of French control. Austria had been forced to capitulate, after a short campaign, by an enemy far from its source of supplies and led by a young and inexperienced general.

The political conditions which rendered Napoleon's wonderful successes possible.

241. After arranging the Peace of Campo-Formio, General Bonaparte returned to Paris. He at once perceived that France, in spite of her enthusiasm for him, was not yet ready to accept him as her ruler. He saw, too, that he would soon sacrifice his prestige if he lived quietly in Paris like an ordinary person. His active mind soon conceived a plan which would forward his interests. France was still at war with England, its most persevering enemy during this period. Bonaparte convinced the Directory that England could best be ruined in the long run by seizing Egypt and threatening her commerce through the Mediterranean, and perhaps ultimately her dominion in the East. Bonaparte, fascinated by the career of Alexander the Great, pictured himself riding to India on the back of an elephant and dispossessing England of her most precious colonial dependencies. He had, however, still another and a characteristic reason for undertaking the expedition. France was on the eve of a new war with the European powers. Bonaparte foresaw that, if he could withdraw with him some of France's best officers, the Directory might soon find itself so embarrassed that he could return as a national savior. And even so it fell out.

Napoleon conceives the idea of an expedition to Egypt.

The French fleet left Toulon, May 19, 1798. It was so fortunate as to escape the English squadron under Nelson, which sailed by it in the night.   Bonaparte arrived at Alexandria, July 1, and easily defeated the Turkish troops in the famous battle of the Pyramids.   Meanwhile Nelson, who did not know the destination of the enemy's fleet, had returned from the Syrian coast where he had looked for the French in

vain.   He discovered Bonaparte's ships in the harbor of Alexandria and completely annihilated them in the first battle of the Nile (August 1, 1798).   The French troops were now completely cut off from Europe.[1]

The Porte (i.e., the Turkish government) declared war against France, and Bonaparte resolved to attack Turkey by land.   He accordingly marched into Syria in the spring of 1799, but was repulsed at Acre, where the Turkish forces were aided by the English fleet.   Pursued by pestilence, the army regained Cairo in June after terrible suffering and loss.   It was still strong enough to annihilate a Turkish army that landed at Alexandria ; but news now reached Bonaparte from Europe which convinced him that the time had come for him to hasten

back.   Northern Italy, which he had won, was lost ; the allies were about to invade France, and the Directory was completely demoralized.   Bonaparte accordingly secretly deserted his army and managed, by a series of happy accidents, to reach France by October 9, 1799.

242.   The Directory, one of the most corrupt and inefficient governmental bodies that the world has ever seen, had completely disgraced itself.[2]   Bonaparte readily found others to join with him in a conspiracy to overthrow it.   A plan was formed for abruptly destroying the old government and replacing it by a new one without observing any constitutional forms.   This is a procedure so familiar in France during the past century that it is known even in English as a *coup d'état* (literally translated, a "stroke of state ").   The conspirators had a good many

[1] Reference, Rose, *Life of Napoleon*, Vol. I, Chapter VIII.
[2] Reference, Rose, *Revolutionary and Napoleonic Era*, pp. 95,96, 104–108, 114, 115.

friends in the two assemblies, especially among the "Elders." Nevertheless Bonaparte had to order his soldiers to invade the hall in which the Assembly of the Five Hundred was in session and scatter his opponents before he could accomplish his purpose. A chosen few were then reassembled under the presidency of Lucien Bonaparte, one of Napoleon's brothers, who was a member of the assembly. They voted to put the government in the hands of General Bonaparte and two others, to be called *Consuls*. These were to proceed, with the aid of a commission and of the "Elders," to draw up a new constitution.[1]

Bonaparte made First Consul.

The new constitution [2] was a very cumbrous and elaborate one. It provided for no less than four assemblies, one to propose the laws, one to consider them, one to vote upon them, and one to decide on their constitutionality. But Bonaparte saw to it that as First Consul he himself had practically all the power in his own hands. The Council of State, to which he called talented men from all parties and over which he presided, was the most important of the governmental bodies. This body and the administrative system which he soon established have endured, with a few changes, down to the present day. There is no surer proof of Napoleon's genius than that, with no previous experience, he could conceive a plan of government that should serve a great state like France, through all its vicissitudes, for a century.

The constitution of the year VIII.

The Council of State.

In each department he put an officer called a *prefect*, in each subdivision of the department a *subprefect*. These, together with the mayors and police commissioners of the towns, were all appointed by the First Consul. The prefects, "little First Consuls," as Bonaparte called them, resembled the intendants — the king's officers under the old régime. Indeed, the new government suggested in several important respects that of Louis XIV.

The administrative system instituted by Napoleon.

[1] Reference, Rose, *Life of Napoleon*, Vol. I, pp. 144–148.
[2] Reference, *Ibid.*, Chapter X.

The new
government
accepted by a
plebiscite.

The new ruler objected as decidedly as Louis XIV had done to the idea of being controlled by the people, who, he believed, knew nothing of public affairs. It was enough, he thought, if they were allowed to say whether they wished a certain form of government or not. He therefore introduced what he called a *plebiscite*. The new constitution when completed was submitted to the nation at large, and all were allowed to vote "yes" or "no" on the expediency of its adoption. Over three million voted in favor of it and only fifteen hundred and sixty-two against it. This did not necessarily mean, however, that practically the whole nation wished to have General Bonaparte as its ruler. A great many may have preferred what seemed to them an objectionable form of government to the risk of rejecting it. Herein lies the injustice of the plebiscite. There are many questions that cannot be answered by a simple "yes" or "no."

Bonaparte
generally
acceptable
to France as
First Consul.

Yet the accession of the popular young general to power was undoubtedly grateful to the majority of citizens, who longed above all for a stable government. The Swedish envoy wrote just after the *coup d'état:* "A legitimate monarch has perhaps never found a people more ready to do his bidding than Bonaparte, and it would be inexcusable if this talented general did not take advantage of this to introduce a better form of government upon a firmer basis. It is literally true that France will perform impossibilities in order to aid him in this. The people (with the exception of a despicable horde of anarchists) are so sick and weary of revolutionary horrors and folly that they believe that any change cannot fail to be for the better. . . . Even the royalists, whatever their views may be, are sincerely devoted to Bonaparte, for they attribute to him the intention of gradually restoring the old order of things. The indifferent element cling to him as the one most likely to give France peace. The enlightened republicans, although they tremble for their form of government, prefer to see a single man of talent possess himself of the power than a club of intriguers."

243. Upon becoming First Consul, General Bonaparte found France at war with England, Russia, Austria, Turkey, and Naples. These powers had formed a coalition in December, 1798, had defeated the armies that the Directory sent against them, and undone Bonaparte's work in Italy. It now devolved upon him to reëstablish the prestige of France abroad, as well as to restore order and prosperity at home. A successful campaign would, moreover, fill the empty treasury of the state ; for Bonaparte always exacted large contributions from the defeated enemy and from those of his allies, like the ephemeral Cisalpine republic, who were under the "protection" of France. Besides, he must keep himself before the people as a military hero if he wished to maintain his supremacy.

Necessity of renewing the war.

Early in the year 1800 Bonaparte began secretly to collect an army near Dijon. This he proposed to direct against an Austrian army which was besieging the French general, Masséna, in Genoa. Instead of marching straight into Italy, as would have been most natural, the First Consul resolved to take the Austrian forces in the rear. Emulating Hannibal, he led his troops over the famous Alpine pass of the Great St. Bernard, dragging his cannon over in the trunks of trees which had been hollowed out for the purpose. He arrived safely in Milan on the 2d of June to the utter astonishment of the Austrians, who were taken completely by surprise.

Napoleon crosses the Alps and surprises the Austrians.

Bonaparte now moved westward, but in his uncertainty as to the exact whereabouts of the Austrians, he divided his force when near the village of Marengo (June 14) and sent a contingent under Desaix southward to head off the enemy in that direction. In the meantime the whole Austrian army approached from Alessandria and the engagement began. The Austrians at first repulsed the French, and Bonaparte saw all

The battle of Marengo, June 14, 1800.

his great plans in jeopardy as he vainly besought his soldiers to make another stand. The defeat was soon turned, however, into one of the most brilliant victories; for Desaix had heard the firing and returned with his division. Meanwhile the aged and infirm Austrian commander had returned to Alessandria, supposing that the battle was won. The result was that the French troops, reënforced, returned to the attack and carried all before them. The brave Desaix, who had really saved the day, was killed; Bonaparte simply said nothing of his own temporary defeat, and added one more to the list of his great military successes. A truce was signed next day, and the Austrians retreated behind the Mincio River, leaving Bonaparte to restore French influence in Lombardy. The districts that he had "freed" had to support his army, and the reëstablished Cisalpine republic was forced to pay a monthly tax of two million francs.

A general pacification, 1801.

A victory gained by the French at Hohenlinden in December of the same year brought Austria to terms, and she agreed to conclude a separate peace with the French republic. This was the beginning of a general pacification. During the year 1801 treaties were signed with all the powers with which France had been at war, even with England, who had not laid down her arms since war was first declared in 1793.

Two most important provisions of the treaties of 1801.

Among many merely transitory results of these treaties there were two provisions of momentous import. The first of these, Spain's cession of Louisiana to France in exchange for certain advantages in Italy, does not concern us here directly.

Bonaparte sells Louisiana to the United States, 1803.

When war again broke out, Bonaparte sold the district to the United States, and among the many transfers of territory that he made during his reign, none was more important than this. We must, however, treat with some detail the second of the great changes, which led to the complete reorganization of Germany and ultimately rendered possible the establishment of the present powerful German empire.

244. In the treaty signed by Austria at Lunéville in February, 1801, the emperor agreed, on his own part and on the part of the Holy Roman Empire, that the French republic should thereafter possess in full sovereignty the territories lying on the left bank of the Rhine which belonged to the empire, and that thereafter the Rhine should form the boundary of France from the point where it left Switzerland to where it flowed into Dutch territory. As a natural consequence of this cession, various princes and states of the empire found themselves dispossessed, either wholly or in part, of their lands. The empire bound itself to furnish the hereditary princes who had lost possessions on the left bank of the Rhine with "an indemnity within the empire."

Cession of the left bank of the Rhine to France and the results for Germany.

This provision implied a veritable territorial metamorphosis of the old Holy Roman Empire, which, except for the development of Prussia, was still in pretty much the same condition as in Luther's time.[1] There was no unoccupied land to give the dispossessed princes; but there were two classes of states in the empire that did not belong to *hereditary* princes, namely, the ecclesiastical states and the free towns. As the churchmen, — archbishops, bishops, and abbots, — who ruled over the ecclesiastical states, were forbidden by the rules of the church to marry, they could of course have no lawful heirs. Should an ecclesiastical ruler be deprived of his realms, he might, therefore, be indemnified by a pension for life, with no fear of any injustice to heirs, since there could be none. The transfer of the lands of an ecclesiastical prince to a lay, i.e., hereditary, prince was called *secularization*. The towns, once so powerful and important, had lost their former influence, and seemed as much of an anomaly in the German Confederation as the ecclesiastical states.

Secularization of church lands.

Reichsdeputationshauptschluss was the high-sounding German name of the great decree issued by the imperial diet in 1803,

[1] See above, § 134.

redistributing the territory so as to indemnify the hereditary princes dispossessed by the cession of the left bank of the Rhine to France. All the ecclesiastical states, except the electorate of Mayence, were turned over to lay rulers. Of the forty-eight imperial cities, only six were left. Three of these still exist as republican members of the present German federation; namely, the Hanseatic towns, — Hamburg, Bremen, and Lübeck. Bavaria received the bishoprics of Würzburg, Bamberg, Augsburg, Freising, and a number of the imperial cities. Baden received the bishoprics of Constance, Basel, Speyer, etc. The knights who had lost their possessions on the left bank were not indemnified, and those on the right bank were deprived of their political rights within the next two or three years, by the several states within whose boundaries they lay.[1]

Disappearance of the imperial cities.

Fate of the knights.

Importance of the extinction of the smaller German states.

The final distribution was preceded by a bitter and undignified scramble among the princes for additional bits of territory. All turned to Paris for favors, since the First Consul, and not the German diet, was really the arbiter in the matter. Germany never sank to a lower degree of national degradation than at this period. But this amalgamation was, nevertheless, the beginning of her political regeneration; for without the consolidation of the hundreds of practically independent little states into a few well-organized monarchies, such a union as the present German empire would have been impossible, and the country must have remained indefinitely in its traditional impotency.

Extension of French territory.

The treaties of 1801 left France in possession of the Austrian Netherlands and the left bank of the Rhine, to which increase of territory Piedmont was soon added. Bonaparte found a further resource in the dependencies, which it was his consistent policy to create. Holland became the Batavian republic, and, with the Italian (originally the Cisalpine)

French dependencies.

[1] Reference, Rose, *Revolutionary and Napoleonic Era*, pp. 132–133.

republic, came under French control and contributed money and troops for the forwarding of French interests. The constitution of Switzerland was improved in the interests of the First Consul and, incidentally, to the great advantage of the country itself.

CHAPTER XXXVIII

EUROPE AND NAPOLEON

The demoralized condition of France, and Bonaparte's reforms.

245. The activity of the extraordinary man who had placed himself at the head of the French republic was by no means confined to the important alterations of the map of Europe described in the previous chapter. He was indefatigable in carrying out a series of internal reforms, second only in importance to those of the great Revolution of 1789. The Reign of Terror and the incompetence of the Directory's government had left France in a very bad plight.[1] Bonaparte's reorganization of the government has already been noticed. The finances, too, were in a terrible condition. These the First Consul adjusted with great skill and quickly restored the national credit.

The adjustment of relations with the pope and the church.

He then set about settling the great problem of the non-juring clergy, who were still suffering for refusing to sanction the Civil Constitution of the Clergy.[2] All imprisoned priests were now freed, on promising not to oppose the constitution. Their churches were given back to them, and the distinction between "non-juring" and "constitutional" clergymen was obliterated. Sunday, which had been abolished by the republican calendar, was once more observed, and all the revolutionary holidays except July 14, — the anniversary of the fall of the Bastile, — and the first day of the republican year, were done away with.

---

1 The roads were dilapidated and the harbors filled with sand; taxes were unpaid, robbery prevailed, and there was a general decay in industry. A manufacturer in Paris who had employed sixty to eighty workmen now had but ten. The lace, paper, and linen industries were as good as destroyed.

2 See above, pp. 572–573, 579–580.

A formal treaty with the pope, the Concordat of 1801, was concluded, which revoked some of the provisions of the Civil Constitution, especially the election of the priests and bishops by the people, and recognized the pope as the head of the church. It is noteworthy, however, that Bonaparte did not restore to the church its ancient possessions, and that he reserved to himself the right to appoint the bishops, as the former kings had done.

The Concordat of 1801.

As for the emigrant nobles, Bonaparte decreed that no more names should be added to the lists. The striking of names from the list and the return of confiscated lands that had not already been sold, he made favors to be granted by himself. Parents and relatives of emigrants were no longer to be regarded as incapable of holding public offices. In April, 1802, a general amnesty was issued, and no less than forty thousand families returned to France.

The emigrant nobles permitted to return.

There was a gradual reaction from the fantastic innovations of the Reign of Terror. The old titles of address, Monsieur and Madame, were again used instead of the revolutionary "Citizen." Streets which had been rebaptized with republican names resumed their former ones. Old titles of nobility were revived, and something very like a royal court began to develop at the Palace of the Tuilleries ; for, except in name, Bonaparte was already a king, and his wife, Josephine, a queen. It had been clear for some years that the nation was weary of political agitation. How great a blessing after the anarchy of the past to put all responsibility upon one who showed himself capable of concluding a long war with unprecedented glory for France and of reëstablishing order and the security of person and property, the necessary conditions for renewed prosperity! How natural that the French should welcome a despotism to which they had been accustomed for centuries, after suffering as they had under nominally republican institutions!

Old habits resumed.

The grateful reliance of the nation on Bonaparte.

One of the greatest and most permanent of Bonaparte's achievements still remains to be noted. The heterogeneous

The *Code Napoléon.*

laws of the old régime had been much modified by the legislation of the successive assemblies. All this needed a final revision, and Bonaparte appointed a commission to undertake this great task. Their draft of the new code was discussed in the Council of State, and the First Consul had many suggestions to make. The resulting codification of the civil law — the *Code Napoléon* — is still used to-day, not only in France, but also, with some modifications, in Rhenish Prussia, Bavaria, Baden, Holland, Belgium, Italy, and even in the state of Louisiana. The criminal and commercial law was also codified. These codes carried with them into foreign lands the principles of equality upon which they were based, and thus diffused the benefits of the Revolution beyond the borders of France.[1]

Napoleon made Consul for life, 1802; and Emperor, 1804.

Bonaparte was able gradually to modify the constitution so that his power became more and more absolute. In 1802 he was appointed Consul for life and given the right to name his successor. Even this did not satisfy his insatiable ambition, which demanded that his actual power should be clothed with all the attributes and surroundings appropriate to an hereditary ruler. In May, 1804, he was accordingly given the title of Emperor, and (in December) crowned, as the successor of Charlemagne, with great pomp in the cathedral of Notre Dame. He at once proceeded to establish a new nobility to take the place of that abolished by the first National Assembly in 1790.

Napoleon's censorship of the press.

From this time on he became increasingly tyrannical and hostile to criticism. At the very beginning of his administration he had suppressed a great part of the numerous political newspapers and forbidden the establishment of new ones. As emperor he showed himself still more exacting. His police furnished the news to the papers and carefully omitted all that might offend their suspicious master. He ordered the journals to "put in quarantine all news that might be disadvantageous or disagreeable to France." His ideal was to

[1] Reference, Rose, *Life of Napoleon*, Vol. I, Chapter XII.

suppress all newspapers but one, which should be used for official purposes.

246. A great majority of the French undoubtedly longed for peace, but Napoleon's position made war a personal necessity for him. No one saw this more clearly than he. "If," he said to his Council of State in the summer of 1802, "the European states intend ever to renew the war, the sooner it comes the better. Every day the remembrance of their defeats grows dimmer and at the same time the prestige of our victories pales.... France needs glorious deeds, and hence war. She must be the first among the states, or she is lost. I shall put up with peace as long as our neighbors

Napoleon on the necessity of war for France.

Napoleon

can maintain it, but I shall regard it as an advantage if they force me to take up my arms again before they are rusted. . . . In our position I shall look on each conclusion of peace as simply a short armistice, and I regard myself as destined during my term of office to fight almost without intermission."

On another occasion, in 1804, Napoleon said, "There will be no rest in Europe until it is under a single chief — an emperor who shall have kings for officers, who shall distribute kingdoms to his lieutenants,. and shall make this one king of Italy, that one of Bavaria ; this one ruler of Switzerland, that one governor of Holland, each having an office of honor in the

Napoleon dreams of becoming emperor of Europe.

imperial household." This was the ideal that he now found himself in a situation to carry out with marvelous exactness.

Reasons for England's persistent opposition to Napoleon.

There were many reasons why the peace with England (concluded at Amiens in March, 1802) should be speedily broken, especially as the First Consul was not averse to a renewal of the war. The obvious intention of Napoleon to bring as much of Europe under his control as he could, and the imposition of high duties on English goods in those territories that he already controlled, filled commercial and industrial England with apprehension. The English people longed for peace, but peace appeared only to offer an opportunity to the Corsican usurper to ruin England by a continuous war upon her commerce. This was the secret of England's pertinacity. All the other European powers concluded peace with Napoleon at some time during his reign. England alone did not lay down her arms a second time until the emperor of the French was a prisoner.

War between France and England renewed in 1803. Napoleon institutes a coast blockade.

247. War was renewed between England and France in 1803. Bonaparte promptly occupied Hanover, of which it will be remembered that the English king was elector, and declared the coast blockaded from Hanover to Otranto. Holland, Spain, Portugal, and the Ligurian republic — formerly the republic of Genoa — were, by hook or by crook, induced to agree to furnish each their contingent of men or money to the French army and to exclude English ships from their ports.

Napoleon threatens to invade England.

To cap the climax, England was alarmed by the appearance of a French army at Boulogne, just across the Channel. A great number of flatboats were collected, and troops trained to embark and disembark. Apparently Napoleon harbored the firm purpose of invading the British Isles. Yet the transportation of a large body of troops across the English Channel, trifling as is the distance, would have been very hazardous, and by many it was deemed downright impossible. No one knows whether Napoleon really expected to make the trial.

It is quite possible that his main purpose in collecting an army at Boulogne was to have it in readiness for the continental war which he saw immediately ahead of him. He succeeded, at any rate, in terrifying England, who prepared to defend herself.

The Tsar, Alexander I, had submitted a plan for the reconciliation of France and England in August, 1803. The rejection of this and the evident intention of Napoleon to include the eastern coast of the Adriatic in his sphere of influence, led Russia to join a new coalition which, by July, 1805, included Austria, Sweden, and, of course, England. Austria was especially affected by the increase of Napoleon's power in Italy. He had been crowned king of Italy in May, 1805, had created a little duchy in northern Italy for his sister, and had annexed the Ligurian republic to France. There were rumors, too, that he was planning to seize the Venetian territories of Austria. Coalition of Russia, Austria, England, and Sweden. Napoleon king of Italy.

War was declared against Austria, August 23, and four days later the army at Boulogne was ordered eastward. One of the Austrian commanders exhibited the most startling incapacity in allowing himself to be shut up in Ulm, where he was forced to capitulate with all his troops (October 20). Napoleon then marched down the Danube with little opposition, and before the middle of November Vienna was in the possession of French troops. Napoleon thereupon led his forces north to meet the allied armies of Austria and Russia; these he defeated on December 2, in the terrible winter battle of Austerlitz. Russia then withdrew for a time and signed an armistice; and Austria was obliged to submit to a humiliating peace, the Treaty of Pressburg. The war of 1805. Occupation of Vienna. Battle of Austerlitz, December 2, 1805.

By this treaty Austria recognized all Napoleon's changes in Italy, and ceded to his kingdom of Italy that portion of the Venetian territory that she had received at Campo-Formio. Moreover, she ceded Tyrol to Bavaria, which was friendly to Napoleon, and other of her possessions to Würtemberg and The Treaty of Pressburg.

Baden, also friends of the French emperor. She further agreed to ratify the assumption, on the part of the rulers of Bavaria and Würtemberg, of the titles of King. Napoleon was now in a position still further to reorganize western Europe, with a view to establishing a great international federation of which he should be the head.[1]

248. Napoleon had no desire to unify Germany; he merely wished to maintain a certain number of independent states, or groups of states, which he could conveniently control. He had provided, in the Treaty of Pressburg, that the newly created sovereigns should enjoy the "plenitude of sovereignty" and all the rights derived therefrom, precisely as did the rulers of Austria and Prussia.

The dissolution of the Holy Roman Empire, 1806.

This, by explicitly declaring several of the most important of the German states altogether independent of the emperor, rendered the further existence of the Holy Roman Empire impossible. The emperor, Francis II, accordingly abdicated, August 6, 1806. Thus the most imposing and enduring political office known to history was formally abolished.

Francis II assumes the title of 'Emperor of Austria.'

Francis II did not, however, lose his title of Emperor. Shortly after the First Consul had received that title, Francis adopted the formula "Emperor of Austria," to designate him as the ruler of all the possessions of his house. Hitherto he had been officially known as King of Hungary, Bohemia, Dalmatia, Croatia, Galicia, and Laodomeria, Duke of Lorraine, Venice, Salzburg, etc., Grand Duke of Transylvania, Margrave of Moravia, etc.

The Confederation of the Rhine.

Meanwhile Napoleon had organized a union of the southern German states, called the Confederation of the Rhine, and had assumed its headship as "Protector." This he had done, he assured Europe, "in the dearest interests of his people and of his neighbors," adding the pious hope that the French armies had crossed the Rhine for the last time, and that the people

[1] Reference, Rose, *Revolutionary and Napoleonic Era*, pp. 148–163.

of Germany would witness no longer, " except in the annals of the past, the horrible pictures of disorder, devastation, and slaughter that war invariably brings with it." [1]

Immediately after the battle of Austerlitz, Napoleon proclaimed that the king of Naples, who had allied himself with the English, had ceased to reign, and French generals were ordered to occupy Naples. In March, 1806, he made his brother Joseph king of Naples and Sicily, his brother Louis king of Holland, and his brother-in-law, Murat, duke of Cleves and Berg. These states and those of his German allies constituted what he called " the real French Empire."

249. One of the most important of the continental states, it will have been noticed, had taken no part as yet in the opposition to the extension of Napoleon's power. Prussia, the first power to conclude peace with the new French republic in 1795, had since that time maintained a strict neutrality. Had it yielded to Tsar Alexander's persuasions and joined the coalition in 1805, it might have turned the tide at Austerlitz, or at any rate have encouraged further resistance to the conqueror. The hesitation of Frederick William III cost him dear, for Napoleon now forced him into war at a time when he could look for no efficient assistance from Russia or the other powers. The immediate cause of the declaration of war was the disposal of Hanover. This electorate Frederick William had consented to hold provisionally, pending its possible transfer to him should the English king give his assent. Prussia was anxious to get possession of Hanover because it lay just between her older possessions and the territory which she had gained in the redistribution of 1803.[2]

Prussia forced into war with France.

Napoleon, as usual, did not fail either to see or to use his advantage. His conduct toward Prussia was most insolent. After setting her at enmity with England and promising that

Napoleon's insolent behavior toward Prussia.

[1] See *Translations and Reprints*, Vol. II, No. 2.
[2] See above, p. 604.

she should have Hanover, he unblushingly offered to restore the electorate to George III. His insults now began to arouse the national spirit in Prussia, and the reluctant Frederick William was forced by the party in favor of war, which included his beautiful queen Louise, and the great statesman Stein, to break with Napoleon.

Decisive defeat of the Prussian army at Jena, 1806.

Her army was, however, as has been well said, "only that of Frederick the Great grown twenty years older"; one of Frederick's generals, the aged duke of Brunswick, who had issued the famous manifesto in 1792,[1] was its leader. A single defeat, near Jena (October 14, 1806), put Prussia completely in the hands of her enemy. This one disaster produced complete demoralization throughout the country. Fortresses were surrendered without resistance, and the king fled to the uttermost parts of his realm on the Russian boundary.

The campaign in Poland. Territorial changes of the treaties of Tilsit, July, 1807.

Napoleon now led his army into Poland, where he spent the winter in operations against Russia and her feeble Prussian ally. He closed an arduous campaign by a signal victory at Friedland (June 14, 1807), which was followed by the treaties of Tilsit with Russia and Prussia (July 7 and 9). Napoleon had no mercy on Prussia. Frederick William III lost all his possessions to the west of the Elbe and all that Prussia had gained in the second and third partitions of Poland. The Polish territory Napoleon made into a new subject kingdom called the grand duchy of Warsaw, and chose his friend, the king of Saxony, as its ruler. Out of the western lands of Prussia, which he later united with Hanover, he created the kingdom of Westphalia for his brother Jerome. Russia, on the other hand, was treated with marked consideration. The Tsar finally consented to recognize all the sweeping territorial changes that Napoleon had made, and secretly agreed to enforce the blockade against England should that country refuse to make peace.

Creation of the grand duchy of Warsaw and the kingdom of Westphalia.

[1] See above, p. 581.

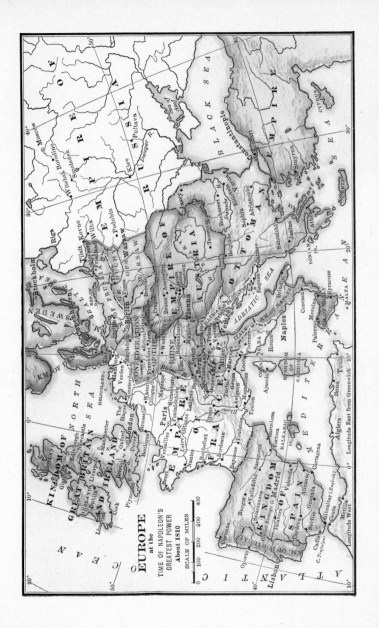

EUROPE
at the
TIME OF NAPOLEON'S
GREATEST POWER
About 1810

SCALE OF MILES
0   100   200   300   400

250. Napoleon's most persevering enemy still remained unconquered and inaccessible. Just as Napoleon was undertaking his successful campaign against Austria in 1805, Nelson had annihilated the French fleet for the second time in the renowned naval engagement of Trafalgar, off the coast of Spain. It seemed more than ever necessary, therefore, to ruin England commercially and industrially, since there was obviously no likelihood of subduing it by arms.

The continental blockade.

In May, 1806, England had declared the coast from the Elbe to Brest to be blockaded. Napoleon replied to this with the Berlin Decree (November 21, 1806), in which he proclaimed it a monstrous abuse of the right for England to declare great stretches of coast in a state of blockade which her whole fleet would be unable to enforce. He retaliated with a " paper "[1] blockade of the British Isles, which forbade all commerce with them. Letters or packages directed to England or to an Englishman or written in the English language were not to be permitted to pass through the mails in the countries he controlled. Every English subject in countries occupied by French troops or in the territory of Napoleon's allies was to be regarded as a prisoner of war and his property as a lawful prize. All trade in English goods was forbidden.

The Berlin Decree and Napoleon's ' paper ' blockade.

A year later England established a similar paper blockade of the ports of the French empire and its allies, but permitted the ships of neutral powers to proceed, provided that they touched at an English port, secured a license from the English government, and paid a heavy export duty. Napoleon promptly declared all ships that submitted to these humiliating regulations to be lawful prizes of French privateers. The ships of the United States were at this time the most numerous and important of the neutral carriers. The disastrous results of these restrictions led to the various embargo acts (the first of

Disastrous effects of the blockades on the commerce of the United States.

[1] That is, a blockade too extensive to be really carried out by the ships at the disposal of the power proclaiming it.

which was passed by Congress in December, 1807), and ultimately to the destruction of the flourishing carrying trade of the United States.

Napoleon's attempt to make the continent independent of English colonial products.

Napoleon tried to render Europe permanently independent of the colonial productions brought from English colonies and by English ships. He encouraged the substitution of chicory for coffee, the cultivation of the sugar beet, and the discovery of new dyes to replace those coming from the tropics. But the distress caused by the disturbance in trade produced great discontent, especially in Russia ; it rendered the domination of Napoleon more and more distasteful, and finally contributed to his downfall.[1]

Napoleon's policy in France.

251. France owed much to Napoleon, for he had restored order and guaranteed many of the beneficent achievements of the Revolution of 1789. His boundless ambition was, it is true, sapping her strength by forcing younger and younger men into his armies in order to build up the vast international federation of which he dreamed. But his victories and the commanding position to which he had raised France could not but fill the nation with pride.

Public works.

He sought to gain popular approval by great public improvements. He built marvelous roads across the Alps and along the Rhine, which still fill the traveler with admiration. He beautified Paris by opening up wide streets and quays, and building magnificent bridges and triumphal arches that kept fresh in the people's mind the recollection of his victories. By these means he gradually converted a mediæval town into the most beautiful of modern capitals.

Reorganization of education.

The whole educational system was reorganized and made as highly centralized and as subservient to the aims of the emperor as any department of government. Napoleon argued

---

[1] Reference, Rose, *Life of Napoleon*, Vol. II, pp. 197-207. For documents relating to the blockade and " the Continental system," see *Translations and Reprints*, Vol. II, No. 2.

that one of the chief aims of education should be the formation of loyal subjects who would be faithful to the emperor and his successors. An imperial catechism was prepared, which not only inculcated loyalty to Napoleon, but actually threatened with eternal perdition those who should fail in their obligations to him, including military service.[1]

Napoleon created a new nobility, and he endeavored to assure the support of distinguished individuals by making them members of the Legion of Honor which he founded. The "Princes" whom he nominated received an annual income of two hundred thousand francs. The ministers of state, senators, members of his Council of State, and the archbishops received the title of Count and a revenue of thirty thousand francs, and so on. The army was not forgotten, for Napoleon felt that to be his chief support. The incomes of his marshals were enormous, and brave actions among the soldiers were rewarded with the decoration of the Legion of Honor.

The new nobility and the Legion of Honor.

As time went on Napoleon's despotism grew more and more oppressive. No less than thirty-five hundred prisoners of state were arrested at his command, one because he hated Napoleon, another because in his letters he expressed sentiments adverse to the government, and so on. No grievance was too petty to attract the attention of the emperor's jealous eye. He ordered the title of a *History of Bonaparte* to be changed to the *History of the Campaigns of Napoleon the Great*.[2] He forbade

Napoleon's despotism in France.

---

[1] See *Readings*, Chapter XXXVIII.

[2] Napoleon was never content with his achievements or his glory. On the day of his coronation, December, 1806, he complained to his minister Decrès that he had been born too late, that there was nothing great to be done any more. On his minister's remonstrating he added: "I admit that my career has been brilliant and that I have made a good record. But what a difference is there if we compare ours with ancient times. Take Alexander the Great, for example. After announcing himself the son of Jupiter, the whole East, except his mother, Aristotle, and a few Athenian pedants, believed this to be true. But now, should I nowadays declare myself the son of the Eternal Father, there is n't a fishwife who would not hiss me. No, the nations are too sophisticated, there is nothing great any longer possible."

the performance of certain of Schiller's and Goethe's plays in German towns, as tending to arouse the patriotic discontent of the people with his rule.

252. Up to this time Napoleon had had only the opposition of the several European courts to overcome in the extension of his power. The people of the various states which he had conquered showed an extraordinary indifference toward the political changes. It was clear, however, that as soon as the national spirit was once awakened, the highly artificial system created by the French emperor would collapse. His first serious reverse came from the people and from an unexpected quarter.

Napoleon's European power threatened by the growth of national opposition to him.

Napoleon decided, after Tilsit, that the Spanish peninsula must be brought more completely under his control. Portugal was too friendly to the English, and Spain, owing to serious dissensions in the royal family, seemed an easy prey. In the spring of 1808 Napoleon induced both the king and the crown prince of Spain to meet him at Bayonne. Here he was able to persuade or force both of them to surrender their rights to the throne; on June 6 he appointed his brother Joseph king of Spain, making Murat king of Naples in his stead.

Napoleon makes his brother Joseph king of Spain.

Joseph entered Madrid in July, armed with excellent intentions and a new constitution. The general rebellion in favor of the crown prince which immediately broke out had an element of religious enthusiasm in it, for the monks stirred up the people against Napoleon, on the ground that he was oppressing the pope and depriving him of his dominions. One French army was captured at Baylen, and another capitulated to the English forces which had landed in Portugal. Before the end of July Joseph and the French troops had been compelled to retreat behind the Ebro River.

Revolt in Spain against the foreign ruler.

In November the French emperor himself led a magnificent army into Spain, two hundred thousand strong, in the best of condition and commanded by his ablest marshals. The

Spain subdued by arms.

Spanish troops, perhaps one hundred thousand in number, were ill clad and inadequately equipped; what was worse, they were over-confident in view of their late victory. They were, of course, defeated, and Madrid surrendered December 4. Napoleon immediately abolished the Inquisition, the feudal dues, the internal customs lines, and two thirds of the cloisters. This is typical of the way in which the French Revolution went forth in arms to spread its principles throughout western Europe.

The next month Napoleon was back in Paris, as he saw that he had another war with Austria on his hands. He left Joseph on his insecure throne, after assuring the Spanish that God had given the French emperor the power and the will to overcome all obstacles.[1] He was soon to discover, however, that these very Spaniards could maintain a guerilla warfare against which his best troops and most distinguished generals were powerless. His ultimate downfall was in no small measure due to the persistent hostility of the Spanish people.

In April, 1809, Austria ventured to declare war once more on the " enemy of Europe," but this time she found no one to aid her. The great battle of Wagram, near Vienna (July 5-6), was not perhaps so unconditional a victory for the French as that of Austerlitz, but it forced Austria into just as humiliating a peace as that of Pressburg. Austria's object had been to destroy Napoleon's system of dependencies and "to restore to their rightful possessors all those lands belonging to them respectively before the Napoleonic usurpations." Instead of accomplishing this end, Austria was obliged to cede more territory to Napoleon and his allies, and he went on adding to his

War with Austria, 1809. Battle of Wagram.

---

[1] "It depends upon you alone," he said to the Spanish in his proclamation of December 7, " whether this moderate constitution that I offer you shall henceforth be your law. Should all my efforts prove vain, and should you refuse to justify my confidence, then nothing remains for me but to treat you as a conquered province and find a new throne for my brother. In that case I shall myself assume the crown of Spain and teach the ill-disposed to respect that crown, for God has given me power and will to overcome all obstacles."

dependencies.   After incorporating into France the kingdom
of Etruria and the papal dominions (1808–1809), Napoleon

Extension of the boundaries of France. was encouraged by his victory over Austria to annex Holland [1]
and the German districts to the north, including the Hanseatic
towns.   Consequently, in 1810 France stretched from the confines of Naples to the Baltic.   One might travel from Lübeck
to Rome without leaving Napoleon's realms.

Napoleon was anxious to have an heir to whom he could
transmit his vast dominions.   As Josephine bore him no
children, he decided to divorce her, and after considering a
Russian princess, he married the Archduchess Maria Louisa,
the daughter of the Austrian emperor and a grandniece of
Marie Antoinette.   In this way the former Corsican adventurer gained admission to one of the oldest and proudest of
reigning families, the Hapsburgs.   His new wife soon bore
him a son, who was styled King of Rome.

Relations between Napoleon and Alexander I of Russia. 253.   Among the continental states Russia alone was entirely
out of Napoleon's control.   There were plenty of causes for
misunderstanding between the ardent young Tsar Alexander I
and Napoleon.   Up to this time the agreement of Tilsit had
been maintained.   Napoleon was, however, secretly opposing
Alexander's plans for adding the Danubian provinces and
Finland to his possessions.   Then the possibility of Napoleon's
reëstablishing Poland as a national kingdom which might
threaten Russia's interests, was a constant source of apprehension to Alexander.   By 1812 Napoleon believed himself
to be in a condition to subdue this doubtful friend, who might
at any moment become a dangerous enemy.   Against the
advice of his more far-sighted counselors, the emperor collected on the Russian frontier a vast army of four hundred

---

[1] Reference, Rose, *Revolutionary and Napoleonic Era*, pp. 193–201.   Louis
Bonaparte, the father of Napoleon III, and the most conscientious of the Bonaparte family, had been so harassed by his imperial brother that he had abdicated
as king of Holland.

thousand men, composed to a great extent of young conscripts and the contingents furnished by his allies.

The story of the fearful Russian campaign which followed cannot be told here in detail. Napoleon had planned to take three years to conquer Russia, but he was forced on by the necessity of gaining at least one signal victory before he closed the season's campaign. The Russians simply retreated and led him far within a hostile and devastated country before they offered battle at Borodino (September 7). Napoleon won the battle, but his army was reduced to something over one hundred thousand men when he entered Moscow a week later. The town had been set on fire by the Russians before his arrival; he found his position untenable, and had to retreat as winter came on. The cold, the want of food, and the harassing attacks of the people along the route made that retreat the most signal military tragedy on record. Napoleon regained Poland early in December with scarcely twenty thousand of the four hundred thousand with which he had started less than six months before.[1]

Napoleon hastened back to Paris, where he freely misrepresented the true state of affairs, even declaring that the army was in a good condition up to the time that he turned it over to Murat in December. While the loss of men in the Russian campaign was enormous, just those few had naturally survived who would be most essential in the formation of a new army, namely, the officers. With their help, Napoleon soon had a force of no less than six hundred thousand men with which to return to the attack. This contained one hundred and fifty thousand conscripts who should not have been called into service until 1814, besides older men who had been hitherto exempted.

254. By the end of February, 1813, the timid Frederick William had been induced by public sentiment in Prussia to

Napoleon's campaign in Russia, 1812.

Napoleon collects a new army

[1] Reference, Rose, *Life of Napoleon*, Vol. II, Chapter XXXII.

break with his oppressor and join Russia. On March 17, he issued a famous address "To my People," in which he called upon them to assist him in the recovery of Prussian independence. Up to the defeat of Jena, Prussia was far more backward in its social organization than France had been before 1789. The agricultural classes were serfs, who were bound to the land and compelled to work a certain part of each week for the lord without remuneration.[1] The population was divided into strict social castes. Moreover, no noble could buy citizen or peasant land ; no citizen, noble or peasant land ; no peasant, noble or citizen land.

The disaster of Jena and the losses at Tilsit convinced the clearer-sighted statesmen of Prussia, especially Stein, that the country's only hope of recovery was a complete social and political revolution, not unlike that which had taken place in France. They saw that the feudal system must be abolished, the peasants freed, and the restrictions which hedged about the different classes done away with, before it would be possible to arouse public spirit to a point where a great popular uprising might expel the intruder forever.

The first great step toward this general reform was the royal decree of October 9, 1807,[2] intended to "remove every obstacle that has hitherto prevented the individual from attaining such a degree of prosperity as he was capable of reaching." Serfdom was abolished and the restrictions on landholding removed, so that any one, regardless of class, was at liberty to purchase and hold landed property of every kind. In some cases the principles of the French Revolution had been introduced by Napoleon or the rulers that he set up. In this case it was the necessity of preparing the country to throw off his yoke and regain its independence that led to the same result.

---

[1] See above, p. 544.
[2] This decree may be found in *Translations and Reprints*, Vol. II, No. 2.

255. Napoleon had therefore to face now, not only the cabinets of Europe and the regular armies that they directed, but a people who were being organized to defend their country. His soldiers were, however, still triumphant for a time. He met with no successful opposition, and on May 14, 1813, he occupied Dresden in the territory of his faithful ally, the king of Saxony. This he held during the summer, and inflicted several defeats upon the allies, who had been joined by Austria in August. He gained his last great victory, the battle of Dresden, August 26–27. Finding that the allied armies of the Russians, Prussians, and Austrians, which had at last learned the necessity of coöperating against their powerful common enemy, were preparing to cut him off from France, he retreated early in October and was totally defeated in the tremendous "Battle of the Nations," as the Germans love to call it, in the environs of Leipsic (October 16–19).

Napoleon defeated by the allied Russians, Prussians, and Austrians, October, 1813.

Battle of Leipsic, October 16-19, 1813.

As the defeated emperor crossed the Rhine with the remnants of his army, the whole fabric of his political edifice in Germany and Holland collapsed. The members of the Confederation of the Rhine joined the allies. Jerome Bonaparte fled from his kingdom of Westphalia, and the Dutch drove the French officials from Holland. During the year 1813 the Spanish, with the aid of the English under Wellington, had practically cleared their country of the French intruders.

Germany, Holland, and Spain throw off the Napoleonic yoke.

In spite of these disasters, Napoleon refused the propositions of peace made on condition that he would content himself henceforth with his dominion over France. The allies consequently marched into France, and the almost superhuman activity of the hard-pressed emperor could not prevent their occupation of Paris (March 31, 1814). Napoleon was forced to abdicate, and the allies, in seeming derision, granted him full sovereignty over the tiny island of Elba and permitted him to retain his imperial title. In reality he was a prisoner on his island kingdom, and the Bourbons reigned again in France.

Occupation of Paris by the allies, March 31, 1814.

Napoleon abdicates and is banished to the island of Elba.

Within a year, encouraged by the dissensions of the allies and the unpopularity of the Bourbons, he made his escape, landed in France (March 1, 1815), and was received with enthusiasm by a portion of the army. Yet France as a whole was indifferent, if not hostile, to his attempt to reëstablish his power. Certainly no one could place confidence in his talk of peace and liberty. Moreover, whatever disagreement there might be among the allies on other matters, there was perfect unanimity in their attitude toward " the enemy and destroyer of the world's peace." They solemnly proclaimed him an outlaw, and devoted him to public vengeance.

Upon learning that English troops under Wellington and a Prussian army under Blücher had arrived in the Netherlands, Napoleon decided to attack them with such troops as he could collect. In the first engagements he defeated and drove back the Prussians. Wellington then took his station south of Brussels, at Waterloo. Napoleon advanced against him (June 18, 1815) and might have defeated the English had they not been opportunely reënforced by Blücher's Prussians, who had recovered themselves. As it was, Napoleon lost the most memorable of modern battles. Yet, even if he had not been defeated at Waterloo, he could not long have opposed the vast armies which were being concentrated to overthrow him. This time he was banished to the remote island of Saint Helena, where he could only brood over the past and prepare his *Memoirs*, in which he carefully strove to justify his career of ambition.[1]

General Reading. — Of the many lives of Napoleon the best and most recent are the following: FOURNIER, *Life of Napoleon* (a translation of this work from the original German, edited by E. G. Bourne, is announced by Holt & Co.); ROSE, *Life of Napoleon the First* (The Macmillan Company, 2 vols., $4.00). The fullest biography of Napoleon is that of SLOANE, *Life of Napoleon Bonaparte* (The Century Co., 4 vols., $18). An excellent sketch of the military history may be found in ROPES, *The First Napoleon* (Houghton, Mifflin & Co., $2.00).

[1] Reference, Rose, *Revolutionary and Napoleonic Era*, pp. 335–361.

CHAPTER XXXIX

EUROPE AFTER THE CONGRESS OF VIENNA

256. There is no more important chapter in the political history of Europe than the reconstruction of the map after Napoleon's abdication. The allies immediately reinstated the Bourbon dynasty on the throne of France in the person of Louis XVI's younger brother, the count of Provence, who became Louis XVIII.[1] They first restricted France to the boundaries that she had had at the beginning of 1792, but later deprived her of Savoy as a punishment for yielding to the domination of Napoleon after his return from Elbe. A great congress of the European powers was summoned to meet at Vienna, where the allies proposed to settle all those difficult problems that faced them. They had no idea of reëstablishing things just as they were before the Napoleonic cataclysm, for the simple reason that Austria, Russia, and Prussia all had schemes for their own advantage that precluded so simple an arrangement.

Problem of the reconstruction of Europe after Napoleon's fall.

The Congress of Vienna began its sessions November 1, 1814. The allies quickly agreed that Holland should become an hereditary kingdom under the house of Orange, which had long played so conspicuous a rôle in the nominal republic. In order that Holland might be the better able to check any new encroachments on the part of France, the former Austrian Netherlands were given to her. Switzerland was declared

Provisions of the Congress of Vienna in regard to the Netherlands, Switzerland, Italy, and Germany.

---

[1] The son of Louis XVI had been imprisoned and maltreated by the terrorists. He died while still a boy in 1795, but nevertheless takes his place in the line of French kings as Louis XVII.

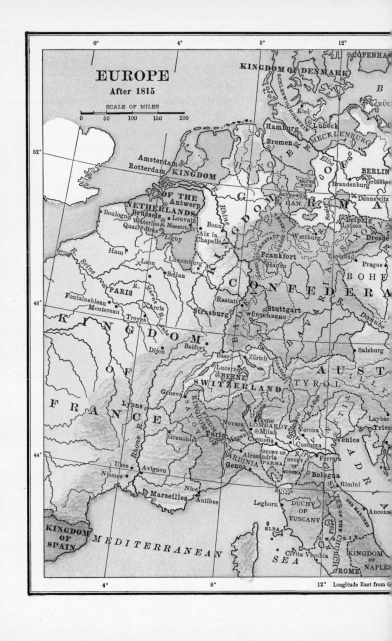

EUROPE

After 1815

SCALE OF MILES
0   50   100   150   200

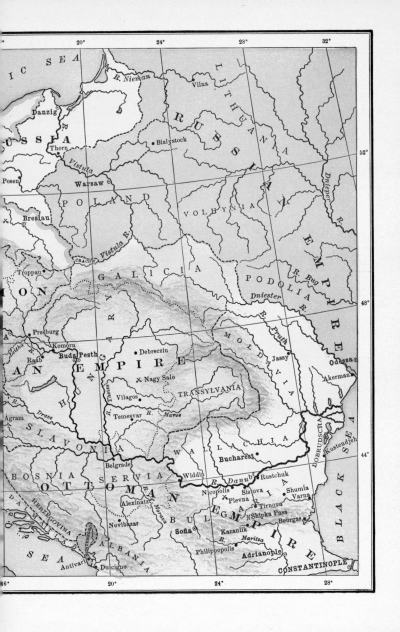

matters to suit themselves. But they were now hopelessly at odds, and Austria and England found France a welcome ally in their opposition to the northern powers. So in this way the disturber of the peace of Europe for the last quarter of a century was received back into the family of nations.

A compromise was at last reached. The Tsar was allowed to create a kingdom of Poland out of the grand duchy of Warsaw, but only half of the possessions of the king of Saxony were ceded to Prussia. As a further indemnity, Frederick William III was given certain districts on the left bank of the Rhine which had belonged to ecclesiastical and petty lay princes before the Treaty of Lunéville. The great importance of this arrangement we shall see later when we come to trace the development of the present German empire.

The compromise.

If one compares the map of Europe in 1815 with that of the present day,[1] he will be struck with the following differences. In 1815 there was no German empire, and Prussia was a much smaller and less compact state than now. It has evidently grown at the expense of its neighbors, as several of the lesser German states of 1815, — Hanover, Nassau, and Hesse-Cassel, — no longer appear on the map, and Schleswig-Holstein, which then belonged to Denmark, is now Prussian. It will be noted that the present German empire does not include any part of the Austrian countries, as did the Confederation of 1815, and that, on the other hand, it does include all of Prussia. The kingdom of Poland has become an integral part of the Russian dominions. Austria, excluded from the German union, has entered into a dual union with Hungary, in which the two countries are placed upon the same footing.

Changes in the map of Europe since 1815.

There was no kingdom of Italy in 1815. Now Austria has lost all hold on Lombardy and Venetia, and all the little states reëstablished by the Congress of Vienna, including the Papal States, have disappeared. A new kingdom, Belgium, has been

1 Compare the accompanying map with that below, pp. 666–667.

created out of the old Austrian·Netherlands which the congress gave to the king of Holland. France, now a republic again, has recovered Savoy, but has lost all her possessions on the Rhine by the cession of Alsace and Lorraine to the German empire. Lastly, Turkey in Europe has nearly disappeared, and several new states, Greece, Servia, Roumania, and Bulgaria, have appeared in southeastern Europe. It is the purpose of the following chapters to show how the great changes indicated on the map took place and explain the accompanying internal changes, in so far as they represent the general trend of modern development or have an importance for Europe at large.

Influence of Napoleon in spreading the reforms achieved by the Revolution.

257. Napoleon had been as thoroughly despotic in his government as any of the monarchs who regained their thrones after his downfall, but he was a son of the Revolution and had no sympathy with the ancient abuses that it had done away with. In spite of his despotism the people of the countries that had come under his influence had learned the great lessons of the French Revolution. Nevertheless, the restored monarchs in many of the smaller European states proceeded to reëstablish the ancient feudal abuses and to treat their subjects as if there had been no French Revolution and no such man as Napoleon. In Spain, for example, the Inquisition and the monasteries were restored and the clergy exempted anew from taxation. In Hesse-Cassel, which had formed a part of the kingdom of Westphalia, all the reforms introduced by Napoleon and his brother were abolished. The privileges of the nobility, and also the feudal burdens of the peasantry, were restored. The soldiers were even required to assume the discarded pigtails and powdered wigs of the eighteenth century. In Sardinia and Naples the returning monarchs pursued the same policy of reaction. The reaction was not so sudden and obvious in the greater European states, — France, Prussia, Austria, and Russia.

Reactionary policy in the smaller states of Europe.

258. The French had aroused themselves in 1793–1794 to repel the foreign powers, Austria and Prussia, who threatened to intervene in the domestic concerns of the country, and to reëstablish the old régime. Twenty years later, in 1814, when the allies entered Paris, there was no danger either of a popular uprising, or of the reëstablishment of the old abuses. It is true that the Bourbon line of kings was restored ; but France had always been monarchical at heart. It was only the ill-advised conduct of Louis XVI in the peculiar circumstances of 1791–1792 that had led to his deposition and the establishment of a republic, which Napoleon had easily converted into a monarchy. The new king, Louis XVIII, left the wonderful administrative system of Napoleon intact and made no effort to destroy the great achievements of the Revolution. He granted the nation a constitution called the "Charter," which is a most interesting document from two standpoints.

The restoration of the Bourbons in France.

Policy of Louis XVIII, 1814–1824.

In the first place, the provisions of the Charter of 1814 furnish us with a statement of the permanent results of the Revolution. The concessions that Louis XVIII found it expedient to make, " in view of the expectations of enlightened Europe," help us to measure the distance that separates his time from that of his elder brother. In the second place, no other constitution has yet lasted the French so long as did the Charter.[1] Although somewhat modified in 1830, it was maintained down to 1848.

The Charter of 1814.

All Frenchmen are declared by the Charter to be equal before the law, and equally eligible to civil and military positions. Personal and religious liberty is insured, and all citizens, without distinction of rank, are required to contribute to the taxes in proportion to their means. In short, almost all the great reforms proclaimed by the first Declaration of the Rights of Man are guaranteed. The laws are to be made by

[1] This document may be found in *Translations and Reprints*, Vol. I, No. 3.

the king in coöperation with a House of Peers and a popular body, the Chamber of Deputies; the latter may impeach the king's ministers.

Policy of the reactionary party in France.

In spite of these enlightened provisions attempts were made by the old emigrant nobles — still led by their original leader, the king's brother, the count of Artois — and by the clergy, to further a reaction in France. This party induced the French *parlement* to pass certain oppressive measures, and, as we shall see, persuaded Louis XVIII to coöperate with the other reactionary rulers in interfering to quell the revolutionary movements in Italy and Spain.

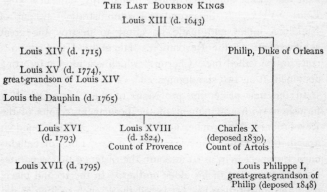

THE LAST BOURBON KINGS

Louis XIII (d. 1643)

Louis XIV (d. 1715)   Philip, Duke of Orleans

Louis XV (d. 1774),
great-grandson of Louis XIV

Louis the Dauphin (d. 1765)

Louis XVI   Louis XVIII   Charles X
(d. 1793)   (d. 1824),   (deposed 1830),
                   Count of Provence   Count of Artois

Louis XVII (d. 1795)   Louis Philippe I,
                                        great-great-grandson of
                                        Philip (deposed 1848)

Charles X deposed in 1830 and replaced by Louis Philippe.

In 1824 Louis XVIII died and was succeeded by the count of Artois, who took the title of Charles X. Under his rule the reactionary policy of the government naturally became more pronounced. A bill was passed indemnifying the nobility for the property they had lost during the Revolution. Other less just measures led to the dethronement of the unpopular king in 1830, by a revolution. Louis Philippe, the descendant of Henry IV through the younger, or Orleans, branch of the Bourbon family, was put upon the throne.[1]

[1] Reference, Andrews, *Modern Europe*, Vol. I, Chapter IV.

259. The chief effects of the Napoleonic occupation of Germany were three in number. First, the consolidation of territory that followed the cession of the left bank of the Rhine to France had, as has been explained, done away with the anomalous ecclesiastical states, the territories of knights, and most of the free towns. Only thirty-eight German states, including four towns, were left when the Congress of Vienna took up the question of forming a confederation to replace the defunct Holy Roman Empire.

Three chief results of Napoleon's influence in Germany.

Disappearance of most of the little states.

Second, the external and internal conditions of Prussia had been so changed as to open the way for it to replace Austria as the controlling power in Germany. A great part of the Slavic possessions gained in the last two partitions of Poland had been lost, but as an indemnity Prussia had received half of the kingdom of Saxony, in the very center of Germany, and also the Rhine provinces, where the people were thoroughly imbued with the revolutionary doctrines that had prevailed in France. Prussia now embraced all the various types of people included in the German nation and was comparatively free from the presence of non-German races. In this respect it offered a marked contrast to the heterogeneous and mongrel population of its great rival Austria.

Advantageous position of Prussia.

The internal changes were no less remarkable. The reforms carried out after Jena by the distinguished minister Stein and his successor, Hardenberg, had done for Prussia somewhat the same that the first National Assembly had done for France. The abolition of the feudal social castes, and the liberation of the serfs made the economic development of the country possible. The reorganization of the whole military system prepared the way for Prussia's great victories in 1866 and 1870, which led to the formation of a new German empire under her headship.

Third, the agitations of the Napoleonic period had aroused the national spirit. The appeal to the people to aid in the

Demand for
constitu-
tional gov-
ernment.

freeing of their country from foreign oppression, and the idea of their participation in a government based upon a written constitution, had produced widespread discontent with the old absolute monarchy.

The German
Confedera-
tion of 1815.

When the form of union for the German states came up for discussion at the Congress of Vienna, two different plans were advocated. Prussia's representatives submitted a scheme for a firm union like that of the United States, in which the central government should control the individual states in all matters of general interest. This idea was successfully opposed by Austria, supported by the other German rulers. Austria realized that her possessions, as a whole, could never be included in any real German union, for even in the western portion of her territory there were many Slavs, while in Hungary and the southern provinces there were practically no Germans at all. On the other hand, she felt that she might be the leader in a very loose union in which all the members should be left practically independent. Her ideal of an international union of sovereign princes under her own headship was almost completely realized in the constitution adopted.

Character of
the German
constitution.

The confederation was not a union of the various *countries* involved, but of "The Sovereign Princes and Free Towns of Germany," including the emperor of Austria and the king of Prussia for such of their possessions as were formerly included in the German empire; the king of Denmark for Holstein; and the king of the Netherlands for the grand duchy of Luxembourg. The union thus included two sovereigns who were out-and-out foreigners, and did not include all the possessions of its two most important members.[1]

The diet which met at Frankfort was composed (as was perfectly logical), not of representatives of the people, but of

[1] Observe the boundary of the German Confederation as indicated on the map, pp. 626–627, above. Important portions of the German constitution of 1815 are given in *Translations and Reprints*, Vol. I, No. 3.

plenipotentiaries of the rulers who were members of the confederation. The members reserved to themselves the right of forming alliances of all kinds, but pledged themselves to make no agreement prejudicial to the safety of the union or of any of its members, or to make war upon any member of the confederation on any pretense whatsoever. The constitution could not be amended without the approval of *all* the governments concerned. In spite of its obvious weaknesses, the confederation of 1815 lasted for a half a century, until Prussia finally expelled Austria from the union by arms, and began the formation of the present German federation.

260. The liberal and progressive party in Germany was sadly disappointed by the failure of the Congress of Vienna to weld Germany into a really national state. They were troubled, too, by the delay of the king of Prussia in granting the constitution that he had promised to his subjects. Other indications were not wanting that the German princes might not yet be ready to give up their former despotic power and adopt the principles of the French Revolution advocated by the liberals. A " League of Virtue " had been formed after the disastrous battle of Jena to arouse and keep alive the zeal of the nation for expelling the invader. This began to be reënforced, about 1815, by student associations organized by those who had returned to their studies from the war of independence. The students anathematized the reactionary party in their meetings, and drank to the freedom of Germany. October 18, 1817, they held a celebration in the Wartburg to commemorate both Luther's revolt and the anniversary of the battle of Leipsic. Speeches were made in honor of the brave who had fallen in the war of independence, and of the grand duke of Weimar, who was the first of the North German princes to give his people a constitution. The day closed with the burning of certain reactionary pamphlets.

Political associations of German students.

This innocent burst of enthusiasm excited great apprehension in the minds of the conservative statesmen of Europe, the leader among whom was the Austrian minister, Metternich. The murder by a fanatical student of a journalist, who was supposed to have influenced the Tsar to desert his former liberal policy, cast discredit upon the liberal party. It also gave Metternich an opportunity to emphasize the terrible results which he anticipated would come from the students' associations, liberal governments, and the freedom of the press.

The 'Carlsbad Resolutions,' 1819.

The extreme phase in the progress of reaction in Germany was reached when, with this murder as an excuse, Metternich called together the representatives of the larger states of the confederation at Carlsbad in August, 1819. Here a series of resolutions were drawn up with the aim of checking the free expression of opinions hostile to existing institutions, and of discovering and bringing to justice the revolutionists who were supposed to exist in dangerous numbers. These "Carlsbad Resolutions" were laid before the diet by Austria and adopted, though not without protest.

Metternich

They provided that there should be a special official in each university to watch the professors. Should any of them be found "abusing their legitimate influence over the youthful mind and propagating harmful doctrines hostile to the public order or subversive of the existing governmental institutions," the offenders were to lose their positions. The general students' union, which was suspected of being too revolutionary, was to be suppressed. Moreover, no newspaper, magazine, or pamphlet was to go to press without the previous approval of government officials, who were to determine whether it contained anything tending to foster discontent with the government. Lastly, a special commission was appointed to investigate the revolutionary conspiracies which Metternich and his sympathizers supposed to exist throughout Germany.[1]

The attack upon the freedom of the press, and especially the interference with the liberty of teaching in the great institutions of learning, which were already becoming the home of the highest scholarship in the world, scandalized all the progressive spirits in Germany. Yet no successful protest was raised, and Germany as a whole, acquiesced for a generation in Metternich's system of discouraging reform of all kinds.

Nevertheless, important progress was made in southern Germany. As early as 1818 the king of Bavaria granted his people a constitution in which he stated their rights and admitted them to a share in the government by establishing a parliament. His example was followed within two years by the rulers of Baden, Würtemberg, and Hesse. Another change for the better was the gradual formation of a customs union, which permitted goods to be sent freely from one German state to another without the payment of duties at each boundary line. This yielded some of the advantages of a political union. This economic union, of which Prussia was the head, and from which Austria was excluded, was a harbinger of the future German empire.[2]

The southern German states receive constitutions, 1818–1820.

Formation of a customs union— zollverein— with Prussia at its head.

261. Metternich had met with signal success in his efforts to keep Germany at a standstill. When, in 1820, the kings of Spain and Naples were compelled by popular uprisings to accept constitutions, and so surrender their ancient right to rule their subjects despotically, it was but natural that Metternich

Metternich opposes revolutionary movements in Spain and Italy.

[1] For the Carlsbad Resolutions, see *Translations and Reprints*, Vol. I, No. 3.
[2] Reference, Andrews, *Modern Europe*, Vol. I, pp. 229–257.

should urge the European powers to unite for the purpose of suppressing such manifestations. He urged that revolts of this kind set a dangerous example and threatened the tranquillity and security of all the other absolute monarchs.

Italy was at this time what Metternich called only "a geographical expression"; it had no political unity whatever. Lombardy and Venetia, in the northern part, were in the hands of Austria, and Parma, Modena, and Tuscany belonged to members of the Austrian family. · In the south, the considerable kingdom of the Two Sicilies was ruled over by a branch of the Spanish Bourbons. In the center, cutting the peninsula in twain, were the Papal States, which extended north to the Po. The presence of Austria, and the apparent impossibility of inducing the pope to submit to any government but his own, seemed to preclude all hope of making Italy into a true nation. Yet fifty years later the kingdom of Italy, as it now appears on the map of Europe, came into existence through the final exclusion of Austria from the peninsula and the extinction of the political power of the pope.

Although Napoleon had governed Italy despotically he had introduced a great many important reforms. He had established political equality and an orderly administration, and had forwarded public improvements; the vestiges of the feudal régime had vanished at his approach. Moreover, he had held out the hope of a united Italy, from which the foreign powers who had plagued and distracted her for centuries should be banished. But his unscrupulous use of Italy to advance his personal ambitions disappointed those who at first had placed their hopes in him, and they came to look for his downfall as eagerly as did the nobility and the dispossessed clergy, whose hopes were centered in Austria. It became clear to the more thoughtful Italians that Italy must look to herself and her own resources if she were ever to become an independent European state.

The downfall of Napoleon left Italy seemingly in a worse state than that in which he had found it. The hold of Austria was strengthened by her acquisition of Venice. The petty despots of Parma, Modena, and Tuscany, reseated on their thrones by the Congress of Vienna, hastened to sweep away the reforms of the Corsican and to reëstablish all the abuses of the old régime, now doubly conspicuous and obnoxious by reason of their temporary abolition. The lesser Italian princes, moreover, showed themselves to be heartily in sympathy with the hated Austria. Popular discontent spread throughout the peninsula and led to the formation of numerous secret societies, which assumed strange names, practiced mysterious rites, and plotted darkly in the name of Italian liberty and independence. By far the most noted of these associations was that of the *Carbonari*, i.e., charcoal burners. Its objects were individual liberty, constitutional government, and national independence and unity ; these it undertook to promote by agitation, conspiracy, and, if necessary, by revolution.

Reaction in Italy after Napoleon's downfall.

The Carbonari.

The Italian agitators had a superstitious respect for a constitution ; they appear to have regarded it not so much as a form of government to be carefully adapted to the needs of a particular country and time, as a species of talisman which would insure liberty and prosperity to its happy possessor. So when the Neapolitans heard that the king of Spain had been forced by an insurrection to grant a constitution, they made the first attempt on the part of the Italian people to gain constitutional liberty by compelling their king to agree to accept the Spanish constitution (July, 1820). However, at the same time that he was invoking the vengeance of God upon his own head should he violate his oath of fidelity to the constitution, he was casting about for foreign assistance to suppress the revolution and enable him to return to his old ways.

Temporary constitutions in Spain and Naples, 1820.

262. He had not long to wait. The alert Metternich invited Russia, Prussia, France, and England to unite in order

Austria intervenes in Italy (1821), in support of absolutism.

to check the development of " revolt and crime." He declared that the liberal movements, if unrestrained, would prove " not less tyrannical and fearful " in their results than that against which the allies had combined in the person of Napoleon. " Revolution " appeared to him and his conservative sympathizers as heresy appeared to Philip II, — it was a fearful disease that not only destroyed those whom it attacked directly, but spread contagion wherever it appeared and justified prompt and sharp measures of quarantine and even violent intervention with a view of stamping out the devastating plague.

To the great joy of the king of Naples, Austria marched its troops into his territory (March, 1821) and, meeting but an ill-organized opposition, freed him from the limitations which his subjects had for the moment imposed upon him. An attempt on the part of the subjects of the king of Sardinia to win a constitution was also repressed by Austrian troops.

Hopeful signs in Italy.

The weakness of the liberal movement in both southern and northern Italy appeared to be conclusively demonstrated. A new attempt ten years later, in Piedmont,[1] Modena, and the Papal States, to get rid of the existing despotism was quite as futile as the revolution of 1820–1821. Yet there were two hopeful signs. England protested as early as 1820 against Metternich's theory of interfering in the domestic affairs of other independent states in order to prevent reforms of which he disapproved, and France emphatically repudiated the doctrine of intervention on the accession of Louis Philippe in 1830. A second and far more important indication of progress was the increasing conviction on the part of the Italians that their country ought to be a single nation and not, as hitherto, a group of small independent states under foreign influence.

[1] The island of Sardinia had, in 1720, been given to the duke of Savoy, who was also ruler of Piedmont. The duke thereupon assumed the title of king of Sardinia, but Piedmont, with Turin as its capital, remained, nevertheless, the most important part of the kingdom of Sardinia.

A great leader arose in the person of the delicately organized and highly endowed Mazzini. He quickly became disgusted with the inefficiency and the silly mystery of the Carbonari, and founded a new association, called "Young Italy." This aimed to bring about the regeneration of Italy through the education of the young men in lofty republican principles. Mazzini had no confidence in princes and treaties and foreign aid. "We are of the people and will treat with the people. They will understand us," he said. He was not the man to organize a successful revolution, but he inspired the young Italians with an almost religious enthusiasm for the cause of Italy's liberation. His writings, which were widely read throughout the peninsula, created a feeling of loyalty to a common country among the patriots who were scattered through the different states of Italy.[1]

Mazzini, 1805–1872.

There was a great diversity of opinion among the reformers as to the best way to make Italy into a nation. Mazzini's party saw no hope except in republican institutions, but others were confident that an enlightened pope could form an Italian federation, of which he should be the head. And when Pius IX, upon his accession in 1846, immediately began to consult the interests and wishes of his people by subjecting priests to taxation, admitting laymen to his councils and tribunals, granting greater liberty of the press, and even protesting against Austrian encroachments, there seemed to be some ground for the belief that the pope might take the lead in the regeneration of Italy. But he soon grew suspicious of the liberals, and the outcome furnished one more proof of the sagacity of Machiavelli, who had pointed out over three centuries earlier that the temporal possessions of the pope constituted the chief obstacle to Italian unity.

Plan of uniting Italy under the headship of the pope.

Early reforms of Pius IX (pope, 1846–1878).

The future belonged neither to the republicans nor to the papal party, but to those who looked for salvation in the

[1] Reference, Andrews, *Modern Europe*, Vol. I, pp. 205–212.

gradual reformation of the existing monarchies, especially of the kingdom of Sardinia. Only in this way was there any prospect of ousting Austria, and without that no union, whether federal or otherwise, could possibly be formed.

Reason of Austria's influence after the Congress of Vienna.

From 1815 to 1848 those who believed in keeping things as they were at any cost were able, under the leadership of Metternich, to oppose pretty successfully those who from time to time attempted to secure for the people a greater control of the government and to satisfy the craving for national life. This did not mean, of course, that no progress was made during this long period in realizing the ideals of the liberal party in the various European states, or that one man can block the advance of nations for a generation. The very fact that Austria had, after the Congress of Vienna, assumed the leading rôle in Europe that France had played during the period following the Revolution of 1789, is a sufficient indication that Metternich's aversion to change corresponded to a general conviction that it was best, for the time being, to let well enough alone.

Creation of the kingdom of Greece, 1829.

Two events, at least, during the period of Metternich's influence served to encourage the liberals of Europe. In 1821 the inhabitants of Greece had revolted against the oppressive government of the Turks. The Turkish government set to work to suppress the revolt by atrocious massacres. It is said that twenty thousand of the inhabitants of the island of Chios were slaughtered. The Greeks, however, succeeded in arousing the sympathy of western Europe, and they held out until England, Russia, and France intervened and forced the Sultan to recognize the independence of Greece in 1829.[1]

Belgium becomes an independent kingdom in 1831.

Another little kingdom was added to the European states by the revolt of the former Austrian Netherlands from the king of Holland, to whom they had been assigned by the Congress

[1] Reference, Fyffe, *History of Modern Europe* (Popular Edition, 1896), Chapter XV.

of Vienna. The southern Netherlands were still as different from the northern as they had been in the time of William the Silent.[1] Holland was Protestant and German, while the southern provinces, to whom the union had always been distasteful, were Catholic and akin to the French in their sympathies. Encouraged by the revolution at Paris in 1830, the people of Brussels rose in revolt against their Dutch king, and forced his troops to leave the city. Through the influence of England and France the European powers agreed to recognize the independence of the Belgians, who established a kingdom and introduced an excellent constitution providing for a limited monarchy modeled upon that of England.

[1] See above, p. 449.

CHAPTER XL

THE UNIFICATION OF ITALY AND GERMANY

The general revolutionary movement in western Europe in 1848.

263. In 1848 the gathering discontent and the demand for reform suddenly showed their full strength and extent; it seemed for a time as if all western Europe was about to undergo as complete a revolution as France had experienced in 1789. With one accord, and as if obeying a preconcerted signal, the liberal parties in France, Italy, Germany, and Austria, during the early months of 1848, overthrew or gained control of the government, and proceeded to carry out their programme of reform in the same thoroughgoing way in which the National Assembly in France had done its work in 1789. The general movement affected almost every state in Europe, but the course of events in France, and in that part of central Europe which had so long been dominated by Austria, merits especial attention.

The revolution of 1848 in France.

The revolutionary movements of 1848 did not begin in France, but in Italy; yet it was the dethronement of Louis Philippe and the establishment of a second French republic that gave the signal for the general European revolt. The Charter of 1814 had been only slightly modified after the revolution of 1830, in spite of the wishes of the republicans who had been active in bringing about the deposition of Charles X. They maintained that the king had too much power and could influence the *parlement* to make laws contrary to the wishes of the people at large. They also protested against the laws which excluded the poorer classes from voting (only two hundred thousand among a population of thirty million enjoyed that right), and demanded that every Frenchman

Unpopularity of Louis Philippe among the republicans.

should have the right to vote so soon as he reached maturity. As Louis Philippe grew older he became more and more suspicious of the liberal parties which had helped him to his throne. He not only opposed reforms himself, but also did all he could to keep the *parlement* and the newspapers from advocating any changes which the progressive parties demanded. Nevertheless the strength of the republicans gradually increased. They found allies in a new group of socialistic writers who desired a fundamental reorganization of the state.

On February 24, 1848, a mob attacked the Tuilleries. The king abdicated in favor of his grandson, but it was too late; he and his whole family were forced to leave the country. The mob invaded the assembly, as in the time of the Reign of Terror, crying, "Down with the Bourbons, old and new! Long live the Republic!" A provisional government was established which included the writer, Lamartine, Louis Blanc, a prominent socialist, two or three editors, and several other politicians. The first decree of this body, ratifying the establishment of the republic, was solemnly proclaimed on the former site of the Bastile, February 27.

The second French republic proclaimed February 27, 1848.

The provisional government was scarcely in session before it was threatened by the "red republic." Its representatives, the social democrats, desired to put the laboring classes in control of the government and let them conduct it in their own interests. Some advocated community of property, and wished to substitute the red flag for the national colors. The government went so far as to concede the so-called "right to labor," and established national workshops, in which all the unemployed were given an opportunity to work.

The social democrats and the 'red republic.'

National workshops established.

A National Assembly had been convoked whose members were elected by a popular vote of all Frenchmen above the age of twenty-one. The result of the election was an overwhelming defeat for the social democrats. Their leaders then attempted to overthrow the new assembly on the pretext that

The insurrection in Paris, June, 1848.

it did not represent the people; but the national guard frustrated the attempt. The number of men now enrolled in the national workshops had reached one hundred and seventeen thousand, each of whom received two francs a day in return for either useless labor or mere idleness. The abolition of this nuisance led to a serious revolt. Battle raged in the streets of Paris for three days, and over ten thousand persons were killed.

Louis Napoleon elected president.

This wild outbreak of the forces of revolution resulted in a general conviction that a strong hand was essential to the maintenance of peace. The new constitution decreed that the president of the republic should be chosen by the people at large. Their choice fell upon the nephew of Napoleon Bonaparte, Louis Napoleon, who had already made two futile attempts to make himself the ruler of France. Before the expiration of his four years' term he succeeded, by a *coup d'état* on the anniversary of the coronation of his uncle (December 2, 1851), in setting up a new government. He next obtained, by means of a plebiscite,[1] the consent of the

Establishment of the second empire, 1852.

people to his remaining president for ten years. A year later (1852) the second empire was established, and Napoleon III became " Emperor of the French by the grace of God and the will of the people."

Austria's commanding position in central Europe.

264. When Metternich heard of the February revolution of 1848 in France, he declared that " Europe finds herself to-day in the presence of a second 1793." This was not true, however. It was no longer necessary for France to promote liberal ideas by force of arms, as in 1793. For sixty years ideas of reform had been spreading in Europe, and by the year 1848 they were accepted by a great majority of the people, from Berlin to Palermo. The Europe of 1848 was no longer the Europe of 1793.

The overthrow of Louis Philippe encouraged the opponents of Metternich in Germany, Austria, and Italy to attempt to

[1] See above, p. 600.

make an end of his system at once and forever. In view of the important part that Austria had played in central Europe since the fall of Napoleon I, it was inevitable that she should appear the chief barrier to the attainment of national unity and liberal government in Italy and Germany. As ruler of Lombardy and Venetia she practically controlled Italy, and as presiding member of the German Confederation she had been able to keep even Prussia in line. It is not strange that Austria felt that she could make no concessions to the spirit of nationality, for the territories belonging to the house of Hapsburg, some twenty in number, were inhabited by four different races, — Germans, Slavs, Hungarians, and Italians.[1] The Slavs (especially the Bohemians) and the Hungarians longed for national independence, as well as the Italians.

On March 13 the populace of Vienna rose in revolt against their old-fashioned government. Metternich fled, and all his schemes for opposing reform appeared to have come to naught. Before the end of the month the helpless Austrian emperor had given his permission to the kingdoms of Hungary and Bohemia to draw up constitutions for themselves incorporating the longed-for reforms (equality of all classes in the matter of taxation, religious freedom, liberty of the press, and the rest), and providing that each country should have a parliament of its own, which should meet annually. The Austrian provinces were promised similar advantages. None of these regions, however, showed any desire to throw off their allegiance to the Austrian ruler.

Overthrow of Metternich, March, 1848.

The rising in northern Italy, on the contrary, was directed to that particular end. Immediately on the news of Metternich's fall the Milanese expelled the Austrian troops from their city, and soon Austria had evacuated a great part of Lombardy. The Venetians followed the lead of Milan and set up a republic once more. The Milanese, anticipating a struggle, appealed

Beginning of Italian war of independence.

[1] See map, p. 649, below.

to Charles Albert, King of Sardinia, for aid. By this time a great part of Italy was in revolt. Constitutions were granted to Naples, Rome, Tuscany, and Piedmont by their rulers. The king of Sardinia was forced by public opinion to assume the leadership in the attempt to expel the interloping Austria and ultimately, perhaps, to found some sort of an Italian union which should satisfy the longings for national unity. The pope and even the Bourbon king of Naples were induced to consent to the arming and dispatch of troops in the cause of Italian freedom, and Italy began its first war for independence.

The liberal movement in Germany in 1848.

The crisis at home and the Italian war made it impossible for Austria to prevent the progress of revolution in Germany. So spontaneous was the movement, that before the fall of Metternich reform movements had begun in Baden, Würtemberg, Bavaria, and Saxony. The opportunity seemed to have come, now that Austria was hopelessly embarrassed, to reorganize the German Confederation.

Frederick William IV (1840-1861) of Prussia takes the lead in the reform movement in Germany.

The king of Prussia, seeing his opportunity, suddenly reversed his policy of obedience to the dictates of Austria, and determined to take the lead in Germany. He agreed to summon an assembly to draw up a constitution for Prussia. Moreover, a great national assembly was convoked at Frankfort to draft a constitution for Germany at large.

265. By the end of March, 1848, the prospects of reform were bright indeed. Hungary and Bohemia had been guaranteed constitutional independence; the Austrian provinces awaited their promised constitution; Lombardy and Venetia had declared their independence of Austria; four Italian states had obtained their longed-for constitutions, and all were ready for a war with Austria; Prussia was promised a constitution, and lastly, the National Assembly at Frankfort was about to prepare a constitution for a united Germany.

The moderate reformers who had gained these seeming victories had, however, only just reached the most difficult part of their task. They had two kinds of enemies, who abhorred each other but who effectually combined to undo the work of the moderates. These were, first, the conservative party, represented by Austria and the Italian rulers who had been forced most reluctantly to grant constitutions to their subjects; and, secondly, the radicals, who were not satisfied with the prospect of a liberal monarchy and desired a republican or socialistic form of government. While the princes were recovering from the astonishing humiliations of March, the radicals began to discredit the revolutionary movement and alienate public opinion by fantastic programmes and the murder of hostile ministers.

Conservatives and radicals both help to frustrate the realization of the proposed reforms.

For the moment Austria's chief danger lay in Italy, which was the only one of her dependencies that had actually taken up arms against her. The Italians had been unable to drive out the Austrian army, which, under the indomitable general, Radetzky, had taken refuge in the so-called Quadrilateral, in the neighborhood of Mantua, where it was protected by four great fortresses. Charles Albert of Sardinia found himself, with the exception of a few volunteers, almost unsupported by the other Italian states. The best ally of Austria was the absence of united action upon the part of the Italians, and the jealousy and indifference that they showed as soon as war had actually begun. The pope decided that his mission was one of peace and that he could not afford to join in a war against Austria, the stoutest ally of the Roman church. The king of Naples easily found a pretext for recalling the troops that public opinion had compelled him to send to the aid of the king of Sardinia. Charles Albert was defeated at Custozza, July 25, and compelled to sign a truce with Austria and withdraw his forces from Lombardy.

Defeat of the Italians under Charles Albert of Sardinia, July, 1848.

The Italian republicans, who had imputed to Charles Albert merely personal motives in his efforts to free Italy, now attempted to carry out their own programme. Florence, as

Policy of the Italian republicans.

well as Venice, proclaimed itself a republic. At Rome the liberal and enlightened Rossi, whom the pope had put at the head of affairs, was assassinated in November just as he was ready to promulgate his reforms. The pope fled from the city and put himself under the protection of the king of Naples. A constitutional assembly was then convoked by the revolutionists, and under the influence of Mazzini, in February, 1849, it declared the temporal power of the pope abolished and proclaimed the Roman republic.

Hostility between the Germans and Czechs in Bohemia.

266. Meanwhile the conditions in Austria began to be favorable to a reëstablishment of the emperor's former influence. Race rivalry proved his friend in his Austrian domains just as republicanism tended to his ultimate advantage in Italy. The Czechs [1] in Bohemia hated the Germans in 1848, much as they had hated them in the time of Huss. The German part of the population naturally opposed the plan of making Bohemia practically independent of the government at Vienna, for it was to German Vienna that they were wont to look for protection against the enterprises of their Czechish fellow-countrymen. The Germans wanted to send delegates to the Frankfurt convention, and to maintain the union between Bohemia and the German states.

The Pan-Slavic Congress of 1848.

The Czechs determined to offset the movement toward German consolidation by a Pan-Slavic Congress, which should bring together the various Slavic peoples comprised in the Austrian empire. To this assembly, which met in Prague in June, 1848, came delegates from the Czechs, Moravians, Ruthenians, and Poles in the north, and the Servians and Croatians in the south. Its deliberations were interrupted by an insurrection that broke out among the people of Prague and gave the commander of the Austrian forces a sufficient excuse for intervening. He estab-

Beginnings of revolt in Bohemia suppressed.

lished a military government, and the prospect of independence for Bohemia vanished. This was Austria's first real victory.

[1] The Slavic inhabitants of Bohemia.

The eastern and southern portion of the Hapsburg domains were not more homogeneous than the west and north. When a constitution was granted to Hungary it was inevitable that the races which the Hungarians (Magyars) had long dominated should begin to consider how they might gain the right to govern themselves. The Slavs inhabiting Carniola, Carinthia, Istria, Croatia, Slavonia, Bosnia, and Servia had long meditated

The Slavic peoples revolt against Hungary.

The Various Races of Austro-Hungary

upon the possibility of a united Slavic kingdom in the south. Both the Servians and Croatians now revolted against Hungary. Like the Germans in Bohemia, the Servians and Croatians were on the whole friendly to the Vienna government, from which they had less to fear than from the establishment of Hungarian independence, which would put them at the mercy of the Magyars. It was, therefore, with the support of the Austrian ministry that an army of Servians and Croatians crossed into Hungary in September.

In October, 1848, the radical party rose in Vienna as it had in Paris after the deposition of Louis Philippe. The minister of war was brutally murdered and the emperor fled. The city was, however, besieged by the same commander who had put down the insurrection in Prague, and was forced to surrender. The imperial government was now in a position still further to strengthen itself. The emperor, a notoriously inefficient

person, was forced to abdicate (December 2, 1848) in favor of his youthful nephew, Francis Joseph I, who still sits upon the Austrian throne. Moreover, a new Metternich appeared in the person of Schwarzenberg.

A vigorous campaign was begun against Hungary, which, under the influence of the patriotic Kossuth, had deposed its Hapsburg king and declared itself an independent republic under the presidency of Kossuth. The Tsar placed his forces at the disposal of Francis Joseph, and with the aid of an army of one hundred and fifty thousand Russians, who marched in from the east, the Hungarians were compelled, by the middle of August, to surrender. Austria took terrible vengeance upon the rebels. Thousands were hung, shot, and imprisoned, and

Final peace-
ful union
between
Austria and
Hungary,
1867.

many, including Kossuth, fled to the United States or elsewhere. But within a few years Hungary won its independence by peaceful measures, and it is now on exactly the same footing as the western dominions of Francis Joseph in the dual federation of Austria-Hungary.

Austria
defeats the
king of
Sardinia at
Novara,
March, 1849.

It remained for Austria to reëstablish her prestige in Italy and in the German Confederation. In March, 1849, Charles Albert renewed the war which had been discontinued after the defeat at Custozza. The campaign lasted but five days and closed with his crushing and definitive defeat at Novara (March 23),

which put an end to the hopes of Italian liberty for the time being. Charles Albert abdicated in favor of his son, Victor Emmanuel, who was destined before many years to become king of Italy.

After bringing the king of Sardinia to terms, Austria pushed southward, reëstablishing the old order as she went. The ephemeral Italian republics were unable to offer any effectual resistance. The former rulers were restored in Rome, Tuscany, and Venice, and the constitutions were swept away from one end of the peninsula to the other, except in Piedmont, the most important part of the king of Sardinia's realms. There Victor Emmanuel not only maintained the representative government introduced by his father, but, by summoning to his councils d'Azeglio and others known throughout Italy for their liberal sentiments, he prepared to lead Italy once more against her foreign oppressors. *Austria reëstablishes the former conditions in Italy, except in Piedmont.*

267. In Germany, as elsewhere, Austria profited by the dissensions among her opponents. On May 18, 1848, the National Assembly, consisting of nearly six hundred representatives of the German people, had met at Frankfurt. It immediately began the consideration of a new constitution that should satisfy the popular longings for a great free German state, to be governed by and for the people. But what were to be the confines of this new German state? The confederation of 1815 did not include all the German inhabitants of Prussia, and did include the heterogeneous western possessions of Austria,— Bohemia and Moravia, for example, where a great part of the people were Slavs. There was no hesitation in deciding that all the Prussian territories should be admitted to the new union. As it appeared impossible to exclude Austria altogether, the Assembly agreed to include those parts of her territory which had belonged to the confederation formed in 1815. This decision rendered the task of founding a real German state practically impossible ; for the new union was to include two great European powers who might at any moment become rivals, since Prussia would hardly consent to be led forever by Austria. So heterogeneous a union could only continue to be, as it had been, a loose confederation of practically independent princes. *Question of the extent of the proposed union.*

Impossibility of a German state which should include both Austria and Prussia.

The Assembly at Frankfurt gives Austria time to recover.

The improbability that the Assembly at Frankfurt would succeed in its undertaking was greatly increased by its unwise conduct. Instead of proceeding immediately to frame a new form of government, it devoted several months to the formulation of the general rights of the German citizen. This gave a fine opportunity to the theorists, of which there were many in the Assembly, to ventilate their views, and by the time that the constitution itself came up for discussion, Austria had begun to regain her influence and was ready to lead the conservative forces once more. She could rely upon the support of the rulers of South Germany, for they were well satisfied with the old confederation and the independence that it gave them.

The Assembly asks the king of Prussia to become emperor of Germany.

In spite of her partiality for the old union, Austria could not prevent the Assembly from completing its new constitution. This provided that there should be an hereditary emperor at the head of the government, and that exalted office was tendered to the king of Prussia. Frederick William IV had been alienated from the liberal cause, which he had at first espoused, by an insurrection in Berlin. He was, moreover, timid and con-

Frederick William IV refuses the imperial crown.

servative at heart; he hated revolution and doubted if the National Assembly had any right to confer the imperial title. He also greatly respected Austria, and felt that a war with her, which was likely to ensue if he accepted the crown, would not only be dangerous to Prussia, since Francis Joseph could rely upon the assistance of the Tsar, but dishonorable as well, in Austria's present embarrassment. So he refused the honor of the imperial title and announced his rejection of the new constitution (April, 1849).

The National Assembly disperses and the old diet is restored.

This decision rendered the year's work of the National Assembly fruitless, and its members gradually dispersed, with the exception of the radicals, who made a last desperate effort to found a republic. Austria now insisted upon the reëstablishment of the old diet, and nearly came to war with Prussia over the policy to be pursued. Hostilities were only averted by the ignominious submission of Prussia to the demands of Schwarzenberg in 1851.

While the revolutions of 1848 seem futile enough when viewed from the standpoint of the hopes of March, they left some important indications of progress. The king of Prussia had granted his country a constitution, which, with some modifications, has served Prussia down to the present day. Piedmont also had obtained a constitution. The internal reforms, moreover, which these countries speedily introduced, prepared them to head once more, and this time with success, a movement for national unity.

Results of the revolutions of 1848.

It will be noted that the revolution of 1848 aimed to do more than the French Revolution of 1789. Not only was the national question everywhere an important one, but there were plans for the economic reorganization of society. It was no longer simply a matter of abolishing the remnants of feudalism and insuring equal rights to all and the participation of the more prosperous classes in the government. Those who lived by the labor of their hands and were employed in the vast industries that had developed with the application of steam machinery to manufacture also had their spokesmen. The relation of the state to the industrial classes, and of capital to labor, had become, as they still are, the great problems of modern times.

In 1851 Austria had once more, in spite of the greatest obstacles, established the system of Metternich. But this victory was of short duration, and it was her last. Five years later the encroachments of Russia in Turkey brought on the Crimean War, of which something will be said later. In this war Austria observed an inglorious neutrality; she thereby sacrificed much of her prestige with both Russia and the western powers, and encouraged renewed attempts to free both Italy and Germany from her control.

Decline of Austrian influence after 1851.

Development
of Piedmont
under Cavour.

268. Under Victor Emmanuel and his great minister, Cavour, Piedmont had rapidly developed into a modern state. It sent a contingent to the aid of the western powers in the Crimean War waged by France and England against Russia (1853–1856); it developed its resources, military and economic, and at last found an ally to help it in a new attempt to expel Austria from Italy.

Position and
policy of
Napoleon III.

Napoleon III, like his far more distinguished uncle, was a usurper. He knew that he could not rely upon mere tradition, but must maintain his popularity by deeds that should

Cavour

redound to the glory of France. A war with Austria for the liberation of the Italians, who like the French were a Latin race, would be popular; especially if France could thereby add a bit of territory to her realms, and perhaps become the protector of the proposed Italian confederation. A conference was arranged between Napoleon and Cavour. Just what agreement was reached we do not know, but Napoleon no doubt engaged to come to the aid of the king of Sardinia, should the latter find a pretense for going to war with Austria. Should they together succeed in expelling Austria from northern Italy, the king of Sardinia was to reward France by ceding to her Savoy and Nice, which both geographically and racially belonged to her.

Victories
of Victor
Emmanuel
and Napo-
leon III over
Austria.

By April, 1859, Victor Emmanuel had managed to involve himself in a war with Austria. The French army promptly joined forces with the Piedmontese, defeated the Austrians at Magenta, and on June 8, Napoleon III and Victor Emmanuel entered Milan amid the rejoicings of the people. The Austrians managed the campaign very badly, and were again defeated at Solferino (June 24).

Suddenly Europe was astonished to hear that a truce had been concluded, and that the preliminaries of a peace had been arranged which left Venetia in Austria's hands, in spite of Napoleon III's boast that he would free Italy to the Adriatic. The French emperor had begun to fear that, with the growing enthusiasm which was showing itself throughout the peninsula for Piedmont, there was danger that it might succeed in forming a national kingdom so strong as to need no French protector. By leaving Venetia in possession of Austria, and agreeing that Piedmont should only be increased by the incorporation of Lombardy and the little duchies of Parma and Modena, Napoleon III hoped to prevent the consolidation of Italy from proceeding too far.

Napoleon III alarmed by the Italian successes.

He had, however, precipitated changes which he was powerless to check. Italy was now ready to fuse into a single state. Tuscany, as well as Modena and Parma, voted (March, 1860) to unite with Piedmont. Garibaldi, a famous republican leader, sailed for Sicily, where he assumed the dictatorship of the island in the name of Victor Emmanuel, " King of Italy." After expelling the troops of the king of Naples from Sicily, he crossed to the mainland, and early in September he entered Naples itself, just as the king fled from his capital.

The formation of a kingdom of Italy, 1860.

Garibaldi now proposed to march on Rome and proclaim the kingdom of Italy from the Quirinal. This would have imperiled all the previous gains, for Napoleon III could not, in view of the strong Catholic sentiment in France, possibly permit the occupation of Rome and the destruction of the political independence of the pope. He agreed that Victor Emmanuel might annex the outlying papal possessions to the north and reëstablish a stable government in Naples instead of Garibaldi's dictatorship. But Rome, the imperial city, with the

Napoleon III intervenes to prevent the annexation of Rome to the kingdom of Italy.

territory immediately surrounding it, must be left to its old master. Victor Emmanuel accordingly marched southward and occupied Naples (October). Its king capitulated and all southern Italy became a part of the kingdom of Italy.

In February, 1861, the first Italian parliament was opened at Turin, and the process of really amalgamating the heterogeneous portions of the new kingdom began. Yet the joy of the Italians over the realization of their hopes of unity and national independence was tempered by the fact that Austria still held one of the most famous of the Italian provinces, and that Rome, which typified Italy's former grandeur, was not included in the new kingdom. Within a decade, however, both these districts became a part of the kingdom of Italy through the action of Prussia. William I and his extraordinary minister and adviser, Bismarck, were about to do for Germany what Victor Emmanuel and Cavour had accomplished for Italy.[1]

William I of Prussia, 1861-1888.

269. With the accession of William I in 1858,[2] a new era dawned for Prussia. A practical and vigorous man had come into power, whose great aim was to expel Austria from the German Confederation, and out of the remaining states to construct a firm union, under the leadership of Prussia, which should take its place among the most powerful of the states of Europe. He saw that war would come sooner or later, and his first business was to develop the military resources of his realms.

William I's plan for strengthening the army.

The German army, which was the outgrowth of the early reforms of William I, is so extraordinary a feature of the Europe of to-day, that its organization merits attention. The war of independence against Napoleon in 1813 had led to the summoning of the nation to arms, and a law was passed in Prussia making military service a universal obligation of every

---

[1] Reference, Andrews, *Modern Europe*, Vol. II, Chapter III.
[2] He ruled until 1861 as regent for his brother, Frederick William IV, who was incapacitated by disease.

healthy male citizen. The first thing that William I did was to increase the annual levy from forty to sixty thousand men, and to see that all the soldiers remained in active service three years. They then passed into the reserve, according to the existing law, where for two years more they remained ready at any time to take up arms should it be necessary. William wished to increase the term of service in the reserve to four years. In this way the state would claim seven of the years of early manhood and have an effective army of four hundred thousand, which would permit it to dispense with the service of those who were approaching middle life. The lower house of the Prussian parliament refused, however, to make the necessary appropriations for increasing the strength of the army.

The king proceeded, nevertheless, with his plan, and in 1862 called to his side one of the most extraordinary statesmen of modern times, Bismarck. The new minister conceived a scheme for laying Austria low and exalting Prussia, which he succeeded in carrying out with startling precision. He could not, however, reveal it to the lower chamber; he would, indeed, scarcely hint its nature to the king himself. In defiance of the lower house and of the newspapers, he carried on the strengthening of the army without formal appropriations, on the theory that the constitution had not provided for a deadlock between the upper and lower house, and that consequently the king might exercise, in such a case, his former absolute power. For a time it seemed as if Prussia was returning to a pure despotism, for there was assuredly no more fundamental provision of the constitution than the right of the people to control the granting of the taxes. Yet Bismarck was eventually fully exonerated by public opinion, and it was generally agreed that the end had amply justified the means.

Bismarck and his struggle with the Prussian parliament.

270. Prussia now had a military force that appeared to justify the hope of victory should she undertake a war with her old rival. In order to bring about the expulsion of Austria

The Schleswig-Holstein affair.

from the confederation, Bismarck took advantage of a knotty problem that had been troubling Germany, and which was known as the Schleswig-Holstein affair. The provinces of Schleswig and Holstein, although inhabited largely by Germans, had for centuries belonged to the king of Denmark. They were allowed, however, to retain their provincial assemblies, and were not considered a part of Denmark any more than Hanover was a part of Great Britain in the last century.

In 1847, just when the growing idea of nationality was about to express itself in the Revolution of 1848, the king of Denmark proclaimed that he was going to make these German provinces an integral part of the Danish kingdom. This aroused great indignation throughout Germany, especially as Holstein was a member of the confederation. Frederick William IV consented to go to war with Denmark, but only succeeded in delaying for a few years the proposed absorption of the provinces by Denmark. The constant encroachments of the government at Copenhagen upon the privileges claimed by Schleswig-Holstein aroused new apprehension and much discontent. In 1863 Schleswig was finally incorporated into the Danish kingdom.

Bismarck's audacious plan for the expulsion of Austria from Germany.

" From this time the history of Germany is the history of the profound and audacious statecraft and of the overmastering will of Bismarck ; the nation, except through its valour on the battlefield, ceases to influence the shaping of its own fortunes. What the German people desired in 1864 was that Schleswig-Holstein should be attached, under a ruler of its own, to the German Federation as it then existed ; what Bismarck intended was that Schleswig-Holstein, itself incorporated more or less directly with Prussia, should be made the means of the destruction of the existing Federal system and of the expulsion of Austria from Germany. . . . The German people desired one course of action ; Bismarck had determined on something totally different ; with matchless resolution and skill he bore down all the opposition of people and of the [European] courts, and forced a reluctant nation to the goal which he himself had chosen for it" (Fyffe).

Bismarck's first step was to invite Austria to coöperate with Prussia in settling the Schleswig-Holstein difficulty. As Denmark refused to make any concessions, the two powers declared war, defeated the Danish army, and forced the king of Denmark

The working out of the plan.

to cede Schleswig-Holstein to the rulers of Prussia and Austria jointly (October, 1864). They were to make such disposition of the provinces as they saw fit. There was now no trouble in picking a quarrel with Austria. Bismarck suggested the nominal independence of the duchies, but that they should become practically a part of Prussia. This plan was of course indignantly

Bismarck

rejected by Austria, and it was arranged that, pending an adjustment, Austria should govern Holstein, and Prussia, Schleswig.

Bismarck now obtained the secret assurance of Napoleon III that he would not interfere if Prussia and Italy should go to war with Austria. In April, 1866, Italy agreed that, should the king of Prussia take up arms during the following three months with the aim of reforming the German union, it too would immediately declare war on Austria, with the hope, of course, of obtaining Venice. The relations between Austria and Prussia grew more and more strained, until finally in June, 1866, Austria induced the diet to call out the forces of the confederation with a view of making war on Prussia. This act

Prussia declares the German Confederation dissolved.

the representative of Prussia declared put an end to the existing union. He accordingly submitted to the diet Prussia's scheme for the reformation of Germany and withdrew from the diet.

War declared
between
Prussia and
Austria.

271. On June 12 war was declared between Austria and Prussia. With the exception of Mecklenburg and the small states of the north, all Germany sided with Austria against Prussia. Bismarck immediately demanded of the rulers of the larger North German states — Hanover, Saxony, and Hesse-Cassel— that they stop their warlike preparations and agree to accept Prussia's plan of reform. On their refusal, Prussian troops immediately occupied these territories, and war actually began.

Prussia
victorious.

So admirable was the organization of the Prussian army that, in spite of the suspicion and even hatred which the liberal party in Prussia entertained for the despotic Bismarck, all resistance on the part of the states of the north was promptly prevented, Austria was miserably defeated on July 3 in the decisive battle of Königgrätz, or Sadowa,[1] and within three weeks after the breaking off of diplomatic relations the war was practically over. Austria's influence was at an end, and Prussia had won her right to do with Germany as she pleased.

The North
German
Federation.

Prussia was aware that the larger states south of the Main River were not ripe for the union that she desired. She therefore organized a so-called North German Federation, which included all the states north of the Main. Prussia had seized the opportunity considerably to increase her own boundaries and round out her territory by annexing the North German states, with the exception of Saxony, that had gone to war with her. Hanover, Hesse-Cassel, Nassau, and the free city of Frankfurt, along with the duchies of Schleswig and Holstein, all became Prussian.

Prussia, thus enlarged, summoned the lesser states about her to confer upon a constitution that should accomplish four ends.

[1] Reference, Fyffe, *Modern Europe*, pp. 954–957.

First, it must give all the people of the territory included in the new union, regardless of the particular state in which they lived, a voice in the government. A popular assembly satisfied this demand. Secondly, the predominating position of Prussia must be secured, but at the same time (thirdly) the self-respect of the other monarchs whose lands were included must not be sacrificed. In order to accomplish this double purpose the king of Prussia was made president of the federation but not its sovereign. The chief governing body was the Federal Council (Bundesrath). In this each ruler, however small his state, and each of the three free towns — Hamburg, Bremen, and Lübeck — had at least one vote; in this way it was arranged that the other rulers did not become *subjects* of the king of Prussia. The real sovereign of the North German Federation and of the present German empire is not the king of Prussia, but "all of the united governments." The votes were distributed as in the old diet, so that Prussia, with the votes of the states that she annexed in 1866, enjoyed seventeen votes out of forty-three. Lastly, the constitution must be so arranged that when the time came for the southern states— Bavaria, Würtemberg, Baden, and south Hesse — to join the union, it would be adapted to the needs of the widened empire.

Requirements of the proposed constitution.

The union was a true federation like that of the United States, although its organization violated many of the rules which were observed in the organization of the American union. It was inevitable that a union spontaneously developed from a group of sovereign *monarchies*, with their traditions of absolutism, would be very different from one in which the members, like the states of the American union, had previously been governed by republican institutions.

272. No one was more chagrined by the abrupt termination of the war of 1866 and the victory of Prussia than Napoleon III. He had hoped that both the combatants might be

Disappointment of the hopes of Napoleon III.

weakened by a long struggle, and that at last he might have an opportunity to arbitrate and incidentally to gain something for France, as had happened after the Italian war. But Prussia came out of the conflict with greatly increased power and territory, while France had gained nothing. An effort of Napoleon's to get a foothold in Mexico had failed, owing to the recovery of the United States from the Civil War and their warning that they should regard his continued intervention there as an hostile act.[1] His hopes of annexing Luxembourg as an offset for the gains that Prussia had made, were also frustrated.

France declares war upon Prussia, July 19, 1870.

One course remained for the French usurper, namely, to permit himself to be forced into a war against the power which had especially roused the jealousy of France. Never was an excuse offered for war more trivial than that advanced by the French,[2] never did retribution come more speedily. The hostility which the South German states had hitherto shown toward Prussia encouraged Napoleon III to believe that so soon as the French troops should gain their first victory, Bavaria, Würtemberg, and Baden would join him. That first victory was never won. War had no sooner been declared than the Germans laid all jealousy aside and ranged themselves as a nation against a national assailant. The French army, moreover, was neither

---

[1] Andrews, *Modern Europe*, Vol. 2, pp. 173-180.

[2] In 1869 Spain was without a king, and the crown was tendered to Leopold of Hohenzollern, a very distant relative of William I of Prussia. This greatly excited the people of Paris, for it seemed to them only an indirect way of bringing Spain under the influence of Prussia. The French minister of foreign affairs declared that the candidacy was an attempt to "reëstablish the empire of Charles V." In view of this opposition, Leopold withdrew his acceptance of the Spanish crown early in July, 1870, and Europe believed the incident to be at an end. The French ministry, however, was not satisfied with this, and demanded that the king of Prussia should pledge himself that the candidacy should never be renewed. This William refused to do. The account of the demand and refusal was given in such a way in the German newspapers that it appeared as if the French ambassador had insulted King William. The Parisians, on the other hand, thought that their ambassador had received an affront, and demanded an immediate declaration of war.

well equipped nor well commanded. The Germans hastened
across the Rhine, and within a few days were driving the French
before them. In a series of bloody encounters about Metz, one
of the French armies was defeated and finally shut up within
the fortifications about the town. Seven weeks had not elapsed
after the beginning of the war, before the Germans had captured a second French army and made a prisoner of the emperor
himself in the great battle of Sedan, September 1, 1870.[1]

The Germans then surrounded and laid siege to Paris.
Napoleon III had been completely discredited by the disasters
about Metz and at Sedan, and consequently the empire was
abolished and France for the third time was declared a republic. In spite of the energy which the new government showed
in arousing the French against the invaders, prolonged resistance was impossible. The capital surrendered January 28, 1871,
and an armistice was arranged. Bismarck, who had been by
no means reluctant to go to war, deeply humiliated France, in
arranging the treaty of peace, by requiring the cession of two
French provinces which had formerly belonged to Germany, —
Alsace and northeastern Lorraine.[2] In this way France was
cut off from the Rhine, and the crest of the Vosges Mountains
was established as its boundary. The Germans exacted, further,
an enormous indemnity for the unjustifiable attack which the
French had made upon them. This was fixed at five billion
francs, and German troops were to occupy France till it was
paid. The French people made pathetic sacrifices to hasten
the payment of this indemnity, in order that the country might

Siege of Paris and close of Franco-Prussian War.

Cession of Alsace and Lorraine to Germany.

---

[1] Reference, Fyffe, *Modern Europe*, pp. 988–1002.

[2] Alsace had, with certain reservations, — especially as regarded Strasburg and
the other free towns, — been ceded to the French king by the treaty of Westphalia
(see above, p. 473). Louis XIV disregarded the reservations and seized Strasburg
and the other towns (1681) and so annexed the whole region to France. The
duchy of Lorraine had upon the death of its last duke fallen to France in 1766.
It had previously been regarded as a part of the Holy Roman Empire. In 1871
less than a third of the original duchy of Lorraine, together with the fortified
city of Metz, was ceded back to Germany.

be freed from the presence of the hated Germans. The bitter feeling of the French for the Germans dates from this war, and the longing for revenge still shows itself. For many years after the war a statue in Paris, representing the lost city of Strasburg, was draped in mourning.

The insurrection of the Paris commune of 1871.

Immediately after the surrender of Paris the new republican government had been called upon to subdue a terrible insurrection of the Parisian populace. The insurgents reëstablished the commune of the Reign of Terror, and rather than let Paris come again into the hands of the national government, they proposed to burn the city. When, after two months of disorder, their forces were completely routed in a series of bloody street fights, the city was actually set on fire; but only two important public buildings were destroyed, — the Palace of the Tuilleries and the city hall.

The French constitutional laws of 1875.

A National Assembly had been elected by the people in February, 1871, to make peace with Germany and to draw up a new constitution. Under this temporary government France gradually recovered from the terrible loss and demoralization caused by the war. There was much uncertainty for several years as to just what form the constitution would permanently take, for the largest party in the National Assembly was composed of those who favored the reëstablishment of a monarchy.[1] Those who advocated maintaining the republic prevailed, however, and in 1875 the assembly passed a series of three laws organizing the government. These have since served France as a constitution.

---

[1] The monarchical party naturally fell into two groups. One, the so-called *legitimists*, believed that the elder Bourbon line, to which Louis XVI and Charles X had belonged, should be restored in the person of the count of Chambord, a grandson of Charles X. The *Orleanists*, on the other hand, wished the grandson of Louis Philippe, the count of Paris, to be king. In 1873 the Orleanists agreed to help the count of Chambord to the throne as Henry V, but that prince frustrated the plan by refusing to accept the national colors, — red, white, and blue, — which had become so endeared to the nation that it appeared dangerous to exchange them for the white of the Bourbons.

While France is nominally a republic with a president at its head, its government closely resembles that of a limited monarchy like Belgium. This is not strange, since the monarchists were in the majority when its constitutional laws were passed. The French government of to-day is therefore a compromise, and since all attempts to overthrow it have proved vain, we may assume that it is suited to the wants of the nation.

Character of the present French republic.

As one reviews the history of France since the establishment of the first republic in 1792, it appears as if revolutionary changes of government had been very frequent. As a matter of fact, the various revolutions produced far less change in the system of government than is usually supposed. They neither called in question the main provisions of the Declaration of the Rights of Man drawn up in 1789, nor did they materially alter the system of administration which was established by Napoleon immediately after his accession in 1800. So long as the latter was retained, the civil rights and equality of all citizens secured, and the representatives of the nation permitted to control the ruler, it really made little difference whether France was called an empire, a constitutional monarchy, or a republic.

Permanent character of the French government in spite of changes in the constitution.

273. The attack of France upon Prussia in 1870, instead of hindering the development of Germany as Napoleon III had hoped it would, only served to consummate the work of 1866. The South German states, — Bavaria, Würtemberg, Baden, and south Hesse — having sent their troops to fight side by side with the Prussian forces, consented after their common victory over France to join the North German Federation. Surrounded by the German princes, William, King of Prussia and President of the North German Federation, was proclaimed German Emperor in the palace of Versailles, January, 1871. In this way the present German empire came into existence. With its wonderfully organized army and its mighty chancellor, Bismarck, it immediately took a leading place among the western powers of Europe.

Final unification of Germany.

Proclamation of the German empire, January 18, 1871.

Predominance of Prussia in the present German empire.

The constitution of the North German Federation had been drawn up with the hope that the southern states would later become a part of the union; consequently, little change was necessary when the empire was established. The king of Prussia enjoys the title of German Emperor, and is the real head of the federation. He is not, however, *emperor of Germany*, for

Proclamation of the German Empire at Versailles

the sovereignty is vested, theoretically, not in him, but in the body of German rulers who are members of the union, all of whom send their representatives to the Federal Council (Bundesrath). Prussia's influence in the Federal Council is, however, secured by assigning her king a sufficient number of votes to enable him to block any measure he wishes.

The unification of Italy was completed, like that of Germany, by the Franco-Prussian War of 1870. After the war of 1866

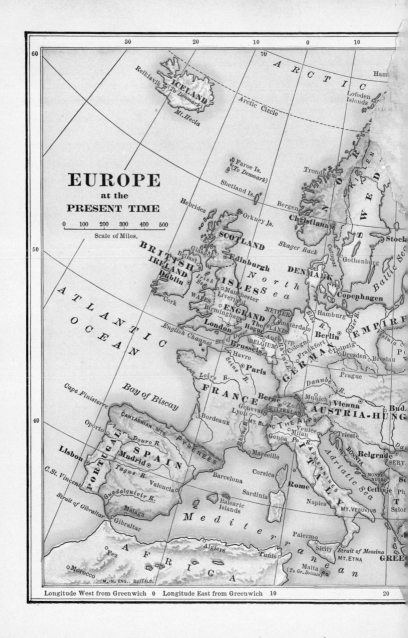

EUROPE
at the
PRESENT TIME

0 100 200 300 400 500
Scale of Miles.

ARCTIC

ICELAND
(To Denmark)
Reikiavik
Mt. Hecla

Arctic Circle

Lofoden
Islands

Faroe Is.
(To Denmark)

Shetland Is.

Hebrides

Trondhjem

Bergen

Christiana

Skager Rack

Stock

Orkney Is.

SCOTLAND

Glasgow
Edinburgh

Belfast

North
Sea

DENMARK

Gothenburg

Copenhagen

Baltic Sea

BRITISH
ISLES
IRELAND

Dublin

Irish
Sea

Manchester
Liverpool

Cork

WALES

ENGLAND
Birmingham

London
The

Hamburg

Amsterdam

Berlin

GERMAN EMPIRE

NETHER-
LANDS
Hague
Antwerp

Cologne

Leipzig

Dresden

Breslau

English Channel

Str.
Dover

Havre

BELGIUM
Brussels

Frankfort

Prague

ATLANTIC
OCEAN

Bay of Biscay

Cape Finisterre

Oporto

Loire
R.

Paris

Seine
R.

FRANCE

Bern

Danube
R.

Munich

Vienna

AUSTRIA-HUNG

Bud

CANTABRIAN Mts.

Douro R.

Bordeaux

Lyon

Geneva
Zürich
SWITZERLAND

THE

ALPS

MT. BLANC

Rhone R.

Venice

Milan

Trieste

Belgrade

SERV

PYRENEES

SPAIN

Lisbon

Madrid

PORTUGAL

Tagus R.

C. St. Vincent

Valencia

Guadalquivir R.

Barcelona

Corsica

Genoa

Po

APENNINES

ITALY

Rome

Adriatic Sea

BOSNIA

MONTE
NEGRO

Cetinje

Naples

MT. VESUVIUS

Malaga

Gibraltar

Strait of Gibraltar

Balearic
Islands

Sardinia

Mediterranean

Palermo

Sicily

MT. ETNA

Strait of Messina

GREE

Fez

Morocco

AFRICA

Algiers

Tunis

Malta
(To Gr. Britain)

Salon

Ph

M.·N. ENG.. BUFFALO.

30   20   10   0   10

60

70

50

40

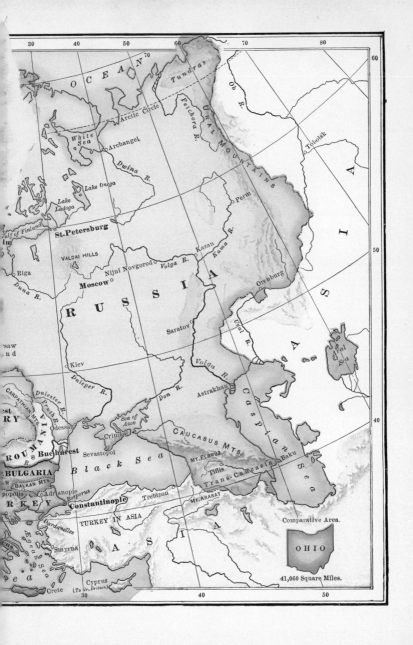

OCEAN

30 40 50 60 70 80

60

70

Tundras

Ob R.

Arctic Circle

Petchora R.

White Sea

Archangel

URAL MOUNTAINS

Tobolsk

Dwina R.

Lake Onega

Perm

50

Lake Ladoga

Gulf of Finland

St.Petersburg

Kazan

VALDAI HILLS

Kama R.

Nijni Novgorod

Volga R.

Orenburg

Riga

Duna R.

Moscow

R U S S I A

A S I A

Saratov

Ural R.

Aral Sea

saw
nd

Kiev

Volga R.

Dnieper R.

Don R.

Astrakhan

40

rsaw

CARPATHIAN MTS.

Dniester R.

Pruth R.

Sea of Azov

Caspian Sea

ry
est

ROUMA

BULGARIA

Bucharest

Odessa

Crim

CAUCASUS MTS.

Sevastopol

BALKAN MTS.

Black Sea

MT.ELBRUZ

Tiflis

Baku

popolis
URKEY

Adrianople

Bosporus

Constantinople

Trebizon

Trans-Caucasia

MT.ARARAT

Dardanelles

TURKEY IN ASIA

A S I A

Comparative Area.

Smyrna

OHIO

Cyprus
(To Gr. Britain)

41,060 Square Miles.

Crete

30

40 50

Austria had ceded Venetia to Italy. Napoleon III had, however, sent French troops in 1867 to prevent Garibaldi from seizing Rome and the neighboring districts, which had been held by the head of the Catholic church for more than a thousand years. In August, 1870, the reverses of the war compelled Napoleon to recall the French garrison from Rome, and the pope made little effort to defend his capital against the Italian army, which occupied it in September. The people of Rome voted by an overwhelming majority to join the kingdom of Italy; and the work of Victor Emmanuel and Cavour was consummated by transferring the capital to the Eternal City.

Rome added to the kingdom of Italy, 1870.

Although the papal possessions were declared a part of the kingdom of Italy, a law was passed which guaranteed to the pope the rank and privileges of a sovereign prince. He was to have his own ambassadors and court like the other European powers. No officer of the Italian government was to enter the Lateran or Vatican palaces upon any official mission. As head of the church, the pope was to be entirely independent of the king of Italy, and the bishops were not required to take the oath of allegiance to the government. A sum of over six hundred thousand dollars annually was also appropriated to aid the pope in defraying his expenses. The pope, however, refused to recognize the arrangement. He still regards himself as a prisoner, and the Italian government as a usurper who has robbed him of his possessions. He has never accepted the income assigned to him, and still maintains that the independence which he formerly enjoyed as ruler of the Papal States is essential to the best interests of the head of a great international church.[1]

Position of the pope.

274. To complete the survey of the great political changes of the nineteenth century, we must turn for a moment to southeastern Europe. The disposal of the European lands occupied by the Turks has proved a very knotty international question.

Southeastern Europe.

[1] See above, p. 75.

We have seen how the Turks were expelled from Hungary by the end of the seventeenth century, and how Peter the Great and his successors began to dream of acquiring Constantinople as a Russian outpost which would enable the Tsar to command the eastern Mediterranean.[1] Catherine II (1762–1796) had extended the Russian boundary to the Black Sea. On the whole, however, the Turks held their own pretty well during the eighteenth century, but the nineteenth witnessed the disruption of European Turkey into a number of new and independent Christian states.

Servia and Greece revolt from the Sultan.

The Servians first revolted successfully against their oppressors, and forced the Sultan (1817) to permit them to manage their own affairs, although he did not grant them absolute independence. Of the war of independence which the Greeks waged against the Turks (1821–1829) something has already been said.[2] The intervention of Russia, England, and France saved the insurgents from defeat, and in 1829 the Porte recognized the independence of Greece, which became a constitutional monarchy. The Turkish government also pledged itself to allow vessels of all nations to pass freely through the Dardanelles and the Bosporus.

The Crimean War, 1853–1856.

Inasmuch as a great part of the peoples still under Turkish rule in Europe were — like the Russians — Slavs and adherents of the Greek church, Russia believed that it had the best right to protect the Christians within the Sultan's dominions from the atrocious misgovernment of the Mohammedans. When in 1853 news reached the Tsar that the Turks were troubling Christian pilgrims, he demanded that he be permitted to assume a protectorate over all the Christians in Turkey. This the Porte refused to grant. Russia declared war and destroyed the Turkish fleet in the Black Sea. The English government looked with apprehension upon the advance of the Russians. It felt that it would be disastrous to western Europe if Russia

[1] See above, pp. 514, 517–518, 535.   [2] See above, p. 640.

were permitted to occupy the well-nigh impregnable Constantinople and send its men-of-war freely about the Mediterranean. England therefore induced Napoleon III to combine with her to protect the Sultan's possessions. The English and French troops easily defeated the Russians, landed in the Crimea, and then laid siege to Sevastopol, an important Russian fortress on the Black Sea. Sevastopol fell after a long and terrible siege, and the so-called Crimean War came to a close. The intervention of the western powers had prevented the capture of Constantinople by the Russians, but very soon the powers recognized the practical independence of two important Turkish provinces on the lower Danube, which were united in 1859 into the principality of Roumania.

Origin of the principality of Roumania, 1859.

The Turkish subjects in Bosnia and Herzegovina naturally envied the happier lot of the neighboring Servians, who had escaped from the bondage of the Turks. These provinces were stirred to revolt in 1875, when the Turks, after collecting the usual heavy taxes, immediately demanded the same amount over again. The oppressed Christians proposed to escape Turkish tyranny by becoming a part of Servia. They naturally relied upon the aid of Russia to carry out their plans. The insurrection spread among the other Christian subjects of the Sultan, especially those in Bulgaria.

Revolt of Bosnia, 1875.

Here the Turks wreaked vengeance upon the insurgents by atrocities which filled Europe with horror and disgust. In a single town six thousand of the seven thousand inhabitants were massacred with incredible cruelty, and scores of villages were burned. Russia, joined by Roumania, thereupon declared war upon the Porte (1877). The Turks were defeated, but western Europe would not permit the questions at issue to be settled without its approval. Consequently, a congress was called at Berlin under the presidency of Bismarck, which included representatives from Germany, Austria, Russia, England, France, Italy, and Turkey.

The Bulgarian atrocities.

The Congress of Berlin determined that Servia, Montenegro, and Roumania should thereafter be altogether independent. The latter two became kingdoms within a few years, Roumania in 1881 and Servia in 1882. Bosnia and Herzegovina,[1] instead of becoming a part of Servia, as they wished, were to be occupied and administered by Austria, although the Sultan remained their nominal sovereign. Bulgaria received a Christian government, but was forced to continue to recognize the Sultan as its sovereign and pay him tribute.[2]

To-day the once wide dominions of the Sultan in Europe are reduced to the city of Constantinople and a strip of mountainous country stretching westward to the Adriatic.

General Reading. — In addition to the works of Andrews and Fyffe referred to in the footnotes, the following are excellent short accounts of the political history of Europe since 1815. W. A. PHILLIPS, *Modern Europe* (The Macmillan Company, $1.50); SEIGNOBOS, *Political History of Europe since 1814,* carefully edited by MacVane (Henry Holt & Co., $3.00), and the readable but partisan German work of Müller, *Political History of Recent Times* (American Book Company, $2.00). For Germany : MUNROE SMITH, *Bismarck and German Unity* (The Macmillan Company, $1.00) and KUNO FRANCKE, *History of German Literature as determined by Social Forces* (Henry Holt & Co., $2.50). For Italy : THAYER, *Dawn of Italian Independence* (Houghton, Mifflin & Co., 2 vols., $4.00); STILLMAN, *Union of Italy* (The Macmillan Company, $1.60); COUNTESS CESARESCO, *Liberation of Italy* (Charles Scribner's Sons, $1.75) and her *Cavour* (The Macmillan Company, 75 cents). For England : MCCARTHY, *History of our Own Times* (issued by various publishers, e.g., Coates & Co., 2 vols., $1.50).

---

1 Herzegovina is a small province lying between Bosnia and the Adriatic. Both Bosnia and Herzegovina appear on the map as a part of Austria, to which they now belong, to all intents and purposes. See map, p. 649, above.

2 In 1885 South Bulgaria (formerly known as Eastern Roumelia) proclaimed itself annexed to Bulgaria. The Sultan, under the influence of the western powers, permitted the prince of Bulgaria to extend his power over South Bulgaria.

CHAPTER XLI

EUROPE OF TO-DAY

275. The scholars and learned men of the Middle Ages were but little interested in the world about them. They devoted far more attention to philosophy and theology than to what we should call the natural sciences. They were satisfied in the main to get their knowledge of nature from reading the works of the ancients, above all of Aristotle. Roger Bacon, as we have seen, protested against the exaggerated veneration for books. He foresaw that a careful examination of the things about us, — like water, air, light, animals and plants, — would lead to important and useful discoveries which would greatly benefit mankind.

He advocated three methods of reaching truth which are now followed by all scientific men. In the first place, he proposed that natural objects and changes should be examined with great care, in order that the observer might determine exactly what happened in any given case. This has led in modern times to incredibly refined measurements and analysis. The chemist, for example, can now determine the exact nature and amount of every substance in a cup of impure water, which may appear perfectly limpid to the casual observer. Then, secondly, Roger Bacon advocated experimentation. He was not contented with mere observation of what actually happened, but tried new and artificial combinations and processes. Nowadays experimentation is constantly used by scientific investigators, and by means of it they discover many things which the most careful observation would never reveal. Thirdly, in

Modern scientific methods of discovering truth.

Experimentation.

order to carry on investigation and make careful measurements and the desired experiments, apparatus designed for the special purpose of discovering truth was necessary. As early as the thirteenth century it was found, for example, that a convex crystal or bit of glass would magnify objects, although several centuries elapsed before the microscope and telescope were devised.

Astrology grows into astronomy.

The progress of scientific discovery was hastened, strangely enough, by two grave misapprehensions. In the Middle Ages even the most intelligent believed that the heavenly bodies influenced the fate of mankind; consequently, that a careful observation of the position of the planets at the time of a child's birth would make it possible to forecast his life. In the same way important enterprises were only to be undertaken when the influence of the stars was auspicious. Physicians believed that the efficacy of their medicines depended upon the position of the planets. This whole subject of the influence of the stars upon human affairs was called astrology, and was in some cases taught in the mediæval universities. Those who examined the stars gradually came, however, to the conclusion that the movements of the planets had no effect upon humanity; but the facts which the astrologers had discovered through careful observation became the basis of modern astronomy.

Alchemy grows into chemistry.

In the same way chemistry developed out of the mediæval study of alchemy. The first experimentation with chemicals was carried on with the hope of producing gold by some happy combination of less valuable metals. But finally, after learning more about the nature of chemical compounds, it was discovered that gold was an element, or simple substance, and consequently could not be formed by combinations of other substances.

Discovery that the universe follows natural laws.

In short, observation and experimentation were leading to the most fundamental of all scientific discoveries, namely, the conviction that all the things about us follow certain natural,

immutable laws. The modern scientific investigator devotes
a great part of his attention to the discovery of these laws and
their application. He has given up any hope of reading man's
fate in the stars or of producing any results by magical combinations. Unlike the mediæval writers, he hesitates to accept as
true the reports which reach him of miracles, that is, of exceptions to the general laws, because he is convinced that the natural laws have been found to work regularly in every instance
where they have been carefully observed. His study of the natural laws has, however, enabled him to produce far more marvelous results than those reported of the mediæval magician.

276. In a previous chapter the progress of science for three
hundred years after Roger Bacon has been briefly noted.[1]
With the exception of Copernicus the investigators of this
period are scarcely known to us. In the seventeenth century,
however, progress became very rapid and has been steadily
accelerating since. In astronomy, for example, the truths
which had been only suspected by earlier astronomers were
demonstrated to the eye by Galileo (1564–1642). By means
of a little telescope, which was hardly so powerful as the best
modern opera glasses, he discovered (in 1610) the spots on
the sun. These made it plain that the sun was revolving on
its axis as astronomers were already convinced that the earth
revolved. He saw, too, that the moons of Jupiter were revolving about their planet in the same way that the planets revolve
about the sun.

Galileo's telescope.

The year that Galileo died, the famous English mathematician, Sir Isaac Newton, was born (1642–1727). He carried
on the work of earlier astronomers by the application of higher
mathematics, and proved that the force of attraction which
we call gravitation was a universal one, and that the sun and
the moon and the earth, and all the heavenly bodies, are
attracted to one another inversely as the square of the distance.

Sir Isaac Newton and his discovery of the law of universal gravitation.

[1] See above, pp. 351–352.

Development of the microscope.
While the telescope aided the astronomer, the microscope contributed far more to the extension of practical knowledge. Rude and simple microscopes were used with advantage as early as the seventeenth century. Leeuwenhoek, a Dutch linen merchant, so far improved his lenses that he discovered the blood corpuscles and (1665) the "animalculæ" or minute organisms of various kinds found in pond water and elsewhere. The microscope has been rapidly perfected since the introduction of better kinds of lenses early in the nineteenth century, so that it is now possible to magnify minute objects to more than two thousand times their diameters.

Advance in medical science.
This has produced the most extraordinary advance in medicine and biology. It has made it possible to determine the difference between healthy and diseased tissue ; and not many years ago the microscope revealed the fact that the bodies of animals and men are the home of excessively small organisms called bacteria, some of which, through the poisonous substances they give out, cause disease. The modern treatment of many maladies, such as consumption, diphtheria, scarlet fever, and typhoid, is based upon this momentous discovery. The success of surgical operations has also been rendered far more secure than formerly by the so-called antiseptic measures which are now taken to prevent the development of bacteria.[1]

Scientific discovery and invention did not affect daily life before the end of the eighteenth century.
277. The discoveries of the scientist and of the mathematician did not begin to be applied to the affairs of daily life until about a hundred and fifty years ago. No new ways had previously been discovered for traveling from place to place. Spinning and weaving were still carried on as they had been before the barbarians overran the Roman Empire. Iron, of which we now make our machines, could only be prepared for use expensively and in small quantities by means of charcoal and bellows.

[1] See *The Progress of the Century*, Harper Bros., pp. 181–188, 232–242.

Manufacture still meant, as it did in the original Latin (*manu facere*), to make by hand. Artisans carried on their trade with their own tools in their own homes, or in small shops, like the cobbler of to-day. Instead of working with hundreds of others in a great factory and being entirely dependent upon his wages, the artisan, in England at least, was often able to give some attention to a small garden plot from which he derived a part of his support. This "domestic system" was displaced by factories, as the result of a series of mechanical inventions made in England during the latter half of the eighteenth century. Through them machinery was substituted for hand and foot power and for the simple implements which had served the world for centuries.

The 'domestic system' of manufacture.

In order that machinery should develop and become widely useful, two things were necessary. In the first place, there must be some strong material available of which to make the machines; for that purpose iron and steel have, with few exceptions, proved to be the best. In the second place, some adequate power must be found to propel the machinery, which is ordinarily too heavy to be run by hand or foot power. This necessary motive power was discovered in steam. The steam engine was devised by James Watt, an English inventor of great ingenuity. He invented a cylinder containing a piston, which could be forced back and forth by the introduction of steam. His progress was much retarded by the inability of the mechanics of his time to make an accurate cylinder of sufficient size, but in the year 1777 the new machine was successfully used for pumping. A few years later (1785) he arranged his engine so that it would turn a wheel. In this way, for the first time, steam could be used to run machinery — the spindles, for example, in a cotton mill.

Cheap iron and adequate power essential to the development of machinery.

Watt invents the steam engine.

A few years before Watt completed his improved steam engine, the old spinning wheel had been supplanted by the modern system, in which the thread is drawn out by means

Steam used for spinning and weaving.

of spindles revolving at different rates of speed. The spindles, which had at first been run by water power, could now be propelled by steam. The old loom had also been improved, and weaving by steam began to become general after the year 1800.

Machinery, however, could not become common so long as iron and steel were expensive. The first use, therefore, to which the crude steam engines were put was to furnish a blast which enabled the iron smelter to employ coal instead of charcoal to fuse the iron ore (1777). Moreover, the steam pumps made it possible for the miners to pump out the water which impeded their work in the mines, and in this way cheapened both the iron and the coal. Soon the so-called "puddling furnace" was

invented, by means of which steel was produced much more economically than it could be earlier. Rolling mills run by steam then took the place of the hammers with which the steel had formerly been beaten into shape. These discoveries of the use of steam and coal and iron revolutionized the life of the people at large in western Europe more quickly than any of the events which have been previously recorded in this volume. It is the aim of the remainder of this chapter to indicate very briefly the variety and importance of the effects produced by modern inventions.[1]

278. Machinery although very efficient was expensive, and had necessarily to be near the boilers which produced the steam. Consequently machines for particular purposes were grouped in factories, and the workmen left their homes and gathered in large establishments. The hand worker with his old tools was more and more at a disadvantage compared with the workman who produced commodities by machinery. The result was inevitable, namely, that domestic industry was supplanted by the factory.

---

[1] Reference, for the development of the inventions, Cheyney, *Industrial History of England*, pp. 199–216.

One of the principal advantages of the factory system is that it makes possible a minute division of labor. Instead of giving his time and thought to the whole process, each worker concentrates his attention upon one single step of the process, and by repeating a simple set of motions over and over again acquires wonderful dexterity. At the same time the period of necessary apprenticeship is shortened under the factory system, because each separate task is comparatively simple. Moreover, the invention of new machinery is increased, because the very subdivision of the process into simple steps often suggests some way of substituting mechanical motion for the motion of the human hand.

An example of the greatly increased output rendered possible by the use of machinery and division of labor is given by the distinguished Scotch economist, Adam Smith, whose great work, *The Wealth of Nations*, appeared in 1776. Speaking of the manufacture of a pin in his own time, Adam Smith says: "To make the head requires two or three distinct operations; to put it on is a peculiar business, to whiten the pin is another. It is even a trade by itself to put them into the paper, and the important business of making a pin is, in this manner, divided into about eighteen distinct operations." By this division, he adds, ten persons can make among them upwards of forty-eight thousand pins in a day. A recent writer reports that now an English machine makes one hundred and eighty pins a minute, cutting the wire, flattening the heads, sharpening the points, and dropping the pin into its proper place. In a single factory which he visited seven million pins were made in a day, and three men were all that were required to manage the mechanism.

Another example of modern mechanical work is found in printing. For several centuries after the development of that art the type was set up by hand, inked by hand, each sheet of paper was laid by hand upon the type and then printed by

Advantages of machinery.

Division of labor.

Examples of the increased production of goods by machinery.

means of a press operated by a lever. Nowadays our newspapers are, in the great cities at least, printed almost altogether by machinery, from the setting up of the type until they are dropped complete and counted out by hundreds at the bottom of a rotary press. The paper is fed into the press from a great roll and is printed on both sides and folded at the rate of two hundred or more newspapers a minute.

New means of communication. 279. The factory system would never have developed upon a vast scale had the manufacturers been able to sell their goods only in the neighborhood. The discovery that steam could be used to carry the goods cheaply and speedily to all parts of the world made it possible for a manufacturer to widen his market indefinitely. Fulton, an American inventor, devised **Steamboats.** the first steamboat that was really successful, in 1807, yet over half a century elapsed before steamships began to supplant the old and uncertain sailing ship. It is now possible to make the journey from New York to Southampton, three thousand miles, in less than six days, and with almost the regularity of an express train. Japan may be reached from Vancouver in thirteen days, and from San Francisco via Honolulu, a distance of five thousand five hundred miles, in eighteen days. A commercial map of the world shows that the globe is now crossed in every direction by definite routes, which are followed by innumerable freight and passenger steamers passing regularly from one port to another. These are able to carry goods for incredibly small sums. For example, wheat has frequently been shipped from New York to Liverpool for two cents a bushel.

Development of the railroad. Just as the gigantic modern steamship has taken the place of the schooner and clipper, so, on land, the merchandise which used to be slowly dragged in carts by means of horses and oxen is now transported in long trains of capacious cars, each of which holds as much as many ordinary carts. A ton of freight can now be carried for less than a cent a mile. In 1825 Stephenson's locomotive was put into operation in England.

Other countries soon began to follow England's lead in building railroads. France opened its first railroad in 1828, Germany in 1835. By 1840 Europe had over eighteen hundred miles of railroad; fifty years later this had increased to one hundred and forty thousand.

Besides the marvelous cheapening of transportation, other new means of communication have resulted from modern inventions. The telegraph, the submarine cable, and the telephone, all have served to render communication prompt and certain. Steamships and railroads carry letters half round the globe for a price too trivial to be paid for delivering a message round the corner. The old, awkward methods of making payments have given way to a tolerably uniform system of coinage. Instead of each petty principality and each town having its own coins, as was common, especially in Germany and Italy, before the nineteenth century, all coins are now issued by the national central governments. Yet the most convenient coins are difficult to transfer in large quantities, and nowadays all considerable sums are paid by means of checks and drafts. The banks settle their accounts by means of a clearing house, and in this way almost no large amount of money need pass from hand to hand.

Startling improvements in the means of communication.

England took the lead in utilizing all these remarkable new inventions, and with their aid became, by the middle of the nineteenth century, the manufacturing center of the world. Gradually the new machinery was introduced on the continent, and since 1850 countries having the necessary coal, such as Germany and Belgium, have developed manufacturing industries which now rival those of Great Britain.

280. The *industrial revolution*, as the changes above referred to are usually called, could not but have a profound influence upon the life and government of Europe. For example, the population of Europe appears to have nearly doubled during the nineteenth century. One of the most startling tendencies

Some results of the industrial revolution of the nineteenth century.

Rapid growth of the towns.

of recent times has been the growth of the towns. In 1800 London had a population of less than one million; it now contains over four million five hundred thousand inhabitants. Paris, at the opening of the French Revolution, contained less than seven hundred thousand inhabitants; it now has over two and a half millions. Berlin has grown in a hundred years from one hundred and seventy-two thousand to nearly two millions. In England a quarter of the whole population live in towns having over two hundred and fifty thousand inhabitants, and less than a quarter still remain in the country. Our modern life is dominated by the great cities, which not only are the center of commerce and manufacturing, but are the homes of the artist and man of letters.

Reasons for the growth of the towns.

There are two obvious reasons for the growth of the towns since the industrial revolution. In the first place, factories are established in places where there is an abundant supply of coal, or where conditions are otherwise favorable; and this brings a large number of people together. In the second place, there is no limit set to the growth of cities, as was formerly the case, by the difficulty of procuring food from a distance. Paris, in the time of Louis XVI, was not a large city in the modern sense of the word; still the government found it very difficult to secure a regular supply of food in the markets. Now grain and even meat and fruit are easily carried any distance. England imports a large amount of her meat from Australia, on the other side of the globe, and even her butter and eggs she gets largely from the continent.

Abolition of most of the restrictions on trade and industry.

281. Before the nineteenth century the European governments had been accustomed to regulate trade, industry, and commerce by a great variety of laws, which were supposed to be necessary for the protection of the public. Of this we find examples in the English Navigation Acts;[1] in the guilds, which under the protection of the government enjoyed a

[1] See above, p. 488.

monopoly of their industries in their particular districts; in the regulations issued by Colbert[1] and in the grain laws in both France and England, which limited the free importation and even the exportation of grain.

The French and English economists in the eighteenth century, like Turgot and Adam Smith, advocated the abolition of all restrictions, which they believed did far more harm than good. The expediency of this *laissez faire*,[2] or free-trade policy, has now been recognized by most European powers. England abolished her grain laws (the so-called Corn Laws) in 1846, and since then has adopted the policy of free trade, except so far as she raises a revenue from customs duties imposed upon a very few commodities, like liquor and tobacco. Low import duties are collected by most of the European powers on goods entering their territories, but all export duties have been abolished as well as all customs barriers within the countries.

A short experience with the factory system showed the need of regulations designed to protect the laborer.[3] There was a temptation for the new factories to force the employees to work an excessive number of hours under unhealthful conditions. Women and children were set to run the machines, and their strength was often cruelly overtaxed. Women and children were also employed in the coal mines, under terribly degrading conditions. One of the great functions of our modern governments has been to pass laws to protect the working men and women and to improve their condition. Germany has been particularly active in this sort of regulation, and has gone so far as to compel workingmen to insure themselves for the benefit of their families.[4] *Government regulations protecting the laborer.*

Another development of the factory system has been the rise of labor unions. These are voluntary associations intended to *Labor unions.*

1 See above, p. 500.   2 See above, p. 553.
3 Reference, Cheyney, *Industrial History of England*, pp. 224–239.
4 For factory legislation in England, see Cheyney, *Industrial History*, pp. 244–262.

promote the interests of their members. They have grown as
the factory system has been extended, and they now enjoy an
influence in certain industries comparable to that exercised by
the craft guilds of the Middle Ages. The governments do
not undertake, however, to enforce the regulations of the
labor unions as they formerly did of the guilds.[1]

The people admitted to a share in the government. 282. The extension of manufacturing industries has had
much to do with the gradual admission of the people to a
share in the government. The life in towns and cities has
quickened the intelligence of the working classes, so that they
are no longer willing to intrust the affairs of government
entirely to a king or to the representatives of the upper classes.
Character of modern constitutions. The result of this was, as we have seen, that constitutions
were, during the nineteenth century, introduced into all the
western European states. While these differ from one another
in detail, they all agree in establishing a house of representatives, whose members are chosen by the people at large.
Gradually the franchise has been extended so that the poorest
laborer, so soon as he comes of age, is permitted to have a
voice in the selection of the deputies.[2] Without the sanction
of the representatives of the people, the king and the upper,
more aristocratic house are not allowed to pass any law or

[1] Reference, Cheyney, *Industrial History*, pp. 277–293.

[2] England, like the continental countries, has gradually, during the nineteenth
century, conceded the right to vote to almost all adult males. Before 1832 a
great part of the members of the House of Commons were chosen, not by the
voters at large but by a few individuals, who controlled the so-called "rotten
boroughs." These boroughs had once been important enough to be asked by the
king to send representatives to Parliament, but had sunk into insignificance, or
even disappeared altogether. Meanwhile great manufacturing cities like Birmingham, Manchester, and Sheffield had grown up, and as there had been no
redistribution of representatives after the time of Charles II, these large cities
were unrepresented in Parliament. This evil was partially remedied by the
famous *Reform Act* of 1832. At the same time the amount of property which
one must hold in order to be permitted to vote was reduced. In 1867 almost
all of the workingmen of the cities were granted the franchise by permitting
those to vote who rented a lodging costing at least fifty dollars a year. This
doubled the number of voters. In 1885 the same privilege was granted to the
country people.

establish any new tax. Each year a carefully prepared list of expenses must be presented to the lower house and receive its ratification before money collected by taxation can be spent.

The French prefaced their first constitution by the memorable words : " All citizens being equal before the law, are alike eligible to all public offices and positions of honor and trust, according to their capacity, and without any distinction, except that of their character and ability." This principle, so different from that which had hitherto prevailed, has been recognized in most of the modern European constitutions. The privileges and exceptions which everywhere existed before the French Revolution have been abolished. Modern European governments are supposed to treat all alike, regardless of social rank or religious belief.

Equality before the law.

At the opening of the nineteenth century England still kept on the statute book the laws debarring Roman Catholics and dissenters from sitting in Parliament or holding any public office. Exceptions, however, were made in the case of the dissenters. Finally, after violent opposition on the part of the conservative party, the Test Act, passed in the reign of Charles II,[1] was repealed in 1828. Next year the Roman Catholics were also given the right to sit in Parliament and to hold office, like the other subjects of the king.

Religious equality in England.

Repeal of the Test Act, 1828.

Education, which was formerly left to the church, has during the nineteenth century become one of the most important functions of government. Boys and girls of all classes, between the ages of four and fourteen or fifteen, are now generally forced to take advantage of the schools which the government supports for their benefit. Tuition is free in France, Italy, Norway, and Sweden, and only trifling fees are required in Germany and elsewhere in western Europe. In 1902 the English Parliament and the French Legislative Assembly each appropriated about forty million dollars for educational purposes. As an example of

Free and compulsory education under the control of the state.

1 See above, p. 492.

the rapid advance in education in recent times, it may be noted that in 1843, among those who married in England and Wales, one third of the men and half of the women were unable to sign their names in the marriage registers. In 1899 all but three men in a hundred could write, and almost as many of the women.

Warfare in recent times.

283. The general advance in education has not yet taught nations to settle all their disputes without recourse to war. It is true that since Napoleon's downfall there have been but three or four serious wars in western Europe, and these very brief ones compared with the earlier conflicts. But the European powers spend vast amounts annually in maintaining standing armies and building battle ships. France and Germany have each a force of over half a million carefully trained soldiers ready to fight at any moment, and two million more who can be called out with the utmost speed should war be declared.[1] The invention of repeating rifles and of new and deadly explosives have, however, rendered war so terrible a thing to contemplate that statesmen are more and more reluctant to suggest a resort to arms.

European colonies in the nineteenth century.

Recent wars and the frequent rumors of war have had their origin mainly in disagreements over colonial matters. The anxiety of the European powers to extend their control over distant parts of the world is now no less marked than it was in the eighteenth century. Modern means of communication have naturally served to make the world smaller and more compact. An event in London is known as promptly in Sydney as in Oxford. A government can send orders to its commanders on the opposite side of the globe as easily as if they were but five miles away. Supplies, ammunition, and arms are, moreover, readily and speedily transferred to remote points.

At the opening of the nineteenth century Spain still held Mexico, Florida, Central America, and most of South America

[1] See Sir Charles Dilke on " War," in *The Progress of the Century*, 333 *sqq.*

except Brazil, which belonged to Portugal. During the Napoleonic period the Spanish colonies revolted and declared their independence of the mother country, — Mexico, New Granada, Chile, and the region about Buenos Ayres in 1810, Venezuela in 1811, etc. By 1826 Spain had been forced to give up the struggle and withdraw her troops from the American continent. In 1822 Brazil declared itself independent of Portugal. After the recent war with the United States Spain lost Cuba, Porto Rico, and the Philippines, the last remnants of her once imposing colonial domains. *The Spanish colonies in North and South America establish their independence, 1810–1826.*

England, on the other hand, has steadily increased her colonial realms and her dependencies during the nineteenth century, and has met with no serious losses since the successful revolt of the thirteen American colonies. In 1814 she acquired the Cape of Good Hope from the Dutch, and since then the territory has been enlarged by adding the adjacent districts. During the last years of the nineteenth century England busied herself extending her power over large tracts of western, central, and eastern Africa. *Expansion of England during the nineteenth century.*

England has secured her interests in the eastern Mediterranean by gaining control of the Suez Canal, which was completed in 1869, mainly with French capital. In 1875 she purchased the shares owned by the khedive of Egypt. Then, since the khedive's finances were in a very bad way, she arranged to furnish him, in the interest of his creditors and in agreement with France, with financial advisers without whose approval he can make no financial decision. Moreover, English troops are stationed in Egypt with a view of maintaining order.

In the southern hemisphere England has colonized the continent of Australia, the large islands of New Zealand, Tasmania, etc. The mother country wisely grants these colonies and Canada almost complete freedom in managing their own affairs. The Canadian provinces formed a federation among themselves in 1867, and in 1901 the Commonwealth of Australia was proclaimed, a federation of the five Australian colonies and the island of Tasmania.

Expansion of Russia since the Crimean War.

France exercises a wide influence in Africa and even Germany has made some effort to gain a foothold there; but the most momentous extension of a European power is that of Russia. Since the Crimean War Russia has pressed steadily into central Asia, so that now her boundaries and those of the English possessions in India practically touch one another. She has also been actively engaged in the Far East. In 1898 she leased Port Arthur from China, and now the Trans-Siberian Railroad connects this as well as Vladivostok on the Pacific coast with Moscow.

The Far Eastern Question.

Recent events have shown that the European powers are likely to come into hostile relations with one another in dealing with China. The problem of satisfying the commercial and military demands of the various nations constitutes what is known as the Far Eastern Question.

General disturbance caused by war in modern conditions.

While all these conquests of the European powers increase the probability of friction and misunderstandings, there is a growing abhorrence of war. It appears more inhuman to men of to-day than it did to their ancestors. Moreover, all parts of the world are now so dependent each on the other that even the rumor of war may produce disastrous results far and wide. The prospect of war frightens the merchants, checks commerce and industry, and causes loss both to the laborer and the capitalist.

The peace conference at The Hague, 1899.

Many difficulties between nations can now be adjusted by the rules of international law. Arbitration is more and more frequently preferred to war. In 1899 an international peace conference was held at The Hague at the suggestion of the Tsar. Its object was to consider how the European powers might free themselves from the burden of supporting tremendous armies and purchasing the terrible engines of destruction which modern ingenuity has conceived. The resolutions of the conference embody rules for adjusting international disputes and prohibiting the use of particularly cruel and murderous projectiles, and for the treatment of prisoners of war, etc.

It has been possible to mention only a few of the startling achievements and changes which the nineteenth century has witnessed. Enough has, however, been said to show that Europe to-day differs perhaps more fundamentally from the Europe Napoleon knew than did Napoleon's world from Charlemagne's. Although civil and religious liberty and equality have been established, and incredible progress has been made in scientific thought, in general enlightenment, and in domestic comfort, yet the growth of democracy, the magnitude of the modern city, and the unprecedented development of industry and commerce have brought with them new and urgent problems which the future must face.

General Reading. — *The Progress of the Century* (Harper & Bros., $2.50), a collection of essays by distinguished writers and investigators, summing up the changes of the nineteenth century. *The Statesman's Year Book* (The Macmillan Company, $3.00) is issued each year and gives much valuable information in regard to the population, constitution, finances, educational system, etc., of the European states. WELLS, *Recent Economic Changes* (D. Appleton & Co., $2.00).

LIST OF BOOKS[1]

ADAMS, GEORGE B., *Civilization during the Middle Ages* (Charles Scribner's Sons, $2.50).

ADAMS, GEORGE B., *Growth of the French Nation* (The Macmillan Company, $1.25).

ANDREWS, *Historical Development of Modern Europe* (G. P. Putnam's Sons, $2.75).

BRYCE, *The Holy Roman Empire* (The Macmillan Company, $1.00).

Cambridge Modern History, Volume I (The Macmillan Company, $3.75).

CESARESCO, *Liberation of Italy* (Charles Scribner's Sons, $1.75).

CHEYNEY, *Industrial and Social History of England* (The Macmillan Company, $1.40).

COLBY, *Selections from the Sources of English History* (Longmans, Green & Co., $1.50).

CUNNINGHAM, *Western Civilization in its Economic Aspects: Volume II, Mediæval and Modern Times* (The Macmillan Company, $1.25).

EMERTON, *Introduction to the Study of the Middle Ages* (Ginn & Company, $1.12).

EMERTON, *Mediæval Europe* (Ginn & Company, $1.50).

FYFFE, *History of Modern Europe* (Henry Holt & Co., $2.75).

GARDINER, *Student's History of England* (Longmans, Green & Co., $3.00).

GREEN, *Short History of the English People*, Revised Edition (Harper & Bros., $1.20).

HASSALL, *The Balance of Power* [Europe in the Eighteenth Century] (The Macmillan Company, $1.60).

HATCH, *Growth of Church Institutions* (Whittaker, $1.50).

HENDERSON, *A History of Germany in the Middle Ages* (The Macmillan Company, $2.60).

---

[1] The works here enumerated are those referred to in the notes throughout the volume. They would form a valuable and inexpensive collection for use in a high school. The prices given are in most instances subject to a discount, often as high as twenty-five per cent.

HENDERSON, *Select Historical Documents of the Middle Ages* (The Macmillan Company, $1.50).

HENDERSON, *Short History of Germany*, 2 volumes (The Macmillan Company, $4.00).

HODGKIN, *Dynasty of Theodosius* (Clarendon Press, Oxford, $1.50).

JESSOP, *The Coming of the Friars* (G. P. Putnam's Sons, $1.25).

JOHNSON, *Europe in the Sixteenth Century* (The Macmillan Company, $1.75).

LEE, *Source-book of English History* (Henry Holt & Co., $2.00).

LOWELL, E. J., *Eve of the French Revolution* (Houghton, Mifflin & Co., $2.00).

MATHEWS, *The French Revolution* (Longmans, Green & Co., $1.25).

MUNRO, *Mediæval History* (D. C. Appleton & Co., 90 cents).

OMAN, *Dark Ages* (The Macmillan Company, $1.75).

PERKINS, *France under the Regency* (Houghton, Mifflin & Co., $2.00).

PHILLIPS, *Modern Europe* (1815–1899) (The Macmillan Company, $1.50).

ROSE, *Life of Napoleon the First*, 2 volumes (The Macmillan Company, $4.00).

ROSE, *Revolutionary and Napoleonic Period* (The Macmillan Company, $1.25).

SCHWILL, *History of Modern Europe* (Charles Scribner's Sons, $1.50).

SMITH, MUNROE, *Bismarck and German Unity* (The Macmillan Company, $1.00).

STEPHENS, *The French Revolution*, 3 volumes (Charles Scribner's Sons, $7.50).

Translations and Reprints from the Original Sources of European History (Department of History, University of Pennsylvania, Philadelphia. Single numbers, 10 cents; double numbers, 20 cents).

WAKEMAN, *Europe from 1598 to 1715* (The Macmillan Company, $1.40).

WALKER, *The Protestant Reformation* (Charles Scribner's Sons, $2.00).

INDEX

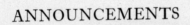

ANNOUNCEMENTS

READINGS IN EUROPEAN HISTORY

By JAMES HARVEY ROBINSON, Professor of History in Columbia
University. Designed to supplement his "Introduction
to the History of Western Europe"

VOLUME I. 12mo. Cloth. 551 pages. List price, $1.50; mailing price, $1.65

VOLUME II. 12mo. Cloth. 629 pages. List price, $1.50; mailing price,
$1.65

ABRIDGED EDITION. 12mo. Cloth. 573 pages. List price, $1.50; mailing
price, $1.65

I T is now generally recognized among teachers of history that
the text-book should be supplemented by collateral reading.
Professor Robinson's "Readings" will supply a need that
has long been felt by those dealing with the general history of
Europe. For each chapter of his text he furnishes from twenty
to thirty pages of extracts, mainly from vivid, first-hand accounts
of the persons, events, and institutions discussed in his manual.
In this way the statements in the text-book may be amplified and
given added interest and vividness. He has drawn upon the
greatest variety of material, much of which has never before
found its way into English.

The extensive and carefully classified bibliographies which
accompany each chapter embody the results of careful criticism
and selection. They are carefully arranged to meet the needs of
students of all grades, from the high-school pupil to one engaged
in advanced graduate work.

Volume I corresponds to Chapters I–XXII of the author's
"History of Western Europe," and closes with an account of the
Italian cities during the Renaissance. Volume II begins with
Europe at the opening of the sixteenth century. The Abridged
Edition is intended especially for high schools.

GINN & COMPANY PUBLISHERS

A
SHORT HISTORY OF ENGLAND

By EDWARD P. CHEYNEY

Professor of European History in the University of Pennsylvania

12mo. Cloth. xvi + 695 pages. With maps and illustrations. List price, $1.40
mailing price, $1.55

THIS short history of England is about midway in length between the shorter school histories and the longer works which are of value chiefly to advanced students or as books of reference. It is admirably adapted for use in colleges and in high schools that offer a rather complete course in English history.

The early period is treated in some detail in the belief that it will be comparatively easy to make clear the later story of the events in the national life, if the foundation is well laid in a knowledge of what kind of country England is, who the English people were, and what were their fundamental customs in language, government, religion, and economic organization.

A great many persons and a great many events often included in text-books have been omitted in order that those which are more significant can be given enough space and attention to show their real character and importance. For the same reason less attention has been given to military than to civil history. For instance, the space given to the Wars of the Roses has been reduced as much as possible in order to give sufficient emphasis to the Reformation.

In choosing the illustrations especial care has been taken that they should be really illustrative of the text, giving visible testimony and reality to what has there been stated in words. Each one of the large number of maps is devoted to the explanation of one particular object, the ideal in text-book maps being illustration rather than use for repeated detailed reference.

GINN & COMPANY Publishers

TEXT-BOOKS ON HISTORY

GINN & COMPANY Publishers

REFERENCE BOOKS IN HISTORY

	List price	Mailing price
Abbott's History and Description of Roman Political Institutions	$1.50	$1.60
Allen's Reader's Guide to English History	.25	.30
Andrews' Droysen's Outline of the Principles of History	1.00	1.10
Brigham's Geographic Influences in American History	1.25	1.40
Channing and Hart's Guide to the Study of American History	2.00	2.15
Davidson's Reference History of the United States	.80	.90
Dyers' Machiavelli and the Modern State	1.00	1.10
Feilden's Short Constitutional History of England	1.25	1.35
Getchell's Study of Mediæval History by the Library Method	.50	.55
Handbooks on the History of Religions :		
Hopkins' Religions of India	2.00	2.20
Jastrow's Religion of Babylonia and Assyria	3.00	3.25
Saussaye's Religion of the Teutons	2.50	2.70
Mace's Method in History	1.00	1.10
Richardson, Ford, and Durfee's Syllabus of Continental European History	.75	.85
Riggs' Studies in United States History	.60	.65
Robinson's Readings in European History :		
Volume I	1.50	1.65
Volume II	1.50	1.65
Abridged Edition	1.50	1.65
Rupert's Guide to the Study of the History and the Constitution of the United States	.70	.75

GINN & COMPANY Publishers

METHOD IN HISTORY

By WILLIAM H. MACE

Professor of History and Political Science in Syracuse University

12mo. Cloth. xvii + 311 pages. List price, $1.00 ; mailing price, $1.10

THE work is designed for teachers and students of history, and aims to make conscious the processes involved in studying and teaching this subject. To this end the work first analyzes events and discovers some of the laws and principles of history, and notes their pedagogical significance. A second part, proceeding in the light of the first, explains and illustrates the processes and products involved in the organization of history into a scientific form. Here the mind is traced in the concrete process of working its way through the subject under the guidance of laws and principles. The educational value of the processes employed and of the products wrought out is also discussed. The third portion is devoted to the organization of the different periods and subperiods of American history. This includes the analysis of the facts of each period till the organizing principle is discovered, and the application of the principle to the interpretation and ranking of events.

The preceding discussions deal with the logical phase of history work, — the phase adapted to the more mature student. The fourth part of the work, holding in view this logical ideal of the subject and the unfolding of the immature mind, treats of the elementary phases of history teaching. As a whole the book presents, in concrete form, a rational pedagogy of history.

GINN & COMPANY Publishers

STUDENT'S AMERICAN HISTORY

REVISED EDITION

A Text-Book for Higher Schools and Colleges

By D. H. MONTGOMERY

12mo. Cloth. 612 + lvii pages. With maps and illustrations. List price, $1.40; mailing price, $1.60

IN this thorough revision of a widely used text-book particular attention has been given to the leading political features, to questions of constitutional history, and to the opening and settlement of the West and its influence on the development of the nation. New maps and illustrations have been added, and the system of cross references has been extended.

The "Student's American History" is more than a mere record of events. It is a philosophical treatment of the rise and development of the nation both socially and politically. It is as attractive in style and as interesting in its manner of statement as the earlier books by this author, and is excellently adapted for the use of advanced students. Especial attention is given to the political and constitutional phases of the subject. Emphasis is laid on cause and effect as illustrated in American history, numerous facsimiles of original documents are shown, and nearly fourteen hundred references to other authorities are cited. The last impression of the book includes a list of important decisions of Chief Justice Marshall and an account of the accession of President Roosevelt.

GINN & COMPANY Publishers